Romans and the Mission of God

Romans and the Mission of God

MARK J. KEOWN

WIPF & STOCK · Eugene, Oregon

ROMANS AND THE MISSION OF GOD

Copyright © 2021 Mark J. Keown. All rights reserved. Except for brief quotations in critical publications or reviews, no part of this book may be reproduced in any manner without prior written permission from the publisher. Write: Permissions, Wipf and Stock Publishers, 199 W. 8th Ave., Suite 3, Eugene, OR 97401.

Wipf & Stock
An Imprint of Wipf and Stock Publishers
199 W. 8th Ave., Suite 3
Eugene, OR 97401

www.wipfandstock.com

PAPERBACK ISBN: 978-1-6667-1944-4
HARDCOVER ISBN: 978-1-6667-1945-1
EBOOK ISBN: 978-1-6667-1946-8

DECEMBER 20, 2021

Scripture quotations marked (ESV) are from The Holy Bible, English Standard Version® (ESV®). Copyright © 2001 by Crossway, a publishing ministry of Good News Publishers. Used by permission. All rights reserved.

This book is dedicated to the God who created the world and is now our Savior, his Son Jesus who came to save us for eternal life, and the Holy Spirit who empowers us to live the life God has for us. It is also dedicated to the apostle Paul who gave his life in the service of this mission and laid the platform for future missional engagement. It is also dedicated to the millions of Christians who have participated in God's mission and will continue to do so until he returns.

Οὐ γὰρ ἐπαισχύνομαι τὸ εὐαγγέλιον, δύναμις γὰρ θεοῦ ἐστιν εἰς σωτηρίαν παντὶ τῷ πιστεύοντι, Ἰουδαίῳ τε πρῶτον καὶ Ἕλληνι.

—Rom 1:16

Contents

Acknowledgments | ix

Abbreviations | x

Introduction | 1

Part One	Background Matters
Chapter 1	Rome and the Roman Empire	7
Chapter 2	The Initial Development of the Roman Church	16
Chapter 3	Authorship, Date, Provenance, Integrity, and Genre	22
Chapter 4	The Purposes of Romans	29

Part Two	Romans and the Content of the Gospel
Chapter 5	Romans as a Gospel Presentation	47
Chapter 6	Romans, Missional Fulfillment, and Salvation History	53
Chapter 7	Aspects of Paul's "Gospel" Presentation to the Romans	59
Chapter 8	Underlying Aspects of the Gospel in Romans	77
Chapter 9	Elements Inimical to God	95
Chapter 10	Salvation Ideas	113
Chapter 11	Human Response	138
Chapter 12	Ethics and Christian Living	148
Chapter 13	The Eschaton	159

Part Three	Romans and the Proclamation of the Gospel
Chapter 14	The Cosmic Scope of Mission and Its Completion	169
Chapter 15	The Power of Salvation	179
Chapter 16	Agents of Evangelism	201

Chapter 17	The Miraculous	237
Chapter 18	Social Justice	249
Chapter 19	Ecological Mission	259
Chapter 20	Social Transformation	269
Chapter 21	Patronage and Hospitality	279
Chapter 22	The Sovereignty of God, Human Volition, and Mission	293
Chapter 23	Missional Prayer	307
Chapter 24	The State and Mission	324
Chapter 25	Culture and Cross-Cultural Mission	336
Chapter 26	Israel in God's Mission	348
Chapter 27	Romans, Mission, Theology, and Apologetics	355

Bibliography | 361

Subject Index | 375

Author Index | 429

Scripture Index | 435

Acknowledgments

As always, I am eternally grateful to my extraordinary wife, Rev. Dr. Emma Keown, for her support, encouragement, and missional example. She is a selfless example of a pastor who serves in the back-breaking work of God's mission day in and day out. I thank Laidlaw College and especially the School of Theology for creating the space for me to write this book and others. I thank those whom God has used to shape me in evangelism and mission; especially, Rev. Graeme Murray, Peter Robertson, Sean and Gillian Pawson, and those many wonderful Christians I have worked with in mission for many years. Thanks to the students at Laidlaw who field-tested this book, encouraged me greatly, and made invaluable suggestions for improvement. I want also to acknowledge the team at Wipf and Stock for accepting this work for publication and partnering to bring it to fruition. You are a pleasure to work with in God's work. Finally, to those who will read this and find some encouragement to participate in God's mission, be strong and courageous, and may the Lord bless you and keep you.

Abbreviations

AB	Anchor Bible
acc.	accusative
ACTMS	Australian College of Theology Monograph Series
AJ	After Jesus
ANRW	*Aufstieg und Niedergang der Römischen Welt*
aor.	aorist
ASMS	American Society of Missiology Series
ATJ	*Ashland Theological Journal*
AYB	Anchor Yale Bible
AYBD	Freedman, David Noel, et al., eds. *The Anchor Yale Bible Dictionary*. New York: Doubleday, 1992.
BA	*The Biblical Archaeologist*
BCBC	Believers Church Bible Commentary
BEB	Ellwell, Walter A., and Barry J. Beitzel. *Baker Encyclopedia of the Bible*. Grand Rapids, MI: Baker, 1988.
BECA	*Baker Encyclopedia of Christian Apologetics*. Baker Reference Library. Grand Rapids, MI: Baker, 1999.
BECNT	Baker Exegetical Commentary on the New Testament
BNTC	Black's New Testament Commentary
BSG	Bible Study Guide
CBT	Counterpoints Bible & Theology
COQG	Christian Origins and the Question of God
CPNIVC	The College Press NIV Commentary
dat.	dative
DBL	Ryken, Leland, et al. *Dictionary of Biblical Imagery*. Downers Grove, IL: InterVarsity, 2000.
DBL Hebrew	Swanson, James. *Dictionary of Biblical Languages with Semantic Domains: Hebrew (Old Testament)*. Oak Harbor: Logos Research Systems, 1997.
DGRBM	Smith, William, ed. *Dictionary of Greek and Roman Biography and Mythology*. Boston: Little, Brown, 1870.

Abbreviations

DJG	Green, Joel B., et al., eds. *Dictionary of Jesus and the Gospels*. Downers Grove, IL: InterVarsity, 1992.
DJG2	Green, Joel B., et al., eds. *Dictionary of Jesus and the Gospels*. 2nd ed. Downers Grove, IL: InterVarsity, 2013.
DNTB	Porter, Stanley E., and Craig A. Evans. *Dictionary of New Testament Background: A Compendium of Contemporary Biblical Scholarship*. Downers Grove, IL: InterVarsity, 2000.
DOTP	Alexander, T. Desmond, and David W. Baker, eds. *Dictionary of the Old Testament: Pentateuch*. Downers Grove, IL: InterVarsity, 2003.
DPL	Hawthorne, Gerald F., et al., eds. *Dictionary of Paul and His Letters*. Downers Grove, IL: InterVarsity, 1993.
EB	*Encyclopædia Britannica*
ECHC	Early Christianity in Its Hellenistic Context
EBD	Easton, M. G. *Easton's Bible Dictionary*. New York: Harper, 1893.
EDEJ	Collins, John J., and Daniel C. Harlow, eds. *The Eerdmans Dictionary of Early Judaism*. Grand Rapids, MI: Eerdmans, 2010.
EEC	Evangelical Exegetical Commentary
EKKNT	Evangelisch-katholischer Kommentar zum Neuen Testament
EJud	Neusner, Jacob, Alan J. Avery-Peck, and William Scott Green, eds. *The Encyclopedia of Judaism*. Leiden: Brill, 2000.
esp.	especially
ESV	English Standard Version
EVV	English versions of the Bible
ExpT	*Expository Times*
FGS	Following God Series
FRLANT	Forschungen zur Religion und Literatur des Alten und Neuen Testaments
gen.	genitive
Gk.	Greek
GLAJJ	*Greek and Latin Authors on Jews and Judaism*. Edited by E. Stern. 3 vols. Jerusalem: Israel Academy of Sciences and Humanities, 1974–84.
HDC	High Definition Commentary
Heb.	Hebrew
HNNTC	Holman New Testament Commentary
HNTC	Harper's New Testament Commentaries
ICC	International Critical Commentary
IDB	*The Interpreter's Dictionary of the Bible*. Edited by George A. Buttrick. 4 vols. New York: Abingdon, 1962.
imper.	imperative
inf.	infinitive

ISPCK	Indian Society for Promoting Christian Knowledge
JETS	*Journal of the Evangelical Theological Society*
Lat.	Latin
LBD	Barry, John D., et al., eds. *The Lexham Bible Dictionary*. Bellingham, WA: Lexham, 2016.
LEB	Lexham English Bible
LES	Lexham English Septuagint
lit.	literature
LSJ	Liddell, Henry George, et al. *A Greek-English Lexicon*. Oxford: Clarendon, 1996.
LXX	The Septuagint
mss.	manuscripts
NAC	New American Commentary
NASB95	New American Standard Bible: 1995 update
NBD	Wood, D. R. W., and I. Howard Marshall. *New Bible Dictionary*. Leicester, UK: InterVarsity, 1996.
NCB	New Century Bible
NCCS	New Covenant Commentary Series
NET	New English Translation Bible
NHC	Nag Hammadi codices
NICNT	New International Commentary on the New Testament
NIDNTTE	Silva, Moisés, ed. *New International Dictionary of New Testament Theology and Exegesis*. Grand Rapids, MI: Zondervan, 2014.
NIGTC	New International Greek Testament Commentary
NIV	New International Version
NIV84	New International Version (1984)
nom.	nominative
NovT	*Novum Testamentum*
NovTSup	Supplements to Novum Testamentum
NPNF[1]	*Nicene and Post-Nicene Fathers*, Series 1
NRSV	New Revised Standard Version
NSBT	New Studies in Biblical Theology
NT	New Testament
NTS	*New Testament Studies*
ONTC	Osborne New Testament Commentaries
OT	Old Testament
OTL	The Old Testament Library
parr.	parallels
PBM	Paternoster Biblical Monographs
PC	The Pulpit Commentary

Abbreviations

PDBS	Patzia, Arthur G., and Anthony J. Petrotta. *Pocket Dictionary of Biblical Studies*. Downers Grove, IL: InterVarsity, 2002.
PDSNTG	DeMoss, Matthew S. *Pocket Dictionary for the Study of New Testament Greek*. Downers Grove, IL: InterVarsity, 2001.
PDTT	Grenz, Stanley, et al. *Pocket Dictionary of Theological Terms*. Downers Grove, IL: InterVarsity, 1999.
pers.	person
pl.	plural
PNM	Publications from The National Museum Studies in Archaeology & History
PNTC	Pillar New Testament Commentary
PTMS	Pittsburgh Theological Monograph Series
SBLDS	Society of Biblical Literature Dissertation Series
SGCS	Study Guide Commentary Series
sing.	singular
SNTSMS	Studiorum Novi Testamenti Societas—Monograph Series
SP	Sacra Pagina
Str-B	Strack, H., and P. Billerbeck. *Kommentar zum Neuen Testament aus Talmud und Midrasch*. 6 vols. Munich: Beck, 1926–63.
TBD	Elwell, Walter A., and Philip Wesley Comfort. *Tyndale Bible Dictionary*. Tyndale Reference Library. Wheaton, IL: Tyndale, 2001.
TDNT	Kittel, Gerhard, et al., eds. *Theological Dictionary of the New Testament*. Grand Rapids, MI: Eerdmans, 1964.
TEE	*Trends in Ecology and Evolution*
TENTS	Texts and Editions for New Testament Study
TNTC	Tyndale New Testament Commentaries
TZ	*Theologische Zeitschrift*
UBSHS	UBS Handbook Series
WBC	Word Biblical Commentary
WMANT	Wissenschaftliche Monographien zum Alten und Neuen Testament
WUNT	Wissenschaftliche Untersuchungen zum Neuen Testament
ZNW	*Zeitschrift für die neutestamentliche Wissenschaft*

Introduction

ROMANS IS A MISSIONAL DOCUMENT through and through.[1] Paul was the first great international missionary of the church, sent by God to the gentiles. He writes from Corinth, where he established the faith with Prisca and Aquila;[2] to Rome, the hub of his world, a place he had wanted to visit multiple times. No doubt, Paul realized that for Christianity to truly flourish, it would have to take root in its purest form in the center of his world. Even if the worst happened and he died in his forthcoming trip to Jerusalem and never made it to Rome, he could die knowing that he had said what he needed to say to them. The gospel is the key theme in the letter, slanted toward matters of righteousness, faith, and culture. His letter calls the church to the gospel of grace through faith with an inclusive vision of a church without elitism, motivated to welcome the world into a new humanity.

Many studies of Paul's mission have been attempted, and that is commendable. However, very few have focused only on the whole letter to the Romans and read it from a missional perspective.[3] Thus, it is justified to devote a whole monograph to mission in Romans considering its setting in the life of Paul and the spread of the gospel in the first century.[4] A look at Romans strictly from a missional perspective is what this book seeks to do.[5] While other passages in Paul will be touched on, the mission-vision of Paul in Romans is allowed to speak.[6] My prayer is that it will be

---

1. "The Letter to the Romans is a missionary charter. . . . Missionary identity, foundation of the mission to the nations, content of the gospel as proposed by this mission, grand coordinates of the missionary strategy—such, then, in a few strokes, is the content of the Letter to the Romans." Legrand, *Unity and Plurality*, 121, 124.

2. As this is a work on the Pauline Epistles, I will use Prisca (*Priska*) rather than the diminutive Priscilla (*Priskilla*), which Luke prefers.

3. Some include Hultgren, *Paul's Gospel and Mission*; Toney, *Paul's Inclusive Ethics*; Panjikaran, *Paul's Concept of Mission*; Magda, *Paul's Territoriality and Mission Strategy*.

4. "A nonmissional reading of the Bible is crippling the church in the West, often fostering self-centeredness and thwarting a missional encounter with our culture." Goheen, "History and Introduction," 27.

5. This seeks to address this apt critique: "Many biblical scholars go on about their business paying little attention to this insight of their missional colleagues: that mission is a central category in the Bible that needs to be taken seriously if our interpretation is to be faithful." Goheen, "History and Introduction," 3.

6. Another area of study that will not be included is Jewish patterns of mission prior at the time of

INTRODUCTION

welcomed into the enormous corpus of literature on Romans as a unique contribution highlighting aspects of mission essential to us today. May it help some believers today to be more committed and faithful to God's mission through understanding Romans better.

For this work, mission is defined as God's vision for the dissemination of the gospel throughout the world so that people have the opportunity to become believers in God and his Son and be joined to God in Christ, the establishment of communities of believers in given geographical locales (churches), and ultimately, the liberation of the world from evil, sin, death, and its consequences. I tend to use "evangelism" of the verbal aspect of this mission, albeit recognizing that the distinction between evangelism and mission is tenuous. I include in mission aspects like social justice, social transformation, ecological mission, signs and wonders, and assume that mission involves the whole life of the church. I will endeavor to show how Romans informs our understanding of such things and how they fit together.

As a male European NT scholar from an evangelical, charismatic, reformed, and evangelistic background, I carry all sorts of biases and blindspots. While I apologize for these and my failure to see them and acknowledging that I am as prone to them as anyone else, I hope my contribution will inspire and challenge others who are determined to take their place in God's mission. I look forward to hearing the critiques and affirmations to deepen my own understanding.

I write as an NT scholar who delights in grappling with the original languages and who can tend to neglect secondary literature. Still, I will seek to add voices of support and question other views as I encounter them. I do not see this work as the final say on Romans and the mission of God but would be delighted if it led to a range of other such writings deepening the understanding of the church in our troubled and challenging times.

Part one of the book focuses on the usual background matters such as the Roman world, the development of the Roman church, authorship, date, provenance, and the integrity of the letter. Special notice is taken of the genre and purpose of Romans as both have critical missional implications.

In part two, Paul's gospel in Romans is considered. Is Romans Paul's gospel? How does he structure the letter and present his material? I will argue that the letter is not a Gospel like the four Gospels, but is a letter in which Paul draws on and articulates aspects of the gospel to those already Christians with an eye on future mission. As such, the core underlying aspects of his "gospel presentation" are explored. The question being asked is, "What is Paul's gospel in Romans?" It is up to us to consider how it might inform proclamation today.

Christ and Paul. See for discussions, Ware, *Mission of the Church*, 23–55; Dickson, *Mission-Commitment*, 11–85; Köstenberger and O'Brien, *Salvation to the Ends of the Earth*, 56–70; Bird, *Crossing Over Sea and Land*. My view is that while there may have been some isolated impulses toward proactive proselytizing in Judaism (Matt 23:15; Rom 2:19; 2 Macc 9:17; Josephus, *Ant.* 20.34–35; Philo, *Spec.* 1.320–23; m. 'Abot 2:14; Horace, *Sat.* 1.4.138–43), the approach was primarily centripetal.

Introduction

Part three considers the proclamation of the gospel. The scope of Paul's mission and its completion is explored. The question of who is to engage in mission is considered from a range of perspectives. A range of questions is then discussed. What is the place of signs and wonders, social justice and transformation, and ecological mission? Themes considered include patronage and hospitality, the sovereignty of God and mission, prayer, the State and mission, culture, Israel, ethics, and doing theology and mission.

Part One

Background Matters

The focus of this part is on those things in the background of Romans that should be discussed before zeroing in on the content of the gospel and its proclamation as found in the letter. The setting is critical for understanding Romans from a missional point of view. What becomes clearly observable is the missional intent of the letter.

1

Rome and the Roman Empire

AT THE TIME OF THE WRITING of Romans, the Roman Empire had been expanding for 250 years. The Empire dominated the world around the Great Sea (The Mediterranean), where the biblical story unfolds. It included large parts of Britain (Britannia), all of Syria, Egypt, northern Africa to Mauretania, and vast areas of Europe bounded by the Rhine and Danube Rivers.

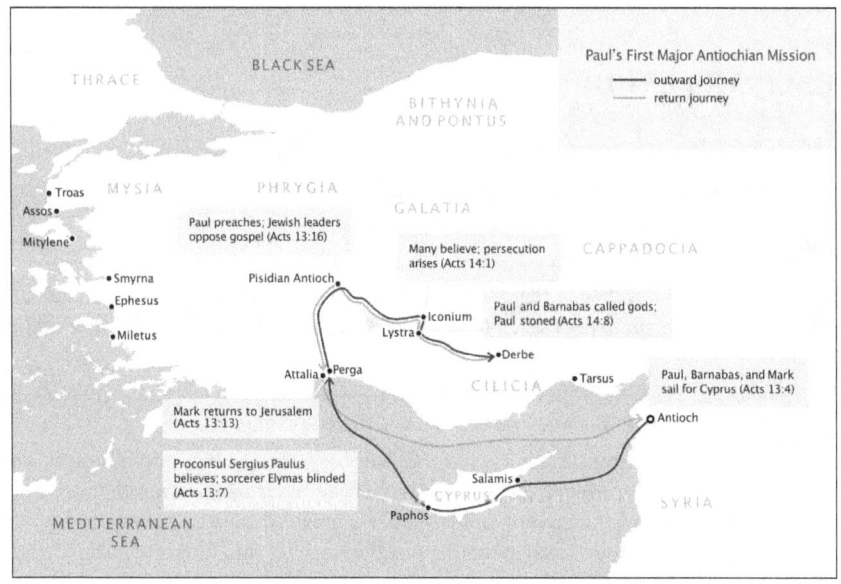

The Roman Empire at the time of Augustus

Before Rome was established, from 3000 BC, Italy was populated by various tribes of Indo-Europeans from Europe and Asia gathered in small towns and farming communities. These included the Etruscans who, according to Herodotus, were from Asia Minor or what we call Turkey.[1]

1. See Encyclopaedia Britannica's entry "Etruscan." They note that Dionysius of Halicarnassus

PART ONE: BACKGROUND MATTERS

The origin of the Italian city-state Rome (Greek: *Rhōmaios; Rhōmē*) is shrouded in legend and uncertainty. Tradition links Rome's origin to a Trojan warrior, Aeneas, who purportedly founded Rome on its "Seven Hills"[2] after the fall of Troy in 1100 BC and, more commonly, to Romulus and Remus in 753 BC.[3] The twins were supposedly abandoned on the Tiber bank and raised by a she-wolf. Whatever the truth of such tales, Rome began as a small farming settlement of Latins near the famous Tiber River. It developed with Sabines and Latins and became *Roma quadrata* ruled by kings over a Senate of heads from families and clans.

MONARCHIAL PERIOD

In the Monarchical Period, Roman citizens (*Quirites*) formed the *Comitia Curiata*, which was both a religious body and municipal council. Around 600 BC, the Etruscans seized the Tiber crossing and then drained large areas of land between the hills to create the forum area as a civic center. They also paved large portions of the city, built a city wall, buildings, and homes, and developed legal and religious systems. Among the buildings on the Capitoline Hill was a temple for Jupiter,[4] Juno,[5] and Minerva.[6] Under the Etruscans, Rome dominated central Italy, and in the Republican period, many Etruscans played a prominent role.

REPUBLICAN PERIOD

The Republican Period began in 510/509 BC (*res publica*) after unified Latin tribes drove out Tarquinius Superbus, the last king of Rome (534–509 BC). This rebellion

---

thought they were indigenous Italians.

2. "The Palatine, the Capitoline, the Aventine, the Caelian, the Esquiline, the Viminal, and the Quirinal. There are really more than seven hills; they are flat-topped spurs." See Comfort and Elwell, "Rome," 1141.

3. One guide on a trip to Rome noted that while this is a legend, it is likely that there was a Romulus behind Rome somewhere. The line between fact and fiction is somewhat blurry.

4. Jupiter was the "the heavenly father" who parallels Zeus. He was the "lord of heaven, the Romans attributed to him power over all the changes in the heavens, as rain, storms, thunder and lightning." He was pictured with a thunderbolt in his hand. He provided rain, protected the city, brought victory, oversaw present and future, had authority over the law, and, with Juno, guarded marriage. See Schmitz, "JU'PITER," 569–60.

5. Juno ruled heaven as queen, matching the Greek goddess Hera. She protected marriage and women throughout their whole lives. She enabled childbearing and was the guardian of finances. There was a temple of the Capitoline hill where coins were made. The month of June is named after her and is supposedly a good time to marry. See Schmitz, "JUNO," 658–59.

6. Minerva was daughter of Jupiter. She was a virgin and linked to Athena. She was creative and invented things like numbers, was the patroness of arts and trades, including "painting, poetry, the art of teaching, medicine, dyeing, spinning, weaving, and the like." She was supposedly an awkward and clumsy but intelligent person; someone today we might call a geek. She gave wisdom in war and invented musical instruments. See Schmitz, "MINERVA," 1090.

established the republic with Rome under the rule of an oligarchy of nobles for almost 500 years.[7] During the Republic, there were two classes of citizens: the patricians (ancient family nobility) and the plebeians (lower class). There were two judges to decide civil cases for the patricians, and the plebeians elected tribunes as political officials. This period included contention between these two classes.

After some time of instability, by the mid-fourth century BC, Rome was unified internally and took control of the whole area of Italy. There were attempts at invasion by the Gauls (mod. France, 390 BC) and the Latin league. However, after 400 BC, Rome was able to extend its power into southern Greece and was greatly influenced by the Greek language and culture. Rome's policy included the absorption of other peoples, the granting of citizenship, and treating them as allies. Such things would play an important role in its later evangelization. Rome was able to gather strength because the Greeks and Phoenicians were preoccupied with the Persian Empire.

Based on a universal draft of citizen-soldiers, Rome gathered a strong army that was well trained. They built roads and aqueducts to supply water to their cities. A treaty was signed with the Ptolemies in Egypt in 273 BC. Rome then turned its attention to Phoenician Carthage in Africa, fighting for a century in three Punic wars, beginning in 241 BC and lasting for around a hundred years.[8] By 200 BC, after finally overcoming Carthage, Rome became ruler over Carthage, Spain, Northwest Africa, Southern Gaul, Sicily, Sardinia, and Corsica. They also took over two major Punic traditions, including the building of enormous plantations worked by slaves and the use of cruelty and force such as crucifixion to control those under its rule. Rome was also heavily influenced by Greek culture with which the Romans were enamored.[9]

Rome's influence was organized into provinces with senatorial proconsuls to ensure justice, peace, order, and taxation. Some areas were organized as provinces and others governed by local client kings subject to the Roman Senate (e.g., Palestine under the Herods). This expansion drew in great wealth to Rome, and so it developed into a cosmopolitan, economic, mercantile power.

During this time, substantial tenement houses[10] appeared that became overcrowded slums (as urban apartments often do). Such places were later ideal for the spread of the gospel. After serving in the military, many Romans and Italians moved

---

7. "Oligarchy" is from the Greek compound *oligarkhía* combining *oligos* ("a few") and *'archō* ("to rule, to govern, to command"). Power is held with a few from the elite based on status, ranks, wealth, family, and religious power. Usually, a few politically powerful families control the State.

8. The three wars ran from 241 to 206 BC; 218 to 201 BC (Hannibal's Defeat); and 149 to 146 BC.

9. E.g., Watson, "Greece and Macedon," 426: "Although Greece was no longer a political power, its cultural influence—the Hellenization begun by Alexander the Great—was a powerful force molding not only Palestinian culture but Roman as well. Greece continued as a cultural and intellectual center during the Roman period, being the location of choice for upper-class Romans to finish their formal education."

10. One guide noted on a trip to Rome that it was the Romans who introduced apartment living to the world. As I traveled Greece and Turkey, I saw that he was right, they are everywhere!

to Rome to enjoy the "good life." This influx contributed to the breakdown of the older *mos mairum* ("custom of the fathers/ancestors"), an upright mode of life.

By the mid-second century BC, Rome had many problems, including lawlessness and crime. Many lost their land to wealthy landowners for the development of plantations or through squandering wealth, and so a poor and unemployed mob developed. These people sold their votes gained through citizenry for patronage. This support was valuable to the ruling elite in a context with intense political rivalry for office. Late Republican Rome saw the ruling elite in constant contention in Senate, the political and legislative assemblies, and in the courts.

The justice system was rife with political manipulation with the use of false accusations and skilled oratory used to attack or defend the Senatorial nobility. Society was split between *Populares* (the people's supporters) and the *Optimates* (supporters of the aristocracy), with factions in the Senate using political and judicial manipulation to give or resist increased rights to the "common" people. Thus, all of Rome's citizens were swept up in factionalism.

> The urban poor clamored for more government supports, Italian allies claimed citizen rights, soldiers insisted upon mustering out benefits, and equestrian businessmen sought a more extensive role in determining fiscal policy. Roman society of the first century BC was segmented into special interest groups whose dictates threatened to destroy the entire community and nearly did.[11]

The military was reformed and forced military service for landowning citizens abolished. This change led to a professional army of soldiers who would serve anyone who would pay them. Money brought political and military power, shifting military power from Rome to individual commanders who could maintain allegiances through recompense. As a result, the military encroached further and further into politics.

There were three civil wars in the century before Christ. First, the "Social War" or "War of Allies" saw the defeat of some seceded Italian allies (*socii*). Second, a political struggle for control between Marius and Sulla in the 80s BC, with Sulla winning power briefly. Third, Julius Caesar fought Pompey and some senatorial oligarchs in the 40s. While Caesar was victorious, he was soon assassinated in 44 BC.

During the late Republican period, there were many building projects (temples, public buildings) and steady population growth. In the period before his fall, Pompey had captured Syria/Palestine, and in 63 BC, stormed Jerusalem, giving Rome control over Judah, Samaria, and Galilee through the period of the NT. This Roman victory ultimately linked the Romans to Jesus, who would become critical in its future story.

Caesar's victory came due to his befriending of tribal peoples on Rome's borders. He was instituted as *dictator perpetuus* ("Dictator Forever") in 49 BC, and this saw the addition of much of Western Europe (e.g., Gaul [France] and Britain) to Roman rule by the first century. It also brought an end to the conflict between *Optimates* and

---

11. Hall, "Rome," 831.

Populares and political stability. After his murder in 44 BC at the hands of Cassius and Brutus, the Roman state was again in political chaos.

After a period of conflict seeing the defeat of Antony and Cleopatra in the Battle of Actium in 31 BC, Julius Caesar's adopted son and heir, Octavian Caesar, took control, with a Senate full of his supporters. Octavian shared power with the Senate and was awarded the title "Imperator Augustus Caesar" and lifetime authority to rule and semi-divine honors. He introduced the *principate* that appeared to follow the old republican order and the power of the Senate but, in reality, brought the republic under Augustus's control. Augustus ruled only a few provinces directly, including Judea, because of its troublesome nature. It was under his reign that Jesus was born and lived his early years.

ROMAN EMPIRE

The period of the Roman Empire ran from 27 BC for 500 years to AD 476. After its inception, propaganda assisted its acceptance by the populace, and a century of peace ensued (*pax Augusta/Romana*). The period was a time of relative political stability, good government, and material prosperity. Rome was transformed with a proliferation of new buildings, temples, and monuments of marble. Augustus boasted of finding Rome built on brick and leaving it made of marble. He built temples for Apollo, "the divine Julius" (Caesar), a senate house, a basilica business hall, a marble speaker's platform, two new forums named after Caesar and Augustus, and a new library near the palace. Augustus restored Rome's ancient religions, building many temples. He built a palace for himself on Palatine Hill.

After Augustus (27 BC–AD 14, cf. Luke 2:1) came a series of Julio-Claudian rulers. These emperors included Tiberius (AD 14–37, cf. Luke 3:1; in whose reign Jesus ministered), Caligula (AD 37–41), Claudius (41–54, cf. Acts 11:28; 18:2), and Nero (who reigned at the time of Romans, AD 54–68).[12] While these emperors, aside from Claudius, were exceedingly indulgent, Rome had a period of relative peace, and the empire expanded. These emperors added to the splendor of Augustus's Rome, including palaces of Tiberius and Caligula, baths, arches, theaters, the Circus Maximus, Circus Nero, a wall, and aqueducts.[13]

At the time of Paul, Rome was the center of the Empire and in full growth. With the influence of Burrus and Seneca still strong, Nero had yet to go off the rails. Rome housed the emperor, senators, administrators, military personnel, and priests. The aristocracy of Rome was highly international due to the Empire's influence and lived in suburban villas and country estates. The Caesars furnished the center of the city with

---

12. Cf. Acts 25:10–12; 27:24; 2 Tim 4:16–17. Unless otherwise stated, all biblical quotes are from the ESV translation.

13. See Hall, "Rome," 829–32; Packer et al., *Nelson's Illustrated Manners and Customs*, 163–74.

astonishing public buildings. The general population experienced generous economic subsidies and entertainment. The city was a hub for the arts and literature.[14]

There were about a million people in the city, mostly gentile. Of these, about half were slaves.[15] They were crowded in multi-story tenement blocks (*insulae*). It was cosmopolitan, with people from every corner of the empire including, of course, Italians, Greeks, and a significant population of people from the East, including Jews.

Rome was highly religious. Roman religion was bound to the State. Priests and priestesses were expected to divine the will of the gods and advise the Senate. It was not uncommon for emperors to visit Delphi in Greece to gain prophetic wisdom from the priestess, the Pythia (oracle of Delphi). Priests purified areas (*augures*), set the calendar, and established religious law (*pontifices*), ensured war was conducted in a religiously correct way (*fetiales*), and kept and interpreted the Sibylline scrolls. Priests also had a role in urging the acceptance of foreign religions in Rome. In the Republican age, the haruspices or "soothsayers" were organized in a priestly college. They divined the will of the gods from the entrails of sacrificial animals.

In Rome, as in the whole ancient world, religion was central to life and the idea of a secular world was nonexistent. There were the dominating temples of Jupiter, Juno, and Minerva on the Capitolium Hill.[16] There were also temples of Saturn (Sun), *Castores* (Castor and Pollux, the *Dioskouroi*, the twin sons of Zeus), Vesta (hearth); offices for the *pontifices* (priest council), and the *rex sacrorum* ("kings of sacred things," a religious post). The whole Forum and Palatine complex was a glorious sight. In homes were found shrines to deceased family members (*lares*) and the gods of the family cupboard (*di penates*).

It was expected that all Romans participated in religious rituals. Adherence to the rituals would ensure peace with the gods (*pax deorum*, cf. 5:1–2). Aside from vocational priests, synagogue, and church, people did not choose to join a religious group by faith. Some *collegia* (guilds) were named after deities, and people joined by common occupation or ethnicity. Roman religion was legal in its focus, and Paul's references to moral law (2:14–16), Torah (3:21; 10:4), and political law (13:1–7) may reflect this in some way. Romans also considered the gods rational. The emphasis on rationality in Romans could indicate that Paul wrote with this in mind (cf. 1:28; 7:20–24; 12:1–2).[17]

Rome's attitude to foreign religions was one of suspicion. No religion could be introduced without the official approval from the Senate. However, Rome was open to accepting them if it was perceived to be of value to the State. For example, the cult of

---

14. See Dunn, "Romans," 850; Judge, "Rome," 1027. The metropolis is about four times bigger than any other city in the Roman Empire; it was not until the industrial era about two centuries ago that any city was that large again.

15. See Easton, "Rome," estimates 1.2m with half slaves.

16. See Reasoner, "Rome and Roman Christianity," 851.

17. See further from Reasoner, "Rome and Roman Christianity," 851–852.

Rome and the Roman Empire

Asclepius (*Aesculapius*), the god of healing, was permitted into Rome in 293 BC to resolve a plague. A temple was dedicated to Asclepius on the island of Tiber, January 1, 291 BC. The State religion remained dominant, however, and the idea of a particular religion or god as found in Judaism and Christianity (or Islam) was not a Roman notion at all. Such exclusivism clashed with Roman (and Greek) polytheism. Suspicion over foreign religions was more pronounced after 186 BC. The cult of Bacchus (cf. Dionysus, the god of wine) was forbidden because adherents engaged in night crime and political conspiracy (*orgia, bacchanalia*). The ban led to violence and crime. The chaos fostered a negative attitude to new religions that were seen as a threat to public order. However, there was a proliferation of eastern religions establishing themselves in Rome. Juvenal famously records:

> the Syrian Orontes has long since poured into the Tiber, bringing with it its language and customs. (Juvenal, *Sat.* 3.62–63; Tacitus, *Ann.* 15.44.4)

Judaism and Christianity, which are both monotheistic, and their people were viewed with suspicion. Jews in Rome can be dated from 139 BC. Pompey brought back a significant number of Jewish captives as slaves in 62 BC after his conquest of Judea the previous year.[18] Most of these were freed, and it appears that by 59 BC, their numbers were significant (Cicero, *Flac.* 66). Jews supported Julius Caesar against Pompey in the civil wars beginning in 49 BC and mourned his death in 44 BC (Suetonius, *Jul.* 84.5). They were granted exemption from Julius Caesar's dissolution of the collegia in the 40s and retained the right to assembly (Josephus, *Ant.* 14.214–215). This right was ratified by Augustus (Suetonius, *Aug.* 32.1).

Augustus also ensured Jews were not missed out in the monthly distribution of food (Philo, *Legat.* 158), which also indicates that some were poor and were Roman citizens.[19] In 4 BC, 8,000 Roman Jews supported the Judean embassy from Judea to petition against Archelaus (Josephus, *J.W.* 2.80–83; *Ant.* 17.299–303). It is estimated that there were 40,000 Jews in Rome at the turn of the first century; a substantial number. Julius Caesar, followed by Augustus, accorded Judaism the status of *religio licita* ("legal religion"). This legal privilege enabled them to observe the Sabbath and principal feast days, gather at the synagogue, eat kosher food, and maintain ritual purity and other rituals.[20]

However, while there was tolerance, Jews also experienced racial persecution, something necessary for understanding the situation in Rome at the time of Paul. Before Christ and Paul's ministries, Jews were expelled from Rome twice, probably for

---

18. For a discussion, see Wiefel, "Jewish Community in Ancient Rome," 85–101.

19. If you visit Rome today, you can still find the Jewish quarter beside the Tiber. Interestingly, the site of Paul's supposed house in Rome is in the neighboring suburb, which makes good sense.

20. There are many kosher restaurants and butchers in this area still today.

Jewish proselytism. The first was in 139 BC (Valerius Maximus, *Fact. ac dict.* 1.3.2). The second was in AD 19, perhaps due to many Romans being attracted to Judaism.[21]

In AD 31, Tiberius reaffirmed the traditional legal rights of the Jews (Philo, *Leg.* 2.159-61) and allowed their return in numbers. Philo writes in AD 38:

> the great section of Rome on the other side of the Tiber is occupied and inhabited by Jews, most of whom were Roman citizens emancipated (Philo, *Leg.* 2.155).

In AD 41, Cassius Dio reports that there were so many Jews in Rome that Claudius withdrew their rights to assembly (*Hist.* 60.6.6.). It seems that there were strong links between Jerusalem and Rome with warm relationships between Herod Agrippa I and Caligula and Claudius in particular. Acts 28:21 indicates correspondence moving between Rome and Jerusalem. Evidence from thousands of Jewish catacombs in Rome suggests ten to thirteen synagogues in existence in the first century AD. It is probable then, at the time of Paul, that there were 40,000-50,000 Jews in Rome, including slaves and freedpeople.[22] It was among these Jews that Christianity took root (see part one, chapter 2).

Through all this, strongly negative attitudes to Jews can be found through the literature of the time. Cicero described Judaism as a "barbaric superstition" that was opposed to all that is Roman (Cicero, *Flacc.* 28.66-69). Seneca called Jews an "accursed race."[23] Tacitus was particularly anti-Semitic, stating that "the Jews regard as profane all that we hold sacred . . . (and) permit all that we abhor" (Tacitus, *Hist.* 5.4.1).[24] Christianity was up against it from the first!

Significantly, in AD 49,[25] Suetonius records the third expulsion of Jews because of unrest among the Roman Jewish community over Christianity. He writes of Claudius that he "expelled Jews from Rome because of constant disturbances at the instigation of *Chrestus (impulsore Chresto)*" (Suetonius, *Claud.* 25.4). It is most likely that *Chrestus* here refers to "Christ" (*Christos*) and so indicates significant disturbances within Judaism with people debating whether or not Jesus is the Messiah. Notably, this expulsion is mentioned in Acts 18:1-2, where Luke explains that Prisca and Aquila were in Corinth because "Claudius had commanded all the Jews to leave Rome." While these were not permanent measures, they demonstrate that Judaism was viewed with intense suspicion and, at times, direct enmity, in Rome.[26]

---

21. See Tacitus, *Ann.* 2.85.5; Suetonius, *Tib.* 36; Dio Cassius, *Hist.* 57.18.5.

22. See Dunn, "Romans," 852; Dunn, *Romans* 1-8, xlv-liv.

23. Seneca the Younger, *De Superstitione* (see *GLAJJ* 1:431).

24. Dunn, *Romans* 1-8, l.

25. A small minority of scholars link this to AD 41 (Cassius Dio, *Hist.* 60.6.6). However, as Dunn notes, this is unlikely. Dunn, *Romans* 1-8, xlix. Thus, there were two actions by Claudius. The first limited their right to assembly; this one was expulsion.

26. Reasoner, "Romans," 852.

This expulsion also indicates that Christianity began in Judaism, was probably initially linked to the synagogue, and made significant inroads into Judaism in its first two decades. For an emperor to make such a move, Christianity must have been making a real impact. At the death of Claudius in AD 54, the edict was rescinded, and Jews were able to return. Among them were Prisca and Aquila, and they were in Rome when Romans was written (16:3, see further part one, chapter 2). Other Jews mentioned in Romans 16 may have done the same.[27]

Dunn notes another vital piece of Roman background that affects Romans 13:6–7 concerning the payment of taxes. Tacitus records that in AD 58, there were vociferous public complaints about indirect taxation. Nero responded by proposing their abolition; however, under pressure from the Senate, he backtracked. As such, taxation was an issue at the time in Rome, and it could be that Jews and Christians were unsure of whether to continue to pay taxes. Paul's response to the Roman Christians is to encourage them to continue to pay them to avoid bringing attention to themselves (see further part three, chapter 24).[28]

At the time of Romans then, early in the reign of Nero and before his later lunacy, the city was densely populated, prosperous, bustling, and impressive. The emperor dominated life as did the gods and goddesses of the pantheon. There were thousands of Jews in the city. Christianity was flourishing. The relationship with Jews and the burgeoning Christian movement was tenuous and dangerous (see part one, chapter 2).

---

27. Jews include Epaenetus (possibly), Mary (possibly), Andronicus and Junia, Aristobulus's household, Herodian, and Rufus.

28. Dunn, *Romans 1–8*, liii–liv.

2

The Initial Development of the Roman Church

PENTECOST

IN ACTS 2:10, Luke records that there were visitors from Rome (*hoi epidēmountes Rhōmaioi*) at Pentecost (March–April, AD 30 or 33). These would have included some of the forty-thousand-or-so Jews in Rome who were pilgrims to Jerusalem to celebrate Pentecost and the Feast of Weeks. Some may have witnessed the aftermath of the coming of the Spirit and were among the three thousand converted and baptized on that day. If so, very early Jewish converts took the gospel back to Rome. As the first converts were Jews, it is likely then that Christianity grew in the context of Judaism with evangelization primarily within the synagogue. It was likely expected that new converts were circumcised and submitted to Torah (Judaizing). Paul assumes knowledge of the LXX in Romans, which supports a Jewish Greek setting for the development of the church.[1]

POSSIBLE CHURCH PLANTERS

Two people we know of from this time are Prisca and Aquila (Acts 18:2). If we are right to read in Romans 16:7 that Andronicus and Junia are apostles (see part three, chapter 16), they may have been key figures in the planting of the Roman church.[2] If the church was planted by Pentecost pilgrims and converts, this could also provide a link to Peter. However, there is no evidence of Peter's (or Paul's) direct influence in the establishment of the church despite Roman Catholic claims.

If the link to Pentecost is correct, then the church in Rome was probably established as early as AD 30 or 33, almost at the same time as the explosion of growth in

---

1. Dunn, *Romans 1–8*, l.
2. See also Bauckham, *Gospel Women*, 172–81; Witherington and Hyatt, *Paul's Letter*, 388–89.

the Jerusalem church. Thus, by the time of Romans, the church would be around a quarter of a century old.

GROWTH

Initially, the church was made up of Pentecost pilgrims and converts made within Roman Judaism, proselytes (Acts 2:11),[3] and some God-fearers.[4] It is likely then that the Roman church initially had a pronounced Jewish feel with any new converts being already Jews, proselytes, or God-worshipers who were then circumcised and expected to adhere to Jewish boundary markers such as eating and purity rituals, and Sabbath. The Claudian edict suggests a strong Jewish core to the church.

Other Jewish influence on Roman Christianity may have come through some of those expelled from Jerusalem by Saul in AD 33 or 35. Over time, through natural movement in and out of Rome, other converts would have entered the Roman church, perhaps influenced by Christianity in Syrian Antioch and Paul's law-free ministry in Syria and Cilicia. Similarly, the gospel no doubt spread into "purely" gentile families. However, this is unlikely to have been significant in the first period in the development of the Roman church. It was initially very Jewish. It was probable that it was viewed within the city as a branch of Judaism.

THE CLAUDIAN EDICT

Claudius's edict in AD 49 appears to have been a turning point in Roman Christianity.[5] As noted above, Suetonius records that the Jews were expelled from Rome at this point, due to conflict within the Jewish community over Christ (also Acts 18:1–2). The edict suggests that the Jewish community in Rome was greatly affected by the Jewish Christian proselytizing. Conflict must have spilled over to the point that the Emperor was moved to act. If so, this suggests a contentious period and significant Christian influence within Roman Judaism.

The effect of this would have been stunning. The expulsion of Jews would have included Christians, such as Prisca and Aquila. If the Roman church had to this point been primarily Jewish in orientation and led by Jewish converts, as is likely, this would have dramatically decreased its size and shifted its emphasis and leadership structures in the direction of a Christianity influenced by Greco-Roman culture. The expulsion could have led to a new impulse toward gentile evangelization.

---

3. Proselytes were gentiles fully converted to Judaism, such as Nicolaus in Acts 6:5 (see also Acts 2:11; 13:43).

4. These were gentiles attracted to Judaism who had not fully converted, e.g., Lydia (Acts 16:14); Titius Justus (Acts 18:17, see also Acts 13:43, 50; 17:4).

5. See on the edict, Wiefel, "Jewish Community in Ancient Rome," 92–94.

PART ONE: BACKGROUND MATTERS

THE JERUSALEM COUNCIL

Significantly, this expulsion fell just after Paul's mission to Cyprus and South Galatia (Acts 13—14) and coincided with the Jerusalem Council at which the Jerusalem Church ruled against Judaizing perspectives on the faith (Acts 15).[6] The expulsion from Rome may have led to intentional attempts from outside of Rome to send gentile Christian support to the Roman Christians to assist the church in crisis (see Rom 16). With general mobility and perhaps intentional attempts to support Rome, Roman Christianity was no doubt influenced by a Pauline law-free perspective of the faith to a renewed level. It is plausible that Paul wished to come to Rome on his second Antiochian mission journey as he traveled with Silas, one appointed to bear the letter.[7] Not able to travel there as he and Silas were Jews, Paul may have sent gentile converts to Rome for this purpose. Luke may have fulfilled this role as he stayed in Philippi as Paul and his team moved on.[8]

GENTILIZATION

It is also likely that in the period after the expulsion, the church became less Jewish in orientation and may have had an increased impact on the Roman non-Jewish population. One can see how the church may have multiplied in this period, with many Greeks and Romans coming to Christ and the church becoming transformed by a gentile perspective of the faith. This process of "gentilization" may have significantly changed the face of Roman Christianity very quickly indeed with less concern for Jewish cultural markers like circumcision, Sabbath, eating rituals, purity, eating meat from temple butcheries, and the like. The gospel was probably increasingly contextualized toward a Roman perspective. The Roman influence may well have brought into the church some of the problems one sees in Corinth and Philippi with Roman attitudes affecting the ethics and values of the church, e.g., selfish ambition, conceit, a love of rhetoric and philosophy (wisdom), rivalry, factionalism, immorality, and debauchery.[9] The ethical sections in Romans 12—13 may have some of these things in mind.

---

6. Those who accept a chronology that integrates Acts and the thirteen-letter corpus usually come up with a date of AD 48 or 49 for the edict. See, e.g., Alexander, "Chronology of Paul," 122–23; Witherington, *Acts of the Apostles*, 82.

7. Rom 1:11; Acts 15:22, 27, 32, 40.

8. We know this from the shift in pronouns from "we" to "they" between Acts 16 and 17, i.e., Luke remained. He rejoined Paul in Acts 20:1–6. On the "we sections" or "we passages" as evidence of Luke as a traveling companion of Paul, see the section "'We' Sections of Acts," in Dicken, "Luke."

9. See the emphasis on humility throughout Rom 12 (esp. vv. 3, 10, 16) and Rom 14–15 (esp. 14:3–5, 10, 13; 15:1). See the critique of false teachers in Rom 16:17–18. See also 1 Cor 1–4 and Phil 2:1–8.

CONFLICT

The return of the Jews would have begun around AD 54 when Claudius died, and the edict lapsed. How many returned we cannot know. Still, it seems fair to assume from the impact of Christianity on Judaism and the city before AD 49 that a significant number returned to Rome, including the founders of the church and other significant leaders. It is possible that on their return, the once-dominant Jews were now in numerical disadvantage, perhaps significantly so.[10] Whether or not this is the case, it is probable at this point that there were ideological and cultural clashes. Fights for power could even have ensued. The church would have had to rediscover its identity.

Romans itself gives evidence of cultural issues. Throughout, Jew and gentile matters are highlighted. In Romans 1:16, the gospel is for the Jew first and also the gentile. In Romans 1–3, Paul carefully demonstrates that both Jews and gentiles are separated from God through sin. In Romans 4, he draws from Abraham's story truth for both Jews and Greeks. He parallels Adam and Jesus in Romans 4. Romans 7 focuses on the law and human failure. In Romans 9–11, he addresses the place of Israel in the purposes of God. Paul is careful in Romans 11 to address gentiles and warn them of the dangers of arrogance and unbelief. In Romans 14–15, he addresses conflict within the Roman church over food rules and Sabbath rituals. Throughout the letter, he draws on the language and ideas of the OT.

Romans 14–15, in particular, suggests a clash between Jews returning to Rome and their more conservative position colliding with a freer perspective on food and special days. In Romans 16, the extent of Paul's greetings indicates that there are many in Rome he knows, possibly some with a law-free perspective. In Romans 16:17–18, there is evidence of some who are divisive and causing division. They appear excessively libertine and concerned for rhetoric.

There were probably many church centers in the metropolis of Rome. Such a proliferation is perhaps indicated in Paul's greeting in Romans 1:7 where, unlike in other Pauline letters which are directed to a church or churches, Romans is addressed to "all those who are in Rome beloved of God, called to be holy ones."[11] As noted above, the extent of Roman Christianity among the Jewish population would have required an assortment of church gathering points before the rupture. Some of these perhaps were initially associated with synagogues. However, the Claudius expulsion and clashes we read of in Acts indicate that these synagogues experienced tremendous conflict with many Jewish Christians driven out into homes.

As the gospel spread among the Romans, this would have grown, although probably centered on Jewish homes. After the return of the exiles, when Paul writes in AD 56–58, there would have been numerous Roman "churches" scattered across the city. Many of these would have been established in the homes of wealthy Romans who had

---

10. Dunn, *Romans 1–8*, liii.
11. Compare with 1 Cor 1:2; 2 Cor 1:1; Gal 1:2; 1 Thess 1:1; 2 Thess 1:1.

converted. Others would have been in Jewish homes as before the rupture. No doubt, the flavor of these gatherings varied, and control would have been difficult. It would seem that there was a range of such groups including traditional Jewish Christianity based perhaps on a Petrine perspective (Pentecost), some with a Pauline libertine perspective, based perhaps on the Jerusalem Council (e.g., Prisca and Aquila, cf. 16:3), and some with a licentious and libertine perspective (cf. 6:15; 16:17–18).

PAUL'S FRIENDS IN ROME

Paul's greetings in Romans 16 indicate he knows many people in Rome. Some would have been traveling Romans he met on his trips. Some would be people who had now settled in Rome. Perhaps, as suggested above, some of these were sent there. These names give insight into such groups (perhaps six), although probably all from the pro-Paul law-free perspective in that he greets them:

- Prisca and Aquila's church (16:3–5): A thoroughly Pauline perspective.
- Andronicus and Junia? (16:7): Possibly Jewish and the church founders.
- Aristobulus (16:10): This group may have had a Jewish perspective as he may have been a grandson of Herod the Great and brother to Agrippa II.[12]
- Narcissus (16:11): This famous Greek name was common among slaves and freedmen and may indicate a pro-Pauline law-free group.
- Asyncritus, Phlegon, Hermes, Patrobas, and Hermas (16:14): These names fit the Roman gentile context and would indicate a law-free group.
- Philologus, Julia, Nereus, his sister, Olympas (16:15): Again, these fit the Roman gentile context as above.

As up to half the population of Rome was made up of slaves, there were undoubtedly many slaves in the Roman church. Dunn notes that fourteen of the twenty-four named have common slave names.[13] The presence of slaves is confirmed in Suetonius's account of Nero's killing of many Christians by crucifixion, which was not usually used to kill freedpeople (Suetonius, *Nero* 16.2; 19:3).[14] The phrase *hoi ek tōn Aristoboulou* (those from [who belong to] Aristobulus), is indicative of some from the servile classes (cf. 16:10–11).[15] Some of these slaves may have been well-to-do, perhaps eight of the twenty-four named.[16] By the time of Nero's persecution in the mid-60s, there is

---

12. Dunn, *Romans 9–16*, 895.
13. Dunn, *Romans 1–8*, lii.
14. "As a result, Roman citizens were generally spared this form of execution. Crucifixion was largely reserved for those of lower status and, above all, for dangerous criminals and insurrectionists." Green, "Crucifixion," 198.
15. Dunn, "Romans," 896.
16. Dunn, *Romans 1–8*, lii.

evidence that Christianity (*Christiani*) was viewed separately from Judaism (Tacitus, *Ann.* 15.44.2–5; Suetonius, *Nero* 16.2). It is described as a new "sect" (Suetonius, *Nero* 16.2) with "a great multitude" (1 Clem. 6:1), of "vast numbers" whose deaths provided long hours of "entertainment" (Tacitus, *Ann.* 15.44.2–4).

3

Authorship, Date, Provenance, Integrity, and Genre

AUTHORSHIP

THE AUTHORSHIP OF ROMANS is not in dispute. It is seen by the vast majority (if not all) scholars as one of the undisputed Paulines. Unlike about half of Paul's letters that mention other senders and possible writers, Romans names Paul exclusively as the author (1:1).[1] However, the letter is the only Pauline letter that explicitly references the use of an amanuensis (secretary) in its production: "I Tertius, *who wrote the letter*, greet you in the Lord" (16:22, cf. 1 Pet 5:12, emphasis and translation mine).[2] Clearly, then, Paul utilized a secretary in the production of at least one of his letters. The content and importance of Romans suggests this was transmitted by dictation rather than a higher degree of freedom sometimes granted amanuenses.[3]

The commendation that begins Romans 16 indicates that the letter-courier was likely Phoebe. She is described as a sister and deacon (masc. *diakonos*) of the church in Cenchreae, one of the ports of Corinth. She is also a generous benefactress of Paul and others. With her responsibility to read out the letter and add an explanation to it, she may have participated in its production. At the least, she would have been familiar with it and Paul's intentions. As such, Phoebe was an important early church female leader (see also part two, chapter 16).

---

1. Compare Gal 1:1; Eph 1:1; 1 Tim 1:1; 2 Tim 1:1; Titus 1:1.

2. This verse could read "I Tertius, who wrote the letter in the Lord, greets you." However, Dunn, *Romans 9–16*, 910 rightly notes that *en kyriō*, "in the Lord," should be taken with *aspazomai*, "I greet" with Tertius using the style of Paul in the greetings of vv. 8, 11, 12, 13.

3. Mounce, *Romans*, 21.

DATE AND PROVENANCE

Romans 15 gives us clues as to its date. Paul speaks in Romans 15:25 (cf. 15:31) of his impending departure (*nyn* = "now") to Jerusalem, having gathered money from Macedonia and Achaia. This passage places Romans at the end of Paul's three months in Achaia after leaving Ephesus and traveling through Macedonia and onto Corinth on his third Antiochian missionary journey (Acts 20:1–3). This trip is the Jerusalem Collection journey with Paul traveling from Corinth to Jerusalem to deliver the collection. The material in Acts 20:1–3 coincides with the data of Romans 15:25–33. Luke records that Paul initially desired to travel directly to Syria from Achaia; however, due to a death threat, he switched his plan to travel back through Macedonia, to Troas, and then to Jerusalem by ship along the coast of Asia Minor.

Mounce notes that it must have been written between AD 51–52 when Gallio was as proconsul of Corinth (Acts 18:12, 14, 17) and the replacement of Felix by Festus in AD 59 as procurator of Palestine (Acts 24:27).[4] This material suggests Romans was written sometime in the period AD 54–58.[5] Scholars are divided concerning where to place Romans in this time frame. Barrett and Morris date the letter in Jan–March 55.[6] More commonly, scholars prefer winter or spring of 55–56 or 56–57.[7] Dunn hedges his bets with 55–57.[8] He suggests that it is most likely written late 55/early 56 or late 56/early 57.[9] Mounce opts for 56,[10] Bruce early 57,[11] Sanday and Headlam, among others, propose 57–58,[12] and Guthrie suggests 57–59.[13] As noted above, this corresponds with taxation being an issue in Rome around 56–58 (Tac. *Ann.* 13). We can be confident that Corinth is the point of origin as indicated by the reference to Phoebe (16:1), Gaius (16:23; 1 Cor 1:14), Erastus (16:23, see also 2 Tim 4:20);[14] and resonances

---

4. Mounce, *Romans*, 25.

5. Mounce, *Romans*, 25.

6. Barrett, *Epistle to the Romans*, 5; Morris, *Epistle to the Romans*, 6–7.

7. Kümmel, *Introduction to the New Testament*, 311; Robinson, *Redating*, 55. Bruce, *Paul*, 324; Cranfield, *Critical and Exegetical Commentary*, 2:12–16.

8. Dunn, "Romans," 838. Some date it as early as 55 and others as late as 58. There is a small minority who follow Lüdemann who dates Romans in the early 50s (51/52) or Knox (54/55); however, these are unlikely. See Lüdemann, *Paul, Apostle to the Gentiles*, 263; Knox, *Chapters in a Life of Paul*, 86.

9. Dunn, *Romans 1–8*, xliii. Similarly, Cranfield, *Critical and Exegetical Commentary*, 1:16.

10. Mounce, *Romans*, 26.

11. Bruce, *Epistle*, 11–12.

12. Sanday and Headlam, *Critical and Exegetical Commentary*, xiii; Black, *Romans*, 20; Fitzmyer, *Romans*, 87; Byrne, *Romans*, 9.

13. Dodd, *Epistle of Paul*, xxvi.

14. This Erastus may be linked to the inscription found in Corinth in 1929 near the theater reading [—] *Erastus pro aedilit[at]e s(ua) p(ecunia) stravit*, "Erastus, in return for the aedileship, laid the pavement at his own expense." While some scholars reject this being from the same person, a good number, like Jewett and Kotansky, accept this is a first-century inscription and correlates with 16:23. He is thus likely "a rich freedman with Roman citizenship who held a responsible office in the city administration." Jewett and Kotansky also postulate that he is mentioned at the conclusion of Romans

between 1 Corinthians 8—10 and Romans 14—15.[15] As such, we can surmise Romans was written between AD 54 and 58 from Corinth. Specifying further the exact date and provenance is not of great importance for this study.

ROMANS 16 AND THE INTEGRITY OF ROMANS

One area of dispute is the placement of Romans 16 in the letter. Some, particularly in the past, have argued that ch. 16 was not original to Romans. This is important, as it has implications for the arguments concerning mission in this book. There are reasonable reasons for believing that the passage may not have been a part of the initial form of the letter.

First, in the second and third centuries, the letter circulated in a shorter form lacking Romans 15—16. Second, some manuscripts place the final doxology of Romans 16:25-27 after Romans 14. Also, P46, the oldest text of Romans (c. AD 200), puts the doxology at the end of Romans 15. Some witnesses have the doxology at the end of *both* chapters 14 and 15.[16] Some witnesses omit "in Rome" in Romans 1:7,[17] 15.[18] These omissions fall in the manuscript that ends at Romans 14:23. Finally, the "grace" found in Romans 16:20 occurs in some manuscripts at *both* Romans 16:20 and 16:24, with some texts omit it at one or the other. Some witnesses place Romans 16:24 after 16:27.

Thus, it is argued that the original Romans ended after chapter 14. Some argue that Paul wrote a shorter form of Romans for general circulation, excluding reference to Rome in Romans 1:7, 15, and that Paul adapted it for the Romans adding these references along with Romans 15—16.

While no extant manuscripts exist in the shorter form, for these reasons, we can surmise that there was a fourteen-chapter version of Romans in existence in the early church. First, earlier Latin chapter headings to Romans list Romans 14:22-23 as Romans 50 and the doxology as Romans 51 with no mention of Romans 15—16. Second, Origen mentions that Marcion dropped out everything from Romans 14, including the doxology. Finally, the church "fathers" Irenaeus, Cyprian, and Tertullian do not quote from Romans 15—16.

Other scholars argue that Paul wrote Romans 1–15 as a general letter. A copy was later sent Ephesus with Romans 16 added—a letter of commendation for Phoebe. This idea takes seriously the Chester Beatty Papyrus (P46) that places the doxology after Romans 15:33. Additionally, it is argued that it is unlikely that Paul would have sent so

---

because he supports Paul's mission to Spain and would alleviate any concerns about the subversive nature of a mission to a sensitive colony. Jewett and Kotansky, *Romans*, 981–83.

15. Dunn, *Romans* 1–8, xliii.
16. See Metzger, *Textual Commentary*, 471.
17. See G 1739mg 1908mg itg Origen.
18. See the bilingual G and the Latin translation of Origen.

Authorship, Date, Provenance, Integrity, and Genre

many greetings to a city he had never visited. On the other hand, as he stayed over two years in Ephesus, he would have known many people in Ephesus, and so it fits better.

Furthermore, evidence places Prisca and Aquila in Ephesus and not Rome. For example, the reference to Prisca and Aquila in Romans 16:3–5 is argued to fit better in Ephesus as in 1 Corinthians 16:19 (written from Ephesus), there is a reference to the church meeting in their house. Moreover, the couple was left in Ephesus in Acts 18:18–19, where they invited Apollos to "their home" (Acts 18:26). Again, in the Pastorals, Paul asks Timothy to greet them in Ephesus (2 Tim 4:19). Placing them in Rome between these events would mean they owned homes in both Rome and Ephesus and moved between Rome and Ephesus freely. Also, supportive of Ephesus is the reference to Epaenetus in Romans 16:5 as "the first convert to Christ in the province of Asia,"[19] where Ephesus was capital. Furthermore, the reference to false teachers in Asia could indicate the problem in Ephesus (Acts 20:28–30, see also 1–2 Tim). Finally, the grace of Romans 15:33 ("Now may the God of peace be with you all. Amen," translation mine) may function as a letter ending.

While these arguments have convinced some scholars (particularly earlier ones), most now hold that Romans is a sixteen-chapter letter.[20] However, doubt remains concerning the authenticity of the final doxology, primarily due to its varied placement.[21] Hence it is probable that rather than an original shorter general letter lengthened for specific use in such places as Rome, early readers shortened the original longer letter to Rome for general use.

There are many reasons for this conclusion:

1. The peace blessing in Romans 15:33 is not used as an ending in Paul's letters. Instead, he uses "grace" (*charis*).[22] The grace benediction comes in Romans 16:20.

2. The *de* (both, and, now) in Romans 15:1 and Romans 16:1 suggests continuity from the previous in both cases.

3. Even more clearly, Romans 14:23 does not read as a letter ending.

4. The long list of greetings is not a surprise considering the centrality of Rome, mobility, and perhaps the intentional sending of leaders to the Roman church after the Claudian expulsion. Their naming may also relate to Paul's trip to Spain;

---

19. Literally, "the first fruit (*aparchē*) of Asia into Christ."

20. Donfried summarizes thus: "it is far more probable that chapter 16 was an integral part of Paul's original edition of Romans and not a late addition for some postulated, but unprovable, letter of commendation to Ephesus." Donfried, "Short Note on Romans 16," 52. Donfried states: "Any study of Romans should proceed on the assumption that Rom. 16 is an integral part of the original letter." Donfried, "False Presuppositions in the Study of Romans," 104.

21. Throughout, I am working with the assumption that the doxology is original, and its various placements are because of different versions sent to different places. For a discussion see part three, chapter 10.

22. See 1 Cor 16:23; 2 Cor 13:12; Gal 6:18; Eph 6:23; Phil 4:22; Col 4:17; 1 Thess 5:28; 2 Thess 3:17; 1 Tim 6:21; 2 Tim 4:21; Titus 3:15; Phlm 25.

he hopes some will join him. Furthermore, there is no other example of such a long series of greetings to a church *Paul did* plant. The closest to the list in Romans 16 is Colossians 4, another church Paul did not plant (Col 1:7).

5. Romans 16:1–23 reads as an epistolary conclusion rather than a standalone letter.

6. The greeting from "all the churches of Christ" (16:16) fits Rome best, where the church was of considerable size and geographical spread (see also "all the churches of the gentiles," 16:4).

7. The personal comments in Romans 1:8–13 fit Rome better than Ephesus or a general letter.

8. The discussion of "weak" and "strong" in Romans 14—15, in light of the historical setting and Jew/gentile relationships in Rome, fits the Roman context better than a general statement.[23]

9. It is not surprising that Aquila and Prisca would have had residences in both Ephesus and Rome as they probably left behind a home when they fled at the edict. According to Luke, they had a home in Corinth (Acts 18:3), suggesting that they were wealthy and purchased properties for their businesses frequently. First Corinthians finds them in Ephesus, after which they would have returned to Rome sometime after Claudius's death. They may have retained their residence in Ephesus and returned at the time of 2 Timothy almost ten years later.

10. A number of the names mentioned in Romans 16 may be cross-referenced to other parts of the NT or other writings (esp. Rufus [cf. Mark 15:21], Aristobulus, Narcissus, Ampliatus, and Nereus).

We can be confident then that Romans is a sixteen-chapter letter from Corinth to Rome, a city he longs to visit at last. Shorter versions found are those created in the early church for general use. The fourteen-chapter version is likely the work of Marcion, who removed them due to the many OT references. Marcion may also have dropped "in Rome" from Romans 1:7, 15, due to the antagonism toward him in that city.[24]

THE GENRE OF ROMANS

More important for this study is the genre of Romans. Romans is undoubtedly written with the desire to persuade the Romans to agree with Paul's perspective. As will be demonstrated, "the gospel" is a core matter in the letter. Hence, his strategy in his letter is important as it gives us a sense of how Paul proclaimed his message on at least this one occasion. Romans is a long letter and as Longenecker says,

---

23. Dunn, *Romans 9-16*, 884; Mounce, *Romans*, 28–30.
24. See Mounce, *Romans*, 27; Dunn, *Romans 9-16*, 884.

Authorship, Date, Provenance, Integrity, and Genre

Romans is not, as is Galatians, a "rebuke and request" letter. Nor is it a strictly "paraenetic" or "hortatory" letter, as is 1 Thessalonians; nor a mixed letter of "response, exhortation, and advice," as is 1 Corinthians; nor a letter of "friendship and advice," as is Philippians; nor simply a letter of "recommendation," as is Philemon.[25]

A range of views of Romans is canvassed across the literature. Moo considers Romans a letter that is also "treatise" or "tractate" and rejects further genre identification.[26] Wuellner sees Romans as a memorandum.[27] Wolter argues it is a friendship letter (which is strained as Longenecker states above).[28]

Some have considered Romans a *Lehrbrief*, "a literary epistle," written to instruct readers. However, this is too broad as all Paul's letters can be seen in this way.[29] Jewett and Kotansky describe it as an "ambassadorial letter of self-introduction."[30] Kim suggests it is a "letter of recommendation" for Paul himself.[31] Longenecker rightly rejects that Romans is a letter of recommendation as, while such letters of recommendation were common, they were written with high praise on behalf of others, which hardly fits Paul's self-description in Romans.[32] Stirewalt considers Romans a "letter essay."[33] Berger sees Romans as a didactic letter from a teacher to students.[34] Bultmann years ago argued it was diatribe, and although scholars reject this designation for the whole letter,[35] it is agreed that Paul used the technique throughout Romans.[36]

Others interpret Romans from the perspective of ancient Greek rhetorical models: forensic (defense and accusation),[37] deliberative (exhortation and dissuasion),[38]

---

25. Longenecker, *Epistle*, 12.
26. Moo, *Letter to the Romans*, 12–14.
27. Haacker, "Exegetische Probleme des Römerbrief," 1–21.
28. Wolter, *Die Brief an die Römer*, 57–61.
29. Longenecker, *Epistle*, 12.
30. Jewett and Kotansky, *Romans*, 44–46.
31. Kim, *Form and Structure of the Familiar Greek Letter*, 150–238.
32. Longenecker, *Epistle*, 12.
33. See Stirewalt, "Form and Function of the Greek Letter-Essay," 147–71; see also Longenecker, *Epistle*, 14.
34. Berger, "Hellenistische Gattungen im Neuen Testament," 1334–35.
35. *PDBS* 36: Diatribe was an ancient rhetorical form used especially by Stoics and Cynics that is marked by "short ethical discourses, rhetorical questions and dialogues, and argumentative speech, in which the author or speaker debates with an imaginary person (interlocutor) in order to instruct the audience" (see Rom 6:1—4; 12—15; Gal 5—6; Eph 4—6).
36. Bultmann, *Der Stil der paulinischen Predigt*.
37. "Forensic speech defends or accuses someone regarding past actions." Hansen, "Rhetorical Criticism," 822:
38. Hansen: "deliberative speech exhorts or dissuades the audience regarding future actions." Hansen, "Rhetorical Criticism," 822.

epideictic (affirmation, praise, blame),[39] or protreptic (hortatory).[40] More recently, a good number of scholars argue that Romans lacks some of the critical aspects of forensic, deliberative, and epideictic rhetoric: an *exordium, narratio,* and *propositio.* Nor does it defend Paul's apostleship and gospel or counter false teaching as in Galatians or 2 Corinthians.[41] They consider that it fits closest to the protreptic model of rhetoric. If so, it is intentionally written as "a type of address intended to win converts and attract people to a particular way of life."[42] This description fits with Paul's missional and pastoral intent in the letter.

It is argued Paul adapts the three main sections of *protreptikoi logoi* (exhortatory messages) with his own material: a negative section (1:16—4:25); a positive section (5:1—8:39); and a hortatory section (12:1—15:13). Longenecker suggests Paul added a fourth focused on Jewish remnant theology, 9:1—11:36.[43]

It is indeed challenging to fit Romans precisely into any of these schemes. Paul also used a range of literary conventions and devices "to get his message across."[44] Still, seeing Romans as an adapted form of protreptic rhetoric seems to fit the letter well. It may also have resonances with an ambassadorial letter; written by the kingdom's leading missionary to the gentiles preparing for his trip to Rome and Spain. As such, Paul, in writing Romans, is seeking to convince the Romans of his understanding of the gospel. His message is genuinely missional with the gospel at its core. He wants the Romans to believe in that same gospel, to imbibe it and live it, and to share it. He wants their support of and active participation in his mission to Spain.

---

39. Hansen: "epideictic discourse affirms communal values by praise or blame in order to affect a present evaluation." Hansen, "Rhetorical Criticism," 822. See, e.g., Wuellner, "Paul's Rhetoric of Argumentation in Romans," 128–46.

40. Fiore: "an exhortation or persuasion to a commonly agreed upon good, associated with *paraklēsis* or exhortation." Fiore, "Parenesis and Protreptic," 5:163. See for a discussion of Romans as protreptic, Aune, "Romans as a Logos Protreptikos," 278–96.

41. Longenecker, *Epistle*, 15.

42. Longenecker, *Epistle*, 14. He notes Berger, *Formgeschichte des Neuen Testament*, 217; Stowers, *Letter Writing in Greco-Roman Antiquity*, 112–14, 128; Aune, "Romans as a Logos Protreptikos," 91–124; Guerra, *Romans and the Apologetic Tradition*, ix; Bryan, *Preface to Romans*, 18–28.

43. Longenecker, *Epistle*, 15–16.

44. Moo, *Letter to the Romans*, 14. See also Schreiner, *Romans*, 23–25.

4

The Purposes of Romans

SCHOLARS REGULARLY DEBATE the primary purpose of Romans.[1] The traditional view is that Romans is "a compendium of Christian doctrine" (Melanchthon),[2] i.e., a timeless expression of the Gospel. Those who argue that Romans 15 or 16, or both chapters are additions to a general letter would be supportive of this view. Bornkamm advocated it being Paul's "last will and testament."[3]

However, these days only a small minority of scholars and many popular-level readers take such perspectives on Romans. Rather than Paul's gospel in general terms, or his final words prior to death,[4] most scholars now view Romans as a letter with a context, and so is a purposeful presentation relevant to Paul's situation and that of the Romans.[5] It is tailormade for the moment rather than a general for-all-time gospel treatise.

The occasional nature of the letter becomes apparent when we consider things that Romans does not cover in detail. These include Paul's pre-Christian life and conversion (cf. Gal 1:14–15), a detailed exposition of the resurrection of Christ (cf. 1 Cor 15), the Lord's Supper (cf. 1 Cor 11), the return of Christ and the day of the Lord (cf. 1 Thess 4—5), marriage and family relationships,[6] eating idolatrous food (cf. 1 Cor 8, 10), tentmaking and matters of money,[7] tongues and a range of other gifts (cf. 1 Cor

---

1. The classic discussion is Donfried, *Romans Debate*.

2. Melanchthon, *Loci communes* of 1521, 2.1, 7.

3. Bornkamm, "Letter to the Romans," 2–28. The view that 1:18—11:36 is Paul's defense in Jerusalem with the collection is unwarranted. Jervell, "Letter to Jerusalem," 53–64.

4. Especially in that Paul had a lot of living to do in his own mind, wanting to come to Rome and then Spain.

5. "Any study of Romans should proceed on the initial assumption that this letter was written by Paul to deal with a concrete situation in Rome." Donfried, "False Presuppositions," 103.

6. Romans 7:1–4 uses the analogy of marriage rather than instructing the Romans concerning marriage.

7. Compare 1 Cor 9; 2 Cor 11–12; 2 Thess 3; Phil 4:10–19.

PART ONE: BACKGROUND MATTERS

12, 14), Christ's humiliation and exaltation (cf. Phil 2:6–11), or a household code (cf. Eph 5:21—6:9; Col 3:18—4:1). As such, there is much theology we have from Paul that Romans does not explore. It hardly qualifies as a theological treatise, systematic theology, or a compendium of his belief.

Rather than seek to find one overarching reason for Romans, it is better to recognize Romans was written for at least three specific and interrelated reasons, all of which are missional in one way or another.

PASTORAL PURPOSE

Romans is written by a Christian leader to a church and has a definite pastoral purpose; namely, to address theological and relational problems between cultural and theological groupings (Jews and gentiles) in the Roman church.

Contemporary Romans' scholarship recognizes that like all letters, Romans is written to address issues in the recipient church. With this in mind, it not likely that Romans is generated with concerns in Corinth or general concerns in the milieu.[8] Rather, Romans addresses differences in theology and praxis between cultural and theological groupings (Jew and gentile) in the Roman church (esp. chapters 9–11; 14–15). Romans then strengthens the case for the law-free gospel and ensures that the Roman church is well established. A strong church in Rome would ensure the future progress of the Christian movement. Christian mission requires unity, and by seeking to ensure harmony in the Roman church, Paul hopes to ensure that the Romans do not self-destruct into conflict but stand united, facing outward to ensure the gospel expands into the world to places like Spain.

Romans 14—15 contains instructions from Paul about how to resolve differences of opinion between the "weak" and the "strong" in the faith (14:1). The issue revolves around eating freely or merely vegetables (14:2). Paul's advice is to the Romans is to respect each other's viewpoints and allow each to live by their conscience in gratitude before the Lord on such non-essential matters as food and holy days (14:3–12). While Paul accepts that no food is unclean, he urges them not to allow such a trivial matter to cause others to fall. Rather, they should walk in love, peace, and edification as Jesus did himself (14:13—15:3).

The situation being addressed can be understood in one of three main ways. First, Paul is speaking of life in Christ in a general sense and citing a typical Christian situation, perhaps linked to his being in Corinth, where he is confronting issues of Christian preferences (cf. 1 Cor 8–10). Second, Paul is speaking of a minor problem

---

8. "There is very little history of religions or exegetical evidence that there were communities of 'the weak' and 'the strong' in Rome. Romans 14:1–15:13 is better explained as general Pauline paraenesis, which is adapted and generalized especially from Paul's discussion in 1 Cor. 8–10 and is addressed to a problem that may arise in the community." Karris, "Romans 14:1–15:13 and the Occasion of Romans," 65–84.

that he has heard about in Rome. Third, these chapters are the tip of the iceberg concerning wider dispute in Rome. Most recent scholars favor the latter view because, alongside this explicit matter in chapters 14 and 15, there is a real concern for matters of the law in Romans (3–7), Jew-gentile relationships, the place of Israel and gentiles in the purposes of God (9–11), and references to contention in the church (e.g., 16:17).

That being said, the exact nature of the matter is not explicit. Most likely, it is a clash between different views of the law without being the full-blown Judaizing heresy. If so, it is a disagreement between those with a Pauline view of freedom from Jewish custom and those who wanted to retain elements of Jewish religious custom (e.g., eating regulations, special days), not for salvation, but as a means of expressing their faith.[9]

Due to the increased gentilization of the Roman church after Claudius's expulsion, the Jewish outlook may have been marginalized. On their return, this would have led to a real culture-clash in the church. If so, the letter to the Romans may be, in part, addressing this clash. Some would see the presentation of the gospel leading to these chapters as slanted toward the issue of Jew-gentile relationships, and in chapters 14–15 we have a practical example of the issue at hand.

PRAYER PURPOSE

Romans is written by a Christian missionary who seeks help from God for the next phase of his mission. One aspect of this support is a request for prayer for his trip to Jerusalem to safely deliver the Jerusalem Collection and then travel unscathed to Rome and onto Spain (15:30–32):

> I urge you, brothers and sisters, by our Lord Jesus Christ and by the love of the Spirit, to contend along with me in prayers to God for me, so that I may be rescued from the disobedient in Judea, and that my service for Jerusalem may be acceptable to the saints, so that when I come to you with joy by the will of God, I might be refreshed together with you.[10] (Translation mine)

---

9. Moo, *Letter to the Romans*, 844 notes seven different views on the passage concerning the weak: 1) non-Christian Jews; 2) gentile Christians influenced by pagan festivals abstaining from meat and perhaps wine especially on "fast" days; 3) Christians practising an ascetic lifestyle; 4) Jewish Christians following Mosaic law for justification; 5) Jewish Christians who followed a "sectarian ascetic program as a means of expressing their piety"; 6) Jewish Christians like some Corinthians who rejected eating meat sold in the marketplace because of idolatry; 7) mainly Jewish Christians who due to Mosaic rules, refrained from particular food maintaining certain holy days. He rightly opts for 7; see his arguments on pp. 845–47).

10. On the textual question concerning whether it is the will of God, or of Jesus Christ, Christ Jesus, the Lord Jesus, which does not affect meaning, see Metzger, *Textual Commentary*, 474. He explains that the absence of *synanapausōmai hymin* in P46 and B may be due to copyist error. The replacement of *synanapausōmai*, by *anapsyxō* in D or *anapsychō* (both meaning "refresh") in G "appears to be a scribal simplification of the syntax."

This prayer request includes three things. First, Paul asks for prayer for protection from non-Christian Jews in Jerusalem who may cause him suffering as an apostate Jew. Second, he requests prayer that the believers in Jerusalem will warmly welcome the collection. Finally, the apostle asks them to pray that he will then be able to, at last, come to Rome. Implied also is that he makes his way to Spain via Rome.

Interestingly, Acts 21—28 tells us that most of these requests were answered positively in one way or another. Paul went to Jerusalem with the gift. He was delivered from great suffering at the hands of his people. He was then able to travel to Rome (albeit as a prisoner of the State). Whether he got to Spain is unclear (see further below).

Importantly, this prayer request is missional. Paul's visit to Jerusalem is an act of social justice he wants to complete. His trips to Rome and Spain are evangelistic in intent. He wants to strengthen the Romans and win more converts. He wishes to establish the faith in Spain. As will be discussed in part three, chapter 23, missional prayer is a crucial aspect of his strategy. As such, we should not downplay this purpose of Romans as secondary. For Paul, prayer is central to Christian mission. It is one of his core reasons for writing.

MISSIONAL PURPOSES

The above two purposes are missional to a degree. Romans also has two main explicitly missional purposes related to the shape and content of the gospel. First, it is written to delineate Paul's gospel in preparation for his visit to preach and teach in the city. Second, he writes to outline his gospel to prepare for his desire to use Rome as a base for further evangelization to the West and especially to Spain.

Paul's Mission to the Point of Writing Romans

By the time of the writing of Romans in the mid to late 50s AD, Jesus's blazing earthly ministry was some twenty-four years past. Culminating in his death and resurrection appearances, including to Paul, Jesus had rocked the Jewish world with his astonishing claims to be the Messiah and Son of Man. With his accursed death by being hanged on a cross, Jesus was largely rejected by Israel's people. However, beginning with 120 men and women, the church in Galilee, Samaria, and Judea had significantly expanded so that by the mid-50s, there were communities of faith sprinkled throughout the region. The gospel was also established in Paul's home area of Cilicia through his mission efforts. The movement had spread into Syria through people Paul had expelled from the church when he was Saul, the Pharisee and persecutor (Gal 1:21; Acts 9:30; 11:25–26).

The Purposes of Romans

By Romans, Paul was a seasoned missionary.[11] He was converted on the road from Jerusalem to Damascus.[12] After this experience that formed a crucial component of his transformation, through Ananias of Damascus, God and Christ commissioned him to be the apostle to the gentiles.[13] Martin cogently writes:

> This Damascus Road experience was decisive and determinative for Paul. His entire ministry was shaped by this initial experience. Always burned into his conscience from this time forward was the realization that he was 'a chosen vessel' to set the name of Jesus before the world.[14]

Paul's call and conversion catalyzed his mission. Hengel rightly states that: "With Paul, for the first time we find the specific aim of engaging in missionary activity throughout the world."[15] Since that time, in his initial years, he had engaged in mission to Arabia (Gal 1:21), Jerusalem (Gal 1:18–19; 2:1–10; Acts 9:28–29), Cyprus (Acts 13:4–12), and Cilicia and Syria (Gal 1:17).

---

11. For a summary of Paul's mission to the writing of Romans, see Barnett, *Paul, Missionary of Jesus*, 76–98, 134–58.

12. In terms of *believing* in God and religious commitment, Paul was not convert. However, he was converted to believing in *Jesus* and, in that God is now revealed in Christ, his transformation is a conversion. He was also converted to a new vocation of preaching this Christ. See for a discussion, Barnett, *Paul, Missionary of Jesus*, 54–75. He discusses the evidence and concludes: "Was Paul 'converted' as well as 'called'? The weight of the evidence from the book of Acts and the specific references, and the identifiable allusions in Paul's letters, leaves no doubt that the Damascus event represented a complete relational and moral turnabout that was accompanied by a radical new vocation as one commissioned to preach to the Gentiles to bring them into the divine covenant." Similarly, Nissen, *New Testament and Mission*, 102; Köstenberger and O'Brien, *Salvation to the Ends of the Earth*, 162.

13. Martin, "Missions in the Pauline Epistles," 83.

14. Martin, "Missions in the Pauline Epistles," 84.

15. See "Origins of Christian Mission" in Hengel, *Between Jesus and Paul*, 52.

Part One: Background Matters

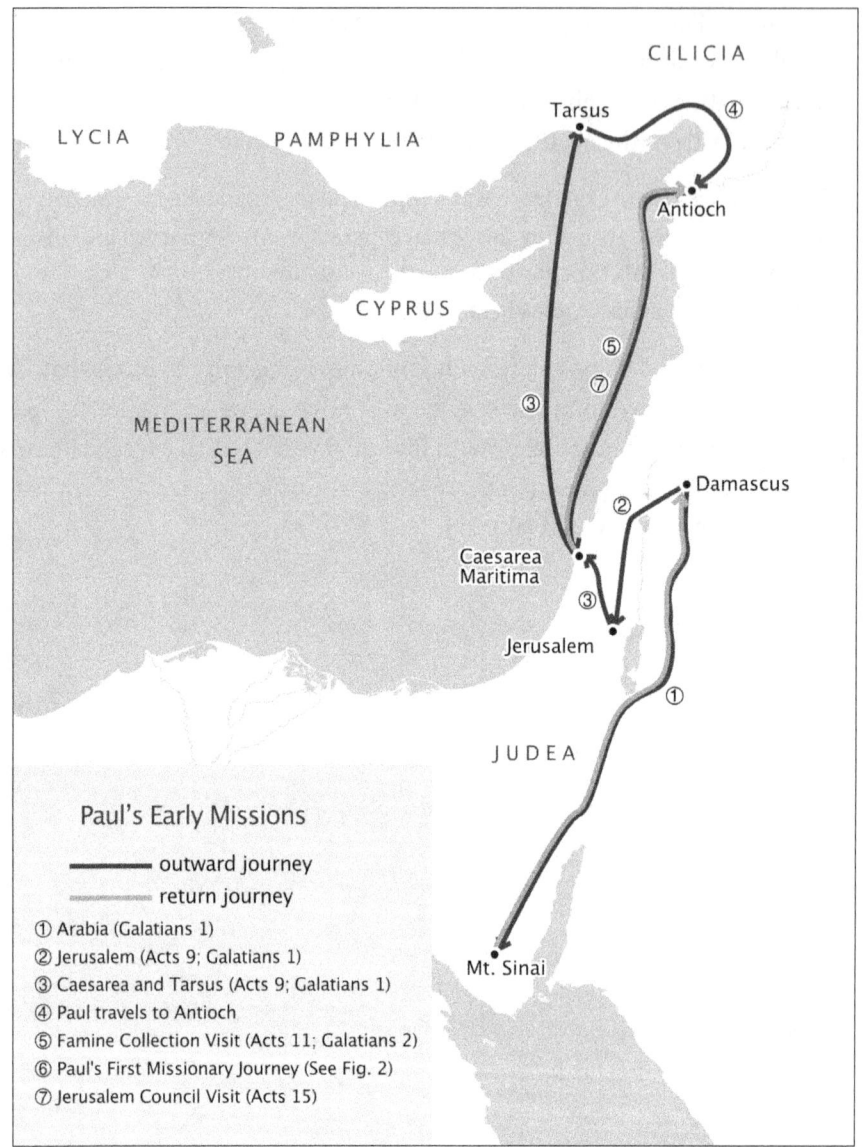

Paul's Early Missions

Having worked with Barnabas in Antioch for a while including a trip to Jerusalem with the first Jerusalem Collection (Acts 11:25–30), set apart by the Spirit, Paul had embarked with Barnabas and John Mark westward to evangelize the regions of Cyprus, Pamphylia, Pisidia, and Laconia (Acts 13:13—14:25).

The Purposes of Romans

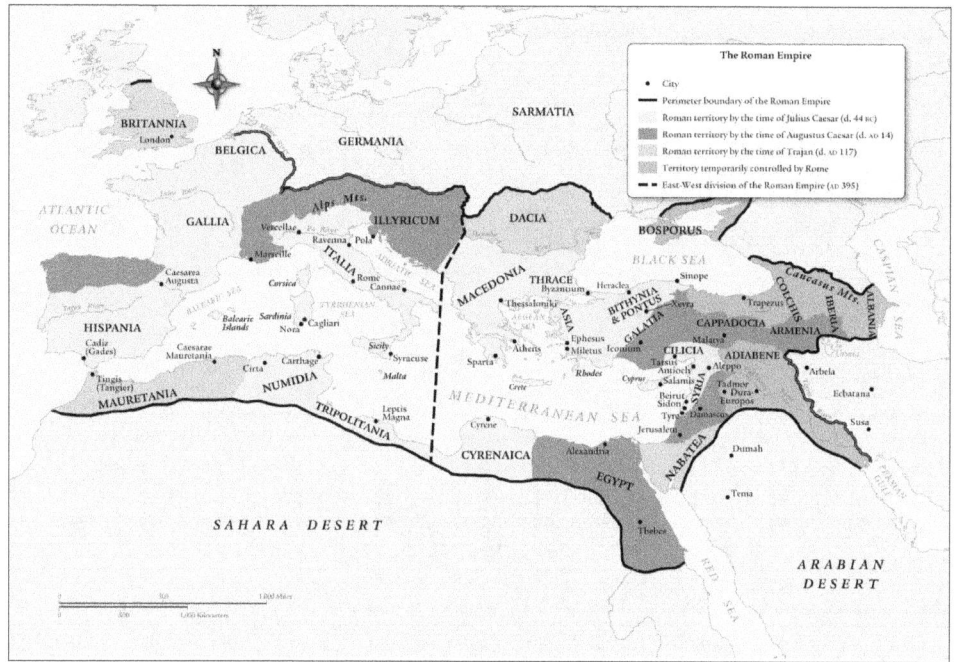

Paul's First Antiochian Mission

After the Jerusalem Council trip and then falling out with Barnabas over John Mark, Paul with Silas had then traveled through the Galatian churches reinforcing the message of Galatians with the Jerusalem Council letter. Led by God away from further evangelism in the western regions of Asia Minor, with Timothy having joined the team, Paul had traveled through Macedonia and Achaia making converts and establishing churches (Acts 16:11—18:17).

Part One: Background Matters

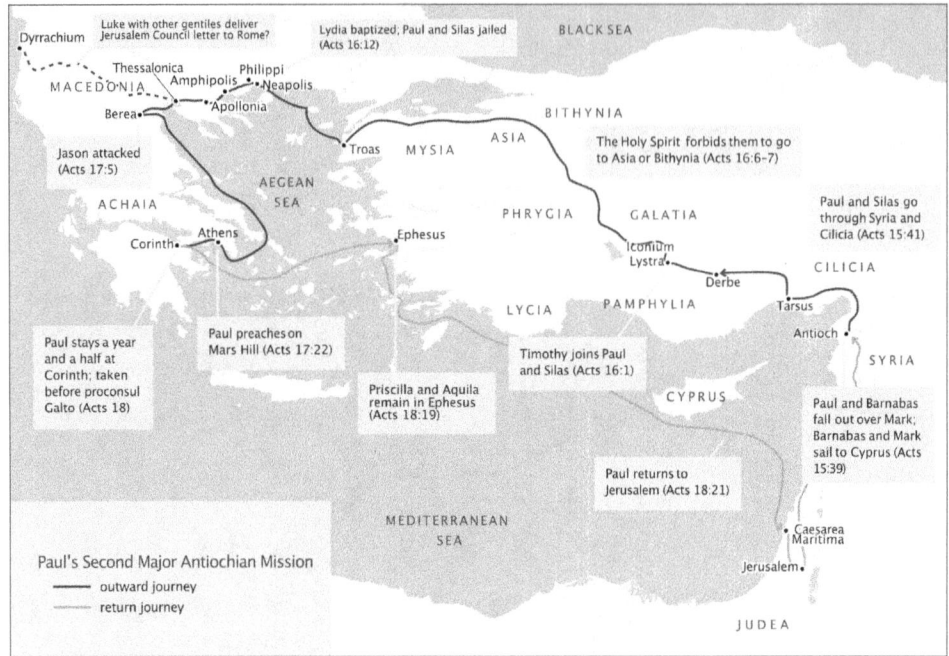

Paul's Second Antiochian Mission

Romans is written on his third great Antiochian mission through the regions previously established, strengthening the churches, evangelizing, and gathering funds for the Jerusalem church (Acts 18:18–21; 19:1–41, see figure below).

In modern terms, he had by this time, either directly, or through members of his team,[16] evangelized the Arabian area, Syria, Cyprus, Turkey, Greece, and areas of the Balkans to the northwest. He had traveled around 11,500 km (7,150 mi), seeking to yield in obedience to God by fulfilling his missional call.[17]

He had planted churches in the main centers of these regions, leaving these churches to continue the mission in their cities and hinterlands. He had written at least six missional letters, including Galatians, two to the Thessalonians, and three to the Corinthians (one of which is lost, cf. 1 Cor 5:9–13). Based on the revelation of Christ, he had developed the law-free gospel of grace and faith. In Syrian Antioch and through his letter to the Galatian churches, ravaged as they were by Judaizers, and with Barnabas at the Jerusalem Council, he had passionately asserted and defended this gospel (Acts 15:1–29).

---

16. The Lycus Valley churches were planted by Epaphras, probably during Paul's two years in Ephesus (Acts 19:10; Col 1:7; 4:13) and as argued, the churches in the western Balkans were evangelized by Luke with Macedonians (see esp. part two, chapter 5).

17. Overall, assuming Paul made it to Spain, Schnabel estimates Paul traveled 25,000 km (15,000 mi) by land and sea. By the time of his third Antiochian mission, he had traveled some 8,000 km (5,000 mi). At the time of his writing, he is in Corinth after traveling about 11,500 km (7150 mi) to this point of his career. Schnabel, *Paul the Missionary*, Table 1.2, Paul's Travels; Schnabel, *Early Christian Mission*, 2:1197–99.

The Purposes of Romans

Romans was penned by Tertius on Paul's behalf (16:22) when the apostle was domiciled in Corinth at the home of a certain Gaius. Gaius himself is a product of Paul's mission, baptized by Paul on his first visit to the city from autumn of AD 50 to spring of 52 (1 Cor 1:14). He was a wealthy man and early church benefactor demonstrated by his hospitality in a home big enough to house the whole Corinthian church (16:23).[18]

Paul is with others from the city, including the local politician Erastus, Quartus (16:23), and a range of other coworkers including at least Timothy, Lucius, Jason, and Sosipater (16:21). Timothy, of course, was also a missionary, having joined Paul in Lystra before the evangelization of Corinth on the second Antiochian mission (ca. AD 49–50, Acts 16:1–3). Indeed, in his first letter to the Thessalonians (AD 50–51),[19] Paul describes him as an apostle (1 Thess 2:6). He is also a "coworker," indicating his active missional engagement (16:21; Phlm 1). Timothy had worked with Paul up to the point of the writing of Romans and would do so beyond Paul's death.[20] Lucius could be Lucius of Cyrene (Acts 13:1),[21] Luke,[22] or, as is likely, another Lucius.[23] Jason could be the Thessalonian (Acts 17:5–9).[24] Jason may have been part of a team that delivered the Jerusalem Council letter to Rome (see part two, chapter 5). Sosipater could be Sopater the Berean mentioned in Acts 20:4.[25]

The presence of these coworkers suggests Paul is in Corinth during the three months covered by Acts 20:3. The year is likely AD 57, although some argue for a few years earlier or a year later (see part one, chapter 3). More important than the date is Paul's intent. He is on what has traditionally been called his third missionary journey, but what is, in reality, his eighth mission.[26]

---

18. Some confuse him with Titius Justus of Acts 18:7 (e.g., Moo, *Letter to the Romans*, 951), but this is pure speculation.

19. Bruce, *1 and 2 Thessalonians*, xxxv.

20. To the time of Romans, see Acts 17:14–15; 18:5; 19:22; 1 Thess 1:1; 3:2, 6; 2 Thess 1:1.

21. Sanday and Headlam, *Critical and Exegetical Commentary*, 432.

22. "But identification with Luke (Λουκᾶς), mentioned in Col 4:14; Phlm 24; and 2 Tim 4:11, and regularly taken to be the author of Luke-Acts, is by no means impossible." Dunn, *Romans 9–16*, 909.

23. This *Lucius* is a Jew, whereas Luke is a gentile (Col 4:10–14). Paul always spells Luke's name *Loukas*. Schreiner, *Romans*, 807.

24. Schreiner, *Romans*, 807.

25. Byrne, *Romans*, 460.

26. His trips include 1) Arabia; 2) Jerusalem; 3) Cilicia; 4) Syria (Antioch); 5) South Galatia (his so-called "first missionary journey"); 6) Jerusalem (the Jerusalem Council); 7) South Galatia, Macedonia, and Achaia (his so-called "second missionary journey").

Part One: Background Matters

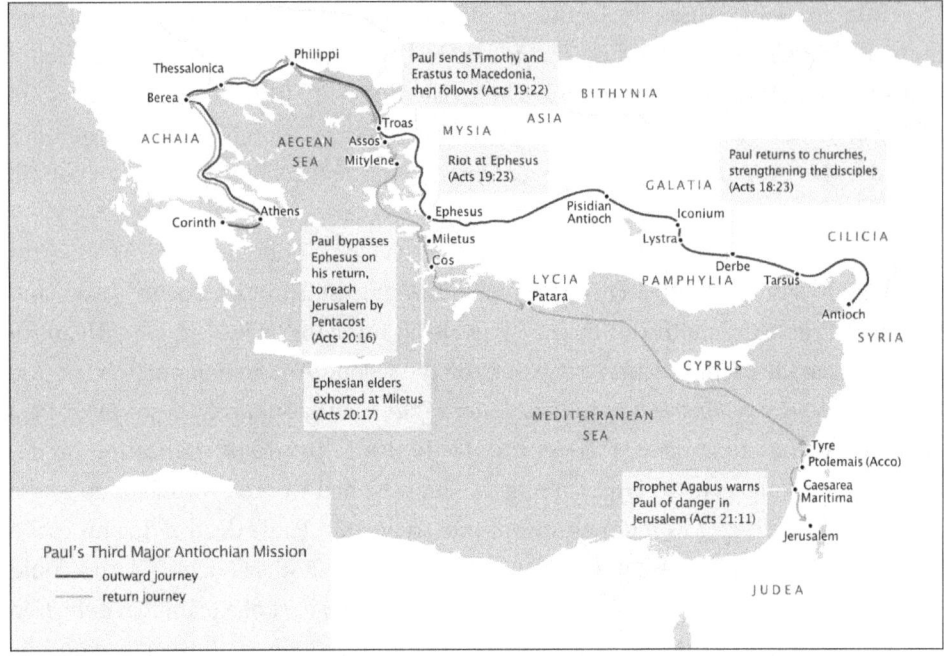

Paul's Third Antiochian Collection Mission

The purpose of his trip is threefold. First, as this is Paul, whose call was to preach the gospel (1:4–5, 14–15; 1 Cor 9:16), as they traveled, he and others under his lead (e.g., Epaphras, Col 1:7; Timothy and Silas, 2 Cor 1:19) engaged in evangelism and planted churches. The most significant evangelistic work on this trip was his time in Ephesus, where Paul and his coworkers evangelized the western regions of Asia Minor in three years (Acts 19).

Second, as was his practice, Paul strengthened the churches previously planted (1:11; Acts 15:41; 16:5).[27] Third, emulating his first financial collection for Jerusalem from Antioch (Acts 11:27–30), and in response to their injunction to "continue to remember the poor" (Gal 2:10, my translation), he had gathered money for the Jerusalem church from the churches of Galatia, Asia, Macedonia, and Achaia.[28] The apostle writes on the verge of leaving Corinth with church representatives and coworkers to Jerusalem. He will follow up the writing of Romans with more mission. Hence, the missional purposes are critical to understanding Romans. In that vein, Howell writes of Romans,

> Romans is first and foremost a written declaration of the self-revelation of God in the person and work of Jesus Christ. But Romans is no abstract

---

27. See also 1 Cor 4:17; Eph 6:22; Col 4:8; 1 Thess 3:2–5.
28. Rom 15:28–30; 1 Cor 16:1–4; 2 Cor 8–9; Acts 24:17.

theological treatise, for here Paul expounds his gospel in the greater context of his apostolic mission.[29]

Mention has been made of the desire for missional prayer to deliver the collection to Jerusalem successfully. There are two overtly missional purposes we can identify in the letter to the Romans.

Preparation for the Mission to Rome

It is argued by some based on Romans 15:24, that Paul's plan was merely to pass through the city to Spain.[30] Paul does use the language of passing through (*diaporeuomai*).[31] His use of this term could be, in part, motivated to ensure that readers know that "Paul is not coming to Rome to 'take charge.' He will not violate his commitment to not build on another's foundation."[32]

While he uses the language of passing through, the first part of the letter indicates that he wants more than just a stopover on his way from Jerusalem to Spain. Indeed, the first stated purpose for Romans was to prepare for his coming to the city to share spiritual gifts with the Romans, strengthen them, to be mutually encouraged with them, and to preach the gospel to win a harvest of converts (1:11–15).[33] Staying long enough to win a harvest and to have that kind of effect on the Romans suggests more than a brief layover. What Paul adds in Romans 15:24 is that he hopes to receive their support and experience refreshment.

As has been discussed, it has been common to see Romans as a dogmatic outline of the gospel. However, it is now generally agreed that this is not adequate. First, while Romans is thorough, it does not fully explain every dimension of the gospel systematically (see part one, chapter 4). Second, the letter is slanted toward relationships between Jews and gentiles, the law, and salvation history. The notion of the righteousness of God dominates the letter. Some jettison the idea that Romans addresses the issue of the gospel at all. However, Romans *is* a presentation of Paul's understanding of the gospel. This gospel presentation is flavored by the issues of Jewish and gentile relationships to law and salvation history, reflecting the problem generally in the early Christian church and specifically in the Roman community of faith. It is pastoral and missional in intent. The particular emphasis within this gospel framework is the "righteousness of God" and "justification by faith."

---

29. Howell, "Mission in Paul's Epistles: Theological Bearings," 93.

30. "Paul's intent was not to remain in Rome for an extended visit." Jewett and Kotansky, *Romans*, 932–24.

31. It means "pass through." BDAG 235.

32. Toews, *Romans*, 353. See 15:20 and 2 Cor 10:13–16.

33. Alexander, "Chronology of Paul," 118 wrongly states that "at this stage Paul feels that his mission in Europe is fully accomplished." This is incorrect. Rome and Spain are in Europe, and Paul wishes to win converts there. Furthermore, later when released from Rome, Paul returns to European areas.

Part One: Background Matters

As a presentation of the gospel, one of the reasons it was written was to probably to establish Paul's credentials to the Romans because it is his stated desire to come to Rome and preach the gospel in that city (1:13–15). It thus defends his apostleship and claims, and is a presentation of his gospel to the Romans:

> I want you to know, brothers and sisters, that I have often intended to come to you (but thus far have been prevented), in order that I may reap some harvest among you as I have among the rest of the gentiles. I am a debtor both to Greeks and to barbarians, both to the wise and to the foolish—hence my eagerness to proclaim the gospel to you also who are in Rome.

His yearning to come to Rome is profoundly missional. He is an apostle set apart for the preaching of the gospel (1:1).[34] He had been commissioned by God's grace to bring about the obedience of faith among all the nations, including the Romans (1:6). As the premier city in the Roman Empire in which he lived his whole life, it is little wonder he longs to see the Romans (1:11a). He desires to strengthen them through the imparting of spiritual gifts among them (1:11b). He wants to see mutual encouragement with both parties experiencing a deepened faith in God (1:12). He thus wants to equip people for the mission of God.[35]

His specific evangelistic desire is that he may reap a harvest among the Romans as he has done among the gentile nations on an arc around the Mediterranean Sea from Jerusalem to the western Balkans (15:19). With his obligation to Greeks and non-Greeks (Barbarians) and to the wise and foolish, many of whom live in the city, he is determined to come to preach to the Romans.

"You" (*hymin*) in Romans 1:15 can be limited to the church in Rome—Paul wanting to strengthen its many believers.[36] However, based on his desire for a harvest (*karpos*, 1:13),[37] his intended mission would have included preaching the word. He would have preached to the saved to deepen their understanding of the gospel (as he does in this letter) *and* to those yet unsaved that they may believe in Christ and receive justification. In other words, he wants to come and take every opportunity to

---

34. "'Gospel' (*euangelion*) here has a verbal nuance to it (as a noun of agency): it is the *act of preaching the gospel* that is in view (emphasis original). "The content of the message and its proclamation are not two distinct meanings of the word *euangelion*, only two sides of one concept." Köstenberger and O'Brien, *Salvation to the Ends of the Earth*, 173–74.

35. Keown, *Congregational Evangelism in Philippians*, 83: "It is possible that this desire to impart to the Romans some spiritual gift could include Paul's supreme gift, the gift of proclamation of the gospel which was central to his gift of apostleship." Support is found in the importance of the gospel and its dissemination in Rome and then in Spain.

36. O'Brien, *Consumed by Passion*, 61–65.

37. *Karpos* here is used in the sense of converts. "Moreover, Paul undoubtedly wanted to engage in initial evangelism while in Rome, for even if a church had been planted he was eager to use every opportunity for winning new converts." Schreiner, *Romans*, 55; Keown, *Congregational Evangelism in Philippians*, 54. See also Phil 1:22. See Keown, *Philippians*, 1:247.

preach in the empire's center. He knows the stronger the Roman church is, the more the gospel will radiate into the empire and beyond to the ends of the earth.

It is possible, too, that Paul was considered with suspicion in Rome. It could be that some of his converts had become dominant in the Roman church since the expulsion and Jerusalem Council and that, after the return of the exiles, tensions existed in the Roman church between those with a "Pauline" point of view and a more Jewish orientation. His presentation may have been in part to defend himself and those with his perspective in Rome. He also challenges the "strong" with a Pauline view to bear with the views of others (Rom 14–15).

It is also likely that Paul wanted to reinforce the law-free perspective agreed to at the Jerusalem Council. After all, if it is not cemented into the Roman church in the center of the Empire, then it may not stand the test of time as the city was so dominant. Paul wants to reinforce that one is justified by faith premised on God's grace, and while subsequent works are vitally important, they play no part in one's justification. A person is justified by faith and faith alone. Romans ensures that this is well understood.

The theme of the epistle outlines the essential feature of the epistle, i.e., the *gospel*. In this good news, the *righteousness of God* is revealed (1:16–17):

> For I am not ashamed of the gospel, for it is the power of God for salvation for all who believe, to the Jew first and also to the Greek. For in it the righteousness of God is being revealed from faith to faith. As it is written, "The one who is righteous by faith, will live." (Translation mine).

Acts records that Paul did preach the gospel in the city, experiencing rejection from many of the Jewish population (Acts 28:15–31). Philippians 1:12–18a also suggests this occurred with some among the Praetorian Guard and others converted (cf. Phil 4:22). It also antagonized some in Rome, leading them to preach to cause Paul suffering. Their malice does not faze Paul; what matters is that Christ is proclaimed, and this brings him joy (Phil 1:18a).[38]

Preparation for the Mission to Spain

Paul's plans do not stop with a desire to evangelize Rome further. After Corinth, with his coworkers and delegates from the churches that had contributed to the Jerusalem Collection, he will travel to Jerusalem (15:25–27). With that in mind, he seeks the prayer support of Rome's Christians that he may be delivered from the unbelievers of Judea and that the believers in the Judean church would find the gift acceptable (15:30–31). Paul knows that prayer is every bit an act of mission as preaching the gospel.

---

38. On Phil 1:12–18a, see Keown, *Philippians*, 1:174–221.

Part One: Background Matters

A second explicit missional purpose of Romans is to gain Roman support for his trip to evangelize Spain for which he is going to use Rome as a base (15:19–29). At the writing of Romans, Paul considers that he has completed his work of preaching the gospel from Israel (Jerusalem) to western Greece and the Balkans (Illyricum, 15:19).[39] He wants to travel across the Adriatic to Rome and then beyond to the west to Spain (15:23–24, 28):

> But now, I no longer have a place in these regions, and I have had a longing for many years to come to see you when I am traveling *to Spain*. For I hope, while I am passing through, to see you and receive assistance from you there, after I have enjoyed your company for a while . . . So after I have completed and sealed for delivery to them this fruit [delivering the Jerusalem Collection to Jerusalem], I will depart by way of you to Spain. (My translation).

The phrase "receive assistance" in Romans 15:24 translates *propempō*, indicating Paul hopes to gain Roman support for the next phase of his mission (see further part three, chapter 11, 21).[40] Hence, just as he used Antioch for a base for the first phase of his missionary work, he now wants to use Rome as a base to go to the virgin mission fields of the west. His wanting to establish a headquarters could also explain the comprehensive nature of Romans.

Why Paul wanted to go to Spain is uncertain. Tom Wright contends it was to fulfill Isaiah's prophetic hope of far-away lands and islands hearing of God.[41] Despite there being few Jews in Spain,[42] he would also be able to use his Roman citizenship and knowledge of koine in Spain.[43] He likely recognized that Spain was the western edge of their known world, and reaching Tarshish would complete one phase of the mission. He would also fulfill Isaiah 66:19.[44] Likely, without any knowledge of the Americas across the Atlantic to the east, it was the logical end of a phase of western

---

39. Illyricum (*Illyrikon*): "Roman Province on the northwest Balkan peninsula, east of the Adriatic Sea, which included modern Croatia, Bosnia-Herzegovina, and Montenegro. The northern limit of Paul's ministry." Guyer, "Illyricum." On Romans 15:19a, see O'Brien, *Consumed by Passion*, 39–43. He sees three possible interpretations: 1) the fulfillment of OT eschatology; 2) fulfilled through his dynamic preaching; 3) fulfilled through the planting of churches through the region. The latter is undoubtedly correct. O'Brien suggests three aspects this includes that primary evangelization is complete, and the churches are nurtured to sustainability. I would add, they have now taken on the mission of self-replication.

40. *Propempō*: "To assist someone in making a journey, send on one's way with food, money, by arranging for companions, means of travel, etc." BDAG 873.

41. Wright notes Isa 11:1; 41:1; 42:4, 10; 49:1; 51:5; 60:9; see also Ps 65:5–8. Wright, "Romans," 755.

42. Bowers, "Jewish Communities, 395–402. Earlier writers wrongly believed that there was a significant Jewish population in Spain. See also Jewett and Kotansky, *Romans*, 75.

43. Wright, "Romans," 755.

44. Aus, "Paul's Travel Plans to Spain," 232–62.

mission beginning in Jerusalem, through Illyricum to Rome, to the western edge of the empire.[45]

We are not sure Paul got to Spain. He may have done so as Clement, writing from Rome (1 Clem. Prol) in AD 95–97,[46] states Paul had "reached the farthest limits of the West" (1 Clem. 5:7), likely meaning Spain. Considering the date of Clement, this is strong evidence Paul got to Spain. This is especially so if this is the Clement of Phil 4:3, which, despite most contemporary scholars ruling it out, is not implausible.[47] The Muratorian Canon, Lines 27–39, assumes he reached there as a well (ca. AD 170–200).[48] Further, Irenaeus (ca. 140–98) and Tertullian (ca. 160–220) also mention that the Christian church extended to Spain.[49] Meinardus has also collected evidence of a range of traditions from the eighth to the sixteenth century related to Paul's evangelization of Spain.[50] So, with such a range, it is not out of the question.

However, we cannot be sure. Philemon 22 and Philippians 1:25–26 suggest that Paul planted to travel to Macedonia and Colossae if he left Roman incarceration. Hence, he may have delayed his plan to get to Spain or never got there as he was martyred in Rome. Whether he did or not, Romans is occasioned in part by Paul's desire to get there in his quest to fulfill the gospel.

Conclusion

Rather than single one reason out over others, it is best to hold these options in tension and not seek to allow one to be read as the dominant reason. Paul then, writes to Rome, to address different views of adopting ritual aspects of Roman law, to reinforce his credentials as the apostle to the gentiles, to ensure that the law-free gospel is cemented in place, and to seek prayer support for his trip to Jerusalem so that he can fulfill his dreams of coming to Rome to preach the gospel there, and then evangelize Spain.

So, it is clear that Romans is fundamentally a missional document. With this in mind, the essays in this book will explore a wide range of missional themes to which Romans contributes. To these, I now turn.

---

45. Jewett and Kotansky, *Romans*, 924.

46. "There is widespread agreement in dating this letter about a.d. 95–97, in the last year of the emperor Domitian or the first of his successor, Nerva." Holmes, *Apostolic Fathers*, 23.

47. Keown, *Philippians*, 2:326–27. He may also have been one of the team that evangelized Illyricum (see part two, chapter 5).

48. Danker, "Spain," 4:592.

49. Irenaeus, *Haer.* 1.10.2; Tertullian, *Adv. Jud.* 7. The Acts of Peter 3 from the late second century details Paul's departure from Ostia to Spain. Meinardus, "Paul's Missionary Journey to Spain," 61–63.

50. Meinardus, "Paul's Missionary Journey to Spain," 62–63.

Part Two

Romans and the Content of the Gospel

PAUL USES THE TERM "my gospel" in Romans 2:16 and 16:25, which could suggest Romans is a once-for-all presentation of Paul's gospel. As has been intimated and will be discussed further, it is not. Still, Romans has a lot to say about the content of Paul's gospel.

This part of the book looks at aspects important to understanding the substance of Paul's gospel that underlies Romans. It begins with a look at how Paul's gospel, at its heart, is a fulfillment of Israel's story and is premised on salvation history. Next, analysis of its structure and genre inform us of at least one of Paul's ways of presenting the gospel, shaped for the Roman church. As we dig into its many themes, many aspects important to Paul's understanding of the gospel become apparent. These elements are helpful for those of us today who are eager to share the gospel so that unbelievers can come to faith in God and experience his salvation.

5

Romans as a Gospel Presentation

IN SOME CIRCLES, Romans is privileged as the quintessential presentation of the gospel that contemporary gospel proclaimers should follow, whatever the situation. With many tracts and approaches drawing on Romans,[1] its influence in gospel proclamation could even be greater than the four "Gospels." This should not be the case, for when the early church wrote down "the gospel," it was the story of Jesus's life, death, and in Luke's case, includes the story of the early church. Nevertheless, Romans informs us how we can evangelize a particular group of Christians on a specific occasion.

In this chapter, the nature of Romans as a gospel presentation will be discussed. Then, its structure as a presentation of the gospel message will be considered. Finally, it will be broken down into the components of the "gospel" *behind* the letter. These are aspects of Paul's gospel, but Romans does not constitute *the gospel* he preached in every situation.

As noted in the introduction to the chapter, Romans is treated by many people (especially non-academic readers) as the fifth gospel. In fact, due to its more propositional nature (when compared to the narratival and biographical Gospels), for some, Romans is the primary pattern by which the gospel should always be preached. Is this justified?

ROMANS—IS IT A GOSPEL?

In short, the answer to the question of whether Romans is a Gospel is "no." There is a range of reasons for this conclusion. First, when an early Christian set out with real intent to write a Gospel, as signaled by Mark 1:1, he wrote a historical *bios* of Jesus's life, declaring that he is the Christ and Son of God.[2] Matthew and Luke amend and

---

1. See Hall, "What Is the Romans Road to Salvation?" For example, the Romans Road: 1) The human problem (3:10, 23; 6:23); 2) humanity's hope in Christ (5:8); 3) sinner's response (10:9–10, 13); 4) the result of salvation (5:1–2; 8:1).

2. While some texts omit "son of God," with the importance of the theme of Jesus's sonship in

adapt Mark with the same intent. John writes with a different style and content, but again, gives an account of Jesus's life.[3] As such, a Gospel narrates the life, death, and resurrection of Jesus.

Unlike the four Gospels, Romans is self-evidently a *letter* written to a particular group of people in a snapshot of time. It is written to *Christians* of Rome, and so is not a once-for-all proclamation of the gospel one should use for *non-believers*, let alone in every situation. In fact, we learn more of gospel proclamation to unbelievers through the preaching ministry of Jesus in the four Gospels and in the speeches of Acts that are invariably spoken to people who *have yet to believe* in Jesus as Messiah.

Romans is a contextual theological reflection on the narrative of the gospel, shaped for a particular context and moment in history: Paul from Corinth, to the Romans facing their challenges, focusing on Jew-gentile relationships, written on the eve of leaving for Jerusalem with his plans to come to Rome and onto Spain. If Romans is to be labeled "a gospel," it is a particular version of the gospel for a set of Christians facing a unique and never-repeatable moment in history. Moreover, these Christians clearly know the OT story that Paul references so often. As such, it is not what one might preach to an unbeliever without a good knowledge of Israel's story. Romans contributes more to the way we should preach the gospel to believers than unbelievers.

Second, as discussed in the first part of this book (esp. part one, chapter 4), the setting of Romans tells us of its multifaceted purposes. We know it is sent to Rome as Paul prepares to leave Achaia to travel to Jerusalem with the collection. Part of its purpose is that the Romans would pray that this collection will be well received, and Paul can come to them in Rome and beyond to Spain. A second purpose regards resolving matters of Jewish law and the Christian faith. The gospel began among Jews having been established in Rome in synagogues by returnees from Pentecost. They had come to believe that Jesus is Messiah, had experienced the Spirit, but remained very Jewish in their worldview. Things like eating the right foods, holy days, circumcision, and other fundamental Jewish laws were not initially questioned. As such, in its first phase, Christianity in Rome was profoundly Jewish in its flavor.

In the meantime, catalyzed by events like the evangelization of Cornelius's family and gentiles at Syrian Antioch, and led by Paul and Barnabas, it was increasingly recognized in the east that the gospel of God did not carry with it many of the cultural demands of the Jewish faith. After serious clashes between Paul and the Judaizers (who saw such cultural demands as integral to the gospel), the letter to the Galatians,

---

Mark, it is likely original (1:1, 11; 3:11; 5:7; 9:11; 13:32; 14:61; 15:39; see Metzger, *Textual Commentary*, 62, who notes that the absence of "son of God" in witnesses include ℵ* Θ 28c, and may be scribal error. It is also included in some important witnesses, including B, D, W, and so gets a {C} rating indicating it is uncertain.

3. John's account of Jesus is usually called a Gospel, although the *euang-* terms are not used in it, and it is written with a different structure and feel to the Synoptic Gospels. The church has since early on designated it as a Gospel, and this is reasonable as, like the others, it is a biography of Jesus.

the Jerusalem Council, and subsequent mission work saw "the gospel of grace through faith" become the official position of the church.

Around the same time as the Jerusalem Council (AD 49), Claudius expelled the Jews from Rome for arguments over *Chrestus* (Christ). What was left of the church was a gentile community. Paul set out on his second Antiochian mission in that year with Silas, and without doubt, the letter from the Council made its way to Rome. As Jews like Paul, Silas, and Timothy could not carry the letter to Rome, it was perhaps carried by Luke (who remained in Philippi) and Macedonian believers. Such Macedonians could include Jason, Aristarchus, and Secundus from Thessalonica,[4] Gaius of Macedonia (Acts 19:29), Epaphroditus (Phil 2:25–30), and the coworkers of Philippi including Euodia and Syntyche (Phil 4:2–3). The tradition that Clement was a bishop of Rome could be linked to this, especially if he were in Rome at the time of the writing of Philippians.[5]

While Claudius's edict was in sway, with the arrival of gentile believers, the non-Jewish church no doubt grew. In AD 54, three to four years before Romans, Claudius died, and some of the Jews like Aquila and Prisca returned. Some other former leaders with a very Jewish perspective were likely among the returnees.

With the growth of the gentile church and return of Jewish leaders, there was likely tension in the Roman church over matters of Jewish culture. This contention would include whether Jewish protocols were necessary at all. Another point of tension may have included how to relate to one another where there are significant cultural differences.

Romans is almost certainly written into such tensions. Romans 16 hints at a range of house churches in Rome. Some were likely Jewish in orientation, some gentile. Great questions would require resolving. What about circumcision? Sabbath observance? Differences in understandings of eating? All of these can be discerned in the letter.

With that in mind, one of the great purposes of Romans is to address such differences in the Roman church. Paul asserts the great principle of justification by faith and not works of the law. Believers are set free from the law. They now live by the Spirit. Romans 12—13 gives general guidelines concerning how to live as a unified, cruciform, and loving Christian church. It gives guidance concerning how Christians should live in relation to the State. Romans 14 and 15 addresses cultural differences more directly; especially where eating and holy days are concerned. Paul sides with those who see them as secondary, the strong. However, where there are differences over such incidentals, they are to hold to their convictions, honor their differences,

---

4. Jason (Acts 17:5–9, cf. Rom 16:21); Aristarchus (Acts 19:29; 20:4; 27:2; Col 4:10; Phlm 24), and Secundus (Acts 20:4).

5. The later traditions of Origen (mid-third century; *Comm. Jo.* 6.36) and Eusebius (*Hist. eccl.* 3.49) suggest he is the writer of 1 Clement and Bishop of Rome in the late first century. I argue that this is possible but uncertain. Keown, *Philippians*, 2:326–27. In my earlier work on Philippians, I had not considered that Clement was in Rome at the time, but it is not implausible.

Part Two: Romans and the Content of the Gospel

not judge each other, and bear with each other. All are welcome, despite cultural differences.

Romans then, at least in part, is a presentation of the gospel to a church that was grappling with matters of law and faith. However, we cannot stop here. As he makes clear in Romans 1:13, Paul wants to come to Rome to preach the gospel in the city. He desires to have a harvest of converts who come to the obedience of faith in the capital of the Roman world, as he has in other gentile settings. So, Romans presents the gospel in part as a preparation for this evangelistic visit to Rome.

Additionally, Paul's desire expressed in Romans 15:24 and 28 is to use Rome as a base for pushing west with the gospel to the yet-unevangelized area of Spain. As such, Romans may, in part, be a presentation of the gospel for that purpose. He wants their support and elicits it with the letter. He wants some to join him as he goes to Spain.

So, in sum, we can say that Romans is not a once-for-all presentation of the gospel that must be emulated in every evangelistic situation. Actually, that is questionable as it could lead to Christians preaching an outdated and contextually disconnected version of the gospel. Hearers without the background understanding of the Roman Christians of the first century will struggle to comprehend such a gospel. The gospel must *always* be contextualized. Paul, himself, appreciates the need to contextualize the gospel as seen in the way he adapted his practice when among different people groups (1 Cor 9:19–22).[6]

Our evidence of Paul's preaching to unbelievers suggests that he greatly varied his proclamation. We see this by comparing his speeches in Acts. In the Pisidian Antioch sermon of Acts 13, with some resonances with Romans,[7] Paul traces Israel's story, landing on Jesus. Nevertheless, this is spoken to Jewish believers and God-fearing gentiles. In Acts 14 and 17, in Lystra and before the Areopagus, preaching to those

---

6. See Longenecker, *Paul, Apostle of Liberty*, 230–44. He writes, "Here is a legitimate flexibility of approach and elasticity of attitude which needs to be more characteristic of every Christian pastor, missionary, scholar, and states[person]" (adapted for inclusive language, p. 244).

7. Aside from both Acts 13 and Romans drawing on Israel's Scriptures and story, some themes common with Romans include election (Acts 13:17; Rom 8:33; 9:11; 11:7, 28), Exodus (Acts 13:16; Rom 9:17), prophets (Acts 13:20, 27; Rom 3:21); Benjamin (Acts 13:21; Rom 11:1); David and Jesse (Acts 13:22–23, 34; Rom 1:3; 15:12); Abraham and Abrahamic descent (Acts 13:26; Rom 4:1–16; 9:7; 11:1); fear of God (Acts 13:16, 26; Rom 3:18); the message sent (Acts 13:26; Rom 10:15); God's message of salvation (Acts 13:26, 47; Rom 1:16); the death of Christ (Acts 13:27–29; e.g., Rom 5:6, 8, 10; 6:6); Christ's burial (Acts 13:20; Rom 6:4); Christ's resurrection by God's agency (Acts 13:30, 33, 34, 37; e.g., Rom 1:4; 4:24; 10:9); gospel (Acts 13:32; e.g., Rom 1:1, 9, 15–16); God's promises to the Patriarchs fulfilled (Acts 13:32–33; Rom 4:13–20; 9:4–5, 8; 15:8); Christ the Son of God (Acts 13:34; Ps 2:7; e.g., Rom 1:4, 9); Christ never to die again (Acts 13:34, 35; Rom 6:9); blessing associated with David (Acts 13:34; Rom 4:6–8); human death (Acts 13:36; Rom 5:12); forgiveness of sins (Acts 13:38; Rom 4:7–8; 11:26–27); faith bringing justification and freedom from law (Acts 13:39; e.g., Rom 3:21–30; 5:1; 7:1–6); the law (Acts 13:39; e.g., Rom 3:28; 7:5, etc.); "word of God" (Acts 13:46; Rom 9:6); to the Jew first and then the Greek (Acts 13:46; Rom 1:16; 2:9–10); Jewish rejection (Acts 13:46; Rom 9:30–33; 11:7–10, 30–32); eternal life (Acts 13:46; Rom 2:7; 5:21; 6:22–23); Paul's mission to the gentiles (Acts 13:46–47; Rom 1:13; 15:16, 18); salvation to the ends of the earth (Acts 13:47; Rom 9:17; 10:18; 11:11).

ROMANS AS A GOSPEL PRESENTATION

with little knowledge of Israel's stories and traditions, Paul appeals to common pagan ideas of God, creation, and humankind. In Acts 22—26, in a series of court appearances, Paul gives testimonies of conversion and his early Christian life. The only letter that approximates Romans is Galatians. The other letters are remarkably diverse; so much so, that many scholars write off Paul being the author of six of them at all! Instead of seeing these as non-Pauline, they show Paul's ability to contextualize his messages for various audiences.

Romans then should never be seen as a one-size-fits-all gospel presentation. It is *a* gospel presented for a moment *to Christians* to gain prayer support, to address cultural and theological differences between Christians in Rome, and to prepare for future evangelization. It is a gospel to believers to cement certain aspects of it in their thinking and cause them to live it and share it more accurately, appropriately, and zealously.

None of this should lead us to the conclusion that Romans has *nothing* to say about evangelism and mission. As this book seeks to demonstrate, Romans is missional to the core. It is evangelistic. The gospel is its central theme, seen in the use of gospel language throughout the letter and the way the gospel and Paul's mission frames the letter.[8] It is certainly one way to preach it in certain circumstances and is replete with a range of aspects of the gospel. These facets will now be discussed, leading into a summary of the "gospel" in Romans.

CONCLUSION

Romans is not *a* Gospel, but its central theme is the gospel (see the next section). It is written to believers to clarify the law-free theology and cultural inclusion that the gospel declares. The central motif is righteousness and justification by faith. The core aspect of the gospel Paul drew out could have been any one of his other metaphors. However, the pressing issue in Roman Christianity was the relationship of faith and the law for salvation, inclusion, and the Christian life.

Romans states that both Jews and gentiles are equally prone to sin and so fall short of God's glory. It states that justification is received by faith in Jesus Christ, whether one is born a Jew or a gentile. It defends the principle of faith throughout the story of God, beginning with Adam, who is contrasted with Jesus, the new Adam. It focuses on Abraham, the gentile who met God who made a covenant with him, and who was *then* circumcised. It defends that faith is enough. It outlines many consequences and concomitants of justification by faith: reconciliation, eternal life and not death, freedom from sin, freedom from the law, life in the Spirit, and hope. It discusses the place of Israel in the purpose of God, now that Christ has come, and the gospel is

---

8. Rom 1:1–17; 15:14–31. *Euangelion* language: Rom 1:1, 9, 15, 16; 2:16; 10:15, 16; 11:28; 15:16, 19, 20; 16:25. *Kēryssō* language: 2:21; 10:8, 14, 15; 16:25. *Rhēma* language: 10:8, 17, 18. *Logos* language (in relation to evangelization): 9:6; *katangellō* language: 1:8; 9:17; 15:21.

Part Two: Romans and the Content of the Gospel

spreading into the gentile world. Israel has the same hope as the gentiles, to believe in Jesus and receive God's justification. It outlines what it means to live as believers in light of the gospel; supremely, love and inclusion. It expounds that there is space for cultural differences within God's people, but advocates love trumping liberty to maintain unity where these nonessentials are concerned. It ends with Paul's passion for the gospel restated and his desire to continue to preach the gospel through Italy to Spain.

6

Romans, Missional Fulfillment, and Salvation History

ROMANS IS A LETTER that proclaims that the mission of God has found its fulfillment and fresh starting point in Jesus Christ. Prior to the coming of Christ, the oracles of God were entrusted to Jews (3:2). The gospel was promised before the coming of Christ by prophets in the Scriptures (1:2). While God's righteousness is revealed aside from the Jewish law, Israel's law and prophets bear witness to it (3:21). The things written in the OT are for Christian instruction. Its writings empower endurance and encourage believers to always have hope (15:4). In what follows, the relationship of Romans to Israel's story and Paul's notion of salvation history will be considered.

OLD TESTAMENT QUOTES, ALLUSIONS, AND ECHOES

It is evident that in Paul's understanding of the gospel (and those of other NT writers), the Scriptures are fulfilled. He employs many OT texts in his argument.[1] His uses show that:

> The OT Scriptures contain the divine promises of the gospel; moreover, they reveal the unfolding purposes of God in significant events of that gospel which are announced, effected and divinely interpreted (*e.g.* the call of Abraham, the exodus from Egypt and that from Babylon).[2]

One aspect is faith, which Paul argues is the only human requirement to be declared righteous by God. So, in Romans 1:17, in the thesis statement of Romans (1:16–17), he cites Habakkuk 2:4, stating that the righteous shall live by faith. The citation speaks of both the initial faith that brings justification and eternal life, and the faith by which that status is maintained.

---

1. Seifrid, "Romans," 607. Paul has roughly sixty OT citations in Romans.
2. Köstenberger and O'Brien, *Salvation to the Ends of the Earth*, 175.

Part Two: Romans and the Content of the Gospel

In his argument on universal sin, Paul cites a range of OT texts. As in the eighth-century BC,[3] in sinful Israel, God's name is being blasphemed among the gentiles by Jews who boast in the law (2:24; Isa 52:5). In Romans 3:10–18, Paul cites a catena of seven OT texts mainly from the Psalter to buttress his argument that all are under sin.[4]

"Righteousness" is revealed apart from the law, but the writings in the law and prophets testify to it (3:21). Righteousness here is the legal status of righteousness before God received by faith. He alludes to the Passover in 3:25.[5] Using the example of Abraham from Genesis 12—25, he argues that faith has always been the basis on which righteousness is declared over a person by God (Romans 4). Specific texts from Genesis are cited as Paul argues for justification by faith for Jew and gentile alike.[6] Abrahamic descent will also feature in Romans 9:6–20. Similarly, LXX Psalm 31:1–2 (32:1–2 EVV) anticipates the forgiveness received in the gospel (4:7–8).

Throughout Romans, Paul assumes the importance, authority, and historical reliability of the OT story. Obviously, the God he has in mind is Israel's God. He refers to God as cosmic creator and to the creation itself (1:20), the history of human idolatry (1:22–24), God as judge (3:6), his judgment (e.g., 2:1–11, 16) and beneficence (2:4), the law (74 times), circumcision (2:25–29; 3:1),[7] including circumcision of the heart (2:29),[8] the Spirit,[9] and the laws of divorce (7:1–3; Deut 24:1) and against covetousness (7:8; Exod 20:17; Deut 5:21). God's justice is exhibited in the gospel (3:4; LXX Ps 50:6 [51:4 EVV]).

Adam is the human starting point for his presentation of Christ in Romans. As in 1 Corinthians 15:42–49, Adam plays a crucial role in his Christology. Adam brought sin into the cosmos, causing death to reign (5:12, 14–15). He is a type of Jesus. Jesus is his antitype, the new Adam, who causes the gift of justification and eternal life by grace to abound to the many (5:15–18, 21). The experience of suffering Roman Christians is likened to Israel's suffering at the hands of foreign nations (8:36; Ps 43:23 [44:22 EVV]).

Romans 9–11 is replete with citations, allusions, and echoes of Israel's story. Their identity as Israelites, descendants of Jacob is affirmed (9:4; Gen 32:28). The covenants are alluded to in general terms, with the focus in Romans (and Galatians) being the

---

3. Or the sixth or fifth centuries BC depending on the date of Deutero-Isaiah, Beaulieu, "Deutero-Isaiah," who notes some date in the sixth to fifth centuries BC. Recent scholars who see it as a unit maintain an eighth-century date. It is unlikely Paul considered Isaiah anything but an eighth-century work by the Prophet.

4. See Ps 5:9; 9:28 (LXX 10:7 EVV); 13:1–3 (LXX 14:1–3 EVV); Ps 35:1 (LXX 36:1 EVV); 139:4 (LXX 140:3 EVV); Prov 1:15; Jer 5:16.

5. The Greek is *paresis* used here means "forgive" but may have an allusion to Passover in its use. Paul does use the Passover in 1 Cor 5:7.

6. Gen 15:6 (4:5, 22–24); 17 (4:10–12); 17:4–6 (4:13, 17); 15:5 (4:18).

7. See also 3:30; 4:9–12; 15:8.

8. See Deut 10:16; 30:6; Jer 4:4.

9. Rom 2:29; 5:5; 7:6; 8:1–17, 26–27.

relationship between the Abrahamic and Sinai covenants, although the Davidic covenant is implied (1:3; 15:12). Quite clearly, Paul also sees in Christ the fulfillment of Jeremiah's new covenant (see esp. 2 Cor 3; Jer 31).[10] He references the giving of the law at Sinai, Israel's cultic worship practices, God's promises, the patriarchs, and their hopes of a Messiah (9:4–5). Israel's patriarchal descent through Abraham and Sarah, Isaac and Rebekah, and Jacob, the line of promise, is affirmed (9:7–12). In so doing, Paul cites a range of Genesis texts.[11] The story of the Exodus is invoked, showing God's freedom to show mercy at his behest.[12] The prophetic potter-clay motif that recalls creation and is utilized by the prophets is invoked to assert God's freedom (9:20, cf. Gen 2:7; Isa 64:8; Jer 18:6).

The ingathering of the gentiles and a remnant of Israel is supported through two passages in Hosea and Isaiah (9:25–29; Hos 2:23; Isa 1:9). Israel's unbelief and rejection of Jesus, the cornerstone of God's renewed temple, is seen as a fulfillment of Isaiah 28:16.

A whole series of OT texts is found in Romans 10. The contrast of doing the law and faith draws on Deuteronomy 30:14, where the gospel is now the word of faith that has come near and should be heeded (10:8). In Romans 10:11, in talking about the requirement of faith, Paul clips out a portion of Isaiah 1:9 referenced earlier in 9:33 (of Israel's unbelief). It is restated as calling on the name of the Lord for salvation from Joel 2:32 in Romans 10:13.

Recalling his use of a string of seven texts in Romans 3, Paul employs another catena of texts in Romans 10:18–21 in answer to the question of whether Israel has heard the gospel. If they have not heard it, they should not be held accountable. However, the gospel *has* gone to the world (10:18 = LXX Ps 18:5 [19:4 EVV]), Israel is uncomprehending and jealous (10:19 = Deut 32:21), and so peoples who did not seek God are finding him (10:20 = Isa 65:1). Still, God invites them to come to him, but they resist in their disobedience and rebelliousness (10:21 = Isa 65:2).

Romans 11 draws on a range of Israel's traditions as Paul recognizes that as always, God reserves a remnant of faithful people, chosen by grace. He warns gentiles against arrogance toward Israel, for just as Israel can be regrafted into God's people by faith, gentile believers can be broken off for unbelief. The apostle yearns for this to happen, hoping the gospel and gentile inclusion will provoke their conversion. He knows that ultimately all God's people will be saved because Jesus has come to take away the sins of humankind (11:26).

---

10. See Shead, "New Covenant and Pauline Hermeneutics," 33–49. He finds four possible points of contact with Jer 31 in 2 Cor 3:1 "All men" (2 Cor 3:2); 2) the contrast of old and new; 3) Paul's argument in 2 Cor 3:12–18 matches Jer 31:31—34; 4) Jeremiah 31 transforms Paul's use of Exod 31 (esp. 2 Cor 3:16).

11. See 9:7 = Gen 21:12; 9:9 = Gen 18:10, 14; 9:12 = Gen 25:23.

12. See especially 9:15 = Exod 33:19; 9:18 = Exod 9:16.

Part Two: Romans and the Content of the Gospel

Paul affirms his own identity as a Benjaminite and a descendant of Israel and Abraham (11:1). He draws on the Deuteronomic account of Elijah, at which time the prophet cried out in despair at being the only one left (11:3 = 1 Kgs 19:10, 14). God's response in 11:4 cites 1 Kgs 19:18, whereby God preserved a remnant of seven thousand, anticipating the remnant of Israel that now yields to Jesus as Messiah. He explains the rejection of Jesus by many in Israel through the words of Isaiah 29:10, likening Israelites who reject Jesus at the time of writing to those of eighth-century Israel who resisted into exile. Paul draws on the LXX of the lament in Psalm 68 (vv. 23–24 [69:22–23 EVV]), reinforcing the pain of Israel's stumbling and blindness (11:9–10). In Romans 15:3, he will cite this Psalm again of Jesus taking the reproaches of Israel's persecutors on himself.

The metaphors of dough and firstfruits draw on bread and harvest from Israel's story.[13] The image of God's people as an olive tree is found in the OT (Jer 11:16; Ps 52:8). Finally, Paul quotes Isaiah 59:20–21 of Jesus as the deliverer from Zion, who will banish ungodliness from God's people and remove their sin (11:26–27).

The ethical sections of Romans include OT promises that find their fulfillment in Christ and his work. A concomitant of Jesus's self-giving is that God's people are to emulate his example. Paul uses Deuteronomy 32:35, urging them not to take revenge, for that belongs to God (12:19). Instead, they are to do as Proverbs 25:21–22 counsels, feeding their enemies (12:20).

The supreme law of neighborly love is invoked as central to their ethic. Drawn from the law itself (Lev 19:18), the virtue of *agapē* sums up the OT law. Specifically, it fulfills the sixth, fifth, seventh, and tenth Decalogue relational commandments (Exod 20:12–17; Deut 5:17–21). His tag "and if there is any other commandment" (my translation) brings the whole of Israel's nomistic tradition into view—it is fulfilled in toto in the law of loving neighbors as oneself, which is restated as doing no wrong to a neighbor.

Romans 14:1—15:7 is backgrounded by Jewish interest in eating protocols (esp. Lev 11) and holy days (esp. the Sabbath and feasts). Paul sides theologically with those who see such things as unimportant. However, building on his injunction for love in Romans 13:8–10, he urges them to accept differences concerning these things, to live out of their convictions, to stop judging each other, and to build each other up.

In Romans 15:3, he cites Isaiah 45:23 (cf. Phil 2:10–11), warning of judgment for all humankind. As he ends the section, he refers to LXX Ps 68:10 (69:9 EVV), of Christ taking on himself the reproaches of those who persecute Israel. Israel's persecutors were gentiles, and Paul, in 15:8–12, will emphasize this gentile dimension to the gospel. He tells the Romans that *everything* written in the OT Scriptures is to instruct them and give them a hope that encourages them to endure (15:4).

Recalling 3:10–18; 9:25–29; and 10:18–21, in Romans 15:9–12, we have a fourth catena of OT references. These focus on Christ's service to Israel to demonstrate God's

---

13. For example, Num 15:18–21; Neh 10:37; Ezek 44:30.

integrity and confirm the promises of God to Israel's patriarchs and that the gentiles will give glory to God for his mercy. Jesus is the fulfillment of God's covenantal promises to Israel so that the gentiles will praise God for his merciful salvation.

Specifically, he recalls David's hope that gentiles will praise and sing to Yahweh.[14] He recalls Moses summoning the gentiles to rejoice with God's people (15:10 = Deut 32:43). Using Psalm 116:1 (LXX [117:1 EVV]), he urges the gentiles to praise and extol *the Lord* (Heb: Yahweh), in context, meaning Jesus—through whom God is praised (15:11). Finally, he remembers the hope of Isaiah 11:10 that a root will spring forth from Jesse, and this Davidic king will rule the gentiles who will put their hope in him (15:12).

These four texts anticipate the world worshiping God and Jesus, who died for them. Significantly, they lead into Paul's final words of his missional plans among the gentiles. Paul saw that through his missional efforts, God was beginning to fulfill the OT hopes of God's savior coming to Zion and salvation to the ends of the earth. The outcome of this is the worship of God in the gentile world. Those of us who are gentiles who worship God alongside Jewish saints today continue this missional story.

He uses Israel's cultic language to describe his work as "the offering of the gentiles" (15:16). He speaks of his passion to take the gospel to yet-unreached groups of gentiles who have yet to hear of God or have perceived or understood him, fulfilling Isaiah 52:15 (15:21). The final destruction of Israel's spiritual adversary, Satan, is foreseen (16:20).

Romans testifies that Paul saw Jesus as the zenith of Israel's stories and hopes, the focus of God's fulfillment. Romans testifies to the continuation of Israel's story in Christ and the mission of God. This mission remains incomplete while one people group has not heard the gospel of Christ and has had the opportunity to respond. Our task is to be inspired by the examples of Christ, Paul, and those who worked alongside him (Rom 16) and continue the work.

SALVATION HISTORY

Linked to the previous discussion of fulfillment is the emphasis on salvation history in Romans.[15] Alongside "the gospel" and "righteousness" as the main themes of the letter, one could add salvation history and, in particular, the relationship of historic Israel and her law to the salvation brought by Christ to *the whole world.*

As will be discussed, righteousness and law are pivotal throughout the letter. So central are they that it is certain Paul's rhetoric is targeting this issue from start to finish, as he outlines his message for the Romans. The emphasis likely relates to questions

---

14. Rom 15:9 = 2 Sam 22:50; Ps 17:50 [LXX 18:49 EVV]).

15. See on the place of Paul in an evangelical biblical theology the essay, Goldsworthy, *Biblical Theology*, 7–18.

Part Two: Romans and the Content of the Gospel

raised in the Roman church living as it is in the shadow of the edict of Claudius, the Jerusalem Council, and the clash of theologies in the NT churches over law and grace.

Without regurgitating all the details above which one can easily piece together, these elements (see the previous section) point in the direction of its importance:

1. The use of the OT.
2. The setting of the gospel of faith against law-observance throughout Romans.
3. The use of types and examples such as Abraham and Adam in Romans 4–5.
4. The devotion of three chapters to the issue of the status of Israel by descent before God and the question of God's fidelity to covenants (9–11, cf. 3:1–5).

As such, alongside righteousness as Paul's dominant theological theme around which he arranges his gospel presentation, we should place the story of salvation. In Christ, the promises of Israel are fulfilled, and in Christ, salvation history now continues. Grace and faith are the principles around which the gospel is now based. Ethics is no longer based on law, but through grace, love, Spirit, Christlikeness, and faithfulness to the gospel.

7

Aspects of Paul's "Gospel" Presentation to the Romans

METAPHOR

ROMANS IS NOT A LETTER full of narratives and stories that are so popular today in a world that seeks stories. Yet, once we know the story behind the letter, the epistle comes alive and informs our reading. Nevertheless, the letter is replete with ideas and images that evoke the imagination of the reader. Mention has already been made of his use of the OT (part two, chapter 6). Aside from this, and with many motifs drawing meaning from Israel's traditions, Paul employs a dazzling array of metaphors drawn from his world to make his appeal.

Some are political, such as reconciliation, peace, and enmity, that all speak of a treaty or covenant (5:1, 10). Covenants which call to mind ancient political treaties are invoked with Abraham (4:1–25; 9:7–13; 11:1), David (1:3), and the new covenant (11:27; 15:12). A range of other political ideas is used, such as "the gospel" (*euangelion*) that speaks of political and military news delivered by the evangel (similarly *kēryssō*), or an apostle (a political envoy, 1:1, 16; 10:14). Titles of Jesus, such as "Lord," "Son," and "Christ" are all political. Both *kyrios* and *huios* were used of Caesar. *Christos* speaks of the Jewish hopes of a messiah (1:4). The kingdom calls to mind the empires of the history and world (14:17) as do notions like dominion, reign, and rule.[1]

The *ekklēsia* politically defined the gathered people in both Greek and Jewish thought.[2] Terms used for praying and intercession are commonly used when petition-

---

1. See 5:17, 21; 6:12; 8:38; 13:3; 15:12.
2. See 16:1, 4, 5, 16, 23. See *NIDNTTE* 2:134–37.

ing superiors.³ Faith language (64x) can mean allegiance to a political ruler.⁴ The government and its rulers and powers (judgment, reward, sword, wrath, taxes) dominate Romans 13:1–7. Some of the terms used for ministry are found in the Greek literature of the State, e.g., *diakonos* (13:4; 15:8; 16:1).⁵ The judgment seat speaks of the *bema* where judicial decisions are made (14:10).⁶

There is some military language including reconciliation, peace, enemies (5:1–10), war (7:23), weapons (6:13), tribulation (8:35), sword (8:35; 13:4), conquerors (8:37), anathema (9:3),⁷ remnant (9:27), and armor (13:12).

Righteousness ideas are legal in origin as are a range of others. Some of these include law concepts (*nomos*, 74x), righteousness and justice (1:16–17), judge (3:6), judgment (2:5), transgression (4:14), trespass (5:15), condemnation (8:1), debt ideas (8:12), witness (1:9), truth (1:18), revenge and vengeance (12:19), fellow-prisoner (16:7), and so on. Inheritance ideas come from family law as do adoption and adultery (4:14; 7:1–4; 8:15). Redemption ideas are drawn from slavery as slaves are purchased and manumitted (3:24). *Kyrios* is also a term used in the *master*-slave relationship (14:4).

Many are cultic, drawn from the religious traditions of Israel and the wider world. Such ideas include God (1:1), spirits and the Spirit (34x), angels and rulers (8:38), Satan (16:20), the Scriptures (e.g., 1:2; 3:2; 11:2), heaven (1:18), the abyss (10:7), covenants (9:4), worship (9:4; 12:1), sacrifice (12:1), holy days (14:5–6), and offerings (15:16). Another example is *hilastērion* in Romans 3:25 that translates the Hebrew for mercy seat (*kăp·pō·rĕṯ*, 3:24). *Christos* (*mā·šîₐh*) is drawn from Israel's tradition of anointing kings. *Sanctification and holiness language* are also cultic (e.g., saints, 1:7; 6:19), as is *leitourgos*, "minister," used to describe Paul's ministry (15:16). Circumcision is essential in Israel's cult (2:25 [also a medical term]), as is the Passover (3:25), baptism (6:4), prayer (1:10), and intercession (8:26–27, 34). Ideas like curse and blessing are general religious ideas with particular nuances for Israel and Christians.⁸

Paul employs a lot of body terminology including the body (13x), flesh (26x); mouth, tongues, lips;⁹ ears and hearing (esp. 10:14–18; 11:8; 15:21); seeing with eyes

---

3. E.g., *entynchanō*, used in Romans 8:27 of the Spirit interceding for the saints, is used of Jacob's sons petitioning Joseph (*Ant.* 2.96). Similarly, *deēsis*, used exclusively of prayer in the NT and Paul (10:1), is used to petition a king (e.g., 1 Macc. 7:37).

4. Gorman, *Becoming the Gospel*, 90–91; Gupta, *Paul and the Language of Faith*, 94. See the monograph, Bates, *Salvation by Allegiance Alone*.

5. See Beyer, "Διακονέω, Διακονία, Διάκονος," 2:82.

6. *NIDNTTE* 1:507.

7. The Greek *anathema* translates *herēm* language in the MT and it is used of the total destruction of enemies (see, e.g., Num 21:3; Deut 13:16). *NIDNTTE* 1:281.

8. See 1:25; 4:6, 8–9.

9. See, e.g., 3:13–14, 19; 10:9–10, 11; 9:3, 5; 12:13; 15:29.

Aspects of Paul's "Gospel" Presentation to the Romans

and blindness;[10] thinking and the mind (prevalent);[11] the heart (15x); necks (16:4); hands (8:34); legs, feet, and toes (3:15; 10:15; 16:20); and backs (11:10). The faculty of speech and the spoken word is critical.[12] Singing, rejoicing, and praise from the mouth also draw on Israel's oral worship tradition (15:9-11).

He employs the language of kinship throughout Romans, including "father" of God and Abraham (1:7; 4:12), sonship and child ideas of Jesus and believers (1:4; 8:16), adoption (8:15, 23), slaves (1:1),[13] servants (14:4), siblings (20x), parents (1:30), mother (16:13), ancestors (4:1; 9:10; 11:28), inheritance (4:13-14; 8:17), marriage (7:2-3), adultery (13:9), firstborn (8:29), kinspeople (9:3; 16:7), offspring (4:13-18; 9:7-8, 29), and possibly "birth certificate" (8:23).[14] Childbirth and conception features in reference to the eschatological woes and the line of promise (8:22; 9:10). Racial terminology is used including Jews (11x), Israel (13x), gentiles (56x), Greeks (6x), and barbarians (1:14).[15] "Strangers" and "neighbors" also speak of the other.[16] Eating together and tables suggest the family meal (11:9; 12:20). The "household" features in Romans 16:5 (cf. 16:10, 11).

A number of geographical places are mentioned including Rome (1:5, 7), Asia, Zion and Jerusalem;[17] west to Illyricum, the western Balkans (15:19); also Spain (15:24, 28), Achaia (15:26), Judea (15:31), Cenchreae (16:1), and Asia Minor (16:5). Phrases describe the full extent of the world, including "all the nations" (1:5; 16:26), "all the world" (1:8), "the creation" or "the whole creation" (8:19-23), "all creation" (8:39), "all the earth" 9:17; 10:18), and "the ends of the world" (10:18).

Some motifs are agricultural such as fruit and harvest (1:13; 6:21-22; 7:4-5). Paul draws on the animal world, speaking of birds, tetrapods, reptiles (1:23), venom and asps (3:13), and sheep (8:36). *Phthora* speaks of decay, including the wider world of flora and fauna (8:21). Firstfruits is a harvest idea (8:23; 11:16). Death and dying come from the world of nature (5:12). Features of the earth like sand and sea (9:27), stones and rocks (9:32-33),[18] and mud are employed (9:21). An olive tree with branches and roots represents God's faithful people of Israel, and orcharding speaks of

---

10. See, e.g., 1:11; 2:19; 3:18; 7:23; 8:24; 11:8, 10; 15:21, 24; 16:17. The term *enōpion*, "before" carries the sense "in the sight of others" (3:20; 11:25; 12:16-17).

11. E.g. 1:28; 2:15, 20; 3:20; 6:11; 7:23, 25; 8:5-7, 18, 27; 10:2-3; 11:7, 33-34; 12:2-3; 14:5, 14; 15:14.

12. Some include 1:1, 8-9, 15-16; 2:16, 21-22; 3:5, 19; 4:1, 3, 6, 9; 6:11; 7:7; 8:31; 9:6, 9, 14, 15, 17, 19, 20, 25, 26, 30; 10:6, 8, 9, 11, 14-17, 19-21; 11:2, 9, 18-19, 28; 12:3, 19; 13:9; 14:11, 16; 15:10, 12, 16, 18-20; 16:25.

13. Slaves were seen as part of the Roman family.

14. *Aparchē* in Rom 8:23 could mean "birth certificate" BDAG 98.

15. See also references to Spain (15:24, 28); Achaia (15:26); Cenchreae (16:1); Asia (16:5).

16. See 12:13 (*philoxenia*, "love of strangers"); 13:9-10; 15:2; 16:23 (*xenos*, "stranger, to host a stranger" and "the whole church" [in Corinth]).

17. See 9:33; 11:26; 15:19, 25-26, 31

18. The term behind "hardening" in 11:25 is used of hard stones such as a bladder stone. *NIDNTTE* 4:196.

God's work as a horticulturist caring for trees (11:16–24). Jesus is also from the "*root of Jesse*" (15:12).

Where food is concerned, the church is also likened to a lump of dough (11:16). Famine speaks of destitution (8:35). Eating and drinking food (meat and vegetables) and drink are important in chapter 14, in particular, and in Romans 12:20.[19]

Transport and movement motifs are commonly used as he mentions language like send;[20] paths, ways, and roads (3:2, 16–17; 11:21); footsteps and following (4:11), walking,[21] stumbling, and obstacles.[22] He employs ideas from the world of work, including work (20x), labor (16:6, 12), and coworkers (16:3, 9, 21). Financial and economic ideas include wages (4:4; 6:23), riches (spiritual),[23] repayments (11:35; 12:17, 19), and poverty and hunger (12:20; 15:26), thirst (12:20), and famine (8:35). Construction terms (temple) include a stone laid (9:33), foundation (15:20), and of building each other up (14:19; 15:2, 20).

He uses a range of binaries, especially life and death.[24] Others include light and darkness (2:19; 13:12), day and night (13:12),[25] height and depth (8:39), peace and enmity (or reconciliation, 5:10; 11:28; 12:18–20), and hate and love (9:13).

Gift language is common whether spiritual gifts (1:11), salvation, justification, and eternal life,[26] or Christ the Son (8:32). The idea of grace implies undeserved giving (22x). Promise language is also prominent.[27]

Suffering concepts can originate from being crushed (*thlipsis*)[28] or being in a tightly confined space (*stenochōria*, 2:9; 8:35).[29] Persecution is *diōgmos* from *diōkō*, "pursue," which was initially a hunting or military term (8:35).[30] The terms snare and trap also come from hunting (11:9). Being poor and threatened is symbolized by nakedness, danger, and sword (8:35; 15:26).

---

19. See 12:20; 14:2, 15, 17, 20–21, 23.
20. See 8:3; 10:15; 15:24.
21. Rom 6:4; 8:4; 13:13; 14:15 (*peripateō*, Paul's favored term for walk, live).
22. See 9:32; 11:9, 11; 14:13, 21; 16:17.
23. See 2:4; 9:23; 10:12; 11:12, 33.
24. 5:10, 17, 21; 6:4, 23; 7:10; 8:2, 6, 38.
25. See also 2:5, 16; 8:36; 10:21; 11:8; 13:13.
26. See 2:7; 3:24; 4:4; 5:15–17; 6:23; 8:11.
27. See 4:13–20; 9:4, 8–9; 15:8.
28. *NIDNTTE* 2:461; see 2:9; 5:3; 8:35; 12:12. See also *lypē*, "grief" (9:2); *odynē*, "pain, distress" (9:2). other ideas
29. *NIDNTTE* 4:368.
30. *NIDNTTE* 1:749.

Other motifs include time ideas,[31] education as in the case of teaching;[32] maths;[33] spatial ideas such as height and depth (8:39); burning and fire (12:11;[34] 12:20); crafts (potter and clay, also creation, 9:20–23); images (1:23; 8:29); choice;[35] mercy, compassion, kindness, love, grace, and other terms;[36] household vessels (9:21–23), table (11:9), and seats ([judgment] 14:10).

Paul's use of a diverse range of contemporary metaphors should challenge those today who share the gospel in church and beyond to not only use the same ideas, but to reframe them, and find new ones to make the gospel come alive in the given context.

RHETORICAL DEVICES

As an accomplished Greek writer and thinker, Paul uses a range of rhetorical devices. Here are some in Romans.[37]

Anthropomorphism (ascribing human characteristics to God) and **Anthropopathism** (ascribing human emotions to God): e.g., God's speech (1:4); God as Father (1:7; 8:15, 21); God's wrath, fury (1:18; 2:5; 5:9); kindness, tolerance, patience (2:4; 11:22); God's love (5:5, 8; 8:39); God's will (8:27; 12:2); God's right hand (8:34); God stretching out his hand (10:21); God's rejection (11:1, 2); God the orchardist (11:21); God's severity (11:22); God's mercies (12:1; 15:9); judgment seat of God (14:10).

Antistrophe (the repetition of a word or phrase at the end of two or more successive clauses or stanzas): 3:30b–c (*pisteōs*, believe).

Antithesis (use of contrast for rhetorical effect): Paul uses these throughout Romans, e.g., grace and sin, Spirit and flesh, etc.

Antinomasia (replacing of one name for another): Adam and Jesus (5:14).

---

31. These include day (2:5, 16; 8:36; 10:21; 11:8; 13:12, 13; 14:5, 6), hour (13:11), time (3:26; 5:6; 7:1; 8:18; 9:9; 11:5; 13:11; 16:25), now (1:10; 4:19, 13.11), until (1:13; 5:13; 8:22; 11:25), future (8:38), present (8:38), always (1:10), age/eternity (1:25; 9:5; 11:36; 12:2; 16:27), and previously (1:2; 3:25).

32. See 2:21; 6:17; 12:7; 16:17.

33. The term *logizomai*, "reckon, count, consider, calculate, think" is mathematical (2:26; 4:3–6, 8–11, 22–23; 9:8).

34. Literally: "burn in [the] s/Spirit."

35. Election (not in a western democratic sense) and choice language is used exclusively of God's sovereign choice (see 8:33; 9:11; 11:5, 7, 28; 16:13).

36. Such ideas are frequent, used over fifty times.

37. Most definitions from *PDSNTG*. See also, Donfried, "False Presuppositions in the Study of Romans," 113–21 for those identified by Bultmann.

Aphorism (a terse statement expressing a truth or defining a principle): used throughout Romans, e.g., 2:2: "We know that the judgment of God rightly falls on those who practice such things."

Aposiopesis (breaking off a sentence to include a grammatically unnecessary element): Romans 7:24; 9:22–23.

Asseverative particle or clause (something that heightens the solemnity of a clause): "as surely as I live" (14:11).

Asyndeton (leaving out a conjunction): commonly, e.g., 1:29–31; 2:19–20; 11:28.

Captatio Benevolentiae (where a writer begins with complimentary words): see, for example, 1:8–12; 7:1; 15:14a.

Catena (a series of words, phrases, verses, quotations, or stories, a "chain"): esp. of OT citations: e.g., 3:10–18; 9:24–29; 10:17–21; 15:8–12.

Cento (a patchwork of biblical quotations): see the same verses listed above.

Chiasm (words, clauses, or themes are laid out and then repeated in reverse order): used regularly, e.g., see 1:16–18; 2:6–11; 7:8–10; 9:6–29; 10:9–10.

Cohortative or Hortatory Subjunctive (first-person plural inclusive subjunctive "let us . . ."): see 13:12 (let us cast off . . .); 14:13, 19.

Conditional sentences (a sentence that presents two situations, one conditioned on the other. Includes an "if" clause [protasis] and a "then" clause [apodosis] Paul uses these throughout Romans, e.g., 2:17–24; 3:5, 7; 4:2.

Deesis (an impassioned plea made in the name of a prominent figure): e.g., 12:1.

Diaphora (repetition of the same word with slightly different significance): e.g., 3:21–26.

Diatribe (ancient literary style employing an imaginary interlocutor for argument's sake): Very important to Romans, Paul uses these: 1) a sudden turn to address an imaginary questioner (e.g., 2:1–5, 17–24; 9:19–21; 11:17–24; 14:4); 2) a response to an immediately preceding objection or false conclusion (e.g., 3:1–9, 31; 4:1–2a; 6:1, 15; 7:7, 13; 9:14, 19; 11:1, 11, 19); 3) a dialogical exchange (e.g., 3:27—4:25).[38]

---

38. Toews, *Romans*, 374.

Aspects of Paul's "Gospel" Presentation to the Romans

Divine Passive (a verb in the passive with God implied as agent): e.g., 1:13; 3:21; 4:20; 8:4; 11:7; 15:22.

Ellipsis (omitting an element of language that renders the sentence ungrammatical but is understood in context): e.g., 9:32; 15:8–9.

Epanalepsis (the repetition of a word or group of words in the same clause), e.g., 8:2b.

Epidiorthosis (a comment that ends with something difficult or unpalatable): e.g., 3:5.

Epimone (repetition of same thought two or more times with a similar word): e.g., 7:18.

Erotesis (affirmative proposition in the form of a rhetorical question), e.g., 8:31–32, 33–34, 35–37.

Hyperbole (exaggeration): 1:8, 32; 15:14; 16:16.

Gezerah shawa (from midrashic interpretation where texts are linked because the same words are present in both): see, e.g., 4:2, 8, 9 (Gen 15:6; Ps 32:2); based on *logizomai*.

Hapax Legomenon (a word found only once in the NT): e.g., *horizō* (1:4), *philostorgos* (12:10).

Hendiadys (use of two words for one concept): e.g., possibly "apostolic commission" (1:5); "drunken revelry" (13:13).

Hypallage (reversal of the normal relationship of two words for rhetorical effect): e.g., 6:17 (*paredothēte typon didachēs*); 9:31 (*nomon dikaiosynēs*).

Hyperbaton (separation of words that naturally belong together): e.g., 1:15; 3:9; 11:13a–b, 31.

Inclusio (framing device): e.g., right thinking in 12:3 and 16; gentile inclusion in 9:24 and 9:30; "accept" in 14:1 and 3.

Irony (humorous or sarcastic statement giving the opposite meaning): e.g., the irony of gentile inclusion and Jewish disobedience in 11:30–31.

Isocolon (two or more coordinate clauses with strong similarities): e.g., 3:25b–26a; 5:19.

Litotes (negation to affirm the opposite, also meiosis): e.g., possibly "I am not ashamed of the gospel," meaning "I am confident in the gospel" in 1:16; "love does no wrong," meaning "love does good" (13:10).

Part Two: Romans and the Content of the Gospel

Makarism (beatitude or blessing): 4:7; 14:22, see also 1:25.

Merism (the juxtaposition of two extremes to suggest everything in between): height and depth in 8:38; Jerusalem to Illyricum in 15:19.

Metonymy (one thing is designated by something associated with it): e.g., circumcised and uncircumcised in 2:26; bellies for self-indulgence in 16:17.

Midrash (Jewish interpretative approach): e.g., Romans 4 as a midrash on Gen 15:6.

Orismus (a definition of a word to support one's argument or giving a specific action, behavior, or event, a name), e.g., "the worker" in 4:4.

Oxymoron (paradoxical statement): e.g., "if we died with Christ, we believe that we will also live with him," in 6:8.

Paradox (a seemingly self-contradictory statement): commonly in Romans, e.g., 8:13; 9:20; 11:28.

Paraenesis (instruction, exhortation, or commands): esp. Rom 12:1—15:7.

Parallelism (parallel statements): commonly in Paul, e.g., 1:1–15; 15:14–33 (inclusio); 6:18–22; 10:9–10; 15:11.

Parataxis (linking clauses and phrases with conjunctions, cf. asyndeton): e.g., 6:17; 8:10.

Parechesis (assonance with different words): e.g., 1:29, 31.

Parenthesis (a short aside in the middle of a sentence): Very common in Paul, e.g., 1:13; 4:13–17a; 11:13–14.

Paranomasia (play on words with similar-sounding words or same word group, punning): e.g., *krinōn . . . krineis . . . katakrineis . . . krinōn* in 2:1; *hyperphronein . . . phronein . . . phronein . . . sōphronein . . .* in 12:3.

Parrhesia (intentional refusal to mince words risking an adverse reaction to get a positive response): 9:1.

Periphrasis (indirect way of saying something, also circumlocution): something common in Paul, e.g., "make mention" in 1:9; "as far as it depends on me" in 1:15.

Pesher (Jewish interpretation stressing present-day fulfillment): common in Romans, e.g., 1:17; 10:5–13.

Aspects of Paul's "Gospel" Presentation to the Romans

Pleonasm (use of superfluous words): e.g., 1:5; 7:12.

Polyplopton (repetition of the same noun or pronoun in different cases in successive clauses): e.g., 11:36; 14:13.

Polysyndeton (superfluous repetition of a conjunction, opposite asyndeton): e.g., 2:17–18; 8:38–39; 9:4; 12:7.

Prolepsis (transfer of a word from a dependent clause to the main clause): e.g., 9–11 (Quintilian); 10:5.

Prosapodosis (mention of two or more ideas and returning to them for repetition or clarification): e.g., "kindness" and "severity" from 11:22a in 11:22b–d.

Prosopopoeia (attribution of speech or personality to nonhumans): e.g., 2:1–17; 7:7–12; 8:19–23.

Qal wahomer (a fortiori, moving from the lesser to the greater): e.g., 5:6–8, 9–11, 12–21; 11:12, 24.

Sorites (sequence of propositions where one established predicate noun becomes subject in the next): e.g., 5:3–5; 10:14–15.

Synecdoche (figure of speech using a more inclusive term is used of a less inclusive one and vice versa): e.g., body in 6:6; members in 7:5; and belly in 16:17.

Synonymia (repetition of though in synonymous terms): e.g., 7:15–16.

Tautology (repetition): e.g., 11:26a; 12:2, 11.

Theologoumenon (a deduction from theological reasoning and truth): e.g., 2:11.

The use of such an array of rhetorical devices should inspire a missionally motivated person to draw innovatively on the many such devices of their own languages as they share the gospel.

STRUCTURE

In Romans 1:1, the theme of the gospel launches the letter. Paul usually anticipates the essential threads of a letter in his prescripts,[39] so this suggests that the gospel is central

---

39. "Paul's letters, which follow the usual Hellenistic letter openings of 'A to B, greetings,' regularly contain expansions of this basic pattern (e.g., Rom 1:1–7; Gal 1:1–5; 1 Thess 1:1; Titus 1:1–4), and these often point to the specific purposes of the letters." O'Brien, "Letters, Letter Forms," 551.

Part Two: Romans and the Content of the Gospel

to understanding Romans. As always, Paul names himself and then describes himself first as a slave of Christ Jesus, then his call to be an apostle. As a "sent one," he is "set apart for the gospel (*euangelion*) of God" (1:1). The *euangelion* becomes antecedent to the next two subordinate clauses that state two enormous premises of the gospel:

- [the gospel] that (*ho*) he promised beforehand through his prophets in the holy Scriptures.
- [the gospel] concerning (*peri*) his Son.

First, the gospel is promised in the Scriptures by the prophets. Their prophetic hopes are finding their fulfillment in the events of the gospel and its message. Second, the gospel concerns God's Son—Jesus is the central content of the gospel.

The second of these two clauses explain further who this Son is.

- [He, Jesus] who (*tou*) was descended from David according to the flesh
- and who (*tou*) was declared to be the Son of God in power according to the Spirit of holiness by his resurrection from the dead, Jesus Christ our Lord.

This Son is the long-awaited Davidic Messiah expected in Israel's story. At the critical moment of his resurrection by the power of the Holy Spirit, God declared his divine sonship to the world. He is Jesus, the Messiah, who is the supreme Lord of the world. The gospel then *is* Jesus, the Christ, who is both Lord and God's Son.[40]

Then, in verse 5, Paul returns to his role (and that of other apostles, "we") in the mission of this Son. Through Jesus, he and those who also work in gospel mission have received grace and apostleship. They are emissaries or ambassadors of the kingdom of the son of David and Son of God. They are to declare this gospel to the world for an express purpose, namely, "to bring about the obedience of faith for the sake of his name among all the nations."

The phrase "obedience of faith" is slippery, but as will be discussed in part two, chapter 11 on human response, it most likely expresses obeying the summons of the gospel *by believing* in God and his Son. It is the obedience of responding to the gospel with faith. This meaning is seen in Romans 10:16, where Paul states that not all of Israel has *obeyed* the gospel. What will bring them salvation and inclusion is to obey it by believing it. Paul's mission is to go to the nations of the world, as he has done to this point and will continue to do after Jerusalem to Rome and Spain, to summon people to believe in Jesus. He does this for the sake of Jesus's name and no other reason: so that Christ's name (and his Father's) may be glorified throughout the world.

In verse 6, Paul brings it all back to the Romans: *they* are included among those called to belong to Jesus Christ. Subtly, Paul tells the Romans that they must listen,

---

40. Hence, we see again that while the gospel is the core theme of the letter (righteousness is the dominant sub-theme in the gospel), Romans is not the gospel or a Gospel. The Gospels tell the story of Jesus; he is the gospel.

for, while he did not start the church there, his commission includes them. He is the apostle to the gentiles of the world, and Rome is the empire's capital. He wants them to respond to the letter with a deepened "obedience of faith," unity in the gospel, and active support for him and God's mission (15:24).

After his usual blessing in Romans 1:8, the gospel again becomes the dominant theme. Paul prays for them with gratitude because their faith is being proclaimed in all the world. Many scholars read the passive tense or *euangelizomai* here as an indication that Paul is speaking of other non-Roman Christians telling the story of the faith of the Roman church to the world. No doubt it includes this.

However, as I have stated before, this verse may include the active role of the Romans themselves in evangelistic engagement in Rome, Italy, and beyond.[41] There are six reasons for this. First, *katangellō* is used for gospel proclamation in Paul.[42] Second, the proclaimers are not specified and could include the Romans. Third, "the faith" (*pistis*) is a parallel term for the gospel on some occasions.[43] Fourth, Philippians 1:14 suggests subsequent evangelistic activity. Fifth, the parallel in 1 Thessalonians 1:8 should be taken actively.[44] Finally, the list of Romans 16 indicates that many Romans were presently active in evangelism (see part three, chapter 16). As such, citing Romans 1:8 and 1 Thessalonians 1:8, Peters is right to say: "Paul commends the churches at Roman Thessalonica for their efforts in evangelizing their communities and beyond their borders."[45]

In verse 9, Paul speaks of his unswerving service of God in his spirit (his inner being) in the "gospel of his Son." Again, Jesus is the content of the gospel. Paul models the ideal attitude of the disciples—wholehearted belief in the gospel and the one who is at its center, Jesus. One facet that flows from such faith is heartfelt prayer, and so he prays for the Romans. Later, he will ask them to pray for him (a prayer inclusio in the letter, 15:30–32). He asks that now, at last, after many times of trying, he can come, share spiritual gifts with them, that they would experience mutual encouragement.

In the *hina* clause of verse 13 he states his purpose: "in order that (*hina*) I may have some harvest (*karpos*, "fruit") in you just as also in the rest of the gentiles" (translation mine). His purpose in coming to Rome is missional. To this point, Paul has evangelized the region from Jerusalem to the western Balkans (Illyricum). Now, continuing his western march with the gospel, he wants to push to Rome. His reason is to have fruit among them. *Karpos* here, as in Philippians 1:22,[46] has that sense of the fruit of new converts, a harvest of those who demonstrate "the obedience of faith."

---

41. Keown, *Congregational Evangelism in Philippians*, 74–75n23.
42. See 1 Cor 2:1; 9:13; Phil 1:17–18; Col 1:28, cf. 1 Cor 11:26.
43. See Gal 1:23; 1 Thess 1:9; 1 Tim 2:7, cf. 2 Cor 4:14; 10:15; Phil 1:27.
44. Keown, *Congregational Evangelism in Philippians*, 250–59.
45. Peters, *Biblical Theology*, 133.
46. In Phil 1:22, *karpos* has the double sense of new converts and the growth of the Philippians.

Part Two: Romans and the Content of the Gospel

In verse 14, his life's call is summed up. As the apostle to the gentiles, he has a divine obligation to preach the gospel to *all* gentiles. Just as Jews tended to divide the world into Jews and gentiles, the Romans identified with the great Greek tradition and divided the world up into Greeks and barbarians. In their own minds, at least, the Greeks (and themselves) represent the wise, the educated, and the philosophically superior. The barbarians are those who babble in other languages and are considered uncivilized and foolish.[47] Formerly, Paul was no doubt similarly racist where gentiles are concerned. Now, rather than partake in such flagrant ethnocentrism, Paul seeks to be impartial as is his God; he is called to preach to men, women, Jews, Greeks, barbarians, Scythians, slaves, and the free (cf. 1 Cor 12:13; Gal 3:28; Col 3:11).

Then in verse 15, this obligation is what generates his passion to come to Rome to preach. "You" here is often read as his desire to preach to the Roman Christians.[48] However, while no doubt Paul does want to travel through the house churches of Rome articulating God's message to strengthen and encourage the Romans (1:11–12); as he does elsewhere, he loves to preach to those yet converted to win fruit for God (e.g., 15:20–21). He wants to evangelize the masses—the elite and the non-elite.

Rightly, many scholars hold that Romans 1:16–17 is the thematic statement of the letter.[49] These verses state the overriding axioms of the letter. Paul begins stating that he is "not ashamed of the gospel." This phrase is not merely a statement of his courage to uphold the gospel but zeroes in on the shameful idea of a crucified so-called Messiah. For Israel, because anyone hanged on a tree is accursed (Gal 3:13; Deut 21:23), Jesus must be so. He has been rejected by his people; shamed and killed by the Roman rulers, and so, for all but a handful of Jewish people, Jesus is *not* Israel's long-awaited Messiah. However, for Paul, in dying on the cross, Jesus bore the shame of humankind, and the gospel declares his glory as the resurrected Son of God.

The gospel then is the power of God for the salvation of all people; Jews and gentiles alike.[50] Paul here speaks of the power of the message to bring people into a saving relationship with God, when heard (10:14–17). The idea of God's word being powerful and active is not new. God's word spoke the world into being at creation (Gen 1). It brings to pass God's purposes (e.g., Isa 55:11; see further part three, chapter 15). The prophets enacted this as they spoke history into being, and now this is culminating in Christ (1:2). Through the gospel, people are called to respond to God's summons.

---

47. See Windisch, "Βάρβαρος," 1:546 who notes that the term "basically means "stammering," "stuttering," or "uttering unintelligible sounds." It has the sense "strange race," or "non-Greek." The barbarians for the Greeks were "the other peoples who are different in nature, poor in culture, or even uncultured, whom the Greeks hold at arm's length, and over whom they are destined to rule, esp. such national enemies as the Persians and the Egyptians etc."

48. O'Brien, *Consumed by Passion*, 61–65.

49. See, e.g., Moo, *Letter to the Romans*, 66–68.

50. "The twenty-first century, no less than the first century, may regard it as a 'stumbling block' or as 'foolishness' (1 Cor. 1:23), but it remains 'the power of God unto salvation' (Rom. 1:16 KJV)." Tennent, *World Missions*, 68.

Aspects of Paul's "Gospel" Presentation to the Romans

The phrase "to the Jew first and also to the Greek" speaks of the sequence of salvation history. Jesus came to the circumcised, summoning Israel to recognize her Messiah, God's Son. A remnant heard and believed (9:27; 11:5). Now, God has sent some of these believers, including Paul and his team, to preach this gospel to the gentiles. Both Jews and gentiles are yielding to Christ as the gospel is preached. Amazingly, as Romans 16 shows, many gentiles are now also proclaiming this gospel (see also Col 4:12–17).

In verse 17, "in *it*" is "in the gospel." There is then a significant shift from the gospel to one aspect of it, "the righteousness of God." "The righteousness of God" is much debated. Does it speak of God's character, his action toward the world, his creative power, or his covenantal faithfulness? Does it speak subjectively of the state of righteousness experienced by people as they hear the gospel and believe—justification by faith? Indeed, here, it is global in its meaning. God is King and Judge, and he is righteous and just. As such, he acts justly in accord with his righteous being, his covenantal relationship with Israel, and the words of his prophets. His salvation is fair, the same for all, for he is impartial (2:11). The status declared over the one—Jew or gentile, barbarian or Greek, slave or free, male, or female—who accedes to the gospel by faith is, "Righteous! Acquitted! Innocent! Not guilty! Pardoned!" (see further, part two, chapter 10).

The basis of this declaration is expounded in a balanced Greek clause: *ek pisteōs eis pistin*, "from faith to faith." This phrase is slippery with a range of potential interpretations.[51] Whichever is adopted, the statement emphasizes the importance of responding with faith (see further part two, chapter 11).

In a sense, every one of these is possible, and perhaps we err in trying to define Paul's thought here precisely. After all, the argument of Romans is that a life of faith is sufficient for salvation, inclusion, and eternal life. It is evident that it is faith on the part of the hearer of the gospel that brings the declaration of being righteous by God. Further, faith is the basis by which a person remains in a state of *being* justified before God.

Paul buttresses the importance of faith by citing Habakkuk 2:4. In the Hebrew the verse reads, "the righteous shall live by his faith/faithfulness" (ESV/NIV). The LXX reads, "the righteous shall live from my faith/faithfulness" (my translation). Habakkuk is told to write down the vision that will come to fulfillment (Hab 2:3). In Habakkuk 2:4, there is a contrast in the wicked in the first half and the righteous in the second. God answers the prophet telling him that "[t]he one whose life is puffed up in pride and arrogance will die; the righteous, in contrast, by his faithfulness will live."[52] The wicked entail those who "rely on something of this earth . . . and not in God."[53]

---

51. See the discussion in Moo, *Letter to the Romans*, 79–82.
52. Barker, *Micah, Nahum, Habakkuk, Zephaniah*, 325.
53. Barker, *Micah, Nahum, Habakkuk, Zephaniah*, 325.

Part Two: Romans and the Content of the Gospel

Conversely, the righteous "accept God's word of promise."[54] In Habakkuk, the term can be translated as faithfulness, which denotes "loyalty as well as truth and trust."[55] Barker summarizes Paul here:

> Paul used this idea as the hallmark of his teaching concerning the primacy of faith in salvation. He took God's message to Habakkuk to its final emphasis: those who are judged righteous as a result of their faith shall live. Habakkuk's questions supplied Paul with his beginning and ending point that faith is the key. God recognizes the faithfulness (faith) of his people and gives life.[56]

Here, in Romans 1:17, both "faith" and "faithfulness" work. Further, the verse can be translated, "the righteous by faith/faithfulness will live," or, "the righteous will live by faith." Although scholars are prone to do so, we need not decide between the two. One begins the journey of salvation coming into that faith, trust, and pledge of loyalty. For Paul, salvation is gifted to the one who continues that journey by faith, faithful to God, to the end.

As we come to the end of the first part of Romans, it is clear that the gospel is the dominant theme in the letter. It is through this gospel proclaimed that people are saved. Two specific aspects of the gospel then take center stage: righteousness/justification and the response of faith. The exposition of the gospel to Rome will focus on those two motifs. Paul could have gone in a range of different directions making the dominant issue reconciliation, redemption, adoption, or sanctification. All of these do feature in the letter but do not lie at its center.

As such, Romans is not a Gospel. The Gospels are narratives of the life of Jesus based on the *bios* genre. Romans does not narrate Jesus's life and, aside from his death and resurrection, has little interest in it. Still, its central theme is the gospel (see the next chapter). It is not a once-for-all presentation of the gospel, but a letter written to Romans Christians with the gospel at its center. It is not a gospel intent on converting unbelievers (although it may do this).

The Christians in Rome were facing unique, contextual-cultural, and theological challenges over matters of Jewish law, justification, and inclusion. It is also written in preparation for future mission. As will be discussed in the next sections, Romans includes many aspects of Paul's gospel. Nevertheless, it is not comprehensive, with a range of things not included (see part one, chapter 4).

In conclusion, then, Romans is not the gospel or a presentation of the gospel to unbelievers. It should not then become the pattern for *all* future evangelization any more than a sermon in Acts or a message by Jonathan Edwards should be assumed as a once-for-all message to be proclaimed today. It is a fantastic example of a message to Christians with the gospel as its core theme and with a focus on righteousness/

---

54. Barker, *Micah, Nahum, Habakkuk, Zephaniah*, 325.
55. Barker, *Micah, Nahum, Habakkuk, Zephaniah*, 326.
56. Barker, *Micah, Nahum, Habakkuk, Zephaniah*, 326.

Aspects of Paul's "Gospel" Presentation to the Romans

justification and faith. We can still learn a lot about shaping a gospel message to a given context from Romans.

After his gospel-focused beginning to the letter, Paul shapes a presentation of the gospel for his hearers in their unique life-setting. Here, I will give a concise summary of the structure of the letter showing the contours of his presentation. Thus far, Paul has told us this about the gospel.

The Gospel of God (1:1)

- The fulfillment of the Prophets in the Scriptures (1:2).
- Concerning God's Son Jesus (1:3–5).
  - A descendant of David (1:3).
  - He was declared so with power by the Spirit at his resurrection (1:4).
  - Through him, people are called to mission and to believe (1:5–6).
- The gospel of his Son (1:9).
- The power of God for the salvation for all (1:16–17).
  - The revelation of the righteousness of God (1:17).
  - Received by the human response of faith (1:17).

We can break down the gospel in Romans in 1:18 onwards.

Universal Sin and God's Wrath (1;18—3:20)

- God's wrath against ungodliness and unrighteousness (1:18).
- The problem of idolatry (1:19–25).
- The consequent problem of sexual immorality (1:26–27).
- Unrighteous attitudes and acts (1:28–32).
- The problem of self-righteous sinfulness (2:1–5).
- God's righteous judgment by works (2:6–11).
- Sinners with or without the law (2:12–16).
- The problem of the self-righteous Jew (2:17–24).
- The impotence of physical circumcision (2:25–29).
- The advantage of the Jew (3:1–2).
- God is faithful, true, and righteous, but his people and all people are not (3:3–8).
- Jews and gentiles alike under sin (3:9–20).

The Righteousness of God Through Faith (3:21—4:25)

- The righteousness of God through faith in Jesus Christ (3:21–31).

Part Two: Romans and the Content of the Gospel

- The example of Abraham (4:1–25).

Consequences and Concomitants of Justification by Faith (5:1—8:39)

- Reconciled to God through faith (5:1–11).
- The sin of Adam undone—death to life (5:12–21).
- Dead to sin, alive to God (6:1–14).
- Slaves of righteousness (6:15–23).
- Set free from the law (7:1–6).
- The struggle the law creates (7:7–25).
- Alive in the Spirit (8:1–11).
- Children and heirs of God (8:12–17).
- Hope in suffering (8:18–39).

The Place of Ethnic Israel (9:1—11:36)

- Israel's blessings (9:1–5).
- Not all Israel are Israel (9:6–33).
  - God's word has not failed (9:6a).
  - Not all Israel are Israel (9:6b).
  - Not all Abraham's children are Abraham's offspring (9:7).
  - The Abrahamic line of promise by election (9:8–23).
  - The line continues in the gentiles (9:24–26).
  - A remnant of Israel (9:27–29).
- Israel's failure—stumbling in unbelief (9:30–33).
- Israel's failure—righteousness by law (10:1–7).
- Faith for salvation (10:8–13).
- Israel has heard the gospel and is accountable (10:14–21).
- A remnant of Israel reserved (11:1–6).
- The remainder of Israel hardened (11:7–10).
- Israel's faithless people can be reintegrated (11:11–24).
- All Israel will be saved (11:25–36).

Living in Light of the Gospel (12:1—15:13)

Aspects of Paul's "Gospel" Presentation to the Romans

- Cruciform living (12:1–2).
- Living out spiritual giftedness with humility (12:3–8).
- Living together as God's people in a heathen world (12:9–21).
- Living in relationship to the State (13:1–7).
- Love and holiness in Christ (13:8–14).
- Welcome one another (14:1—15:7).
- As Prophesied, the Gentiles are Worshiping God (15:8–13).

From Romans 15:14 to the end of the letter, Paul returns to the same kind of material we find in Romans 1:1–18 as he speaks of his ministry in the gospel. By the grace of God, Paul is a minister of Jesus to the gentiles (15:15–16). For Paul, this is a priestly service, and the gentiles are an offering to God,[57] now sanctified by the Spirit (15:16).[58] Paul speaks of his pride in his mission, not because of his personal accomplishments, but based on what Christ has done in and through him in bringing the gentiles to the obedience of faith (15:18, cf. 1:5).

In Romans 15:18–19, we get a sense of Paul's approach. He engages in preaching and teaching (by word), good works (deeds such as the Jerusalem Collection), and miracles (by the power of signs and wonders), all done through the power of the Spirit. In Romans 15:19b, Paul neatly summarizes the geographical scope of his mission. To this point, he has evangelized from Jerusalem, through Syria, Asia, to the western Balkans. He has sufficiently established the Christian church in an arc from Israel along the coast of the Mediterranean to the Adriatic Sea.

Paul then expresses his passion for preaching in areas in which Christ has not yet been named (preached). He wants to establish churches where no one else has begun the work of planting the seed of the gospel (15:20, cf. Isa 52:15). In what follows, we read of his travel plans. First, he will leave Corinth and go to Jerusalem with the collection (15:25–28a, 30–31). Then, he hopes to come and experience refreshment and mutual encouragement in Rome (1:12; 15:32). He wants to share spiritual gifts among those in the church and preach in the city, winning converts (1:11, 13–15). He wants then to garner their support for his push west to Spain to preach the gospel (15:24, 28).

Romans 16 tells us of a range of coworkers in the gospel, which will be discussed in due course (see part three, chapter 6). Suffice to say at this point, that it indicates

---

57. The offering can be the people or the gift. Both may be in view. O'Brien, *Consumed with Passion*, 31, 50–51. I prefer to see it as the gentile converts and if both the gentiles and gifts are in view, the financial gifts are secondary.

58. "Paul describes his evangelistic mission as his 'priestly duty.' Immediately he refers to the the same double direction of movement—bringing the gospel to the nations and bringing the nations to God (Rom 5:16)." Wright, *Mission of God*, 333.

.Paul's approach is not a one-person mission but involved partnership with many others in his quest to see the gospel penetrate the world.

Paul's final doxology, if original as is likely, again focuses on the gospel. The gospel declares that God will strengthen the Romans (16:25). The gospel is a revelation of the long-veiled mystery of salvation through a crucified Messiah. Now, what was disclosed but not fully understood in the prophetic writings "has been made known to all nations, according to the command of the eternal God." The purpose of this unveiling is to "bring about the obedience of faith" (1:5).

We can sum this up:

The gospel

- The preaching about Jesus Christ.
- The revelation of a long-held secret mystery that is disclosed in the Scriptures.
- It is revealed to the gentiles by God's command.
- To bring about the obedience of faith.

8

Underlying Aspects of the Gospel in Romans

THE CENTRAL THEME—THE GOOD NEWS OF GOD

WHILE ROMANS IS NOT a Gospel nor the gospel we should preach every time we share Christ, the central theme of Romans *is* the *euangelion* of God. There are four main reasons for this conclusion. First, the dominant motif in the prologue of the letter is *euangelion* (1:1–4, 8, 10–15). Second, the gospel is the central motif in the thematic statement of the letter in 1:16–17:

> For I am not ashamed of the gospel, for it is the power of God for salvation for all who believe, to the Jew first and also to the Greek. For in it the righteousness of God is being revealed from faith to faith. As it is written, "The one who is righteous by faith, will live." (Translation mine)

So, while righteousness is the core aspect of the *euangelion* that will dominate the letter, it is in fact, only one (albeit important) element of the gospel of Paul. In other letters, righteousness is far from dominant. Third, the content of the letter is a theological presentation of the gospel set in a given context, i.e., first-century Roman Christians. Therefore, theology and mission are central to the purposes of Romans. The prominence of the gospel makes sense as Paul is planning to come to Rome to preach to strengthen the church at the center of the empire, to gain a harvest of people who believe in Jesus, and then to evangelize Spain from Rome. He seeks their support for his Spanish mission. As such, all that is said in the letter falls under this governing rubric. Fourth, the gospel as a theme dominates 15:14–33, which, with the Prologue, frames the letter. Gospel work is also central to Romans 16, as a series of workers are greeted and send greetings.

As previously argued, Romans *is* not an exposition of the gospel of Christ but is a letter that presents the gospel to the Roman Christians and is more a contextual theological reflection premised on the gospel, shaped for a particular context and moment in history. Still, it is crystal clear that the core theme of the letter is the "gospel." Consequently, attention is now given to the emphases of the letter, aspects that grow out of Paul's gospel which he deemed important that the Romans fully understood in that historic moment.

THE TRIUNE GOD, FATHER, SON, AND SPIRIT

While it would be a few hundred years before the Trinity was formalized and adopted as orthodox theology, Paul has a rich understanding of the Triune God in Romans.

God the Father

The Romans (and Greeks) were polytheistic,[1] explaining reality through a pantheon of gods associated with all aspects of life. In radical contrast and consistent with the rest of the Bible, Romans speaks of *one* God (*Theos*, 3:30).[2] This Being is in control of all reality, is loving yet just, and the One from whom the whole story of Jesus comes. Jews are radically monotheistic, vehemently protective of the idea that there is one God (esp. seen in the Shema, Deut 6:4–5). Paul retains this emphasis.

However, Paul has been apprehended by Jesus (Gal 1:14–15) and is now convinced that Jesus Christ is God's Son, and the Spirit is the presence of both Father and Son in this age (8:9). As such, his letters give evidence of a dramatic transformation in Paul's understanding of monotheism. His view of God is still profoundly monotheistic, yet his vision has expanded to a God who is triune; three in One. Later Trinitarian formulations will draw on the threeness of the One God acting within history found in Romans and the other NT writings.

Aside from the widespread use of the personal pronoun, "he, his" of God, the Greek *Theos* is found 151 times in Romans. Moreover, *kyrios* is used of God nine times.[3] He is "Father" (*patēr*) four times.[4] While much is said about Christ, the Spirit, and humans, it is God who is the beginning, the end, and the everything-in-between of Paul's gospel.

---

1. Technically, Roman and Greek polytheism is henotheism, which has a chief God, i.e., Zeus or Jupiter. Geisler, "Polytheism," 602.

2. See also 1 Cor 8:4, 6; Gal 3:20; Eph 4:6; 1 Tim 2:5.

3. See Rom 4:8; 9:28, 29; 10:16; 11:3, 34; 12:19; 14:11; 15:11. Some of these may refer to Jesus but seem in context to be God the Father.

4. Rom 1:7; 6:4; 8:15 (also *Abba*); 15:6. As God was defined by the masculine, I will retain the masculine pronoun throughout this book aware that God is not male; both men and women are made in his image (Gen 1:27).

Underlying Aspects of the Gospel in Romans

In these texts, God is the author and pioneer of every aspect of existence. He is the content, author, and source of the gospel (1:1; 15:16). He is eternal and wise and brings his salvation in Christ (16:26–27). He is the father of Jesus (1:4; 15:6). God loves believers (1:7), and he welcomes all (14:3). As the God of peace (15:33; 16:20), he bestows peace (1:7) and will ultimately crush Satan, who brings chaos (16:20). He is the object of prayer,[5] service and worship,[6] thanksgiving (6:17; 7:25; 14:6), and obedience (11:30)

Idolatry—the failure to worship him exclusively—is humankind's central problem that has caused the defilement of God's world.[7] God's will *is* what matters (1:10). He is almighty and, through the gospel, expresses his absolute power in saving people who believe (1:16). God is immortal in contrast with the mortality of humanity and the natural world (1:23). He is the Creator (1:19–20, 25).

God is righteous/just and expresses his righteousness/justice in the gospel.[8] He is wrathful against evil,[9] an expression of his justice.[10] In Christ, God demonstrates his justice (3:24–26; 9:14). In accordance with his righteous character and rule, he will judge the world.[11] As those created by him, charged with the responsibility for his world, all people are accountable to him (3:19; 14:12). All must stand before him and give account (14:10). He will grant reward to those who live out of faith and righteousness (2:29).

He is glorious in his holiness and purity, something that no human (aside from Christ) can attain (3:23). Paul believes God can be perceived through what he has made in creation (1:19–20). God created everything out of nothing (4:17). He is the giver of the law (1:32; 7:22, 25), a law he bestowed on Israel (3:2), and that Israel has broken, and in so doing, has brought disgrace to his name (2:23–24). He is faithful to Israel, who has been unfaithful (3:3–4) but he has *not* rejected his people (11:1–2); instead, they have rejected him.

He is not only Israel's God, but is the God of all people (3:29). The gospel is about his determination to reconcile all humankind through the salvation found in Jesus. As such, he is kind to all humanity, bringing people deserving of destruction to salvation through his mercy and patience (2:4; 11:32; 12:1). Humans should praise him for this

---

5. See 1:8, 21; 10:1; 15:5, 6, 30.

6. See 1:8, 21, 25; 4:20; 5:11 [Greek = "boast"]; 9:5; 10:1; 11:33; 14:11; 15:5, 6, 30—remembering service and worship language significantly overlap.

7. See 1:21, 25, 28–32; 3:11, 18. "Writing to Christians, and speaking of idolatry objectively as a phenomenon, Paul pulls no punches. In his sharp analysis of human rebellion against God in Romans 1:18–32, he sets idolatry firmly within the realm of that which incurs the wrath of God.... It involves the inversion of the creation order." Wright, *Mission of God*, 179. See also his comments on p. 186 of Paul's "searing" and "prophetic" exposure of idolatry in 1:18–32.

8. See 1:17; 3:21, 22; 10:3.

9. See 1:18; 2:3, 5.

10. Cf. 1:24, 26, 28; 3:5.

11. See 2:2, 5, 13, 16; 3:6.

mercy (15:9). He is impartial, showing no favoritism to any ethnicity or group—a truly multicultural God (2:11; 3:29).[12] He is truthful (3:7), a truth expressed in the gospel of Christ (15:8).

In salvation history, he is the God of the Jews (2:17). As a demonstration of his justice and righteousness, he sent Jesus to save the world through his death (3:25–26). He declares righteous—announcing them not guilty, justified, pardoned, and acquitted—all people (Jew and gentile), not based on righteous works of the law or any other works, but through faith. Prior to Jesus, this involved faith in God, as in Abraham (4:3). Now that Jesus has come, it requires faith in Jesus as resurrected Lord (3:26; 4:2, 3).

Believers must remain in a faith-based relationship with God (11:21, 23). He bestows righteousness on the saved (4:6) and raises the dead (4:17). He is a God of promise who is faithful to his promises found in the Scriptures (4:20). In the gospel, the wrath of God is averted, and by faith in Jesus Christ, people are reconciled to God and share in his glory as God always intended (5:1–2, 10, 11).

God is characterized by love, and this *agapē* is poured into the hearts of all believers through his Spirit, who indwells their beings (5:5). The death of Jesus is not only a demonstration of his justice (3:25–26), but it is also a display of his love (5:8). He is full of kindness leading to salvation (2:4; 11:22). He is merciful by his sovereign choice (9:15–18, 23). This mercy is bestowed on those formerly disobedient who respond with the obedience of faith (11:30–32; cf. 1:5). To his mercies, believers should react with worshipful self-giving (12:1), acts of mercy (12:8), and praise (15:9). The Spirit is the presence of God in the believer (8:9). He is the same power that raised Jesus from the dead (1:2–4; 10:9). It is by the power of the Spirit of God that Paul ministers (15:19). God thus fills his people with love, hope, joy, and peace (5:5; 15:13).

The Spirit-presence of God in believers gives them hope in present suffering (5:5). Nothing can separate them from his love, which is unconditional and unstoppable (8:39). Knowing they are loved brings great solace to believers, no matter what they face. Their God is a glorious God who is on their side! (8:31). They are more than conquerors against whom nothing can stand (8:37), even if their bodies are beaten to a pulp.

Another feature of God is his grace, whereby he gives freely to humankind through Jesus (5:15). This grace is seen in spiritual gifts, including Paul's own commission (12:3–6; 15:15). Through Jesus, God bestows life, resolving the problem of physical and eternal death (6:11, 22, 23). The Christian life is living to please God in love as led by the Spirit (6:12–23; 7:4; 8:14). Failure to do so and to prefer the desires

---

12. "The Apostle Paul does insist that 'God shows no partiality' (Romans 2:11). Notice, however, the character of the divine 'impartiality.' God is impartial, argues Paul, because 'anguish and distress' due to 'everyone who does evil' will befall 'the Jew *first*' just as the 'glory and honor and peace' due to 'everyone who does good' will come to 'the Jew *first*' (vv. 9–10). God's 'impartiality' as Paul understands it *entails* the priority of the Jews. Formulated paradoxically, God is impartially partial. Volf, *Exclusion & Embrace*, 222n6.

of the flesh is to live in enmity to God and to fail to please him (8:7, 8). In the gospel, through Jesus whom he sent, he has resolved the problem of sin, setting humanity free from its power and consequences (8:3).

God is the head of the family of God. He is the father (1:7; 6:4), the paterfamilias of all humanity. Believers can confidently cry out to him, "Abba!" as did Jesus (Mark 14:36). This freedom indicates that he is their father, and they need not fear him, having been adopted by God into his cosmic family (8:15). Actually, as Romans 8 unfolds, he is a fiercely jealous father who protects his own (cf. 8:28-36). He, and not the emperor or Jupiter (Zeus), the father of the gods, heads the cosmic family as its *paterfamilias* under the leadership of his Son, Jesus Christ, and including humanity by faith indwelt with his presence, i.e., "the children of God."[13]

God's election by grace received with faith is, and always has been (4:3-8), the principle of entry into the family of God (9:8). As children, believers are heirs of God, meaning that they are in, under, and with Christ, and as such, with him, they will inherit all things. However, this "in Christness" includes the full experience of Christ, including participation in the suffering that blights all creation because of corruption through sin (8:17, 19). Nevertheless, as Christ's death is meaningful for human salvation, in Christ, God turns the horrors of suffering to the overall good, using it for his purposes as people expend themselves for God. Ultimately, God will release creation from its bondage, and all creation and his children will be free (8:21).

The Spirit of God leads the believer and intercedes for them (8:14, 27). God is sovereign, moving all of history toward his purposes, a source of deep comfort for believers he called and loves (8:28). God will give ultimate victory for believers; this is assured, and so in the present, they can live in complete confidence and without fear (8:31). Based on his mercy, God elects those who believe, and they are irreproachable in Jesus.[14] Jesus is his appointed regent, who sits at his right hand (8:34).

God has given Israel his word (9:6), to which he is faithful (11:29). However, most of Israel has failed, with a false zeal for God (10:2). Zeal for God is good, but it must be based on knowledge. God's will is found through a person giving her or himself over to God entirely, and through a mind renewed in Christ, the gospel, and Spirit; that is, to live out the cruciform pattern lived fully by Christ (12:2). This life of worship will involve service and suffering on behalf of others, by the power of the Spirit.[15]

Paul himself lives to obey God's will (15:32). God assigns to believers their function (12:3-6). He is sovereign over governments that he establishes and that serve him, even if unwittingly (13:1-6). As such, believers should submit to their governments,

---

13. Rom 8:14, 16, 19, 26.

14. Rom 8:33; 9:11, 16, 20, 26.

15. See Tennent, *World Missions*, 97–98. He comments, "For Paul, suffering is a normal expectation for Christian witness." See also Hafemann, "'Because of Weakness' (Galatians 4:13)," 131–46. He notes "Paul's apostolic ministry of missionary suffering and his gospel theology were an inseparable unity" (p. 140).

Part Two: Romans and the Content of the Gospel

even one like that of Rome (13:1–2). Nevertheless, they should do so without violating their first allegiance—to God and his Son. God reigns through his Son, and God's kingdom is supreme (14:17). God is at work in the human heart, bringing salvation, something believers must not destroy in others through petty judgmentalism (14:20). They must live in all things to see God glorified through their acceptance, unity, and worship (15:5–9). Christian work is work for God, who is their Lord, master, employer, and rewarder (15:17). Romans, it must be said, is *all about God*.

Jesus Christ Lord

If Romans is all about God, the center of God's gospel story in Romans (and the NT and the whole Bible! And creation!) is Jesus. God runs the show in Romans, but the whole letter and gospel revolve around Jesus, who is the royal agent through whom God works. As with the rest of the NT, Paul uses four main terms for Jesus.

Jesus

Iēsous is Jesus's earthly name. More fully, he is "Jesus of Nazareth," although this formula is not in Romans or any of the NT letters or Revelation. The name is derived from *yehô-šûaʿ*, the later form of Hebrew *yē-šûaʿ*, a name that incorporates the divine name and means ""Yahweh helps / is salvation.""[16] While the name invokes a number of OT figures, it calls to mind the first Joshua, the son of Nun, who led Israel into the land, overcoming the Canaanites.[17] Jesus is the new Joshua, bringing a conquest of the world in a completely different way. He did not conquer with violence but was crucified and rose from death. In his apparent defeat, he triumphed over the real enemies of humankind: sin, death, and destruction. The name also places Jesus in the historical setting of the world and Israel (9:30–32; 10:17–21; 11:26). He died on a cross and rose again as Lord. As his name suggests, he brings God's salvation.

Messiah, the Christ

Jesus is called *Christos* sixty-five times in Romans. Throughout his letters, it is Paul's favored term for Jesus. The name indicates he is the long-awaited anointed Davidic king, the Messiah. He has come to Israel as its peoples' anointed King and Savior. He is

---

16. Schneider, "*Iēsous*," 2:181.

17. Aside from the son of Nun (Neh 8:17), there are is a priest (1 Chr 24:11); a Levite in the days of King Hezekiah (2 Chr 31:15); an ancestor of exile returnees (Ezra 2:2, 6; 4:3; Neh 7:7, 11; 12:1); the high priest in the days of Zerubbabel (Ezra 3:2, 8; 10:18; Neh 12:26); an ancestor of returnees (Ezra 2:36; Neh 7:39); another ancestor of returnees (Ezra 2:40; 3:9; Neh 7:43; 9:4, 5; 12:8); a father of a Levite in Ezra's days (Ezra 8:33); a father of a wall builder (Neh 3:19); a Levite expositor of Torah (Neh 8:7); a signer of a covenant (Neh 10:10 LXX [EEV 10:9]). See *DBL Hebrew* #3800 (noting that identification in these texts is challenging).

the Son of David dreamed of by many in Israel.[18] He is also the "root of Jesse" (David's father), fulfilling the hopes of Isaiah and Israel (15:12 = Isa 11:10).[19] The rock laid in Zion is Jesus, who honors believers but who has become a stone of stumbling and rock of offense for Israel (9:33 = Isa 28:16). The savior from Zion has come who banishes Israel's ungodliness and forms the basis of a covenant of forgiveness (11:26–27 = Isa 59:20–21).

As such, while Jesus is a man who dies for the world, he is more than a man, a teacher, or a prophet. He is the Messiah of Israel (esp. 9:3, 5, see also 1:4). He is not only Christ but a crucified Messiah who blows to smithereens the expectations of Israel and the paradigms of power of the gentile world.[20] He has entered history, not in power to rule by might and sword, but in kindness, mercy, grace, and love, to die on a cross and through that death, to save the world and lay down a pattern for life that his people are, by the power of the Spirit, to emulate.

Lord

Kyrios is used thirty-three times of Jesus in Romans (forty-three times overall). As Lord, Jesus is not only Israel's Christ, but he also reigns over the world and all creation. Through him, a new creation is planted within a fallen world, and ultimately all creation will finally be healed (8:19–22). He is thus Savior of people, without favoritism, but on the same basis: grace and faith, not works and law. All other claimants, whether Nero, who reigned at the time in Rome over his vast empire, any other rulers, or the gods and goddesses of Rome and other nations whose temples are found throughout the city and empire, are subjugated to him as Lord of lords. It is through him that Yahweh has finally spoken, and the world is saved in and through him alone.

Paul's use of *kyrios* of Jesus also implies Christ's divinity.[21] *Kyrios* is used some 6156 times for God in the LXX.[22] By utilizing the term, Paul is identifying Jesus with God's self. This identification of Jesus with God is especially noticeable where he quotes OT verses that were initially related to God and now apply to Jesus.[23] These

---

18. See Isa 9:7; 16:5; 23:5; 33:15, 17; 34:23–24; 37:24–25; 55:3; Hos 3:5; Amos 9:11; Zech 12:7, 10–12; 13:10; 1 Macc 2:57; 2 Esdr 12:32; 3 En. 45:5; Sib. Or. 6:16; 7:31; 8:252; 4 Ezra 12:32; Mart. Ascen. Isa 11:2; 4Q161 Frags. 8–10:18; 4Q174 Frags. 1:1, 21; 2:11–13; 4Q252 Col. 5:2–4; 4Q285 Frag. 5:3; 4Q504 Frags. 12, 4:6–8; 11Q5 Col. 27:2; 11Q14 Frag. 11:12–13.

19. See also 4Q161 Frags. 8–10:11; 4Q285 Frag. 5:2; 4Q522 Frag. 9, 2:33; 11Q14 Frag. 1 1:11.

20. "Equally fundamental and equally shattering for Paul's world-view was the conviction that Jesus the Christ exercised his messianic function preeminently through his death and resurrection. *Nothing in Jewish tradition had prepared Paul for this paradoxical fact.*" Senior and Stuhlmueller, *Biblical Foundations for Mission*, 174 (emphasis mine).

21. See the nuanced discussion of Hurtado, *Lord Jesus Christ*, 108–18. He notes the early use of *marana tha* (1 Cor 16:22).

22. Witherington, "Lord," 485. Overall, *kyrios* is used 9000 times.

23. See Rom 4:8 = Pss 32:1–2; possibly 9:27–28 = Isa 10:22–23; 10:13 = Joel 2:32; 9:29 = Isa 1:9; 10:16 = Ps 19:4; 11:34 = Isa 40:13; 12:19 = Deut 32:35; 14:11 = Isa 45:23 (cf. Phil 2:9–11); 15:11 = Ps

indicate Jesus is God's divine Son and regent ruling on his behalf; he is Yahweh with us (cf. *Immanuel*, Matt 1:23).[24]

The Son

Less often (but equally significantly),[25] Jesus is *the* Son (seven times: "his son" six times; "Son of God" once). As the sent Son, his preexistence is implied.[26] As it was for the Roman centurion at the cross, for Paul "Truly this man was the Son of God" (Mark 15:39). In a dynastic world, this speaks of Jesus as God's heir. Sonship language was also used of Caesar—yet now, there is only one true Son, Jesus, and not Caesar. "Son of God" is thus a politically subversive name, especially in Rome, where Caesar rules. It is also used in the LXX of Israel and the King. Jesus is God's appointed and anointed King; he is Israel embodied, the climax of her story. Through him, God functions. He is the head of humanity, and in him, younger sons and brothers are joined to the family of God.

Christological Combinations

Paul uses a range of combinations of names. "Jesus Christ" is found seventeen times. The epithet is a fuller name of Jesus: "Jesus the Messiah (Israel's King)." While it is a name for Jesus, we must not fall into the trap of thinking that it is just a name.[27] It *is* the name of Jesus *because* he is Israel's king, the culmination of God's promise to Israel, the anointed one who has come to rule as Lord.[28] Paul reverses this as "Christ Jesus" fifteen times. The combination is used interchangeably with "Jesus Christ." There is no discernible reason for the shift of order. Many textual variants shift the order of these combinations. He uses "Lord Christ" once in Romans 16:18 (cf. Col 3:24), a sequence that emphasizes the two great christological notions—the Lord Messiah of Israel and the cosmos.

117:1. See also 12:19 = Deut 32:35. See further Hurtado, *Lord Jesus Christ*, 112–13.

24. See Wright, *Mission of God*, 106–9, "Jesus Shares the Identity of YHWH," for a similar perspective.

25. "Bousset was surely correct in seeing Jesus' divine sonship as central to Paul's beliefs." Hurtado, *Lord Jesus Christ*, 102. See Boussett, *Kyrios Christos*. He claims Paul drew his ideas from the Jewish milieu.

26. Hurtado, *Lord Jesus Christ*, 119. He powerfully and rightly critiques Dunn's view of adoptionism. Dunn, *Christology in the Making*, 113–28, 176–96 (pp. 119–26).

27. This is a common mistake in Pauline scholarship. Many scholars only consider the term has messianic connotations when it has the article. See, e.g., the discussion in Hurtado, *Lord Jesus Christ*, 99–101.

28. See Wright, *Climax of the Covenant*, 41–55.

Underlying Aspects of the Gospel in Romans

Christ, Jesus, and Lord are used in combination ten times, including "Christ Jesus our Lord" (6:23); "Jesus Christ our Lord" (three times: 1:4; 5:21; 7:25); and "Lord Jesus Christ" (seven times).[29] These three titles are the full name of Jesus.

In the Roman world, citizens usually had three names (*Tria Noma*), including the *praenomen* (given name), *nomen* (or *nomen gentile* or simply *gentilicium*, the name of the *gens*, or clan), and *cognomen* (name of a family within the *gens*).[30] So, for example, Nero was born Lucius Domitius Ahenobarbus (his full title was longer: Nero Claudius Caesar Augustus Germanicus). Emperor Titus was Titus Caesar Vespasianus. Jesus Christ Lord and variants appear to be Paul's full title for Jesus. So, Jesus is his given name (*praenomen*); he is the Christ (*cognomen*), and the Lord (*nomen*).

The numbers above reveal that his favorite designation for Jesus is "Christ," and combinations of "Christ Jesus" and "Jesus Christ" are split evenly. He is occasionally called "Son" and is never designated savior in Romans.[31]

Interestingly, the terms "Lord," "Son," and "Savior" were all used of the Emperor, so Paul's preference for *Christos* is vital in a Roman setting—it is Israel's *Christos*, who is the true Roman Lord, not Caesar. Christ's supremacy applies to any other sovereign or deity other than the God of Israel himself. The Lord of the world is *the* Christ, and despite being crucified, he remains the Christ. A crucified Christ ensures false understandings of power are not made, i.e., through sword and spear; instead, it is power through Spirit, gospel, and love (cf. Zech 4:6). Note too, that Jesus is defined at the core of the gospel in Romans 1:2–4 from the start:

> Paul, a slave of *Christ Jesus*, called to be an apostle, having been set apart for the gospel of God, which he promised beforehand through his prophets in the Holy Scriptures concerning *his Son*, who as to the flesh, was a *descendant of David*, and *who* through the Spirit of holiness was declared the *Son of God* with power by the resurrection from the dead: *Jesus Christ our Lord* (translation and emphasis mine).

As such, for Paul, one could say that Christ is the central theme in his gospel presentation in Romans. This remains so throughout his letters. It is through him that God's righteousness and justice are expressed.

The Stone

Jesus is also likened to a stone in Romans 9:32–33, where Paul cites Isaiah 28:16. As Assyria threatened Judah, Isaiah 28:1–13 declares God's judgment on the northern kingdom.[32] In Isaiah 28:14, the prophet shifts his attention to Jerusalem, who, in

---

29. See 1:7; 5:1, 11; 13:14; 15:6, 30; 16:20.
30. Bennett, *New Latin Grammar*, 300.
31. Paul entitles Jesus "savior" in Eph 5:23; Phil 3:20; 2 Tim 1:10; Titus 1:4; 2:13; 3:6.
32. Meeks, "Ephraim, Son of Joseph": "'Ephraim' then became a metonym for the north, or for any

making a covenant with Egypt against Assyria, assumed they were protected; however, for Isaiah, this is a covenant with death.[33] Isaiah declares that God will lay a tested and precious stone of foundation in Zion so that those who believe "will not be put to shame" (*kataischynō*, LXX). Now that he has come, the Sinai covenant has become a covenant of death for Israel, where an Israelite rejects the one who fulfills the law.

Reference to Zion speaks of a Davidic Messiah. As a result of this stone laid, justice and righteousness (Heb) or judgment, hope, and mercy (LXX) will be established. Smith explains that there are six options for this and prefers that this stone refers to God's promises.[34] However, Watts argues that this is the foundation of the Temple.[35] Interestingly, it is read messianically in the Targums.[36] Briley suggests, "more specifically, to the embodiment of covenant promises in the Davidic messiah."[37] Paul sees Jesus as the messianic fulfillment of this Isaianic text and likely the foundation of a new temple (cf. 1 Cor 3:16; 6:19; Eph 2:19–22).[38] In Christ, God has laid the foundation of a new temple held together by the cornerstone: Jesus.

For Israel, he is a stone that causes them to stumble and an offense. The stone refers to a crucified Messiah, which is anathema to Israel. Conversely, those who believe in Christ will never be put to shame (10:11). In this life, whatever shame they face at the hands of others (Jew or Greek), they will never be humiliated by God. Instead, they will experience hope because of God's love poured into their beings by the Spirit (5:5). Moreover, at the final judgment to come, those who trust in him have been justified before God and will experience honor rather than shame (see Phil 1:20).[39]

The Deliverer

While *sōtēr*, "savior," is not used of Jesus in Romans,[40] Paul draws on Isaiah 59:20–21, indicating that Jesus is *Ho Rhyomenos*, "the Deliverer" that Isaiah predicted would come from Zion.[41] The mention of Zion again asserts Jesus's Davidic and messianic credentials.[42] He will banish ungodliness from Israel, will be the basis for a new

---

of the 10 northern tribes" (Isa 28:1).

33. Smith, *Isaiah 1–39*, 486. The other five options are "the cornerstone of the temple building;" "the law of God;" "the faithful people who were the pillars of the community;" Jerusalem; or the Davidic monarch.

34. Smith, *Isaiah 1–39*, 487.

35. Watts, *Isaiah 1–33*, 437.

36. "I am about to appoint in Zion a king, a strong king, powerful and terrible." Childs, *Isaiah*, see Tg. Isa. 28:18.

37. Briley, *Isaiah*, 20.

38. See also Eph 2:20, where Jesus is the *akrogōniaios*, the cornerstone or capstone (BDAG 40).

39. Compare Mark 8:38 and parr.

40. See Eph 5:23; Phil 3:20; 2 Tim 1:10; Titus 1:4; 2:13; 3:6

41. On this being Jesus rather than God, see Jewett and Kotansky, *Romans*, 704.

42. Jewett and Kotansky, *Romans*, 704.

covenant with them, and take away the sins of her people (11:26–27; Isa 59:20–21). In context, this new "Israel" includes Jews by faith and the many gentiles being grafted into "the circumcision" (Phil 3:3), "the Israel of God" (Gal 6:16), the renewed temple of God's people (1 Cor 3:16; Eph 2:19–22, see further part three, chapter 26).

THE NEW ADAM

Another aspect of Romans is Jesus as the new Adam, the progenitor of a renewed humanity. This is important, as it shows that while Abraham is important, Paul's gospel story begins before Abraham, at the creation of the first human beings.[43] It begins with the whole world of humans in relationship with God and the gospel reaches all humankind, through Jesus, the zenith of Israel's covenantal hopes.

The Adam-Jesus typological relationship is seen mainly in Romans 5:12–21, where the two men are contrasted. Through Adam, death entered God's world, condemning all humanity to be universally bound in sin, decay, mortality, and ultimately, eternal condemnation and destruction (5:12, 15). Through Jesus's righteous act and obedience, grace and eternal life has come for many (5:15–20).

In 1 Corinthians 15:45–49, Jesus, the new Adam, is contrasted with the mortal, natural, earthly, and dusty Adam who is perishable and mortal and subject to death. The "last Adam" is spiritual, from heaven, and he gives eternal life. People are borne in the image of Adam, but having believed, the called will ultimately bear the image of the Adam of heaven.

In Romans 8:29, the children of God are being conformed to the image of this heavenly Adam. Jesus is thus the new Adam, who inaugurates God's new creation and redeems them out of the consequences of Adam's sin. These people do not form a "new humanity" so much as a "renewed humanity," full of gentiles grafted into historic Israel by faith since the first Adam (cf. Rom 4; 11).

GOD OVER ALL

While some dispute this,[44] the Greek of Romans 9:5 strongly suggests that Paul entitles Jesus "God."[45] It reads (my translation):

> to whom [the Israelites] are the patriarchs also, from whom [the Israelites] is the Christ according to the flesh, *who* [*ho*] *is God over all things blessed into the ages, amen.*

---

43. Paul also mentions Eve elsewhere: 2 Cor 11:3; 1 Tim 2:13–14.
44. See, e.g., Dunn, *Romans 9–16*, 535–36.
45. See Moo, *Letter to the Romans*, 586–88; Jewett and Kotansky, *Romans*, 567–69.

The *ho* leads the clause, and its natural antecedent is *ho Christos* in the previous clause.[46] Hence, we see a decisive moment in which Paul attributes the divine name to Jesus, something found in Titus 2:13 and, in different ways, at other points in his letters (Phil 2:6–11; Col 1:19; 2:9).

Jesus Through Romans

Through Romans, Jesus is the Son of God, Christ (Messiah), and Lord (above). Through his resurrection, he who *always has been* God's Son has been publicly declared[47] Son of God and Lord (1:4, see also 4:24; 8:11). Paul speaks of Jesus as God's Son, or "his son" a number of times. Jesus is not merely a son of David; he is God's *own* (*heautou*, *idios*) son (8:3, 32). This reference to God's "own son" has almost a Johannine notion of "only" or "unique" son (*monogenēs*).[48] It also has royal overtones in Israel where *huios* was used of the king (e.g., Ps 2:7), and in the Greco-Roman world, where Caesar was a son of the gods (1:4, 9; 5:10).

Jesus is the son whom God sent with the specific purpose of dealing with sin, condemning it in his death (8:3). This condemnation of sin and its consequences was achieved by God by not only sending his Son but also giving him up for humanity (8:32). God is thus the Missionary who sends and is prepared to sacrifice his Son so that he will gain many sons and daughters from all over the world. This Son is the image of God into whose *eikōn* (image) believing humanity is being formed, and so God's family of sons and daughters is being established in, through, and by Jesus (8:29). It is God the Father through the Son who sends the church into mission.[49]

Jesus is the essential content of the gospel message (1:2–4; 16:25). It is this Christ that Paul preaches (15:19).[50] He desires to take the message of Christ to places where he is unknown; hence, his desire to go to Spain (15:20). Believers belong to Jesus (1:6). With the Father, Jesus grants grace and peace to believers (1:7; 16:20). God will judge the world through Jesus (2:16).

---

46. See for a full exposition and defense of Jesus being defined as God here, Harris, *Jesus as God*, 143–72. See especially pp. 157–59.

47. He was not then appointed the Son of God, for he was always God's Son. Such an idea is adoptionism: "A teaching in the early church period that claimed that Jesus became God's Son through adoption during His earthly life (whether at His baptism, resurrection, or ascension) and denies the preexistence of Jesus. The early church condemned Adoptionism, though it was revived in 8th-century Spain." Mangum, *Lexham Glossary of Theology*, n.p. See also Moo, *Letter to the Romans*, 46.

48. John 1:14, 18; 3:16, 18; 1 John 4:9.

49. "So, in human history it is Jesus who sends the church, but from the deeper perspective of the inner nature of the Triune God, it is God the Father who is the source of all sending." Tennent, *World Missions*, 76.

50. See also 1 Cor 1:23; 2 Cor 4:5; Phil 1:15, 17; Col 1:28.

Now that Jesus has come and where he has been proclaimed and heard (10:14–17),[51] people are saved and justified exclusively through faith in Jesus Christ (3:22).[52] It might be that Paul here means "faith (or faithfulness) of Jesus Christ," and as such, believers are saved through Jesus's faith or faithfulness to God (e.g., Hays against Dunn, who goes the other way, see further part two, chapter 11). Either way, as these disputed texts make clear, it is faith in Jesus that saves (e.g., "for all who believe," 3:22).[53] People are justified by faith (5:1). More fully, this would say: "people are justified by God as a gift based on believing in Jesus." Their justification is not contingent on any works whether the works of the law or otherwise.

God's righteousness is expressed in and through Christ, and this righteousness is granted to believers as a status (3:22). Redemption from enslavement to sin, death, and wrath come through Jesus (3:24) as does peace with God, or reconciliation (5:1, 11). Christ's death is for the ungodly (5:6; 14:11) and a visible demonstration of the love of God (5:8). Through his death, Jesus became Lord of the living and the dead (14:9), and God reconciles to himself those who believe in him (5:10). Paul uses Christ's death for all as a basis for believers doing everything that they can to ensure *others* do not fall; specifically, they are not to become divided over non-essentials but should allow each other liberty to disagree in love (14:15).[54] Christ is welcoming to all; thus, believers should welcome one another (15:7).[55]

Through Jesus, God's grace has come, is coming, and will continue to come (5:15). He brings life, whereas Adam brought sin and death (5:17)—a new creation and a new Adam and renewed humankind. This life is eternal and gifted to those justified by faith (5:21; 6:23). Believers are "in Christ" and "in the Lord" at the moment of faith,[56] of which water baptism is a visible symbol of participation. As such, they are dead in Christ, baptized into his death spiritually and visibly in the waters of baptism (6:3). Just as believers have died with and in Christ, they will be raised as he was resurrected (6:4, 8, 9). Now they are spiritually alive in God and dead to sin and its power (6:11). They have also died to the law (7:4), something that is a present reality (8:1).

---

51. The logic of Romans 4, when read alongside Romans 10:14–17, is that a person who has not heard the gospel is justified by faith in God that parallels that of Abraham (who was a gentile at the point of faith). From the point of hearing the gospel of Christ, they are justified through faith in the Son of God.

52. See also John 14:6; Acts 4:12.

53. See also, "so we also have believed in Christ Jesus" (Gal 2:16); "to those who believe" (Gal 3:22); "that is based on faith" (Phil 3:9, my translation).

54. On Paul's understanding of *adiaphora*, "non-essentials," in mission, see Longenecker, "'What Does It Matter?," 147–60.

55. Or as Volf, *Exclusion & Embrace*, 29, puts it, "embrace" one another. He aptly comments in regards to the theme: "The metaphor seems well suited to bring together the three interrelated themes that are central to my proposal: (1) the mutuality of self-giving love in the Trinity (the doctrine of God); 2) the outstretched arms of Christ on the cross for the 'godless' (the doctrine of Christ); (3) the open arms of the 'father' receiving the 'prodigal' (the doctrine of salvation)."

56. See 16:5, 7, 8, 10, 11, 12, 13.

Because of being in Christ, believers are saved from wrath and so experience freedom; there is no condemnation (before God [guilt] and before others [shame]) in Christ Jesus (8:1). Further assurance comes from Jesus presently interceding for believers before God, ensuring that they need not fear condemnation whatever befalls them (8:34). They are set free through the Spirit of life from sin and death, and from the law that arouses sin (8:2).

The Spirit who raised Christ will also give life to the believer. Believers must live in and by this Spirit (8:11). This Spirit is the Spirit of God and Christ, and thus is God and the Son's very presence as they mutually indwell the believer (8:9, 10). As children of God alongside Jesus, believers are heirs of all that is Christ's, i.e., the world (not some future away-from-earth-heavenly experience, 8:19–23). However, this will involve participation not only in the glory of the resurrection but the struggle of being human and Christian in a fallen world, i.e., suffering (8:17).

Prayer is made to the Father *through* Jesus Christ (1:8; 7:25; 16:27). Believers are to boast in Jesus above all else (5:11) and glorify Christ (15:6). God loves humankind, and this motivated his sending of his Son for them. Jesus demonstrates that love in his death for the sinful and ungodly (5:6, 8). God's love for his children, expressed through and in Jesus, is unconditional and unbreakable. There is *absolutely nothing* in the created order that can separate a believer from this love (8:35, 39).

Jesus is the Messiah of Israel. Paul yearns for Israel that her hardened people would recognize her Messiah and believe in him (9:3). In Romans 9:5, Paul describes Jesus as "God over all." Jesus is the completion, fulfillment, end, and culmination of the law (10:4). Justification is now found in faith in Jesus and not law fulfillment.

Salvation comes through the confession of the lordship of Jesus (Jesus is Lord) and the belief that God raised him from the dead (10:9). This confession is a heartfelt acknowledgment that Jesus is Lord when the message of Christ is heard and believed (10:14–17). An ongoing life of virtue is defined by Christ's pattern of life expressed in different ways. One is to clothe oneself in the Lord Jesus Christ. The appeal for unity and love over liberty is rooted in the example of Christ (15:3, 5). To give oneself as a living sacrifice recalls Christ on the cross (12:1).

Jesus is the one Paul and others serve and in whom and for whom they minister in God's mission.[57] What believers achieve is, in fact, the work of Christ in and through them. As such, until God affords each person his praise at the judgment,[58] God through Christ receives all praise for achievements performed on his behalf (15:18). Service of Christ brings approval of God and others (14:18). Christ's own service is the foundation and example to believers as they serve God, Christ, and others (15:8). Christ's service calls to mind the suffering servant of Isaiah and the servant motif that undergirds the Synoptic Gospels (esp. Isa 53). Clearly, for Paul, even if he does not say a lot about it, the gospel narrative we find in the Synoptics is foundational

---

57. See 1:1; 14:18; 15:16; 16:3, 18.
58. See 1 Cor 3:12–15; 4:5; Phil 2:16.

to his Christ upon whom he meditates theologically. Christ is the content of the proclamation that lies at the heart of mission (1:4; 15:19–20).

The church is the one body of Christ, and all individual members are unified within it (12:5). Writing from Corinth, Paul can speak of "all the churches of Christ," indicating that in Romans (unlike Ephesians and Colossians with the cosmic/heavenly church), the church is defined by locality, and Paul can thus greet the Romans from all these church contexts (16:16).

Sometimes Paul uses Jesus's name to add authority or solemnity to a statement or appeal (9:1; 14:14; 15:30). He uses "in the Lord" in terms of an action that pleases God (16:2, 22).

In sum, Romans presents Christ as God's divine Son and God in person (9:5; his use of *kyrios*). However, Jesus is also very much an image-bearing human who suffered and died for the world. We have a balanced Christology in Romans.

The Holy Spirit

Paul refers to *pneuma* thirty-four times in Romans, of which all but five refer to the Spirit of God. The others are used to describe the human spirit[59] or of a spiritual influence ("to fear," 8:15; "of stupor," Rom 11:8).[60] For Paul, while the Trinity may not be yet philosophically defined, God the Father, Christ the Son, and the Spirit, are separate persons who are intertwined as One. He can thus interchange the "Spirit of Christ" and the "Spirit of God" (8:9).

As elsewhere in the NT, the Spirit is the *Holy* Spirit (or Spirit of *holiness*, 1:4), referring to the Spirit's undefiled purity, reflective of God's otherness and purity (1:4). As such, the Spirit sanctifies converts making them an acceptable offering to God (15:16). The Spirit's role is essential for ethics, and contemporary believers need to reclaim the seemingly outdated notions of holiness, for those who are imbued with the Holy Spirit are called to live in step with the Spirit: to be holy.

The Spirit of God is the power by which God raised Christ from death (1:4). The Spirit is the agent of heart-circumcision, which Paul contrasts with the circumcision of the body (2:29). New uncircumcised believers do not need to be physically circumcised, shedding their own blood (Lev 17:11), as the blood of Jesus has sanctified them. They are "circumcised of the heart." Such a circumcision refers to the inward transformative work of the Spirit in the human heart, the "cutting off the foreskin of the heart" as a metaphor for faith (cf. Deut 10:16). The concept elides into a metaphor of cutting sin and mortality from the inner being. Piecing together Paul's understanding of salvation, this work is found among those who have faith in God (cf. Rom 4). A faithful follower of God is one whose heart is being transformed by the Spirit of God

---

59. See 1:9; 8:10, 16 (2nd use).

60. Rom 12:11 can be translated "be fervent in spirit" (ESV and most translations). However, in my estimation, *pneuma* here is best translated "Spirit," with Paul appealing them to "burn in the Spirit."

who dwells within the believer, and they increasingly conform to the patterns of life in God led by the Spirit (8:1–17).

In Romans, as in Galatians chapters 3, 5, and 6, the Spirit is central to Paul's ethical vision. The ethics of the believer is Spirit-impelled virtue. In Romans 5:5, after waxing lyrical on the gospel and speaking of the peace with God found in Jesus, Paul speaks of the present reality of suffering. He puts an educative spin on it: suffering produces character and hope within believers (5:3–5). While living in Christ, the Spirit is the basis for hope in the inevitable suffering that comes with being human and a follower of Jesus.

Through the Spirit, God has poured love into the human heart. This inseparable love saves, heals, transforms, encourages, impels, and flows over as love to others (cf. 13:8). Paul's appeal in Romans is driven by this same love, by which he appeals to the Romans to join him in prayer for his upcoming trip to Jerusalem (15:30). The connection between the Spirit and love is crucial. Believers are filled with God's Holy Spirit to be holy and love impelled in all that they do (cf. 2 Cor 5:14).

Paul contrasts life in the Spirit with life in the flesh. Life in the flesh is lived outside of faith in Christ, governed by God-given desires (such as eating, drinking, sexuality, pride, and the like) that are distorted into lusts and addictions through sin's corrupting effect. Paul links the law to the flesh as the law excites and reveals sin and sinfulness that hold captive the human heart. The law, although holy and good (7:12), enslaves believers to a written code and corruption (7:6). The Spirit brings new life and freedom from law, guilt, and condemnation (7:6; 8:2). The cross has opened the way for all believers to receive God's presence in the form of the Spirit. They are set free from sin and death (8:2).

Ethics for Paul is walking in the Spirit, being led by the Spirit, and obeying the Spirit. The Spirit is the inner impulse of God's being in the human heart. Imperatives, injunctions, commands, and demands do not drive authentic Christian living, whether from Jewish law or otherwise.[61] Instead, it is generated from allowing the Spirit to have the lead (8:4). It is a life of yielding, and then Spirit-activated being.

By living according to the Spirit, believers have an enhanced capacity to take control of their desires, resist temptation, and live the life God wants for them (8:13). Those who are led in this way by the Spirit are children of God (8:14). Genuine *koinōnia* then is a product of the Spirit. The alternative is to be led by the flesh and its lusts.

To live by the Spirit is to have one's mind transformed and focused on the Spirit, rather than selfish and warped desires (8:5). Following the Spirit is the path to life and peace (8:6, 10), even during times of severe struggle (5:3–4; 8:17–23). Having the

---

61. Any ideological system can become a ruler in this sense. Paul speaks of the *stoicheia* in Gal 4:3, 9; Col 2:8. These forces rule people in their idolatries. It can come through any political, economic, religious, or philosophical ideology which enslaves people to its rules and regulations. Today, in the west, we are swamped with them, and this is why so many people are drowning under "law." Keown, *Galatians*, 559–72.

Spirit marks one as God's; indeed, without the Spirit, one does not belong to God or Christ (8:9).

In Romans 14:17, Paul urges the Romans to move beyond the debate over issues of eating and holy days toward the essential matters of the kingdom: "righteousness and peace and joy in the Holy Spirit." Again, the Spirit is the source of a righteous, peaceful, and joyful life. God's *pneuma* (Spirit) is the basis for *koinōnia* (community). In Romans 15:13, Paul prays that the Lord will fill the Romans with joy, peace, and hope by the Spirit. His prayer is interesting as he does not assume that because they received the Spirit at conversion, they do not need a fresh experience of the Spirit. Instead, they *have* received the Spirit, but Paul knows that people can know the Spirit's presence in fresh ways when believers pray for them (also Eph 1:17; 5:18).

The Spirit is the power of the Christian life. Just as the Spirit raised Christ (1:4), so *pneuma* gives life to the mortal body (8:11). That is, despite physical life ebbing away as people age and struggle with suffering (cf. 2 Cor 4:7–18), the Spirit gives believers life, peace, and hope amid suffering. Present hope is found through the Spirit along with the future hope of glory that sustains God's people (8:18).

The Spirit is the defining dynamic that marks off people as God's children. Elsewhere, Paul speaks of the Spirit as a seal and guarantee (2 Cor 1:21–22; Eph 1:13–14). In Romans 8:17 (see also Gal 4:5–6), he writes of the Spirit of adoption who binds people to God's family and leads them to cry out, "Abba! Father!" This outburst is a glorious cry of love and intimacy of people who are God's children. Believers are thus set free from fear despite all that Satan, the world in its fallen sense, their own sin, and others throw at them. Knowing one is a child of God is a spiritual notion; the inward impulse and "voice" of the Spirit whispers to the human spirit of a believer's status in Christ (8:16). So, whereas the "voice" of the flesh condemns, the murmurs of the Spirit console. They declare within believers their status of freedom and justification. For Paul, knowing one is saved means, "I know, because I know."

In Romans, Paul speaks of believers having the first fruits (*aparchē*) of the Spirit. It is like a deposit and foretaste of things to come. Alternatively, it is a birth certificate that seals citizenship, family status, of redemption (8:23).[62] The role of the Spirit in suffering is powerful in Romans 8:26–27. The Spirit intercedes on behalf of God's people in their moments of weakness. This speaks of the *pneuma* of God leading believers in prayer, interceding in and through them on our behalf. These groans are not speaking in tongues, as the context speaks more broadly of the inward voice of the Spirit expressing himself through God's children in their frustration as does creation.[63] The link here between God and Spirit is again pronounced; God searches the heart while knowing the mind of the Spirit, and the Spirit intercedes for God's people according to God's will.

---

62. BDAG 98.

63. See also Fee, *God's Empowering Presence*, 584–85.

While Romans 12:11 could refer to "ardent in spirit," alternatively, and more likely, it is an appeal to the Romans to "burn (*zeō* = "boil") in the Spirit" as they zealously serve the Lord (cf. Acts 18:25).[64]

Pauline Christianity is a pneumatic, charismatic faith, but not in a narrow sense of tongues, miracles, and gifts, as is seen in many charismatic and Pentecostal traditions.[65] *All of life* is Spirit-inspired; the Spirit-impelled life. Authentic Christian relationships, inwardly with oneself, with God, with each other, and with creation, are transformed to their ideals by the Spirit within believers. Characters are Spirit-transformed as people yield to God's impulses. Christian mission is Spirit-impelled and guided by the Spirit who goes ahead of us in the *missio Dei*. All of life is to be governed by the Spirit.

Conclusion to Triune God

Paul may not develop a robust theology of the Trinity or perichoresis,[66] but both are implied throughout Romans. His theology is built on the Father, the Son, and the Spirit. The three are unified as one, sovereign over creation, working in it with perfect harmony and love in line with God's purposes.[67] They demonstrate what it means to experience genuine unity. Those who believe join the *koinōnia* of the Godhead in Christ, and through the Spirit, *agapē* flows creating a countercultural and intercultural community of God's people who give witness to the world. The three persons of the Godhead worked together in creation, history, and Christ's death and resurrection. As One, they continue to work together in history, in personal transformation, in forming and building the church, in ethics, in all of life, mission, and the transformation of communities and the world.[68]

---

64. Dunn, *Romans 9–16*, 742.

65. I say this with humility as one who identifies with the NZ Presbyterian evangelical and charismatic tradition.

66. *PDTT* 26 describes "perichoresis" or "circumincession" as "the theological concept . . . affirming that the divine essence is shared by each of the three persons of the Trinity in a manner that avoids blurring the distinctions among them. By extension, this idea suggests that any essential characteristic that belongs to one of the three is shared by the others. Circumincession also affirms that the action of one of the persons of the Trinity is also fully the action of the other two persons."

67. Romans justifies the view of Goheen: "A missional hermeneutic begins with the Triune God and his mission to restore the world and a people from all nations." Goheen, "History and Introduction," 15.

68. On a Trinitarian Missiology, see Tennent, *Invitation to World Missions*.

9

Elements Inimical to God

ONE DIMENSION OF THE GOSPEL Paul does not skirt around is the problem of evil in his rich theology of human sin, corruption, God's wrath, and destruction.[1] His diagnosis of sin and evil forms the backdrop against which the "good news" is presented, i.e., what people are saved *from*. Paul's emphasis on these "negative" aspects of the gospel is likely due to his genuine concern that as in Galatia (although without the same immediate urgency), the gospel of grace is under some threat.

Paul is warning readers of the consequences of failing to seek righteousness before God based on anything other than the initiative of God's grace and the human response of faith. To fail to do so leaves a person in sin, exposed to God's wrath, and destined for destruction. The good news for readers is that as Romans unfolds, Paul's emphasis becomes that into which people are saved. In this section, however, the focus will be those aspects of Romans that speak of enmity to God and its consequences.

SIN

Clearly, for Paul, the fundamental human problem is sin. Sin entered the world through Adam's sin (5:12); commonly called the fall. While Paul does not use the phrase in his writings, "the fall" is one good way of describing his theology as, for Paul, sin and human death came through Adam. His reliance on the Adam narrative presupposes his acceptance of the Genesis accounts of Adam and Eve falling from the glory of eternal existence through the tree of life.[2] At another level, it is the "the

---

1. I have included law in this chapter recognising that the law gifted by God to Moses is not inimical to God, it is holy and good (7:12). However, due to sin and false understandings, the law became something that enslaved people and shut them off from God.

2. This can be either 1) losing their pre-fall status of immortality; or 2) remaining mortal and cut off from the source of immortality; the Tree of Life. The latter fits with evolutionary theism and the former with traditional renderings of the gospel.

rupture," in that the decay and death unleashed through Adam's sin also corrupted the whole cosmos.[3]

At one level, the sin of Adam speaks of original sin—people are guilty because of the sin of Adam. However, the final *eph hō* clause in Romans 5:12 gives an additional reason that people are responsible for Adam's sin: it is "*because* all have sinned."[4] Paul, then, neatly balances the problem of the inevitability of sin with people's own guilt for sin. That is, as Adam sinned, all humanity has also sinned, and so all, without exception, are subject to death (5:12–14). They are prone and subject to sin through Adam but are at fault because of their personal sin.

In Romans 1:18—3:20, Paul establishes the human condition and problem—all have sinned.[5] It is not as if only the gentiles are guilty before God, and the Jewish people are righteous based on their election and law (as many in Israel believed). Instead, *all people* stand before God on the same basis.

Romans 3:23 is a crisp summary of the argument of 1:18–3:20: "for all have sinned and fall short of the glory of God."[6] A similar statement is made in 3:9; "we have already made the charge that *Jews and gentiles alike are all under sin*"(emphasis mine). They are under sin's dominion. Sin is a power that holds them in captivity. Indeed, sin as a personified power is a distinctive aspect of Paul's theology especially in Romans.[7]

The catena of verses that follow in 3:10–18 reinforces this from the Hebrew Scriptures.[8] This problem of universal sin lays the foundation for the gospel that deals with the problem of sin in Jesus's atoning death.

Paul uses a range of notions for sin in Romans. These include:[9]

- ***Hamartia* Terms**: The essence of *hamartia* is to "miss the mark."[10] The study of sin is sometimes called hamartiology. Overall, the language is found sixty-one times, including 1) *Hamartia*: noun, "sin" (48x);[11] 2) *Hamartolos*: noun "sinner,

---

3. Keown, *What's God Up to on Planet Earth*, 31–46.

4. Dunn, *Romans 1-8*, 273–74.

5. "Romans 1—2 is Paul's incisive commentary on the universal reign of sin in human life and society." Wright, *Mission of God*, 430.

6. Volf, *Exclusion & Embrace*, 82 describes this as "solidary in sin."

7. Schreiner, *Romans*, 304 says of Rom 6:2 notes that most scholars, "rightly describe sin as a power" in the passage. He notes Rom 5:21 where sin reigns. Similarly, speaking of the Adamic sphere, Käsemann speaks of "the forces of sin and death which have invaded the world." See Käsemann, *Romans*, 147.

8. See also 1 Kgs 8:46; Prov 20:9; Eccl 7:20; Jas 3:2; 1 John 1:8, 10.

9. These meanings are drawn from BDAG.

10. BDAG 49.

11. See 3:9, 20; 4:7, 8; 5:12, 13, 20, 21; 6:1, 2, 6, 7, 10, 11, 12, 13, 14, 16, 17, 18, 20, 22, 23; 7:5, 7, 8, 9, 11, 13, 14, 17, 20, 23, 25; 8:2, 3, 10; 11:27; 14:23.

Elements Inimical to God

sinful" (four times);[12] 3) *Hamartanō*: verb, "to sin" (7x);[13] 4) *Hamartēma*: noun, "a sin, transgression" (3:25); and 5) *Ta pathēmata tōn hamartiōn*, "the sinful passions" (7:5).

- *Asebeia*: "ungodliness, impiety" (1:18; 11:26).
- *Adikia*: "unrighteousness, wickedness, injustice, wrongdoing."[14] *Adikia* is the opposite of righteousness/justice (*dikē, dikaiosynē*).
- *Kakos*: "evil, wickedness."[15]
- *Ponēria*: "wickedness, baseness, maliciousness, sinfulness" (1:29).
- *Pleonexia*: "greed" (1:29).
- *Parabatēs nomou*: "transgressor, violator of the law" (2:24).
- *Parabasis*: "transgression" (2:23; 4:15; 5:14).
- *Paraptōma*: "offence, wrongdoing, sin, trespass."[16]
- *Akathasia*: "immorality, vileness, uncleanness" (1:24; 6:19).
- *Anomia*: "lawlessness" (4:7; 6:19).
- *Ta erga tou skotous*: "works of darkness" (13:12).

The problem of sin is linked to false, corrupted thinking (1:18, 28), and turning away from God toward idolatrous worship (1:21–24). Idolatry is humankind's central problem. As Cranfield says,

> So we understand these verses as the revelation of the gospel's judgment of all [people], which lays bare not only the idolatry of ancient and modern paganism but also the idolatry ensconced in Israel, in the Church, and in the life of each believer.[17]

In Romans 1, Paul identifies a set of sins stemming from this failure of thinking, including sexual immorality, which violates God's ideal for marriage and family (1:24–27), and a range of other false attitudes that shatter human relationships such as wrong behaviors and speech patterns (esp. Rom 1:29–31). Sin is driven from impulses that are corrupted by fallenness (1:24). These basic human desires are not wrong in and of themselves; they are God-given. However, these desires have become distorted and controlling because of the corruption of the human being under sin's reign. What are authentic needs have been warped into lusts and addictions. In Romans 1:31, sin

---

12. See 3:7; 5:8, 19; 7:13.
13. See 2:12; 3:23; 5:12, 14, 16; 6:15; 14:23.
14. 1:18; 2:8; 3:5; 9:14. Elsewhere, Paul uses *adikos*, "unrighteous," of people (1 Cor 6:1, 9). In Romans, he only uses it in a question concerning God being unrighteous (3:5).
15. See 2:9; 7:19; 12:17, 21; 13:4, 10.
16. See 4:25; 5:15, 16, 17, 18; 11:11, 12.
17. Cranfield, *Critical and Exegetical Commentary*, 1:106.

is found not only in acting or thinking wrongly, but approving others who transgress. This speaks of corporate sin in corrupted contexts where people sin and others spur them on and sin and its devastation becomes exponential.

In Romans 2:1–2, sin is seen in the self-righteous, hypocritical judgment of others who sin. These sins are a danger to all humanity and, in particular, the likes of Israel with her election presumption and perceived moral superiority.[18] Such sin is very much a danger to Christians who can easily become arrogant in their own self-righteousness, when in fact, we Christians are no better than others, in many instances.

Sin is also linked to one's inner heart attitude, driven out of "your stubbornness and unrepentant heart" (2:5, translation mine). Central to sin in Romans is self-seeking rather than the pursuing good of others (2:6). Sin is the rejection of the truth (i.e., God's truth).

Sin angers God, leading to wrath (2:5). For Paul, God is utterly righteous and pure and repulsed by the evil and corruption that defiles his creation, shatters relationships, and destroys people made in his image. Due to his holiness, God's wrath rightly leads to condemnation and destruction. For God to be God, he must act in line with his holy character and ultimately act to cleanse his world of all sin and evil, even if he dreams that all are saved and pass through that destruction to eternal life.[19] Indeed, his judgment is an act of love for the oppressed and his world. However, as will be discussed, salvation will not come to pass for many people. Where someone does not desire life with God, God grants that person their desire for eternal separation from him.

Death entered humankind through sin and reigns because of sin. Sin itself reigns as a power under which humanity is held secure (Gal 3:22) and hopeless without intervention; Jesus is the solution who saves. Sin is thus almost personified as a demonic force holding captive humanity. Thus, sin reigns as a dominion inimical to God (5:21). Humanity then is "under (*hypo*) sin" (3:9). Consistent in the honor-shame cultures of the ancient world, sin brings shame (6:21).

The law, although good (7:7, 12, 16), rather than saving from sin, serves to intensify sin in that it reveals right and wrong and so has the effect of illuminating evil (3:20; 7:8–11, 13). The illuminatory power of the law is the same problem the tree of the knowledge of good and evil caused for Eve and Adam; the prohibition against eating excited their desire for the forbidden fruit, and deceived, they ate (2 Cor 11:3; 1 Tim 2:13). The law is not the problem; sin is, and the law reveals sin (7:14). However, now that Christ has come, the law becomes redemptive not as the basis for salvation,

---

18. Some commentators see this as focused on Jewish presumption, e.g., Cranfield, *Critical and Exegetical Commentary*, 1:137–40. However, Paul likely has in view anyone with such arrogant thoughts toward God and judgment, e.g., Barrett, *Epistle to the Romans*, 43. Still, undeniably, Jews are at the forefront of his critique.

19. Keown, *What's God Up To*, 69–71.

but knowing the law leads them to recognize their sin and seek Jesus rather than rely on obedience to the law or other works for salvation. Sin brings condemnation (5:16).

The diatribe of Romans 6 deals with arguments made by his opponents that Paul's logic inexorably leads to the conclusion that believers can and should sin more, as to do so reveals more grace from God (6:1, see also 3:8; 6:15).[20] However, Paul emphatically writes this off as false logic, arguing that believers are dead to sin, and as such, should no longer live under its power (6:1–2). Baptism into Christ's death puts to death sin, and so believers live in the newness of life (6:4). They are no longer enslaved to sin but are set free to live lives of love and goodness. They are still subjugated by their own volition to be "slaves of righteousness" (6:6–10). Hence, they are set free from sin not to sin more, but to live the life of service for which they were created (cf. Gal 5:13). Believers, then, should not allow sin to reign but live righteously (6:11–23).

Romans 8 resolves the dilemma of the means of empowerment to live a life that pleases God; namely, by the Spirit. The law has no compelling force except external pressure that relies on personal self-effort (which is tenuous because people are universally sinful). Such self-effort to please often generates failure, fear, shame, and guilt. The only power that enables transformation is the Spirit; God's gift of himself to those in Christ to sanctify them (as a status) and to empower sanctification and every aspect of life.

The Spirit is received by faith and not works of the Law (10:17, cf. Gal 3:3, 5). Hence, when people turn to the law, they rely on their own devices to overcome sin, and they fail as everyone does, excluding Jesus. Faith brings a person into a relationship with God in Christ, and that person receives the Spirit. God's indwelling power enables believers to overcome fleshly desires where previously they could not. This is not a perfection but being increasingly transformed into the image of Christ (8:29).

The Spirit has set believers free from sin and death (8:2). Jesus achieved this by being a sin offering and, unlike the temporary solution in the Jewish sacrifice system, solved the problem of sin completely through his redemptive death (8:3). The requirements of the law are completed in his life and death. The Spirit will only live in perfect receptacles. Because Christ has died for sins (1 Cor 15:3), and as people are joined to him by faith[21]—meaning they are dead to sin with their lives hidden in Christ (Col 3:3)—they are fitting vessels for God to fill with his presence. As such, believers should live by the Spirit (8:4).

The Spirit then empowers the believer for a new life that enhances the capacity to overcome sin (8:5–14). Believers are to put behind them "deeds of darkness" such as orgies, drunkenness, sexual immorality, debauchery, dissension, jealousy, and the

---

20. Jas 2, Jude, and 2 Pet 2–3 appear to be dealing with a similar issue. People feel they can claim faith in Christ and salvation but abuse the grace of God by participating in gross sin. They are profoundly warned otherwise, especially in Jude and 2 Pet 2.

21. See 3:25, 28, 30; 5:1; 9:30.

like, and live righteously (13:12–13).²² Such behaviors were common in the Roman world, and Christians who had previously lived in this way are now to remain in the world but are not to join in the revelry of their pagan neighbors.

The pattern of the life of Christ is essential to Paul's ethic, i.e., a Spirit-led and Spirit-empowered Christlikeness. Another dimension of sin is found in Romans 14:23, where Paul states, "everything that is not from faith is sin" (translation mine). That is, all acts that violate a Spirit-filled conscience are sinful. Such things include eating or drinking what a person believes in the Lord they should not.

FLESH

Sometimes Paul uses *sarx* in a neutral sense of the human body (2:28; 3:20), life in the flesh (4:1; 8:3), and genealogical descent.²³ More often, however, in Romans and elsewhere, Paul uses it to speak of that aspect of humanity that is corrupted by sin due to Adamic failure (5:12–21) and stands opposed to God and especially life in the Spirit. *Sarx* should not be defined as "the sinful nature" (e.g., NIV84), as if people are divided beings, but the flesh describes the corruption of every aspect of a person: their bodies, mind, heart, soul, and spirit.

For Paul, the inner person is weak in that it is prone to sin and enslaved to it (6:19; 7:18, 25). It is held captive to its corrupted desires. Life under the power of sin outside of Christ is life in the flesh (7:5). The law is unable to release people from sin in that all humankind is weakened by sin (8:3). Only Jesus, who was found in the likeness of human flesh, but overcame sinful desire and died having overcome *sarx*, can deal with sin, condemning it in his flesh (8:3, cf. Phil 2:7; 2 Cor 5:21). As such, believers must live not by the impulses of the fallen flesh but in obedience and submission to the Spirit (8:4–13). They must set their minds on the things of the Spirit and not the flesh (8:5), and if they do, they will find life and peace and not death and enmity with God (8:6–8).

Paul contrasts two modes of being: 1) in the flesh (8:9); or 2) in the Spirit (8:9). Believers are to live in the Spirit and not the flesh, a pneumatic existence. Because of what Christ has done, they are indebted to the Spirit and not the flesh (8:12–13). If they live according to the Spirit, they will live eternally (8:13). Believers are to renounce the licentiousness that comes from feeding the desires of the flesh and live Christlike lives (13:14).

---

22. See also Rom 1:18–32; Gal 5:19–21; 1 Cor 6:9–11.

23. See, e.g., 1:3; 9:3, 5, 8; 11:14. Although, even in these texts, there is a taint of Paul's understanding of *sarx* as fallen, mortal, and merely human.

WORLD, AGE, CREATION

The Greek *kosmos* is used fourteen times in Romans. God created the world; hence, it has value (1:20). Tragically, it is rife with sin, and its God-appointed rulers—humans—have consistently violated what the creator requires. The people of the entire world are sinful, and because of this, sin has spread to all humankind (5:12–13). They are accountable to God (3:19) and will be judged by a righteous God (1:25). Ultimately, the world will be liberated from sin, and the descendants of Abraham by faith will inherit it (4:13). This inheritance will be shared as the gospel is proclaimed through the world (1:8). The rejection of the gospel by Israel has caused the gospel to explode into the gentile world, bringing reconciliation of people to God (11:14) and so has brought "riches for the gentiles" who people the wider world (11:12).

Paul uses *aiōn* once of the present age in 12:2. The age refers to the period between creation (or better the Fall) and the consummation. This verse implies that the present era stands in opposition to God, warped as it is by corruption. Believers are not to be conformed to its brokenness but are to be renewed mentally in line with the gospel and God's intention in creation. His theology of God's sovereignty implies a period "before the ages," referring to the time before creation, in which God shaped his purposes.[24] In the age to come (Eph 1:21), after the consummation, the earth will be renewed. This renewal is *aiōnios*, "forever" for which God is blessed and glorified (1:25; 9:5; 11:36; 16:27).

Creation (*ktisis*) is not evil in and of itself; instead, it is glorious and very good (1:19–20; Gen 1:31), created by God from nothing (4:17). In creation, God's "invisible attributes," including his omnipotence and divinity, should be easily perceived (1:20). The created order is replete with creatures and humans created to reflect God's glory (1:23). The creation narrative includes God as the Potter forming people from dirt, a clear allusion to the creation of Adam in Genesis 2 (9:20–23).

Sadly, the gentiles have chosen to create idols shaped in their own form or of creatures and now worship them, rather than give God the glory and honor he deserves (1:23–25). God's jars of clay (2 Cor 4:7) should be grateful for their createdness and respect God's freedom in making them as they are. They should not question their creator's choices (9:20). They forget that an artist, like an earthly sculptor or potter, has complete freedom in creating things for his or her pleasure. Some of the potter's work is destined for destruction, and that is his prerogative (9:21–22). Nor is this capricious, as "to make known the riches of his glory," God intended to create "vessels of mercy, which he has prepared beforehand for glory" (9:23–24). Those he created include Jews and gentiles on the same basis, for God shows no favoritism (2:11). Moreover, as will be discussed in the next sections on salvation, this mercy is available to all.

In 8:19–23, Paul personifies creation. Sadly, because of human sin causing the world to be infected with rotting and death, like a woman yearning to give birth,

---

24. "Before the ages" is confirmed at other points in Paul's letters (1 Cor 2:7; 2 Tim 1:9; Titus 1:2).

creation groans in longing to be set free from its bondage to decay at the revelation of God's children at the judgment. Creation itself will be set free from its captivity to corruption and will experience the same liberation humans do. This emancipation is cosmic renewal and resurrection. In the meantime, the creation is a dangerous place that brings decay and death, as seen in events like Covid-19. Thankfully for believers, nothing in creation can separate believers from God's love now that Christ has come, and righteousness is gifted where faith is found.

Human beings are universally sinful, as are human-made institutions. Where sinful humans come together with evil intent, sin is corporate and amplified. The exponential power of corporate sin is seen in fallen human institutions like the Caesars and, last century, Nazism (among many other such expressions).

Sin cannot be limited to individual guilt for sins committed. People have also been sinned against, as is creation itself. In a corrupted context, people are more and more broken as their humanity is violated by others, and the world's corruption is amplified. People violate themselves psychologically and bodily (e.g., 1:27), their relationships are torn apart as in a divorce (e.g., 7:1–4), whole societies are wrecked (e.g., 13:14), and the creation itself is violated (8:19–22). Sin's effect is more sin as damaged people are prone to the indulgences of the flesh to bring relief for their guilt and shame. They get trapped in addictions that, if not dealt with, become demonic. The human problem is not merely personal sin; they are the victims of sin, and society and the world are perverted. The work of Christ is to redeem all people, all human institutions, and the whole of creation. In the meantime, God works in and through fallen institutions, even Nero's despotic regime (13:1–7).

WRATH, JUDGMENT, CONDEMNATION, DESTRUCTION

Paul's God, while characterized by love, mercy, kindness, and grace, consistent with OT pictures of God, is also a God of wrath.[25] Wrath (*orgē*) is "anger." Indeed, Paul's gospel presentation to the Roman Christians begins with this: "the *wrath* of God is being revealed" (1:18). The present tense of the verb *apokalyptō* (revealed) here speaks not only of God's wrath that culminates in eternal destruction but in immediate consequences of sin such as his giving them over to sin (1:24, 26, 28). So, chaos on earth is one expression of God's wrath. Chaos begets chaos as God allows humankind the outcome of its sinful desires—more profound fragmentation. God's fury is directed against sin; specifically, ungodliness, wickedness, and idolatry.

---

25. See, e.g., Exod 22:24; 32:10–11; Num 13:18; 16:46; Deut 9:7–8; 29:28; Josh 22:20; 1 Sam 28:18; 2 Kgs 22:13, 17; 2 Chr 19:2, 10; 29:8; 34:21; Ezra 8:22; Job 19:11; 21:20; Pss 21:9; 78:21, 59; 89:38; 110:5; Isa 9:19; 13:13; 51:22; 63:5; Jer 7:20; 10:10; 21:20; 30:23; Lam 2:2; Ezek 7:8; 21:31; 36:18; Mic 5:15; Nah 1:2; Zeph 1:15; Zech 8:2.

Elements Inimical to God

In Romans 2:5, Paul warns that all people regardless of race (3:10, 23) are storing up wrath for judgment (cf. 9:22).[26] This outworking of wrath will occur on the Day of Judgment when God will treat each justly ("God's righteous judgment"). Paul does not mince words at the consequences of sin: those who seek self, wickedness, and disobedience to God will experience God's wrath and fury! (2:8).

Paul defends the justice of God, arguing that the problem is not God's injustice or unfairness but human failure (3:5). Controversially for a first-century Jew, Paul argues that law does not bring salvation; instead, it generates wrath as it reveals sin and human failure (4:15). The glorious story of the gospel is that God in Christ is saving the world from this wrath through declaring righteous by faith those who believe in Jesus, his death propitiating God's wrath (5:9).

Paul gives no support for Christians to use this as a justification for them meting out vengeance or violence; they are to leave it to God to deal with wrongdoing (12:19). So, unbelievers are also given time to heed the gospel and be saved by Jesus's propitiatory death. However, in Romans 13:4, the State serves God in executing some aspects of wrath against people for their wrongdoing.

In Romans, God is judge and his judgment is based on truth on truth (2:2). His judgment is righteous (2:5, see also 11:33) and impartial; he will treat all people in the same way (2:11–12). Indeed, this is a central theme of Romans: God is just toward all people; therefore, people are not to stand in arrogant judgment over one another. Instead, they are to accept one another in Christ and be one unified people.

In Romans 2, one of Paul's core points is that Jews and gentiles are in the same boat. The law gives no advantage in terms of judgment to Jews; they too are condemned before God because they fail to live the law that was entrusted to them (3:2) and because of their election presumption and self-righteousness. Gentiles, although not having the law, face the same plight for the law is written on their hearts, and God should be known from creation (see also 1:18–21).

As elsewhere in his letters and the Bible, Paul speaks of a "day" of judgment (2:5, 16, see also 13:12). On this day, God will judge even the deepest thoughts of all. The judgment is "through Jesus Christ," indicating a primary role for Christ in sentencing humankind. Paul here refers to the day when all people will face God. Human sin serves to store up wrath for people when they face God (2:5). This judgment is based on works, with God rewarding and punishing people, whether Jew or gentile, in response to their lives (2:5–11). There will be wrath for those who pursue evil; there will be the reward of eternal life for those who do good.

"Wrath" in Romans 2:5, 8–9 is God's eternal condemnation of those who sin. Paul's language is cumulative and vivid: "wrath and anger . . . trouble and distress." The apostle here reflects the horror of being condemned by God. All will stand before

---

26. On judgment, see also part two, chapter 13.

God, who is judge (14:10–11).²⁷ Paul uses this as a basis for calling the Romans to stop judging each other on non-essentials (below).

The notion of "death" (*thanatos*) in Romans is not merely concerned with physical death, but spiritual and eternal death (cf. 5:12, 21). Sin leads to this death (6:21, 23; 7:5). Another way of saying this is that life in the flesh culminates in death (8:6, 13).²⁸ By contrast, by grace, God gives believers eternal life and immortality. The law is holy and good, but it serves to lead to sin and death by revealing and "exciting" sin (7:12–13).

The term *katakrima* (condemnation) in some verses also carries that sense of eternal "condemnation" before God, the judge (5:16, 18; 8:1). Christ's death deals with this condemnation, death, wrath, and destruction. His death is a *hilastērion*, indicating a propitiation of God's wrath and arguably also an expiation (cleansing) from sin. As a *hilastērion*, Jesus's death deals with sin as he stands in place of humans before God and receives God's wrathful judgment. He condemned sin in his flesh (8:3). Believers in Christ are saved through his death.

Water baptism symbolizes and enacts this participation (6:4, 5). Believers will experience future resurrection and eternal life rather than eternal destruction. As such, Paul can say, "there is therefore now no condemnation for those who are in Christ Jesus" (8:1). This liberation is objective; believers are absolutely freed from God's condemnation due to sin. It is also subjective and existential; they can live experiencing freedom without guilt, shame, and fear before God. Moreover, they should yield to the Spirit, who wants them to live this way.

They are free from the "law of sin and of death" (8:2). *Nomos* here can refer to the Torah that functions to condemn or the "law" that sin leads to death.²⁹ That is, sin no longer leads inevitably to death; instead, it leads to life because Jesus has dealt with sin. In Romans 8:34–39, Paul brings this home, stating that Jesus is the one who condemns, and he will not condemn his own who are loved. Consequently, they can live in the freedom of knowing that nothing can separate them from the love of God (8:34–39). This freedom is the liberty to love and serve the other.

Paul also uses "destruction" ideas (see further part two, chapter 13). In Romans 2:12, he employs *apollymi* ("destroy, perish"); those who sin will perish. The verb refers to eternal destruction (cf. 14:15).³⁰ In Romans 9:22, Paul utilizes the cognate *apōleia*, rhetorically asking whether God has the right to create people for destruction, implying the eternal destruction of some people.³¹

---

27. See also Isa 45:23; Phil 2:9–11.

28. Paul goes further in Eph 2:1

29. See Moo, *Letter to the Romans*, 496–500 for a full discussion.

30. See also 1 Cor 1:18, 19; 8:11; 15:58; 2 Cor 2:15; 4:3, 9; 2 Thess 2:10, cf. 1 Cor 10:9, 10 (where it is used in the OT of people dying).

31. See also Phil 1:28; 3:19; 2 Thess 2:3; 1 Tim 6:9. While Paul uses *phthora* in 8:22 of creation's bondage to corruption, he does not quite use it in the sense of eternal destruction as in Gal 6:8 (cf. 2 Pet 2:12). Neither does he employ *olethron*, "destruction," in Romans (cf. 2 Thess 1:9; 1 Tim 6:9).

Elements Inimical to God

As God is the only righteous judge, people themselves are not to stand in place of God and judge one another in an ultimate sense (2:1–3). Instead, believers should judge themselves with humility and authenticity (12:3, cf. 2 Cor 13:5). In Romans 14–15, believers are not to stand in judgment over each other on non-essentials such as eating and sacred days (14:3–5, 10–13). In making judgments over each other in this way, they may cause others to fall away from the faith. Instead, each person must live by their faith convictions (14:13, 22, cf. 1 Cor 8:11). In other words, they must judge themselves according to their God-informed consciences while allowing others to live according to their own perspectives (14:23). Of course, this is not a license to participate in sin or teach false doctrine (Galatians; 2 Cor 10–13; Phil 3) but applies to the non-essentials of the faith.

Another angle is the role of the State in "judgment." Paul supports his call for submission to the governing authorities with a warning of their "judgment," i.e., punishment (13:2). Paul here vindicates the role of the governments of the world in executing judgment on God's behalf. Still, the governments of the world are also under God's watchful eye and will fall if they violate his intent for them.

SATAN AND HIS MINIONS

As with all of Paul's letters, there are sparing references to Satan and demons. For Paul, while Satan and fallen angels exist, the real problem he highlights in his letters is people and their sin. One of the core messages of both Galatians and Romans is that while Satan and evil spirits exist and are oppressive and dangerous, humans are primarily responsible for the state of the world.

The one unambiguous reference is in Romans 16:20: "The God of peace will quickly crush *Satan* under your feet" (my translation, emphasis mine). This verse appears to speak of the imminent destruction of Satan.[32] Interestingly, this verse immediately follows his warning against false teachers who cause divisions, create stumbling blocks, teach falsely, and are licentious, rhetorically masterful, and deceitful. It could be that the defeat of such enemies is in purview. In support of this, the contrast of "peace" and "division" is suggestive. Alternatively, and most likely, it includes these teachers but is broader in scope, and speaks of the ultimate destruction of Satan and evil.[33]

"Crush" is *syntribō*, a powerful term suggesting, "shatter, smash, crush, annihilate," i.e., comprehensive destruction.[34] It is used of the demoniac's destructive behavior and the smashing of a jar (Mark 5:4; 14:3, see also Rev 2:27). "Quickly" is *en taxei*, and this could point to Paul's view of an imminent Parousia ("soon"); however, more

---

32. An unlikely possibility here is that "Satan" is a euphemism for the Roman Empire, and Paul is portending the fall of Rome or the Julio-Claudian dynasty that ended in AD 68.

33. Cranfield, *Critical and Exegetical Commentary*, 2:803. Schreiner, *Romans*, 805.

34. BDAG 976.

likely, it implies "quickly" speaking of Satan's quick destruction at the consummation (cf. Net Bible). As I have argued elsewhere, as Paul recognized that the gospel had to go to all nations before the return of Christ, it is not an imminent parousia that is in mind for he realized there was much work to do before that date. The language used speaks of urgency and not immediacy.[35]

His crushing is the ultimate fulfillment of Genesis 3:15. As elsewhere in the NT, Satan's destruction is certain (Matt 25:41; Rev 20:10). The defeat of opponents calls to mind Psalm 110:1, where God's enemies will be placed under the Messiah's feet (itself fulfilling Gen 3:15).[36] Implicitly, by saying "under your feet," he implies that believers "in Christ" who share in Christ's inheritance of all things, also share in the judgment of evil. Overall, this verse speaks of the certainty of the destruction of evil forces.

It is likely that *archai* (pl. *archē*, "ruler"), as it is balanced with angels in Romans 8:38, refers to demons. Similarly, powers (pl. *dynamis*), height (*hypsōma*), and depth (*bathos*) may speak of powerful spiritual forces that inhabit the world above and below.[37] Whatever power exists among forces that inhabit the occult and dark side of creation, which first-century people fervently believed in and feared,[38] they can never separate a believer from God's immense love for them.

Here, their destruction is inevitable. Paul's interest in Romans is not primarily demonic forces or Satan, but the problem of human failure and sin and its power to bring death and destruction. However, he recognizes the existence of Satan and the demons and their role in attacking Christians. His tactics include disrupting their faith through false teaching.[39] However, ultimately, all of God's enemies will be destroyed.

LAW

The Jewish law is central to Romans. Paul's presentation of justification by faith and the Christian life is set against the backdrop of the role of the Jewish Torah. In Galatians and Romans, Paul gives a fresh second temple interpretation of Jewish law in the light of Christ.

---

35. Keown, "Imminent Parousia and Christian Mission," 242–63.

36. Image bearing is a royal notion. "Humankind is *in* the image of God but also serves *as* the image. Humans have resemblance to God, even if limited, but stand in God's place in the administration of God's creation." Merrill, "Image of God," 444 (emphasis original). Subjugation of the serpent by Adam can be extended to the messianic hope. On the subjugation of enemies, also see Pss 2:8–9; 21:8–12; 45:5; Josh 10:24.

37. Morris notes that the terms height and depth were used in astrology. It is possible "powers" refers to a magician's capacities. Morris, *Epistle to the Romans*, 341–42. See also Käsemann, *Romans*, 251–52. They are not merely spatial, as Moo claims (although he contradicts himself by including in heights and depths, heaven and hell. Moo, *Letter to the Romans*, 568.

38. See, e.g., Arnold, *Ephesians*, 14–29.

39. See esp. Eph 6:10–17, see also 1 Cor 5:5; 7:5; 2 Cor 2:11; 11:14; 12:7; Eph 4:27; 1 Thess 2:18; 2 Thess 2:9; 1 Tim 1:20; 3:6, 7; 5:15; 2 Tim 2:26.

Elements Inimical to God

Before his conversion, as a Pharisee, the law would have been his delight and focus.[40] Salvation for a Jew meant not to rely on one's election, but to maintain one's position in God's covenant people by living according to the law (covenantal nomism).[41] Salvation for a gentile meant converting to Judaism and coming under Torah with its rituals and regulations; most notably, the badges or boundary markers of Jewish national identity—things that mark them off from the gentiles: especially circumcision, food laws, and Sabbath.[42]

Now that he has met Jesus on the road to Damascus,[43] Paul has had a radical about-face. As we see in Romans (who are probably living in some confusion over law after the impact of the Claudian edict and Jerusalem Council), he reinterprets the law. The law is not the means of getting into the covenant people (for the gentile proselyte) or even staying in (for the Jew born into the covenant community by election and a proselyte once converted). The law's function is not to save *at all* or the basis of justification before God. Indeed, Paul now knows the law was never designed for justification before God. Rather, justification was, is, and until Christ returns, always will be, credited on the basis of *faith* (1:17; Rom 4; Gal 2—3).

The law, while good (7:12), reveals the problem that blights all people: sin. The commands of the law designed to enable a person to know God's righteous requirements and live them out serve to illuminate sin as humans in their sin fail to uphold the law. As such, the law becomes a means to lead a person, Jew or otherwise, to know their need of Christ, and serves the great goal of God; salvation by grace, through faith, and not by works (Eph 2:8).[44]

For the believer, then, ethics is no longer living by the law as an external code. Instead, it is seeking Christlikeness, through the power and leading of the Spirit, and supremely, living from the inside out, the command found in the law that sums the intention of the law, love.[45] There will be continuity with the legal requirements of Mosaic law that came from the righteous God is now "etched" on the circumcised hearts of people. While there is still great value in the written law as a guide to understanding the character and desires of God, the Christian ethical life is an inside-outside life empowered by the Spirit rather than living by an external code. The latter inevitably

---

40. See, e.g., Phil 3:6; Gal 1:14, esp. Ps 119.

41. "Covenantal Nomism" was coined by E. P. Sanders and emphasizes "the primacy of the covenant (God's gracious election) for 'getting in' along with obedience to the Law for 'staying in.'" Yinger, *New Perspective on Paul*, 10.

42. Dunn writes: "three of Israel's laws gained particular prominence as being especially distinctive—circumcision, food laws, and Sabbath." Dunn, *Romans 1–8*, lxxi. Others include festivals, ritual purity, sacrifices, pilgrimage, synagogue, and Israel's worship.

43. See Gal 1:11–12; Acts 9:1–19; 22:1–21; 26:12–18.

44. "For the law cannot overcome sin and death, or lead to true righteousness and to life, but is destined to do nothing but drive [people] still more deeply into sin and to bring them to realize that as long as they depend on themselves they are lost." Hahn, *Mission in the New Testament*, 101.

45. See 13:8–10; Gal 5:14; Lev 19:18, 34.

leads to things like self-righteousness, condemnation, a critical spirit, judgmentalism, hypocrisy, failure, death, and destruction.

Paul's first mention of the language of works and law is Romans 2:6, where he states the principle of salvation by *works*: "he [God] will give to each person according to his/her *works*" (translation and emphasis mine). Thus, it is by works that a person will be judged. Notably, Paul uses "works" here and not law. As such, he sets the broader scope of the debate on law into a works-faith debate, not merely one about works *of the law* and faith.

In Romans 2:12–15, Paul develops this premise in the direction of the law. He argues gentiles without the law will perish (eternal destruction) apart from the law (2:12). Gentiles will be judged by the law that is upon their heart (moral law) and they too will be found wanting (2:14–15).

Some read 2:14–15 positively arguing Paul holds that gentiles *can* uphold the requirements of God, this moral law,[46] or that Christians are in mind here.[47] However, this being Christians is ruled out by 3:9, 19–20, and 3:23, where Paul's argument climaxes with statements that *no one*, whether Jew or gentile, is righteous *by the law*. Further, no one, whether a Christian or otherwise, can fulfill the law. Only Jesus did this, and believers can achieve this *in* Christ, who has fulfilled the law (while believers remain sinners and lawbreakers). Indeed, Romans 2:15 highlights that "their conflicting thoughts accuse or even excuse them," showing that they too are accused despite having the law.[48] He shows readers how gentiles can be justified with the example of the "gentile" Abraham who is justified by faith (4:3, 9–11).

On the other hand, Jews who live under the law (all faithful Jews) and others who come under the law (as would a proselyte or Judaizing "Christian") will accordingly be judged by it (2:12). That is, their status, righteous or otherwise, before God, will depend on their having fully lived the law. Paul then states that merely hearing the law, as all Jews have done since childhood at synagogue and home, will not bring a favorable verdict; instead, *doing* the law will bring a declaration of innocence (2:13). Elsewhere, Paul applies this to himself, the Jew of Jews—even he, the great persecuting Pharisee, though blameless according to the law, can have no confidence in his flesh (his capacity to fulfill the law, Phil 3:3–6).

Romans 2:13–14 could be read as Paul stating that some will indeed be declared innocent on this basis.[49] However, as with other attempts to read parts of Paul's argument positively in this section of Romans, it is ruled out by his summative comments in 3:9, 19–20, and 23 that each state all (Jew and gentile) are sinners, and the law can

---

46. Some hold that these are gentiles who fulfill the law and are saved through it, e.g., Snodgrass, "Justification by Grace," 72–93.
47. E.g., Wright, "Romans," 441.
48. See, e.g., Moo, *Letter to the Romans*, 158–64.
49. Some think Paul has Christians in mind, e.g., Wright, "Romans," 440.

Elements Inimical to God

justify no one.[50] Such a positive interpretation is also countered in chapter 4, where faith is given as the basis for God's judgment before the law was given. The problem with the law and works is that they cannot be lived out because of sin. No one other than Jesus can do it. The dilemma of being human is that no one is righteous before God, whether by law or other means (other than faith in the Righteous One).

In Romans 2:17–29, Paul powerfully targets Jewish views of law, clarifying the argument he began in Romans 2:12–16. He challenges Jews who "rely on the law" (2:17), are "instructed in the law" (2:18), have "in the law the embodiment of knowledge and truth" (2:20), and who "boast in the law" (2:23). Scholars are divided over whether this means all Jews or only a section of Jews at the time. Likely, these people are representative of all.[51] This conclusion is likely because Paul's summation is that all are under sin and fall short of God's glory. Hence, his argument is targeting all, and these are representative sins of the extremely pious Jew. Indeed, this is who he once was. He is almost certainly speaking of himself as he was in his pre-Christian state.[52]

He asks the Jewish interlocutor, "do you dishonor God by breaking the law?" Paul presupposes that that person must answer, "yes, indeed!" Jewish views of the law acknowledge this fact; they did not see themselves as perfect before God and relied on sacrifice and atonement (esp. the Day of Atonement). Paul goes on in Romans 2:25, striking at the distinctive boundary marker where men are concerned, circumcision. Rather than being a decisive entry point that guarantees right status before God, Paul controversially argues that circumcision is valueless unless one obeys the law. On the other hand, if one does not (as all do not), one's circumcision is valueless.

He then states that where an uncircumcised man keeps the law, they are effectively circumcised. If so, such people will judge Jews in their failure (2:26–27). While some scholars see this positively as if some can fulfill the law or that Paul here is speaking of Christians, in the flow of his argument and overall theology, we know that he does not believe this is possible (again, see 3:9, 20, 23).[53] This inability is explicit in Romans 9:31: "but, *Israel*, pursuing the law of righteousness [Jews who do not believe in Christ], *did not attain* the law" (my translation). The reason for their failure is given in the next verse, "For what reason? Because [they did] not [pursue it] *from faith*, but as from works" (9:32, my translation and emphasis).[54]

---

50. See also Moo, *Letter to the Romans*, 157–58.

51. Moo, *Letter to the Romans*, 169.

52. Perhaps his comment on robbing of temples refers to his plundering of the church, imprisoning the people of the temple of God (Acts 8:3; 22:4), and perhaps taking their possessions. Alternatively, it speaks of stealing temple articles (Dunn, *Romans 1–8*, 114); robbing the Jerusalem temple through failing to pay the Temple Tax (suggested in Moo, *Letter to the Romans*, 173, e.g., Pss. Sol. 8:11–13; T. Levi 14:5); or "to involve various acts (or attitudes) of impiety toward the God of Israel" (Moo, *Letter to the Romans*, 173).

53. Wright, "Romans," 448–50.

54. "Nevertheless, while some allusion to Christians is clear, we think Paul is still setting up a straw man to contest Jewish claims of exclusive access to God's saving grace in their covenant." Moo, *Letter*

Overall, Paul's argument is clear: righteousness by law is antithetical to grace and the governing principle of righteousness by faith because works cannot achieve it. The point throughout this is that no one has kept the law, and circumcision of the heart is what matters and, as he will outline, this comes from faith, whether past (Abraham), present (e.g., Paul and the Romans), or future (in Christ).

Paul's view of the law is summed up in 3:19–31. *No-one* can be justified before God by the Jewish law. Through the law comes the knowledge of sin (3:21). This deepened awareness of sin will form a key focus in Romans 7. Salvation (righteousness) has now come aside from law but was predicted within the Jewish writings (law and prophets, 3:21, see also 1:2). This righteousness is from faith in Christ (3:22–26).

Romans 3:27 makes clear that Paul sees the issue of law as a broader works/boasting issue rather than merely a question of Jewish boundary markers. He asks, "then what becomes of boasting? It is excluded! By what kind of law? By a law of works? No, but by the law of faith." Paul writes off any self-reliance for salvation, whether law or works-righteousness of any sort. In stating "the law of faith," he uses *nomos* ironically (as he will do in Romans 8:2). Faith is not a law; instead, it is willing assent to God's gracious offer of salvation, a belief in and submission to his Son. Still, it is legally axiomatic for Paul that justification and salvation are by faith and faith alone.

Romans 3:28 sums up his view, "for we consider that a person is justified by faith *apart from works of the law*" (translation and emphasis mine). This position does not mean the law is thrown out (3:31). He will uphold its sanctity and goodness in Romans 7:12; instead, the law has a different function in the new era of salvation in Christ (cf. 9:4). In Romans 4:15, Paul sums it up again, "For the law generates wrath; but where there is no law, neither is there violation" (my translation). Sin is seen for what it is where law is found, as it exposes sin (5:13), and so in a sense, sin is multiplied (at least seen to be more prevalent, 5:20). Put another way, law arouses sin because of sinful tendencies in humanity, by bringing awareness (7:5). In Romans 7:7, Paul illustrates this with the law "do not covet." The tenth and summative commandment makes one aware of covetousness as a problem, and so, ironically, in that the law is good, a law-aware person is more prone to fall prey to it! (7:7–9). This is another problem of law that Jesus comes to save people from.

Romans 4 is vital in showing again that the issue for Paul over law is part of the broader question of salvation by any works, as his argument concerning Abraham relates to life *before* the Mosaic law (4:13), and so contrasts heathen or gentile works and faith. The gift of God justifies Abraham (grace, 4:16), a declaration of righteousness received by faith and not *any works* and so he has no boast before God (4:2, 4, 5, see also 3:27). Similarly, David sang of righteousness *apart from works,* and so implied in context, by faith (4:6, see also Ps 32:1–2). For Paul, to attribute salvation to anything other than grace through faith is to completely empty the cross of its power (cf. Gal

---

to the Romans, 180.

2:21). This sentiment is seen in Romans 4:14; "faith is null and the promise is void" (4:14).

Again, in Romans 11:6, Paul writes: "but if it is by grace, it is no longer on the basis of *works*, otherwise *grace would no longer be grace*" (emphasis mine). For Paul, you cannot have it both ways; it is either law and works (which end with wrath), or it is grace and faith (which end in salvation). Grace is God's initiative and action. Faith is the only right human response. Law/works and grace and faith are mutually exclusive notions where justification is concerned. They cohere in the Spirit who enables increasingly righteous living from the inside out according to the law inscribed in the heart.

It is fair to suggest that Paul's argument in Romans—that centers on ethnic issues in the first century and supremely, whether a gentile must not only believe in Jesus but become a Jew (Judaize) to be justified—is not precisely the same as later works-faith debates. Each debate had its particular context and nuance. However, the argument is analogous with and anticipates the later Augustine-Pelagius and Reformation works-faith debates, and other such controversies. The contexts and details differ, but the situations have equivalence.

In Romans 6–7, Paul explains that believers are no longer under law. Just as a person is set free from marriage at death, so they are set free from law through Christ's death (7:1–4). They are under grace. They are set free from law's dominion (6:14). Believers then are dead to law and sin in Christ's death (7:6). Their new life *must* not lead to licentiousness, as this is to misunderstand salvation (as some of Paul's opponents misunderstood his theology). A believer is not a servant of sin (Gal 2:17), but a servant of grace, righteousness, love, God, Christ, and the Spirit.[55]

The problem with the law is not the law itself but people's inability to live lives free of sin (which is required for eternal life outside of faith). While Paul did not view the law this way as a Pharisee who focused on living it faithfully (Phil 3:6), as a believer who has discovered God's grace in Christ and the "law of faith," he looks back at the law with different eyes. He realizes that seeking to live the law creates for the Jew and proselyte a cognitive dissonance and struggle leading to a deep desire for freedom from law (7:14–25).

Now that Paul has met Jesus and worked through the implications of his coming, Jesus is the power that sets people free from this struggle (8:1–4). Jesus alone satisfied the requirements of the law, as he was born under the law (Gal 4:4) and died an innocent, sinless man who never broke God's law (2 Cor 5:21). In his resurrection, gifted because he had not sinned, he blazed a path to freedom people can follow if they are joined to him by faith (Gal 5:1). God brings people of faith into this liberty. They receive the Spirit who sets them on a new road; not of a new law, but of love and grace (8:4–17). By the impulse of the Spirit (not external command of the law), they turn from sin to goodness.

55. See Rom 6:15; 7:6; 8:4–16; 13:8–10.

The culmination of Paul's argument is Romans 10:4: "Christ is the *telos* of the law." *Telos* carries the sense of completion and fulfillment, as well as the sense of "end." In Christ, the law is fulfilled, and thus, he ends life *under* the law. The salvation-historical era that was a shadow of the Christ-era has come to an end, completed in Christ.[56] Life is now lived by faith as led by the Spirit. Aside from the law to love God, which gets little attention in Paul, the law that fulfills all other relational laws is "love your neighbor as yourself" (13:8–10; Lev 19:18). This law is the sum of all law and should not be applied as a law, but as a precept worked out in the Spirit in any and every situation.

CONCLUSION

In Romans, Paul clearly tells readers that while there are demonic beings, the problem all humans face, whether Jew or gentile, is their sin. God is holy and righteous to the core, and his ultimate purpose in creation is a world free of evil. This sin means God has consigned them to physical death. Indeed, death is required to eradicate sin from God's world. All of creation is blighted with the same problem, and all flesh and living things must be freed from corruption. God will renew creation. However, humans are sinful, and they must be freed from corruption to inherit the renewed creation that will come to pass at the end of the age when God destroys evil and corruption. Gentiles are under sin. Jews, despite the law, are in the same place. Even though the law is holy and righteous, it cannot make people righteous and holy. It illuminates right and wrong and shows humans the poverty of their existence and failure. Thankfully, throughout Romans, he gives the solution: Jesus. God's salvation will be the next focus of this look at the components of Paul's gospel that can be gleaned from Romans.

---

56. Moo, *Letter to the Romans*, 658.

10

Salvation Ideas

GLORIOUSLY, THE FINAL WORD in Romans and the gospel is not sin, death, condemnation, or destruction. It is the salvation of people into eternal life and the liberation of the creation in Christ. Here, "salvation" is used in the broad sense of the term—saved into *agapē*-relationship with God, his people, and his creation. Law, sin, flesh, death, condemnation, and other destruction ideas are the dark backdrop against which the light of Christ's salvation is beamed. Christ is the glorious center of Romans (see also part four, chapter 4 on Jesus). The salvation of humankind and the world is the *telos* of the letter.

GOD'S BENEFICENCE

For Paul, in Romans and elsewhere, salvation is the work of God. It is born out of God's character to save. Paul uses a range of words of God that speak of his attributes that lead to him acting to save, including grace (*charis*),[1] mercy (*eleeō*),[2] kindness (*chrēstos, chrēstotēs* [2:4; 11:22]), love (*agapē*),[3] patience (*makrothymia* [2:4; 9:22]), and forbearance (*anochē* [2:4; 3:25]). These are, of course, all fruits of the Spirit expressed in God's character, Christ's ministry, and experienced through the Spirit. These flow from human hearts forming strong Christian relationships within the community of faith and with others in the world (Gal 5:22–23).[4] They come from God's essence. A good example is Romans 2:4:

---

1. Twenty-four times overall. In regard to salvation, see 3:24; 4:16; 5:2, 15, 17, 20, 21; 6:1, 14, 15; 11:5, 6.

2. Six times: 9:15, 16, 23; 11:30, 32; 12:1.

3. *Agapē* (love), *agapētos* (beloved), and the associated verb *agapaō* (to love) are used twelve times of the love of God, Father, Son, and Spirit, in 1:7; 5:5, 8; 8:28, 35, 37, 39; 9:13, 25; 11:28; 12:19; 15:30.

4. The lists are not exhaustive and such things should be recognized as fruit of the Spirit. Fee, *God's Empowering Presence*, 444–45.

Or do you despise the riches of his kindness and forbearance and patience. Do you not realize that *God's kindness* is meant to lead you to repentance?" (translation and emphasis mine).

The character of God in expressing his unmerited favor to humanity in the gospel is the basis for ethics.

SALVATION

The actual language of salvation (*sō-* terms) is used thirteen times: (the noun *sōtēria* five times and the verb *sōzō* eight times).[5] The importance of the theme is stated with the use of *sōtēria* in the thematic verse for Romans, "For I am not ashamed of the gospel, for it is the power of God for *salvation* for all who believe, to the Jew first and also to the Greek" (translation and emphasis mine). Salvation is thus a governing motif in the letter within the overall theme of the gospel. Other ideas such as righteousness as a status, reconciliation with God, adoption, and so on, fall within its orb.

Salvation comes to a person through faith in Jesus (5:9). One is saved from wrath in him, i.e., released from the sentence of eternal destruction for sins committed (5:9). Paul links salvation to other more technical metaphors, including being justified (5:9–10). In Romans 8:24, one is saved in hope, referring to the anticipation of future salvation found in Christ and that is yet unseen in ultimate terms (cf. Heb 11:1). Paul speaks of his desperate desire for the Jews to "be saved" (10:1).

Salvation comes through faith in the resurrected Jesus and acknowledgment of his lordship (10:9–10). In Romans 10, salvation by faith and profession of Christ's lordship stand in contrast to "by works" or "by law," which, as discussed above, fail to save. For Paul, the gospel of Christ fulfills Joel 2:32 whereby the one who calls upon the name of the Lord (i.e., Christ; one who has received the Spirit, cf. Joel 2:28–29) will be saved (10:13). In Joel, this speaks of gentile inclusion.[6] In Christ, salvation has come to the gentiles, something Paul hopes will cause Jews to become jealous (11:11, 14). Sadly, this hope remains unfulfilled.

In Romans 13:11, salvation has a future edge as Paul speaks of it being nearer for the Romans than when they first came to faith. It has a past dynamic in Romans 8:24: "we were saved." This is intriguing because one is saved in *the past* in the hope of a future that is yet unseen, i.e., the consummation. Consistent with the Jewish Scriptures (Isa 10:22–23),[7] Paul holds a remnant theology of salvation. As in Israel's history, a remnant of Israel will be saved as in the past at the exile (9:27). Such a Jewish remnant

---

5. The language is found in early Greek with the senses: 1. "to deliver from a direct threat," 2. "to bring safe and sound out of a difficult situation." Foerster, "Σῴζω, Σωτηρία, Σωτήρ, Σωτήριος," 7:965.

6. "This is as close as Joel came to opening the doors of salvation explicitly to Gentiles." Garrett, *Hosea, Joel*, 375.

7. See, e.g., Gen 45:7; 2 Sam 14:7; 2 Kgs 19:31; 2 Chr 36:20; Isa 10:20–23; 11:11; 28:5; 37:32; 46:3; Jer 23:3; Mic 2:12; 4:17; 5:7–8; Zeph 2:7, 9; Zech 8:6, 12; Amos 9:12.

could explain what Paul means by "all Israel will be saved," i.e., all Jews and gentiles in the olive tree of Israel by faith in history, in the present, and the future through the gospel (11:26).[8] Others believe that this points to all Jews being saved per se, or a great turning before Christ's return or after. The latter view is preferable because of the inexorable logic of salvation by faith alone (see part three, chapter 26). In Romans, then, people are saved from sin and its devastating consequences into the life God has for them, a life that flowers to eternal life.

One feature of Paul's salvation metaphors is their realized and future aspects. Paul speaks of having been saved (8:24),[9] being saved presently (1 Cor 1:18; 15:3; 2 Cor 2:15), and future salvation (5:9, 10; 9:27; 10:9).[10] Many of his metaphors have this already-not yet eschatology.

CHRIST'S DEATH AND RESURRECTION (PROPITIATION, EXPIATION)

Clearly, the center of Paul's theology of salvation is Christ, and in particular, his death and resurrection.[11] This focus is clearest in Romans 3:24–25, where Paul responds to the plight of humanity locked up in sin by declaring that a righteousness from God is now revealed, based around Christ. He writes of Jesus: "God presented him as a sacrifice of atonement (*hilastērion*), through faith in his blood" (NIV84). Here, Paul uses the language of sacrifice.

Hilastērion features in the LXX of the most important cult object in the holy of holies in God's tabernacle and temple, forbidden to all except the high priest on the Day of Atonement: the mercy seat of God (*kibbāret*). The *kibbāret* was the gold plate that sat atop the Ark of the Covenant flanked by the cherubim whose wings covered God's throne and abode. On the Day of Atonement, it was sprinkled by the high priest with the blood of the young bull, a sin offering that atoned for the sins of the community.[12]

By using the term here, Paul is saying that Jesus is now the final and ultimate mercy-seat of God, the sacrifice itself, and it is his blood that atones. In Greco-Roman literature, *hilastērion* refers to an instrument for regaining the goodwill of a deity, i.e.,

---

8. Wright, "Romans," 688–90.

9. See Eph 2:5, 8; 2 Tim 1:9; Titus 3:5.

10. See also Rom 10:13; 11:26; 1 Cor 3:15; 5:5; 7:16; 1 Tim 2:16. See also Colijn, "Three Tenses of Salvation in Paul's Letters," 29–41.

11. See 3:25; 5:6, 8–10; 6:3, 5–6, 8–10; 8:34; 14:9, 15. See also 1 Cor 1:13, 17–18, 23; 2:2, 8; 8:11; 10:16; 11:25–26; 15:3; 2 Cor 4:10; 5:14–15; 13:4; Gal 2:21; 3:1; 5:11, 24; 6:12, 14; Eph 1:7; 2:13, 16; Phil 2:8; 3:10, 18, 20; Col 1:20, 22; 2:14, 20; 1 Thess 4:15; 5:10; 2 Tim 2:11.

12. Exod 25:17–22; 31:7; 35:12; 38:5–8; Lev 16:2, 7, 13–15; Num 7:89; Ezek 43:14, 17, 20; Amos 9:1, see also 4 Macc 17:22.

a "means of propitiation or expiation, gift to procure expiation," often in the form of a consecrated stele.[13]

Scholars unnecessarily debate whether propitiation or expiation is in view here. Propitiation speaks of "an offering that turns away the wrath of God directed against sin."[14] Wrath is a dominant aspect of the picture Paul paints of human wickedness in Romans 1:18—3:20; God's anger fueled by human depravity will ultimately bring the destruction of all that defies God.[15] As such, *propitiation* is unquestionably in Paul's mind here.

Expiation is "[t]he belief that sin is canceled out by being covered over."[16] Earlier, Paul wrote that God has given over idolatrous humankind to "impurity" or "uncleanness" (*akatharsia*, 1:24). He will soon describe them as slaves to impurity (6:19). As David sang a thousand years before Christ, by God's grace, lawless deeds are forgiven, and sins are covered over (4:7; Ps 32:1–2).[17] Paul also cites Isaiah's hope of a deliverer from Zion and the taking away of Israel's sins (11:26–27; Isa 59:20–21). As such, expiation and cleansing from impurity is also an aspect of thought in Romans, even if wrath language is used more frequently.

Consequently, Christ's death is both a propitiation of God's wrath and an expiation (cleansing) from the defilement of sin. Christ's death resolves the problem of sin, wrath, and impurity before God. Jesus is the atoning sacrifice for sin. "Faith in his blood" (referring to his redemptive death) brings salvation in both a propitiatory and expiatory sense.

The salvific death of Christ features through the epistle in different ways. "Christ died for the ungodly," at just the right time—while humanity was powerless, trapped in sin (5:6). His death is a demonstration of God's love (5:8). Believers are "justified by his blood" and are saved from God's wrath (5:9), and reconciled to God through the death of his Son (5:10).

In Romans 6, believers are baptized into Christ's death, i.e., they participate in his death that satisfies God's wrath and justice. Baptism symbolizes and enacts their death, burial, and resurrection in him (6:1–4). They are thus crucified in Christ, a statement of identity and status, despite their sinful reality (6:6, cf. Gal 2:20; 6:14), and so are freed from sin. In Romans, resurrection is a future hope rather than a present reality (6:8). However, spiritual resurrection is a present experience by the Spirit. Spiritual rebirth is the starting point for ethics; believers are now to live as slaves of righteousness, counting themselves as dead to sin (6:11–18). They have also died to the law in the death of Christ (7:4). Christ fulfills the law, and believers now live in love by the power of the Spirit (7:6).

---

13. See Roloff, "*hilastērion*," 2:186; BDAG 474.
14. *PDTT* 96.
15. See 1:18; 2:5, 8; 3:5.
16. *PDTT* 50.
17. See also Rom 11:26–27 = Isa 59:20–21.

In Romans 8:3–4, Paul again refers to Christ's death as a sin offering that is a propitiation and expiation for sin; he is the mercy seat of God. In ultimate terms, he completes the requirements of sacrifice for sin. In Christ, sin is condemned; the righteous requirements of obedience to the law are fully met due to what Christ has done.

The injunction to "present your bodies as a living sacrifice" in Romans 12:1 should draw the readers to Christ's death, for he is the example par excellence of doing so. They are to take on his mindset and emulate his life of service, culminating in death on a cross. As in Philippians 2:5–11, the sacrificial life of service and voluntary self-humbling in crucifixion Christ becomes the pattern to which God's people are to conform (cf. 8:29).

In Romans 14:9, Paul refers again to Christ's death and resurrection and adds, "that he might be the Lord of both the dead and living." He then discusses judgment. Christ's faithful death and resurrection led to his exaltation as cosmic Lord and judge. In Romans, Christ's death is the center of Paul's theology of salvation and Christian living (see elsewhere, esp. 1 Cor 2:1–4; 15:3–5).

INCORPORATION IN CHRIST

In recent times, there has been a definite move from seeing justification as the center of Paul's theology to the notion of participation "in Christ." There is a tendency to reduce the importance of justification to a subsidiary crater of Paul's thought.[18] I would agree with the first point that "in Christ" is Paul's primary descriptor of Christian life for the saved. However, I would not want to relegate justification to a subsidiary crater but see it as an essential and crucial way of describing salvation and one's status in Christ alongside others like redemption, reconciliation, and adoption, among others. One enters Christ at the moment of the declaration, "righteous!" based on faith.

"In Christ" (*en Christō*) language comes up seventy-six times in the Paulines, and thirteen of these are in Romans. He also uses "in the Lord" forty-six times, including eight in Romans and "in him" of "in Christness" some sixteen times (especially in Ephesians and Colossians, although not in Romans). Overall, there are around 140 uses of the idea.

Somewhat unusually, "in Christ" language is not used until Romans 3:24. The delay in its use is likely intentional with Paul laying out the problem of sin and faith as the only means of entry into Christ *before* coming to discuss the salvation that is *en Christō*. In Romans 3:24, using this in- language, Paul speaks of believers being justified by the gift of God's grace that has come about by the redemption that is "in Christ Jesus." Here, justification and redemption are in Christ and received through incorporation into him.

---

18. An idea first propagated by Schweitzer, *Die Mystek des Apostels Paulus*, 220.

PART TWO: ROMANS AND THE CONTENT OF THE GOSPEL

Although some theologies such as Barthianism consider people in Christ objectively despite unbelief, for Paul, an unsaved person is "in Adam" and this inclusion comes at the moment of faith when the universally efficacious atoning work of Jesus is made actual in the life of the believer. At this moment, her or his sins are dealt with, and God's wrath propitiated (3:22, 25–31, cf. Eph 1:13). Believers are included in Christ (cf. Eph 1:13) and can rightly be said to be "in Christ" or "in the Lord" (16:11). At this moment they are "alive to God in Christ Jesus"—brought into relationship with God the Father, in Christ the Son, who is perpetually in union with God (6:11). Believers are connected to God "in Christ Jesus." This relationship guarantees them the eternal life Jesus has "in Christ Jesus our Lord" (6:23).

In Romans 6, the believers' "in Christness" is the basis for ethical behavior. They are "in Christ" and so should live the Christ-life well, clothed in Christ (13:13). Paul himself functions "in Christ," a status that governs his speech and moves him to truthfulness (9:1). Generally, Paul renounces boasting, but where he does so, he does so "in Christ," i.e., he brags about what Christ has achieved in him and through him. Alternatively, and better, what he has achieved is *in Christ* (15:17).

The participatory relationship sets believers free from the hold of the law and the angst of failure so that there is "now no condemnation for those who are in Christ Jesus" (8:1). They are now imbued with the Spirit that is in Christ and are enveloped in Christ, filled with his presence, and are set free from bondage to the law that excites the sin that brings death (8:2). Those in Christ Jesus are safe in God's love within the life of the Son, who is perpetually loved by the Father. Therefore, nothing can separate the believer from God's love that is *in Christ Jesus* (8:39).

The believers' "in Christness" is not merely a vertical God-human connection point, but the point of the interconnectedness with other believers. "In Christ" is an ecclesiological concept in which believers are bound together to Christ, God, the Spirit, and to each other in Christ's "body" (12:5). Having died to law, sin, and death through the actual deceased body of Christ (7:4), raised in him, they are one "body of Christ" and members of one another (12:5). There is a new spiritual and ontological reality. It cannot be overstressed how important it is that individualistic and narcissistic westerners grasp this truth: we are bound "in Christ" *together*!

As such, believers should greet one another and welcome one another "in the Lord" (e.g., 16:2, 8, 22). "In Christness" is the basis for unity. However, within this unity is room for diversity of members and gifts (12:5–8). There is also space for differences of opinion over non-essential matters such as cultural protocols (Rom 14–15). Paul's theological and ethical thinking is now shaped "in the Lord." Christ is at the center of his theological decision making, including his shift from concerns over ritual purity found in the law to freedom from such concerns in Christ (14:14).

Mission is also an "in Christ Jesus" activity whereby God through his Son, by the power of the Spirit, continues his work in the world through men and women who are "in Christ" and "in the Lord." These people include women and men like Paul (15:17),

Prisca and Aquila (16:3), Andronicus and Junia (16:7), Urbanus (16:9), Apelles (16:10), Tryphaena and Tryphosa (16:12), and Rufus (16:13).

In conclusion, for Paul, becoming a Christian is more about believers being incorporated into Christ than Christ incorporated into a person's life. A believer's primary identity is "me in Christ," not "Christ in me" (although the latter is still valid, Christ in believers, by the Spirit). Such an understanding protects believers against an idolatry of self and merely adding Jesus to the pantheon of our own idols, interests, and preferences.

His people are "in him." *He* is Lord. People do not invite Christ into their lives; instead, he invites them into his. This truth should lead gospel preachers to proclaim salvation as Christ's invitation to unbelievers to enter God's life in Christ less than for people to invite Jesus into theirs. When a person says, "yes," this demonstrates that she or he is called and elect, swept up into his being, people, and purposes. "In Christ" is a profoundly soteriological idea—people are saved "in Christ" and are gifted the status of children of God in *the* Child (Son) of God. They are now in union with the Father "in Christ."

There is a kind of derived theosis here, whereby people are in Christ and so a part of the Godhead in the sense that they are in him. Christians never become deities; they are in the Deity and participate in his life. Further, it is a corporate concept whereby believers are ontologically joined to others in Christ. They are joined and are one church, whether they like it or not. Local churches are visible expressions of this unity of being in Christ. They are the "body of Christ" and part of the cosmic, heavenly, and universal body of Christ. Such knowledge should lead to people living lives of faith and love.

While there is room for diversity of faith expression and gifts in Christ, oneness unites God's people. "In Christness" also has ethical consequences whereby believers, being "in Christ," now live the Christ-life. Being in Christ means they should not countenance any sin that offends and violates their spiritual savior and host. Believers are to seek to live out the Christ-life every moment of every day in a faithful relationship with God, each other, and the world. This life is the eschatological life of the "man of heaven," Jesus, a life that has broken in and has the power to transform relationships.

Finally, importantly, as noted, "in Christness" in Romans is also a missiological idea—God's people are swept up in the glorious mission of God to redeem a cosmos and all people. Hence, to be "in Christ" is to be missional. Indeed, there is no such thing as an "in Christness" that is not missional for God wants all to hear his gospel so that Christ is filled up.

PART TWO: ROMANS AND THE CONTENT OF THE GOSPEL

RIGHTEOUSNESS AND JUSTIFICATION

Many would argue that righteousness is *the* core theme of Romans, e.g., Wright.[19] The language is prevalent, occurring fifty-six times, including the noun "righteousness" (*dikaiosynē*) thirty-four times, the verb "justify/declare righteous" (*dikaioō*) fifteen times, and "righteous/just" (*dikaios*) seven times.

Whether or not it is *the* theme of Romans, it is critical, featuring in the thematic statement of Romans 1:16–17: "For I am not ashamed of the gospel . . . in it the *righteousness* of God is being revealed from faith to faith." It is righteousness in particular that Paul draws out as the critical aspect of the gospel that he develops ("in it [the gospel]," 1:16–17). The exact meaning of Paul's use of *dikaio-* language is disputed. What I will do here is work through each reference to see if his main point(s) can be discerned.

The first reference to *dikaiosynē* is Romans 1:17. The first thing to note is that *dikaiosynē* carries in it the sense of justice and righteousness. It is debated whether the righteousness of God should be taken as:

1. An attribute of God, i.e., a possessive genitive "God's own righteousness": His justice (*iustitia distributive* ["distributive justice"]): a common view in the early church due to the Latin context, but rare today.[20]

    a. His faithfulness to the covenant promises of salvation that takes "from faith to faith" with the verb "is being revealed," which is common today (e.g., Wright, Jewett and Kotansky).[21]

2. An activity of God, i.e., a subjective genitive ("the righteousness that is being shown by God"), the dynamic sense of "establishing right," e.g., Psalms, Isaiah. As such, it is "the saving action of God."

3. "God's salvation creating power" to bring the world back under his lordship, i.e., an activity and status (e.g., Käsemann).[22] These are not mutually exclusive. For example, Moo opts for a blend of status and activity in 1:17.[23] Schreiner opts for a forensic status involving transformative power.[24]

4. A status given by God, i.e., a gift, forensic, a genitive of source: "a righteousness that is from God" (Luther). This view also includes taking "from faith to faith" with righteousness as a declaration of one's righteous status before God.

---

19. Wright, "Romans," 396–406.

20. Moo, *Letter to the Romans*, 73, although he does not subscribe to this view.

21. Wright suggests Romans 1:17 is "about God and God's covenantal faithfulness and justice, rather than simply about "justification." Wright, "Romans," 403. See also Jewett and Kotansky, *Romans*, 144.

22. Käsemann, *New Testament Questions of Today*, 168–82.

23. Moo, *Letter to the Romans*, 77.

24. Schreiner, *Romans*, 66.

Salvation Ideas

Before discussing the meaning of righteousness in the programmatic verse of 1:16–17, it is essential to explore the LXX and background in Romans.

Dikaiosynē in the LXX

In the LXX, *dikaiosynē* is found 351 times. In these references, we see that the righteousness of God is more of an attribute of God expressed in his action on behalf of Israel in covenant relationship. The idea of righteousness as a status is rare. An analysis of the term reveals these details:

Righteous living according to the Covenantal Requirements of Torah.

Righteousness, in this sense, is human attitudes, actions, and speech that is in line with the expectations of the covenant. It involves worship and, more importantly, social justice. Righteousness is not so much a status as something Israel does or does not live up to.[25] Often this righteous and just living relates to living according to the ordinances of the law, i.e., legal, forensic (e.g., Deut 33:21; Ps 4:6: "righteous sacrifices," cf. Ps 50:21). The law itself is righteous and reflects God's righteousness, as in Psalm 119.[26] At times, it involves a person to person forensic justice/righteousness (Lev 19:15) and justice in terms of the law and people (Deut 33:21). At other times we have "right sacrifice," i.e., something legal (Deut 33:19). Sometimes it relates to the king ruling justly.[27]

Dikaiosynē in the LXX often translates *ḥĕ·sĕḏ* (steadfast love) and is often linked to the Hebrew justice, *miš·pāṭ* (e.g., Amos 5:24). It is also related to judgment and justice with reciprocity involved, God repaying the righteous in kind.[28] It is contrasted with evil (Ps 51:5). In Proverbs, righteousness is linked to wisdom, fear of God, and the law; and in the main, is attitudinal and behavioral. It is the path to life, prosperity, and peace. It is contrasted with wickedness.[29] In the Prophets, it is often related to

---

25. See, e.g., Gen 15:6; 18:6; 20:5, 13; 21:23; 24:29; 30:33; 32:11; Deut 9:4–6; Josh 24:14; Judges 5:11; 2 Sam 22:25; 1 Kings 8:32; 1 Chr 29:17; 2 Chr 6:23; Neh 2:20; Job 8:6; 22:28; 24:13; 27:6; 29:14; 33:26; 35:8; Pss 4:2, 6; 5:9; 14:2; 16:15; Ps 22:3; 35:11; 36:6; 37:21; 51:5; 71:3; 93:15; 105:3; 105:31 (of Phinehas: "reckoned to him as righteousness"); 117:19; 131:9; Eccl 5:7 (justice for the poor); Isa 1:21; 5:7; 26:2, 9, 10; 32:16–17; 33:15; 39:8; 46:12; 48:1, 18; 54:14; 56:1; 57:12; 58:2; 58:8; 59:9, 14; 60:17; 61:3, 8 ("I the Lord, love justice"), 11; 62:1–2; 64:5; Jer 4:2; 22:3, 13; 27:7; Ezek 3:20; 45:9; Dan 6:23; 8:12; 9:18; Hos 10:12; Amos 5:7, 24 ("let justice roll down like waters, and righteousness like and everflowing stream;" Amos 6:12, also Zeph 2:3; Mal 3:3).

26. E.g., Pss 118:7, 40, 62, 75, 106, 121, 123, 138, 142, 144, 160, 164, 172; Isa 33:6.

27. 1 Sam 26:23; 2 Sam 8:15; 1 Kgs 3:6, 9; 10:9; 1 Chr 18:14; 2 Chr 9:8; Pss 71:1, 2, 7; Prov 8:15; 16:12; 17:14; 20:28; 25:25; Jer 22:15.

28. E.g., Job 33:26; Pss 17:21, 25; 37:21.

29. See Prov 1:3, 22; 2:9, 20; 3:9; 8:8, 18, 20; 10:2; 11:5, 6, 21, 30; 12:28; 13:2, 6; 14:34; 15:6, 9, 29; 16:8, 11, 17, 31; 17:23; 20:7; 21:16, 21.

injustice, i.e., the failure to live the relational standards of the covenant.[30] This more ethical type of use is found in Romans 6, in particular, of ethical living in accordance with the new covenant in Christ, serving righteousness, especially love, in the power of the Spirit (Rom 8).

God's Righteousness

Often *dikaiosynē* is attributive and speaks of God's righteousness seen in his action (an emphasis Wright will note),[31] i.e., his faithfulness to his people according to his promises to Abraham and the Patriarchs, the Mosaic and Davidic covenants, and promises in the Scriptures.[32]

There is a pattern, God repaying humanity in kind for righteousness and lack thereof. Sometimes it translates *ḥĕ·sĕḏ*, which refers to God's "steadfast love." At other times it is linked to *ḥĕ·sĕḏ*.[33]

It often relates to judgment; God judges justly.[34] It is an attribute of God; he is righteous and delights in righteousness. For example, Psalm 10:7 LXX: "For the Lord *is* righteous and loves righteousness; his face beholds uprightness" (emphasis mine). Negatively, it is associated with exile as an expression of God's justice for Israel's unrighteousness/injustice (Isa 10:22).

God's righteousness is to be proclaimed. For example, in Ps 34:28: "Then my tongue shall tell of your *righteousness* and of your praise all day long."[35] It is thus missional, and contemporary Christians fulfill this summons as they share the gospel. It is linked to God's kingship (suzerain-vassal covenant). God reigns righteously.[36] The numerous references in the Psalms (thirty-four times) indicates it is a critical reason for praise.[37] There is a moral element; God is morally righteous, i.e., holy (e.g., Pss 64:5; 68:28). It is sometimes linked to God's deliverance of his people in distress.[38]

---

30. E.g., Isa 1:21; 5:7; 33:15; 59:9, 14.

31. Wright, "Romans," 403.

32. So see Gen 19:19; 24:27; Exod 15:13; 34:7 ("Thou hast guided in thy righteousness this thy people whom thou hast redeemed, by thy strength thou hast called them into thy holy resting-place"); 1 Sam 2:10; 1 Sam 12:7 ("righteousness of the Lord"); 1 Sam 26:23 ("And the Lord shall recompense each according to his righteousness and his truth"); Ps 7:18; Ps 21:32; 30:2 (righteousness and deliverance linked); 34:24 (character of God basis of prayer appeal); 34:27; Ps 35:7 ("'your righteousness is like the mighty mountains, your judgments are like the great deep"); 39:11; 47:11; 49:6; 64:5; 68:27; 70:2, 15, 16; 84:11–14; 87:13; 97:2; 102:17; 110:3 ("his righteousness endures forever"); 111:3, 9; 142:1; Isa 5:16; 33:5; 38:19; 42:6; 45:19, 23, 24; 51:8; 59:17; 63:1, 7; Jer 9:23; Dan 9:7, 9, 16; Hos 2:21; Joel 2:23; Mic 6:5; 7:9; Mal 2:17.

33. E.g., Exod 15:13; Ps 102:17; Isa 63:7; Hos 2:21.

34. Pss 7:9; 9:5, 9; 16:1; 49:6; 57:2 (unlike the other gods); 95:13; 97:9.

35. Cf. Pss 21:32; 39:10; 70:18, 24.

36. Pss 44:6–7; 88:15; 95:13; 96:2; 98:4.

37. E.g., Pss 70:16; 88:17; 96:6; 144:7.

38. E.g., Pss 30:2; 70:2; 142:11; Isa 41:2; 45:13.

Salvation Ideas

The hope of a coming Davidic king involves his acting in righteousness and justice.[39] The eschatological age will be characterized by justice and righteousness. For example, Isaiah 61:11: "the Lord God will cause *righteousness* and praise to sprout up before all the nations" (emphasis mine).[40] In Second Isaiah, at times, it speaks of God's salvation of Israel from exile and in eschatological terms.[41]

If we put all this together, righteousness in the LXX is:

- Founded in God's utterly righteous/just character and being.
- Exercised in the kingship of God as righteous and just.
- Expressed in the covenant relationships, promises, blessings, and curses.
- sourced in his steadfast love and mercy.
- Documented in the Law (which is righteous and the basis for justice).
- Decided in his righteous/just judgment that is based on covenant and law.
- Seen in God acting to save in Israel's story.

Paul adds to this OT picture. For him, righteousness is now:

- Fully satisfied in his Son, who died to propitiate God's wrath.
- Received as a declaration of righteousness and justification as a gift where there is heartfelt faith in the Son.
- Generated in the life of the believer by the Spirit as God empowers to live righteously in accordance with the heart of the law.

As such, based on the LXX, one might argue that God's righteousness is an attribute and speaks of his resultant action in terms of the covenant. However, this is not conclusive as Paul's use of righteousness ideas in Romans needs to be explored.

Righteousness in Romans

Aside from Romans 1:17, initially discussed above and to which we will return, Paul uses *dikaiosyne* thirty-three times. In that the theme verses of 1:16–17 anticipate the content of the letter, we need to explore how he uses the idea in these verses.

In Romans 3:5, *dikaiosynē* is an *attribute of God* demonstrated in his *action* on behalf of Israel. It is God's complete and utter righteousness/justice in contrast to human unrighteousness and injustice. One must also agree with Wright and see it as

---

39. Isa 9:6; 11:5; 16:5; Jer 23:5.
40. Cf. Isa 32:16, 17; 54:14; 58:8; 60:17; 61:3; 62:1–2; Dan 9:24; Zech 8:8; Mal 3:20.
41. See Isa 45:8; 46:13; 51:5, 6.

effectively covenantal faithfulness to Israel.[42] However, it transcends an Israel-focus, as it speaks of God's righteousness in contrast to all humankind and so speaks of his righteousness in relation to Jew and gentile alike (cf. 3:9).

Romans 3:21 is especially important as, in this passage, Paul gives the solution to the problem of human failure and so, in a sense, returns to 1:17 after the "detour" of 1:18—3:20. Here, the righteousness of God is most definitely *a status conferred on believers through the work of Christ*. It is disclosed (cf. "revealed" in 1:17), anticipated in the law and the prophets, based around faith and not law (faith in Jesus Christ, cf. "faith to faith" in 1:17), and is for all people, Jew and gentile. All people are trapped in sin and declared righteous (justified) by his grace through the redemption that is in Christ Jesus, whose salvific death brings righteousness. It is then a status conferred because Christ died for the sins of people (cf. 1 Cor 15:3).

In Romans 3:25–26, it is an *attribute of God* seen in his *action* to save, in the righteousness that came by faith through Christ's salvific death. Christ's atoning sacrifice *demonstrates* God's righteousness. One could link this to the covenant; however, it reaches back before the covenant to Adam—it is both his faithfulness to his covenant, and his faithfulness to all people who are made in his image (creational).[43]

Through Romans 4, *dikaiosynē* is again a *status* conferred. Righteousness is conferred on Abraham by God based on his trust in God (cf. Gen 15:6). His faith is counted as righteousness.[44] In Romans 4:6, premised on Psalm 32:1–2, again, it is a status conferred through faith, i.e., sins are forgiven and not counted against believers because of faith and not through works. This counting of righteousness does not need to quantify righteousness as something able to be measured and literally given. It is a status and identity conferred by God by grace as a gift (below). It is a result of being "in Christ" because of the work of Christ.

In Romans 5:17, Paul uses the language of *gift*, i.e., "the *gift* of righteousness" (emphasis mine). Again, it is a *status* conferred on believers, not through their works, but faith in Jesus Christ. In Romans 5:21, it is a status that offers eternal life where saving faith remains. All uses in Romans 8–10 relate to the *status* of believers declared righteous by faith and not law.[45]

In Romans 6, Paul uses *dikaiosynē* differently. He does not use it as a status, although it is implied that the believer is under the realm of righteousness and dead to sin. Rather, he personifies righteousness as a master to whom Christians should submit. Righteousness is then the personification of right living or goodness. It is effectively equivalent to God and/or Jesus, and/or the gospel, and/or the Spirit. One

---

42. Wright, "Romans," 403.

43. If we accept the view that there is an Adamic covenant, it is covenantal in an all-of-humankind sense.

44. Cf. 4:3, 5, 9, 11, 13, 22.

45. Cf. 8:10; 9:30, 31; 10:3, 4, 5, 6, 10.

might say, it aligns with God's righteousness embodied in Jesus, experienced in the Spirit, and expressed in the gospel.

The standard of righteousness is not the Jewish law but the gospel and its life of faith and especially the love that sums up and fulfills all law. More detail will be given on the specifics of this in Romans 8 and especially in Romans 12—15. In a sense, then, "righteousness" functions as a synonym for God himself as revealed in Christ and the Spirit. By doing this, Paul intimates that God's righteousness is an attribute of his being (and Christ and the Spirit). Believers are to be "instruments for righteousness" (6:13), obedient (6:16), and "slaves of righteousness" (6:18, 19). They are transformed to be like God and his Son who are righteous. There is some overlap with the notion of righteousness by faith and grace as believers live by grace rather than law. However, the emphasis here is primarily ethical, which, as was discussed earlier in this chapter, is a pervasive thread in the LXX.

This ethical emphasis is again found in Romans 14:17, where righteousness is a pattern for living. Righteousness language used ethically illustrates the problem with classic Protestant thinking where justification relates to the moment of salvation, and sanctification defines Christian growth. It is not as simple as that as sometimes righteousness is ethical. Similarly, sometimes sanctification speaks of the moment of salvation (see below on sanctification).

Pulling these threads together, in Romans, Paul uses *dikaiosynē* in three main ways.

1. God's Character Expressed in Action toward Humankind and the World

As often in the LXX, righteousness is ontological, used of God's character of righteousness and justice. He existed prior to creation and *is* righteous and just to the core. Supremely, this is reflected in his righteous and just action to save through Jesus Christ his Son (3:5, 25–26). It is thus covenantal, God is righteous in his love (cf. ṣeḏā·qā, ḥě·sěḏ) and justice (cf. *miš·pāṭ*) and is faithful to his covenantal promises to Israel. However, God's righteousness also precedes the covenants with Abraham and is creational, God putting right the world and humankind (cf. Käsemann). Through Israel's Christ, the personified and embodied Israel, God's Son, God is faithful to all humanity, for it is through this Israelite that the world will be made right. Righteousness also extends to all of creation in Romans 8:19-22—God will make his world right, releasing the cosmos from its bondage to decay.

2. As a Conferred Status

In Romans, Paul also uses *dikaiosynē* in the Lutheran sense of the righteous status conferred on believers through faith in Jesus Christ. Jesus Christ's righteousness is gifted or conferred on believers. This subjective use is dominant in Romans and other salvation and ethical ideas are linked to it. Romans 3:21 is expounded as a status received by faith. This status is expressed concerning Abraham in Romans 4. Romans

5 then flows from the summative statement in 5:1, "therefore, having been justified by faith" (my translation). Romans 8 begins with a declaration that there is now no condemnation for those in Christ Jesus. Life in the Spirit flows from this status of being free from condemnation (8:1). Israel's failure in Romans 9–11 is seeking the status of righteousness through legal observance and not faith (esp. 9:30–32; 10:3–6, 10).

The ethical use in Romans 6 is derived out of right standing before God, symbolized by death to sin in baptism (6:3–4). The empowerment for this is the Spirit, who is touched on in Romans 5:5 and 7:6 and expounded in Romans 8:1–17. The attributive use in Romans 3:5 and 25–26 again flows from the action of God in Christ to bring the righteousness that is by grace and faith and not law.

3. Ethical Righteousness

Righteousness language is also used ethically of righteousness as something to be served as people live righteously. Righteousness here is the personification of goodness and so is virtually synonymous with God himself, the Spirit, the gospel, and righteous living (6). It is then ethical; a life lived out for God according to the grace of the gospel and not law. It springs from the status one has in Christ.

Righteousness in Romans 1:17

Returning to Romans 1:17, the idea of righteousness as a conferred status is dominant in Romans despite *dikaiosynē* being used in the LXX ethically and of God's character and action on behalf of the covenant. Good arguments can be made for the righteousness of God in the verse being creational/covenantal and attributive/active. First, the genitive can be possessive "the righteousness God possesses."

Second, the clause *ek pisteōs eis pistin* can be "from God's faithfulness to human faith response" or "from the faithfulness of Christ to the human faith." If so, then we have a movement from God's faithfulness to the covenant through Christ toward the human response of faith.

Third, if we also attach "from faith to faith" to "has been revealed" (*apokalyptetai*) to "righteousness of God," this shifts the emphasis toward righteousness as an attribute/action of God.

Finally, the uses of the righteousness of God in a character sense in 3:5 and 25–26 could lead to this conclusion, i.e., God's righteousness is being revealed in this gospel of salvation by faith.

On the other hand, a good case can be made for the Lutheran view "righteousness of God" as a status conferred on believers. It can be a genitive of production ("a righteousness God produces") or source or origin ("the righteousness sourced in God"). "From faith to faith" can be seen to be emphatic to reinforce that it has been faith in the past (cf. Abraham), and it is faith in the present. Further, the quote from Habakkuk 2:4 can support this reading, "the one who is righteous will live by faith" (or "the one who is righteous by faith will live"). Finally, the movement in the next section from universal human corruption to a righteousness that is by faith and not law, could lead in this direction.

Dikaioō, "Justified," in Romans

Before a final decision, we also need to explore *dikaioō* and *dikaios* language in Romans. The verb *dikaioō* is used fifteen times and the noun *dikaios* seven. The verb is used of being justified before God. It is a forensic idea of being declared righteous before God. It is one of a range of metaphors Paul uses of salvation (cf. reconciled, redeemed, adopted, and so on). In Romans 2:13, it is those who not only hear the law but do the law who are justified.

As noted previously, the summative texts in 3:9, 19–20, 23 indicate that Paul believes only Christ has done this. Thus, being justified here is the conferring of a status by God. In Romans 3:20 and 28, Paul uses it in this sense, stating that justification through law is not possible (3:20). Instead, they are justified through the gracious gift of redemption in Christ Jesus (3:24). Further, in Romans 3:26, God is righteous in that he justifies believers. So, whether a person is Jewish or gentile, they are justified by faith alone (3:30).

In Romans 4, justification is a status of righteousness conferred on the ungodly based on faith and not works in the old covenant (4:2, 5). Similarly, in Romans 5:1, Paul states, "we are justified by faith," again a status conferred. In Romans 5:9, he speaks of being justified "by his blood," centering justification on the death of Christ whose shed blood deals with sin. In Romans 6:7, one is justified "from sin," reinforcing the freedom justification brings. In Romans 8:30, the believer is justified. The final use in Romans 8:33 declares that "it is God who justifies."

Paul applies *dikaioō* to God once, in Romans 3:4, where he quotes Ps 51:4 of God being justified in his words. Thus, it is more related to God's character and subsequent action. Hence, we can say that "justification" is overwhelmingly related to the status of having been declared righteous by God through his grace and the saving work of Jesus Christ.

The noun *dikaios* ("righteous") is used in Romans 1:17 from Habakkuk 2:4: "and, the righteous one from faith will live." Leaving aside the complex debate about Paul's use of versions here,[46] there are two main ways of reading this. We can take *ek pisteōs* ("from faith") with *dikaios,* and so it means "the righteous one on the basis of faith will live," referring to salvation.[47]

46. There are four versions of this we know of including, 1) MT: "the righteous by his faith(fullness) shall live"; 2) LXX: "the righteous out of *my* faith/faithfulness shall live"; 3) Paul here and in Gal 3:11: "the righteous out of faith/faithfulness shall live"; 4) Heb 10:38: "the righteous one out of faith/faithfulness shall live." However, whatever source Paul is using, the text in 1:17 is not disputed.

47. See NEB, NET, NASB 95, ESV. See also, e.g., Barrett, *Epistle to the Romans*, 31–32; Käsemann, *Romans*, 30–32, Cranfield, *Critical and Exegetical Commentary*, 1:99–10; Dunn, *Romans 1–8*,

Alternatively, we can take *ek pisteōs* with *zēsetai* ("will live"), and so it reads, "the righteous will live from faith," i.e., more the transformative process.⁴⁸ As noted above, the overwhelming emphasis in Romans in terms of righteousness language is toward the conferring of status and faith. That being the case, it seems highly likely that the first of the two options, "the righteous by faith will live," is correct, even if Habakkuk's original context supports the latter. Alternatively, the idea "the righteous will live by faith" may be preferred as it encompasses both coming to faith and living by faith.

Other uses of *dikaios*, where humanity is concerned, relate to the status of being right with God, based on faith rather than law (2:13; 5:19). No one reaches this status aside from faith in Christ (e.g., 3:10: "no one is righteous, not even one"). In Romans 3:26, it is used of God who is righteous, as seen in the justification brought in Christ. In Romans 5:7, Paul uses it ethically and generally, while he uses it of the law in Romans 7:12. As with other *dikaio*-terms, it is primarily related to the status of being right with God.

CONCLUSION

Based on this discussion, it seems that while the Jewish background would suggest the "righteousness of God" refers to God's character and action to save, it is more likely that in Romans, Paul has more in mind a righteousness of God conferred on believers through the work of Christ. Such a conferral does not necessarily mean that some part of God is infused into believers, i.e., imputed righteousness in a concrete sense (see Wright's critique in *Justification*).⁴⁹ Instead, it is the declaration of God, the judge that a person is right with God. It is a present reality that will find its completion at the consummation of history and the final transformation of the believer. It is thus the moment of salvation where a sinner is declared righteous. If there is any imputed righteousness, it is not received by the declaration of righteousness, but when God enters the believer by the Spirit. His Spirit brings righteousness into the human heart and begins the work of transforming people to be increasingly righteous (if they continue to yield).

It is certainly fair to argue that righteousness is the dominant motif in Romans *within* the overall threads of the "gospel" and salvation (1:16). The theme of the gospel is established in the prologue, in which *dik-* language is not employed. It features twice in 1:16–17, righteousness as Paul transitions from the "gospel" to righteousness as the core focal-point of his letter ("in *it*").⁵⁰ Righteousness language then features

---

44–46; Moo, *Letter to the Romans*, 80–82; Thielman, *Romans*, 81–84.

48. See NIV84, NIV, NRSV. See also, e.g., Wright, "Romans," 425; Hendriksen, *Romans*, 64; Jewett and Kotansky, *Romans*, 145–47; Mounce, *Romans*, 74; Longenecker, *Epistle*, 185–86.

49. Wright, *Justification*, 29–30, 133–35.

50. 6x Rom 1 (1:17 [2x], 18 [2x], 29, 32); 5x Rom 2 (2:5, 8, 13 [2x], 26); 17x Rom 3 (3:4, 5 [3x], 8, 19, 20, 21, 22, 24, 25, 26 [3x], 28, 30); so 17x in Rom 1:18—3:20; 11x Rom 4 (4:2, 3, 5 [2x], 6, 9, 11, 13,

SALVATION IDEAS

seventy-seven times through the letter. As such, Luther's view that "justification by faith" or "righteousness by faith" is the dominant theme of the letter is not without warrant.[51]

However, whether it is the dominant idea in all of Paul's writings is tenuous. It is undoubtedly one of the core threads of Romans (above) and Galatians (14x), featuring in the propositional verses in Galatians 2:15–16. However, the language is not used as broadly and in the same central way in the other letters.[52] More prominent is "in Christ," "in him," and "in the Lord" language, suggesting that this is closer to the center of Paul's theology, used some 123 times.[53]

In my view, Christ is the center of Paul's theology, theologically and existentially. Christ and believers being in him dominate his understanding of salvation and inclusion. Experiencing this inclusion as he did on the Damascus Road, is the center of his experience. All believers experience this by the Spirit. Hence, the Spirit is also an essential aspect of Paul's theology.

In sum, justification is the dominant soteriological concept in Romans. The language is, at its essence, forensic, drawn from the law-court motif, speaking of *"be found in the right, be free of charges"*[54] and relates to the judgment language that dominates Romans. Aside from Romans 3:4, where it speaks of God being vindicated, the verb speaks of the declaration by God the judge of the innocence of believers, i.e., acquittal, pardoned, declared innocent, or *Gerechtfertigt*! It is one of Paul's favorite ways of describing salvation.

Paul's righteousness language has the same already-not yet eschatology we see with his salvation language. A person is justified at the point of faith.[55] They are also being justified, as indicated by the present passive participle of *dikaioō* (3:24). They are to live out their righteous status as slaves of righteousness, seeking to be righteous and just in every aspect of their lives (6:16, 18). If they persevere in faith, they will

---

22, 25); so 20x Rom 3:21—4:25; 9x Rom 5 (5:1, 7, 9, 16, 17, 18, 21); 7x Rom 6 (6:7, 13, 16, 18, 19, 20); 1x Rom 7 (7:12); 5x Rom 8 (8:4, 10, 30 [2x], 33); so 22x Rom 5–8; 5x Rom 9 (9:14, 30, 31); 7x Rom 10 (10:3 [3x], 4, 5, 6, 10); 0x Rom 11; so 12x Rom 9–11; so 3x Rom 12:1—15:13; 2x Rom 12 (12:19 [2x]); 1x Rom 13 (13:4); 1x Rom 14 (14:17); 0x Rom 15–16.

51. By comparison, "in Christ" (13x), "in him" (1x), and "in the Lord" (8x) are used only twenty-two times.

52. Righteousness language is used seventy times from 1 Cor to Phlm: 1 Cor (9x); 2 Cor (13x); Eph (4x); Phil (6x); Col (2x); 1 Thess (2x); 2 Thess (6x); 1 Tim (3x); 2 Tim (5x); Titus (4x); Phlm (1x).

53. 60x "in Christ," 23x "in him," 40x "in the Lord." "In Christ": 1 Cor (11x); 2 Cor (6x); Gal (6x); Eph (9x); Phil (10x); Col (3x); 1 Thess (3x); 2 Thess (0); 1 Tim (2x); 2 Tim (7x); Titus (0x); Phlm (3x); "In him": 1 Cor (2x); 2 Cor (4x); Gal (0x); Eph (6x); Phil (1x); Col (8x); 1 Thess (0x); 2 Thess (1x); 1 Tim (1x); 2 Tim (0x); Titus (0x); Phlm (0x). "In the Lord": Romans (8x); 1 Cor 9x; 2 Cor 2x; Gal 1x; Eph 7x; Phil 9x; Col 4x; 1 Thess (3x); 2 Thess (2x); 1 Tim 0x; 2 Tim 0x; Titus 0x; Phlm 0x.

54. BDAG 249 (emphasis original).

55. See 4:2; 5:1, 9; 8:30; 1 Cor 6:11; Gal 2:16 [2nd use]; Titus 3:7.

experience the final verdict, "justified," at the judgment.[56] They will be fully righteous for eternity.

REDEMPTION

Redemption language (*apolytrōsis*) is used twice in Romans. It has its origins in slavery and the "'buying back' a slave or captive, i.e., 'making free' by payment of a ransom."[57] In Romans 3:24 it refers to the work of Christ as a redeeming work, a ransom paid setting believers free. We do not need to be distracted by pondering to whom the payment is made, as were earlier scholars.[58] Instead, it is a metaphor that relates to manumission or emancipation—humans are set free from slavery to sin and its consequences because of Christ's death.[59] In Romans 8:23, it is used in a future sense of the redemption of the body at the second coming, i.e., bodily transformation and being set free from sin and death—total redemption of the being (not merely spiritual status as at present).

We see that Paul's redemption language has the same now/not yet eschatological tension. Redemption is gifted through Jesus (3:24).[60] Ultimately, believers will experience the redemption of their bodies (8:23) on the day of redemption (Eph 4:30). In the meantime, believers are to live out their freedom in Christ in service and not sin (Gal 5:1, 13).

RECONCILIATION

A salvific notion Paul does not use frequently is reconciliation, a highly relational and political metaphor speaking of enmity overcome, and the relationship restored. Paul considers all humanity sinful and recipients of God's wrath, and destined for destruction, i.e., in a state of enmity to God.

In Romans 5:1, Paul speaks of justification by faith, because of which, believing humanity is now at *peace* with God: "we have peace with God through our Lord Jesus Christ." The broken relationship between God and humanity caused by the Edenic rebellion is overcome; a treaty (covenant) is signed because of Christ (cf. 11:27), and believers and God are one where faith is found. Paul picks up this notion in Romans 5:10–11, where he describes sinful humanity as "enemies" of God. However, in Christ,

---

56. See 2:13; 3:20; Gal 2:16 (3rd use).

57. BDAG 117.

58. See, e.g., "Origen (c. 185–254), a theologian of Alexandria, maintained that the ransom was paid to the devil. Origen's form of the theory was that Christ cheated the devil by escaping through his resurrection." Elwell and Beitzel, "Ransom," 1822.

59. "The point of the New Testament teaching on redemption is not that Jesus paid someone, but that our redemption came at a high cost." Grindheim, *Introducing Biblical Theology*, 132.

60. See also Gal 3:13; Eph 1:7.

they are reconciled to God through Christ's death and are saved by his life. Believers have received reconciliation through Christ.

In Romans 11:15, Paul speaks of "the reconciliation of the world." While the notion of cosmic reconciliation is found in Ephesians and Colossians and could be argued to be relevant based on the renewal of creation in Romans 8:19–23,[61] it is not clear that we should read it into this verse in Romans. Paul's focus in Romans 11:15 is the reconciliation of God and *people* in the gospel. In the letter, he uses reconciliation language in Romans of *people* restored from enmity to peace with God. Still, the reconciliation of all things is a Pauline theme, especially in Colossians.

Peace in interpersonal relationships is an aspect of his paraenesis (14:17, 19), including maintaining good relationships with unbelievers (12:18). This concord is no doubt derived from divine-human reconciliation; humans should be reconciled to one another as a visible manifestation of the work of the God of peace (15:33; 16:20) who generates peace in human lives by the Spirit.[62] Harmonious relationships flow from the reconciliation people have with God in Christ. God's people are one, Jew, and gentile, male and female, slave and free (cf. Gal 3:28). There can be no arrogance, inferiority, and hostility in God's people. As Governor Hobson is reputed to have said at the Treaty of Waitangi signed between Māori and the British Crown in New Zealand in 1840, "*He iwi tahi tatou*" (we are now one people).[63]

Through Paul's letters, reconciliation carries the same temporal eschatological tension we have seen with salvation, righteousness, and redemption discussed above. Believers are presently reconciled to God (5:10, 11). In a realized sense, all things are reconciled to God now (Col 1:20, 22). Nonethless, believers like Paul and his team have a "ministry of reconciliation" summoning people into that reconciled status (2 Cor 5:18, 20). They are to live at peace with God and one another in the present (12:18; 14:17, 19).

SANCTIFICATION

Holiness is a neglected notion in today's world and parts of the church obsessed with antinomian and individualistic love and freedom. However, the language of holiness is used regularly in the Scriptures, which are, for Paul, themselves holy (1:2). The law is holy, despite its failure to regulate unholy humans (7:12). The term is frequently used of the Spirit, who is the holiness of God and fills people with it.[64] Where people are concerned, it is utilized of people giving themselves to God as holy sacrifices (12:1).

---

61. Eph 1:10; 2:16; Col 1:20, cf. 1 Cor 7:11; 2 Cor 5:18–20.
62. See 1:7; 5:1; 8:6; 15:13; Gal 5:22.
63. See Simpson, "William Hobson."
64. See 1:4; 5:5; 9:1; 14:17; 15:13, 16 (the "Holy Spirit" sixteen times overall in Paul).

They are to greet one another with a holy kiss (16:16). People are described as *hagiois*, "holy ones" or "saints" eight times in the letter.[65]

The descriptor "Holy Spirit" alerts us to the importance of holiness as the by-product of God dwelling in believers' hearts—the Spirit works holiness in the lives of believers as they accede to God's *pneuma*. Indeed, in that "Holy" is used adjectivally to describe the Spirit more than any other descriptor, the primary function of the Spirit in one's life is to sanctify people.

Sanctification is not merely moral holiness but is a relational, social, and missional holiness that permeates all of life, whether one's private thoughts, sexuality, social relationships with believers or those outside the church, and relationship with creation.

By describing believers regularly as "holy ones," Paul sees holiness as a status. Previously unholy, the death of the Holy One, Jesus,[66] in peoples' stead, sees them declared holy or sanctified by God. This holiness is a status but not completed, for they remain sinful. However, it is an act of grace whereby Christ's holiness is attributed to the believer. Further, the power to be holy is gifted via the Holy Spirit. Then, believers are charged to be holy because he is holy, has declared them holy, and has empowered them to be holy.[67]

In Romans 6:19–20, it is used of the process of sanctification (*hagiasmos*) whereby believers seek to live righteous lives. The endpoint is the complete sanctification of the whole being and eternal life (6:22–23). Eternality will only be granted to that which is entirely holy.

Sanctification then is a declared state that should flow increasingly into sanctified living as, by the Spirit of holiness, believers become more and more like Jesus, the image of the invisible God (8:29). This transformation will come to pass as people yield to the Holy Spirit. Christians are to live out of their identity as those declared holy, becoming more and more holy in our thinking, behavior, and speech.

Again, we have the now/not yet tension in Paul's use of sanctification language. Believers are saints now, declared holy, sanctified (1 Cor 1:2; 6:11; 2 Thess 2:13), and recipients of the Holy Spirit. They are to live holy lives in the present, submitting to the promptings of the Spirit, and renouncing the works of the flesh for the life of the Spirit (12:1).[68] At the eschaton, they will be sanctified entirely in that glorious moment when their bodies are finally set free from sin's corruption (1 Cor 15:50–54). They will be God's holy people with their holy Triune God in a completely holy creation.

---

65. See 1:7; 8:27; 12:13; 15:25, 26, 31; 16:2, 15; see also 11:16 (thirty-nine times overall in Paul).
66. See Mark 1:24; Luke 4:34; John 6:69; Acts 2:7.
67. An adaption of "be holy, for I am holy" (Lev 11:44, 45; 19:2; 1 Pet 1:16).
68. See Eph 1:4; Col 3:12; 1 Thess 4:3–8; Titus 1:8.

ADOPTION

For Paul, the fundamental metaphor to describe God's people is not "the body of Christ," "the bride of Christ," or "the temple of the Spirit" (vital though they are), it is the "family of God." A claim like this can sound questionable as explicit statements using familial notions of God's people are rare in his letters. He speaks in Galatians 6:10 of the "household/family of faith," and in 1 Timothy 3:15 of "the household of God, which is the church of the living God." Nevertheless, the *idea* is dominant in his letters where God is Father (four times Romans),[69] Jesus is the Son (seven times Romans),[70] and believers are frequently addressed as *adelphoi*, an inclusive term indicating "brothers and sisters."[71]

This kinship language is a fictive extension of the household as the primary political unit of the Roman world.[72] Paul uses adoption language to describe the inclusion of people into God's family. Adoption is likely drawn from a Roman rather than a Jewish setting.[73] In some cultural settings, adopted children can be considered to have less status than children born children into a family unit. However, the Romans thought no such thing, and it describes people's complete inclusion in God's family with full inheritance rights. We see its importance in that some Roman emperors were adopted, including four of the five Julio-Claudian emperors relevant to NT times: Augustus (by Julius Caesar), Tiberius (by Augustus), Caligula (by Tiberius), and Nero (by Claudius).[74]

Paul uses the term *huiothesia* of Israel's adoption as God's people before Christ (9:4). Otherwise, Paul employs it twice and in two ways. First, he utilizes it of conversion when believers receive the Spirit of adoption and become his children. By the Spirit, believers join Jesus (Mark 14:35), crying out to the God who is now their

---

69. God is "Father" forty-one times.

70. Jesus is "Son" seventeen times.

71. *Adelphos* is used nineteen times in Romans. Ten times he uses the plural as his epistolary address to the Romans (1:13; 7:1, 4; 8:12; 10:1; 11:25; 12:1; 15:14, 30; 16:17). Otherwise, believers are brothers of Christ, the firstborn (8:29) or of fellow Christians (14:10 [2x], 13, 15, 21; 16:14, 23). Once, he uses *adelphos* of Israelites who are "brothers" by descent (9:3). Twice, he uses *adelphē* of "sisters" including Phoebe and the sibling of Nereus (16:1, 15). Overall, Christians are addressed as *adelphoi*, "brothers and sisters," sixty-three times with Paul using *adelphos* ninety-two times and *adelphē* six times.

72. "The basic unit of the Greco-Roman society in which Paul lived and ministered was the household (*oikos, oikia*). Its importance was such that secular ethicists saw the stability of the city-state as dependent upon the responsible management of the household. The foundational nature of this institution is further seen in the pattern it provided for the structure and definition of larger political institutions." Towner, "Households and Household Codes," 417.

73. Scott, "Adoption, Sonship," 16–18 argues for a Jewish background to Paul's adoption metaphor. However, *huiothesia* is not used in the LXX, it was in the Roman world that adoption was legal, and it is likely Paul drew his understanding from the Roman legal practice. Longenecker, *Epistle*, 702–6.

74. Some of the emperors in the second century were also adopted, including Trajan (by Nerva), Hadrian (by Trajan), Antonius Pius (by Hadrian), Lucius Verus (by Antonius Pius), and Marcus Aurelius (by Antonius Pius).

Father, "Abba! Father!" Whereas Jesus cried out in desperate travail as he faced the coming cross (Mark 14:36), believers cry out fearlessly and joyously because they are included in God's great global family (8:15). In the present, believers live by the Spirit, spiritually bound to God the Father in Christ.

Second, Paul uses *huiothesia* of the final redemption when believers experience the fullness of their bodily and spatial adoption as God's children (8:23). This moment comes at the consummation where his children will no longer be separated from him physically but will be in his presence, their bodies free from sin and death, his forever. Like creation trapped in its bondage to sin and death as people are, they groan and yearn for this. These two uses show that Paul uses adoption with the same now/not yet tension seen in other metaphors. Believers are adopted now (8:15; Gal 4:5; Eph 1:5) to be fully incorporated into God's family at the eschaton (8:23).

NEW LIFE

The contrast of life and death flows through Romans. Humanity is lost in sin and death, not only meaning physical death and decay, but spiritual death ultimately culminating in eternal destruction. The promise of eternal life is central to the gospel. Sometimes he speaks of "eternal life,"[75] and at others "life."[76] This life is that of the resurrection, as we see in Jesus's being raised from death (5:10, 17; 7:10). It is the gift of God in Christ (6:23). Christ's work sets believers free from law, sin, and death and into life (8:1–2). Living by the Spirit brings life (8:6, 10).

IMMORTALITY

Associated with resurrection and eternal life is immortality. In Romans 1:23, immortality is an attribute of Paul's God. Conversely, humans are mortal, as are the animals of the world (1:23). Their bodies are destined for corruption, beset with passions morphed by sin into lusts and addictions (6:12). Jesus was also mortal, as seen in his death (the humanity of Christ). Still, immortality is possible and is granted to a person who lives a life entirely devoted to seeking glory, honor, and immortality from God (2:7). Sadly, no one can reach this standard, other than Jesus, the sinless one. Faith in him brings the defeat of sin and death. The Spirit who raised and restored Jesus's bloody crucified corpse also gives life to believers (8:11). Immortality is planted in the believer's heart by the Spirit.

We have to look elsewhere in Paul's writings to understand the consummation of this process (again showing that Romans is not Paul's full gospel). In 1 Corinthians 15, at the end (15:24), God's final enemy in the cosmos, death, will be defeated (15:26).

---

75. See 2:7; 5:21; 6:22, 23.
76. See 5:18; 6:4; 8:1, 6; 11:15.

SALVATION IDEAS

As he says in Romans 8:21, creation will be emancipated from decay and death. In an instant, mortal and perishable bodies of humiliation will be changed to be like the body of glory Jesus has, seen in his resurrection appearances (1 Cor 15:6–8)—spiritual bodies, glorious, immortal, and imperishable (1 Cor 15:42–54; Phil 3:21). Presently, believers are renewed by the Spirit inwardly as they live out their lives in frail jars of clay facing suffering to death. Ultimately, these bodies will be fully transformed into heavenly eternal dwellings. What is mortal will be swallowed up by life (2 Cor 4:7–5:5). People will be immortal, never to die again. From an individualistic point of view, immortality is the ultimate outcome of the gospel.

FREEDOM AND DELIVERANCE

Another word group Paul utilizes are the freedom terms found six times in Romans.[77] This language includes the verb "to set free" (*eleutheroō*), the nouns "free, independent" (*eleutheros*), and "freedom" (*eleutheria*). Akin to manumitted slaves, believers are free from sin (6:19, 22; 8:2), not in the sense of never sinning again, but are liberated from its power and consequences (death, wrath). Like a widow who is free from the law of marriage, a believer is free from the law (7:3).

This freedom is a release to be image bearers who are increasingly like Jesus by the Spirit. They are freed into the humble service of God, Christ, and others (Gal 5:13) and the receipt of eternal life. It is a freedom to live righteously.[78] Believers are released from hate to love. They are liberated from living for the flesh to living by the Spirit, from law to grace and the Spirit-life. The deliverance of the gospel is also cosmic in scope. The creation remains bound to decay and death; however, it will be set free from its frustration at the consummation (8:21).

Paul also utilizes the language of deliverance, i.e., *rhyomai*, meaning "save, rescue, deliver." Jesus is "the Deliverer" from Zion to set people free from ungodliness and sin (11:26; cf. Isa 59:20–21). He rescues believers from sin and death (7:24).[79] In Romans 15:31, Paul prays that Jesus will deliver him from Judean unbelievers when he arrives with the collection.[80] He will do so as later he came to Rome (as a prisoner).

FORGIVENESS

Although Paul does not stress the language of forgiveness in Romans or elsewhere,[81] the idea is found in the letter. In his argument that the people of Israel have always

---

77. See also 1 Cor 7:21–22, 39; 9:1, 19; 10:29; 12:13; 2 Cor 3:17; Gal 2:4; 3:28; 4:22, 23, 26, 30, 31; 5:1, 13; Eph 6:8; Col 3:11. *Apeleutheros*, "freedman," is used in 1 Cor 7:22.

78. See 6:18, 22; 8:2, see also 6:20; 7:3.

79. See also Col 1:13; 1 Thess 1:10; 2 Tim 4:18.

80. See also 2 Cor 1:10; 1 Thess 3:2; 2 Tim 3:11; 4:17.

81. See Eph 1:7; 4:32; Col 4:10. Paul also uses the language of interpersonal forgiveness in 2 Cor

been justified by faith and not law, Abraham's faith takes center stage. Nevertheless, in Romans 4:7–8, he cites the Davidic Psalm 32:1–2 that stresses the blessedness of those "whose lawless deeds are *forgiven*, and whose sins are *covered*" (emphasis mine). By doing so, he links forgiveness to justification. Where a person is declared righteous by God, she or he is forgiven for their sins, that person's transgressions are covered, and they are blessed. Their sins are no longer counted against them.

There is then an expiatory aspect to Christ's death—he cleanses people from sin. Statements like Romans 4:25 ("who was delivered up for our trespasses") imply that Christ was "delivered for the *forgiveness* of our trespasses." Where a person is "free from sin" (6:7, see also 6:18, 22), they are forgiven of sin. The citation of Isaiah 59:20–21 also stresses forgiveness, speaking of the banishment of ungodliness and the taking away of the sins of God's people through Zion's Deliverer, Jesus. Although not a major Pauline theme, for Paul, forgiveness is an important aspect of the new covenant established in Christ (11:26–27).

IMAGE BEARING AND NEW CREATION

As in 1 Corinthians 15:22, 45–49, Paul uses Adam typology of Christ in Romans 5. Paul has a robust theology of what some call "the fall," or, as I call it, "the Rupture."[82] Through Adam, the first "head" of humanity, the original "man," sin entered the world.[83] Through this sin came death to all people (Gen 3). Paul neatly balances the notion of original sin with personal responsibility in Romans 5:12: "Therefore, just as sin entered the world *through one man*, and death through sin, so death spread to all people, *because*[84] all sinned" (translation and emphasis mine). Death entered through Adam. All people die because of Adam's sin and because all sin. Cranfield is right to argue that we should understand *hēmarton* here "to refer to [people] sinning in their own persons but as a result of the corrupt nature inherited from Adam."[85] As such, in that all have sinned, sin and death have reigned since Adam (5:13–14).

Adam is expressly stated to be a type (*typos*) of the one who was to come, i.e., Jesus. In Jesus comes grace, justification, and life. He is undoing the effects of Adam's sin. Jesus is thus the new Adam, and, in his work, God is forming a new/renewed

---

2:7, 10.

82. Keown, *What's God Up To?*, 31–46. See Fitzmyer, *Romans*, 408–9. Fitzmyer refutes that there is a fall from grace in the story but "the loss of God's trust and friendship by Adam and Eve because of their transgression and disobedience." I would go further and say that not only was the relationship with God ruptured, but a person's psychological state was fractured, interpersonal relationships were ruptured, and humankind's relationship with creation was tragically shattered.

83. Fitzmyer, *Romans*, 409. He notes that the idea of "Original Sin" is developed by Christians based on this passage. Although later writers sought to do so, he rightly avers that "Paul never explains how that causality works or how Adam's sin is transmitted."

84. Cranfield, *Critical and Exegetical Commentary*, 1:274.

85. Cranfield, *Critical and Exegetical Commentary*, 1:274 (adapted for inclusive language).

humanity, and so in Jesus is the genesis of God's renewed people and creation. Romans 5:12–21 read with Romans 8:19–23 gives a rich picture of cosmic recreation, which has begun in the work of Christ.

In Romans 8:29, believers are foreknown and predestined "to be conformed to the image of his Son." The use of predestination and foreknowledge language shows that, for Paul, the election of God's people was decided before creation. Now that he has come, Jesus is the firstborn among many siblings. Paul neatly summarizes the process by which God's image bearers believe in him, the image of the invisible God (Col 1:15), and are adopted as God's children and siblings of Jesus (8:15; Gal 4:5). They receive his Spirit (8:11) and are progressively transformed to be more and more like him. The process of this is summarized in believers putting to death the misdeeds of the flesh by the Spirit, giving themselves as living sacrifices, and being transformed through the renewal of the mind (8:13; 12:1–2).[86]

HONOR AND GLORY

Unlike western individualistic cultures where wrongdoing often generates a sense of guilt, ancients (and moderns in more collective cultures) more commonly experienced shame (6:21). God is full of glory and honor (6:4; 9:23). His salvation brings the believer the converse, honor. Hence, there will be glory and honor for all who do good (2:10). While no human can achieve this in their own capacity (for all fall short of his glory, 3:23), due to Christ's goodness and sacrificial death, believers will experience glory and honor. This glory will transcend human suffering (8:18) and bring freedom from sin and its cosmic consequences (8:21). Conversely, having been prepared beforehand for glory (9:4), believers "will not be put to shame" (9:33; 10:11; Isa 28:16). Paul knows this and can declare "I am not ashamed of the gospel," despite it being the story of God's Son who is killed in the most shameful way imaginable in that context (1:16). Hence, believers boast in the hope of the glory of God (5:2). With such a hope, believers are to respond by glorifying and honoring God in worship (11:36) and social relationships (14:6). They are to outdo one another in honoring each other (12:10) and those in governance (13:7). Such things glorify God (15:7). Little wonder Paul ends the letter ascribing glory to God through Christ (16:27).

---

86. While an important salvation motif in Romans is election, that is discussed in part three, chapter 22.

11

Human Response

WHEN CONSIDERING PAUL'S GOSPEL undergirding Romans and expressed in the presentation to Rome, what is required for salvation is critical. Hence, in this chapter, Paul's understanding of the right response to the gospel is considered. Four ideas, in particular, are considered: faith, repentance, confession (professions), and obedience.

FAITH

For Paul (and John and Peter), "faith" language is his favorite way of speaking of the human side of the relational experience of turning from sin, coming to know God, and walking in relationship with him ("we walk/live by faith," 2 Cor 5:7). God summons through the proclamation of the gospel; people respond by faith and acceptance of the message, or unbelief and rejection (esp. 10:14–17, see part three, chapter 15).

The language of faith dominates Romans, featuring sixty-six times.[1] Faith language is found in the prologue and thematic statement, indicating its importance (1:1–7, 16–17). In Romans 1:5, Paul speaks of his apostolic commission "for the obedience *of faith* (*hyperkoēn pisteōs*) among all the gentiles" (translation and emphasis mine).

This phrase, "obedience of faith," is also found in the final doxology (16:26), the inclusio demonstrating its importance (assuming the originality of this disputed text, see part three, chapter 23). The exact meaning of the phrase is disputed, but considering Paul's theology of faith and not works, it may be a genitive of production, i.e., "the obedience produced by faith." If so, preaching Christ for the response of faith leading to obedience is the heart of Paul's commission. Alternatively, and more likely, as suggested earlier in this work (see part two, chapter 11), it is the obedience of believing whereby a hearer obeys the summons of the gospel and *believes* in God and his Son.

---

1. The noun *pistis*, "faith," forty times, *apistia*, "faithlessness, unfaithfulness" four times; the verbs, *pisteuō*, "believe, trust" twenty-one times, *apisteō*, "unfaithful" (3:3).

Human Response

That person is justified by the obedience of believing, the obedience of faith. Paul's preaching is aimed at obtaining from his hearers true obedience to God, the essence of which is a responding to His message of good news with faith."[2]

The thematic text Romans 1:16–17 also emphasizes faith. Salvation comes to "all who believe, to the Jew first, and also to the Greek." This anticipates the argument of Romans 4 that faith and not works or law sparks a person's salvation, and that it has been this way from the beginning.

In Romans 1:17, the righteousness is revealed "from faith to faith" (*pisteuōs eis pistin*). There is a range of ways to interpret this, including:

- From God's faithfulness to a person's faith.
- From Christ's faith/faithfulness to the believers' faith (esp. for those who translate *pisteōs Iēsou Christou* as "faith/faithfulness of Jesus Christ" as opposed to the usual "faith in Christ").
- From faith in the old covenant (e.g., Abraham and other pre-Christ believers) to faith in the new (Christian believers).
- From the faith of the Jews to the faith of the gentiles.
- Saved by faith to live by faith.
- From salvation faith to deepened faith.
- From the preacher's faith to the hearer's faith.
- For emphasis, "faith from first to last" or "faith and faith only."[3]

While all ideas have merit and cannot be equivocally ruled out, the final is to be preferred as the whole premise of Romans and Galatians is to assert that salvation and justification comes from than faith and not works, whether works of the law or otherwise. Galatians makes the same point with even more force: justification stems from God's grace and received by faith alone. Hence, this seems best understood as an emphatic statement.

In whatever way we interpret *ek pisteōs eis pistin* in Romans 1:16, the clause emphasizes the role of faith in salvation and the Christian life. Similarly, the proof text, Habakkuk 2:4, reaches back into the OT and demonstrates that it is faith that saves, and it is by faith people are to live. Abraham serves as Paul's primary example of this (Rom 4; Gal 3:8–9).

---

2. Cranfield notes a range of possibilities of which he prefers vii. These include objective genitive solutions: i) "obedience to the faith" (i.e., to faith in the sense of *fides quae creditor*, the body of doctrine accepted); ii) "obedience to faith" (i.e., to the authority of faith); iii) "obedience to God's faithfulness attested in the gospel"; subjective genitive solutions: iv) "the obedience which faith works" (or a genitive of production); v) "the obedience required by faith"; vi) "believing obedience"; a genitive of apposition or definition: vii) "the obedience which consists in faith." Cranfield, *Critical and Exegetical Commentary*, 1:66.

3. See the discussion in Moo, *Letter to the Romans*, 79–82.

Part Two: Romans and the Content of the Gospel

In the central passage stating justification by faith in the letter (3:21–26), in which Paul answers the problem of universal human sin he has just laid out, faith dominates. In Romans 3:22, the righteousness of God is *dia pisteōs Iēsou eis pantas tous pisteuontas*. *Pisteōs Iēsou Christou* is traditionally taken objectively as "faith in Jesus Christ."[4] Others read it subjectively as "the faith/faithfulness of Jesus Christ."[5] Another group sees it as ambiguous, encompassing both ideas.[6] If the subjective reading is to be preferred, the emphasis falls on Jesus's faith in God or his faithfulness to God that saves those who place their faith in him. However, as with Romans 1:17, the traditional interpretation is best, and so this is another emphatic statement highlighting that it is faith and faith alone that justifies.[7]

Either way, faith in Jesus still saves for the Jew and the gentile alike. The salvific power of Christ's death is made effective in an individual's life through the response of faith (3:25). One is justified by faith.[8] Put another way, using *dikaio-* language, justification is by faith and not law or any other works (9:30, 32). Law and works cannot save or justify, for they have no power in and of themselves except the power to reveal sin and bring condemnation. It is faith that justifies (3:27, 28). Israel's problem is a lack of faith and a rejection of their Messiah and reliance on law and so self for salvation.[9] Christ then is the endpoint of the law, its culmination, completion, and fulfillment. He has been faithful to the law and God, and now, salvation is not through any law but is found in Christ and Christ alone (10:4). Confession of Christ's lordship and faith in him as the resurrected one saves (10:9–11).

As noted above, in Romans 4, Abraham's example is key to Paul's demonstration that it is faith and always has been faith, i.e., "faith was credited to Abraham for righteousness" (LEB, Gen 15:6; Rom 4:9; Gal 3:6). Abraham demonstrates the principle that one is not declared righteous by works, but by trust in God who justifies the ungodly (4:5).

Paul argues that Abraham was declared righteous based on faith *before the law as an uncircumcised man*, i.e., a gentile. He was not an Israelite or Jew, for Israel was his grandson and Judah his great grandson. Then, after believing, God made the covenant with him (Gen 15:7–21), and he was circumcised (Gen 17). As such, Abraham

---

4. All earlier writers up to Barth (Barth, *Epistle*, 96–97: "through his faithfulness in Jesus Christ") and more recently, e.g., Cranfield, *Critical and Exegetical Commentary*, 1:203; Käsemann, *Romans*, 94; Morris, *Epistle to the Romans*, 175; Dunn, *Romans 1–8*, 166–67; Fitzmyer, *Romans*, 344; Newman and Nida, *Handbook*, 65; Cottrell, *Romans: Volume 1*; Barrett, *Epistle to the Romans*, 70; Schreiner, *Romans*, 181–86; Mounce, *Romans*, 114; Boa and Kruidenier, *Romans*, 106; Moo, *Letter to the Romans*, 243–46; Osborne, *Romans: Verse by Verse*, 98–99; Keener, *Romans*, 57–58; Thielman, *Romans*, 204–5.

5. E.g., Toews, *Romans*, 99–100; Witherington and Hyatt, *Paul's Letter*, 101; Wright, "Romans," 470; Longenecker, *Epistle*, 408–13.

6. E.g., Jewett and Kotansky, *Romans*, 277–78, although leaning toward the objective view.

7. See for a fuller argument, Keown, *Philippians*, 2:155–61; Keown, *Galatians*, 331–40.

8. See 3:26, 28, 30, 31; 5:1.

9. See 9:32–33 (Isa 8:14; 28:16); 11:20.

is the archetype of faith for *all* who believe, whether Jew (circumcised) or gentile (uncircumcised, 4:11–13, 16). Paul rejects any other means of salvation; specifically, in Romans, Jewish law. If it is through the law, then it is not through promise, and faith is not salvific (4:14).

We have some understanding of what saving faith looks like for Paul as he describes the faith of Abraham and uses him as an example. Although he was a flawed man as the Genesis narrative shows,[10] Abraham held firm to his relationship with God and trusted God's promise of an heir despite it seeming impossible (4:17–20). Faith then is trust in God to fulfill his word. Additionally, if "faithfulness/faith of Jesus Christ" is the right translation of Romans 3:22 and 26, then we see what authentic faith is in the faithful life of Jesus.

For Paul, faith lays the foundation for salvation. The moment of inward faith response and outward profession (10:9) brings union with Christ, justification, reconciliation, redemption, adoption, and the receipt of the Spirit, and all else that flows from a relationship with God in Christ (cf. 5:1–21). Moreover, ongoing life is lived by faith, the only boundary marker. Rather than a covenantal nomism, there is for Paul a "covenantal pisticism."[11]

For Paul, faith is also linked to the proclamation of the message to whoever is listening. Through the preaching of the message, God works in the human heart, and people respond by rejection, indifference, or faith (10:17).[12] Many in Israel have rejected the message, and so they are cut off from the people of God through unbelief (11:20, 23). In Romans 11:21–24, Paul warns the gentile readers that they too could be snapped from the tree of God's people if they waver into unbelief. This passage is one of the many texts in Paul that are a problem for the once-saved-always-saved theology (14:15, 20).[13] Thankfully, those cut off can be reintegrated by faith.

Paul links his theology of *charismata* (spiritual gifts) to faith, speaking of the "measure of faith that God assigned to you" (12:3, see also v. 6). In Romans, it is not that people have varying degrees of faith gifted by God, but a faith that is expressed in different ways through their God-given giftedness.[14] As such, they should be humble and encourage others to serve with their gifts.

---

10. Examples of this include sexual immorality with Hagar (Gen 16:4), lying to Pharaoh and Abimelech (Gen 12:10–20; 20:2).

11. Covenantal nomism indicates staying in the covenant people of God through law obedience, particularly boundary markers. Covenantal pisticism means getting in and staying in the people of God through one means, faith (from the human perspective). I adopted this some time ago. Independently, Gupta argues similarly. Gupta, *Paul and the Language of Faith*, 141–43.

12. See also the Parable of the Sower (Mark 4:1–20 and parr.).

13. See also 1 Cor 3:17; 6:9; 8:11; 9:27; 10:1, 9–10, 12–13; 15:2; 2 Cor 6:1; 11:3; 13:5; Gal 1:6; 2:2; 3:4; 4:11; 5:1–4, 19–21; Col 1:21–23; 1 Thess 3:5; 2 Thess 2:3; 1 Tim 1:6; 3:6–7; 4:1–4; 5:15; 6:20–21; 2 Tim 3:5–7; 4:3; Titus 1:16.

14. In 1 Cor 12:9, faith is a gift, but the context does not suggest initial saving faith, but an extraordinary level of faith (cf. 1 Cor 13:2). See, e.g., Fee, *First Epistle to the Corinthians*, 658. In Philippians 1:29, while faith appears to be a gift as is suffering, just as the agent of their suffering is *not* God

Part Two: Romans and the Content of the Gospel

Similarly, Paul relates differing faith levels to views of law and grace in Romans 14–15. He describes those who are concerned about non-essentials as weak in faith (14:1). That is, their faith can be quickly brought down by those who have a recognition that such non-essentials are not of the substance of the faith (the stronger). Those who are stronger in faith must take care not to cause the weaker to stumble.

The distinction between stronger and weaker faith shows that among believers saved by faith in Christ, there are various degrees of faith. At a personal level, believers are to live by their faith convictions whatever they are as led by their conscience informed by the Spirit and word (14:22). Paul allows for differing understandings, i.e., diversity within unity. Christians then are to live by their Spirit-informed conscience (14:22–23).

Faith is anchored in Christ's work that gives believers future hope of eternal life and present hope of his guidance and strength (cf. 6:8). Faith should also lead to ethical living as believers move closer to their final salvation (13:11). True faith-life will be virtuous, with the supreme virtue, love.

Sometimes faith takes on a more static content notion such as "your faith" or "my faith," i.e., the content of belief (1:8, 12). At other times Paul speaks of *pistis* as "faithfulness," e.g., 3:3: "What if some were unfaithful? Will their faithfulness nullify the faithfulness of God?" Thus, to live by faith is to be faithful. God, of course, is always faithful. Paul can also use *pistis* of being "entrusted" with something to which one is to be found faithful, e.g., "Jews have been entrusted with the oracles of God," i.e., his Holy Scriptures (3:2). This use speaks of human faithfulness leading to God trusting a person to do his work, the highest honor for any Christian.

If faith is so important, what is faith? We can draw together some threads from the letter to the Romans.[15] First, it includes belief in every aspect of Jesus mentioned in Romans, including at least his pre-existence and then humanity (8:3); his identity as the Christ, the Son of God, Lord, Deliverer, and God over all (1:4; 9:5; 11:26); his life of service (15:3, 8); his atoning death for sins (3:24–25; 5:8–9), his resurrection (10:9), his ascension to absolute cosmic rule (8:34); that he is judge (2:16).[16]

Second, in that Jesus is the Son, it includes belief in the Father who sent him, including every aspect of God referenced in Romans. Some will include his eternality, supremacy, that he is to be worshiped alone, and that he is creator and sovereign over history.[17]

---

himself, but the Roman authorities, faith being a gift does not rule out the Philippians' own agency (see Keown, *Philippians*, 1:314).

15. See also Keown, *Galatians*, 330 where I adapt the classic reformed understanding of faith to include *notitia* (intellectual belief in the elements of the gospel); *assensus* (a yielding "yes" to God initially and in an ongoing sense); *fiducia* (trusting God and Christ no matter what); and *affinitas* (a relational knowing of God).

16. See the full discussion of Christ in Romans in part two, chapter 8.

17. See the full discussion of God in Romans in part two, chapter 8.

Third, in that Jesus is the fulfillment of the promises of God, it is a belief and confidence in the OT Scriptures leading to him.

Fourth, considering that Abraham's unwavering trust in God's promises is paradigmatic (4:16), true faith trusts the promises of God to Christians in Romans: justification by faith, reconciliation with God, adoption into God's family, freedom from sin, the flesh, the law, death, and destruction and the promise of resurrection, eternal life, immortality, and the redemption of the cosmos. Further, if we accept Romans 3:22 and 26 should be rendered subjectively, it is emulating Christ's life of faith and faithfulness.

Fifth, faith for Paul is not premised on *anything* a person does; it is a trust coming from the heart and enacted by a public acknowledgment of the lordship of Christ (10:9). Presumably, a key marker of this is water baptism (6:1–3). However, to say that water baptism is a condition of justification distorts Paul's theology away from faith alone, creating a new boundary marker other than faith.

Sixth, faith becomes allegiance in some contexts and so it speaks of yielding completely to God and his Son as his appointed world ruler.[18]

No works, whether Torah-based or otherwise, are included in the faith that sees one justified. A person prior to faith may be a fine person. However, like all people, they fall short of the glory of God. Works will follow as a believer yields to the Spirit, but it is not anything based on human effort and merit. Indeed, it is likely that Paul would agree with James that faith without works is dead (Jas 2:17, 26). Still, it is faith and faith alone that sees a person declared righteous and ultimately saved.

Finally, the acknowledgment of the exclusive lordship of Christ suggests all other allegiances are now secondary to yielding to him. He is Lord.[19]

REPENTANCE

The language of repentance is infrequent in Paul. However, it is mentioned in Romans 2:4, where he speaks of God's kindness and mercy that leads a person to repentance. Its use in this verse suggests that the idea of a change of mindset (*metanoia*) is an essential aspect of his understanding of faith. Repentance is also implied in Romans 6 and 8, where he speaks of denying the flesh and being a slave of righteousness living by the Spirit. Paul's notion of "faith" should be understood to include the idea of turning *to* God, which implies repentance: a turning *from* all other false allegiances, behaviors, attitudes, idolatries, and actions. Faith is a term inclusive of turning from all idolatries and desires that divert a person from God to live the life he has for them.

---

18. Gorman, *Becoming the Gospel*, 90–91; Gupta, *Paul and the Language of Faith*, 94.

19. "Faith is not the work of the human will, a creation of the human mind, or a result of human experience. It is a dynamic, all-inclusive personal response to the grace of God revealed in Christ Jesus and made possible by the gracious application of the dynamic, living Word of God by the Holy Spirit." Peters, *Biblical Theology*, 70.

PART TWO: ROMANS AND THE CONTENT OF THE GOSPEL

CONFESSION

Another notion used rarely, but still of significance, is confession or profession (*homologeō*). In Romans 10:9–10 (cf. 1 Tim 6:12), Paul speaks of faith and confession as the markers of salvation:

> because, if you *confess* (profess, acknowledge) with your mouth that Jesus is Lord and believe in your heart that God raised him from the dead, you will be saved. For with the heart one believes and is justified, and with the mouth one confesses and is saved (emphasis mine).

This passage suggests heart belief is to be partnered with verbal confession or perhaps better, "acknowledgment" or "profession" of Christ's lordship. The content is "Jesus is Lord." This acknowledgment carries Jewish and Greco-Roman resonances. *Kyrios* is used of Yahweh over 6000 times in the LXX, and so, from a Jewish point of view, it speaks of Jesus being in some sense divine. Secondly, it speaks of Jesus's supremacy over Greco-Roman gods and Caesar. It is thus a statement of his universal rule and divine supremacy.

In Romans 14:11, all will bow and confess this lordship. As with Philippians 2:9–11, Paul takes Isaiah 45:23, where this cosmic submission is applied to Yahweh and applies it to Jesus. Jesus thus has the fullness of deity within him (cf. Col 1:15–20; 2:9). Confession for Paul is not merely a momentary initial decision at an altar call or something a person does at baptism. It is a lifetime of confessing Jesus *is* Lord in a person's attitudes, relationships, witness, treatment of brothers and sisters in Christ, and whole life in church and world. It means denying all idolatries (1:21–25) and is expressed in worship as people from the nations sing praises (*exomologeō*) to God (15:11; 2 Sam 22:50; Ps 18:49). It cannot be limited to worship contexts but is missional whereby God and his Son as is professed before others as believers encounter others in the world.

OBEDIENCE

Obedience language is infrequent in Romans, perhaps because Paul is arguing against law and works-observance that naturally ally with such terminology. Still, obedience terminology is not absent. Sinful people are disobedient (*apeithēs*)[20] to their parents (1:30). Whereas Adam's disobedience (*parakoē*)[21] brought sin and death, the hyper-obedience (*hypakoē*)[22] of Jesus has brought justification to the many (5:19). In Romans

---

20. *Apeithēs* means "disobedient," and is used in 2 Tim 3:2 also of being disobedient to parents. In Titus 1:16 and 3:34, it speaks of disobedience to God. BDAG 99.

21. From the *akouō*, "hear," family, *parakoē* means the "refusal to listen and so be disobedient, *unwillingness to hear, disobedience.*" See also 2 Cor 10:6. BDAG 767–78 (italics original).

22. Another word related to *akouō*, "hear," *hypakoē*, "obedience," may here be intensive (when compared to Adam's *parakoē*). Jesus is hyper-obedient! For the term *hypakoē* see also 1:5; 6:16 [2x];

11:32, God has consigned all humankind to disobedience that he may have mercy on all.

Just as Jesus was obedient and because believers are being conformed to his image (8:29) and summoned to put on Christ (13:14), obedience is a goal of the Christian life. Paul uses what seems an intentional inclusio of the phrase "the obedience (*hypakoē*) of faith" in Romans 1:5 and 16:26.[23] Such obedience is the required response of people to the gospel. As has been mentioned several times thus far, this is "the obedience of believing" in the gospel.[24] It is to "obey (*peithō*) the truth" rather than emulate those who "do not obey (*apeitheō*) unrighteousness" (2:8). Alternatively, as Paul puts it in 2 Thessalonians 1:8, it is obeying "the gospel of our Lord Jesus Christ." It differs from obeying the law, which requires perfection and is implausible (2:25).

The obedience of believing is not measurable in behavior and all fall short of full obedience; still, God knows whether a person has believed, and it is that faith that justifies. Despite this, the believer is to seek to be obedient to God and his righteousness, refusing to obey (*hypakouō*) the passions of the flesh (6:12). They are not to be like the many in Israel who do not obey (*hypakouō*) the gospel (10:16). Whereas formerly, they were slaves to flesh, law, and sin, now they are to be obedient (*hypakoē*) to God, leading to righteousness (6:16). This response is heartfelt obedience (*hypakoē*) to the teaching of God in the gospel (6:17).[25] As Romans develops, it is the Spirit who produces the capacity to live in obedience.

Paul's goal in mission is that the gentiles receive the mercy of God that has, in a sense, come to them due to Israel's disobedience (*apeitheia*, 11:30). Paul wants the formerly disobedient (*apeitheō*) gentiles to come to the obedience of faith (1:5). He hopes this will lead to obedience from disobedient Israel (11:31). The obedience of faith springing forth into obedience to God's desires (15:18). The Romans themselves are known for such obedience (16:19).[26]

While Romans is clear, no one can receive righteousness through flawless obedience to God's law, obedience is critical to understanding its message. Sinful humankind is under wrath due to universal disobedience. Believers are justified through obeying the gospel by believing it. They are then summoned to live obediently to God in Christ by the Spirit.

15:18; 16:19, 26; 2 Cor 7:15; 10:5, 6; Phlm 21. BDAG 1028.

23. Similarly, O'Brien, *Consumed by Passion*, 32.

24. This interpretation resonates with John 6:28, where Jesus responds to those who want to know what the works God requires, to which Jesus replies, "This is the work of God, that you believe in him who he has sent."

25. See also 2 Cor 10:5–6, where every thought is to be brought into obedience to Christ.

26. See also 2 Cor 2:9; 7:15; Phlm 21. The Philippians were renowned for their obedience (or working out their own salvation), which they are to continue by the power of God (2:12–13).

PART TWO: ROMANS AND THE CONTENT OF THE GOSPEL

CALLING ON THE NAME OF THE LORD

In Romans 10:12–14 Paul thrice refers to people calling on God or his name.[27] "Call on him" appears to be another way of describing the required response of a believer to the summons of God through the gospel. However, it takes faith and profession a step further to active worship, prayer, and praise of Christ *because* one believes.[28] Paul speaks of believers as those called by God. Calling on God could be misunderstood as God inviting people, and they responding to his call by calling on him in response; hence, they are his people. However, this misunderstands Paul's thinking on election. People are called where they also respond to God by calling on him. God's call is effectual. Where they do not call on God's name in response, they are not the called or elect of God. At the same time, such thinking can be misunderstood to rule out human response. People "obey" the gospel with faith or do not. If they do not, they are accountable and are not among the called. Where they do, they are also accountable, but they are then described as "the called."

The notion of calling upon God or his name is first found in Genesis 4:26. Wenham states that this "is an umbrella phrase for worship, most obviously prayer and sacrifice."[29] It is then found commonly in the OT as a formula for those who believe in God and worship him appropriately.[30] Paul uses it elsewhere of all Christian believers in 1 Corinthians 1:2 (see also Acts 9:14). Where God is concerned, it is neatly summed up in the cry "Abba, Father," as the Spirit fills the believer (8:15; Gal 4:5). Such a cry also goes up to Jesus, who, in being faithful to his Father after crying out to God, "Abba," became the recipient of the cries of worship of those who believe in him and profess "he is Lord" (Mark 14:36).

In verse 13, Paul draws on one of the OT uses, emphatically stating that "everyone who calls on the name of the Lord will be saved." The citation is from Joel 2:32 EVV (3:5 LXX) that comes near the end of Joel's vision of God pouring his Spirit out on all flesh, causing his servants to prophesy and of wonders in the skies leading to the day of the Lord (Acts 2:17–21). There are some people of Jerusalem that God calls who escape his judgment. Paul does not appropriate this text of God's deliverance of his people from attackers, but of eschatological salvation.

---

27. The idea of calling on God and his name are synonymous with "the name" in Semitic thought representing the person and being of the Lord. Newman and Nida, *Handbook*, 203.

28. "Therefore, in this verse, Paul commends prayer to Christ." Schreiner, *Romans*, 562. Similarly, Fitzmyer rightly says, "Verses 12–13 thus become an eloquent witness to the early church's worship of Christ as *Kyrios*" (emphasis his). Moo, *Letter to the Romans*, 593.

29. Wenham, *Genesis 1–15*, 116. See his discussion on debates over this statement because it predates the revelation of the divine name.

30. See, e.g., Gen 12:8; 13:4; 21:33; Deut 4:7; 1 Sam 12:17–18; 18:24–25; 2 Sam 22:4, 7; 2 Kgs 5:11; 1 Chr 16:8; Pss 4:1, 3; 14:4; 17:6; 18:3, 6; 28:1; 31:17; 53:4; 55:16; 79:6; 80:18; 86:5, 7; 88:9; 99:6; 105:1; 116:2, 4, 13, 17; 141:1; 145:18; Isa 12:4; 41:25; 55:6; 64:7; Jer 10:25; Lam 3:55, 57; Zeph 3:9; Zech 13:9; Jdt 6:21; 8:17; 9:4; 16:2; 2 Macc 3:22, 31; 4:37; 7:37; 8:2; 12:6; Pss. Sol. 2:36; 9:6; T. Jud. 24:6; T. Dan 5:11; 6:3. See also Dunn, *Romans 9–16*, 610.

Human Response

The right response of a person who believes in God and confesses Christ's lordship is to call out to him in worship and prayer. As will be seen, Paul creates a sequence in 10:9–17 whereby a preacher is sent, the gospel is preached, it is heard, a person believes, he or she professes Jesus is Lord, and the believer calls on the name of the Lord in prayer (see part three, chapter 15). Prayer is a natural consequence of becoming a believer. The importance of calling on the Lord in prayer is seen throughout the letter as Paul prays frequently. He urges the Romans to do the same on his behalf (see part three, chapter 23).

12

Ethics and Christian Living

ROMANS, WITH ITS INTEREST in matters of the Jewish law, is weighted heavily toward matters of ethics.[1] In the Jewish world, ethics was based around adherence to Torah.[2] In the Greco-Roman world, for many writers, ethics was based around virtues such as the four cardinal virtues: courage (*andreia*), wisdom (*phronēsis/sophia*), prudence (*sōphrosynē*), and justice (*dikaiosynē*).[3] For Romans, the State was supreme, and the maintenance of social order through these virtues was critical.[4]

However, in Paul's case, while submission to the State is endorsed, it is the ethic of the kingdom that is to be lived above all else. This chapter also doubles as a discussion of missional ethics, as the ethic Paul espouses is not something lived just when among believers (although this is to be taken for granted), it is to be taken into the world as believers give witness to Christ (ethical witness)—it is a twenty-four-seven ethic.[5]

---

1. Although this is not the place to discuss this, I am perplexed by this comment by Hill: "[i]t is universally agreed that Paul was not an ethicist. He was a theologian." Hill, "Theology and Ethics in the Letter to the Romans," 249. This to me shows a blindness to the ethical vision of Paul through his letters. In Romans 1:18—11:36, Paul lays a foundation for an ethical vision, and in 12:1, launched by "therefore," Paul gives a profound vision for Christian living—as outlined in this essay.

2. "That humans are created in the image of God makes it possible for the Torah to command that Jews walk in God's ways, i.e., practice the imitation of God." See Kellner, "Ethics of Judaism," 1:252.

3. The ideal society is "wise, brave, sober, and just"; see Plato, *Resp.* 4.427e. Aristotle unpacks them and contrasts them with vices. See Aristotle, *Rhet.* 1.6.1362b; 1.9.13.13666b.

4. "Nor is the attaining of that goal a matter, as it is in Aristotle, of the 'self-made man' producing the cardinal virtues of courage, justice, temperance and prudence that were required for a soldier or statesman in ancient Greece." Wright, *Paul and the Faithfulness of God*, 1116.

5. On the relationship of Paul's theology and his ethics, see Hays, *Moral Vision*, 16–59. "His ethical teachings are rooted in his theological thought" (p. 18).

Ethics and Christian Living

ETHICAL FAILURE (1:18—3:20)

A failure of ethics is core to the problem of the world in Romans. Pagan humanity, in its rejection of God and its idolatry, is characterized by a range of unethical behaviors that corrupt self, human relationships, and God's world. These are attitudinal, behavioral, and speech acts that demean self and others. They violate God's creation intention (1:19–32). Because of these prevalent vices, the entire gentile world stands condemned before God, who will deal with the problem of the corruption of his glorious creation (2:1–11).

Jews are also condemned on the same basis for their sin and, in particular, their failure to live the Torah granted them by God, and their unjustified and hypocritical ethical self-righteousness (2:1–29). The universal inability of people to live by God's relational laws is a failure of ethics and they will be judged on this basis. So, in Romans 2:6: "he [God] will give to each person according to his/her works" (translation mine). As such, based on ethical works, *no one* is righteous before God (esp. 3:9, 19–20, 23, emphasis mine). In a sense, then, it is ethical failure that spurs salvation and mission. Humankind is universally unethical. God desires that his created beings are transformed to live ethically according to his ideals. Only those who are ethically flawless will live forever. Jesus resolves the problem of failed ethics. Mission flows from humankind's failed ethics to God's ethic. The end result of mission is ethically pure people living eternally with God.

CHRIST, THE SOLUTION TO FAILED ETHICS

In sending his Son (mission), God has resolved the problem of the separation that this ethical failure has brought.[6] Jesus came and lived under the law (Gal 4:4) and lived the perfect ethical life according to common morality and the law (2 Cor 5:21).[7] He fulfilled the law and became the unblemished sacrifice for sin in his death. Believers are saved through his work by placing their trust in him. The law as a means of justification is of no value.

Paul goes further; he explains that believers are now completely set free from the Jewish Torah. That is, the Torah no longer rules their ethical life. Paul is not saying

---

6. Although not developed in Romans, Paul's idea of a new creation is important to his ethics. He hints at this in 8:18–25. See Hays, *Moral Vision*, 19–27.

7. See also Rom 5:18–19 where Jesus's one act of righteousness and obedience likely indicates his sinlessness. On "one act of righteousness" see Moo, *Letter to the Romans*, 367. Similarly, "obedience to the point of death" indicates the same (Phil 2:8). Witherington and Hyatt, *Paul's Letter*, 213 find Christ's sinlessness is implied in the use of *homoiōma*. Jewett and Kotansky, *Romans*, 484 reject this. However, while agreeing that *homoiōma* does not necessarily indicate Christ's sinlessness, Cranfield, *Critical and Exegetical Commentary*, 1:381, correctly argues that Christ's sinlessness is implied in Rom 8:3b. Christ's obedience to the point of death is also implied in Phil 2:8 (Keown, *Philippians*, 1:418). Boa and Kruidenier, *Romans*, 111 rightly see sinlessness implied in Christ as an sacrifice bringing propitiation in Rom 3:25a.

that the Torah is bad. Indeed, he is at pains to defend the holiness and goodness of the law (7:12–13). As will be discussed further below, the love command in the law is his most important ethical precept. However, the law's function is now different. It serves to point to a person's failure and need of Jesus and does not have value to save. He seems to be saying that Torah, while great and clearly a reflection of the ideals of God, as an external ruling code, is not the ethical basis for life in Christ. The rejection of the law as the basis for ethical life raises a huge question (especially for first-century Christians joining what began as a primarily Jewish movement). By what standard are they to live?

The rhetorical questions in Romans 6 anticipate this question with objections: "What shall we say, then? Shall we go on sinning so that grace may increase?" (6:1, NIV). Similarly, "What then? Shall we sin because we are not under law but under grace?" (6:15, NIV). In both cases, his answer is *mē genoito*, which is an emphatic, "no way!" (my translation). He then, in Romans 6–8, outlines a theological basis for ethics. In Romans 12—15, he will give more specific instructions as to how he reads ethics working off this theological base. Ethics is arguably the dominant issue in these six chapters of Romans.

ETHICAL RATIONAL (6:1—8:17)

In Romans 6–8, he introduces a number of ideas that lead to and undergird ethical behavior.

Participation in Christ's Death as the First Basis for Ethics

Paul responds to the rhetorical question in Romans 6:1 with a set of counter questions: "we died to sin; how can we live in it any longer?" "Or don't you know that all of us who were baptized into Christ Jesus were baptized into his death?" (6:3). That is, believers have died and risen in Christ and are no longer bound by the ways of the world. Instead, they have risen into a "new life" (6:5) of goodness and righteousness. As such, it is inconceivable that they would consider going back to a life of sin; to do so violates their relationship with Christ. Despite living in their mortal, fleshly bodies, and continuing to be prone to sin, believers are now united in Christ and have begun resurrection life. They are to live this life free from sin, because—at least spiritually and theologically speaking—their old bodies are dead, and they are no longer slave to its impulses. Hence, they are now freed from sin (6:6–8). They are thus to live to God, not allowing themselves to be enslaved to sin.

In Romans 6:11–14, Paul appeals to them on this basis to refuse to yield to the pull of sin in the world and their corrupted inner desires. They are to devote their whole beings to the one who saved them, out of grace and not external legal imperatives (6:14), i.e., gratitude, not law. They no longer live by "I must" or "I should," in a direct sense, but instead, "I *want to* please God *because* he has saved me." It is a willing devotion to righteousness and good. It is an inside-out life where from a believers heart, mind, and will, goodness in attitudes, actions, and speech radiates outward. The believers' relationships with friend and foe alike are shaped by love, freely given out of gratitude to God. It is not merely conformity to an external rule. As he will espouse, it is the law of love lived in yielding to the Spirit (below).

In Romans 6:15, Paul persists with more rhetorical questions: "What then? Shall we sin because we are not under law but under grace?" Again, he answers with the emphatic *mē genoito*, "no way!" Believers, who were unavoidably slaves of sin, are now, willingly, slaves to God, purchased by Christ out of enslavement to sin and into goodness and righteousness. They have a new master who is the God of love, and who would not want to live to please such a master (6:16–19)? To this point, arguably, there is still a problem in Paul's argument: how? If humanity, before coming to Christ, was unable to live good lives, why and how can they now? He has touched on the answer in 5:5, will do so again in Romans 7:6, and will deal with the answer thoroughly in Romans 8—the Spirit.

In Romans 7, Paul continues using the analogy of marriage to illustrate that believers are released from the law at the death of a spouse (notably, he draws on the *law* of marriage here, implying divorce and adultery violate God's ethics). Just as a woman is released from the bond of marriage at death, so Christians are released from the bond to law through death in Christ. They are no longer "married" to the law, for they have died to the law, and the law has died to them (7:1–3). He repeats that they now belong to a new master Christ.

In Romans 7:4–5, he asserts that although believers are dead to sin and are to bear fruit to God, the law is not the basis for doing this. He introduces two linked ideas. First, they are to "bear fruit (*karpos*) to God" (7:4). Here, as in Galatians 5:22–23, *karpos* is ethical, reflecting attitudes of the heart that shape behavior. Fruit, of course, grows "naturally," which for Paul is supplied by God, and so this implies God's creative power.

Second, anticipating Romans 8, in Romans 7:6, he refers to the key that unlocks Christian ethics; namely, *the Spirit*: "But now, we have been released from the law because we have died to that by which we were bound, so that we *serve as slaves in the new way of the Spirit* and not the old way of the written code" (translation and emphasis mine). We can observe here the joining of the two words essential to the shaping of Christian virtue: "serve" (as slaves, *douleuō*) and "Spirit." That is, Christian ethics is love-impelled voluntary enslavement to God and others by the power of the Spirit of God. This little verse then is a neat summary of Christian ethics (cf. Gal 5:13–25).

Paul has already anticipated the Spirit's ethical power in Romans 5:5, where he writes regarding the problem of human suffering, "And hope does not bring shame on us, because the love of God has been poured out into our hearts *through the Holy Spirit*, who he has given to us" (translation and emphasis mine). Now he is moving beyond people merely receiving God's love by the Spirit; they will live out this love by the same Spirit. This love restores believers, and through them, others.

This thinking leads into another question which is effectively,

> wait a minute Paul, are you saying that the glorious law, given at Sinai by angels, written on tablets of stone, which sustained Israel, is the basis of the covenant, and which is wonderful in every way, is corrupt? Is it sin?

Again, Paul states in his emphatic manner, "no way!" (*mē genoito*). He then explains that "the law is *holy*, and the commandment is *holy and righteous, and good*" (esp. 7:12, emphasis mine). However, of itself, law has no power to stop sin; rather, God's flawless law serves to illuminate and excite sin because of human subjugation to sin's power. He then illustrates this illuminatory power of the law using the injunction "do not covet," the final summative commandment from the Decalogue (7:6–11). Law reveals sin as it creates boundaries between right and wrong and so "the knowledge of good and evil."[8]

In Romans 7:13, he responds to another possible objection: "did that which is good, then, become death to me?" Again, he responds: "no way!" (*mē genoito*). Instead, sin brings death, not the law, but sin is amplified and revealed for what it is through God's holy law.

Paul responds with a hypothetical or personal testimony of the struggle law brings; one knows what one ought to do in one's mind, but one cannot do it! The Jewish law causes cognitive dissonance, something Paul realizes looking back through the lens of faith in the Messiah Jesus (7:13–23).[9] While he himself did not experience it in this way prior to his conversion (cf. Phil 3:6), looking back as a Christ-believer, he now sees the power it has over those who seek to live it (and that it had over him). The problem, however, is not the law, but the human inability to live it out (something Paul hammered home in Romans 1:18—3:20, 23).

So, Paul cries out desperately in verse 24: "Wretched man I am! Who will rescue me from this body of death?" (my translation). The answer is found in verse 25: "But thanks be to God through *Jesus Christ* our Lord!" (translation and emphasis mine). That is, God has acted in history to send Jesus to save by grace through faith and not through law or any works. Such faith will lead to works, but, important though they are, these works are not salvific in themselves.

---

8. The principle of the first law, "do not eat," continues in the later laws—they reveal good and evil.

9. See Wright, "Romans," 551–55. Although Christians can identify with the angst of Paul in this passage, Paul is not "referring to the 'normal Christian.'" (p. 551). Paul has in view those under the law, "Jews, and by extension, those who attach themselves to Israel, i.e., God-fearers and proselytes" (p. 552). To these groups I would add former Christians who Judaize, and who by doing so, sever themselves from Christ (Gal 5:4) and place themselves under the law. "Though in a sense this is Paul's own story, as a Jew who had lived under the Torah himself, it is not a transcript of 'how it felt at the time'" (p. 552); "those who embrace the Torah find that Torah turns and condemns them." (p. 553).

The Power of the Spirit as the Second Basis for Ethics

Having touched on the Spirit in Romans 5:5 and 7:5 as the basis for Christian ethics, he now picks the theme up and drives it home. First, he restates the freedom from law and sin that believers have in Christ. He adds condemnation; believers need not fear judgment by works (2:6). They are in Christ and so will not face the consequences of sin. Christ's work is sufficient for sin (8:1–3).

In Romans 8:4–16, Paul outlines a theology (or pneumatology) of ethics; a "Spirit-led ethic." Paul contrasts two ways of living: life in the flesh and life in the Spirit. Believers must not allow themselves to fall back into life in the flesh as its end is destruction, death, and does not please the master who saved them. On the other hand, living by the impulse of the Spirit brings "life and peace" with God *now*, with others similarly redeemed, and a life of eternal peace in the future (8:4–8).

In Romans 8:9–11, Paul assures the Romans that they have the Spirit.[10] He states their obligation more directly in 8:12–13: having received salvation in Christ, the Romans and all Christians must now live according to the Spirit and not their faulty fleshly impulses. Led by the Spirit, they are to put sin to death (8:13–14). This Spirit-focus provides one of the critical keys to the Christian life; it is a Spirit-led life. This presupposes the presence of God in the believer. So, ethics is now relational and moving from the inside out, the believer responding to the inner direction and leading of the Spirit.

Paul then shifts the discussion from the Spirit and ethics to the Spirit and status and identity: believers are children of God and so need not fear God. Thus, Christian ethics is not guilt-driven, but is premised on freedom, flowing out of gratitude and familial relationship rather than fear, guilt, and shame (8:15–16). Hence, believers can live out their father's ideals gratefully, joyfully, and hopefully. The filial relationship with God also indicates that the work of the Spirit is to conform the children to the Father. Hence, it is a pneumatological ethic in which, by the Spirit, believers become more and more like God their Father.[11] Later, he will mention conformity to the image of God, who is Christ—hence, it is a Christological ethic (8:29, see also 12:1). Paul's ethics are profoundly Trinitarian!

In Romans 8:17–25, Paul moves the conversation into the direction of present-day suffering in a corrupted world. He then comforts them through the Spirit and the victory and love of God.

---

10. Translating *eiper* in v. 9b as "if after all" or "if, as is indeed the case" (Wright, "Romans," 584), Wright rightly states, "Paul clearly believes that his readers are 'in the Spirit,' no longer 'in the flesh.' The evidence for this is that the Spirit of God dwells in them." Wright, "Romans," 583.

11. Kellner, "Ethics of Judaism," 1:252: "the single most important ethical doctrine of the Hebrew Bible, that of *imitatio Dei*, the imitation of God." Similarly, in Jesus's teaching see Matt 5:48; Luke 6:36, and in Paul, Eph 5:1–2.

PART TWO: ROMANS AND THE CONTENT OF THE GOSPEL

The Law of Love: The Third Foundation for Ethics

The third foundational aspect of Paul's ethics is found in Romans 13:8–10, and that is love. Consistent with Rabbinic Judaism and other NT writers, his most important ethical precept is from the law—Leviticus 19:18: "love your neighbor as yourself" (e.g., 13:8–10, see also Gal 5:14).[12] This command is found in the Torah and its importance for Paul shows that while believers are not under the law and their ethic is not generated by law, the law is important to inform believers of right behavior. In the initial context, the command seems limited to Jews loving other Jews. Nevertheless, later in Leviticus 19:34, this love is extended to those who sojourn in Israel, immigrants.[13] They are to be loved as Israel themselves were strangers in the land of Egypt and enslaved. God redeemed them. God's people are to emulate God's love for them as foreigners in Egypt in their treatment of sojourners among them.

In the Good Samaritan, Jesus interpreted Leviticus 19:18 with 19:34 in mind—universally—including "love your enemies" (e.g., Luke 6:27, 32–35). Undoubtedly, Paul understood it in the same way now that he believes in Christ. As such, the law, in a sense, still stands, but all law must be outworked through the prism of love, as led by the Spirit at that moment. It must be led from the heart and mind, informed by the Spirit, producing a Spirit-empowered life of love. As such, while love does have specific content (which is found in the Jewish law and Christian ethical principles), love will determine the best course of action in a given moment.

For Paul, then, love for other people is the sum of all. Love is *the* law that is expressed by Spirit producing Christlikeness and humble service. Hence, we might call Paul's approach an *agape*-ethic. However, to define what the most loving thing is in every situation is complex as "love" is an elastic idea that has a degree of relativity (situational ethics). So, someone like Fletcher developed his ethics around the exercise of love in a particular context. That is, it is not always easy to know what the most loving act is in a situation.[14]

---

12. Outside of Romans in Paul: Gal 5:13–14; Eph 4:2; 1 Thess 3:12; 4:9; 2 Thess 1:3. In Judaism, see e.g., Sifra 7:4 where in answer to the question "What is the greatest maxim of the Torah?" Aqiba responded: "Thou shalt love thy neighbor as thyself" (Lev 19:18). Similarly, when Hillel summarized the Torah in this way: "What you dislike do not do to others; that is the whole Torah. The rest is commentary. Go and learn" (b. Shab. 31a). See Kellner, "Ethics of Judaism," 1:253. See also Mark 12:31, 33 and parr.; Matt 5:43; 19:19; Luke 10:27; John 13:34–35; 15:12, 17; Heb 10:24; Jas 2:8; 1 Pet 1:22; 4:8; 1 John 3:11, 23; 4:7, 11, 12; 2 John 5.

13. Schreiner says, "In Lev. 19:18 the "neighbor" is doubtless the fellow Israelite, and Lev. 19:34 exhorts Israel to love sojourners (cf. T. Gad 4:1–7; 6:1–7)." Schreiner, *Romans*, 691. "Some Jews understood *gēr* in the narrower sense, 'fellow Israelite' (see the targum and Sipre on Lev. 19:18), while others applied it more broadly (see Lev. 19:34; T. Zeb. 5:1; T. Ash. 5:7; T. Naph. 5:2). Moo adds, "The interchange between a lawyer and Jesus in Luke 10:25–29 implies that many teachers of the law in Jesus's day held to a 'narrow' meaning of the term." Moo, *Letter to the Romans*, 832n396

14. Fletcher, *Situational Ethics*. While I do not always agree with Fletcher's reasoning and conclusions, his overall premise is correct—the law of love tells us that the right thing to do in the situation is the most loving (as defined by God's definition of love, which is primarily seen in the cruciform Son).

ETHICS WORKED OUT (12:1—15:13)

After his long detour into the place of Israel in the purposes of God considering the axiom of righteousness by faith, Paul returns to ethics in Romans 12:1 and what follows. This time, Paul is more direct, giving specific injunctions to the Romans concerning what such a Spirit-led, grace-motivated, and law-free service of righteousness will look like in the real world. We should not read Romans 12—15 in abstraction from the theological ethical undergirding he has already established in Romans 5–8. This section should also be read with an eye on mission, as his ethics are missional to the core.[15]

Christ-Emulation: The Heart of Ethics

In Romans 12:1–2, premised on the many mercies of God that punctuate Romans 1–11, Paul urges the Romans to:

> offer your bodies as a living sacrifice, holy and pleasing to God—this is your logical[16] act of service. Do not conform this age but be transformed by the renewal of your mind so that you will be able to approve what the will of God is—what is good and pleasing and perfect (my translation).

This summative statement gives the foundation for what will follow. The first thing to note is that the clause concerning the offering of bodies as sacrifices points back to the supreme example of Christ.[17] He gave his body and self for the world in his ministry of humility, self-emptying, service, obedience (esp. Phil 2:5–8), and as the once for all sacrifice for sin (cf. 3:21–24).[18] It is thus an appeal for Christlike service and sacrifice for the world. Later, in Romans 13:14, he will say, "clothe yourselves with the Lord Jesus Christ" (NIV), meaning that believers are to live within the cruciform shape of Jesus's life.

---

15. See Barram, *Mission and Moral Reflection*, 175 who argues that as an apostle, Paul "considers the ongoing nurture of established communities to be a vocational requirement." As such, "Paul's moral reflection must be seen in terms of the larger mission that characterizes his vocation" and every text should be read as a 'mission' text." He argues behavior has an evangelistic function (pp. 149–73).

16. I choose "logical" not merely because it sounds like *logikos*, but Paul's point is that the right consequential and logical response of any human to the amazing mercies of God (see through Rom 1–11), and seen supremely in Jesus giving his body and life over to death to save sinners, rightfully understood, is to present their bodies and beings into the service of this amazing, loving, and gloriously generous God. *Logikos* is a term derived from *logos* and speaks of reason, intellect, and rationality. "Logical" is one meaning, see LSJ 1056 meaning 2. "Body" is used, I believe, because it draws our thoughts to Jesus's sacrifice of his body on the cross. Our summons is to emulate him to the point of death, however that comes.

17. Hays, *Moral Vision*, 27–32. For him, the cross is the "paradigm of faithfulness" believers are to emulate.

18. See also Heb 7:27; 9:12, 26; 10:10.

Paul will mention Jesus as an example in Romans 15:3 and 15:7–8 of selfless service for the good of others. As such, "what would Jesus do?" is found in Paul's ethics. However, this is not sufficient in and of itself; it must be Spirit-led. The more profound question is, "what would Jesus feel, think, be, do, and say if he was you and here in this given moment led by God's Spirit (as he was for the period of his earthly life)?" The reference to a transformed mind in Romans 12:2 then points to the renewal of the mind in the direction of the pattern of Christ and away from self-interest (cf. esp. Phil 2:1–11). Notably, it is a Christ-conformed life that is not living in accordance with the false values of this present age. Cruciform ethics are foundational to all mission.

Using Gifts in Humility

In Romans 12:3–8, Paul continues with ethics urging Christians to exercise their spiritual gifts in humility in the sense of a realistic view of oneself, and of using one's gifts to serve God and others. Not only so, but they must allow others the freedom to do the same. Thus, ethics and Christian living is not uniformity but diversity within the unity of being united in Christ, led by the Spirit, and the gospel.

Core Virtues

In Romans 12—15, Paul gives a string of guidelines, some ethical and relational, others liturgical (worship), and some missional. These ethics include love (12:9, 10; 13:8–10), goodness (12:9), honoring others (12:10), service with zeal and spiritual fervor (12:11), joy (12:12, 15), hope (12:12), patience (12:12), prayer (12:12), material generosity and hospitality (12:13), blessing enemies (12:14), empathy (12:15), unity (12:16), humility (12:16), renouncing status distinction (12:16), nonviolence/retribution and cultivating peace (12:17–21), submission to the State (13:1–7), the renunciation of licentiousness (13:11–14), Christlikeness (8:29; 12:1; 13:14), non-judgmentalism, mutual acceptance, allowing diversity over non-essentials, and living by a Spirit-informed conscience (Rom 14–15). These virtues encourage the Romans to be a countercultural community in Rome, living out of the ethics of the gospel in the church and world. In 13:8–10, love as the basis for the Christian ethic is articulated. Believers are obligated to all people for all time to love them. All that a believer does is to be motivated by love and is exercised with love (1 Cor 13:1–3).

As will be discussed in more detail in part three, chapter 24, Paul's ethic of the State in Romans 13 is astonishing, considering the power and attitude of Nero. While this is in the earlier part of his reign before his madness had taken full control, even relatively benign Roman rulers were ruthless and powerful. In our modern world, at their best, they can be likened to brutal communist, Islamic, or fascist states.

Nevertheless, Paul urges submission to such a government, seeing rulers in providential terms as God's servants. As such, believers should pay taxes and submit to its rule (if not absolutely, for Jesus is Lord!). Interestingly too, Romans 13 follows the end of the previous chapter in which Paul urges non-retribution (perhaps with the State in mind) and to leave room for God's justice. Besides, he speaks of the State as the administrator of wrath on God's behalf. Is Paul suggesting that believers must renounce all use of coercive force and leave it to the State? Whatever Paul precisely means, believers should submit to the governing authorities and continue to pay taxes.

Along with 1 Corinthians 8—10, Romans 14—15 is critical for realizing that there is room in the church for varying ethical views on non-gospel essential matters, without people tearing themselves apart over their different opinions. In the Roman church, there were different views on eating certain foods and holy days. The discussion is probably indicative of differing understandings of the law in the Roman church after the death of Claudius and the return of Jewish Christians in the mid-50s. Finding such unity is critical for successful mission—God's servants lay aside differences over relatively unimportant matters of the faith to join together to share Christ to the world.

Paul urges emulation of Christ:

> In Romans 15, Paul takes Christ's death as an example that should constrain the behavior of "the powerful," who might otherwise be inclined to despise those who are "weak in faith."[19]

With Christ's example undergirding his ethical thought, Paul advocates for mutual acceptance, non-judgmentalism, love over liberty, seeking the best for one's neighbor, unity in diversity, and living by one's conscience (a person's understanding based on their faith in Christ). Such ethical precepts are critical in a world and church where we do have different positions on minor ethical issues.

All of this tells us that the unity of the church is of great importance to Paul. We do not all have to agree with one another on everything. On non-essentials, we should love each other and defer to one another when we do. As the old saying goes, "In essentials unity, in non-essentials liberty, in all things charity."[20]

Of course, this is tricky when we hit issues that clash with clear Scriptural injunction or those that some believers consider essential, whereas others do not. Paul deals with things he considers essential to the gospel in places like Galatians; Philippians 3; 1 Corinthians 5; 2 Corinthians 10—13; and the Pastorals (esp. 1 Tim 1, 4; Titus 3). In such texts, he pulls no punches urging authentic believers to disassociate from others who claim the name of Christ but violate the gospel and its ethics to the very core. In

---

19. Hays, *Moral Vision*, 28.

20. "It was during the fiercest dogmatic controversies and the horrors of the Thirty Years' War, that a prophetic voice whispered to future generations the watchword of Christian peacemakers, which was unheeded in a century of intolerance, and forgotten in a century of indifference, but resounds with increased force in a century of revival and re-union." It originated in a tract from Rupert Meldenius, *Paraenesis votiva pro Pace Ecclesiae ad Theologos Augustanae Confessionis, Auctore Ruperto Meldenio Theologo*. Schaff and Schaff, *History of the Christian Church*, 7:650–53.

such instances, the good of the gospel mission and church is paramount over unity, even if unity is critical.

However, in non-essential matters, unity is primary for Paul. The problem is discerning whether the issues that divide believers are of the substance of the faith. In some instances, it is self-evident, e.g., Jesus rose from the dead/Jesus did not rise from the dead. However, in other situations, it is difficult, such as, is gay marriage a central matter for the gospel? Some will say no and be more open to gay marriage. Others, in my view rightly, will argue that heterosexuality lies at the center of human ontology and that sexual immorality is a result of the Rupture, and the church should stand against it (1:26–27, cf. Gen 1:26–27; 2:24, see part three, chapter 20).[21] However, others will say, not in the church, but if people in broader society want such things, let them do it, we do not control the world. The church must work these things out in love, community, and dialogue. Still, Paul urges Christians to have room for diversity on many ethical matters.

CONCLUSION TO ETHICS

In conclusion, ethics is of massive importance in Romans. Human failure is tied to ethics. His analysis of law and grace leads to questions of how his people should live. His answer is to live out one's "in-Christ" life knowing that one is dead to sin, in yielding to the Spirit and living out of love. Believers will never be perfect in their ethics, and they remain people who fall short of God's ethical ideals;[22] yet, with attitudes of grace, they are to continue to grow. It is never good enough to stop and say, "that is just the way I am, live with it." Instead, knowing that God cherishes us even with our foibles, we are to work out our salvation with fear and trembling, with the power of God surging in our inner beings (cf. Phil 2:12–13).

---

21. See Keown, "Is the Gay Issue a Secondary Theological Issue?"

22. Luther's doctrine, *simul justus et peccator*. Witherington and Hyatt note, "There is nothing quite like Luther's later concept of *simul justus et peccator* in Paul, nor would we expect one from early Jewish discussion of such matters. There is however the issue of the "inclination to do evil" which is affirmed in various places in the early Jewish literature, and also in Paul. Paul speaks of it at some length in Galatians 5 and sees the work of the Spirit as more powerful and as pulling a person in the opposite direction." Witherington and Hyatt, *Paul's Letter*, 248.

13

The Eschaton

UNLIKE THE THESSALONIAN LETTERS that focus on eschatology, the emphasis in Romans is not so much of the future, but life in the present. The core question is how believers are to live *now* in relation to the law and the Spirit. The eschatological emphasis is the inbreaking of God's salvation in Christ Jesus and the present work of the Spirit, who is generating the life God wants in his people. To get a full understanding of Paul's futuristic eschatology requires consideration of other passages in Paul.[1] Still, there is much to observe in his understanding of the consummation and what follows in Romans. Some of the ideas here have been previously discussed, and these discussions will not be repeated in full here. So, what can we grasp from Paul's understanding of the eschaton in Romans?

LEADUP TO THE CONSUMMATION

Concerning the lead-up to the consummation, Paul hints at travail, the "woes of the Messiah," in Romans 8:19–23. The imagery of birth pains preceding the consummation of history comes from Jewish apocalyptic. "The created order is going through the 'messianic woes,' the tribulations ending the present age and introducing the age to come."[2] Still, some scholars question whether the "woes of the Messiah" are being mentioned here at all. Fitzmyer writes:

> Whether there is a reference here to the "woes" of the messianic times is debatable. The idea of *heblôšel māšîaḥ*, "woes of the Messiah," is known from later rabbinic literature (Str-B 1.950), but whether it was current in the first century or known to Paul is hard to say.[3]

---

1. Especially 1 Cor 15; 2 Cor 5:1–10; 1 Thess 4—5; 2 Thess 1—2.

2. See Dan 7:21–22, 25–27; 12:1–3; 4 Ezra 5:1–13; 6:13–24; 9:1–3; 2 Bar. 25:2–3; 27:1–15; 48:30–41; 70:2–10; Rev 6:12–17; 1 En. 62:4; 1QH 3:7–18; 4 Ezra 10:6–16; Mark 13:8 and parr.; John 16:21). Toews, *Romans*, 224.

3. Fitzmyer, *Romans*, 509.

Fitzmyer is right to say that Paul does not directly mention increased suffering, but the idea of a woman's birth pains naturally evokes an increase in intensity as birth approaches. It is likely, then, that Paul does here have in view messianic woes.[4] This idea fits with the birth of the new creation being preceded by increased suffering in 2 Thessalonians 2, in which, consistent with other NT texts,[5] Paul mentions a rebellion and the "man of lawlessness" and "son of destruction" who usurps God (2 Thess 2:3–4).

THE RETURN OF CHRIST

In Romans, he does not use *parousia* (coming) nor give any pictures of the return of Christ, such as in 1 Thessalonians 4:13–18. There is certainly no rapture, secret or otherwise, in the letter.[6] He gives no details around the point at which the enemies of God are defeated and Jesus's subjugation to God so that God is all in all (cf. 1 Cor 15:24–28). However, there is clearly a terminus to the age. It is the "day of God's wrath" (2:5), "that day" (2:16), the end (*telos*, 6:22), the end of "the night," and the dawn of "the day" (13:12). The absence of references to the second coming shows that one can preach the gospel without emphasizing the second coming, even if it is integral to the Christian story.[7]

UNIVERSAL JUDGMENT

Unsurprisingly, in that *dikaio-* legal language dominates Paul's gospel presentation to the Romans, judgment is an important motif in the letter. His theology of justification speaks of God as the judge declaring a believer innocent *in the present* (e.g., 5:1). However, he also looks forward to the final day of judgment which is universal in scope.

No one will escape this judgment (2:3). It is "the day of wrath" when "God's righteous judgment will be revealed," and for which people store up wrath for themselves (2:5). Sadly, because all have sinned, there will be wrath and fury for people at this time (2:8). Those under the law (Jews, proselytes, Judaizers) will be judged by the law, or better, their failure to do it (2:12–13). Gentiles, too, will be judged, even if *at times* they live by the law inadvertently (2:14–15).[8] The secrets of human hearts will

---

4. Similarly, Käsemann, *Romans*, 232.

5. See especially Mark 13:14–25 and parr.; 1 John 2:18; Rev 13:1–18.

6. While some scholars see some kind of rapture in 1 Thess 4:13–18, it is certainly not *secret* but occurs dramatically at the return of Christ (cf. 1 Thess 1:8).

7. This is confirmed in the sermons of Acts where there are sparing references to the end with the messages in Acts 3, 7, 13, 14, 22, and 26 lacking any mention. The only verses that allude in some way to a futuristic eschatology are Acts 2:20; 3:21; and 17:31. John's Gospel also has a muted futuristic eschatology.

8. Their consciences sometimes accusing or excusing them in 2:15 rules out perfect obedience.

be judged by Christ Jesus, indicating that Jesus will stand in God's stead as Judge of the world (2:16).

As the judge, God and his Son are impartial and just (3:4). As humans are without exception unrighteous, God is righteous to inflict wrath (3:5). It is on this basis that he judges the world (3:6), including those who obnoxiously argue that people should do evil so that good may come from it (3:8).

Although judgment is based on works (2:6), no one will be justified by works of the law or any such thing on the day of judgment (3:20). They are justified by God's grace through faith in God (prior to hearing the gospel) or through Christ Jesus (after hearing the gospel) during their lives. Christ's works satisfy the demands of God's justice (3:21–24, 28). This principle applies to Jew and gentile alike (3:30). Law illuminates sin and brings wrath (4:15). However, Jesus died for peoples' transgressions and was raised for their justification before God the Judge (4:25).

So, on the day of judgment, having been justified through his blood, believers will be saved from God's wrath—a reference to the final verdict, "Final justification; justified! Saved!" (5:9). They will receive absolute justification and eternal life (5:18). The status of the person in Christ by faith is freedom from condemnation on the day of God's wrath; his wrath is propitiated through Christ's atoning death (8:1). Instead, the faithful will be justified and glorified (8:30). This outcome is guaranteed because Jesus sits at God's right hand, interceding for them (8:34). Still, some who do not believe will be destroyed (9:22).

As Isaiah 45:23 states and Romans 14:10 and Philippians 2:9–11 confirm that all people will stand before the judgment seat of God (14:10). They will bow to God and acknowledge him (14:11). For believers, this is a joyous thought, for as they willingly yield to Christ again (as they first did at their conversion and continue to do through their lives), they will know that they are his forever. For those who have rejected him, this will be a day of abject terror as they realize their eternal fate before God the consuming fire (Heb 12:29; Deut 4:24).[9] Nevertheless, both believers and unbelievers will give an account of their lives to God (14:12).

Judgment is a governing theme in Romans with Paul emphasizing present justification and pointing forward to the ultimate verdict. He hopes that readers respond with yielding to Jesus in the present with faith and hearing God declare them righteous.

ETERNAL DESTRUCTION

Destruction language is not common in Romans. The destination of the dead without faith is not mentioned frequently in any of his letters. He does not mention core

---

9. Keown, *Philippians*, 1:431.

NT Greek terms and phrases describing the eternal destination of the condemned: *geenna*,[10] *tartaroō*,[11] *hades*,[12] "the lake of fire,"[13] or darkness.[14]

Hypsōma (height) *and bathos*, in Romans 8:39, while likely referring to the threat of demons,[15] are mentioned regarding a *current* danger to God's people. Hence, they do not refer to eternal destruction. The *abyssos* (abyss) in Romans 10:7 speaks of the world of the dead to which Jesus went.[16] *Abyssos* likely parallels "the lower parts of the earth" in Ephesians 4:9. Elsewhere, Paul may have the place of eternal destruction in mind as he mentions "the world below" (*katachthonios*) in Philippians 2:10.

The most unambiguous reference in Paul is 2 Thessalonians 1:9, where those who reject the gospel "will pay the penalty of eternal destruction away from the presence of the Lord and from the glory of his might" (my translation). Elsewhere, Paul speaks of this eternal destruction without describing it in detail.[17]

Still, the destruction of the ungodly is not absent from Romans. It is bound up in his use of the language of wrath, death, condemnation, and the one or two explicit references to destruction. Paul's presentation of the gospel in Romans does not seek to scare people into the kingdom with horrific images of destruction but to woo them with the wonders of God's salvation in Christ and its magnificent eternal consequences. His presentation and the evangelistic messages of Acts show that while destruction is a core aspect of the gospel, it does not have to dominate every message.[18]

At times, Paul describes this fate merely as wrath (*orgē*) and God unleashing his fury (*thymos*, 2:8) at the failure of his created image bearers and cosmic rulers to live out their divine calling (1:18). This destruction will occur on the day of wrath (2:5); something believers are spared from (5:9).

At times, the outcome of unbelievers is merely described as God's judgment (*krima*) with a negative outcome condemnation implied but not described (2:3). This condemnation by a righteous God against human unrighteousness is just (3:5).

---

10. *Geenna*, Gehenna, is found in Matthew seven times (5:22, 29, 30; 10:28; 18:9; 23:15, 33); Mark three times (Mark 9:43, 45, 47), and in Luke and James once each (Luke 12:5; Jas 3:6).

11. *Tartaroō*, a derivative of *tartaros*, Tartarus, is found once in 2 Pet 2:4.

12. *Hadēs*, Hades, is found twice in Matthew (Matt 11:23; 16:18); four times in Luke's writings (Luke 10:15; 16:23; Acts 2:27, 31), and four times in Revelation (Rev 1:18; 6:8; 20:13, 14).

13. See Rev 19:20; 20:10, 14, 15; 21:8.

14. "The outer darkness" (see Matt 8:12; 22:13; 25:30); "the gloom of darkness" (Jude 13).

15. Käsemann, *Romans*, 251.

16. *Abyssos* is found once in Luke (Luke 8:31) and three times in Revelation (Rev 9:11; 11:7; 20:3).

17. See 1 Cor 1:9; 3:17; 5:5; 6:13; 8:11; 10:9–10; 15:26; Gal 6:8; Phil 1:28; 3:19; 1 Thess 5:2; 2 Thess 1:9; 2:3; 1 Tim 6:9.

18. Indeed, the destruction of the ungodly is not mentioned in any sermon in Acts. Hints include Hades as the abode of the dead (Acts 2:27, 31, Peter); destruction of those who do not listen to God's prophet (Acts 3:23, Peter); God judging the world (Acts 17:31, Paul); and "the coming judgment" (Acts 24:25, Paul). Nor is eternal destruction explicitly stated in John's writings (see John 3:16, 36; 5:22–30; 10:28; 12:48; 17:12; 1 John 4:17). However, John shows that eternal destruction is pivotal to his theology in Revelation (e.g., Rev 20:11–15).

THE ESCHATON

Krima is sometimes translated as condemnation—the negative outcome of judgment; again, without description (3:8; 5:16, 18). Believers are set free from this condemnation (8:1). The term "death" (*thanatos*) at times carries that sense of the final eternal outcome contrasted with "eternal life."[19]

Paul does use his more common *apōleia*, "destruction" language in Romans. It is the outcome of the life of "vessels of wrath" God has endured for the sake of his purpose of saving his elect people (9:22). The context implies those who have failed to respond to God or his Son with faith. The cognate verb *apollymi* is used in Romans 14:15 as Paul warns the strong Roman Christians not to cause their fellow believer to be destroyed eternally by such an insignificant thing as the choice of food. He uses *katalyō* in the same manner as *apollymi* in 14:20. The term carries the various senses of "destroy, demolish, or dismantle, tear down, end."[20] Both Romans 14:15 and 20 speak of the potential of a believer to undermine the faith of another Christian and bring them to the point of destruction.

Eternal destruction is not a significant theme of Paul's letter to the Romans, but it is undoubtedly one aspect of it. There is no definition of it to give us clarity as to whether Paul considered it means that people are destroyed for eternity or experience eternal torment. It is assuredly eternal in one sense or another.[21] If annihilation is in view, there is no clarity as to how God destroys or causes eternal suffering after judgment.[22] People's perspectives on such things tend to be driven by their theological agendas.

RESURRECTION, IMMORTALITY, AND ETERNAL LIFE

As discussed earlier when considering Paul's array of salvation notions, even if there is nothing akin to his brilliant exposition of resurrection in 1 Corinthians 15 in Romans, Paul assumes the resurrection of Christ,[23] a general resurrection to face judgment (above), and the eternal resurrection of believers. God will give life to their mortal bodies (8:11). Whereas God is immortal, all living flesh, including people, is mortal (1:23; 6:12). God has the power to give life to the dead (4:17). However, the

---

19. See Rom 6:21, 23; 7:5; 8:2, 6.

20. BDAG 521.

21. Commenting on Phil 1:28, formerly I have written: "This text [which applies equally here], alongside many others, emphasizes the eternal lostness of those who reject the gospel in Paul and shows that Paul is no soteriological universalist—the enemies of God's people are destined for eternal destruction. This and other Pauline texts call into question the rising tide of contemporary claims that universalism is consistent with evangelicalism. Keown, *Philippians*, 1:310. See also I. Howard Marshall, "New Testament Does Not Teach Universal Salvation," 55–76.

22. Fire is arguably implied in the use of *thymos* as it has senses of heat and smoke. *NIDNTTE* 2:474. The use of forensic metaphors implies punitive justice. The use of wrath language of God and the State implies this as well. Still, Paul's precise understanding of eternal destruction is not explicit.

23. See Rom 1:4; 4:24; 6:9; 7:4; 8:34; 10:9.

faithful seek immortality and will experience resurrection, immortality, and eternal life.[24] Eternal life is implanted into believers by the Spirit at the moment of faith and comes to full expression in the eschaton. As will be discussed in the next section, the world will be free of death and will be transformed into the eternal resurrection freedom of God's children.

COSMIC RESTORATION

Unique to Romans among Paul's letters is some development of the idea of the ultimate restoration of the creation. The dominant Jewish understanding of the eschaton is that evil will be defeated, and the conditions of Eden fully realized. The most precise articulation of this in the OT is the vision of the new heavens and new earth in Isaiah 65—66. We glean from Romans 8:19-23 that Paul holds the same hope as did Jesus (Matt 19:28), Peter (Acts 3:21; 2 Pet 3:1-13),[25] and John in Revelation 21—22. Paul hints at this in a range of texts including Romans 4:13 where believers will inherit the world and Romans 8:32 where God gives believers "all things." Again, in 1 Corinthians 15:26-28, it is implied as Paul predicts the defeat of God's final enemy, death, and the subjection of all things to God.[26] References to Jesus seated at the right hand of God, drawing on Psalm 110, imply the ultimate subjugation of his enemies (8:34; Eph 1:20; Phil 3:21; Col 3:1). God's plan to unite all things in Christ and the reconciliation of all things speak of the same hope of the earth's redemption (Eph 1:10-11; Col 1:20).

Elsewhere in Romans, Paul affirms the creation of the world by God, the creator.[27] The problem of the world is sin, which blights every human being aside from Jesus (1:18—3:20). Because of sin, death has spread to all people because they participate in sin, as did Adam (5:12). In Romans 8:19-22, Paul speaks of the broader impact of sin. Sin has corrupted all of creation with decay and death. In this passage, he speaks of the creation's pain and its yearning for release. What follows is a brief summary of the argument that will be discussed more fully on Romans and ecology (part three, chapter 19).

Ktisis is used four times in Romans 8:19-22, where the creation is personified as a being suffering immensely and yearning for release (like a woman in childbirth). *Ktisis* here speaks of the world (and perhaps the universe). In verse 19, the *ktisis* waits longingly for God's children to be revealed. In other words, it waits for the consummation and the outcome of the judgment.

---

24. See 2:7; 5:18, 21; 6:22-23; 11:15.

25. While some see in 2 Peter 3 the dissolution of the cosmos, in my view, it is better interpreted as the restoration of the cosmos through judgment (symbolized by fire). It parallels the recreation after the flood (2 Pet 2:5). Earlier scholars who held this view include Irenaeus and Origen (Thiede, "Pagan Reader of 2 Peter," 83-91). See for a contemporary perspective, see also Heide, "What Is New," 37-56.

26. The redemption of the cosmos is also implied in Eph 1:10-11, 22; 4:10; Phil 3:21; and Col 1:20.

27. See Rom 1:20, 23; 4:17; 8:39; 9:20-23.

In verse 20, Paul explains why: the creation is subjected to futility by God. However, in verse 21, creation lives in hope, waiting for the day when it is "set free from its bondage to corruption." It will then obtain "the freedom of the glory of the children of God." This verse implies that just as Paul anticipates the resurrection of believers, he looks forward to the renewal of the whole creation.

In verse 22, he speaks of the shared knowledge he and the Romans have: the creation is like a woman in the severe pain associated with childbirth. Just as people wait for their full bodily redemption at the consummation, the creation will undergo the same.

Undoubtedly, we see here that Paul's vision of salvation transcends humankind and encompasses the world itself. This period is not a millennial reign, which is never mentioned in Paul's letters, but is the final, complete liberation of the cosmos. This restoration of the world is the outcome of God's work on earth. God's beautiful creation will be liberated from evil, Satan, demons, decay, human opponents, and death, and will fully be what God created it to be. God's children will live in it with God forever. Such a message is worth proclaiming to the world.

CONCLUSION

Paul does not mention a rapture, and while the "woes of the Messiah" are hinted at in Romans 8:19–23, there is no mention of a great tribulation and an antichrist in Romans. However, the second coming is assumed, with a focus on judgment (in line with the theme, "justification by faith"). The destruction of the ungodly is apparent as is the resurrected, eternal, and immortal destiny of believers in God (before hearing the gospel of Christ, e.g., Abraham), and people who have heard the gospel of Jesus and believed. The ridding of the cosmos of decay and death, the consequence of Adam's sin, is also evident. What happens next is anyone's guess, but as God's people will live on in a world free of evil, no doubt, it will be great.

Part Three

Romans and the Proclamation of the Gospel

This third and final part of the book focuses on questions that can be asked concerning the proclamation of the gospel. It will look at the scope of gospel proclamation and to what extent Paul's vision for the evangelization of the world is complete. Other matters relevant to those who engage in mission will be approached. Such things include whose responsibility it is to preach the gospel, signs and wonders, social justice and transformation, ecological mission, patronage and hospitality, the sovereignty of God in evangelism, prayer, the State, culture and cross-cultural mission, and the place of Israel in God's mission purposes. The final chapter considers Romans as a superb example of the use of theology in mission and the importance of apologetics.

14

The Cosmic Scope of Mission and Its Completion

THIS CHAPTER CONSIDERS THE NT understanding of the scope of God's mission, Paul's perspective on the same, and the progress of the gospel mission by the time of the writing of Romans in light of the first-century understanding of the world as they knew it. It is here argued that the NT and Paul envisaged the whole world being evangelized before the end and that by the time of Romans, the job had barely begun. There is no expectation of an imminent parousia in Paul, for Christ had not been named in most of the known world.

THE SCOPE OF MISSION IN PAUL

The Worldwide Mission in Romans

It is not difficult to demonstrate that the writers of the Gospels and Acts vividly recall Jesus commissioning the first believers to tell the message of salvation to peoples in every part of the world.[1] Paul's understanding of the scope of God's mission is the same: all humankind on planet earth.[2]

This cosmic vision is reflected in Romans 1:5, where Paul and other gospel preachers (we) are commissioned as apostles to reach "all nations" (or all the gentiles) with the gospel (1:5).[3] It is also seen in the faith of the Romans being "proclaimed in all the world" (1.8). He feels obligated to preach to Greeks, Barbarians (all non-Greeks

---

1. See, e.g., Matt 8:11; 24:14; 25:32; 28:18–20; Mark 13:10, 27; 14:9; Luke 13:29; 21:24; 24:46–49; John 1:29; 4:42; 20:21; Acts 1:8.

2. "*All*, in fact, are ungodly, and *all* are called to experience God's justice in Jesus Christ. The saving death of Jesus is for *all* Jews and Gentiles alike." As such, "it is the 'justification of the godless', the justification by faith, that opened the road to the nations." Nissen, *New Testament and Mission*, 104.

3. Wright, *Mission of God*, 247–48 calls this "the universality of God's mission" (p. 247). He recognizes this in 1:5 and 16:26; 3:29—4:25 (in relation to Abraham), and 10:12–13 (also Gal 3:26–29).

and Romans), the wise, and the foolish, which simply means "all races and classes within the Gentile world" (1:14).[4] The gospel holds power to bring salvation to Jews and Greeks (used in the sense of gentiles), and so again, all peoples (1:16).[5]

The logic of Paul's gospel also implies his desire to see all people from all nations hear the gospel, something seen powerfully in Romans. Through Romans 1:18—3:20, *all* individuals and races are under God's wrath, and so *all* will perish without God's intervention to save.[6] God is a God of the gentiles as well as the Jews, and the righteousness of God by faith revealed in Jesus is for the world (3:29–30). Sin has triggered death which has spread all humankind (5:12), and so the message of life needs to be proclaimed to all.

Several OT texts cited in Romans allude to the cosmic scope of mission. Exodus 9:17 speaks of God raising Pharaoh "so that my name might be proclaimed in all the earth." Paul, here, anticipates the story of God being shared throughout the world, including the account of the Exodus. This proclamation is coming to pass in the Christian era through the likes of Paul. As Jewett and Kotansky say,

> The phrase [*en pasē tē gē*] ("in all the earth") resonates with the global sweep of the gospel seen throughout Romans.[7]

In Romans 10:18, in his argument that Israel has heard the gospel, Paul cites Psalm 19:4. The verse speaks of the voice of the heavens and sky declaring the glory of God and his handiwork "through all the earth" and "to the end of the world." Paul appropriates this for Christian mission. "Every knee" and "every tongue" in the quote of Isaiah 45:23 in Romans 14:11 speaks of all humankind being judged before God. This universal judgment implies the cosmic scope of mission. Paul here is not saying the gospel has gone to all places[8]; it is anticipatory of the mission that has begun.[9] It is thus prophetic,[10] yet incomplete.

---

4. Dunn, *Romans 1-8*, 33.

5. "Paul did not entertain a moment's doubt that the gospel must be preached in the whole world." Hahn, *Mission in the New Testament*, 97.

6. See esp. 1:18; 2:12; 3:9, 19, see also 3:23.

7. See Rom 1:5, 16, 18; 2:1, 9, 10; 3:4, 9, 12, 19, 20, 22, 23; 5:12, 18; 8:22, 28; 9:5; 10:12, 13, 18; 11:32, 36; 12:18; 14:11; 15:11, "where the universal scope of divine sovereignty advanced by the gospel is lifted up." Jewett and Kotansky, *Romans*, 585.

8. *Contra* Käsemann, *Romans*, 296. He wrongly writes, "In fact, he already sees the whole world filled with Christian proclamation. He undoubtedly thinks above all of his own work (Asmussen), although he speaks of the apostolic activity in general. Thus, he sees himself close to the goal envisioned in Mark 13:10, and with it to the parousia." This is utterly flawed; Paul was not stupid. See Keown, "Imminent Parousia and Christian Mission."

9. Moo notes that he may mean the whole Roman Empire or every nation. Yet, the gospel has not reached the fullness of either of these by the time of Romans, as evidenced by his desire to go to Spain where Christ is not named. He suggests this is hyperbole. Rather, this text is anticipatory and ongoing—it is being fulfilled and as with all God's promises, it will be. Moo, *Letter to the Romans*, 685.

10. On this point, agreeing with Käsemann, *Romans*, 296.

The Cosmic Scope of Mission and Its Completion

The quartet of OT citations in Romans 15:9–12 each speak of the "the gentiles" responding to God in worship.[11] Psalm 117:1, in particular, emphasizes "all the gentiles" and "all the peoples (pl. *laos*)" praising and extolling God. Such texts imply that the mission requires the gospel extending to every nation, something that had begun to occur in Paul's time, and will ultimately be complete (11:25).

Israel's partial hardening means "riches for the world" and "the reconciliation of the world" indicating the cosmic benefits of the gospel as it spreads (11:12, 15). Romans 11:25 implies that the mission will reach its conclusion when "the fullness of the Gentiles has come in." This statement speaks of the day in the future when God completes his mission to the nations of the world beyond Israel.[12] The gospel brings God's "mercy on all," implying all the peoples of the world (11:32).

Paul's ministry as the apostle to "the gentiles" indicates all nations beyond Israel (11:13; 15:16, 18). He speaks of his completion of this mission from Jerusalem to Illyricum in Romans 15:19. Illyricum at the time of Paul, was on the northwest Balkan peninsula, east of the Adriatic Sea, potentially meaning that Paul and his team had preached the gospel in modern Croatia, Bosnia-Herzegovina, and Montenegro.[13]

As mentioned earlier, this likely occurred during the period of Jewish expulsion through gentiles from Macedonia. It is possible Luke led a team of gentiles during Paul's second Antiochian mission to deliver the Jerusalem Council letter to Rome. Paul moved from Philippi to Thessalonica and then to Athens, leaving Luke behind in Philippi (Acts 16:40—17:1). On this trip, Luke and others like Jason, Aristarchus, Secundus, Gaius, Epaphroditus, Euodia, Syntyche, Clement, and others established the faith in the western Balkans (see part two, chapter 5).

Whenever this evangelization occurred in this way, Paul states that he has fulfilled his mission in his allotted field (cf. 2 Cor 10:12–15).[14] He has established self-supporting Christian communities through the regions of Syria, Asia, Greece, and the Balkans.[15] He next wants to push west to Rome and then Spain. The apostle finishes Romans stating that the mystery of the gospel is now made know to "all nations" (16:26),[16] pointing to the cosmic scope of God's mission. Again, this does not suggest the near completion of the mission but is ongoing and prophetic.

---

11. 2 Sam 22:50/Ps 18.49; Deut 32:43; Ps 117:1; Isa 11:10.

12. Witherington and Hyatt, *Paul's Letter*, 273: it refers "either to all the Gentiles who will be saved or to the additional number of Gentiles yet to be saved after Paul wrote. It does not mean the Gentile world as a whole."

13. Guyer, "Illyricum."

14. Belleville, "Authority," 56.

15. "Paul claims that he has brought to completion in the regions designated his own special apostolic task of planting strategic churches." Moo, *Letter to the Romans*, 912.

16. Rather than "all the gentiles" (e.g., Cranfield, *Critical and Exegetical Commentary*, 2:812), as Israel should be included. Jewett and Kotansky, *Romans*, 1009.

Part Three: Romans and the Proclamation of the Gospel

The Worldwide Mission in the Other Paulines

The global vision of Paul's mission is amply supported throughout the rest of his letters. In 1 Corinthians 9:19–22, his pattern of culturally assimilating with recipients of his ministry is to win as many as possible to Christ from "all people" (v. 22). In 2 Corinthians 4:4, he understands the world to be under Satan's domination (cf. Eph 2:2). Elsewhere, he speaks of unbelieving Jews and gentiles alike under the *stoicheia*, which are elemental religious, political, and philosophical ideologies and associated spiritual powers that bind them (Gal 4:3, 9; Col 2:8, 20).[17] The gospel sets people free from them. His understanding of a world held captive to such forces implicitly suggests God's mission to all nations so that they may be released. Of course, the same applies to sin (3:23), the problem of the flesh (3:19), death (5:12; 1 Cor 15:26), and the fallenness of this age (12:2) and the world (1 Cor 7:31).

In line with Romans 2:5–11 and 14:10–13, 2 Corinthians 5:10 refers to universal judgment. Knowing this and motivated by the fear of the Lord and God's love, Paul is determined to preach the gospel of reconciliation (2 Cor 5:11). As in Romans 11:15, in 2 Corinthians 5:19, God in Christ is reconciling *the world* to himself.

Of importance is Galatians 2:7–10, where the leading Jerusalem missionaries acknowledge that Paul and Barnabas are commissioned to go to the gentile world with the gospel, while they evangelize the Jewish world. Their acknowledgment of the ministry of the pair indicates that they also accepted that all nations are to be evangelized.[18]

As in Romans 4:13, the Abrahamic promise that in him "shall all the nations be blessed" (Gen 12:3) is now being fulfilled in the seed of Abraham, Christ, and through the international proclamation of the gospel (Gal 3:7–29). In Ephesians, the mission to all nations is presupposed in God's overall purpose: "to unite all things in him, things in heaven and on earth" (Eph 1:10). The text implies not only evangelism to win people,[19] but God's broader mission to transform a world. In Ephesians, this is fulfilled by all believers equipped by vocational leaders and clothed in God's armor doing the good works of service prepared for them.[20]

Paul's allusions to the OT passage most oft-cited in the NT, Psalm 110:1, implies a mission to the whole world.[21] Jesus must reign above *everything* (Eph 1:21) until God has placed *all* enemies under his feet. In the era of the gospel, this is achieved through the proclamation of the gospel and willing submission to Jesus as Lord (Phil 2:10–11; cf. Isa 45:23; Rom 14:10–12). The logic of Romans 10:14–17 and Ephesians

---

17. In a world where sacred and secular were intertwined, these are ideologies and the spiritual powers that inhabit them. See further, Keown, *Galatians*, 559–72.

18. Keown, *Galatians*, 280.

19. See in Eph 1:13–14; 2:14–17; 3:1–10; 4:11; 6:15, 17.

20. Eph 2:10; 4:11–12; 6:15, 17.

21. Rom 16:20; 1 Cor 15:25, 27; Eph 1:22.

The Cosmic Scope of Mission and Its Completion

1:13, where faith is born from hearing the gospel, implies that the gospel is to be preached to all peoples so that they can willingly yield.

In Colossians, all things are created for Jesus and sustained by him—the image of the invisible God, the head of everything, within whom the fullness of God's deity dwells (Col 1:15–17; 2:10). Through him, God has reconciled all things to himself (Col 1:20). The gospel—which is Jesus—has been preached to all creation (Col 1:23). While Paul describes these things as already complete, still, the gospel must be proclaimed to make actual what is already realized in theological terms (Col 1:6).

Notably, as in Ephesians, the Colossians' vision encompasses all things, and so mission is evangelism plus so much more. At its center are evangelism and discipleship, as Paul makes known to the gentiles the great and mysterious gospel that includes them (Col 1:27). So, he is devoted to proclaiming Jesus and presenting all people mature in Christ (Col 1:28). This mission includes the whole world of Greek, Jews, Barbarians, and Scythians (Col 3:11).[22]

The cosmic mission is implied in 1 Thessalonians 2:15–16, where Paul speaks of Jewish persecution as opposition to God and "all humankind" as they hindered Paul and others preaching to the gentiles so that they may be saved.

Some of the clearest cosmic theology is in the Pastorals, which I consider Pauline.[23] In 1 Timothy 2:4, "who [God] desires *all* people to be saved and to come to the knowledge of the truth" (emphasis mine; cf. 1 Tim 2:6). In 1 Timothy 4:10, God is "the Savior of all people," premised on faith. Similarly, the grace of God is bringing salvation "for all people" in Titus 2:11. Crucially, Paul's final words include mention of "all the Gentiles" hearing the gospel (2 Tim 4:17).[24]

The Progress of the Mission by the Time of Romans

We know that, by the time of Romans, Christianity was established in the arc from Jerusalem to the Balkans (15:19) and had reached Rome. As noted earlier in this chapter, it was established to some extent in North Africa, likely through the Ethiopian eunuch and other Africans named in the NT. While some early writers like Clement believe so (Clement of Rome, Irenaeus, Tertullian, Muratorian Canon), we cannot be sure Paul fulfilled his hope of reaching Spain (see part one, chapter 4).

Having established that Paul and the other NT writers recognized that Christ had commissioned them and others to evangelize the whole world, it is intriguing to consider how far they had got by the time of Romans. It is assumed by some Romans

---

22. Scythia was the region around the Black and Caspian Seas, possibly including parts of Bulgaria, Romania, Moldova, Ukraine, western Turkey, Georgia, Armenia, Azerbaijan, southern Russia, Kazakhstan, Uzbekistan, Turkmenistan, and northern Iran.

23. See the summary in Lea and Griffin, 1, 2 *Timothy, Titus*, 23–40.

24. Other references in the NT aside from the Gospels and Acts (see this chapter, note 1) that imply cosmic mission include: Heb 1:2; 2:8–15; 7:27; 8:11; 2 Pet 3:9–10, 13; 1 John 2:2; 4:17; Rev 1:7; 5:9–13; 7:9–11; 11:15; 12:5; 13:7–8; 14:6, 15–19; 16:14; 21:1–15.

scholars that Paul believed that the mission to the gentiles would be completed when he had evangelized Spain. James Dunn considers so, arguing that Paul's desire to go to Spain "reflects his conviction of the pressing imminence of the parousia, leaving all too little time to take the gospel to where it had not so far been heard"[25] and "is informed by the eschatological vision of a pressingly short time in which the gospel can be preached."[26]

As stated earlier, by the time of Romans, while Paul (likely in his fifties) may have been nearing the completion of *his* missionary work, the mission to the world was far from complete.[27] From Acts and Paul's letters, we know that the gospel had potentially spread through Pentecost pilgrims in some way to the regions immediately east of Israel, including the Arabian Peninsula, Iraq, Iran, and the regions around the Black and Caspian Seas. It had penetrated to some extent into North Africa to Egypt, parts of Libya, and Ethiopia. Syria, what we call Turkey, Greece, and the Balkans were potentially reached. Clearly, the letter shows that a church was established in Rome. Spain remained unevangelized.[28]

Early church tradition gives some indication of further evangelization. 1 Clement 42:3 (ca. AD 90–100) tells readers that the apostles "went forth with the firm assurance that the Holy Spirit gives, preaching the good news that the kingdom of God was about to come." In the Preaching of Peter 3a (AD 100–120), Jewish believers will "after twelve years go out into the world,"[29] and in verse 3b, the faithful apostles were sent "into the world to preach the gospel to people throughout the world."[30] In the Epistle to the Apostles, 30 (AD 100–150?), Jesus tells the Twelve to:

> Go you and preach to the twelve tribes and preach also to the gentiles and to the whole land of Israel from sunrise to sunset and from South to North, and many will believe in the Son of God.

While this is suggestive of the Twelve intending to evangelize the world, it says nothing about the completion of the cosmic mission.[31] Similarly, later traditions do not give clear evidence of the completion of the Christian mission in the first century.

25. Dunn, *Romans 9–16*, 864. See also Käsemann, *Romans*, 313.
26. Dunn, *Romans 9–16*, 871. See also Käsemann, *Romans*, 316, 395; Schreiner, *Romans*, 16.
27. Morris argues there is nothing of an imminent parousia in Romans. He adds, "it comes up against the fact that the apostle must have been conscious that there were many nations, such as the Parthians and the German tribes, where he had not been and had no prospect of going. He was not doing something to bring about the parousia but discharging his obligation to plant churches in virgin territory." Morris, *Epistle to the Romans*, 517. "But nowhere does he predict a near return; and, more importantly, he does not ground his exhortations on the conviction that the parousia would take place very soon but on the conviction that the parousia was always imminent—its coming certain, its timing incalculable." Moo, *Letter to the Romans*, 839.
28. See further Keown, "Imminent Parousia and Christian Mission," 257–59.
29. Agraphon 10, in Clement of Alexandria, *Strom.* 6.5.43.
30. Agraphon 9; in Clement of Alexandria, *Strom.* 6.648.
31. Keown, "Imminent Parousia and Christian Mission," 259.

The Cosmic Scope of Mission and Its Completion

- Acts of Peter 5 (ca. AD 180–190) suggests Peter was instructed to travel to Rome.

- Apollonius (ca. AD 200) held that Jesus had told the apostles not to leave Jerusalem for twelve years (Eusebius, *Hist. eccl.* 5.18.14).

- Acts of Thomas 1:1 (ca. AD 200–240): the apostles "portioned out the regions of the world in order that each one of us might go into the region that fell to him by lot, and to the nation to which the Lord sent him" (Eusebius, *Hist. eccl.* 5.18.14).

- Origen (AD 185–254) in Vol. 3 of his Genesis commentary suggests that the apostles drew lots and "were scattered throughout the whole world." They were associated with different locals: Thomas—Parthia, Andrew—Scythia, John—Asia, and Peter—the dispersion of Asia and then Rome (Eusebius, *Hist. eccl.* 3.1.1.).

- Acts of Peter and the Twelve Apostles 1:9–20; 5:11–14 (second/third century; NHC 6.1) states the apostles took ships "to spread the word of God in every city harmoniously."

- The Letter of Peter to Philip 134:18–26; 140:7–15, 23–27 (second/third century; NHC 7.2): "the apostles parted from each other into four winds in order to preach. And they went by the power of Jesus, in peace."

- Didascalia Apostolorum 23 (ca. AD 250): they "divided the world into twelve parts, and were gone out to the gentiles into all the world to preach the word."

- Acts of Philip (fourth century): Jesus "divided the apostles according to city and country, so that each one would depart to the place that had been allotted to him." They went to these places: Peter—Rome; Thomas—Parthia and India; Matthew—innermost Parthia, Bartholomew—Lycaonia, Simon Cananaeus—Spain, Andrew—Achaia, John—Asia, and Philip—to the Greeks.

- Fragments of Polycarp a. 5–12 (third century): people (probably the apostles) went out in the whole inhabited world so that each one of them might complete his course within the regions which were assigned to them, while they completed the preaching about the kingdom of heaven throughout the whole of his creation, according to the testimony of the apostles.

- *Acts of John* (ca. AD 500): the apostles each "travelled to the country and the region for which he had received responsibility through the grace."

This material confirms that the early missionaries of the church believed in a cosmic mission and intentionally sought to complete it. The references perhaps indicate that each apostle had a particular geographical calling. However, only the Fragments of Polycarp suggest that they completed the commands of Jesus to take the gospel, preach, and make disciples *throughout the whole world*. This one late reference is hardly sufficient to argue that they had completed the gospel mission. There is little evidence that the fullness of the gentiles (or Jews) had come in (11:12, 25).

Furthermore, as will be discussed below, these texts do not include many other parts of the then known world.

Schnabel raises the possibility that this evidence indicates a conference in Jerusalem twelve years after Christ (AD 41/42), at which the apostles divided the world up for missional purposes. He ponders whether they left Jerusalem at the time of Agrippa's persecution to fulfill their calls.[32] However, the late and inconsistent accounts call this into question.[33] Even if they did engage in such mission (e.g., Thomas in India),[34] we know little about their effectiveness and whether they evangelized the whole world as they knew it. With the immense distances involved and the dangers of first-century mission, it is exceedingly implausible that they did. Overall, as I have previously argued:

> We can conclude then that there is good evidence that the early Christians understood that the gospel would go to all nations and that the apostles were prominent in this mission. However, there is sparse evidence that it was believed that this mission was complete in the NT or the early church.[35]

THE FIRST-CENTURY UNDERSTANDING OF THE EXTENT OF THE NATIONS

In considering the scope of their completion of the mission, it is essential to consider how the writers of the NT documents understood the extent of the nations. What they would have known can be discerned from early church writings. Aside from the obvious places they were aware of, Acts and Paul's letters suggest familiarity with Ethiopia (Acts 2:10; 8:27, cf. Acts 13:1), Arabia (Acts 2:11; Gal 1:17), Scythia (Col 3:11), and barbarians (1:14, cf. Diogn. 5:1–5).

Schnabel has discussed the geographical understanding of people in the biblical world in the first century.[36] He examines Greek sea voyages (*periploi*) from as early as the fifth century BC showing Greek awareness of Sierra Leone in West Africa to the south; Britain, Iceland, and the Baltic Sea to the north; to the east, the Black and Caspian Seas, the Arabian Peninsula, Pakistan (the Indus River), India, the northern Indian Ocean (Erythraean Sea), and the Mediterranean ("Inner Sea").[37]

---

32. Schnabel, *Early Christian Mission*, 1:530–33. He bases this on the Indian nature of the *Acts Thom.* and Rom 15:20; 1 Cor 9:5; 15:5, 7; Gal 6:13. However, this only confirms apostolic missionary activity. The level of gospel penetration is uncertain.

33. See Schnabel, *Early Christian Mission*, 1:530 for a summary of the objections to the historical credibility of these traditions.

34. See Schnabel, *Early Christian Mission*, 1:880–95 argues that the tradition stands up to scrutiny. I consider this possible, but tenuous.

35. Keown, "Imminent Parousia and Christian Mission," 261.

36. Schnabel, *Early Christian Mission*, 1:444–99.

37. Schnabel, *Early Christian Mission*, 1:444–46.

The Cosmic Scope of Mission and Its Completion

The *Peutinger Table*, perhaps from the first century, extends from Britain to China.[38] The Greek geographer Strabo (64 BC–AD 21) and earlier works show knowledge of Syria, Europe to Britain, east to Arabia, India, Asia (Turkey), the Persian Gulf, Assyria, and China (*Seres*),[39] and south to Egypt, Libya, and Mauretania.

Pliny the Elder (AD 23/24–79) was aware of Europe, including Spain, Gaul, and Germany; the Scythians of the Russian Steppe area around the Black and Caspian Seas, North Africa; and west to India, China, and the Malay Peninsula.[40]

Josephus references European regions of Gaul, German Spain, African Libya, and east to Persia (Iran), and the Scythians of the Russian steppes.[41] Josephus also defines the "ends of the earth," which included the Germans and Scythians to the north, west to the Atlantic edge of Spain, Ethiopia in the south, and east to China.[42]

Schnabel argues that the "nations" include all known peoples (and unknown if they existed). The "ends of the earth" would include south to Ethiopia, east to India, north to Scythia, and to Spain in the west.[43] Yet, as I have argued, this does not go far enough. There is good evidence that they knew of the "silk people" of *Seres* (China) and in the second century BC with imports from the area in the first century BC.[44] Since Caesar, they were fully aware of all or most of western and central Europe, including at least Gaul,[45] Germany,[46] and Britain (which Caesar visited and Claudius conquered in AD 43).[47] If the Greeks were cognizant of the Baltic Sea, as seems likely, then Scandinavia (at least Denmark) would be known.[48] Knowledge of Ethiopia and Sierra Leone for centuries would suggest they knew of many people south into Africa.

Bringing this back to Paul and Romans, by the time of Romans, considering the extent of their knowledge of the world, the mission was barely getting going. The

---

38. Schnabel, *Early Christian Mission*, 1:447. Schnabel, *Early Christian Mission*, 1:448–52 also mentions other maps.

39. See Strabo, *Geogr.* 11.11.1. Strabo also mentions the Roman poet Virgil (70–19 BC) referring to silkworms from China. Virgil, *Georg. Lib.* 2.121.

40. Schnabel, *Early Christian Mission*, 1:452–63.

41. Germany (e.g., *J.W.* 1.672), Gaul (e.g., *J.W.* 1.5, 397), Spain (e.g., *J.W.* 2.374), Libya (e.g., *J.W.* 1.99), Persia (*J.W.* 1.143), and the Scythians (*J.W.* 7.90).

42. Schnabel, *Early Christian Mission*, 1:468–69. Gades (Cádiz) in Spain (*J.W.* 2.363); Ethiopia (e.g., *J.W.* 2.382); India (*J.W.* 2.385); and China (*Ant.* 1.147).

43. Schnabel, *Early Christian Mission*, 1:470.

44. Schnabel, *Early Christian Mission*, 1:495–97.

45. Rome's contact with Gaul can be dated from the third century BC; see "Gaul" in the *Encyclopedia Britannica*.

46. Rome's contact with Germanic tribes can be dated from the first century BC; see "Germany" in the *Encyclopedia Britannica*.

47. Roman contact with Britain can be dated from the mid-first century BC. with its conquest in the mid-first century AD. See "United Kingdom," in *Encyclopedia Britannica*.

48. Some scholars argue that Romans made direct contact with people in Denmark in the early first century. See Jørgensen, "Warriors, Soldiers and Conscripts," 9–19. See also "Denmark and the Roman Empire."

PART THREE: ROMANS AND THE PROCLAMATION OF THE GOSPEL

whole of Europe, Britain, and Scandinavia were largely unevangelized. There was a church growing in North Africa in Libya, Egypt, and Ethiopia with an awareness that Africa had many peoples yet unreached. To the east, China and Southeast Asia remained unreached. The work had just begun. It remains incomplete today, and this should spur us on to evangelize the world.

15

The Power of Salvation

IN THE PREVIOUS CHAPTER, it was established that Paul and other first-century Christians believed they were charged with taking the gospel to every person in the world so that they may be saved. Completion of the task required traveling to "the ends of the earth," and with our knowledge of the first-century geographical self-understanding, they had barely begun this work. In this chapter, I will look a little closer at how Paul's understanding of mission centers on the gospel and its proclamation.

THE POWER OF GOD FOR SALVATION

Paul begins Romans stressing his enslavement to Christ and his commission to preach the gospel of God promised in the Scriptures (1:1–2). The focus of this gospel is Jesus, the son of David (Christ, Messiah) and Son of God (1:3–4). By grace, Paul was chosen as an apostle to preach to the people of the world so that they may obey the gospel by believing it (1:5). He lived out this call, serving God "with his Spirit in the gospel of his Son" (1:9). As he is the apostle to the gentiles, and as Rome was the capital of one of the leading empires in the then-known world, he writes of his yearning to come to Rome to win converts as he has done from Jerusalem to the Balkans (1:13, 15; 15:19). His gospel call includes an obligation to preach to all gentiles, from the "civilized" wise Greeks (Greeks and Romans in this context), and the seemingly "uncivilized" and "foolish" barbarians (1:14).

In Romans 1:16, Paul states that he is not ashamed of the gospel.[1] His lack of shame resonates with 2 Timothy 1:12, where he says, "But I am not ashamed, for I know the one in whom I have believed" (translation mine). He summons Timothy to

---

1. Moo, *Letter to the Romans*, 68 notes this may be an example of litotes. The Greek *litotēs* means "simplicity," and as a literary device is "[t]he negation of something in order to affirm the opposite; or understatement in order to give emphasis"; see *PDSNTG* 81. If so, Paul is declaring "I have great confidence in the gospel."

be similarly unashamed of "the testimony about our Lord" and of Paul (2 Tim 1:8; cf. 1:16).

In the ancient world, there is a range of reasons one might be ashamed of the message.[2] First, the story of Jesus is full of cultural and social anomalies. Jesus was from insignificant beginnings, from the non-descript Nazareth in isolated Israel (cf. John 1:46). He was not a Roman citizen and merely a humble carpenter. He is a Jew, and many Romans reviled Jews.[3] He was crucified; publicly humiliated before the world in what was designed to be the most demeaning death possible (Gal 3:13; Deut 21:23). For his people, in his crucifixion, he was a God-accursed man. His own people rejected him. The Romans killed him. The gods of Rome conquered the God he supposedly represented in the world. His followers claimed he rose from the dead and appeared, which for a Roman, is laughable.[4] He did not appear to anyone in the Jewish world that "mattered," hence, his resurrection was written off as a fanciful construct. Little wonder that the message of the cross is a stumbling block to Jews and foolishness to gentiles (1 Cor 1:22; Gal 5:16).

Nevertheless, Paul is unashamed of the gospel of this Jesus. Similarly, in 2 Timothy 1:12, after summoning his deputy not to be ashamed of the gospel or Paul (2 Tim 1:8), Paul states that he is not ashamed despite his suffering. He is confident because he knows Christ, the object of his belief, and knows Christ will guard him to the end (whatever happens). He is then unashamed to believe in this gospel and to proclaim it. As Cottrell puts it,

> He is ready to preach it anywhere, even and especially in Rome itself, the very center of human power and pomp and presumptuousness, the crossroads of worldly wealth and wisdom and sophistication.[5]

His confidence is "because (causal *gar*), it [the gospel] is the power of God for salvation" (*dynamis . . . Theou estin eis sōterian*).[6] The "gospel" (*euangelion*) here picks up the Jewish idea of God's divine word (*dābār*), which, because the God of the

---

2. Further on objections to the faith in the early church, see Green, *Evangelism in the Early Church*, 49–57.

3. See Keener, *Gospel of John*, 1:1121, who notes Horace *Sat.* 1.5.100–101; Juvenal *Sat.* 14.96–106; Quintilian 3.7.21; Tacitus, *Hist.* 5.1–5; Persius, *Sat.* 5.179–84.

4. "Lots of things could happen to the dead in the beliefs of pagan antiquity, but resurrection was not among the available options." On the evidence, see Wright, *Resurrection of the Son of God*, 32–84, esp. 38.

5. Cottrell, *Romans: Volume 1*, "The Glory of the Gospel" (1:16a). See also Schreiner, *Romans*, 60: "The asseveration that Paul is not ashamed in Rom. 1:16, therefore, refers both to his willingness to confess the gospel in public and the overcoming of fear."

6. "The gospel is divine power that results in, or brings about, the salvation of everyone who believes in it. Here the gospel is described not simply as the content of what Jesus has done to bring about salvation, but is actually the effective 'power' which applies that salvation to believing Jews and Gentiles." Plummer, *Paul's Understanding*, 52.

The Power of Salvation

cosmos speaks it through human agency, has the power to bring into being that which is spoken.[7]

This power to enact through divine fiat is seen in creation where God speaks, and creation comes into existence (e.g., Gen 1:3–5; Ps 33:6). It is invoked when Moses speaks to Pharaoh and Yahweh did as Moses spoke on his behalf (Exod 8:13). The power of the word is seen in God's promises to Abraham that he would inherit the land. Against all the odds, God brought this to pass through Moses and Joshua. So, in Joshua 21:45, we read:

> Not one word (*dābār*) of all the good promises (*dābār*) that the Lord had made
> to the house of Israel had failed; all came to pass.[8]

The prophetic tradition of Israel is premised on God putting his words into the mouth of his prophets and prophetesses, his words are listened to, and his or her veracity is demonstrated by the word coming to pass (Deut 18:18–22; cf. Amos 3:7). So, in the case of Samuel, "the Lord was with him and let none of his words (*dābār*) fall to the ground" (1 Sam 3:19; cf. 2 Kgs 10:10). Later, prophets anticipated the exiles of the north and south, and these also came to pass (e.g., 2 Chr 36:21–22). So, the Psalmist writes, "He sends out his command to the earth; his word (*dābār*) runs swiftly" (Ps 147:15).[9]

The idea of God's word as power is captured best by Isaiah. For him, God's word is like precipitation that waters the ground and generates the life on earth that feeds people; similarly, the word that goes out from God's mouth feeds people (cf. Deut 8:3; Matt 4:4; Luke 4:4). When spoken, "it shall not return to me empty, but it shall accomplish that which I purpose, and shall succeed in the thing for which I sent it" (Isa 55:11).

Jeremiah speaks of God "watching over [his] word to perform it" (Jer 1:12). Again, in Jeremiah, God asks, "Is not my word (*dābār*) like fire, declares the Lord, and like a hammer that breaks the rock in pieces?" (Jer 23:29). In the context, the power of God's word to invoke judgment is highlighted with images of war and destruction. In Ezekiel, God says,

> None of my words (*dābār*) will be delayed any longer, but the word (*dābār*)
> that I speak will be performed, declares the Lord GOD (Ezek 12:28).

The prophet Joel says,

---

7. "This notion of the message being an effective power (cf. 1 Cor 1:18) is to be understood in the light of such OT passages, concerning the divine word as Gen 1:3, 6, etc.; Ps 147:15; Isa 40:8b; 55:10–11; and Jer 23:29." O'Brien, *Consumed with Passion*, 71.

8. Cf. Josh 23:14.

9. See also Isa 45:23; 46:10; 48:3; Esth 7:8. Compare 2 Thess 3:1.

> The LORD utters his voice before his army, for his camp is exceedingly great; he who executes his word (*dābār*) is powerful. For the day of the LORD is great and very awesome; who can endure it? (Joel 2:11).

In each of these passages, God's word has the power to bring to pass what God wants.[10] Hence, his words are fulfilled in history.

For Paul, God's word has that kind of power. In and through his Son, God has spoken, and the good news of God's salvation is now in effect (cf. John 1:1; Heb 1:2). Like the prophets of old, couriers of God's message, he carries a message infused with the power of God to effect salvation for those who believe. Elsewhere, Paul describes the word of God as a sword, wielded by the Spirit in the hands of believers whose feet are always ready to move (Eph 6:15) to speak God's lovely *rhēma* (Eph 6:17; cf. Heb 4:11–12; Isa 52:7). The image of the sword speaks of the word's cutting power of salvation and judgment, both in defense and attack.[11]

Jesus's notion of the word of God as a seed carrying power to produce life within the believer also suggests extension (Mark 4:1–20, 26–32). Luke's agricultural understanding of the word of the Lord growing (*auxanō*) is synonymous (Acts 6:7; 19:10). For Luke, "God's word is an active agent of the mission of God."[12] In Colossians 1:6, Paul invokes a similar concept of plant growth whereby the gospel is "bearing fruit (*karpophoreō*)[13] and increasing (*auxanō*)" in the whole world. The word of God is a living power that cannot fail (9:6). In 2 Thessalonians 3:1, like a brilliant athlete from the games or a runner carrying a message, it has the power to run or race (*trechō*) ahead. This recalls Ps 147:4 LXX [147:15 EVV] where

> In the context of the psalm, God sends his word to the earth and, just as God is in control of the seasons such that he sends snow, hail, and wind and nothing can stop him, so he is in control of his word such that nothing can hinder it from "running" or spreading swiftly.[14]

In Philippians 1:12–14, despite the apostle and gospel being chained, the gospel is advancing like a military power through the Praetorian Guard and into the city.[15] Later, again writing from Roman chains, he speaks elsewhere of the impossibility of harnessing the power of the gospel (2 Tim 2:9). Indeed, it is true that "Paul speaks of

---

10. See also Wis 18:14–16: "For while gentle silence enveloped all things, and night in its swift course was now half gone, your all-powerful word leaped from heaven, from the royal throne, into the midst of the land that was doomed, a stern warrior carrying the sharp sword of your authentic command, and stood and filled all things with death, and touched heaven while standing on the earth."

11. Keown, *Congregational Evangelism in Philippians*, 292–96.

12. Walton, "Ascension of Jesus," 61.

13. See Rom 1:13; Phil 1:22 where *karpos*, "fruit," includes converts.

14. Weima, *1–2 Thessalonians*, 586.

15. Further, see Keown, *Philippians*, 1:184–87.

the gospel as a force or agency able to accomplish something, and which has a purpose toward which it moves."[16]

Another statement similar to Romans 1:16 is 1 Corinthians 1:18. Paul writes,

> For the word of the cross is folly to those who are perishing, but to us who are being saved (*sōzō*) it is the power (*dynamis*) of God.

The "word of the cross" is synonymous with "the gospel" but focuses on its central redemptive moment, the crucifixion of Jesus. Paul notes the two possible effects of the proclamation of the gospel of a crucified Messiah. For some whose destiny is destruction, it is foolishness. It further hardens them for judgment (cf. Mark 4:12; Isa 6:9–10). For those being saved, God's power is unleashed as it is preached, and their hearts melt in faith. As Garland puts it,

> In this case, "power" refers to the effectiveness of the cross to make God known to humankind, to accomplish salvation, to defeat evil, and to transform lives and values.[17]

Here, in Romans 1:16, the power of salvation is for *everyone* who believes. As such, the power inherent to the gospel is unleashed or actualized when it is received *with faith*. The preposition *eis* carries the sense of "for [the] salvation" as in most translations,[18] but equally, can be translated "to salvation" (NKJV), "into salvation," "produces salvation," or "brings about salvation." The power of salvation is universal in effect but does not always save; sometimes, it leads to destruction. The soteriological effect is not universal; it is activated when there is a faith on the part of the recipient. As will now be discussed, such faith comes through hearing the message of the gospel.

FAITH COMES FROM HEARING

Justification requires faith, and faith involves the hearing of the message. The link of justification, faith, and hearing is pronounced in Romans 10:5–17. Paul is explaining the righteousness that is by faith that stands in contrast to the righteousness based on the law that hardened Israel is pursuing (10:5–7).

As in Galatians 3:12, in Romans 10:5, Paul cites Leviticus 18:5 stating the fundamental premise of righteousness by the law: "the person who does the commandments shall live by them" (translation mine). To gain righteousness through the Torah requires flawless fulfillment of the laws of Israel.[19]

16. O'Brien, *Consumed with Passion*, 113.
17. Garland, *1 Corinthians*, 62.
18. E.g., ESV, NET, LEB, NRSV, NIV84, NRSV, NASB95.
19. See also Gal 3:10 = Deut 27:26. Moo notes three possibilities for the righteousness based on the law: 1) It is the same as the righteousness by faith; 2) It is about Christ who did the law; 3) It is negative speaking of failure to achieve righteousness through law compared to by faith. As he argues, 3) is in mind. Moo, *Letter to the Romans*, 663–67. However, 2) is also implied as Jesus the "end of the

Part Three: Romans and the Proclamation of the Gospel

In Romans 10:6, using the Hebrew *pesher* approach,[20] Paul personifies "the righteousness from faith"[21] and imagines it as an interlocutor speaking into the debate on the basis for righteousness. It continually speaks (present tense). The message of the righteousness of faith speaking calls to mind 1:16, where the gospel is God's power for salvation. The message here becomes the messenger.

The words the righteousness from faith speaks are a composite of Deuteronomic texts (Deut 8:17; 9:4; 30:12–14). The introductory formula, "do not say in your heart," draws on Deuteronomy 8:17 and 9:4. In the first setting, Israel is not to say to itself that it gained its status and wealth from its own power, forgetting from whence it came; God. If they do, they will perish through disobeying the voice of God (Deut 8:17–20). The second text, similarly, warns them that they should not claim it was their own righteousness that gained them the land; it was due to Canaanite wickedness. Implied here is a warning to Israel that the same could happen to them (Deut 9:4–5). A few years later it did, as Jerusalem fell to Rome. Paul likewise warns contemporary Israel that even worse could happen to them if they do not hear the preaching of the righteousness by faith—eternal destruction.

Deuteronomy 30:12–13 comes immediately after the pronouncements of the blessings and curses associated with the covenant requirements.[22] By using the Deuteronomic text of the righteousness of faith, Paul cleverly shows the power of the word of God to continue to speak, now in the Christ-era. Indeed, his appropriation of OT texts to argue his point in the present throughout Romans demonstrates this power. The power of the word of God is also evident in what follows in Romans 10:18–21.[23]

In Deuteronomy 30:1–10, Israel is promised restoration when in exile (Deut 30:1) if it returns wholeheartedly to God, obeying his commands (Deut 30:3). God will bring in her outcasts from "the uttermost parts of heaven" (Deut 30:4) to their land and into prosperity. While it originally had in mind the return from exile, now, through Christ, this is happening in a fresh way as the gospel is preached to the world (10:18). Israelites, too, can be grafted in where she or he believes in Jesus (11:23–24).

God then circumcises their hearts, recalling Romans 2:25–29,[24] causing them to love God with all they have (Deut 30:5–6). Their enemies will experience the curses

---

law" in that he fulfilled it and so Jesus can be the object of the faith that justifies those "in Christ." To say "[t]he formulation of v. 5 is not polemical" is mistaken and misses the point. Jewett and Kotansky, *Romans*, 624.

20. Pesher is a Jewish approach to interpretation that stresses present-day fulfillment of OT texts. See Brook, "Pesharim," 778–82.

21. For more on this Moo, *Letter to the Romans*, 667. He compares this to the personification of wisdom in Prov 8 and the word in Isa 55:10–11. "Righteousness" is personified in Ps 85:10–13 and Isa 45:8. Greek rhetoric also used such personification. Jewett and Kotansky, *Romans*, 625.

22. Jewett and Kotansky note that Deut 30:12–14 was important in second-temple Judaism (Bar 3:29–30; Philo, *Post.* 84–85; Tg. Neof. Deut 30:11–14). Jewett and Kotansky, *Romans*, 626.

23. See also, esp., 1:17; = Hab 2:4; 4:3 = Gen 15:6; and the strings of OT texts in 3:11–18; 9:25–28; 11:7–10; 15:9–12.

24. Showing that while Romans 2:25–29 was a part of Paul's argument that all have sinned, it

(Deut 30:7), while Israel will be obedient (Deut 30:8) and will prosper under God's delight as they obey him (Deut 30:9–10).

The citation Paul uses involves Moses telling Israel that the commandment they are required to obey is not too difficult for Israel nor far off. The command is not in heaven as if Israel has to ascend to get it and preach it to them that they may hear (Deut 30:12). Nor does anyone need to go and get the message and bring it to Israel that they may listen and obey (Deut 30:13). Instead, it is "very near you. It is in your mouth and in your heart, so that you can do it" (Deut 30:14).

Paul applies these ideas here of the gospel. In verse 6, just as Moses said of God's commands to Israel as they prepared to enter the land, no one needs to travel into heaven to get this word, for the Christ has come and embodied God's word and preached it among them.[25] There is not a requirement to bring the Messiah down, his coming as a human was enough.[26] He has sent his Spirit into his preachers, and they are sent to declare the gospel (10:18).

In verse 7, Paul adapts the Hebrew and Greek OT focus on crossing the sea to find God's word to going into the abyss to get the word of God and bring it up. The abyss is a play on the idea of the sea, as it was used of its depths.[27] *Abyssos*, in the NT, is used exclusively of the place of demonic forces.[28] The term invokes pagan ideas of divination, fortunes, omens, sorcerers, charmers, mediums, and necromancers, as Samuel did with the witch of Endor (1 Sam 28). Doing such things is forbidden in Israel's story (e.g., Deut 18:10–11).[29] While this could then be a reference to Jesus going to hell between his death and resurrection,[30] more likely, however, abyss here refers to the world of the dead (Sheol, Hades).[31]

---

shows that heart-circumcision is possible. It requires faith and not law-observance. Now that Christ has come and been declared, through faith in him and his Father God.

25. Fitzmyer, *Romans*, 590 notes this is the closest Paul comes to speaking of the incarnation.

26. Barrett notes the contemporaries hoping to hasten the coming of the Messiah at the time through obedience to the law. It is not needed: "the Messiah has appeared, and it is, therefore, impossible to hasten his coming (as some devout Jews thought to do) by perfect obedience to the law and penitence for its transgressions." Barrett, *Epistle to the Romans*, 199.

27. Thielman notes Strabo, *Geogr* 1.6.6 and Job 41:23 LXX use *abyssos* of the deep. Thielman, *Romans*, 493. See Deut 8:7; Pss 33:7; 77:17; 107:26.

28. See Luke 8:31; Rev 9:1, 2, 11; 11:7; 17:8; 20:1, 3.

29. See also Gen 44:5; Lev 19:26, 31; 20:6; Num 22:7; Josh 13:22; 2 Kg 17:17; 21:6; 23:24; 2 Chr 33:6; Isa 8:9; 19:3; Jer 14:14; Ezek 12:24; 13:7, 23; 21:21–23; Mic 3:11; 5:12.

30. "For the first time in the NT the message of Christ's ascension is linked here with the descent into Hades, thus with the descent into the realm of the dead." Käsemann, *Romans*, 288.

31. It is sometimes used of the place of the dead (Euripides, *Phoen.* 1605; Diogenes Laertius, *Lives* 4.27. For Thielman, this "is how Paul uses it here." Thielman, *Romans*, 493. Jewett and Kotansky note Jewish expectations of Elijah, Enoch, and others like Moses returning during the messianic age. Paul may be aware of these. Jewett and Kotansky, *Romans*, 628.

Part Three: Romans and the Proclamation of the Gospel

Paul is saying, quite brilliantly, that no one needs to go into the world of the dead, Sheol, to bring Christ up from the dead, because Jesus has risen! He has spoken God's word and is raised, vindicating him as Messiah.

As Moo puts it,

> As he could use the fact of the incarnation to suggest the foolishness of "going into heaven" to bring Christ down, so now he can use the fact of the resurrection to deny any need to "go down to the abyss" to bring Christ up from "the realm of the dead."[32]

Moreover, Jesus has ascended, is in heaven, and has poured his Spirit into his people, filling his people with his word, which they are now proclaiming (as did Moses). Moses, of course, is also dead, and now his words are completed, interpreted, and fulfilled, transcended by the life, death, and words of the risen one. He is the long-awaited Mosaic prophet they must listen to—the one Moses pointed to, and who Moses himself would demand they hear and heed (Deut 18:15–18, cf. Mark 9:7 and parr.).[33] To prefer Moses over Jesus is to violate God's prohibition against consulting spirits and the dead and is virtually no different to pagan necromancy (cf. Gal 4:3, 8–9). It is also to disobey Moses, who they venerate.

As such, the word of God found in the gospel is near to Israel. It is, in fact, here, having come in Jesus and is now in the mouths of Paul and other preachers. In verse 8, Paul continues his personification of "righteousness by faith" and asks what it says. He cites Deuteronomy 30:14: "the word is near you, in your mouth and in your heart."[34]

"In your mouth and in your heart" is a little elusive in context. It could be psychological, referring to it being within each person in Israel, if they will only grasp it. However, a better reading is that it is in the hearts and mouths of Spirit-empowered Jewish missionaries like the apostles and Paul. The word of faith is implanted among the people of Israel, first in Jesus, and now in Spirit-filled, God-appointing proclaimers, and they are declaring it. All that Israel must do now is what they were required to do when Moses first preached it to them: listen and obey. They failed the first time and went into exile. They are doing so again. Noticeably, the gospel here is described as the "word of faith that we proclaim." This descriptor applied by Paul effectively says, "the word of God and his Son received by faith," emphasizing the importance of believing the gospel.

Verse 9 begins with a *hoti* that can be causal, "because . . . "[35] However, it is better read as a "marker of narrative or discourse content . . . *that*."[36] It gives content to the

---

32. Moo, *Letter to the Romans*, 674.
33. See also John 1:21, 25; 6:14; 7:40; Acts 3:22–24; 7:37.
34. This all calls to mind Jesus's words: "The kingdom of God is near" (Mark 1:14, NET).
35. Moo, *Letter to the Romans*, 657; rather than "that" (NIV).
36. See BDAG 731, meaning 1 (emphasis original).

verb *kēryssomen* that ends the previous verse, i.e., it is the content of "the word of faith."

The substance is one of the crispest summaries in the NT of what it means to be a Christian. It draws on the terms "mouth" and "heart" in 10:8 from Deuteronomy 30:14. It is couched as a third class conditional sentence that speaks of the uncertainty of fulfillment.[37] It refers then to what *could* occur in the future (if Jews [and anyone else for that matter] heed the gospel).[38]

The protasis describes two conditions required for salvation, and the apodosis states the outcome: "then you will be saved" (my translation). The emphasis is on future salvation, meaning here Paul is speaking of a future event experienced in that moment of belief, or of the final state of salvation. Both aspects, of course, need to apply for it to be fulfilled. A person needs to confess and believe, and they are justified and saved at that moment. They continue being saved as they persevere in faith and will be saved if they continue to believe to the end.[39]

The protasis has two elements of the condition. First, a person must "confess (*homologeō*) with (*en*, in) your mouth that Jesus is Lord." *Homologeō* in the LXX has a range of senses.[40] In the wider NT, amongst a range of meanings,[41] it is not uncommonly used of acknowledging or professing something where Christ is concerned. An example is someone acknowledging Jesus before others, so that Christ, in turn, acknowledges that person before God (Matt 10:32; Luke 12:8).[42]

Paul uses *homologeō* twice here and two other times. In 1 Timothy 6:12, it is used of Timothy making the good profession or confession before witnesses, which likely

---

37. Wallace, *Greek Grammar*, 696.

38. Wallace, *Greek Grammar*, 696. Alternatively, it could mean it is likely to occur. It is hardly hypothetical. He lists Rom 10:9 as a third class condition on p. 699.

39. See under salvation, part two, chapter 10.

40. LXX uses include to praise or bless God (1 Esdr 4:60; 5:58); to confess something such as a crime (Esth 1:10); to confess (Sir 4:26; Jer 51:25; Apoc. Sedr. 13:4; T. Gad 6:3), to rejoice over someone's death (T. Dan 1:4), or to desire to kill someone (T. Gad 2:1); to admit something such as one's ethnicity (2 Macc 6:6); to acknowledge something including the dominance of reason (4 Macc 6:34), someone's blessed self-restraint (4 Macc 13:5), that God's hand is able to save (Job 40:14), that Israel is God's son (Wis 18:13), a reputation for justice (Let. Aris. 24); and to agree to do something such as to eat (4 Macc 9:16).

41. NT uses include to praise God's name (Heb 13:15); to declare something, e.g., that Jesus never knew evildoers (Matt 7:23); to promise with an oath (Matt 14:7); to grant a promise (Acts 7:17); to confess sins (1 John 1:9); to confess as did John that he is not the Christ (John 1:20); to acknowledge the existence of spirits (Acts 23:8), that one is a stranger or alien in a land (Heb 11:13); and Jesus acknowledging a person before God (Matt 10:32; Luke 12:8) or his acknowledging a faithful person's name before the Father (Rev 3:5).

42. Also to acknowledge Jesus as the Christ and be expelled from a synagogue (John 9:22); to acknowledge faith before antagonists (John 12:42); Paul acknowledging before Felix that he is a follower of the way (Acts 24:14); to acknowledge rather than deny the Son (1 John 2:23); to acknowledge that Jesus has come in the flesh (1 John 4:2; 2 John 7) while a spirit that does not acknowledge him is not from God but is antichrist (1 John 4:3); and to acknowledge Jesus is the Son of God (1 John 4:15).

refers to his profession of faith at baptism.[43] In Titus 1:16, it is used of people falsely professing to know God, but denying him with their works.

Here, it has the common NT sense referred to above whereby a person verbally (mouth) confesses, professes, or acknowledges that Jesus is Lord. The aorist could lead to seeing this as the initial profession, perhaps at baptism or worship.[44] Such an interpretation makes sense, but in perfective aspectual terms, the aorist can speak of a whole life given over to such an acknowledgment.[45] So, it includes the initial profession of faith and continuing to do so in all situations, especially where a person faces antagonism for one's faith. As Dunn says,

> As a "slogan of identification" it would no doubt be used at baptism, but also much more widely in worship (1 Cor 12:3), evangelism (2 Cor 4:5), and parenesis (Col 2:6).[46]

The confession "Jesus is Lord" is the central profession of the early Christians (1 Cor 12:3; Phil 2:11). In Jewish circles, this is controversial because Yahweh alone is Lord, Jesus is a false claimant.

In the Roman world, Caesar is lord, and there are many deities whose lordship is also recognized. Indeed, the formula *Kaisara despotēn homologeō* ("profess Caesar is supreme ruler" [translation mine]) was demanded of rebels as an essential oath of loyalty. In *Jewish Wars*, Josephus refers to Egyptian Sicarii, who were forced to say this but refused under torture (*J.W.* 7.418). Intriguingly, Paul was accused of being their leader in Rome (Acts 21:37–38).[47] Later, in the Pliny-Trajan exchange, this demand became the means of deciding whether a Christian should die or not (Pliny the Younger, *Ep.* 10.96–97).[48]

To be a Christian is to be prepared to admit, acknowledge, confess, or profess at all times and in all situations that Jesus is the exclusive Lord of the world. Jesus and Paul give space to other political and familial allegiances (13:1–7; Eph 5:21—6:9); however, they are all subordinate to Christ's lordship, and obedience to him is primary (see further part three, chapter 11).

The second part of the protasis to "believe in your heart that God raised him from the dead." Here, to believe is not a general trust or confidence in God or Jesus but means to accept as true or be sure of something particular: that God raised Jesus

---

43. See Marshall and Towner, *Critical and Exegetical Commentary*, 661.

44. Käsemann, *Romans*, 291.

45. Porter, *Idioms*, 21: "*Perfective aspect is the meaning ('semantics') of the aorist tense: the action is conceived of by the language user as a complete and undifferentiated process. This is regardless of how in actual fact the action occurs, that is, whether it is momentary or lasts a significant length of time.*" (Emphasis original).

46. Dunn, *Romans 9–16*, 607.

47. Jewett and Kotansky, *Romans*, 629. He also states, "The acclamation "Lord Jesus!" was a very early expression of allegiance to Christ, as the parallels in Phil 2:11; 1 Cor 1:2 and 12:3 indicate."

48. Ford, "Pliny the Younger."

The Power of Salvation

from the dead. The resurrection of Jesus is the central aspect of belief. Faith in his resurrection presupposes that one believes in the God of the biblical story, in Jesus, that he died, and that God raised him.

Notably, it is a belief "in your heart (*kardia*)." *Kardia* here is not to be distinguished from the mind as if it is just a feeling of the affections or passions; instead, it is used in the sense of the "seat of physical, spiritual and mental life."[49] One wholeheartedly believes that God raised Jesus. It seems that Paul here renders variants of the Christian faith false, such as Protestant liberalism that rejects the resurrection of Christ.

We can also see here the link between internal faith and outward profession. Both are required. Dunn states, "Inward belief and outward expression of the word [are] inextricably linked, the two sides of one coin."[50] So Lenski rightly draws out the implication: "True faith is never silent; it always confesses."[51] Cottrell, similarly, proffers that "faith without confession is simply unthinkable."[52]

Verse 10 continues the emphasis on belief and profession. With the heart (mind and inner being),[53] a person believes. At that moment of faith, she or he is justified. That person confesses, professes, or acknowledges this with the mouth, i.e., verbally, and openly. That person is saved. These are not two separate events, but the point of full acknowledgment with mind, heart, and mouth. As noted above, while this includes baptism,[54] this profession transcends this one moment that is integral to the launching of the Christian life. As Morris says, "We need not doubt that such a confession was made at baptism, but it cannot have been confined to it."[55]

So, one believes and acknowledges from that first day to one's final breath and is justified and saved before God. In fact, such a statement challenges *all* believers to acknowledge their faith as they encounter unbelievers.

In verse 11, to support the link between faith and salvation, Paul again reaches into the Jewish Scriptures drawing on the final clause of Isaiah 28:16, a verse he used in 9:33 to support his preceding statements (see also 1 Pet 2:6). Isaiah 28:16 speaks of

---

49. BDAG 508.

50. Dunn, *Romans 9–16*, 609.

51. Lenski, *Interpretation of St. Paul's Epistle to the Romans*, 655.

52. Cottrell, *Romans: Volume 2*, "Saving Righteousness Comes through Trusting Christ's Works, Not Our Own (10:6–10)."

53. "As a rule, the term denotes the center of intellectual and spiritual life, the inner life in opposite to external appearance. . . . The powers of the spirit, reason, and will, as well as the movements of the soul—the feelings, the passions, the instincts—have their seat in the heart. One may say that the heart stands for the individual ego: it is simply the person (cf. 1 Pet 3:4, ὁ κρυπτὸς τῆς καρδίας ἄνθρωπος, lit., "the hidden man of the heart" [NIV and NRSV, "inner self"])." *NIDNTTE* 2:625.

54. Many find here a credal statement.

55. Morris, *Epistle to the Romans*, 385.

God laying a precious tested cornerstone as a sure foundation of Zion. In the original setting, this has a range of meanings.[56]

For many Jews, this is a messianic prediction.[57] For Paul, Jesus is that Messiah. The citation here is very close to the LXX,[58] stating that "everyone who believes (*pisteuō*) in him will not be put to shame" (*kataischynō*). "Shame" here is used in the eschatological sense and speaks of judgment, at which time the believer will not experience shame (see also 1 Cor 1:27; Phil 1:20).[59] Instead, they will be blessed with honor, glory, immortality, and peace (2:7, 10, cf. 5:5). This promise resonates with Mark 8:38 and parallels where Jesus is unashamed before the Father of those who unashamedly profess him as Christ.[60] Paul is this type of believer, stating in 1:16 that he is unashamed of the gospel. Jesus has taken the believer's shame on himself in the cross (cf. Heb 12:2). Inverted, God honors those who honor his Son.[61] This latter idea is drawn out in Peter's use of Isaiah 28:16—"the honor is for you who believe" (1 Pet 2:7).

In verse 12, Paul states again that God shows no favoritism between Jew and Greek. Unlike 1:14, where Greeks are distinguished from Barbarians, "Greek" (*Hellēn*) here has the inclusive sense of every person who is not a Jew, i.e., a gentile (cf. 1:16; 2:9, 10; 3:9).[62] "Lord" here can be God or Jesus. In favor of "Lord" here indicating God is that God is clearly in view in the OT quote.[63] Yet, commonly, Paul substitutes Jesus for God in OT texts. Furthermore, he has just emphasized the confession "Jesus is Lord." Hence, this is most likely Jesus.[64] Still, the difference is minimal, for God is exercising his reign through his Son, so if Jesus enriches those who call in him, God does so through him.

Assuming this is Jesus, he is Lord over both Jew and Greek, the same Lord of all. As in the profession, "Jesus is Lord," he, rather than Caesar and the gods, rules over

---

56. See Smith, *Isaiah 1–39*, 487 who notes these options: "(a) the cornerstone of the temple building; (b) the law of God; (c) the faithful people who were the pillars of the community; (d) Jerusalem, God's chosen dwelling place; or (e) the Davidic monarch (like Hezekiah)." He argues that the best option is "(f) to understand God and his promises as the secure foundation of the nation." He notes that while the Hebrew has anomalies and appears to be best translated "has established," documents in Qumran suggest that it should be read "surely I am establishing/will establish."

57. "Other 'stone' references in the OT would almost certainly attract messianic interpretation in Jewish circles, particularly Dan 2:34. . . . And at Qumran, Isa 28:16 was taken as referring to "the council of the community" (1QS 8:7; cf. 1QH 6:26–27). Dunn, *Romans 9–16*, 584.

58. The LXX has the double negative *ou mē*, whereas Paul just has *ou*. Paul also adds *pas*, "everyone" which emphasizes what is already present in the LXX.

59. Dunn, *Romans 9–16*, "It means that the one who puts his faith in Christ will be vindicated in the judgment."

60. See also Heb 2:11; 11:16; 1 Pet 1:7.

61. See also 1:21 where sinful humankind does not honor God. Compare John 12:26. See also John 5:23, where those who honor the Son, honor the Father.

62. See also Rom 3:29; 9:24. Mounce, *Romans*, 210–11 observes: "God does not have alternate methods of salvation for groups from diverse ethnic backgrounds."

63. See, e.g., Gaston, *Paul and the Torah*, 131.

64. See, e.g., Moo, *Letter to the Romans*, 678.

all humankind. It is an absolute statement. Jesus rules over all people, the godly and ungodly; however, this does not mean they know it nor that their fates are identical. Those who believe in the risen Jesus and recognize and acknowledge his lordship receive the Spirit and eternal life (5:5; 6:23). Others remain in sin and death, under wrath, and await eternal destruction.[65]

As the Lord, he enriches (*plouteō*) those who call on him. This promise is not prosperity theology—Paul's theology of inevitable suffering rules that out (5:3; 8:17–18)[66]—but the spiritual blessing of his people. Although being God's Son, with all the riches that entails, Jesus assumed material poverty, so that through his poverty to the point of death, believers may become spiritually enriched in him in the present, and prosperous in every way in the eschaton (2 Cor 8:9). Believers share the blessing of Christ (15:29). David sang of this blessedness based on faith in Psalm 32:1–2, which Paul refers to in 4:7–9. In the gospel-era, gentiles are sharing in this blessedness with the remnant of Israelite Christ-followers (15:27). These riches include the presence of God with the believer by the Spirit, to be fully realized in the eschaton.

As discussed in part two, chapter 11, calling on God is the right response of a believer who professes Jesus as Lord. Calling on God is found across Israel's writings as "a technical expression for praying and expressing allegiance to God or Christ."[67] Paul uses Joel 2:32 EVV (3:5 LXX) to speak of doing so as the right response that brings salvation.

In Romans 10:14–15a, Paul moves into diatribe, asking a series of four questions that can be raised by an interlocutor to query his argument for righteousness by faith. They overlap, and so form a sorites in which the questions end with a verb that begins the next question.[68] In context, "they" refers to Israel in particular and so virtually reads, "How can Israel call on him . . ." However, the passage has universal application to all contexts now that Christ has come. The same principles apply without distinction to everyone, Jew and Greek, who call on the name of the Lord. So, those in Spain who have yet to hear the gospel cannot be expected to call on Jesus, for he has not yet been named there (15:20–24). This challenges readers to join Paul in taking the gospel to them to initiate mission to other yet-unreached places. It should summon modern Christian readers to ongoing mission in the same way.

---

65. See 1:18; 2:5; 5:9; 9:22.

66. See also Paul's ironic critique of the Corinthians who claim to be rich in the present when presently suffering is to be expected, and such blessings are for the eschaton (1 Cor 4:8). Similarly, Paul challenges those who seek riches that this ends in destruction (1 Tim 6:9). See also Rev 3:17–18.

67. Jewett and Kotanksy, *Romans*, 633.

68. See earlier on "Rhetorical Devices," in part two, chapter 7. See also Spence-Jones, *Romans*, 294. Paul also uses a sorites in Romans 5:3–5. Keener, *Romans*, 71. See note 4, where he includes a number of examples from Greek writings including Jewish Greek sources: Wis 6:17–20; Sipre Deut. 161.1.3; b. 'Abod. Zar. 20b. Jewett and Kotansky, *Romans*, 635 also notes that: "This series of four rhetorical questions opens a powerful syllogism, starting with the presence of saving faith and moving chronologically backwards through hearing, preaching, and sending of preachers."

Recalling Romans 8:30, the questions neatly overlap and begin by picking up this emphasis on calling on God in verses 12–13. They work backward from calling on God to someone sent to preach. They "invite a crescendo of negative responses from the audience: 'It is impossible!'"[69] They also reverse the sequence of missional sending. The purpose is to move from Israel's failure to call out to Christ the Lord for his salvation to God's sending of people to preach to them.

Paul begins with the logical inferential conjunction, *oun*, here meaning, "so then . . . " Each subsequent question begins with *pōs de*, which can be consecutive "and how," or adversative, "but how . . . " The latter brings out the strength of each of the interlocutor's questions better.

The first asks: "How then can they call on him in whom they have not believed?" As noted above, to call on God or Christ is to worship him. However, "him" (*hon*) is Christ, not God, as it was a given that all Jews would call on Yahweh. Similarly, non-Jews would call on any number of deities (e.g., 1 Kgs 18:14, 25; Matt 4:10), but balked at the exclusive worship of Jesus (e.g., John 5:18; 8:58; 10:31). So, how can Israel possibly worship Jesus as Lord if they have not believed in him as such? Indeed, they should not! Exclusive worship of Yahweh is axiomatic to their existence, enshrined in the first commandments to have no other gods and bow down to any images (Exod 20:2–3; Deut 5:6–8). The Shema recited everyday declares God is one, and he is to be loved wholeheartedly (Deut 6:4–5). They do not believe in Jesus, so of course, they refuse to worship him. However, for Paul, who used to think the same; sadly, they err by failing to do so.

The second question overlaps, beginning with *pisteuō* giving the verb prominence, and poses the question of whether they have heard of Jesus the Lord: "but how can they believe in him of whom they have never heard?" (my translation). The immediate answer is that it is impossible to believe in something about which they know nothing. Still, Paul is tacitly asking whether they have heard of Jesus, something he will deal with in verse 18. The link between believing and hearing is essential to Paul's missiology, as he will make connection explicit in verse 17.

Question three overlaps picking up the verb *akouō*, "hear," asking: "but how are they to hear without someone preaching?" (my translation). Again, one cannot hear without someone communicating the message to them. If believing comes from hearing, then this presupposes someone preaches the message of the gospel audibly so that it can be heard.[70] In context, he is effectively asking whether someone has gone to Israel to preach to them so that they can hear and believe (again, see v. 18; the answer, "yes"). Again, the principle holds for all evangelism: someone communicates (preach), people receive (hear), they believe (or do not do so, as in the case of hardened Israel

---

69. Jewett and Kotansky, *Romans*, 637.

70. With the advent of technologies such as the printing press, clearly one could substitute "read" here or even "watch." Indeed, Romans is a letter written through which the gospel can heard. Still, someone has to be "sent to write the material or create the digital material for people to "hear."

and gentile rejectors). The Romans are implicitly summoned into the task of ensuring the evangelization of all people so that the full number of gentiles and Jews can come in (11:12, 25).

The final question creates the final chain in the evangelistic sequence: "But how can they preach unless they are sent?" (my translation). They cannot! Someone preaching the gospel presupposes that someone sends them. In the case of the Christian message, people are sent from God and Christ. Paul is asking whether anyone has been sent to Israel by God to preach to them so that they can hear, believe, and call on the name of Jesus Christ as Lord. In verse 18, he will emphatically state that they have. Again, the principle holds for evangelism, and so an evangelistic sequence is created. The diagram below shows the sequence found in Romans 10.

The Sequence of Evangelism

Evangelistic mission requires a sender and a person sent. They find people and preach. The gospel is heard. Hearers either believe or reject the message. By the Spirit, the one who believes cries out to God "Abba, Father" (8:15; Gal 4:5), confesses Christ's lordship (10:9–10), and calls on his name (10:13).

This sequence of questions highlights the critical necessity for gospel preachers in *every* context. Preachers are *always* required to proclaim God's gospel and reinforce it in fresh and creative ways, strengthening God's people for the many challenges of faith. Such evangelists are required in every pulpit of every church in the world (the intra-church aspect of evangelism). Equally, gospel preachers are required with the skill of reaching those who are yet to believe in God (what is commonly called "evangelism," but is merely the outward-facing aspect of the evangelism task). Such people can be Billy Graham-like proclaimers to the multitudes, Timothy Keller-like preachers in huge churches, people who welcome small groups or individuals into their company and share Christ with them, or those who correct a straying Christian or who bring home a lost sheep. There is no status differentiation in God's mission.

In verse 15b, Paul again turns to the OT with a kind of parenthetical exclamation that highlights the principle that God has sent people to preach his "good news" in the past, and it is a beautiful thing. The particular text is Isaiah 52:7: "How lovely are the feet of those who preach the good news" (my translation). The term for "lovely" (or "beautiful") is *hōraios*, from *hōra*, "hour," and can mean "timely."[71] However, the original Hebrew term is *nā·' ā(h)*, which in the Qal means "be beautiful" in the sense of "lovely, fitting."[72] Furthermore, *hōriaos* is overwhelmingly used in Jewish Greek literature of something beautiful, pleasant, lovely, or delightful.[73] Hence, as Schreiner says, "here it means 'beautiful' which is what the Hebrew word נָאווּ (*nā'wû*) means in Isa. 52:7."[74]

The verb "to be" (are) is required. "The feet of those who preach the good news" uses the plural of *pous* (feet) as synecdoche,[75] whereby the feet of the preacher are representative of the whole person traveling with the good news. Using feet is entirely appropriate, for, in Paul's and Isaiah's world, communiqués were carried by couriers from sender to recipient. By such people, the gospel advances (Phil 1:12) and races to the world (2 Thess 3:1). Feet are generally not beautiful, especially in the ancient world where they did not have the footwear that we have today that protects our feet. However, the gnarled and hard feet and person of an ancient gospel communicator is still a beautiful thing because of the beauty of the news conveyed.

The good news is the verb, the middle of *euangelizō*, and a verb in its own right, *euangelizomai*. In the Greek and Roman traditions, the herald (*euangelos*) transmitted the good news to the people of the empire, and it was received with grand celebrations and joy.[76] In the OT, it has that same sense of a courier taking good news.[77]

In the original context, it is the prophet Isaiah declaring God's coming victory, when Babylon will fall to Cyrus and Medo-Persia, and God's people are released to return to their land.[78] In a world where religion and politics were fused, it speaks of a

---

71. E.g., Jewett and Kotansky, *Romans*, 640; Fitzmyer, *Romans*, 598.

72. *DBL Hebrew* #5533.

73. Uses include: Lovely vegetation or produce (Gen 2:9; 3:6; Lev 23:40; 2 Macc 10:7; Ps 64:13; Joel 1:19, 20; Jer 11:16; 1 En 24:5; T. Levi 8:16; Jos. Asen. 2:19; 4:4; Liv. Pro. 4:3; *Ant.* 2.64; *Sac.* 25), Eden itself (Odes Sol. 11:16), a beautiful or lovely person (Gen 26:7, 17; 39:6; 2 Kgdms 1:23; 3 Kgdms 1:6; Jdt 8:7; Ps 44:3; Song 1:16; 6:4; Sir 25:1; Isa 63:1; 1 En 6:1; T. Sim. 5:1; T. Jos. 9:5; T. Sol. 26:5; Jos. Asen. 1:6, 8; *Ant.* 6.296; 19.33; *Leg.* 1.56, 58; 3.177) or bodily features (Song 2:14; 4:3; Job 18:13), speech (Song 6:7), something desirable or lovely (1 Kgdms 9:20; 1 Esdr 4:18, 19), praise (Sir 15:9), wise judgment (Sir 25:4–5), lovely vessels (2 Chr 36:19), beautiful feet of a construction (Sir 26:18; *Ant.* 12.65), God's mercy (Sir 35:24), a rainbow (Sir 43:11), beautiful things Aaron brought (Sir 45:13), beautiful dwellings (Lam 2:2), Rome (Sib. Or. 8:124), gates (3 Bar. Pro. 2), heavenly beings and spirits (3 Bar. 9:6; T. Reu. 3:4; T. Ab. (A) 16:6), Israel (T. Jos. 18:4), lovely temple curtains (*Ant.* 3.126), beautiful things in a city (*Ant.* 8.153). It is possibly used of something timely in Sir 20:1, although "pleasant" also fits the context. It can have the sense "ripe" (Josephus, *Ant.* 2.83; 4.65, 234, 241; *Spec.* 2.250), although that could equally mean pleasing to eat or timely.

74. Schreiner, *Romans*, 568.

75. *PDSNTG* 119 notes that synecdoche is "figure of speech whereby a more inclusive term is used for a less inclusive term, or vice versa." So, for example, in "all hands on deck," "hands" refers to the whole person.

76. Friedrich, "Εὐαγγελίζομαι," 2:710–12; O'Brien, *Consumed with Passion*, 77–80.

77. Friedrich, "Εὐαγγελίζομαι, 2:708–10.

78. In 1 Kgdms 31:9; 2 Kgdms 1:20; 4:10, it is used of "good news" to the Philistines of Saul's death. Otherwise it is the "good news" of Absalom's death (2 Kgdms 18:19, 20, 26, 31; 1 Chr 10:9); the "good

The Power of Salvation

political, military, and religious victory. Now, for Paul, Christ, the Lord of the cosmos, has won the victory over the real forces that rail against humankind—sin, decay, death, and eternal destruction—and people with "lovely feet" are proclaiming this beautiful message throughout the world. The defeat of death and consequent hope of resurrection and eternal life is a beautiful thing then, and it remains so now. The gospel here is "the good things" (*ta agatha*).[79] The use of this general term for "good" speaks of the range or good things for this life and the life to come that the gospel declares.

With the stronger of the usual adversatives, *alla* (rather than *de*), verse 16 abruptly declares Israel's problem: "but not all have obeyed the gospel" (my translation). Put another way; they have not responded with "the obedience of faith" (1:5; 16:26). "They," here, is first and foremost, the people of Israel. Yet, again it can have a general impact as people rejected the message in the ancient Roman world and subsequently across the generations. A large portion of Israel has not called on the name of the Lord and experienced his salvation. They refuse to believe Jesus has been raised from the dead nor acknowledge his cosmic lordship.

Paul, in verse 16, again turns to Isaiah, who says, "Lord, who believed what they heard from us?" (my translation). This quote is from the fourth of Isaiah's servant passages (Isa 52:13—53:12). By choosing Isaiah 53:1, as does John in John 12:38, Paul brilliantly cuts to the heart of Israel's failure. The passage speaks of a suffering servant who dies for the sins of the nation and yet is vindicated. While Israel *did not* associate the servant of Isaiah with the Messiah before and in the first century AD,[80] for Paul and the early Christians, this servant is Jesus, who is the Messiah, Son of God, and Lord (cf. 15:8, 21).[81]

---

news" of Solomon's coronation (3 Kgdms 1:42); the "good news" of righteousness amongst God's people (Ps 39:10 [40:9 Heb]); women giving the "good news" of enemies fleeing (Ps 67:12 [68:11 Heb 7 Heb]); the "good news" of the birth of a child (Jer 20:15); and as here, a prophetic proclamation of God's triumph (Joel 3:5; Nah 2:1; Isa 40:9; 52:7; 60:6; 61:1). See also Pss. Sol. 11:1.

79. While a range of texts lacks the article, it is likely original as it is found in important MSS, 𝔓 46 ℵ* D1 K L Ψ 33.

80. Bailey notes that the two main candidates in Isaiah for the Servant "are the exiled nation of Israel or an anonymous individual, the prophet whom modern scholarship knows as Second Isaiah." He goes on: "The motif of vicarious suffering in Isaiah 53 was enormously influential in Christian tradition, which applied it to the ministry and passion of Jesus (e.g., Rom 4:25; 1 Cor. 15.3b)." While he finds some echoes in Dan 12:3b; Wis 5:2-6; 4Q491c Frag. 1 (= 4Q491 Frag. 11); 1QH^a 12:22-23; 1 En. 38:2-3; 39:6-7; 48:1; etc., he rightly says: "*In pre-Christian Judaism, however, Isaiah 53 was not understood in terms of vicarious suffering*" (emphasis mine). While the *Targum of Isaiah* (second century BC) links the Servant to the Messiah (Tg. Isa. 52:13; cf. 53:10; 42:1 mss.; 43:10), he states: "The targum, however, rejects the notion of a *suffering* Messiah. Vicarious sin-bearing is reserved for the Gentiles (53:8), or indeed for the Temple itself, which was 'handed over' for Israel's iniquities (53:5). The singular 'man of sorrows' applies collectively to the Gentile nations (Tg. Isa. 53:3). Other statements of individual suffering are also read collectively, recast as plural, and applied to the members of the house of Israel (Tg. Isa. 52:14; 53:4; 53:10)." Bailey, "Suffering Servant," 1257-58.

81. See, e.g., Matt 8:17; 12:18-21; Mark 1:11; 10:45 and parr.; Luke 2:29-32; 9:35; 22:20; John 3:14; 8:28; 12:32; Acts 3:13, 26; 4:27, 30; 8:32-33; 13:47; Rom 5:16; Phil 2:7; 1 Tim 2:6; 1 Pet 2:23-25.

Unlike Israel, "Gentiles will see and understand the message about the suffering servant of the Lord" (Isa 53:13-15).[82] Contrastingly, Jews at the time could not associate this figure with the Messiah for the Servant was a prophet, Isaiah himself, or Israel. This text predicts such unbelief, and it has come to pass, as has the death of the Servant and his vindication to achieve God's purposes. For Christians, the Servant figure is the dominant OT text for understanding a crucified Messiah, a stumbling block for the Jews. Paul once saw Jesus this way; now, he is unashamed of the gospel (1:16) and shapes his life on Christ's example (Phil 3:10).

Verse 17 concludes.

> "Therefore (*ara*) faith (*hē pistis*) is from hearing (*akouē*), and (*de*) hearing (*hē akoē*) is through (*dia*) the word (*rhēma*) of Christ" (my translation).

Here, "hearing," is not merely "listening to," but is more akin to the Jewish notion of šā·măʿ, a verb that carries the sense of "hearing, understanding, *and heeding*." So then, Paul is speaking of people hearing, understanding, and experiencing faith burst forth in their hearts and minds causing them to yield to God as they hear the gospel, so that they profess his lordship and call on his name.

In Romans, since Abraham, faith has activated God's declaration "justified" over a person. Hence, a person, gentile or Jew (remembering Abraham was a gentile at the moment of faith and justification, cf. 4:9–12), before hearing the message of Christ, is justified by faith in God as God has revealed himself to that person. Abraham's justification by faith raises the possibility that other gentiles from God's world have been justified by faith, even if under other religious systems. They are not justified by participation in their cult or the works expected of them in their religious law (any more than a person today is justified by participating in church life), but by their faith in the one true God. Before his call, Abraham was probably a polytheist (Gen 31:19–35; Josh 24:2, 14) including belief in El, a generic Semitic term of divinity found at Ugarit and the head of the Canaanite pantheon.[83] However, based on his faith in God-revealed, he is justified by faith by Yahweh (4:3). Similarly, Melchizedek served the "God (El) Most High" and is considered by the writer of Hebrews to be superior to Abraham.[84]

However, where Jesus as Christ, Son of God, Son of Man, God's Servant, and Lord, crucified, risen, and exalted, has been proclaimed and the message heard; the hearer is justified by faith in *him*, Jesus, God-revealed. Rejection of him is a rejection of the one who sent him (God, cf. Luke 10:16), and the declaration of justification is not heard, salvation is not received. Hearing the gospel *generates* faith. This work is from the Spirit, who empowers the message, akin to God plunging a sword into an

---

82. Schreiner, *Romans*, 570.

83. Backlund, "El, Deity."

84. See Gen 14:18; Ps 110:4; Heb 5:6, 10; 6:20; 7:1–17. In the NT, other examples include those named in Luke's genealogy prior to Abraham (Luke 3:34–38); Abel, Enoch, Noah, and Lot (Matt 23:35; 24:37–38; Luke 11:51; 17:26–29; Heb 11:4–7; 12:24; 1 Pet 3:20; 2 Pet 2:5, 7; Jude 14), and their families.

The Power of Salvation

enemy. The word cuts the heart and mind (Eph 6:17). Where it is rejected, that person remains "perishing" (1 Cor 1:18).

The link between hearing and faith is found elsewhere in Paul. Twice in Galatians 3:1–5, Paul reminds the Galatians that they received the Spirit and saw God work miracles among them because of "the hearing of faith," which has the sense, "believing what they heard" (Gal 3:2, 5).[85]

In Ephesians 1:13–14, we see a neat sequence of salvation in his description of the conversion of his recipients:

> and you were included in Christ when you heard the word of truth, the gospel of your salvation, in which you believed and were sealed with the promised Holy Spirit (NIV).

Here the sequence can be outlined.

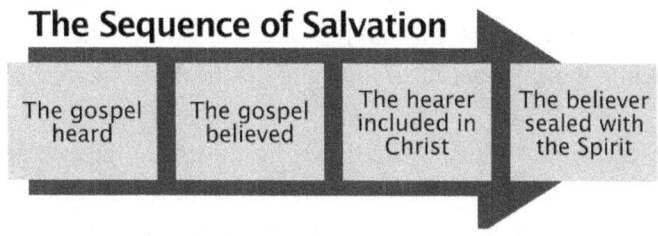

The Sequence of Salvation

Figure 1 The Sequence of Salvation

When we blend this with Romans 10:9–14, it yields a fuller picture:

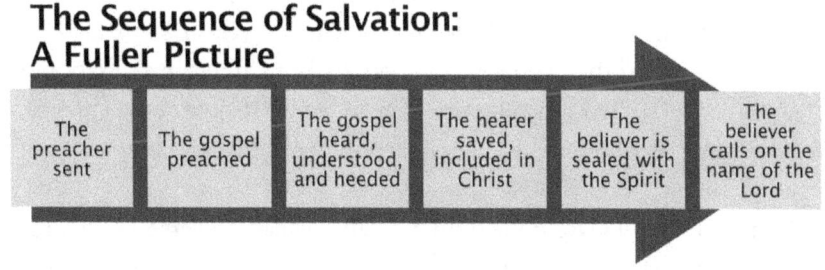

The Sequence of Salvation: A Fuller Picture

Figure 2 The Full Sequence of Mission

---

85. See Moo, *Galatians*, 183, who discusses the genitive phrase *akoēs pisteōs*. While the phrase may mean "hearing of the faithful one," it almost certainly refers to human faith. *Akoē* can mean "what is heard," or "the message." It can be an objective genitive, "the message that evokes faith," loosely attributive yielding "believing what you heard" or attributive of a "hearing" that "involves" faith or that is "accompanied by faith" (attributive genitive), or, "the 'hearing' that Christians call faith."

197

Part Three: Romans and the Proclamation of the Gospel

Paul, then, understands conversion as a *moment* of hearing, comprehending, and believing. In that instant, God pours his Spirit into the heart. Such a momentary view of conversion does not preclude a process in the life of the person converted as God engages with that person in the lead-up to the moment. This can be through spiritual experiences and encounters with Christians that have prepared that person for conversion. Such engagement could include love and other godly attitudes, good deeds (e.g., acts of justice), and gospel-sharing. Nor does it mean that faith comes at the exact moment of hearing. Conversion could come later, as one ruminates on the message preached (even multiple times to the same person). Yet, it appears that Paul understands conversion to come when faith is birthed through the hearing of the message.

In what follows in 10:18, Paul resumes his diatribe, posing another question from his imaginary interlocutor. He asks whether Israel has heard the gospel. He answers with the emphatic particle *menounge*,[86] "indeed!" The world that has yet to hear the gospel is without excuse because God's glory is displayed in creation for them to observe (1:20).

However, unlike the wider world, Israel *has* heard the gospel, and so is even more culpable (as are people today who have heard the gospel and rejected it). Jesus has been sent to them, has preached throughout the land, and was rejected and killed. Apostles and others, like Stephen and Philip, empowered by the Spirit, have preached in Jerusalem, all Judea, and Samaria (Acts 1:8—12:25). Apostles and others have taken the gospel to diaspora Jews across the world, as in Rome.[87] However, aside from a remnant chosen by grace (11:6), they have been rejected. Indeed, Paul himself had opposed them seeking their imprisonment and had driven them from the city (Acts 8:1–3). Paul the Christian had returned to preach in Jerusalem, and he too had been expelled.[88] Others remained in the city ministering (Gal 1:8-19; 2:7-10). Right up to AD 57, Jesus's brother James and others had remained in the city preaching Christ (Acts 21:18). In a few years, he would be killed for it (Josephus, *Ant.* 20.9). Still, most rejected the gospel. However, this rejection is not because they had not heard the gospel.

In Romans 10, Paul gives none of that detail. Instead, in verse 18, he draws on a catena of four OT texts to make his point. First, he cites Psalm 19:4, a verse focused on the voice of God spoken through the heavenly bodies: "Their voice has gone out to all the earth, and their words to the ends of the world." Prior to Christ, God spoke

---

86. BDAG 630. *Menoun, men oun, menounge,* and *menounge* are particles primarily used in answers to questions "to emphasize or correct." Here, it is emphatic, "indeed!" (cf. Phil 3:8). In Romans 9:30, it is an emphatic "but."

87. See for examples of people traveling with the gospel, e.g., Rom 16:1–16; Acts 2:8–11; 8:4; 18:2, 18, 24—19:1; 20:4; 1 Cor 1:12; 3:4–6, 22; 4:6; 9:5; 16:12, 16, 19; Gal 2:1–9; Col 4:7–17; 2 Tim 4:19–21; Phlm 23–24; 1 Pet 1:1; Jas 1:1; 2 Pet 3:2; Jude 17.

88. See Gal 1:18–19; 2:1–10; Acts 9:26–30.

to the nations through the creation and where he chose to reveal himself with special revelation (1:19–20). Now, he speaks to the nations through his missionaries.

This verse can be misread to think Paul is stating that the mission is complete (see the previous chapter).[89] However, this speaks of the activity that is underway and will continue in his ministry and others that will follow until the world has heard.[90] What it does declare is that Israelites who have rejected the revelation of God in Christ, his Servant, are no better than pagan humanity in rejection of God their Creator.[91]

Another question from his interlocutor follows in 10:19: "But I ask, did Israel not understand?"[92] Here, Paul states directly who the "they" have been through the section: Israel. Clearly, some did believe, for he himself is an Israelite (11:1) as were all from the first generation of believers. Still, most Israelites clearly did not understand. For if they had, they would surely have heard and heeded, faith would have been born, and God would have declared them righteous through Jesus. They would have professed his lordship and called on his name and been saved.

Still, again, Paul says none of this. Instead, he cites Deuteronomy 32:21. The passage falls in the Song of Moses. In Deuteronomy 32:7–14, Moses sings of Israel's election and God's blessing and protection of her. In Deuteronomy 32:15–18, Israel rebelled with complacency and idolatry. Their rebellion led to Israel's punishment as his children, including a foolish nation making them angry and jealous. Paul appropriates this part of the song, adapts its language, and applies it to the nations who are coming to Christ, causing Israel's anger and jealousy (11:11, 14). History is being repeated with Israel still in spiritual exile as she has rejected her Messiah.[93] Israel simply does not understand what God is doing through Jesus and in the nations. Paul yearns that they will become jealous and convert (11:11, 14).

---

89. "Thus he sees himself close to the goal envisioned in Mark 13:10, and with it to the parousia." Käsemann, *Romans*, 296.

90. "His meaning is rather what Bruce calls 'representative universalism'; the gospel had been widely enough preached for it to be said that representatives of Judaism throughout the known world had heard it." Morris, *Epistle to the Romans*, 393. See Bruce, who links this to Col 1:5–27, 23, where Paul, on the one hand, says, the gospel has been proclaimed to every creature under heaven, yet sees the mission as incomplete. Bruce, *Epistle*, 209.

91. See Tennent, *World Missions*, 191–226 for a discussion of religions from an evangelical point of view. He suggests four views: 1) exclusivism or replacement/partial replacement; 2) inclusivism/new fulfillment; 3) pluralism or mutuality; 4) postmodern or acceptance. It is my view in Romans that Paul affirms an exclusivist view based on faith. First, where a person lives in a non-biblical religious paradigm but believes in that God as did Abraham, they will be justified by faith. Their religion is not the point, their faith in God is. God knows who these people are. Second, where a person has heard the gospel and genuinely believes in Jesus, that person is justified by faith. Positions 1) and 2) have merit.

92. The Greek is *gnōskō* here used with the sense "to grasp the significance or meaning of something, understand, comprehend" (BDAG 200 meaning 3).

93. "Even though Israel returns to the land, the New Testament finds a situation in which Israel remains in spiritual exile within the land, with the pious still yearning for the 'consolation of Israel' (Lk 2:25), the 'redemption of Jerusalem' (Lk 2:38)." Ryken et al., *DBL* 187.

He then cites Isaiah 65:1–2 in verses 20–21. In Isaiah, the passage heads an oracle of judgment against Israel. Paul sees the salvation of the gentiles in Christ as a fulfillment of God's declaration through the prophet that he would reveal himself and be found by those who did not seek him or ask after him. He concludes with the tragic statement that he has held out his arms all day to Israel, but they are a disobedient and contrary people. Preachers have been sent repeatedly, but Israel has not heeded them. A few have responded with faith and received justification and salvation. Most have refused to respond with the obedience of faith and have persecuted Christians. They are indeed a "disobedient and contrary people." Aside from a remnant, they remain so today.[94] Still, the gospel is for Jews and gentiles, and mission to Israel's people must continue.

Similarly, as I ruminate on these verses, I cannot help thinking about European cultures in recent years. Faithful Christians continue to share the gospel among the Europeans of the world. However, forgetting how God has been the spiritual power behind our dominance for centuries, and enamored with our scientific prowess and ignorant of our colonial mistakes, many of us in the West raised in the Christian faith have become a disobedient and contrary people. God's people in the West are summoned not to fall prey to this rebellious spirit. We are commanded to continue to proclaim to them. Sadly, I am not sure it will have much effect at this point in history. Some kind of suffering and exile may be required, perhaps. It could be that world events percolating as I write may be a factor in this and provoke a renewal. Who knows? But, may the people of the West (and all people) hear and heed God's message.

---

94. Two percent of Israeli Jews are Christian. Lipka, "7 Key Findings," para. 7.

16

Agents of Evangelism

JUST WHO PAUL IMAGINED doing evangelism is an ongoing debate in NT scholarship. Broadly speaking, there are two schools of thought. Some consider that he imagined the work being done only by specialists with the church supporting them with prayer and finance, and the church giving ethical and apologetic witness.[1] Others, including myself, argue that Paul envisaged the church doing these things but also, having been equipped by apostles and evangelists (Eph 4:11), having an active role in evangelization.[2] Romans is not devoted to the question of who does evangelism, but there is data that helps us answer the question for today.

GOD

First, undoubtedly God is the initiator and enactor of mission in the letter—the mission is indeed the *missio dei*.[3] For Paul in Romans, all things exist from, through, and to God (11:36). He gives witness to his glorious power and divine existence through creation so that failing to believe in him is inexcusable (1:19–20, cf. 4:17).

He is King, and the kingdom Jesus establishes is concerned about righteousness, peace, and joy in the Spirit, rather than minor issues like any particular food or

---

1. The fullest articulation of this is Dickson, *Mission-Commitment in Ancient Judaism*. See also Bowers, "Church and Mission in Paul," 89–111.

2. Key writings defending this position include Keown, *Congregational Evangelism in Philippians*; O'Brien, *Consumed with Passion*, also published as *Gospel and Mission in the Writings of Paul*; Köstenberger and O'Brien, *Salvation to the Ends of the Earth*, 191–299; Marshall, "Who Were the Evangelists?," 251–64; Schnabel, *Early Christian Mission*, 2:1451–65; Plummer, *Paul's Understanding* (see especially his literature review, pp. 1–42).

3. See Bosch, *Transforming Mission*, 289–93. "God is a missionary God" (p. 390); "the church is missionary by its very nature" (p. 391). He adds, "Mission is, primarily and ultimately, the work of the Triune God, Creator, Redeemer, and Sanctifier, for the sake of the world, a ministry in which the church is privileged to participate. Mission has its origin in the heart of God. God is a fountain of sending love. This is the deepest source of mission. It is impossible to penetrate deeper still; there is mission because God loves people" (p. 392).

Part Three: Romans and the Proclamation of the Gospel

special days (14:17). With the riches of his unsearchable and inscrutable wisdom and knowledge, God's will and purpose for good are exercised in creation. He works all things for his people who are called and loved (8:27–28; 9:19; 12:1). He foreknows and predestines all things (8:29), even where there is rejection (11:8). He has commanded that the mystery of his gospel is known to all nations to bring about the obedience of faith and thus a people for himself (16:26).

Even deeply flawed governments like the Roman imperium serve him and his purposes, exercising approval and wrath on his behalf (13:1–6). As an aspect of their mission, his people are to be submissive to the government, responding with blessing and not curse, good and not evil (12:14). God has subjugated the cosmos to death and consigned all to disobedience (11:32). Of course, he has done so to ensure sin, death, and evil do not live on forever, and he has, at the same time, provided salvation. He is patiently holding back his wrath for the day when he calls time.

The gospel is his (1:1; 15:16), and he empowers it to save (1:16). His righteousness and justice are revealed in it (1:17; 3:21). This righteousness is received as a status by grace and as a gift through faith in his Son Jesus (3:22, 24, 26). It is God who justifies (8:33). Those justified by faith are reconciled to God (5:1, 11) and have access to his grace (5:2). They are saved from the wrath of God (5:9, 11). God's grace abounds in Christ (5:15)

He promised the gospel through his prophets in the Scriptures (1:2), through which he speaks (9:25), and that are entrusted to Israel (3:2). His word has not failed but is fulfilled in Christ (9:6). His wrath is also revealed in it against sinful people (1:18). His wrath and severity will see some destroyed (9:22; 11:22) for vengeance is the Lord's (12:19).

However, Jesus is God's Son (1:3, 4; 8:29). Just as God gives sinful people over to their desires (1:24, 26, 28), he gave his Son over to death to bring them back to him (4:25; 8:32).[4] God sent him to condemn sin in his flesh (8:3). He did not spare Jesus but gave him up for believers (8:32). He put him forth as a propitiation for sins through his shed blood (3:25). God raised him (10:9) through his glory (6:4) by his Spirit (8:11).

God postpones "the full penalty due sins in the Old Covenant, allowing sinners to stand before him without their having provided an adequate 'satisfaction' for the demands of his holy justice" (3:25).[5] However, where there is faith in God before Christ, or in Christ, when the gospel is heard, he forgives sin (4:6). From all over the world, people become his children adopted into his great family (8:16, 19; 9:26). As his children, they are heirs to all things with Christ, after suffering for him to death (8:17, 32). His creation, which he subjugated to death and decay that evil would not be eternal (8:19), will be liberated into the same freedom (8:21).

---

4. Paul plays on the Greek *paradidōmi*, "give over." People are given over *to* their sins. Jesus is given over *for* our sins.

5. Moo, *Letter to the Romans*, 261.

His love, kindness, forbearance, patience, mercy, and faithfulness to his covenant promises motivate mission.[6] The giving of Jesus to die for sinners demonstrates this love (5:8). A believer cannot be separated from this love (8:35–39).

God has not rejected his people, but by grace, as in times past, he preserves a remnant, saving them from total destruction (9:29; 11:1–6). He does not spare those who reject him (11:21). However, he has the power to graft them back into his people if they believe in him (11:23).

He calls (1:7; 9:11, 24), and his summons is irrevocable (11:29). He is the source of grace and peace (1:7). He gives his Spirit to believers (8:9) and, by the Spirit, gives them gifts. As in the case of Paul, set apart as an apostle by grace, he gives missional gifts to grow his church.[7] His Spirit empowers mission (15:19). He is for his people (8:31) and enables them to conquer in all situations (8:37).

He is impartial in terms of the peoples of the world. All can come and are judged on the same basis, faith. He welcomes everyone that believes despite cultural and ethnic differences (14:3). Hence, mission must be genuinely multicultural and the church intercultural (2:11; 3:29). While people can legitimately have cultural differences (14:22–23), Paul warns severely against people who cause others to fall away through cultural prejudice. Believers are severely warned against racism, sexism, ageism, and all such elitist attitudes (14:20). God enables such cultural harmony (15:5).

Mission culminates in judgment where humankind is judged concerning their response to God's existence.[8] All will bow before him and give account (14:10–12). With impeccable justice (2:2; 3:5–6), he declares people righteous on the same basis: perfect fulfillment of the requirements of God (2:13). No human other than Christ has achieved this,[9] so all are accountable for their sins before him (3:19). Alternatively, they are justified not by works, but with a trust in God like Abraham's (4:1–6, 18–22). The same applies to Jew and gentile (4:10–16). Now that Christ has come and has been preached, this faith is directed toward his Son (3:21–25, 30) and the one who raised him from the dead (4:24).

God raises his people of faith from death (4:17), judges them innocent in Christ, and gifts them immortality and eternal life (2:7; 6:23; 8:11). He will liberate the cosmos from ungodliness, death, and decay (8:19–22; 11:26) and will crush Satan under his Son and his peoples' feet (16:20).

Alive to him, Christians live for God in everything with all they are and have (6:10–12). They serve him (6:22), including working in their particular vocations in him (1:9; 15:17). Such people are acceptable to him (14:18), bear fruit for him (7:4), and living rightly, they are led by his Spirit (8:14). They are to be knowledgeably zealous for him (10:2). They are to give themselves sacrificially as their logical worship

---

6. See 1:7; 2:3; 3:3; 8:37; 9:15–18; 11:22, 30, 33; 12:1; 15:9.
7. See 1:4; 11:29; 12:3–8; 15:15.
8. See 2:2, 3, 5–11, 16; 9:28.
9. See 3:11, 18, 20, 23; 8:7–8.

of him, ever transformed with renewed minds, living by his will (12:1–2). This transformed life is the missional calling of the people of God.

The goal of mission is people worshiping God, calling on his name, and the end of idolatries and the hatred of God.[10] He is worshiped as "Abba, Father" (8:15), and prayed to (1:8–10; 10:1), including missional prayer (15:30). Believers in Christ boast in God (5:11) and give him thanks (6:17; 7:25; 14:6). They accept what he has made them to be (9:20). His glory is to be honored by all nations forever (9:23; 15:6, 9; 16:27). People are to praise him with joy (15:10–11).

Finally, Gorman argues that a central theme of Romans is theosis—"becoming like God by participating in the life of God—and that theosis is inherently missional."[11] Mission then is participation in God's great mission, in Christ, and by the Spirit.

CHRIST

If God is the Missionary par excellence, Jesus is the central agent of God's mission. "The Son *is*, in person, the mission of God, in Israel and for the world."[12] Witherington rightly notes that in the "larger story of God," the "cosmic mission is also intertwined with the story of Christ as redeemer of humankind."[13] While it is God's gospel, it is as much Jesus's (1:9; 15:16).

Jesus is God's Son (1:3–4), sent by God (8:3), given to die to save people from sin, death, and wrath, and the cosmos from decay and death (8:3, 19–21, 32). He is the Son of David, the fulfillment of the messianic hopes of Israel (1:3). Jesus is Lord of the world; the living and the dead (14:9). Zion's deliverer has come to forgive sins and establish God's covenant with his people (11:26–27). Not only is he the Christ, but he is God (9:5).

Lost in sin, trapped in mortality and the inevitable destiny of death, people cannot save themselves. They are subject to wrath and destined for destruction. Jesus came to die for them in their hapless state (5:6, 8). He was raised and is Jesus Christ the Lord (1:4; 6:9; 8:11).

Righteousness is declared over all who believe in him (3:22, 26) and his Father, who raised him (4:24). These are those who confess his lordship and believe God raised him, who call on his name, and never face his shame (10:9–13). They call on his name (10:13). They are justified by his grace through his redemptive death (3:24). He came in the likeness of sinful flesh and condemned sin in his flesh as he died (8:3). God did not spare him but gave him for the world (8:32). His blood propitiates the wrath of God (3:25). Those justified by his blood (5:9) have peace with God and access to his grace (5:1–2). They are saved from wrath into his life (5:9–10). He is the new

---

10. See 1:21–22, 25, 30; 4:20; 10:13.
11. Gorman, *Becoming the Gospel*, 261.
12. Wright, "Reading the New Testament Missionally," 179. Emphasis original.
13. Witherington, "Christology," 105.

Adam, whose grace abounds in justification, salvation, and eternal life for many (5:15, 17).

Believers are baptized into his death and burial and will rise to a resurrection like his (6:3–6). They are crucified in him and set free from sin (6:6) to live for him (6:8). In Christ, they are dead to sin but alive to God (6:11). Moreover, they have died to the law (7:4), for he is the end of the law (10:4). They are free from condemnation set free from sin and death in him (8:1–2).

Those saved receive him by the Spirit and belong to him (1:6; 8:9–10). They receive eternal life through him (5:21; 6:23). He is the heir of the cosmos, and believers who share in his sufferings inherit the world with him (8:17, 32). Nothing can separate them from his love (8:35–39).

He is the supreme image of God (cf. Col 1:15), and believers are being transformed to be conformed to him, their big brother (8:29). Put another way; they are clothed in him, now repudiating works of unrighteousness (13:14). They live for him (14:8). They are to emulate his attitude of service, his refusal to live for himself, never to retaliate, and always to welcome others (15:3–8). Together, they form his body on earth, diverse, yet joined as one (12:5). This people are the churches of Christ (16:16).

He is the conduit for prayer to God (1:9) and worship (5:11). Astoundingly, he is God-facing on our behalf, his death always interceding for people's sin and Christ himself praying for us (8:34). God also judges by him (2:16). Nevertheless, they also call on him in prayer and worship (10:13). He is the object of thanksgiving (7:25), and God is glorified through him (16:27).

He sets apart people for mission, and they are his slaves (1:1). This is not coerced bondage as in human slavery, but voluntary submission because of the greatness and goodness of the one served. Mission is enacted for his name's sake (1:5). His people serve him in this gospel (1:9), as did Paul (15:16), and others (16:2, 8–10, 12). Sadly, some feign doing this but merely serve their own desires (16:18). However, God's missionaries are motivated to go to places where Jesus is not known and preach him (15:20; 16:25) so that converts are made (16:5). The things achieved in mission are done through and by him (15:17–18). They do so with a fervent Holy-Spirit zeal (12:11) and are acceptable to him (14:18). They are sent by him so that people hear of the good news of him, believe in him, and call on him (10:14–17). They know Jesus died for others and walk in love, seeking never to destroy them with their prejudices (14:15).

The *missio dei* is very much the *missio Christi*, "the mission of Christ." God is bringing the people of the nations into his family through the work of his Son.

PART THREE: ROMANS AND THE PROCLAMATION OF THE GOSPEL

THE SPIRIT

Robert Meye has correctly observed:

> Paul's proclamation of salvation and his instruction regarding the mission of God in the world is predicated on the understanding that the Holy Spirit, promised in the OT as a decisive aspect of the eschatological time of salvation, is powerfully at work in the world.[14]

As such, the *missio dei* is also the mission of the Spirit, although this dimension of the Spirit's work is not strongly highlighted in Romans or the other Pauline letters. It is Luke's writings where we find this highlighted.[15] Still, there is enough data to tell us that the mission of God and his Son is the *missio Spiritus*.

In Romans, it is the Spirit by whom God raised Jesus from the dead (1:4), showing the Spirit's divine power to bring life to the physically dead. The Spirit brings alive the believer, lost in sin and decay, destined for death and destruction. Hence, the Spirit is the power that unleashes what we call conversion.

A person believes, is justified, and instantaneously, God's love is poured from heaven into his or her heart (5:5). In that instant, as they are flooded with God's love and despite remaining in a dangerous world, fear is swept away as they are adopted as God's children with full rights. The Spirit of love cries out in and through their mental and speech faculties, "Jesus is Lord" (10:9), "Abba, Father!" (8:15), and in prayer (10:13) as the Spirit floods their hearts with God's love.

The heart is then circumcised (2:29). Just as a priest circumcised a boy on the eighth day, where faith springs up in the heart, the Spirit takes a short sword to the human heart (Eph 6:17). The image also speaks of cutting off sin. They are instantly set free from sin, decay, and death by the Spirit of life (8:2). The Spirit brings assurance and comfort, testifying with whispers into the human spirit that they are God's children (8:16). They are declared holy and begin the journey of sanctification (15:16).

The Spirit empowers the subsequent life of the believer. They do not live in submission to the law and its commands but live by "the new way of the Spirit" (7:6). Rather than the lusts of the flesh, they yield to the internal nudging of the Spirit so that they experience God's life and peace, as they put to death the flesh's misdeeds (8:4–13). They are led by the Spirit and are God's children (8:13–14). At all times and especially in times of weakness, the Spirit prays from within the believer to their *Abba* with wordless groans according to God's will (8:26–27). By the Spirit, the believer is ever in communion with God experiencing righteousness, peace, joy, and hope (14:17; 15:13).

---

14. Meye, "Spirituality," 907.

15. See especially Acts 1:8. See also Acts 4:8, 31; 7:55; 8:29, 30; 10:19, 38 (cf. Luke 4:14, 18–19), 44; 11:12, 28; 13:2, 4, 9; 15:28; 16:6–7; 19:8–10, 21; 20:22, 23; 21:4, 11.

Agents of Evangelism

Ultimately, they will die and be raised (8:11). The firstfruits of the Spirit given to them will ripen to the full transformation of the human body free of sin and its destructive consequences (8:23).

There are some notes of mission. If Romans 12:11 should be translated, "do not be slothful in zeal, be fervent in the Spirit,[16] serve the Lord" (my translation), this would include a passion for mission. Paul's mission of traveling through the nations, preaching (word), doing good (deed), performing miracles, and planting churches, is "by the power of the Spirit of God" (15:18). In doing this, Paul lives out his spiritual gift, "the grace given to him [us, me]" (12:3; 15:15).[17] In Romans 12:6, Paul refers to the various gifts of graces received by every one of the Romans. They are to live these out with the same kind of spiritual fervor as Paul (12:6–8). While mission is not specified in this list, missional gifts feature in other ones.[18] As such, Romans, exceptionally gifted in mission, should serve God passionately with those gifts. They should equip others to grow in their missional capacities (Eph 4:12).[19]

The love produced by the Spirit prompts prayer for his mission and his specific concerns that the collection will be received in Jerusalem, and that he can come to Rome and onto Spain (15:30).

The *missio dei* was personified in space and time in the person of Jesus whose flawless life and his death and resurrection pathed the way of eternal life. Now, it is the Spirit through whom God via the Son leads the mission.[20] God, in Christ, and by the Spirit, calls people to faith, enacts their conversion, shapes that person into the image of his Son, grants gifts to them, and sends into their particular missional vocation.

---

16. Alternatively, it refers to the human spirit and so would be rendered something like "enthusiastic in spirit" (LEB) or "fervent in spirit" (ESV). Both are probably implied here. Schreiner rightly observes that most of in Paul, *pneuma* refers to the Holy Spirit (e.g., Rom 1:9; 1 Cor 5:4; 14:14, 15; Gal 6:18; Phil 4:23; 1 Thess 5:23) and "boiling" fits with the association of Spirit and fire (Isa 4:4; 30:27–28; Matt 3:11; Luke 3:16; Acts 2:3; 1 Thess 5:19; Rev 4:5). However, such passion also implies fervency in the believer's spirit. He writes, "Believers are to burn and seethe in their spirits, but the means by which this is done is the power of the Holy Spirit." Schreiner, *Romans*, 665.

17. See also 1 Cor 3:10; Gal 2:9; Eph 3:2, 7–8, cf. Phil 1:7.

18. Including the gift of apostleship (1 Cor 12:28–29; Eph 4:11), evangelist (Eph 4:11), miracles and healings (1 Cor 12:28–29, cf. Rom 15:19; 2 Cor 12:12; Gal 3:5), prophecy within the church where unbelievers are present (1 Cor 14:20–25. See Keown, *Congregational Evangelism in Philippians*, 197, 248–49). The "word of wisdom" could also include a missional declaration of the wisdom of the cross. Keown, *Congregational Evangelism in Philippians*, 142.

19. Keown, *Congregational Evangelism in Philippians*, 285–92.

20. "Gravity is an almost imperceptible power; yet it is vital to the flowing of water. Likewise, the Spirit of God is the power (sometimes perceived only by the spiritually discerning) driving forward the mission of God. In the analogy of a spring the Holy Spirit is God's empowering agent, propelling the living water to the world." Van Rheenen, *Missions*, 27.

Part Three: Romans and the Proclamation of the Gospel

PAUL

Now, people involved in mission will be discussed. After the preceding three sections, it goes without saying that in Paul's thinking, anyone who is a Christian is summoned to participate in some way in the mission of God. They do so in Christ, whose missional work established the pathway to righteousness before God. Moreover, they participate in this mission by the power of the Spirit of God and Jesus, who inspires their service and enacts God's will in and through them as they are prepared to yield to him. God's mission comes to pass as people believe and are swept up into the mission of the Triune God. In this section, however, we will discuss the question of whether all are to share the gospel and if so, how.

The most prominent person in mission in Romans is, of course, Paul. The letter, as with his others, is an essential part of his mission strategy. We have thirteen letters with his name and know of at least one other that is lost (1 Cor 5:9–13). Where Paul could not travel to speak into a situation, he sent letters with couriers who delivered the letter, read it out, and added commentary.[21] Phoebe most likely played this role with Romans (further below, 16:1–2).[22]

Paul begins by describing himself as Christ's slave, who has been called by God to be an apostle and set apart for the proclamation of God's good news to the world (1:1). Paul here recalls his sensational conversion where he was transformed from being a destroyer of the Christian church to the one set apart by God to launch and develop his mission to the gentiles. As Witherington notes, "it is clear that Paul did not see his commission, mission and essential message as deriving from a human source."[23]

Apostolos is a diplomatic term used infrequently in the Greco-Roman world. Even rarer is its use of a single apostle. It has military and political connotations, and so an apostle of Jesus is a diplomat or ambassador (cf. 2 Cor 5:20; Eph 6:20). It also fits neatly into Israel's tradition of God sending prophets to declare his word to Israel and the nations.[24] The other use in Romans is 11:13, where Paul is "the apostle to the gentiles" (my translation). I have translated it with the definite article as in Galatians 2:7–10, Paul is charged with leadership of *the* gentile mission. As such, Paul is effectively the "foreign secretary" (UK), "the minister of foreign affairs" (NZ), or "secretary of state" (US).

In Judaism, the term:

---

21. Reed, "Epistle," 171–92.

22. Other possible bearers include: 1 Corinthians: Stephanas, Fortunatus, and Achaicus (1 Cor 16:15, 17); 2 Corinthians: Titus and three other significant missionaries who are unnamed (2 Cor 8:16–24); Ephesians, Colossians, and Philemon: Tychicus and Onesimus (Eph 6:21; 2 Tim 4:7, 9); Philippians: Epaphroditus (Phil 2:25–30; 4:18); and Onesiphorus? (2 Tim 1:16). It is uncertain who bore Galatians; 1 and 2 Thess; 1 Tim; and Titus.

23. Witherington, "Christology," 101.

24. See Rengstorf, "Ἀποστέλλω (πέμπω), Ἐξαποστέλλω, Ἀπόστολος, Ψευδαπόστολος, Ἀποστολή," 1:400–402.

Agents of Evangelism

appears to resemble the šālîaḥ of later rabbinic writings who might be sent on a mission from Jerusalem to synagogues of the Diaspora.[25]

Certainly, it has resonances with Israel's prophets sent by God to preach his word to Israel.

In the NT, the term has its origins in the selection of the twelve apostles of Jesus (Mark 3:13–19 and parr.). They were sent to Israel by Jesus to preach the good news of the kingdom and minister in his name (Mark 6:7–13 and parr.). After the fall of Judas and the resurrection, Matthias was added to their number. At the selection of Judas's replacement, the *apostolos* had to be someone who had been with Jesus from the beginning of his ministry and a witness to his resurrection (Acts 1:22). However, Paul is an apostle without that full experience, based on his Damascus Road experience of the risen Christ. The Galatians 2 meeting saw Paul and Barnabas's (see below) appointment by Jesus as his chief ambassador to the nations ratified. The Jerusalem apostles continued in their ambassadorial role among Jews not only in Israel but the diaspora.

There is evidence in Acts and Paul's letters that there were others recognized as apostles. In Romans, Junia and Andronicus are labeled as such (16:7, see next section). In Acts 14:4, 14, Luke uses the plural *apostoloi* of Paul and Barnabas. The plural suggests that Barnabas was by now one of the Twelve, perhaps appointed to replace James. If so, he may have been an eyewitness to Jesus and one of the seventy-two (Luke 10:1). Alternatively, and more likely, his role with Paul was recognized by Luke as apostolic, perhaps based on the Spirit setting Paul and Barnabas apart for their mission (Acts 13:1).[26] Barnabas's apostolic role may have been recognized even earlier in the Jerusalem meeting when the Jerusalem leaders, offered both Barnabas and Paul the right hand of fellowship releasing them to go to the gentiles while they went to the Jewish people (Gal 2:9, cf. Acts 11:28–30).[27]

Paul uses the plural *apostoloi* of himself, Timothy, and Silas in 1 Thessalonians 2:6. Two unnamed emissaries on Paul's third mission (on which he writes Romans) are labeled *apostoloi* (2 Cor 8:23). While this is usually translated "messengers,"[28] Paul is comfortable to use the somewhat controversial term of them. Likely then, they were

---

25. Barnett, "Apostle," 47; Rengstorf, "Ἀποστέλλω," 402–3.

26. Bruce, *Acts of the Apostles*, 271 rejects that Luke saw Paul or Barnabas as apostles, seeing this as a clip from a travel document. This suggestion is tenuous and lacks evidence. Schnabel's view is preferable. He sees a distinction between the Twelve and Paul and Barnabas, understanding v. 4 as "a hint that he saw Paul and Barnabas having a role similar to that of the twelve apostles." Still, that does not go far enough. Both Paul and Barnabas are full apostles to Luke, showing that the church extended its understanding beyond the Twelve over time for international missionaries. See Keown, *Congregational Evangelism in Philippians*, 172. See also Dickson, *Mission-Commitment*, 139–40.

27. While the singular is used in Gal 2:7 of Paul, the plural in vv. 9–10 may mean Barnabas was recognized to carry the same ministry.

28. Here, I am pushing back against the common view that Paul uses the term in two senses: a messenger and in the technical sense of "specially-recognized leaders in the early Christian movement." See, e.g., Plummer, *Paul's Understanding*, 45–46.

seen by Paul as apostles, even if not from the Twelve.[29] Epaphroditus is also called "your apostle" in Philippians 2:25. Again, this is often translated "messenger," but as I have argued elsewhere, this epithet suggests Epaphroditus was an apostle appointed in the Philippian church.[30]

Paul also lists *apostolos* in his spiritual gift lists of 1 Corinthians 12:28–29 and Ephesians 4:11, which seem to refer to present active ministries in the church (as with the other three or four gifts).[31] We can surmise then, that as time went on, the church recognized the ministry of apostle as something not only limited to the Twelve and Paul. It was used for those with a special call from God for missionary engagement and particularly the establishment of the Christian movement in new territories.

Paul's apostleship was challenged, especially in Corinth, where he had to defend it in both his letters (1 Cor 4:9; 9:1–22; 15:8–9) and confronted others who falsely claimed the title while preaching a flawed gospel (2 Cor 11:13; 12:11). Still, these latter references to "pseudo-apostles" and "super-apostles" of Jewish preachers (2 Cor 11:22) also confirm that the term was used more broadly than the Twelve and Paul (cf. Rev 2:2). They show it is possible to claim the term and not be an apostle, something the church today needs to consider as it uses the term. It should do so advisedly.

The specifics of Paul's particular ministry are given through the apostolic inclusio of Romans 1:1–15 and 15:14–33. Paul was commissioned to preach the gospel to the gentiles, summoning people to the obedience of believing the gospel (1:2, 4). This ministry was his spiritual and priestly service (1:9; 15:16).[32] He has a particular desire to come to Rome, which is hardly surprising, as it was the center of his world (1:10–12, 15). He had the task of imparting spiritual gifts, undoubtedly through the laying on of hands (1:11),[33] and encouraging others in their faith (1:12).

He sought new converts in all the nations he visited, committed to preaching to all cultures and mindsets (1:13–15). Nevertheless, he did not neglect his own people,

---

29. Keown, *Congregational Evangelism in Philippians*, 171–73.

30. Keown, *Congregational Evangelism in Philippians*, 158–84; Keown, *Philippians*, 2:38–44; Dickson, *Mission-Commitment*, 139–40; 315–17.

31. "The ἀπόστολοι are probably those who first took the gospel to the Gentiles—people such as Barnabas, Timothy, Silvanus, Apollos, and, preeminently, Paul himself (Acts 14:1, 4; 1 Thess. 1:1; 2:7; 1 Cor. 4:6–9; 9:5–6; Rom. 11:13; 15:18–21; Eph. 3:4–9; 1 Tim. 2:7)." Thielman, *Ephesians*, 180 (commenting on Eph 2:20, but equally applicable to 4:11). Ephesians 4:11 can indicate four gifts, the last being "prophets who teach." However, the shift from the *tous* to *kai* in the final gift is likely due to it being the final element in the list rather than the *tous* governing both *poimenas* and *didaskalous*. However, as the final two elements are not outwardly missional, this debate is not vital for this discussion. See also Thielman, *Ephesians*, 275.

32. "With a concertation on Old Testament cultic terminology that is quite remarkable, Paul refers first to the content of that ministry to which he was called (he is a *leitourgos*), as 'the priestly duty (*hierourgounta*) of proclaiming the gospel of God', and then to the purpose of this commissioning—and thus of his whole missionary career—as 'so that the Gentiles might become an offering (*prosphora*) acceptable (*euprosdektos*) to God, sanctified (*hēgiasmenē*) by the Holy Spirit' (Rom 15:16)." Köstenberger and O'Brien, *Salvation to the Ends of the Earth*, 168 (emphasis original).

33. See 1 Tim 4:14; 5:22; 2 Tim 1:6; Acts 9:12, 17; 13:3; 19:6; 28:8.

preaching in their synagogues (Acts 17:2),[34] praying for them, and yearning for their salvation (9:2–3; 10:1). He saw the gentiles as a priestly offering to God (15:16). He preached, did good works, and performed miracles, all by the Spirit (15:18–19). He had by this time finished his work of establishing the faith from Israel to the Balkans, and now yearned to come to Rome and then to the virgin fields of Spain (15:19–28).

Paul was a preacher of the gospel, especially set aside for mission leadership. He was an ambassador of the King and his kingdom, sent to the world, to tell them the good news that God's Son has come, that he is Lord, and that he has died and risen to save the world. Since the ministries of Jesus and Paul, mission leaders would rise up bringing church renewals, saving the church from apostasy, evangelizing new areas and countries, planting churches and denominations, building seminaries, hospitals, schools, and universities. God calls such people and will do so until his mission is complete.

Paul's example shows that some people are called to make their primary vocation preaching the gospel. Assuming their call is recognized, they preach the authentic gospel, and have godly character, they should be supported financially by God's church for their missional engagement.[35] As with Paul, however, they may voluntarily choose not to make a living from this, preferring to support themselves.[36]

OTHER MEN AND WOMEN

Others engaged in evangelistic mission are suggested in Romans 1:5, where Paul uses "we" of those who have received grace and apostleship. "We" can be an epistolary plural,[37] a plural of self-reference, or as is likely, it points to others.[38] Some consider this refers to Paul's team, yet this is unlikely as he specifies an apostolic calling, which was not universal to his team. As such, he has in mind apostles, as apostleship was a particular calling.[39] From the discussion above, we can identify at least the Twelve, James brother of Jesus and perhaps his other brothers (Gal 1:19), Barnabas (Acts 14:4,

---

34. Even if Paul does not mention synagogue proclamation, there is no reason to dispute Luke's frequent mention of his synagogue ministry (Acts 13:5, 14–15, 43; 14:1; 17:1, 10, 17; 18:4, 19; 19:8).

35. See especially 1 Cor 9:1–27; 2 Cor 2:17; 11:7–9; 12:14–16; 1 Thess 2:9; 1 Tim 5:18 (see also Matt 10:10; Luke 10:10; Acts 18:3).

36. Paul was not fully self-supporting, accepting the gifts from Macedonians and Philippians (2 Cor 11:8; Phil 2:25–30; 4:10–19), and the hospitality of the likes of Phoebe (16:2), Rufus's mother (16:13), Gaius (16:23), and Philemon (Phlm 7, 22). He also sought support for his Spanish mission, which may include finance (15:24).

37. E.g., Cranfield, *Critical and Exegetical Commentary*, 1:65, and especially note 6 for a list of others.

38. E.g., Dunn, *Romans 1–8*, 16 (others who preach to the gentiles including the likes of Barnabas, Silas, Timothy, and others associated with him); Longenecker, *Epistle*, 78.

39. "I infer that Paul wishes to convey solidarity with the apostles whose emissaries had established the house and tenement churches in Rome in the decades before the writing of this letter." Jewett and Kotansky, *Romans*, 109.

Part Three: Romans and the Proclamation of the Gospel

14), Timothy and Silas (1 Tim 2:6), the two of 2 Cor 8:23, and Epaphroditus (Phil 2:25). Based on the spiritual gift lists, there may be others recognized as such (1 Cor 12:28–29; Eph 4:11). There were also false "super" apostles, at least in Paul's purview (2 Cor 11:5, 13; 12:11).

In Romans 1:8, Paul writes,

> First, I thank my God through Jesus Christ concerning all of you because your faith is being proclaimed (*katangellō*) into the whole world" (my translation).[40]

My interest in this verse falls on *katangellō*. The verb is one of many Greek *angel*-words which speak of messages and their dissemination. The term is mostly found in Jewish Greek literature of proclamation, including dreams,[41] a political or religious declaration,[42] a religious or prophetic proclamation.[43]

In early Christian writings, it is employed for prophetic proclamation (Acts 3:24; Ign. *Phld.* 5:2; 9:2). Most commonly, it describes Christian proclamation.[44] Paul uses it of Christian preaching,[45] and of the Lord's Supper as a visual proclamation of Christ's death (1 Cor 11:26). The verb is not to be translated by something as mundane as "spoken of" or "indicates that Paul is consciously striving for effect."[46] It speaks of unspecified people *declaring* the faith of the Romans.

Here, while the form can be middle, the subject of the verb "your faith" (nom. *pistis*) indicates the verb is passive ("your faith is being proclaimed into the whole world"). Most interpreters note this but then assume then that the speakers are traveling preachers telling others of the faith of the Romans. They usually take 1 Thessalonians 1:8 in the same way; however, in that context, it is probable that the Thessalonians are the agents of the proclamation.[47] Here, in Romans 1:8, at the least it is general and includes others like Paul, who are well aware of the Roman situation, as the long list of greetings in Romans 16 makes clear.[48] Some like Prisca and Aquila have traveled with Paul in mission.

---

40. Käsemann, *Romans*, 17. This is a *captatio benevolentiae*, where the author begins with complimentary words (see also part two, chapter 7).

41. Political: *Ant.* 1.183, 284; 2.86, 175; dreams: *Ant.* 2.10, 15; *Ios.* 92; religious: 2 Macc 9:17; *Ant.* 3.206; 5.345.

42. 2 Macc 8:36; *Ant.* 6.203; 11.8, 222, 229; 15.269; 16.237; 20.72, 82; *J.W.* 1.581; 2.203; 4.582; *Aet.* 68.

43. *Ant.* 8.199; 9.92; 10.61, 92; *J.W.* 6.286; *Abr.* 261. Other uses include a symbolic signification (*Opif.* 106), an announcement of immortality (*Migr.* 189), an inward mental announcement (*Prob.* 64), and an ethical assertion (*Prob.* 71).

44. See Acts 4:2; 13:5, 38; 15:36; 16:17, 21; 17:3, 13, 23; 26:23; Pol. *Phil.* 1:2.

45. See 1 Cor 9:14; Phil 1:17, 18; Col 1:28.

46. Dunn, *Romans 1–8*, 28.

47. See Keown, *Congregational Evangelism in Philippians*, 250–59; Ware, "Thessalonians as a Missionary Congregation," 126–31.

48. Those who take it generally include Dunn, *Romans 1–8*, "because your faith is spoken of in all the world" (which downplays the declaratory force of *katangellō*).

Agents of Evangelism

"Your faith" is literally "the faith of yours," and is another way of describing "the Christian faith" or the gospel. The same kind of construct (*pistis* with the article) is found in Jesus's teaching and is common through the biblical narrative,[49] including Romans.[50] Some think this speaks of the beginning of the faith,[51] others the state of their faith.[52] Such a distinction is too nuanced as both aspects would be shared. Additionally, "your faith" is equivalent to "the gospel of yours (and ours)," cf. "my gospel." Likely, those sharing of the Romans, including the Romans themselves, told the whole story of Roman Christianity meshed into the gospel narrative.

"Your faith" is probably chosen, rather than the gospel, as "faith" is one of the central themes of Romans. Like Galatians a decade earlier, the letter is written to reinforce that justification is by faith and not by works of the law. Hence, essentially calling the gospel "the faith" highlights the required human response to the gospel that has saved Abraham and others in Israel's story, early Christians, the Romans, and others throughout the world. This "faith" advances through the world.

There is nothing here that rules out the verb being inclusive of the active agency of the Romans. In fact, "your faith" draws attention to the Romans, not others. Furthermore, the observation of Witherington and Hyatt also suggests Roman active agency.

> Since Rome was the center of the social networks of the empire and since communication went out from Rome throughout the empire, it is not surprising that Paul writes that the Romans' faith has been "proclaimed" in the whole empire.[53]

Barrett notes too that this fits with the Claudian edict whereby Roman Christian Jews had been expelled from the city and they took the gospel to the world.[54] As such, there are likely some from within the Roman church engaging in evangelistic mission spreading their faith. In the next section, some of these people become evident.[55]

---

49. "The faith of yours" or "the faith of theirs" (Matt 9:29; 15:28; Mark 2:5; 5:34; 10:52 and parr.; Luke 7:50; 8:25; 17:19; 22:32; 1 Cor 2:5; 2 Cor 10:15; 13:5; Col 1:23); "the faith" (Acts 3:16 [2x]; 6:7; 13:8; 14:22; 15:9; 16:5; 24:24; 1 Cor 3:2; 15:14, 17; 16:13; 2 Cor 1:24; 4:13; Gal 3:14, 23, 25, 26; Phil 2:17; 1 Thess 1:8; 3:2, 5; 3:7, 10; 2 Thess 1:3; 3:2; Phlm 6; Jas 1:3; 1 Pet 1:7, 9, 21; 2 Pet 1:5; 1 John 5:4; Jude 20); "household of the faith" (Gal 6:10). See also Eph 3:17; 4:13; 6:12; Phil 1:25, 27; 3:19; Col 1:23; Col 2:7, 12; 1 Thess 1:2; 3:6; 1 Tim 1:9; 3:9, 13; 4:1, 6; 5:8; 6:10, 12, 21; 2 Tim 3:8, 10; 4:7; Titus 1:3; 3:3; Phlm 5; Heb 2:1, 14, 17, 20, 22, 26; 4:2; 5:15; 11:39; 12:2; 13:7; 1 Pet 5:9; Rev 2:13; 13:10; 14:12; See also "that faith in him [or, the faithfulness of him]" (Eph 3:12).

50. Rom 3:25, 30, 31; 4:5 (his faith), 9, 11, 14, 19, 20; 5:2; 10:8, 17; 11:20; 12:6; 14:1.

51. Bultmann, "Πιστεύω, Πίστις, Πιστός, Πιστόω," 212.

52. Käsemann, *Romans*, 17.

53. Witherington and Hyatt, *Paul's Letter*, 42.

54. Barrett, *Epistle to the Romans*, 25. This would include Prisca and Aquila (Acts 18:2). See also Suetonius, *Claud.* 25.4). We can compare how the Jerusalem Christians took the gospel with them when driven out by Saul (Acts 8:1–4).

55. "Go where he will, in Asia, in Macedonia, in Achaia, in Illyricum, he meets believing 'strangers from Rome,' with spiritual news from the Capital, announcing, with a glad solemnity, that at the

Part Three: Romans and the Proclamation of the Gospel

"Into the whole world" can be translated "in the whole world," but that could suggest that Paul considers that the world is now evangelized, with Jesus's return imminent. Some avoid this by seeing here hyperbole.[56] However, as has been discussed, the gospel had barely begun its journey through the world at this point. Consequently, translating *en* "into," which is a legitimate translation,[57] avoids this problem. The gospel is being proclaimed into the world, and the mission goes on. Soon, hopefully, it will reach Spain. Ultimately, it will be proclaimed in the whole world so that the fullness of Jews and gentiles has come in, and then the end will come.[58] While this "reflects the missionary concern of Paul,"[59] here, it speaks more of the missionary concern of those who took the stories of Rome to the world.

Romans 16:19 is similar to Romans 1:8, which suggests an intentional inclusio. Paul writes, "For your obedience is known to all."[60] "Obedience" here can be general,[61] but in light of the letter's focus, includes the idea of Romans 1:5: their obedience of believing in Jesus. "All" again can be hyperbole but still speaks of the broad impact of the belief and fidelity of the Romans. How this became known requires travelers communicating the details, including the Romans themselves. This is evangelistic work.

Romans 16 gives a list of others who are engaged in gospel work. Phoebe is named first in 16:1–2 and is commended, likely because she is carrying the letter to Rome.[62] As hinted earlier of Paul's involvement in evangelism, with Tychicus, the slave Onesimus may have carried Ephesians, Colossians, and Philemon to the Asian cities (Eph 6:21; Col 4:7–9; Phlm 10). Paul says of these letter bearers that he or they will make known to the readers "everything" (Eph 6:21), "all my circumstances" (Col 4:9, LEB), and "all the circumstances here" (Col 4:9, LEB). Hence, the bearer was intimately involved in the situation around the letter at its point of production.

If Phoebe is the letter bearer, as is likely, she may have been a participant in its writing. She definitely knows and understands its contents so that she can read it and

---

great Centre of this world the things eternal are proving their power, and that the Roman mission is remarkable for its strength and simplicity of '*faith*,' its humble reliance on the Lord Jesus Christ, and loving allegiance to Him. Such news, wafted from point to point of that early Christendom, was frequent then; we see another beautiful example of it where he tells the Thessalonians (1 Thess. 1:8–10) how everywhere in his Greek tour he found the news of their conversion running in advance of him, to greet him at each arrival. What special importance would such intelligence bear when it was good news from Rome!" Moule likens this to the news of the distress of Ugandan Christians in 1892 extending into England by a Ugandan. Moule, *Epistle to the Romans*, 24.

56. E.g., Witherington and Hyatt, *Paul's Letter*, 42; Bauckham, *Bible and Mission*, 21 (among many others). There is no reason "the whole world" should be limited to the churches of Paul from Jerusalem to Illyricum. Schreiner, *Romans*, 49.

57. BDAG 327.

58. Rom 11:12, 25, also Mark 13:10; Matt 24:14.

59. Schreiner, *Romans*, 49.

60. Utley, *Gospel According to Paul*, n.p.

61. Thielman, *Romans*, 75.

62. E.g., Dunn, *Romans 9–16*, 886.

speak to its message in Rome. She must, therefore, have been a highly competent theological and missional thinker. Paul's preparedness to entrust her with the task of delivering what is clearly one of his most important letters, written as it is to the Roman capital, speaks of the esteem he had for her. The involvement of a woman and slave bearing a letter also speaks volumes of Paul's desire for others to engage in missional activities. Reading the letter is evangelistic work, and so we have a woman actively trusted to be involved in evangelism and pastoral care in early Christianity.

The use of the masculine *diakonos* rather than the feminine suggests she is a deacon of the church at Cenchreae.[63] She is described as a "sister" (*adelphē*). The label can merely indicate her missional kinship with Paul or may have the more technical sense of "coworker" here (see also Apphia, Phlm 1).[64] She is also a patroness of Paul and others,[65] perhaps indicating that she financed mission (see further part three, chapter 21). The specific term *prostatis* may also indicate a role in leadership, which accords with using *diakonos*.[66]

Next, two of Paul's regular partners in mission are named Prisca and Aquila (16:3–5). They are both designated "coworkers." A catacomb has been discovered that may indicate their noble origin.[67] The term *synergos* is used of people who work (*ergos*) with (*syn*) Paul in the mission of the gospel.[68] The exact roles of the coworkers are uncertain, but in Timothy's case (16:21), it included the full range of missional activities. It at least included preaching and evangelizing (2 Cor 1:19; 2 Tim 4:1–5), traveling on Paul's behalf with responsibility to enact his desires and teaching,[69] co-writing or co-sending letters,[70] and leading churches through false teaching (1 Tim 1:2–11).

Titus was also sent as Paul's emissary to Corinth and to lead the church of Crete (2 Cor 8:23; Titus), and Philemon led a church, probably with his wife Apphia (Phlm 1). Epaphroditus traveled from Philippi with gifts for Paul (Phil 2:25). As such, coworkers like Prisca, Aquila, and Urbanus (16:9) were active missionaries. Some of his workers are Jews and some gentiles, again showing Paul's inclusive attitude to others in mission (Col 4:11).[71]

---

63. E.g., Fitzmyer, *Romans*, 729.

64. Ellis, "Paul and His Co-Workers," in *Prophecy and Hermeneutic*, 9.

65. Patronesses are well attested, especially Junia Theodora of Corinth. Witherington and Hyatt, *Paul's Letter*, 383. See also Thielman, *Romans*, 712.

66. Fitzmyer, *Romans*, 731.

67. It was found in the country estate of the Acilian family. Jewett and Kotansky state that Tacitus and Dio Cassius indicate that the M. Acilius Glabrio later in the first century was killed for his faith. Jewett and Kotansky, *Romans*, 955.

68. See also 1 Cor 3:9; 2 Cor 1:24. Jewett and Kotansky tell us that *synergos* "is technical language for missionary colleagues." Jewett and Kotansky, *Romans*, 957.

69. See 1 Cor 4:17; 16:10; Phil 2:19–23; 1 Thess 3:2–6.

70. See 2 Cor 1:1; Phil 1:1; Col 1:1; 1 Thess 1:1; 2 Thess 1:1.

71. Jews include Aristarchus, Mark, and Jesus Justus. Gentiles include Tychicus, Onesimus, Epaphras, Luke, Demas (Col 4:7–17; Phlm 23–24). The only use of *synergos* outside of Paul is 3 John 8.

Here, the naming of Prisca immediately after Phoebe and before Aquila shows the importance of women to Paul's missional vision. Two other women of significance assigned the term *synergos* are Euodia and Syntyche (Phil 4:3). As I have argued elsewhere, this is unsurprising as the world was largely bifurcated along gender lines, and evangelization of women required female coworkers.[72]

While Prisca is not always named first (Acts 18:2; 1 Cor 16:19), most often she is,[73] and this could indicate her significance to the mission. Aquila was from Pontus, and he and Prisca left Rome when expelled by Claudius and traveled to Corinth, where they met Paul and worked with him as tentmakers and in mission (Acts 18:2). Prisca and Aquila are pictured here as people of real courage, having put their lives of the line to save Paul.[74] Their service is such that the gentile churches are grateful to them. The wider gratitude is not surprising as they have a church in Rome (16:5), in Ephesus (1 Cor 16:19; 2 Tim 4:19), and perhaps Corinth (Acts 18:2). They are an international missionary couple, both of whom should be recognized as church planters with Paul in Corinth, where they got to the city ahead of him. They were also left in Ephesus by Paul when he left for Jerusalem after some preaching in the synagogue (Acts 18:18–23). Hence, they should also be credited with being among those who planted the church in Ephesus. Together, they trained the firebrand Apollos and encouraged him in his evangelism (Acts 18:24—19:1).[75] Because they are always named together, they were clearly a husband-and-wife team, something not uncommon in the NT.[76]

Andronicus and Junia are also greeted in Romans 16:7. Like Herodian in Romans 16:11 and Lucius, Jason, and Sosipater in Romans 16:21, Paul describes them as his kinsmen. This moniker could be literal, referring to their being blood relatives (Acts 10:24), their fellow Jewish heritage (9:3),[77] close friends,[78] or as another way of describing their partnership with him in the gospel. They are likely another

---

72. Keown, *Philippians*, 2:316–29.

73. Acts 18:18, 26; Rom 16:3; 2 Tim 4:19.

74. Perhaps this occurred during Paul's Corinthian evangelization (Acts 18:12–18); during the riots in Ephesus (Acts 19:24—20:1, e.g., Moo, *Letter to the Romans*, 936); or the more recent death plot against Paul in Corinth (Acts 20:3). There was also suffering in Corinth (1 Cor 16:9) and Asia (1 Cor 15:32; 2 Cor 1:8). Rather than risking their lives, "to lay down one's neck" can indicate merely "placing one's self under a burden or submitting one's self to some duty" (see 1 Clem. 63:1; Epictetus, *Diatr.* 4.1.77). Whether this was neck risking or merely submission service, it involves great sacrifice. Thielman, *Romans*, 716.

75. The plural of *ektithēmi* used in Acts 18:26 suggests they together explained or expounded (BDAG 310, cf. Acts 11:4; 28:23) for Apollos "the way of God more accurately."

76. Junia and Andronicus (Rom 16:7); Philemon and Apphia (Phlm 1); see also the wives of James, Jude, and the other brothers of Jesus (1 Cor 9:5). I enjoy such a missional relationship with my wonderful wife and minister, the Rev Dr Emma Keown.

77. Thielman, *Romans*, 742.

78. Michaelis, "συγγενής, συγγένεια," 7:742.

husband-and-wife team.[79] They are "fellow prisoners," indicating that they were in prison with Paul at some point.

While earlier scholars assumed *Ionias* was male, it is almost universally accepted that this is a woman.[80] It is disputed whether they are "well known to the apostles" (ESV)[81] or "well known among the apostles." The latter is almost certainly correct, with early interpreters taking it that way and a more likely translation of *en*.[82] If so, we have a female apostle and an apostolic couple. They were important kingdom diplomats sharing the good news and planting churches.[83] They, along with Prisca and Aquila, could be key figures in the group spreading the gospel referenced in Romans 1:8. Bauckham's suggestion that Junia is Joanna of the Gospels may have merit (Luke 8:3; 24:10). They may have been instrumental in planting the Roman church.[84]

The naming of others indicates that they are important missional figures. Urbanus is termed as a coworker (16:9). Apelles is "approved (*dokimos*) in Christ." *Dokimos* and others in the word group in such a context speak of someone tested and approved.[85] The term is sometimes used of a person proven by testing in the furnace of mission, and this could be the sense here.[86] Herodian, in 16:11, is also a kinsman of Paul, perhaps indicating a fellow worker or that he is a Jew. His name may suggest he is from the family of the Herods.

In Romans 16:6 and 12, Paul commends Mary, Persis, Tryphaena, and Tryphosa for their labor (*kopiaō*). The verb and associated noun *kopos* are commonly used of gospel work.[87] Rufus could be the son of Simon of Cyrene, who bore Jesus's cross and is now in Rome (Mark 15:21).[88] His naming in Mark could be due to his renown in the church and perhaps he itinerated in the gospel ending up in Rome. Reference to

---

79. Dunn, *Romans 9–16*, 894.

80. Considering that the name Junia is found over 250 times in the feminine and never the masculine, Dunn, *Romans 9–16*, 894 rightly asserts, "The assumption that it must be male is a striking indictment of male presumption regarding the character and structure of earliest Christianity." See also Lampe, "Roman Christians of Romans 16," 223.

81. E.g., Moo, *Letter to the Romans*, 937–40.

82. E.g., Dunn, *Romans 9–16*, 894–95; Mounce, *Romans*, 275. See also Keown, *Congregational Evangelism in Philippians*, 82n59.

83. "Andronicus and Junia may have travelled together as a married missionary couple." Lampe, "Roman Christians of Romans 16," 225–26.

84. Bauckham, *Gospel Women*, 109–202. See also Witherington and Hyatt, *Paul's Letter*, 388.

85. BDAG 256.

86. See 1 Cor 9:27; Phil 2:22; 1 Thess 2:4; 2 Tim 2:15, cf. 1 Cor 3:13.

87. See 1 Cor 3:8; 15:10, 58; 16:16; 2 Cor 6:5; 10:15; 11:23, 27; Gal 4:11; Phil 2:16; Col 1:29; 1 Thess 1:3; 2:9; 3:5; 5:12; 1 Tim 4:10; 5:17. Lampe rightly says, "*kopiaō* is a technical term describing the labors of a missionary." Lampe, "Roman Christians of Romans 16," 223.

88. See, e.g., Jewett and Kotansky, *Romans*, 969. He notes the term *eklektos* (elect) was used of handpicked soldiers (Ep. Arist. 13; Sib. Or. 3:521) or very gifted religious people (Wis 3:14; 2 John 1; Ignatius, *Phld.* 11.1). He notes Mark was written for a Roman audience. The term *eklektos* may indicate his direct link to "the historical Jesus." He wonders whether they met when Rufus was expelled from Rome by Claudius.

his mother's care of Paul indicates her importance for missional patronage (see part three, chapter 21).

Some of the other groups in Romans 16 may indicate house-church communities. The naming of particular people could suggest both their importance and their acquaintance with Paul. It is then likely that Aristobulus and Narcissus are key missional people (vv. 10–11).[89] The reference to "the brothers who are with them" in verse 14 could indicate that the group named are coworkers of Paul: Asyncritus, Phlegon, Hermes, Patrobas, and Hermas.[90] The mention of "all the saints who are with them" in verse 15 could imply that Philologus, Julia, Nereus and his sister, and Olympas all represent missional leaders.

Romans 16:17–18 mentions licentious false teachers who cause divisions, obstacles, and preach a false message using rhetoric and flattery. They are to be avoided. Hence, while there are authentic Christian missionaries in Rome, there are false ones who are to be challenged. Such people are refuted all over Paul's letters.[91] One aspect of mission is dealing with challenges to the content and ethics of the gospel. Romans may be, in part, occasioned by their poison.

Some in Corinth are likely coworkers, including the educated and erudite Tertius, Paul's amanuensis for the letter (16:22). Penning a letter for Paul was an essential function of early church mission, as are administrative tasks today.[92] Other potential coworkers include Lucius (of Cyrene and Antioch, Acts 13:1?), Jason (probably of Thessalonica, Acts 17:5–9), Sosipater, Gaius (a wealthy Christian with a house large enough to host the whole Corinthian church), Erastus (the Corinthian local politician with a financial portfolio, 2 Tim 4:20),[93] and Quartus.

MISSION ASSISTANCE

In Romans 15:24, Paul speaks of his hope to get help from the Romans for his evangelistic mission to Spain. The particular term is *propempō*, compounding *pro* (before)

---

89. Aristarchus may have come to Rome in the 40s with Aristobulus, grandson of Herod the Great and the brother of Herod Agrippa I. This may refer to one of his family or slaves who remained in Rome. Witherington and Hyatt, *Paul's Letter*, 393; Josephus, *Ant.* 18:273–76; *J.W.* 2.221. Narcissus is likely a member of the family of Narcissus who was an important advisor to Claudius in the early fifties (Juvenal, *Sat.* 14.329–31). He was part of Nero's retinue and fell to Agrippina (Tacitus, *Ann.* 13.1). Witherington and Hyatt, *Paul's Letter*, 394.

90. Ellis, "Paul and His Co-Workers," 3–22.

91. See especially 2 Cor 10–12; Galatians; Phil 3; Col 2; and the Pastoral Epistles.

92. It is unclear who penned Paul's other letters. There are indications he used amanuenses by his comments in 1 Cor 16:21; Gal 6:11; Col 4:18; 2 Thess 3:17. The only certain person is Tertius. It is possible those mentioned in prescripts functioned in this regard: Sosthenes (1 Cor 1:1); Timothy (2 Cor 1:1; Phil 1:1; 1 Thess 1:1; 2 Thess 1:1; Phlm 1); Silvanus (1 Thess 1:1; 2 Thess 1:1), especially noting that he likely penned 1 Peter (1 Pet 5:12). Alternatively, the amanuensis is among those whose greetings are sent as in Romans.

93. In contrast to the Macedonian Erastus (Acts 19:22).

and *pempō* (send), so strictly means "send before."[94] As Morris rightly notes, "Paul does not explain what this means, but his verb is one which can be used for sending one forward on a journey with a variety of pieces of assistance."[95] BDAG suggests that it could indicate he wants company for the trip, or assistance "with food, money, by arranging for companions, means of travel, etc."[96] Consideration is now given to such possible aspects of support. Among other possibilities, I will argue that Paul wanted the Romans to join him in the mission to Spain.

Prayer

One uncontestable aspect of missional support Paul seeks is prayer; in the passage in question, for his trip to Jerusalem (15:30–32). He prays for his deliverance from unbelievers in Judea so that the offering he is bringing might be acceptable to the Jerusalem saints, with the result that (*hina*), he may come to Rome with joy. In his other letters, he frequently seeks prayer support for his mission, and no doubt he hoped for such prayers from the Romans (see further part three, chapter 10).[97]

Hospitality

Paul, second, hoped for hospitality from the Romans during his time there. Hospitality could be an aspect of his desire for mutual encouragement in Romans 1:12. He also mentions, in Romans 15:24, that his trip to Spain would come "after I have enjoyed your company (*empiplēmi*) for a while." The verb *empiplēmi* refers to being full and often in relation to food as in all other NT uses.[98] In verse 24, it likely includes Roman hospitality that satisfies body and soul: physical and spiritual nourishment. As Cottrell puts it, "it is appropriate to interpret it (as does the *NIV*) to mean something like 'filled full with the pleasure of your company.'"[99] As such, this could refer to some of those named in Romans 16, who will house and care for him as has Gaius in Corinth (16:23). Such hospitality could potentially come from the likes of Prisca and Aquila, with whom he has worked before (16:3–5), and Rufus's mother, who has helped him previously (16:13).

---

94. See for this usage, Macc 12:4; *Ant.* 1.328; 12.165; 14.84, 447; *Life* 90; *J.W.* 1.162, 177, 230, 250, 298, 305, 381; 2.83, 290, 298, 319, 334, 507, 513; 3.458; *Spec.* 3.111.

95. Morris, *Epistle to the Romans*, 518.

96. BDAG 873.

97. See 2 Cor 1:11; Eph 6:18; Phil 1:19; Col 4:3–4; 1 Thess 5:25; 2 Thess 3:1; Phlm 22.

98. See Luke 1:53; 6:25; John 6:12; Acts 14:17 (food and gladness). See also, e.g., LXX Gen 42:25; Lev 26:26; Deut 6:11; 8:10; Ruth 2:14; Ps 21:27 (22:26); Prov 6:30; Eccl 5:11; Job 38:39; Wis 13:12; Hos 13:6; Mic 6:14; Isa 58:10.

99. Cottrell, *Romans: Volume 2*, "His Plans for the Future (15:23–29)." Emphasis original.

PART THREE: ROMANS AND THE PROCLAMATION OF THE GOSPEL

Financial Support

The third aspect of support he may have wanted was financial and material. Some writers even limit the support Paul implies with the term *propempō* to such material support for the Spanish mission.[100] *Propempō* in Jewish Greek sources, at times, carries the meaning of ensuring someone's safe conduct (1 Esdr 4:47; Jdt 10:15). It can be used of someone sent forth in a good manner (*Ant.* 20.50; *J.W.* 1.614).

Such material provision is probably the sense in 1 Corinthians 16:6 where Paul wants to be sent on his way by the Corinthians wherever he goes. Similarly, in 1 Corinthians 16:11, the Corinthians are to send Timothy on his way back to Paul in peace. Again, in 2 Corinthians 1:16, he wants the Corinthians to send him on his way to Judea with the collection. Titus is instructed to send Zenas and Apollos on their way, ensuring they lack nothing (Titus 3:13). 3 John 6 instructs the recipients to do this for unnamed brothers. Paul's support could come from the same sources mentioned above.

However, a caveat is required where financial support is suggested. Elsewhere, at times, Paul is extremely reticent to take the money of other Christians. In Thessalonica, he provided for himself and accepted Philippian material gifts, rather than relying on the Thessalonians (1 Thess 2:9; 3:6–12, also Phil 4:16). It is particularly to the Corinthians that Paul passionately defends his right not to take Corinthian patronage (1 Cor 9). His reluctance is likely to avoid being caught up in the petty political attachments to preachers in the church (1 Cor 1:10–12).

A year or so before he wrote Romans, while taking up the Jerusalem Collection, Paul wrote 2 Corinthians with a focus on fending off critics claiming that he and his coworkers are peddlers of the gospel, something Paul strongly refutes (2 Cor 2:17).[101] He asserts that he and his team operate with utmost integrity (2 Cor 2:18—7:16), pleads with the Corinthians to contribute to the collection generously (2 Cor 8–9), and defends his strategy of self-support (2 Cor 11:7–11; 12:14–18). Still, at other times, he does receive material support from others (2 Cor 11:8–9; Phil 4:15–16), accepted Philippian provision later in Rome (Phil 2:25–30; 4:10–13, 17–20), and does rely on hospitality (16:2, 13, 23). Hence, it could be that financial support is included in the range or *propempō*.

However, with strong rumors circulating of his financial corruption, it could be that his reference to "passing through" could be, in part, motivated to ensure they know he is not there for their money. Moo ponders how to reconcile Paul's desire to preach in Rome with what seems to be a hint at a short stop in 15:24. He suggests:

---

100. Jewett and Kotansky, *Romans*, 926; Moo, *Letter to the Romans*, 918; Cottrell, *Romans: Volume 2*, "His Plans for the Future (15:23–29);" Keener, *Romans*, 177 suggests provision and ship fare to Spain; Thielman, *Romans*, 690 suggests food, money, and provision for sea travel (and companions).

101. For my argument concerning this reading of 2 Corinthians, see Keown, *Discovering the New Testament: Paul and His Letters* (Bellingham, WA: Lexham, forthcoming), Chapter 5.

"The best explanation for the difference in emphasis between these two statements is Paul's sensitivity about financial matters."[102]

Witherington and Hyatt write:

> Paul consistently refused patronage from new converts, had only a parity reciprocity relationship with the Philippians, and otherwise accepted only either hospitality or traveling funds from churches like that in Corinth, or in this case in Rome. It would have been especially unlikely that Paul would accept patronage or even parity from the Roman church for it was not one he had founded, and he was only just now establishing some kind of personal contact and influence over the Christians in Rome.[103]

Witherington and Hyatt go on to suggest Paul may have accepted money from Rome to use in a setting outside the giving church (as with the Philippians).[104] His doing so is possible but only appropriate where he had complete confidence in those giving, namely, that they gave with the Greco-Roman expectations of patronage (without putting Paul in their debt). In that Paul had yet to acquaint himself with the Romans fully to gain confidence in their motives for supporting him, it is unclear whether at this stage money is in view.

Additionally, he already has substantial potential support from Phoebe (16:1–2), Gaius and Erastus in Corinth (16:23), and the Macedonians (2 Cor 11:9). Jewett and Kotansky suggest "that Phoebe had agreed to underwrite a project of vital significance to Paul and to the letter he is writing."[105] As such, we cannot just assume that Paul wanted their financial support.

Rome as a Base

A fourth possibility relevant to this study is that Paul wanted to use Rome as his base for the Spanish mission, as he has used Syrian Antioch for his mission into the west to Illyricum.[106] As such, the people of Rome would pray for him, supply him in various ways for the trip, he would give an account of his mission, and as will be argued in what follows, support him with coworkers.

Missional People

A fifth possibility is that Paul wanted not only to use Rome as a base but wanted people to join him for the mission to Spain. The verb *propempō* is used of people

---

102. Moo, *Letter to the Romans*, 918.
103. Witherington and Hyatt, *Paul's Letter*, 363–64.
104. Witherington and Hyatt, *Paul's Letter*, 364.
105. Jewett and Kotansky, *Romans*, 947.
106. Morris, *Epistle to the Romans*, 518; Witherington and Hyatt, *Paul's Letter*, 363.

joining Paul three times in Acts. While Acts 15:3 may include material provision for Paul and Barnabas, equally, it could involve their sending a retinue of locals to support them. So, in Acts 20:38, the Ephesian church leaders accompanied Paul to the ship. In Acts 21:5, a great group of believers in Tyre accompanied the Jerusalem Collection group outside the city.

The verb elsewhere also carries the idea of people joining others. Jesus is sent forth from God into his mission (Poly. *Phil.* 1:1).[107] In actual fact, in wider Greek Jewish sources *propempō* is most often used of people conducted (sent forth) on a journey with an escort.[108] Hence, it potentially means that Paul "may well have hoped that one or more of the Roman Christians who knew Spain would accompany him there."[109] They would join him in his mission, conducting him to Spain.

Jewett and Kotansky ponder the challenges of the Spanish mission.[110] While earlier writers assumed a strong Jewish presence in Spain, meaning that Paul could begin as usual in synagogues, Bowers has shown that there was not a strong Jewish presence until the third and fourth centuries.[111] This is supported by the absence of Spain among the nations in Acts 2:9–10 and that, unlike Rome, Christ has not yet been named there.

The absence of Jews, proselytes, and God-fearers would mean making converts would be more challenging. The absence of Jews and synagogues would also create social and economic challenges because the usual business and informal contacts and starting points would be lacking. Thus, there would logistical challenges—setting up bases for Paul's tentmaking business, patronage, and starting points for mission.

While Spain in parts was highly Latinized, large parts, especially in the north, were relatively untouched by Greek and Roman culture.[112] Greek was only spoken in some parts of Spain with Latin used in main centers and in the southern central area of Baetica (*Hispania ulterior*), with most locals speaking their own languages.[113]

---

107. See 2 Macc 6:23; Wis 19:2; *Ant.* 1.91, 325; 7.188; 14.103; *J.W.* 2.631; 3.400; 4.3, 10, 640; 5.383, 389; 7.9; *Leg.* 3.21; *Mos.* 1.195)

108. See Let. Aris. 172; Jos. Asen. 22:7; *Ant.* 4.3; 24; 5.99; 6.53, 254, 272; 9.251; 11.59, 67, 135; 13.105; 14.151, 156, 342, 375; 15.103, 363; *J.W.* 1.201, 255, 278, 362, 456, 512; 2.104, 282, 480; 7.356; *Mos.* 1.227. It is also used of the soul escorted by angels to the grave (Hist. Rech. 15:8) or to God at death (*Ant.* 1.230).

109. Dunn, *Romans 9–16*, 872. See also Schreiner, *Romans*, 774: "Paul wanted the Roman church to support his mission to Spain financially, in prayer, and possibly also with personnel."

110. Jewett and Kotansky, *Romans*, 74–79.

111. Bowers, "Jewish Communities," 395–402.

112. Rostovtzeff, *Social and Economic History of the Roman Empire*, 211–15. Jewett and Kotansky, *Romans*, 75. See Jewett and Kotansky, *Romans*, 76n515 for other studies supporting these perspectives.

113. Rostovtzeff, *Social and Economic History of the Roman Empire*, 213; Jewett and Kotansky, *Romans*, 75. In the west and northwest of Spain Indo-European languages; in the south and east, Iberian dialects on the east coast; on the southern coast, the Punic languages and a wide range of other languages of obscure origin. "[I]n three small pockets Greek was used on the east coast where colonies had been established in an earlier period." Jewett and Kotansky, *Romans*, 76. In the other two provinces, Lusitania and Tarraconensis (*Hispania citerior*), were Latinized in coastal areas, river

Establishing the gospel among these Greeks centers might be possible, but how effectively it could then spread is questionable.[114] There was no Latin equivalent to the LXX, and further spread would require Latin translators.[115] The Cantabrian War of 29–19 BC was caused by locals in Lusitania and Tarraconensis who had been forced to abandon worship of local deities for Roman deities. Local patrons could also come under fire. Such a history suggests that Paul and others could face severe persecution from locals when they preached Christ.

With all these things above in mind, it would at least require "finding logistical support for their travels and lodging and recruiting translators capable of moving from Greek to Latin as well as other languages."[116]

Some of these may be the many coworkers named in Romans 16, perhaps specifically named because Paul wants their support and involvement (see the previous section). Further, the reference to the proclamation of the faith and obedience in Romans 1:8 (although couched in the passive), and Romans 16:19, may indicate his hope that some who had been active previously will join him in the announcing "their faith" to new fields in Spain.

THE MISSIONAL RHETORICAL FORCE OF ROMANS

Romans lacks any prohibition from preaching the gospel.[117] This is critical as one of the starting premises for arguing Paul did not envisage local churches being proactive evangelistically is a lack of an imperative to churches or converts to proactively evangelize.[118] The absence of an explicit imperative is dubious as the converse can be argued. Hence, we need to assess the cumulative evidence to see whether it is more likely Paul did want them to evangelize, or not.

---

valleys, military, and mining colonies.

114. Jewett and Kotansky, *Romans*, 79.

115. Jewett and Kotansky, *Romans*, 79. Jewett and Kotansky also aver that "the church in Rome remained Greek speaking until the mid-third century."

116. Jewett and Kotansky, *Romans*, 90.

117. There are a few examples of God or Christian leaders prohibiting preaching the gospel. One is Acts 16:6–10, where the Spirit stopped Paul preaching in Asian areas. He was led to preach somewhere else, Macedonia. Later, he would come to these areas and thoroughly evangelize them (Acts 19:1–20). Hence, this is not a prohibition but about the right time. In 1 Pet 3:1, Peter instructs Christian wives not to continue to use words in evangelizing their unbelieving husbands who have rejected the gospel. However, he still wants them evangelized (won) through the quality of their witness (1 Pet 3:1–7). Prohibitions in most of the NT are viewed negatively, and Christians refuse to yield to them (see, especially Acts 4–5). Or, they move on to another context and continue to evangelize, as we see in the Sauline persecution (Acts 8:4) and during Paul's missions (e.g., Acts 13:51).

118. The only absolutely unambiguous imperative is to Paul's right-hand man and coworker, Timothy, in the disputed 2 Tim 4:2: "*kēryxon* (aor. imper. sing. 2nd pers. *kēryssō*) *ton logon*, "preach the word"; 2 Tim 4:5: *ergon poiēson* (aor. imper. sing. 2nd pers. *poieō*) *euangelistou*, "do the work of an evangelist."

Elsewhere, limitations are placed only on women in two passages. The command to women to be silent in 1 Corinthians 14:32–34 is not relevant to this discussion, as Paul specifies "in the church" and so at the most, these verses preclude women from speaking in Corinthian church gatherings. Anyway, a complete prohibition is unlikely as he states in 1 Corinthians 11:5 that women can prophesy in the church (with appropriate attire). So, the prohibition does not forbid a woman bringing a prophecy that strengthens another believer or causes an unbeliever to worship God (evangelistic prophecy).[119] However we interpret the passage, the verse places no limit on women sharing the gospel to unbelievers outside the church gatherings (or within churches via prophecy).

The context for the prohibition in 1 Timothy 2:11–12 is also church gatherings. The women of the Ephesus churches can learn and are to be in submission.[120] They cannot teach or dominate men. In whatever way we interpret this difficult text, it is does not forbid women sharing the gospel with others outside of church gatherings. Indeed, it would be very surprising if it did as Prisca the coworker is addressed in the Timothy letters (2 Tim 4:19). This then is not a prohibition of women evangelizing men *outside the church*. They can evangelize women *in any situation*.

The absence of an imperative to evangelize is sometimes used as a hermeneutical lens to interpret other texts that have ambiguity. As intimated, one can reverse this and say that the absence of a prohibition, along with Paul's passion for preaching the gospel, which is strongly evident in Romans 1:1–15 and 15:14–33, suggests that he wants *all* other Christians to grow in their capacity to communicate the gospel. There are, of course, provisos—they must preach the authentic gospel of Christ (e.g., 1 Cor 10–12; Galatians; Phil 3). They should not do peddle the gospel for money (2 Cor 2:17). Neither should they grossly violate the ethics of the gospel or its unity (e.g., 1 Cor 5–6).[121]

Another premise employed by advocates of passive evangelization and support of specialists is the backreading of later ecclesiastical structures into the NT period. At the time of the letters of Paul, there is no clear delineation of specialists and non-specialists, what we might call "clergy" and "laity," or "the ordained" and non-ordained.

---

119. Throughout 1 Cor 14 to v. 34, Paul addresses the whole church without limit. All are to desire spiritual gifts, especially prophesying. Prophecy upbuilds, encourages, and consoles (v. 3). Prophecy builds the church up (1 Cor 14:5). All are to strive to excel in building up the church (vv. 12, 17). It stands to reason, in light of 1 Cor 11:5, that the hope of vv. 24–25 applies to any who prophesy, women or men. There is no gender limit in v. 26 ("brothers" is inclusive as in every other use in 1 Corinthians). Women are to bring the fruit of their gifts and speak in tongues, interpret, and prophesy in order (vv. 26–32).

120. Just what they are to be in submission to is not specified.

121. Even where someone is not completely immoral, Paul is permissive. Those preaching Christ at the point of his imprisonment (Rome, and perhaps Ephesus) seek to cause Paul suffering and preach from false motives but merely cause Paul to rejoice that Christ is proclaimed (Phil 1:14–18a).

Certainly, the letter endorses that some are set apart for mission by God, most notably Paul (1:1–2). Other apostles are acknowledged (1:5;[122] 16:7). We know of Jesus's commissioning and sending the Twelve (Mark 3:13–19; 6:7–13), the replacement of Judas (Acts 1:12–26), and the appointment and commissioning of the Seven (Acts 6:1–6). Elders and deacons were established in churches (Acts 14:23; 20:17). They were required to have specific godly attributes (1 Tim 3:1–13; Titus 1:5–9). There is evidence of the laying on of hands, commissioning, the impartation of the Spirit and spiritual gifts, and healing.[123] So, there seems to be some recognition of a process toward leadership within the church.

Coworkers could be seen as those commissioned to participate in gospel proclamation (16:3, 9, 21). Nevertheless, at the points they are designated, there is no process explained whereby an "ordinary" Christian becomes a "vocational missionary." They are simply Paul's coworkers.[124] At the same time, at least in Acts, the likes of Apollos came from nowhere, and rather than his being forbidden from preaching, he was equipped to do so better by two of Paul's identified coworkers (Acts 18:24—19:1).[125]

By this early stage, we have no specified process of ordination or the commissioning of people into roles. The church was not organized to that level or joined into denominations. It was and was spreading spontaneously, quickly, dynamically, and organically. The movement was Spirit-led and charismatic with some degree of formal structure (as in the case of Jesus's selection of the Twelve and the Jerusalem apostles appointing the Seven). As such, a coworker may have been *appointed* to the role. Alternatively, they were people passionate about mission and so were *recognized* as coworkers.

With the above two thoughts in mind, it is interesting to consider the evangelistic and mission rhetorical force of Romans. I contend that first-century hearers open to the message of Paul in Romans would be inspired to want to evangelize by its message and Paul's example.

Paul's Example

Unsurprisingly, in that the Romans were not Paul's converts, he does not include any of his characteristic imitatory texts in Romans.[126] Still, as with all letters that seek to persuade people to align with the gospel and Paul's perspective, as Paul speaks of his

---

122. I am assuming "we" speaks of the apostolic group including the Twelve and others recognized as such.

123. Acts 6:6; 8:17; 9:12, 17; 19:6; 28:8; 1 Tim 4:14; 5:22; 2 Tim 1:6.

124. They are simply designated *synergos* (see also 1 Cor 3:9; 2 Cor 1:24; 8:23; Phil 2:25; Col 4:11; 1 Thess 3:2; Phlm 1, 24).

125. See also 1 Cor 1:12; 3:4–6, 22; 4:6; 16:12; Titus 3:13.

126. Compare 1 Cor 4:16; 11:1; Phil 3:17; 4:9; Eph 5:1–2; 1 Thess 1:6.

PART THREE: ROMANS AND THE PROCLAMATION OF THE GOSPEL

life and mission, Romans has an implicit and imitatory rhetorical power to summon people to mission effort.

Romans 1:1–17 and 15:19–31 speak powerfully of Paul's passion for the gospel.[127] He is set apart by God for it (1:1), having by grace been called to be an apostle preaching the gospel to the gentiles so that they might be saved by faith.[128] Hearers would surely be challenged to seek God's purpose for themselves and their place in God's mission.

Paul's endorsement of the Roman church's engagement in evangelism would encourage further engagement. The church itself was not founded by those designated apostles by Christ (the Twelve), and testifies to "nobodies" engaging in evangelism, church planting, and discipleship. Furthermore, as argued, Romans 1:8 potentially includes their involvement in mission, as does Romans 16:19. Romans 16 refers to evangelistic people he greets. These references have an inspirational power for a Christian seeking to please God and would surely motivate them to do the same.

The Romans would have been fully aware that the whole world (1:8) needs evangelizing, and one man or group of people cannot do it alone. Others would surely be drawn to emulate Paul's example of serving God wholeheartedly in preaching the gospel as his priestly service (1:9).[129] His fervent, constant prayers that he can travel land and sea to Rome and beyond would also inspire them to do the same (1:10). His eagerness and determination to win converts in Rome would motivate them to prepare to invite people to hear the gospel from Paul (1:13, 15). His obligation to Romans and non-Romans would cause them to look out at the one million people from across the world living in the city and become increasingly active in evangelization (1:14).

His confidence in God to work in him, empowering his speech, through him performing signs and wonders, and filling his heart with desire for good deeds such as the Jerusalem Collection would be inspirational to many (15:14–19). His consuming passion for preaching in places yet unreached, like Spain, would surely encourage others to look at the world and consider where they might go with God's word (15:20–24). As argued, he requires help for the Spanish journey (15:24), and some would be inspired to join him in this venture.

His amazing travels back and forth evangelizing the 2,500–3,000 km (1553–1,860 mi) region from Jerusalem to Illyricum, his determination to travel some 11,500 km (7,150 mi) to Corinth where he writes Romans,[130] and to travel some 2,371 km (1473 mi) from Corinth to Jerusalem (15:28–30),[131] would inspire others to want to travel

---

127. See especially 1:9, 14. See also 1 Cor 9:16; Phil 1:14–18.

128. Romans 1:5, 13–14; 11:13; 15:16, 18; Gal 1:16; 2:2, 7, 9; Eph 3:1, 8; 1 Tim 2:7; 2 Tim 4:17.

129. On the priestly aspect of 1:9 and *euangelion* as a noun of agency, see Köstenberger and O'Brien, *Salvation to the Ends of the Earth*, 174.

130. Schnabel, *Paul the Missionary*, "Paul's Travels: statistics;" idem, *Paul and the Early Church*, 1197–99. See earlier part one, chapter 1, "Missional Purposes."

131. Schnabel, *Paul and the Early Church*, 1199.

with the gospel to far-flung places. Those reading it would hope he would come to Rome as expected, which he did just a few years later, traveling some 3,100 km (1,930 mi) from Jerusalem.[132] They know he then plans to travel another 2,800 km (1740 mi) to Spain (15:24, 28). If he had one more journey, he would travel another 4,020 km (2500 mi) on his last missions.[133]

His determination to twice travel enormous distances to gather financial support for the beleaguered Jerusalem Christians would motivate others to care for those in need in their orb and to emulate his concern for worldwide social justice. His commendation of patrons and others who provide hospitality and house Christians and churches would indeed invoke a desire to do the same among readers. Where hearers and readers of the letter were filled with God's missional Spirit, they would hear, understand, and desire to emulate Paul's example.[134]

Ancient Hero Cultures

The impact of Paul's example and that of others positively affirmed in the letter, especially in Romans 16, would be far greater knowing that the ancient Greek and Roman world was what might be labeled a "hero culture." This is not unusual. As Spence-Jones writes, "Nations pride themselves most on the heroes of their history, and they delight to trace their descent from [people] of renown."[135]

Bowley notes that the first century was a time of intellectual upheaval and engagement across the Greek, Roman, and Jewish cultures. "Such cultural intercourse encouraged the practice of relating and comparing the narratives and heroes of one culture to those of another."[136] Ancient heroes like Achilles from the *Iliad* remained important. Hesiod, for example, found heroes in the Fourth Age of "men" before the fall of Troy. Pindar saw heroes as demigods. The term *hero* was used of local gods and city founders. The most prominent was Heracles.[137] In the preceding century, Julius Caesar was the paradigm of a Roman hero.[138] At the time of the NT, Augustus was

---

132. Estimated using measure distance on Google Maps.

133. Schnabel, *Paul and the Early Church*, 1288.

134. "The Christians of the Four Provinces were certainly zealous in propagating the faith., and apparently needed no exhortation on the subject. This surprises us; we are not always accustomed to find our converts so zealous. Yet it is not really surprising. Christians receive the Spirit of Jesus, and the Spirit of Jesus is the missionary spirit, the Spirit of Him Who came into the world to bring back lost souls to the Father." Roland Allen, *Missionary Methods*, 125–26; idem, *The Spontaneous Expansion of the Church*, 8–9.

135. Spence-Jones, *Romans*, 278 (adapted for inclusive language). Spence-Jones then mentions Abraham and the Patriarchs (see below).

136. James E. Bowley, "Heroes," in *DNTB* 494.

137. Bowley, "Heroes," 495.

138. "Romans also traced their origins back to the Trojan hero Aeneas, who was the son of the goddess Venus (Aphrodite). Julius Caesar himself claimed to be a direct descendant of Aeneas." Winn, "Son of God," 887.

Rome's great hero, having ended years of war and establishing the *pax Romana*.[139] Others were viewed as heroes who died "for the honored fatherland."[140] Those who gained victory in politics and the military were viewed as heroes with *gloria*.[141]

Bowley notes that during the Hellenistic era, Jewish writings showed a greater interest in heroes such as Noah, Abraham, Moses, David, and Solomon.[142] Bible stories were embellished, such as Abraham being responsible for teaching the Egyptians astronomy (Josephus, *Ant.* 1.165) and a philosopher's hero (Philo, *Abr.* 66, 84). In particular, apocryphal and pseudepigraphal writings, in common with heroic literature, idealized Israel's key figures (e.g., Sir 44—50).[143] Such an interest is demonstrated in an interest in Enoch and Melchizedek and the pseudonymous authors of pseudepigraphal works.[144]

Undoubtedly, for Christians, God and Jesus are the heroes of the NT story. Jesus, in particular, is presented by Paul in heroic terms. Still, Bowley finds a tendency toward idealizing figures as heroes and heroines.[145] The best example is the "Faith Hall of Fame" in Hebrews 11,[146] which resembles Sir 44—50.[147] In Romans, implicitly, OT

---

139. See Bowley, "Pax Romana," 771–75. See also Jewett and Kotansky, *Romans*, 48. They cite Virgil, *Ecl.* 4.11.48: "He shall have the gift of divine life, shall see heroes mingled with gods, and shall himself be seen of them."

140. Jewett and Kotansky, *Romans*, 361.

141. Jewett and Kotansky, *Romans*, 50.

142. Bowley, "Heroes," 495–96.

143. Bowley, "Heroes," 495. He mentions the song of Sir 44:1–3: "Let us now sing the praises of famous men, our ancestors in their generations. The Lord apportioned to them great glory, his majesty from the beginning. There were those who ruled in their kingdoms, and made a name for themselves by their valor; those who gave counsel because they were intelligent; those who spoke in prophetic oracles" (NRSV).

144. Bowley, "Heroes," 496. He notes especially, Adam, Enoch, Abraham, Jacob, Joseph, David, Solomon, Ezra, and others. We can add Job, Daniel, Judith, and the twelve sons of Jacob. Strangely, Toews claims, "There are no heroes in the Hebrew Bible, no moral paragons, only failures; Moses, David, and Solomon, as examples, come under the judgment of God." Toews, *Romans*, "The Family Debate," 3:19, n.p. While it is true that these leaders failed and were judged, as Bowley has shown, many OT figures were idealized and honored. While there is truth in their failure, many are presented as paradigms of faith to be emulated. In Romans, especially Abraham, despite his failings. As Dunn says, "Israel's great heroes honored by the title [slave] precisely because of the unconditional quality of their commitment to Israel's God and of their part in maintaining the covenant between God and his people." Dunn, *Romans 1-8*, 7.

145. Bowley, "Heroes," 496.

146. Rasnake, *Book of Romans*, 62. He cites Charles Swindoll, who calls Hebrews 11 "faith's Hall of Fame." Swindoll, *Faith That Endures*, 2.

147. Other notable examples include Rahab (Matt 1:5; Heb 11:1; Jas 2:25), Melchizedek (Heb 7), David (Matt 12:3-4 and parr.), Noah (Matt 24:37-38; Luke 3:36; 17:26-27 ; 1 Pet 3:20; 2 Pet 2:5), Lot (Luke 17:28-29; 2 Pet 2:7); Enoch (Luke 3:37; Heb 11:5; Jude 14); Solomon (Matt 1:6, 7; 6:29; 12:42; Luke 11:31; 12:27; John 10:23; Acts 7:47), Joseph (34x NT), Abel (Matt 23:35; Luke 11:41; Heb 11:4; 12:24), Aaron (Luke 1:5; Acts 7:40; Heb 5:4; 7:11), Jonah (Matt 12:39-41; 16:4, 17; Luke 11:29-32), Joshua (Luke 3:28; Acts 7:45; Heb 4:8), and Samuel (Acts 3:24; 13:20; Heb 11:32).

figures are presented favorably as examples, while others are types or negative.[148] "The prophets" as a group are implicitly commended as are individual prophets, Isaiah, Hosea, David, Moses, and Elijah.[149] Abraham is the dominant "hero" of Israel's faith.[150] For Paul, he is the hero of the faith for his faith (4:1–25).[151]

With the "hero-culture" of readers in mind, Romans would invoke a desire among members of the church to emulate Jesus, who is the hero of all Paul's writings.[152] In Romans, this is particularly so in Romans 5:6–7, where. After stating that Christ died for the ungodly, Paul notes that it is rare indeed for someone to dare to die for a good person.[153] Christ's example of sacrifice calls others to emulate him in giving their lives for God and his mission.[154]

Aside from Jesus, Paul himself is the hero of Romans with his massive sacrifice for the cause. (Even if Paul did not want things to be all about him but about Jesus and the gospel).[155] His letter summons people to "Christian heroism," including mis-

---

148. Such as Adam (5:14, see also 1 Cor 15:22, 45; 1 Tim 2:13–14) ["Adam the tragic hero, and Christ the redeemer hero," Dunn, *Romans 1–8*, 288] and Esau (9:13), and Pharaoh (9:17, cf. Acts 7:10, 13, 21; Heb 11:24). Some others include Eve (2 Cor 11:3; 1 Tim 2:13) and Cain (Heb 11:4; 1 John 3:12; Jude 11), Balaam (2 Pet 2:15; Rev 2:14); Jezebel (Rev 2:20), and Korah (Jude 11).

149. See 1:2; 3:21; 4:6; 5:14; 9:15, 25, 27, 29; 10:5, 16, 19, 20; 11:2, 3, 9; 15:12. Jesse is also mentioned in regards to David in 15:26. Moses is mentioned mostly as the counterpart to the righteousness by faith, but this does not mean Paul denigrates him. Overall, his regular citations of the Pentateuch, which was ascribed to Moses, indicate that Paul saw Moses as a hero of the faith. Isaiah is mentioned 22x in the NT, David (59x), Moses (80x), and Elijah (29x).

150. Jewett and Kotansky, *Romans*, 308 describes Abraham as the religious hero of the people in later Judaism. Also, Phinehas (Num 25:10–13) and Mattathias (1 Macc 2:19–26, 54, 58). Dunn, *Romans 9–16*, 587, 595.

151. See also Gal 3:6–29; Jas 2:21. Overall, "Abraham" is mentioned 72x in the NT. Others in the patriarchal era are mentioned, albeit in regards to God's election: Isaac (9:7, 10, 22x NT), Sarah (9:9, cf. Heb 11:11; 1 Pet 3:6), Rebekah (9:9), Jacob (9:13; 11:26; twenty-six times NT).

152. Nothing much has changed. Rasnake writes: "There's no substitute however, for good examples to follow. We need the squires God places around us, but for truly admirable knights, we look to the heroes of Scripture. The apostle Paul can serve well as a spiritual Sir Galahad, setting a high standard and laudable model to which we may aim." Rasnake, *Book of Romans*, 164. "We remember with genuine reverence the long succession of heroes and saints, martyrs and prophets." Morris, *Epistle to the Romans*, 478n5.

153. Barrett, *Epistle to the Romans*, 99: "For scarcely will anyone die for a righteous man, who might be expected to merit such heroic action? [sic.]; "The analogy pushes Christ's death into the sphere of the heroic." Käsemann, *Romans*, 137.

154. "Christ has exalted self-sacrifice into a heroism that charms the beholder, as he realizes the true glory of an intelligent will, that wins life by losing it, and imparts instead of egoistic happiness a Divine blessedness." Spence-Jones, *Romans*, 402.

155. Luke's writings arguably demonstrate the growing early church hero culture (Fitzmyer, *Romans*, 229). Part one (Luke) is totally dedicated to Jesus and has a range of subsidiary heroes. Acts focuses on Peter and Paul and to a lesser extent, Philip.

sion.¹⁵⁶ Indeed, knowing God sent Jesus (8:3) and Paul (1:1, 5), and others (see below), including those who established the faith in Rome, would inspire desire.¹⁵⁷

Further, the many named affectionately and positively would summon hearers to "be like them." These would include the OT figures of faith mentioned (above). Others mentioned in Romans have already been mentioned earlier in the chapter. In terms of potential "heroes,"¹⁵⁸ others in Paul's team would be prominent (esp. Timothy, 16:21). Lucius, Jason, and Sosipater were traveling with Paul and the collection at great personal expense to ensure the delivery of the gift to Jerusalem. Tertius would be a hero to scribes who could copy the LXX, Paul's letters, and others of Paul's writings (which within a few years were seen as Scripture and put together as a collection, 2 Pet 3:16).¹⁵⁹

The amazing women of Romans 16 would inspire the women of Rome to be deacons (Phoebe), be patrons and provide hospitality (Phoebe, Rufus's mother), preach and plant churches (Junia), be hosts of churches either alone or with their husbands (Prisca), and work hard for the church and Lord (Mary, Tryphaena, Tryphosa, Persis).

The wealthy men of the church and those with political power would see in Gaius and Erastus potential heroes of the faith. Such is the power of NT documents today. For hearers and readers, they are God's word, and by the Spirit, God speaks, often through godly examples that inspire us to be like them.¹⁶⁰ It is never easy: "We are taking the same journey as ancient heroes, and share their perplexities and convictions."¹⁶¹ Still, God is with those who hear and go. Further, it is true that "[n]o act of heroism is unregistered in heaven."¹⁶² While all NT documents do this, arguably alongside the Gospels, Romans has the most missional rhetorical force. May we hear its summons!

The Gospel, Its Content, and Its Power

The content of the letter summons readers to evangelize. In Romans 1:18—3:20, Paul outlines that all humankind is under sin's power and facing inevitable wrath. This sin leads to death (5:12) and eternal destruction (2:6–10). The world has been infected

---

156. The phrase "Christian heroism" is used by John Chrysostom (347–407). John Chrysostom. "Homilies of St. John Chrysostom, Archbishop of Constantinople, on the Epistle of St. Paul to the Romans." *NPNF* 1 11:426, 508, see also 4:409, 511, 552.

157. "All work is honourable to which God has appointed us. To receive a commission from an illustrious sovereign lends dignity to a task, and it is this thought of a Divine mission which has upheld many a hero at his post of toil and peril." Spence-Jones, *Romans*, 334.

158. Longenecker, *Epistle*, 1070 posits that Paul lists these "heroes of faith" to illicit support for him. Possibly, but I contend he also hopes that people emulate them.

159. This assumes the authenticity of 2 Peter. See Schreiner, *1, 2 Peter, Jude*, 255–77.

160. "Christian heroism cheerfully underwent the loss of goods, stripes, and imprisonment; it converted jails into holy fanes resounding with praise and prayer." Spence-Jones, *Romans*, 254.

161. Spence-Jones, *Romans*, 451.

162. Spence-Jones, *Romans*, 473.

with sin's cancer and is subject to decay (8:19–22). All who do not bow the knee to God and his Son will be destroyed eternally.[163]

Paul explains how, stunningly, God has sent his Son Jesus (8:3) to die for the sins of the world (6:10), to be raised from the dead (4:24), and to be exalted to cosmic lordship (8:34). He expounds that those who believe in him and acknowledge his lordship are guaranteed redemption from sin and its consequences (3:22–24). They, too, will be raised and gifted eternal life and immortality (6:4).

Furthermore, the gospel is the power of God for salvation (1:16; 1 Cor 1:18). Where it is preached to an open and comprehending heart, it is welcomed with faith and allegiance. This person is then God's child, reconciled to him (5:10), adopted (8:15), and they receive the Spirit (5:5). The gospel must be preached and heard for this to occur. The logic of Romans 1:16 calls all Christians to recognize that they are summoned into this mission.

The Salvation Sequence

While Romans 10:14–17 speaks first to Israel's rejection of the gospel, a Spirit-filled and open-hearted believer cannot help but be encouraged to share his or her faith, due to the content, scope, power, of the gospel and the sequence of conversion.[164] While the passage speaks first of Israel's rejection, the evangelistic progression of Romans 10:14–17 provides a precise sequence of evangelism: a person is sent, they preach, the gospel is heard and believed, the convert confesses and calls on the name of the Lord, and as Ephesians 1:13–14 tells us, the Spirit is received. The passage calls believers to ensure that all people have opportunity to hear the gospel. Then the process begins again.

Romans 16 speaks of a range of other preachers who live among the Romans. The letter was carried to Rome by a woman, Phoebe, who added to the letter details and information (16:1–2). The people named include men, women, Jews, gentiles, slaves, and freedpeople (see above). People are praised for their courage (16:4), their patronage (16:5, 13), their work for the church (16:6), and in the Lord (16:12). Again, the rhetorical impact is to excite missional zeal among others.

By AD 57 or 58, moreover, the Romans were well aware of Jesus's life through the likes of Pentecost pilgrims (Acts 2:10) and Jews like Prisca and Aquila, Junia and Andronicus, Herodian, Rufus and his mother, and other travelers to and from Rome. In fact, within a few years, two Gospels will be written from the city by John Mark and

---

163. Peters notes eight missional aspects of Paul's logic in Romans that would motivate mission. 1) God over creation and history; 2) humanity in Adam; 3) universal sin in Adam; 4) all have sinned; 5) Christ representative of all people; 6) Jesus the only way of salvation; 7) salvation revealed by God through his word; and 8) Paul's apostolic self-awareness. Peters, *Biblical Theology*, 149.

164. "We cannot read Romans 10:12–18 and not think missions." Peters, *Biblical Theology*, 133.

Luke.[165] As such, they also know that preaching the gospel was also central to the life of Christ (cf. Eph 2:17).

Christlikeness

Paul writes in Romans 8:29 that believers are predestined to "be conformed to the image of his Son," becoming more and more his brothers and sisters. Paul places no limit on this transformation. In that Jesus was the evangelist par excellence, without any limitation, this conforming should include missional zeal (especially with no prohibition to preach the gospel in Paul).

Believers are also to put on Christ Jesus (13:14). This injunction is set in the context of relationships with people of wider society. The saints are not to conform to their corrupted values but are to be clothed in Christ. One aspect is appropriate evangelistic zeal with the ethics of Romans 12:13–21 and 13:8–10.

Spirit-Empowerment

Elsewhere, Paul wants them to burn in the Spirit as they serve the Lord (12:11). This clause should not be interpreted only in terms of worship and internal relationships. It surely includes readers being spiritually passionate as they face a hostile world, loving strangers, blessing and feeding persecutors, refusing to curse and take revenge, and yielding to the State's rulers (12:13–14, 19–21; 13:1–10).

The Romans had all received the same Spirit as Paul, and the Spirit is the power of Christ and Paul's missions (15:19). The Spirit takes the God-breathed words of letters like Romans and generates missional desire. Indeed, Romans 1:16 applies here. Just as the gospel is the power of God for salvation, it is the power of God to generate evangelism that brings salvation. Romans itself is the word of God (for the faithful) and would have this effect implicitly.

Of course, Romans gives testimony to varying spiritual gifts, as seen in Paul's own call and commission.[166] Romans 12:4–8 lists a few of these gifts, including proclamation gifts of prophecy, teaching, and exhortation. These three speech gifts are neatly balanced by gifts that speak of humble and less visible things like serving others and social justice: service, generosity, and mercy. The other gift is leadership. Many Christians and scholars see such gifts and immediately localize them to service within churches. However, there is no limit placed on where and how these gifts are expressed. Members of the body of Christ are to employ them in the church and in the

---

165. See Keown, *Discovering the New Testament*, 1:139–40, 224–25.
166. See 1:1, 5–6, 14–15; 11:13; 15:15–32.

world for the common good and to build up the church both in terms of maturity and new converts (1 Cor 12:7; Eph 4:12).[167]

We know from Paul's other letters that there is a range of other gifts, including the "word of wisdom," which, in 1 Corinthians, is a message of the wisdom of the cross (1 Cor 12:8). As I have noted elsewhere, this would include such a message within the Christian community or outside.[168]

There are the gifts of apostolicity and evangelism, which are both inwardly and outwardly focused (1 Cor 12:28–29; Eph 4:11).[169] Some are gifted, and their role is to outwork their gifts in the world and to equip other Christians for works of service (Eph 4:11–12).[170] According to Paul, believers are right to desire spiritual gifts, especially those that build up the church (1 Cor 12:31; 14:1). While he focuses on prophecy in 1 Corinthians 14 (because the key issue in Corinth is tongues),[171] all gifts that cause growth (whether extensive or intensive) to God's church, build it up. Evangelism is undoubtedly one of these gifts. Working with Paul's logic, apostles and evangelists

---

167. The verb *sympherō* used in 1 Cor 12:7 speaks of advantage or benefit for the church without specifying the detail. Most commentators stop at the benefit to the community without any interest in extensive growth (e.g., Fee, *First Epistle to the Corinthians*, 654; Garland, *1 Corinthians*, 578–79; Ciampa and Rosner, *First Letter to the Corinthians*, 571; Thiselton, *First Epistle to the Corinthians*). Yet, surely, *sympherō* would include benefit to grow the church intensively *and extensively* with new converts (esp. apostles, workers of miracles, and healings [1 Cor 12:28–30]). Paul is thus gifted and does all things to win *as many as possible* (1 Cor 9:19–22; 10:31—11:1). Similarly, in Eph 4:11–16, the vocational leaders of the church equip others to build up the church in maturity (especially prophets, teachers, and pastors) and *further growth* (especially apostles and evangelists).

168. Based on wisdom in 1 Cor 1:17—2:16, Fee argues this "is the recognition that the message of Christ crucified is God's true wisdom, a recognition that comes only to those who have received the Spirit.... Spirit-inspired utterances that proclaim Christ crucified *in* this highly 'wisdom'-conscious community." Fee, *First Epistle to the Corinthians*, 656–67 (emphasis mine). But why should it be limited to "in this ... community?" Instead, it would be a message of the wisdom of the cross *in any situation*. Better is Thiselton, who says, "it is the articulate utterance of this wisdom. Hence it relates to 'God's plan of salvation' and its articulation or communication." Thiselton, *First Epistle to the Corinthians*, 939. *Logos* plus the genitive is always used of gospel proclamation. See further Keown, *Congregational Evangelism in Philippians*, 142.

169. "'Evangelists,' then, are probably those whom God has especially equipped to travel from place to place with the good news of peace through Christ." Thielman, *Ephesians*, 274. On Eph 4:15: "It is the Church's own growth, both in the quality of its corporate life and in the number of its adherents (cf. 1 Cor. 3:9), which is the author's chief concern in this passage and the reason for his insistence on the need for unity; so the intransitive is probably correct." Muddiman, *Epistle to the Ephesians*, 207. See further Keown, *Congregational Evangelism in Philippians*, 180–82.

170. Dickson limits the role of the evangelist to the restoration or the completion of the church (is a church ever complete?); a commissioned office; and work for its "construction." Dickson, *Mission-Commitment*, 327–28. However, as Thielman says: "The different types of leaders have been granted, not to enhance their own prestige or power, but to equip, serve and build up the whole community." Thielman, *Ephesians*, 200.

171. "It is clear from Paul's way of addressing the issue that some Corinthians were seeking or eagerly desiring what they considered to be the greater gifts (esp. tongues) and that that had created problems in the community." Ciampa and Rosner, *First Letter to the Corinthians*, 615.

should equip all the saints for the task of evangelism. Conversely, believers should seek missional spiritual gifts due to their importance.

A believing husband or wife is to be motivated to save their unbelieving spouse (1 Cor 7:12–15).[172] Believers who eat among unbelievers are to do nothing to offend but seek to act in the best interests of their salvation.[173] Interestingly, for Paul, the gift of prophecy itself is evangelistic. When outsiders and unbelievers hear God's word clearly, they are potentially converted (1 Cor 14:20–25).[174] In 1 Corinthians 14, in fact, Paul tacitly endorses sharing the gospel and in an appropriate way (not in untranslatable babble). Prophecy, as Paul understands it, has evangelistic power on visitors.

Hence, the thrust of Paul's view of who does evangelism is participation, not prohibition (because there is no imperative). Rather than inhibiting others, I find the very converse—all roads lead to Paul wanting others to take up the challenge of sharing their faith. All believers open to the message of Romans will be inspired to share the gospel as able wherever they encounter others: to build up other Christians and to see those who are yet to believe given opportunity to be saved. They will be passionate to embody the attitudes of Christ and do good to all they meet. Notably, even when motives are flawed, Paul is joyful when the gospel is preached. What matters for him is that Christ is proclaimed in every way (Phil 1:18).[175] Of course, it should always be done in an appropriate and timely way.

In Paul and the wider NT, there are also no limits placed on women or men serving God in his mission. No one is prohibited from sharing their faith, although it must always be done with warmth and grace (12:13–21; 13:8–10). Sometimes it must or must not be done at a particular time as the Spirit directs (Acts 8:26–40; 10:1–48; 16:6–10),[176] and at times, one must do it through attitudes and actions rather than direct speech (cf. 1 Pet 3:1–6). Indeed, Paul's hindrances from coming to Rome earlier prove the point: many times he has wanted to come, but God has intervened (1:8–15).[177] Ultimately, in God's time, he did come to Rome, and not only did he preach (1:15), evangelistic fervor broke out afresh (Phil 1:12–18a).[178]

---

172. On this passage, see Fee, *First Epistle to the Corinthians*, 328–38.

173. Keown, *Congregational Evangelism in Philippians*, 243–49.

174. Keown, *Congregational Evangelism in Philippians*, 248–49.

175. On Phil 1:18, see Keown, *Congregational Evangelism in Philippians*, 71–106, where I argue that "what counts is that Christ is proclaimed in every way" is an axiom of Paul's life.

176. Interestingly, Paul is directed away from Asia Minor in Acts 16:6–8. Guided by a vision to Macedonia, he goes and wins many converts through Macedonia and Achaia (Acts 16:9). Later, he comes to Ephesus, and an amazing work of the Spirit leads to Asia Minor hearing the gospel in two years (Acts 19:1–20). The conversions of the first gentiles in Acts were also catalyzed by the Spirit.

177. Whether the hindrance is Satan (1 Thess 2:18), opponents, or political circumstances (e.g., the Claudian Edict), or as is most likely, the urgency of other mission opportunities (Moo, *Letter to the Romans*, 63 and most commentators), for Paul, God is ultimately sovereign over the timing of his mission to Rome as seen in his use of "God's will" in 1:10; 15:32.

178. On a Roman provenance for Philippians, see Keown, *Philippians*, 1:24–32. On Phil 1:12–18a, see Keown, *Philippians*, 1:174–275.

The example of Paul, the Romans themselves, the shape of the gospel, the scope of mission, and Paul's pneumatology and understanding of God's sovereignty all summon people to yearn to join God's mission and share the gospel in lives, attitudes, deeds, in community, and with words full of grace and seasoned with salt (Col 4:5–6). In this way, the elect will be saved.

The debate over who does evangelism is false by assuming the negative and then imposing on the later church institutional structures such as ordination and the false dichotomy of clergy and laity. In the early days of the Christian movement, such things were not yet set. The gospel was spreading spontaneously and quickly through whoever would carry it. This expansion was more dynamic and charismatic than today's dying, cumbersome, ecclesiological institutions of the west. It was more akin to the rapid spread of the gospel in non-European settings where all are engaged in evangelization.[179] It is axiomatic in such contexts and should be in all.

God, the Father, the Son, and the Holy Spirit together are, "*The* Evangelist." People are saved from sin, death, and destruction, not to hold onto our faith in holy huddles, but to be gripped by the gospel, build one another up with it, and tell it to the world. The church is the body of Christ charged to give witness to God in the world. Believers are to follow the example of Jesus, Paul, and the outstanding workers of Romans 16 and preach the word to the world in lives given over to God, in deeds, in community, and word.

CONCLUSION

So, I surmise that Romans supports the notion of a whole people of God equipped and inspired by the Spirit to join God in his mission. The Spirit uses Romans and other texts to generate desire in God's people. The gospel summons peoples to share their faith with the lost. It urges churches to be bound together in the one Spirit, fearlessly standing and contending for the faith of the gospel, and holding forth the word of life (Phil 1:27–30; 2:16).[180] The power of God must be unleashed. Indeed, it will be, for it cannot be contained (2 Tim 2:9). If some will not hear the call, others will be raised by God. God will do this because people *must* hear his gospel. New converts must then be inspired to share it with those in their orb. Yes, specialists are required to lead the mission and equip the saints (Eph 4:11). Of course, the church is to support them financially and prayerfully (which they do poorly in my context; yet another problem

---

179. I recall a friend in Hong Kong sharing with me a trip to a Chinese underground house church. Upon entering, he asked who established it. He was pointed to a middle-aged woman and told, "She has planted 10,000 of these." He became a believer in women in ministry on the spot. In this manner, the gospel spread in the early church.

180. On Phil 1:27–30, see Keown, *Congregational Evangelism in Philippians*, 107–24; idem, *Philippians*, 1:276–326. On Philippians 2:16a in context, see Keown, *Congregational Evangelism in Philippians*, 125–47, 449–513; Keown, "ΛΟΓΟΝ ΖΩΗΣ EPECHONTES," 98–117. Similarly, see Ware, *Mission of the Church*, 215–23, 237–84.

of the Western church). Indeed, the church is to give witness in its life, worship, ethics, relationships, and in gracious, confident response to inquiries.[181] However, surely, the church and its people are all called to preach the gospel to those in its world. The gospel is not just the power of salvation; it has within it the power to inspire evangelism. If the church stops preaching, the church dies.[182]

Reflecting on the expansion of the gospel in non-Western countries, Stephen Niell writes,

> In the days of St. Paul those who were given to the Church were not the wise or the mighty or the influential; the poor, the simple and the disinherited were the instruments whom God was pleased to use for the accomplishment of His great work.[183]

It is time for Western biblical scholarship to recognize that in contexts where the gospel is establishing and expanding, as in the early church, it was not merely vocational missionaries who did the work. The whole church was mobilized in mission led by the Spirit.

---

181. Dickson, *Mission-Commitment*; Bowers, "Church and Mission in Paul," 89–111; Bosch, *Transforming Mission*, 133–39.

182. Similarly, see Plummer, *Paul's Understanding*.

183. Neil, *Unfinished Task*, 115. He notes this is what happened in India as the mission grew.

17

The Miraculous

IN OUR SCIENTIFIC WORLD, miracles are contentious, and many people rule them out as evidence of an ancient mythological worldview. Everything is explainable scientifically, and science supposedly rules out miracles. Of course, this is curious in that the origin of the universe is unknown and that and the complexity of existence demands some kind of creative force. Furthermore, we still have no idea how to generate life, prolong it indefinitely, or raise the dead.

Conversely, ancient people hoped for and believed in the possibility of the miraculous. They experienced great suffering.[1] They lacked our medical advances and were vulnerable, with a life expectancy of thirty to forty.[2] They believed that deities and spirits influenced the world with what we call the sacred and secular fused. Their gods and these spiritual forces were assumed and were capable of intervention.[3]

Romans, like all NT documents, challenges contemporaries to consider the place of the miraculous in mission. Although it is fair to say the miraculous is not a dominant thread in Romans, there is evidence that miracles were a part of Paul's worldview and missional approach. This material will now be considered.

CREATION

As has been discussed, Paul is convinced that God is the Creator who made the universe (1:25). The world is labeled "the creation" (8:19–23, 39). Paul does not mention seven days or describe the scientific process. He simply assumes the veracity of the Genesis narrative. It is an important aspect of his theological thinking, that shaped

---

1. See Keown, "Notes of Hope in the Face of Suffering," paras. 8–10.

2. Jones, "Paleopathology," 5:67.

3. Kee, "Medicine and Healing," 659–62; Keown, *Gospels & Acts*, 469–70. For Ephesus as an example, see Arnold, *Ephesians*, 14–29.

and other Jewish and Christian believers.⁴ We are left to speculate on what he would say about evolution.⁵ In terms of the miraculous, creation by evolution or divine fiat (over whatever period) is equally miraculous.⁶

Although Paul probably did not encounter what we call an atheist and naturalist who completely rejects the divine, he likely had little time for such a person's view. For him, God's incredible character and power are plain and able to be recognized through what has been made. A person who fails to perceive this is without excuse (1:19–20). The creation of Adam is affirmed with the image of God as potter and people as vessels formed from clay (9:20–23, cf. 5:14). As the creator and the one who "calls into existence the things that do not exist," God is a God of the miraculous (4:17).

God's creative work extends beyond the physical world into history as he forms Israel and works out his salvation in space and time. His work in people, flooding them with his Spirit, and bringing them alive spiritually is creative work, something Paul stresses elsewhere (2 Cor 5:17; Gal 6:15). Indeed, believers are the firstfruits of a new creation launched at the resurrection. Their spiritual rebirth will culminate in their complete redemption at the consummation (1 Cor 15:50–54). He will then renew creation, liberating it from its bondage to decay and death (8:19–23).⁷

THE PROPHETIC

Romans is premised on God fulfilling prophecies made by his chosen prophets in former times. God himself is the Prophet who existed before time, foresaw, foreknew, and predestined history (8:29–30), who speaks through people and his Son in any genuine prophetic utterances, and who enacts what is predicted in space and time in Jesus and by his Spirit. He has spoken in the past, making promises through his prophets. These are recorded in the Holy Scriptures (1:2). The righteousness of faith fulfills these hopes (3:21). Indeed, the whole eschatological eon launched by the coming of God's Son is fulfilling the OT prophecies to the end (part two, chapter 6). At the heart of this is his Son, who descends from David, fulfilling the promise of an eternal

---

4. Discussing Rom 5:15–19, Schreiner astutely comments: "Finally, it is debated whether Adam is a historical or a mythological figure here. There is little doubt that Paul believed he was historical. He did not confront the theory of evolution, which has caused people to reconsider the historicity of Adam. The question of Adam's historicity, therefore, relates more to the area of apologetics than it does to exegesis." Schreiner, *Romans*, 292–93.

5. "Polygenism is thus a modern development of teaching about evolution. It goes far beyond Paul's perspective; hence what Paul says in 5:12–21 cannot be used to solve such a problem." Fitzmyer, *Romans*, 410. Where evangelism is concerned, evolution is neither here nor there. The story of human-God engagement begins at the moment the first people met God. The biblical narrative holds true whatever process God used.

6. If God put in process evolution and guided the billions of mutations that led to the creation of humankind, our world remains an amazing miracle full of myriads of signs and wonders..

7. See also 1 Cor 15:26; Eph 1:11; Col 1:20.

It Is Written

The formula "it is written" (*gegraptai*), which is used by Paul thirty-one times, with just over half of these in Romans (16x).[8] It is in the perfect passive of *graphō*, "write." The passive speaks of God writing by his Spirit through a human agency (2 Tim 3:16, see also Eph 3:5). Wallace describes the traditional understanding of the perfect tense:

> The force of the perfect tense is simply that it describes an event that, completed in the past (we are speaking of the perfect indicative here), has results existing in the present time (i.e., in relation to the time of the speaker).[9]

Others, like Porter, take the perfect tense in this way:

> The perfect and pluperfect tense-forms occur in contexts where the user of Greek wishes to depict the action as reflecting a given (often complex) state of affairs.[10]

In the case of *gegraptai*, whether we take it statively or in the traditional manner, Paul is using the perfect tense to speak of something written in the past by an OT writer, empowered by the Spirit, and that continues to speak into the present (and beyond). A look at Paul's use of *gegraptai* in Romans shows how the prophetic voice of God in the Scriptures is being fulfilled in the present. It is another example of the miraculous in Romans.

He uses it first of, "the righteous will live by faith," first declared by God through Habakkuk (1:17; Hab 2:4). This covenantal axiom is being worked out in the present by faith in Christ, the Son. The prophets testified to this righteousness of God through faith (3:21). Now, the principle of Genesis 15:6 spoken over Abraham that faith is counted as righteousness is being worked out for humankind through Christ (4:4, 23). David's dream of God blessing his people with forgiveness and the covering of sin is being shared to all humankind in Jesus, David's descendant (4:7–8; Ps 32:1–2, cf. 1:3; 15:12).

Similarly, Isaiah's critique of Israel's self-righteousness and blaspheming of God among the nations goes on as Israel continues to violate God's commands up to the time Romans was written (2:24; Isa 52:5). David's prophetic song of contrition after his sin highlights God's justice that finds its fulfillment in Christ, the righteousness of God (3:4; LXX Ps 50:6 [51:4 EVV]). Universal human depravity remains the same as

---

8. Rom 1:17; 2:24; 3:4, 10; 4:17; 8:36; 9:13, 33; 10:15; 11:8; 12:19; 14:11; 15:3, 9, 21. See also 1 Cor 1:19, 31; 2:9; 3:19; 4:6; 9:9; 10:7; 14:21; 15:45; 2 Cor 8:15; 9:9; Gal 3:10, 13; 4:22, 27.

9. Wallace, *Greek Grammar*, 573.

10. Porter, *Idioms*, 39.

when the prophets David and Isaiah prophesied.[11] Israel's persecution at the hands of enemies continues in the suffering of God's church (8:36; Ps 44:22).

Just as God chose Jacob over Esau (9:13), he elects to continue his line in Christ. Isaiah's vision of a cornerstone of God's people causing Israel to stumble in unbelief is fulfilled in Christ (9:33; Isa 28:16). The beauty of the prophet crying the good news to Israel is now fulfilled and transcended in Christ and his sons and daughters who are carrying the news of God's victory over sin, death, and destruction to the world (10:15; Isa 52:7).

Isaiah's experience of Israel's stupor and spiritual blindness has come to pass again as hardened Israel rejects Jesus (11:8; Isa 29:10). God's deliverer from Zion, who will deal with sin, has now come (11:26–27; Isa 59:20–21). Isaiah's vision of the people of the world on their knees in full submission to God is approaching. Ultimately, they will yield to the Lord his Son at the judgment and face the consequences of rejecting him (14:11; Isa 45:23). As David sang, Jesus has died on a cross, taking the reproaches of the world onto himself (15:3; Ps 69:9). Now, as David, Moses, and Isaiah predicted, the nations are praising God.[12] They do so because Isaiah's hope of those of the world who have never heard of God are now hearing and understanding (15:21; Isa 52:15). In *gegraptai* alone, we see how the prophetic and its fulfillment lies at the heart of Paul's understanding of the gospel.

Other Prophetic Aspects

Other aspects of God's prophetic brilliance coming to fulfillment are found throughout Romans. God's promises to Abraham that he would have a myriad of offspring (Gen 15:5) and would be the father of many nations (Gen 17:5) is being fulfilled in Christ and the yielding of gentiles to God's Son (4:17).

While now that Christ has come, believers are free from the Jewish Torah and no longer live under it (6:15), the law is not overthrown but upheld in Christ and righteousness by faith (3:31).

The first Adam is now trumped by the new Adam, who brought death and condemnation (5:12, 16). The new and better Adam, the authentic and complete image of God (8:29), graciously gives righteousness and eternal life (5:16–21). Believers are conformed into his image (8:29). Isaiah's dream of the new heavens and new earth is becoming a reality in Christ (8:19–22; Isa 65:17–25).

Just as not all people born into Abraham's family, Israel, are God's people and Abraham's children, having rejected God's word, so the family of Abraham goes on and extends now that Christ has come (9:6–7). God's sovereign choice of the line of Abraham, Isaac, and Jacob has come to its climax in Christ and continues by faith in him (9:6–24). The dreams of the prophets that the gentiles will be God's people

---

11. See 3:10–18; Pss 5:9; 9:28 [LXX]; 14:1–3; 36:1; 140:3; Isa 59:7–8.
12. See 15:9–13; 2 Sam 22:50; Pss 18:49; 117:1; Deut 32:43; Isa 11:10.

and Israel's sad rejection and stumbling over Jesus is being fulfilled.[13] As in the days of Elijah, God has chosen a remnant by grace, the people of the Son (11:3-6; 1 Kgs 19:10-14).

Whereas in Israel prior to Christ, God's vengeance was exercised through Israel, now Moses's hopes of God's people laying aside revenge, leaving it for God, is fulfilled (12:19; Deut 32:35). Christ's death deals with God's vengeance for those who believe (13:5). For those who do not, time is given for them to yield (cf. 2 Pet 3:9, 15). The governments of the world function on his behalf, maintaining order (13:1-6). Now that God's love has been demonstrated in Christ (5:8), every one of God's laws are now swept up into one governing imperative: love others! (13:8-10).

Romans itself is a prophetic document with Paul, God's prophet, looking forward to the future fulfillment of his promises. Like Mark and Matthew (Mark 13:10; Matt 24:24), Paul looks forward to the day that the mission is complete (11:12, 25). He will work until his final breath, taking Christ to new territories to hasten that day (15:20-24). While he only hints at Christ's return in Romans (13:12), he looks forward to all facing judgment (2:5-11; 4:10-12). He looks forward to the destruction of decay, death, and evil (8:19-22; 9:22), and the eternal life and immortality of God's people (6:23). Satan will be crushed under the feet of the son of Adam and God (16:20). By showing how God has been faithful in the past to Israel, readers can be confident that God will fulfill his promises into the future. Indeed, believing in these promises is an essential aspect of the faith that justifies (cf. 4:20).

Aside from the OT prophets and Paul's prophetic gift, Romans endorses the spiritual gift of prophecy. Contemporary Christians are, in many instances, reticent about prophecy, often because of bad experiences and false prophetic claims. Some theological constructs like Cessationism consider that such prophetic gifts are limited to the apostolic period.[14] Others, like the Reformers, limit prophecy to the exposition of the Scriptures.[15] Some limit it to inspired preaching, speaking into the present prophetically without the element of foretelling.[16]

However, the NT, including Paul, is clear: the gift of prophecy should be a part of the life of the church within worship. It also has a missional function to convict and convert unbelievers (1 Cor 14:24-25). Paul's interest in the prophetic has already been demonstrated in Paul's view of fulfillment and his prophetic perspective on the future (above). For Paul, God chooses to communicate his word through people gifted in

---

13. 9:25; Isa 1:9; Hos 1:10; 2:23; Isa 28:16.

14. See Gaffin, "Cessationist View," 23-64.

15. "The Reformers, Luther and Calvin, limited the spontaneous character of prophecy by defining this gift as the proper exposition of the Scriptures, hence, they popularized the idea of prophecy as preaching." Robeck, "Prophecy, Prophesying," 761.

16. "The New Testament prophet is to be distinguished from the Old Testament prophet both as one situated in a different dispensation and as more committed to forthtelling than to foretelling." Chafer, *Systematic Theology*, 4:268.

this way. They should do so as God calls some to be prophets in his church (12:6).[17] Elsewhere, we learn more. They are permitted to prophesy one at a time, three at the most, and in order (1 Cor 14:29, 31). Both women and men can prophesy in the appropriate cultural attire (1 Cor 11:4–5). Believers should indeed earnestly desire the gift of prophecy (1 Cor 14:39).

Paul's interest in the prophetic punctuates Luke's account of his life. Paul was imbued with the Spirit and commission for his ministry through the prophetic word and consequence act of Ananias, an "ordinary" disciple of Damascus (Acts 9:10–19). It was Agabus who sparked his first Jerusalem Collection and, subsequently, his second (Acts 11:26; Gal 2:10).[18] His great missions from Antioch were sparked by the Spirit (Acts 13:2, 4). His mission was subsequently guided a number of times by prophetic experiences.[19] It seems that looking at Paul's letters and Acts, prophecy could include both forthtelling and foretelling dimensions.

However, prophecies are to be weighed by others carefully (1 Cor 14:29, 32; 1 Thess 5:21).[20] Where it is assessed to be the voice of God, his people should act. Where not, it is to be rejected. Believers are at the same time to have an anticipatory openness to prophecy and a healthy skepticism that sees them test every such claimed utterance. Still, Western Christianity needs to rediscover the gift of the prophetic. God still speaks. As such, Romans shows us that the prophetic is integral to the Christian mission. Believers must not "despise prophecies" (1 Thess 5:20). Equally, they must test everything (1 Thess 5:21).

RESURRECTION

At the heart of Romans is the miracle of resurrection. God is not merely the Creator, but he is the one who "gives life to the dead" (4:17). The pivotal miraculous moment in Romans is the resurrection of Jesus by the agency of the Spirit.[21] By this resurrection, Christ's eternal sonship was declared to the world (1:4). People who place their trust in him are crucified and buried in him. That is, his death becomes their death, and

---

17. See 1 Cor 12:10, 28–29; 13:9; 14:5–6, 24–25, 29–39; Eph 3:5; 4:11; 1 Tim 4:14.

18. In part, Paul's second collection mentioned in Romans 15:28–32 was a fulfillment of his promise to continue to remember the poor (Gal 2:10)—he was in Jerusalem because of Agabus (Gal 2:2). On Gal 2 = Acts 11:26–30, see Longenecker, *Galatians*, lxxvii–lxxxiii. See also Keown, *Galatians*, 16–32.

19. Acts 13:9–11; 16:6–10; 18:9; 20:22–23; 21:4, 11; 27:23–24 (telling him he would go to Rome, fulfilling his hopes in Rom 1 and 15). The believers' concerns and Agabus's prediction of Paul's suffering in Jerusalem were correct, yet Paul had already been told to go to Jerusalem by the Spirit (Acts 20:22–23; 21:11). There are also prophets in Antioch (Acts 13:1), a false prophet in Paphos (Acts 13:6), Judas and Silas were prophets, and the latter traveled with Paul, preaching and co-sending letters (Acts 15:32; 2 Cor 1:19; 1 Thess 1:1; 2 Thess 1:1). Paul stayed with Philip; whose four daughters prophesied (Acts 21:9).

20. In 1 Cor 14:29, 32, it is implied that others with the prophetic gift participate in the testing of prophecy. In 1 Thessalonians 5:21, it seems general.

21. See 1:4; 4:24, 25; 6:4, 9; 7:4; 8:11, 34.

death has no hold on them. They will also be raised from the dead to eternal life.[22] The same Spirit who raised Jesus will raise the faithful (8:11).

This eternal life is the gift of God based on faith and not works (6:23). At the center of this faith is the belief that God raised Jesus from the dead (10:9). Where such faith is found, and Christ's lordship acknowledged, believers will experience a resurrection like his. Their perishable and mortal bodies of humiliation will be transformed in an instant to be imperishable and immortal bodies of glory (6:5).[23] Just as Jesus will never die again because death has no dominion over him, so it will be for God's people (6:9).

The central problem that humankind faces is death. Romans tells us that death is caused by sin, and both sin and death are unavoidable human conditions (3:23; 5:12). Jesus's redemptive death solves the problem of sin and his resurrection resolves death. Although many scientists are now being charged to solve the physical problem of death,[24] they have yet to resolve it. God has. Jesus is the solution. The miracle of resurrection lies at the heart of the faith. People are summoned to hope for resurrection in Christ.

MIRACLES IN MISSION

The gospel is the declaration of repeated miracles. God created the world and shapes history — miracle upon miracle. He sent his Son into the world to perform miracles, to die, and to rise from the dead—an astonishing reversal of death. Paul and his readers (and Christians today) believe in these miracles and hope for the same in our lives. That this is so was all predicted and is coming to pass. The gospel is premised on the miraculous.

Miracles in Paul's Mission

Paul tells us in Romans that miracles were an essential feature of his mission strategy. He speaks of his ministry "by the power (*dynamis*) of signs (pl. *sēmeion*) and wonders (pl. *teras*)" in Romans 15:19. The terms are unsensational with *sēmeion* meaning

---

22. See 5:18, 21; 6:4, 22; 11:15.
23. See also 1 Cor 15:50–54; Phil 3:21.
24. See, e.g., Gabbatt, "Is Silicon Valley's Quest for Immortality."

"miracle,"[25] and *teras*, "something that astounds... prodigy, portent, omen, wonder."[26] The terms are paired sixteen times in the NT, three times in Paul.[27] "'Signs and wonders' was a traditional way of speaking of the exodus miracles."[28] As such,

> Paul's missionary calling and work among the nations stand within a salvation-historical framework—especially related to the exodus—with which the purposes of God for the saving of both Jew and Gentile are closely bound.[29]

Sēmeion is used of the miracles of Moses (Acts 6:8), Jesus (Acts 2:22), apostles,[30] and of other early Christians including Stephen (Acts 6:8), Philip (Acts 8:6), and Paul and Barnabas (Acts 14:3; 15:12). Paul uses *sēmeion* of the Jewish demand for signs (1 Cor 1:22) and in 2 Cor 12:12, where miraculous signs are one of the signs (*sēmeion*) of true apostleship.[31] *Teras* is used of counterfeit miracles (2 Thess 2:9), of miracles in the early church (Heb 2:4), and of those of Moses (Acts 7:36), Jesus (Acts 2:22), apostles (Acts 4:30; 5:12), Stephen (Acts 6:8), Paul and Barnabas together (Acts 14:3; 15:12), and Paul himself (15:19; 2 Cor 12:12).[32]

The genitive phrase *dynamei sēmeion kai teratōn* may be attributive: "powerful signs and wonders performed in the power of the Spirit of God." The double use of power here speaks of Paul's belief that God's supernatural strength empowers his ministry. He is not merely a public speaker using the power of persuasion; God is truly with him. The gospel he proclaims *is* the power of salvation (1:16). He lays hands on those in need, and God acts.

---

25. BDAG 920. See Mark 16:17, 20. *Sēmeion* features in requests for a sign that Jesus refused (Matt 12:38–39; 16:1–4; Mark 8:11–12; Luke 11:16, 29–30; 23:8; John 2:18; 6:30) and the Jewish demand for signs in general terms (John 4:48). They can be false, meaning their source is demonic or magic (Matt 24:24; Mark 13:22). *Sēmion* is John's favored term for the miracles of Jesus (John 2:11, 18, 23; 3:2; 4:54; 6:2, 14, 16, 30; 7:31; 9:16; 11:47; 12:19, 37; 20:30, see also John 10:41). It can be broadercomma signifying a sign pointing to the consummation (Matt 24:3, 30; Mark 13:4; Luke 21:7); a sign marking a person or something, e.g., by a kiss (Matt 26:48), or a baby in a manger (Luke 2:12); Jesus himself as a sign (Luke 2:34); amazing sights in the skies (Luke 21:11, 25; Acts 2:19); signs in the heavens in Revelation (Rev 12:1, 2; 15:1); fake miracles by the beasts (Rev 13:13, 14) and demons (Rev 16:14; 19:20).

26. BDAG 999. *Teras* is also used of false wonders (Matt 24:24; Mark 13:22); the Jewish demand for wonders (John 4:48); wonders in the heavens (Acts 2:19). He also uses it of counterfeit signs and wonders by the lawless one (2 Thess 2:12).

27. Matt 24:24; Mark 13:22; John 4:48; Acts 2:19, 22, 43; 4:30; 5:12; 6:8; 7:36; 14:3; 15:12; Rom 15:19; 2 Cor 12:12; 2 Thess 2:9; Heb 2:4; Rev 15:1.

28. Köstenberger and O'Brien, *Salvation to the Ends of the Earth*, 169.

29. Köstenberger and O'Brien, *Salvation to the Ends of the Earth*, 169.

30. See Acts 2:43; 4:16, 22, 30; 5:12.

31. Paul also uses it of the mark of circumcision, which signifies inclusion in the covenant community (4:11), tongues as a sign for believers (1 Cor 14:22), a signature as a mark of authenticity of his letters (2 Thess 3:17).

32. With the language used almost exclusively in Paul and the NT, Betz's claim that these are "are not only charismatic miracles but also missionary successes visible in the life of the congregation (cf. 2 Cor 3:2)" is unlikely (even if such things are miraculous in the broader sense of the term). Betz, "σημεῖον," 241. The broader notion of the power of God could relate to conversion (cf. 1:16).

Paul does not emphasize the miraculous dimension of his ministry, perhaps because there were triumphalist early preachers who were critical of his theology of suffering and focused on the miraculous (see 2 Cor 10–12).[33] Still, somewhat reluctantly, he speaks of the marks of a true apostle, including "signs, wonders, and miracles" (2 Cor 12:12). He also reminds the Galatians of their experience of miracles when he was amongst them (Gal 3:5).

In Acts, Luke mentions miracles associated with Paul. His conversion included the miracle of his blinding and then his healing through Ananias, perhaps also signifying the healing of his spiritual blindness (Acts 9:9, 18). He himself commanded blindness on Elymas in Cyprus (Acts 13:9–12), healed a disabled man in Lystra (Acts 14:10), delivered a demon in Philippi (Acts 16:18), and healed the father of Publius in Malta (Acts 28:8). He may have been raised from the dead in Lystra (Acts 14:20) and miraculously survived a snake bite in Malta (Acts 28:3–6). Luke gives neat summaries of other signs and wonders he performed, especially in Ephesus.[34]

The partnership of speaking the gospel and the miraculous is etched into the missional practice of Jesus (e.g., Matt 4:23; 9:35), other preachers in the Gospels, Acts, and the letters.[35] They did not conceive of a missional approach that was purely people proclaiming God's salvation verbally; they understood that God was active in the present and could perform miracles. Paul is no different from these other preachers, with signs and wonders a feature of his approach.

The Place of Miracles in Mission

Nevertheless, more can be said about miracles. First, as with Jesus, Paul condemns the seeking of signs and wonders before they can believe (1 Cor 1:22).[36] Jesus refused, only performing miracles where there was a genuine need. Non-Christians are prone to this, and so sadly are some Christians who demand God do miracles to vindicate himself. God the Creator, sovereign over history, the sender of his Son, transformer of the world, and savior of souls, empowerer by the Spirit, has surely done enough. Seeking miracles for anything other than legitimate human need is greed and arrogance.

Second, especially in Corinth, Paul was challenged by false apostles who made much of their supernatural powers.[37] Paul's boast is suffering and not any miracles, although he had done them. While praying for those in need is central to mission,

---

33. See Dunn, *Romans 9–16*, 863: "The point is rather that too much weight could be placed on such 'signs' and undercut the primary theology of the cross."

34. See Acts 14:3, 12; 19:11; 28:9.

35. For example, Luke 9:6; Acts 2:43; 3; 5:12; 6:8; 8:5–7; Heb 2:4.

36. See Matt 12:39; 16:4; Mark 8:12; John 4:48; 6:26.

37. "The rivals may also have cast doubt on Paul's spiritual power because of a perceived shortage of the signs of the true apostle, 'signs and wonders and mighty works' (12:12)." Garland, *2 Corinthians*, 441.

suffering is real, death is inevitable, and we should not demand signs or expect them to a ludicrous degree. The life expectancy of the ancients was thirty-five to forty, and while God intervened on occasion, we should not overstate miracles. They all subsequently died and often when still young. Indeed, Paul himself left Trophimus sick in Miletus, demonstrating that God had not healed him (2 Tim 4:20).[38]

Third, when we consider the timespan of Paul's ministry in Acts (ca. AD 33–61) and his letters (ca. AD 48–66), in actual fact, there are not that many miracles mentioned. There were indeed moments where God acted more dramatically, especially at the inception of the gospel in Jerusalem, Samaria, and with Paul in Ephesus (Acts 5:12–16; 8:7; 19:10–20). Aside from this, we have edited highlights from over thirty years.[39]

Furthermore, miracles are mentioned only once in Romans, 2 Corinthians, and Galatians, and the gift of the miraculous only in 1 Corinthians (1 Cor 12:10, 29; 13:2). As such, eight letters make no mention of them. They are not mentioned in the spiritual gifts in Romans nor Ephesians (12:4–8; Eph 4:11). Christian miracles do not dominate the other letters and Revelation either. There is a summary of early miracles in Hebrews 2:4, and prayer for the sick is mentioned in James 5:14–16 but with no mention of the certainty of healing.[40]

Fourth, for Paul, miraculous powers and healing are spiritual gifts that not all believers are given (1 Cor 12:9–10, 29–30).[41] He seems to consider them a mark of an apostle (2 Cor 12:12).[42] As such, there was no rampant expectation in Paul that every Christian would perform miracles if only they have enough faith. This heresy is rejected and challenged by Paul.

---

38. Garland, *1 Corinthians*, 582. Garland also mentions Epaphroditus as evidence Paul did not see himself as a healer (Phil 2:27). This suggestion is flawed as we do not know how Epaphroditus was healed. Paul may have been the agent, and there is ample evidence that Paul had the gift of healings. Still, he is right to argue that we should not overstate healing.

39. I like to ask my students how many miracles would be attested from the last thirty years if we were to travel throughout all New Zealand's churches interviewing Christians asking them what they have witnessed. I posit that there would be many more than in Acts. I myself can testify firsthand to at least ten unexplainable occurrences in my thirty-six-year Christian life to this point.

40. Perhaps miracles are implied in Heb 6:2. Revelation is full of apocalyptic signs, including those attributed to evil sources (Rev 13:3, 12). The ultimate healing of believers is implied in Rev 2:7; 21:4; 22:2, 14, 19.

41. Some take the plural to indicate that people are not healers, so the gift is the healing. E.g., Ciampa and Rosner, *First Letter*, 578. Yet, the gifts in 1 Cor 12:28–30 are possessive (apostle, prophet, teacher, miracle-worker, healer, tongues-speaker). So Thiselton says, "the plural becomes a device for carrying the notion of *more than one kind* of what the word represents" (emphasis original). He goes on, "Justin, writing in the second century, alludes to the ministry of Christian persons who 'perform exorcisms in the name of Jesus Christ . . . who have healed and do heal . . . those who could not be cured . . . by those who use incantations and drugs.'" Thiselton, *First Epistle*, 946.

42. Further, in Acts, miracles are only performed by Moses (Acts 7:36), Jesus (Acts 2:22; 10:38), apostles (Acts 2:43; 5:12), especially Peter (Acts 3:1–10 [and John]; 5:15–16; 9:32–43]), and Paul (Acts 14:3, 8–10; 15:12; 19:11–12; 28:8), two of the seven (Stephen [Acts 6:8] and Philip [Acts 8:5–7]), and Barnabas (Acts 14:3; 15:12). There is no evidence other Christians did them from the text.

Fifth, counterfeit miracles are mentioned across the NT, indicating that a miracle does not immediately demand that God is the actor.[43] Just as early Christians believed in miracles, they recognized that their source could be malicious and deceitful. Hence, care needs to be taken where they are observed.

Sixth, any discussion on the miraculous in Paul cannot ignore the "thorn in his flesh" (2 Cor 12:5–9). We are not sure what the thorn was with a range of ideas that can be broken down into three real possibilities.[44] First, it could be spiritual or psychological anxiety. Two options here are the pain of his former persecution[45] or Israel's stubborn disbelief.[46] Second, it could be some opposition Paul experienced. These could be general,[47] a single opponent,[48] or opposition in Corinth.[49] Third, it could be a physical ailment, whether unknown,[50] malarial fever,[51] Malta fever,[52] migraine headaches,[53] or defective vision.[54] It may well be some kind of visible disability that led to the criticism "his bodily presence is weak" (2 Cor 10:10).

Whatever his problem was, it was for Paul a weakness (vv. 5, 9), something that prodded into him in his body literally or figuratively (v. 7), and a messenger of Satan that harassed him (v. 7). He asked three times for healing (v. 8). Nonetheless, he was told, "My grace is sufficient for you, for power is made perfect in weakness" (v. 9, my translation). In other words, while it was a weakness, God's grace in all that he had given Paul was enough, and his power was perfected in him through it. As such, the thorn strengthened his ministry, even if it weakened him personally.

Paul also interpreted it as a gift to stop him from falling into arrogance due to the unique revelation of heaven he received (vv. 1–4, 7). As such, he boasts in his weaknesses as God's power is on him (v. 9), and he states that he is content with his various sufferings, for when weak, he is strong in Christ (v. 10).

Paul knew the value of prayer as he prayed three times for deliverance from the thorn. He then accepted Christ's rejection of his request, finding that the problem he

---

43. Matt 24:24; 13:22; 2 Thess 2:9; Rev 13:13–14; 19:20.

44. Taken from Harris, *Second Epistle to the Corinthians*, 858–59.

45. Schlatter, *Paulus, der Bote Jesu*, 667.

46. See "Thorn in the Flesh and Satan's Angel (2 Cor. 12:7)," in Menoud's book, *Jesus Christ and the Faith*, 19–30.

47. See, for example Barnett, *Second Epistle to the Corinthians*, 570, who sees it as Judaizers.

48. A single opponent, e.g., Forbes, "Comparison, Self-Praise and Irony," 1–30.

49. Harris notes three options: the "false apostles" (11:14, Binder, "Die angebliche Krankheit des Paulus," 1–13); an accusation he was an angel of Satan (Thierry, "Der Dorn im Fleische (2 Kor. xii 7–9)," 301–10); and the rejection of his apostolicity (McCant, "Paul's Thorn of Rejected Apostleship," 550–72).

50. E.g., Fee, *God's Empowering Presence*, 352–53; Harris, *2 Corinthians*, 859.

51. Ramsay, *St. Paul the Traveller*, 94–97.

52. Alexander, "St. Paul's Infirmity," 469–73, 545–48.

53. E.g., Thrall, *Commentary on II Corinthians VIII–XIII*, 818.

54. Nisbet, "Thorn in the Flesh," 126.

had amplified God's power in and through him and kept him humble. Such a rejection had also been Christ's experience in the Garden of Gethsemane when he also prayed three times to be delivered from crucifixion, including thorns in his head (Mark 14:32–42).[55] We see here a balanced Paul emulating Christ: he prayed passionately for healing and deliverance; he accepted the answer from his sovereign God. He got on with his ministry with joy and confidence in God. This approach believers should emulate.

The final aspect of the value of suffering in Romans is in Romans 5:1–5. Just as Paul boasted in his thorn, believers are also to boast in their sufferings. They do so as those justified by faith who have peace with God and access to his throne room. Further, they know that the suffering generates endurance, which in turn produces character, which then engenders hope. This hope will not bring them disappointment because of the presence of the Spirit and God's love in their hearts. Furthermore, suffering is the inevitable path to glory that believers, as heirs of the cosmos, must tread (8:17). However, God is with them in their sufferings, especially present with the Spirit (8:26–27).[56]

CONCLUSION

In conclusion, it is evident that Paul was committed to praying for those in need and was open and hopeful of God's intervention. As he preached the gospel, no doubt prayer for healing was offered, and so it should be today. However, we must take extreme care not to tip the balance from the proclamation of the gospel in godly attitudes, words of grace, and good deeds to the demand and hyper-expectation of miracles. Overemphasizing miracles empties the gospel of its power as people seek miracles and do not recognize the miracle of Christ and believe in him for salvation. Conversely, we must not fall into the trap of Cessationism as if miracles ended at the death of the apostles and the period of the writing of the NT. Doing this neglects the great truth that God is a God of miracles, as is his Son, who is the same throughout time (Heb 13:8).

---

55. Not that I think the two ideas are actually related.
56. See Keown, "Notes of Hope in the Face of Suffering."

18

Social Justice

As discussed, Paul's approach to mission involved the proclamation of the gospel and miracles. These elements do not exhaust Paul's vision of mission. Romans gives ample evidence that he was also committed to social justice.[1] Social justice in this section speaks of actions to stand against and seek to put right the injustice and oppression found in all parts of the world since humans were expelled from Eden. It encompasses care for the poor, the needy, the vulnerable, and the marginalized.[2] It has two dimensions: social justice within the church and toward the world.

Remembering that *dikaiosynē* language dominates the letter and that *dik*- language can be translated with "justice" terminology, it becomes clear that social justice is a big theme in the letter. Indeed, in the gospel, "the *justice* of God" is revealed (1:17). The focus in this short chapter will be on justice in terms of social relationships, as justice in terms of God and human relationships is well covered earlier when looking at righteousness in Romans.

---

1. Bosch avers, "Although evangelism may never simply be equated with labor for justice, it may also never be divorced from it." Bosch, *Transforming Mission*, 400. See his discussion on pp. 403–8. He notes in *A Response to Lausanne*: "there is no biblical dichotomy between the word spoken and the word made visible in the lives of God's people . . . we must repudiate as demonic the attempt to drive a wedge between evangelism and social concern" (p. 406). See also the *Wheaton '83 Statement*, para. 2: "We must therefore evangelize, respond to immediate human needs, and press for social transformation" (p. 407).

2. On care for the poor in Paul, see Longenecker, *Remember the Poor*, 279–97. He notes that this is implied in 12:4–5 (pp. 281–83). He rightly avers, "Paul seems to have imagined that, while alleviating the needs of the poor within communities of Jesus-followers was never to be compromised, neither was that practice to be set in opposition to caring for those beyond Jesus-communities" (p. 292).

Part Three: Romans and the Proclamation of the Gospel

THE UNIVERSAL HUMAN PROBLEM OF SOCIAL INJUSTICE

Social injustice is a feature of sinful humankind and leads to terrible consequences.[3] In fact, God's wrath is specifically against humanity's injustice (1:18) as people are filled with all manner of injustice (1:29). Postures that cause oppression and injustice are listed. Such attitudes include covetousness (greed), envy of what others have, the murder of others, creating strife, acts of deceit, hostile attitudes, gossip and slander that maligns the other, violence, arrogance (haughty, boastful), disobedience to parents (fragmenting families), heartlessness, and ruthlessness (1:29–31). People not only commit injustice; they approve of others acting unjustly toward others, perhaps because they benefit from it (1:32).

In Romans 2:1,[4] the emphasis falls on Jews and others who are arrogantly confident in their justice toward others and condemn the injustice to others; yet they are no better. Such people also face the wrath of God (2:2–3). In contrast, God is kind and patient toward sinful humankind (2:4) and will repay each person with perfect justice and impartiality—according to his or her works (2:6, 11).[5] Where a person, Jew or gentile, lives with perfect justice toward God and others, they will receive eternal life. Where a person does not, they will receive wrath and fury (2:7–11).

The critique of the failure to be socially just in 1:18—2:1 is resumed in 2:17. The self-righteous Jew who claims to be just is challenged on their theft, adultery, and robbery of temples (2:22). They are unspecific and difficult to place in context, but each speaks of acts of injustice. Theft robs others of what is rightfully theirs. Adultery violates marriage commitments and leads to poverty (mainly where women and their children were concerned in the ancient world). Robbery of temples destroys cultures and robs objects held sacred by others (even if the worship is idolatrous).

Injustice then is the human condition, and it illuminates God's perfect justness (3:5). The citations of Romans 3:10–18 declare that no one is just (3:10, cf. Ps 14:1–3), all speak words of oppression,[6] and all run to commit violence, causing destruction and misery (3:15; Isa 59:7–8).

Paul's critique in Romans 1:18—3:20 reveals the justice of God in exercising wrath toward sinful humanity. People are unjust,[7] and God, in his perfect justice, must

---

3. "As Romans 1:18–32 teaches, profound misunderstandings of God lead to horrific consequences for the mistreatment of other human beings." Thielman, *Romans*, 217.

4. Osborne contends that "the absolute justice of God is the core theme throughout 2:1–3:8." Osborne, *Romans: Verse by Verse*, 86.

5. "Every person will be judged by the same impartial criteria of divine justice." Osborne, *Romans: Verse by Verse*, 62.

6. See 3:13–14, cf. Pss 5:9; 9:28 [LXX]; 140:3.

7. "No amount of human justice or goodness can begin to compare." Lopez, *Romans Unlocked*, 108. "Solidarity in sin" is disturbing because it seems to erase distinctions and unite precisely where the differences and disjunctions matter the most—where dignity is denied, justice is trampled underfoot, and blood is spilled." Volf, *Exclusion & Embrace*, 82.

ultimately act to deal with injustice for the sake of all humankind. As such, Boa and Kruidenier are correct:

> Humans, Paul said in Romans 3:10–18, are not righteous, do not understand or seek God, have turned away and become worthless, lie and practice deceit, murder, and cause ruin and misery. This puts us all, proverbially, "at the mercy of God." Is justice negated by mercy? Absolutely not. Justice is served in the condemnation of all according to our sins. If God, in his mercy, chooses to extend mercy to some to accomplish his purpose of bringing salvation to many, justice has still been served to all by condemning their sin to begin with.[8]

GOD'S JUSTICE IN CHRIST

As the embodiment of God, "[l]ove and justice meet in Jesus (cf. v. 26)."[9] His death satisfies God's justice.[10] The justice of God, received by faith in Jesus Christ for Jew and gentile alike in 3:21–31, deals with the problem of injustice at a heart level and in terms of relationship with God. God's justice is satisfied in Christ's redemptive death, and people are put right with God through faith in him.[11] This redemption demonstrates the justice of God, who passes over sins committed before Christ, allowing Christ's redemptive death to deal with them where faith is found (e.g., Abraham, 3:25; 4:3). Similarly, anyone with faith in Jesus now that he has come, has been preached, and heard, receives right standing (3:26).

God's justice is shown to be merciful, loving, gracious, just, and kind. His character and action are the theological foundation for social justice between believers. Believers are forgiven, recipients of forbearance, kindness, grace, love, and mercy, and so they should treat others in this way (esp. 12:9–21; 14:1—15:12).

God's actions in Christ recall his gracious salvation of Israel from slavery in Egypt. His saving work in the Exodus became the foundation for them treating others with love and mercy and never themselves enslaving others (Lev 19:34; 25:42; 26:13). Indeed, the Decalogue begins with a reminder of this and is followed by a set of injunctions including the interpersonal commands five to ten. In these injunctions, God calls for honoring of parents (Exod 20:12), prohibits murder (Exod 20:13), adultery (Exod 20:14), theft (Exod 20:15), bearing false witness (Exod 20:16), and coveting

---

8. Boa and Kruidenier, *Romans*, 283.

9. See Utley, *Gospel*, "Romans 3:25: Word and Phrase Study."

10. Commenting on Romans 3:25–26, Schreiner rightly comments: "God's justice (εἰς τὸ εἶναι αὐτὸν δίκαιον) is satisfied in that the death of his Son pays fully for human sin." Schreiner, *Romans*, 198. "Through our Lord Jesus Christ. Christ satisfied the claims of justice."

11. Morris writes, "When believing sinners are tried at the bar of God's justice they will be acquitted because of Christ's saving work which they have appropriated by faith." Morris, *Epistle to the Romans*, 178. Witherington and Hyatt aver, "So what Paul has in mind is that Christ's 'act of justice' wiped the slate clean, and thus life was set right." Witherington and Hyatt, *Paul's Letter*, 149.

what others have (Exod 20:13–17). The gospel's central event, God's giving of his Son to die for humankind to enact his justice, calls believers to a love-based social justice toward all, even (and one might say, especially) enemies.

SOCIAL JUSTICE IN ROMANS 6—8

After he discusses Abraham's justification by faith, reconciliation with God, and Jesus the new Adam (Rom 4—5), Paul turns to social justice in Romans 6. Believers are baptized into Christ's death and are raised to a new life in which they serve God's justice. They are not to yield to the desire to oppress and cause injustice toward others, despite their very selves being warped in this way (6:12). They are now recipients of grace and so instruments of God's gracious justice (6:13–14).[12] The outcome of their lives is to be justice, for they are slaves of justice (6:16–17, 19). Indeed, their sanctification is enacting justice as slaves of God (6:20).[13]

Here, in Romans 6, Paul treats *dikaiosynē* as the equivalent of the goddess *dikē* (cf. Acts 28:4) or the Roman *Iustitia*, "Justice."[14] Christians are slaves to justice, which, of course, is personified in Jesus but is, in reality, Yahweh, who *is* justice. As Justice, "[t]he law reflects God's justice in that those who follow its commandments will also be conforming their actions to the perfect norm of God's nature."[15]

Unsurprisingly (in light of God's mercy and perfect justice), at the heart of the law is a call for social justice. In his impartiality toward humankind, God "takes the side of the weak" (e.g., LXX Ps 81:1–3 [82:1–4 EVV]).[16] Israel is to love God and to love their neighbors, including the immigrant, as themselves (Deut 6:4–6; Lev 19:18, 34). Provisions are made for the poor (e.g., Exod 23:11; Lev 19:10), widows and orphans (e.g., Exod 22:22; Ps 68:5; Isa 9:17), immigrants (e.g., Deut 16:11; 24:17, 19), and others in need. Israelites are to be impartial (e.g., Exod 23:3, 6; 2 Chr 19:7). Justice is not to be perverted (e.g., Exod 23:2; Lev 19:15; Deut 16:19).[17] Such attitudes are all

---

12. "Since believers are united with Christ's life and not with the sin that put him to death, their abilities and opportunities should not promote sin and injustice but should advance God's desire to establish justice and equity in the world through his people." Thielman, *Romans*, 310.

13. As Thielman says, "It is more likely, however, that Paul uses 'righteousness' here to mean justice, fairness, and uprightness, since this ethical sense of the term dominates the immediate context (6:18–20)." Thielman, *Romans*, 320. It looks to "a decidedly new way of living a life of righteousness and justice, both before God and among people in society." Longenecker, *Epistle*, 638.

14. Jewett and Kotansky tell us that *Iustitia/Dikaiosynē* "surfaces in the Augustan period in celebrations of the Roman imperial cult. The Roman gods generally promoted justice through reward to the Roman world." Jewett and Kotansky, *Romans*, 276.

15. Cottrell, *Romans: Volume 1*, 7:12: "Does Grace Mean That Law is Bad? No! (7:7–13)."

16. Jewett and Kotansky, *Romans*, 281. "God demanded worship to Him in the form of social justice and compassion to the needy (Isa. 58:6–7; Mic. 6:8)." Utley, *Gospel*, esp. "15:26: Word and Phrase Study." God "calls for justice that stands with the marginalized." Toews, *Romans*, 75.

17. "It is this kind of evenhanded justice that Paul ascribes to God." Morris, *Epistle to the Romans*, 121.

Social Justice

premised on God as the creator of all people (Job 34:19) and his justice toward the marginalized (e.g., Deut 10:18; 24:17, 19): "for all his ways are justice" (Deut 32:4; cf. Ps 9:7).

The prophets critiqued Israel's failure to enact the social justice of the covenant and urged Israel to seek justice.[18] Nonetheless, they recognized that a day was coming when the Servant would bring God's justice, establishing it through the earth (Isa 42:3–4). For early Christians, this is fulfilled in Jesus God's Servant. He proclaimed justice (Matt 12:18, 20), demanding it of his people (Matt 23:23). He preached good news to the poor and called believers to care for them (e.g., Matt 11:5; Luke 12:33).

For Paul, this day of justice has come in Christ. Believers are not under the law, but the Spirit is in them to generate the life of justice that God envisages for his people (7:6). People formerly constrained by sin and the flesh are liberated to live by the Spirit producing works of justice (7:7—8:10).[19] A core aspect of the Spirit's role in the life of a believer is to spur them on to attitudes of compassion and mercy, which generate acts of social justice.

Witherington and Hyatt comment on today's western context:

> It is part of the American pledge that we affirm "one nation, under God, with liberty and justice for all." There is in this pledge some sense or awareness that freedom and justice in a dark world are ultimately provisions of God. They are perhaps the two things besides love that the human heart most cries out for in the modern era. However, the freedom (and justice or righteousness) Paul is referring to is not merely freedom from things like slavery or addictive behavior, but freedom for doing righteousness. While there is always a legitimate cry for justice in a world full of injustice, Paul is more concerned to focus on our contribution to setting the world right, our attempt to manifest the righteousness of God in our character and behavior. He places the onus on believers to do so. Paul never gives way to the spirit of victimization and retaliation that so often permeates our world.[20]

SOCIAL JUSTICE IN ROMANS 12—15

Paul fills this picture of just living out in Romans 12:1—15:13. God's mercies toward unjust humanity are the basis for their lives. They are to give themselves for his service with minds shaped by the Spirit and his virtues and not the injustices of the world (12:1–2). They are to renounce all notions of self-pride and live humbly using their gifts in his service. They are to allow others to do the same, serving each other, God, and the lost zealously (12:3–8, 9).

---

18. See, e.g., Isa 1:17, 21, 23; Jer 5:28; 7:5; Ezek 22:29.

19. Cranfield rightly observes that "the intention of doing justice to a vital element of the truth which certainly ought not to be obscured." Cranfield, *Critical and Exegetical Commentary*, 1:277.

20. Witherington and Hyatt, *Paul's Letter*, 178.

The dominant virtue, of course, is *agapē* toward one another (12:9, 10).[21] Believers are to contribute to those among God's holy people who are in need and show hospitality to strangers (12:13). They are to demonstrate empathy where there is pain (12:15) and live in unity (12:16). There can be no elitism among them, always prepared to associate with the seemingly lowly (12:16).

Recipients of God's mercy and grace, despite their sin, are to respond to persecutors with blessing (12:14), repaying evil and overcoming it with good (12:17, 21). As far as they are able, they are to live at peace honorably before unbelievers and at peace with them (12:17–18). They are never to avenge themselves but leave that to God for the day of wrath (12:19; Deut 32:35).[22] They are to show hospitality to enemies, even providing them food and drink (12:20).

Paul does not explicitly link Christian ethical engagement to evangelism here or elsewhere in Romans. However, with his link between ethics in mission in other places,[23] he may also have in view the Romans responding with goodness, peacefulness, and hospitality as ways of attracting unbelievers to faith.[24] This may be what he has in mind when mentions the role of deed (*ergon*) in his own mission in Romans 15:18. His concern that the "strong" Romans be tolerant and gracious to the "weak" on non-essential matters to ensure they do not stumble is also missional (14:13, 20, 21). Christians behaving in a way that does alienate other believers is another aspect of ethical witness.

Even though the Roman state was unjust in many ways under Nero, they are to be submissive to the State as the instrument of God's justice (13:1–4) and pay taxes to be used by the government (13:7). As Longenecker says,

> Christians are not to take retributive justice into their own hands, but rather are to submit to the God-established governmental authorities in these matters.[25]

---

21. "The obligation to love others is constant, however, as the Mosaic law demonstrates with its focus on showing justice and kindness to others." Thielman, *Romans*, 612.

22. "When we leave the hurt and vengeance with God, knowing that justice will indeed be done, we find the strength to forgive those who do not deserve it and to free ourselves from a life of bitterness." Osborne, *Romans: Verse by Verse*, 403.

23. Compare, e.g., 1 Cor 6:6; Phil 2:14; 1 Thess 4:12, also 1 Cor 7:12–15; 10:27—11:1; 14:24–25.

24. Similarly ethical (and evangelistic) witness is potentially encompassed in presenting members as instruments for righteousness (6:13), obedience (6:16), being slaves of righteousness (6:18), slaves of God (6:22), fruit that leads to sanctification and eternal life (6:22), living according to the Spirit (8:5), set the mind on the Spirit (8:6), being led by the Spirit (8:14), presenting bodies as a living sacrifice (12:2), the use of gifts (12:6–8). The love command has no limit (13:8–10), living in the armor of light and Christ and refusing to engage in common Greco-Roman sins (13:12–14), emulation of the service of Christ (15:8), and Paul's example (15:18).

25. Longenecker, *Epistle*, 961. Witherington writes, "Paul believes that authorities do have a limited right to exercise force and do so as agents of God, but he does not believe that private individuals, in particular Christians, should try to take justice into their own hands." Witherington and Hyatt, *Paul's Letter*, 296. Similarly, Schreiner states, "believers are liberated from taking justice into their own hands and are free to do good because they know that God will right all wrongs in the end." Schreiner, *Romans*, 675.

However, this need not be read as complete passivity. Keener rightly states,

> Most likely, Paul would have applied 13:1–7 as the norm where possible, living in a respectable manner in society but allowing dissent where necessary and political participation for justice when possible.[26]

In Romans 13:8–10, the lead virtue love is unpacked with the Romans called to show love toward all people, and in so doing, they will sum up the relational laws of the decalogue mentioned earlier.[27] With the urgency of the parousia always with them, they are to repudiate the debauched wasteful life of their generation and the violations of God's sexual ethics prevalent in the Greco-Roman world. They are to put on Christ Jesus living for his vision of justice and not the desires of the flesh (13:9–14).[28]

Romans 14–15 instructs readers concerning how to treat one another across cultural divides with differences in terms of eating and holy days.[29] Such things are not to divide believers. They are not to despise each other, judge one another for such differences (14:1–4, 13). Each is to live out of their conviction before the Lord, knowing they will face judgment (14:5–12). They are to walk in love, determined not to destroy each other over differences on such small things (14:13–16). They do so because "the kingdom of God is not a matter of eating and drinking but of justice and peace and joy in the Holy Spirit" (my translation). God accepts those who serve Christ in this way and is approved by others. They are to pursue peace and building one another up (14:18–19). They are to live by their faith-based conscience before God, not passing judgment nor causing others to stumble (14:20–23).

A central principle of Christian justice is stated in Romans 15:1: those who are strong are to bear with the failings of the weak, and not live to please themselves. The strong have a particular call to care for those who are weaker socially, spiritually, physically, intellectually, emotionally, or relationally. The strong are responsible for the weak (an underlying premise of gospel ethics). Still, all are called to live to build up their neighbor as did Jesus (15:2–3). God will enable such harmonious living and unified worship as they welcome one another as Christ has welcomed them (15:5–7).[30]

---

26. Keener, *Romans*, 156. He says this with an eye on such things as the abolition of slavery, Nazism (Bonhoeffer), apartheid, Chinese communism, and other contexts.

27. "Justice is the bond of human society. To do to others as we may reasonably expect them to do to us is indeed the golden rule which conserves all security and peace among men. To be just towards them is to respect their rights. And what are the rights of man? God has set them forth strongly, in their essentials, in that Decalogue which was the Divine code of justice for a barbarous nation." Spence-Jones, *Romans*, 398.

28. Thielman suggests, "it is time to throw the covers off the bed, pull on some clothes, and pick up the weapons of justice, peace, and love with which to fight for the purposes of God." Thielman, *Romans*, 615.

29. Utley, *Gospel*, "2:11: Word and Phrase Study," correctly suggests that Christians then should "[s]upport legislation and legislators in the passing of laws promoting racial justice and oppose those who exploit prejudice for political gain."

30. "One day his justice would obviously prevail. In the way they handle social tensions within

Paul here has a particular interest in Jew and gentile unity, as he has through the whole passage. The desire for racial harmony will be discussed in more depth in part three, chapter 12; suffice to say here that the two cultural collectives are to welcome one another and be one people before the Lord, despite their differences. This dream of harmonious unity applies to all ethnic and cultural groups.

ENACTED GLOBAL SOCIAL JUSTICE: THE JERUSALEM COLLECTION

We think of Paul as a church planting evangelist, and for a good reason, as this was at the heart of his missional vision. However, while he evangelized Asia Minor in this period, a core purpose of Paul's present journey at the time of writing is social justice. His third great Antiochian mission was to collect money for the saints of Jerusalem (15:28–32).[31]

Paul describes this with the word *diakoneō*, "a service" (15:25). The gifts gathered from Macedonia and Achaia are a *koinōnia*, an act of fellowship (15:26). They are collected "for the poor among the saints at Jerusalem" (15:26). Paul is seeking to alleviate their poverty with the wealth of others (without them becoming poor, 2 Cor 8:13). Inadvertently, Paul commends the Macedonians and Achaians: "for they were pleased to do it" (v. 27, cf. 2 Cor 8:1–5). Both Paul and these generous Christians embody the attitude of 12:13, where Paul urges them to "contribute (*koinōneō*) to the needs of the saints, pursuing love toward strangers" (my translation). Paul also sees their response as fitting as they, as gentiles, have come to share in the spiritual blessings of Israel in Christ (15:28).

Paul's commitment to such an act of social justice is seen in him delaying his mission trip to Rome, even though he has longed to come there many times (1:13). He is also deferring his trip to Spain, even though he similarly longs to preach Christ, where he has not yet been named (15:20). He is determined to complete the mission to the poor of Jerusalem. He thus embodies the principles of social justice that are in God and Christ, and that he is encouraging of the Romans: a preparedness to sacrifice one's desires and purposes for the good of others. He is also placing social justice over his evangelistic goals, at least for the time being, showing his preparedness to do so at times. This determination to go to Jerusalem is all the more remarkable in that he anticipates danger from the unbelieving Jewish community in Jerusalem. He shows that, like Prisca and Aquila (16:4), he is prepared to risk his life to complete it (15:31, cf. Phil 2:25–30). He then emulates Christ's preparedness to go to the cross to make rich those who are poor (2 Cor 8:9). Later readers know that Paul did follow through on this

---

their own believing community, they should work for peace and they should build up one another, accepting one another as Christ accepted them (14:1—15:13)." Thielman, *Romans*, 563.

31. See also Acts 24:17; 1 Cor 16:1–4; 2 Cor 8–9.

SOCIAL JUSTICE, PRAYER, AND ROMAN PEOPLE

Paul's appeal for prayer in 15:30–32 is another aspect of social justice we cannot neglect. Sometimes believers can do nothing to help others. However, they can always pray for their fellow believers and others in desperate situations. Notably, he also prays for them (1:8–10) and finishes his prayer request with a blessing; this is mutual prayer (15:33).

He then expects to come to Rome to "be refreshed in your company." "Refreshed" is a *hapax legomenon*, *synanapauomai*, formed with *syn* (with) and *anapauō*, meaning "cause to rest, give rest, refresh, revive."[32] *Anapauō* is used in Jesus's memorable promise to give rest to those who labor and are heavy laden (Matt 11:28). Paul uses it of generous Corinthians who have refreshed his spirit and those of the Corinthian church (1 Cor 16:18), the Corinthians refreshing Titus's spirit (2 Cor 7:13), and Philemon refreshing the hearts of the saints (Phlm 7) and Paul himself (Phlm 20).[33] *Synanapauō* then speaks of Paul coming to Rome and being refreshed through the hospitality of the Romans.

Finally, Romans 16 gives evidence of social justice at work in the churches of Corinth and Rome. Paul is in Corinth and gives hints of the incredible generosity of his present hosts and hostesses. He commends Phoebe, a deacon in Cenchreae, and "patron of many and of myself as well" (16:1–2). Paul likely stayed with her on his trips. He also recalls the hospitality of Rufus's mother (16:13). Tertius has served in penning the letter for Paul (16:22). Gaius is presently hosting Paul and uses his wealth to host the whole church (16:23). As an important Roman civil servant, Erastus is wealthy. If he is the same figure referenced in the Erastus inscription as is probable, he was a generous benefactor to the city (see part one, chapter 3). There are clearly Corinthians that Paul commends and who embody the Christian call to care for those in need.

Where the Romans are concerned, Paul urges them to treat Phoebe with appropriate social justice. She is to be welcomed in the Lord in a way worthy of the saints and helped in whatever way she needs them, speaking of rich hospitality and Christian fellowship (16:2). Prisca and Aquila have risked their lives to save Paul and use their home in Rome as a base for the church (16:3–5). Elsewhere we read that they have done and will do the same in Corinth (Acts 18:2) and Ephesus (1 Cor 16:19; 2 Tim 4:19). They are wealthy Christians using their resources to build the church and host others in worship. Others, among those named in the greetings, are no doubt, generous benefactors as well, although the details are lacking.

---

32. BDAG 69.
33. See also Matt 26:45; Mark 6:31; 14:41; Luke 12:16; 1 Pet 4:14; Rev 6:11; 14:13.

PART THREE: ROMANS AND THE PROCLAMATION OF THE GOSPEL

CONCLUSION

Even if not immediately apparent because English translations use righteousness language in most translations, social justice is an important theme in Romans. It is also essential to Paul's missional understanding. Social concern begins among the Christians of the church as they turn away from socially unjust attitudes and love one another. They bear with each other's varied perspectives, attitudes, and weaknesses. When in need, they share with each other. Social justice is also crucial as Christians face the world. They are to bless persecutors (12:13), never cursing, retaliating, or avenging those who hurt them (12:17, 19). They are to do their utmost to live at peace with unbelieving neighbors (12:18). Enemies are welcomed into family meals (12:20). They are to submit to the governing authorities (13:1–6).

Evangelism, the miraculous, and social justice are always intertwined. Certainly, one cannot be justified through acts of social justice, no matter how generous and impressive. Nevertheless, one is justified by faith *to do* works of justice, expressing their faith in love (Gal 5:6). As James puts it, true faith is expressed in social justice (Jas 1:26—2:26). Authentic mission has social justice at its very core as God undoes our injustices, declares us righteous and justified before him, and propels us into the world to bring his justice to the nations. As Thielman says, "Christians should be at the cutting edge of showing how well a society functions where kindness, respect, love, and justice are equally distributed to all."[34]

I will leave the last word to Toews.

> The righteousness of God is a question again in our world, although in a different way than in Paul's time. Religious and racial wars abound—Auschwitz, Bosnia, Congo, Rwanda, Congo, Iraq—all of which raise questions about God and God's justice. September 11, 2001, raised profound questions about God. The mission of the church is to proclaim the gospel of God's righteousness through the faithfulness of Jesus for the purpose of creating one people out of many peoples, one human community that welcomes "the other" just as Jesus "welcomed us." The Creator God is the Righteous God who is "making right" people and creation in order to renew and restore the whole.[35]

---

34. Thielman, *Romans*, 730.
35. Toews, *Romans*, 63.

19

Ecological Mission

ONE OF THE GREAT MOVEMENTS in modern times has been the green movement. During the industrial revolution, the desire for progress and economic prosperity has seen increasing devastation of the world. This ecological crisis manifests in a range of issues such as global warming, air and sea pollution, the extinction of species, the accumulation of waste on land and sea, the depletion of resources, threats to the supply of food and freshwater, extreme meteorological phenomena, deforestation, soil degradation, and overpopulation.[1]

Christianity itself has been used in the Western pursuit of progress, creation seen as something to be subdued, dominated, and used for economic gain.[2] Some Christians are not concerned, especially those influenced by theologies that see God's people raptured and this world demolished as God exercises his wrath on the world.[3] Ecological carnage is supposedly not an issue; it is just a sad sign of human depravity and a marker that the rapture is imminent. Others are global warming deniers, evangelistically resisting the green movement. While I fully accept that humankind is responsible to a significant degree for the current crisis, in one sense the cause of global warming is should not change our attitude to the environment. Any Christian who knows the Scriptures and the heart of the Creator should be passionate about reducing the many pollutants that are spoiling God's world, making species extinct, and threatening our existence.

---

1. See, e.g., Bredin, *The Ecology of the New Testament*, Chapter 1, "The Ecological Crisis;" Hughes, "Biological Consequences of Global Warming," 56–61; Boston, "Hope in the Face of Ecological Disaster," 5; Frances, "Laudato Si," Chapter One, 20–52.

2. Ploutz, *Global Warming*, 46; Pope Francis describes this as "the charge that Judaeo-Christian thinking, on the basis of the Genesis account which grants man "dominion" over the earth (cf. Gen 1:28), has encouraged the unbridled exploitation of nature by painting him as domineering and destructive by nature. This view is not a correct interpretation of the Bible as understood by the Church. "Laudato Si," 67.

3. Veldman, *The Gospel of Climate Skepticism*, 25–46, 69–85.

Part Three: Romans and the Proclamation of the Gospel

The good news is that in recent times, many Christians have chosen to rethink their story and consider what the Scriptures say to the church concerning the devastation of the environment.[4] Missiologists ponder whether there is an ecological mission mandate or not, and if so, how does it mesh with other elements of mission such as evangelism, church planting, and social justice.[5] A quick look at Romans suggests that ecological mission *is* a critical aspect of a missional mandate. However, its place in the mission of God, as conceived by Paul in premodern times, needs consideration.

THE INITIAL GLORY OF CREATION

Creation is a significant theme in Romans.[6] God is the creator (1:25) who formed the world. Animals are mentioned, recalling their origins in Genesis 1. They are part of God's "very good" creation (Gen 1:31), but Paul does not dwell on this. Instead, he first mentions them in terms of idolatry, whereby people falsely build idols shaped like birds, reptiles, and other creatures (1:23). People fail to recognize the utter supremacy of God over creation. He compares people with sinful speech to asps and their poison (3:13). The suffering Roman church, as with Israel, is likened to sheep ready for slaughter (8:36; Ps 44:22).[7] Still, none of these should be misunderstood to think Paul does not value animals. As a man immersed in Israel's Scriptures, no doubt, he loved them as part of God's good creation. What he despises is their elevation above God and the worship of their images.

Recalling Genesis 2, where God shaped Adam from mud, humans were created by God the potter (9:20–23). He created the first Adam, a prototype of the new Adam to come who would save his world (5:13–21). This new Adam is the image of God into whose life and character believers are being conformed (8:29). The contrast between Adam and Jesus should not lead us to think Paul devalues Adam and other humans. He does not, for they are worth saving and made in the image of God. While their sin has wrecked the world, they are a part of God's good creation.

---

4. See, e.g., European Christian Environment Network, "Bibliography of Christian Theology (Resources in English)"; Bakken and McDuffie, "Bibliography," in *Yale Forum on Religion and Ecology*.

5. E.g., Ruether, "Ecojustice at the Center of the Church's Mission," 111–21; DeWitt and Prance, eds., *Missionary Earthkeeping*, passim; Roberts, *Patching God's Garment: Environment*, passim; Daneel, *African Earthkeepers*, passim; idem, "Earthkeeping in Missiological Perspective," 130–88.

6. See also part two, chapter 9; part three, chapter 19.

7. Elsewhere Paul mentions the different flesh God gifted to domesticated animals (*ktēnos*), birds, and fish (1 Cor 15:39); allowing an ox to feed as it works likened to gospel workers being fed (1 Cor 9:9; 1 Tim 5:18); Jesus as the Passover lamb (*pascha*, 1 Cor 5:7); a flock of sheep cared for compared to gospel workers (1 Cor 9:7); and snakes that killed Israelites in the wilderness (1 Cor 10:9). Negatively, Satan is defined as "the serpent" (2 Cor 11:3); Cretans are described as "evil beasts (*thērion*)" (Titus 1:12); Nero is likened to a lion (*leōn*, 2 Tim 4:17); Judaizers are described as dogs (*kyōn*, Phil 3:2); the serpent who tempted Eve, i.e., Satan (2 Cor 11:3); and opponents who persecute Paul are likened to wild animals (*thēriomacheō*, 1 Cor 15:32).

Indeed, the beauty and grandeur of creation are implied in Romans 1:19–20. Paul considers that creation's wonders are such that an observant human should recognize God's greatness. What can be known about God is plain and evident to them. It is revealed by God, who has "shown it to them."

Mounce writes of these verses,

> Seeing the beauty and complexity of creation carries with it the responsibility of acknowledging the Creator both as powerful and as living above the natural order. Disbelief requires an act of rebellion against common sense. It displays fallen humanity's fatal bias against God. Although the created order cannot force a person to believe, it does leave the recipient responsible for not believing.[8]

So, Paul here clearly implies that enough can be discerned concerning God's eternal character and power from creation that humankind is without excuse if it fails to worship the one who made them and the world.

ECOLOGICAL CARNAGE

Romans also paints a vivid picture of creation as frustrated, in bondage to decay, and yearning for release (8:19–22). If we track Paul's logic in Romans, the core problem of the world is universal human wrongdoing (1:18—3:20). Writing in his world, he lays out characteristic problems of gentiles (1:18–32) and Jews (2:1–25). Where gentiles are concerned, he focuses on characteristic vices such as idolatry (1:19–25), sexual immorality (1:24, 26–29), and a range of relational evils that destroy families and societies (1:28–31). He equally challenges Jewish presumption, self-righteousness, hypocrisy, and failure to keep the law (2:1–29). He says little about ecological destruction. However, were he writing today, while he would note many of the same sins today, he would surely add a range of attitudes, false desires, and actions that are destructive to the world.

Of course, in Romans, Paul does not stop with sin. The contagion sin has infected humanity, causing death to spread to all people (5:12). Moreover, this death has invaded and contaminated all of life in the creation (8:19–22). All things decay and die because of humanity's ultimate enemy and the last to be destroyed, death (1 Cor 15:26). Indeed, people continue to reproduce, but all that has life is mortal; it decays and dies.[9] As such, creation is a dangerous place that can threaten human

---

8. Mounce, *Romans*, 78.

9. Chris Wright observes that "the Bible unequivocally states that the Fall radically distorted and strained our human relationship with the earth itself and also frustrated creation's primary function in relation to God . . . We live in a cursed earth (since Adam) as well as a covenanted earth (since Noah). Our mission theology needs to take full account of the radical realism of the former and the limitless hope of the latter." Wright, *Mission of God*, 433.

existence even if it cannot separate a believer from the love of God that is in Christ Jesus (8:35–39).

For Paul, while he mentions Satan and demons and attributes some responsibility to them (8:38–39; 16:20, see part two, chapter 9), humankind is to blame for all of this. In his time, he understandably could not yet conceive of people filling the earth to the point where megacities abound, and humanity in its greed is prepared to destroy the world for its advance. Still, our destruction of the cosmos is a natural extension of the sins he identifies in humankind; especially idolatry (1:21–25), greed or covetousness,[10] the love of money (1 Tim 3:3; 6:10; 2 Tim 3:2), and the desire to simply satiate the flesh (7:18; 8:4–8; 13:14). Much of human "progress" is produced by their rampant worship of self and desires, their desire for more and more, and for pleasure.

THE LIBERATION OF CREATION

Romans 8:19–23 is critical for understanding the cosmic scope of God's redemptive work.[11] The passage will now come under consideration from an ecological missional perspective. While it is not focused directly on a concern for the environment, Paul's eschatological perspective has enormous implications for present-day mission. Before coming to this, some comments need to be made on the Jewish eschatological vision and several other NT passages.[12]

The Jewish Vision of Restoration

The central hope of Israel was for a restored world ruled from a theocratic state centered in Zion (Jerusalem). The most explicit statement is found in Isaiah 65—66. Through Isaiah, God declares that he will create the new heavens and new earth (Isa 65:17). There is continuity, as Jerusalem will be a joy (Isa 65:18–19) and will be at peace (Isa 66:10–12). However, in this renewed world, while people will live for a long time, they will still die (Isa 65:20). They will be at peace and blessed with wild animals no longer a threat (Isa 65:21–25). The nations will come and see God's glory (Isa 66:18–23), and all rebels will be destroyed (Isa 66:24). The vision of the new heavens and earth features in later Jewish apocalyptic writings, many of which include the complete removal of corruption and death.[13] Romans 8:19–23 continues this tradition.

---

10. See 1:29; 7:8; 5:3; 1 Cor 5:11; Col 3:5.

11. Concerning the restoration of the cosmos, Peters writes, "Romans 8 is the classic presentation of this matter." Peters, *Biblical Theology*, 74.

12. Some of the material here is drawn from Keown, "Apostolic Green Imperative," 33–39.

13. See 1 En. 91:16, see also 1 En. 45 4–5; 72:1; LAB 3:10; 37:17; Sib. Or. 5:212; Jub. 1:29; 4:26; Apoc. El. 5:38; 2 Bar. 32:6; 44:12; 49:3; 57:3; 4 Ezra 7:30–31, 75; Tg. Jer. 23.23; 1QS 4:25. See Aune, *Revelation* 17–22, 1116–17.

Romans 8

The wider NT gives ample evidence that God's purpose is to restore this cosmos. In John, the divine word and creator became flesh to redeem what was rightfully his, the world (John 1:1–5, 14; 4:42). The parable of the weeds pictures God ripping the weeds out of his garden, ridding it of evil (Matt 13:36–40, cf. Gen 2—3). In Matthew 19:28, Jesus talks of the *palingenesia*, the "creation (*genesis*) again (*palin*)" (re-creation) of the world: "the restoration, resurrection, or rebirth *of all things, the cosmos*, after the consummation."[14] The sheep inherit this kingdom in Matthew 25:31–46. The parallel with the flood in 2 Peter 3:5–6 suggests that images of fire speak not of the actual dissolution of the cosmos, but its judgment and renewal.[15] The healing of the nations in the vision of a new heaven and new earth in Revelation 21—22 points to the renewal of this world to Edenic conditions (Rev 22:2).

Romans 8:19–23 shows that Paul agrees with this picture of cosmic restoration. As Wright cogently states, "The creator God has promised to renew his whole creation."[16] In the wider Pauline corpus, Jesus is co-creator (1 Cor 8:6; Col 1:16–17). However, the creation is defiled as, through sin, death has infected the cosmos (5:12). It is subject to the frustration of decay (*phthora*). Creation is personified as a person longing for a future unveiling of God's children. It is subjugated to frustration by God because of Adam's sin, for fallen flesh cannot live forever, and it must be renewed. The world is in bondage itself, yearning for the same freedom God's redeemed people will experience in the new heavens and earth. It is like a mother in the pains of childbirth, desperate to finally give birth.

The problem of the world in Romans 8:21 is *phthora*. In wider sources, it is used of decaying or decomposing flesh.[17] Paul employs it of the perishability of humankind (1 Cor 15:42, 50). In Romans, this is a consequence of the sin of Adam (5:12), and *phthora* continues until things die and are fully decomposed.[18]

Paul looks to the day when creation will be "*set free* from its bondage to *phthora*" (8:21, emphasis mine). This release parallels the transformation of people from

---

14. In Judaism, the term is used of resurrection (Philo, *Cher.* 114; *Post.* 124), the recreation of the world after the flood (Philo, *Mos.* 2.65), and restoration after the exile (Josephus, *Ant.* 11.66). In Titus 3:5, it speaks of a person's spiritual renewal. Later Christian writings apply it to the recreation after the flood (1 Clem. 9:4) and resurrection. Keown, "Apostolic Green Imperative," 36.

15. Chris Wright notes that "whatever the language of fiery judgment and destruction will actually mean in relation to our physical universe, God's purpose is not the eternal obliteration of the created order but its eternal restoration to his glorious purpose for it." Wright, *Mission of God*, 409.

16. Wright, "Reading the New Testament Missionally," 177.

17. See, e.g., Galen, *Nat. Fac.* 2.4; Plutarch, *Adv. Col.* 11; Pss. Sol. 4:6. It can also have the sense "destroy" (2 Pet 2:12, see also Sib. Or. 2:9; 3:336).

18. Fitzmyer, *Romans*, 507 correctly says, "Paul speaks of 'corruption,' even though he did not have in mind what modern industry and technology have done and are doing to the universe and Earth's ozone layer. Yet his words somehow ring true even in this century with its ecological concerns."

perishability to imperishability and from mortality to immortality.[19] This creation will be renewed.

Beale asserts,

> God's intention as the Creator is one day to fill every part of his creation with his presence. God's holy presence could not dwell fully in the old creation because it was a sin-tainted and idolatrous world, which we have also seen is an implication of Isaiah 66:1–2. Hence, his special revelatory presence dwelt in a limited and temporary manner in human-made structures. But when he would fully redeem the world and recreate it (so Rom. 8:18–24), he would dwell in it in a fuller way than ever before.[20]

Jewett and Kotansky rightly note that,

> Overcoming ecological disorder is depicted here as a divine gift enacted as a result of God's restoration of humanity to its position of rightful dominion, reflecting God's intended glory.[21]

And as Jonathan Moo says,

> The implication of Romans 8:19–22 is that it must be fundamentally the same created world that finds its purposes fulfilled and its hopes realized when it is released from its slavery to ruin and brought into the "freedom of the glory of the children of God."[22]

The end of decay and death parallels 1 Cor 15:26, where death is the last enemy to be destroyed. Still, while all this is future, this restoration of our created glory begins at conversion, and so our desire to participate in God's redemption of the cosmos should begin now.

Again, Jewett and Kotansky are correct to say of believers restored to their rightful dominion over creation,

> in more modern terms, their altered lifestyle and revised ethics begin to restore the ecological system that had been thrown out of balance by wrongdoing (1:18–32) and sin (Rom 5—7).[23]

As I wrote elsewhere:

> However, in the meantime the Gospel calls God's people to be God's co-workers in the pursuit of "God's Great Project." While it is evident that Paul has a dream of people saved, of churches planted, and of justice, his long-term hope

---

19. "God will do for the whole creation what he did for Jesus at Easter." Wright, "Reading the New Testament Missionally," 177.
20. Beale, *Temple and the Church's Mission*, 152–53.
21. Jewett and Kotansky, *Romans*, 515.
22. Moo, "Environmental Unsustainability and the Biblical Vision," 260.
23. Jewett and Kotansky, *Romans*, 513.

is a whole world transformed by God's power. Our mission encompasses all such dimensions.[24]

Paul's understanding of the gospel cannot be reduced to evangelism, planting churches, or social justice and transformation (all of which are critical to the mission). It envisages the renewal of the created order. At one's conversion, one becomes a new creation (2 Cor 5:17; Gal 6:15). This renewal is not just something for believers as individuals. They become part of the new creation while still living in a world writhing in pain. Jesus is Lord over all creation, and his people are to live in it, seeking to bring to pass in the present what will be fully realized in the future. We join God in his great mission of putting right the world.

As Osborne rightly says,

> In recent years our society has realized how important ecological concerns are for our future. Here we see the ultimate ecological recovery, as all of creation joins us in awaiting our deliverance from all the evils human sin has visited upon our environment.[25]

ECOLOGICAL MISSION

Does this picture painted in Romans lead us to see the care of creation as an aspect of Christian mission? Unquestionably, the answer is "yes!"

> In that Christian mission is joining God in this Great Cosmission, Christian concern for the environment flows from this notion. Ecological concern should be axiomatic for all God's people.[26]

People who come to Christ become agents of God's transformation. They are then participants in the renewal of every aspect of God's world, beginning with each person and including the whole creation. Christians should have a love of creation that transcends even that of those who participate in the green movements that dot the political landscape.

The biblical story that shapes Paul's worldview began in a garden. However, they sinned and were shut out of God's garden and eternal life. Those who believe receive the same Spirit that hovered over creation (Gen 1:2), and they are in the Christ who created the world. Their job is to do what the first Adam failed to do, "work it and keep it" (Gen 2:14). They are to do so walking with God as he paces the garden and seeks to

---

24. Keown, "Apostolic Green Imperative," 37.
25. Osborne, *Romans: Verse by Verse*, 256.
26. Keown, "Apostolic Green Imperative," 36. The term "Great Cosmission" comes from Keown, *What's God Up To*, 65–69. The neologism is a play on "the Great Commission," which focuses on the conversion and discipleship of individuals. The Great Cosmission speaks of God's Great Project to restore the world. It combines *kosmos* (Gk. "world, universe") and *missio* (Lat. "sent"), i.e., "sent to build/restore the world."

undo the carnage of ecological destruction (Gen 3:8). Christians invite others into the garden of delight that has been vandalized. There they have access to the tree of life, are healed, and join with others to care for it.

THE PLACE OF ECOLOGICAL MISSION

While ecological mission should go without saying for Christians, a few caveats must be added. First, without doubt, the focus of mission in Romans and the whole NT is the redemption of *people* from sin and its consequences. The Adams and Eves of the world are "shut out of the garden." For them to find salvation and be released into their Spirit-led roles in God's mission, they must first hear the gospel, believe, profess Christ's lordship, and call on his name (10:14–17). They "enter the garden" and receive the Spirit (5:5) so they can live the life of the new creation. So, while believers must join many others in the world concerned for ecological renewal, the redemption of creation, and give this a high priority, it cannot be the church's primary focus.

Longenecker rightly observes:

> In days when many of the cultural, societal, psychological, and ecological ramifications and benefits of the gospel have taken center stage in Christian preaching and counseling, it is well to remind ourselves of the centrality of the gospel message itself. For though the Christian gospel has implications for all of life—and though as God's people we are called by God to work out these implications in our own lives, in the lives of people individually, and in society corporately—it yet remains true, as Paul says only a few verses later in this same letter to Rome, that it is "the gospel" that is "the power of God for the salvation of everyone who believes" (1:16). All-too-often contemporary Christian preaching and counseling have turned the gospel into some form of "religious humanism," which only uses Christian imagery and Christian jargon in a humanistic fashion for motivational purposes. But it is the gospel message of what God has done "in Christ" in "reconciling the world to himself" (cf. 2 Cor 5:19), as illumined and applied by God's Spirit, that changes our sinful human condition and that alters our confused human circumstances.[27]

Still, an ecological concern must remain an emphasis, or God's people are failing their Creator who put us here to rule creation for him. God's people are in the new Adam, and they must do better in caring for the garden. So, in their quest to win people to Christ, they must not do so in a way that further degrades the planet's resources. Indeed, believers give witness to the world as they advocate and care for the environment. Ecological concern and evangelism should not be seen as two separate things. Christians believe in ecological evangelism (evangelizing through environmental concern) and ecologically responsible evangelism.

---

27. Longenecker, *Epistle*, 96.

Second, believers must not morph their passion for creation into idolatry. The worship of the created rather than the Creator is the central human problem (1:21–25). Such idolatry is a subtle danger when the situation is so urgent. Creation is not our god, nor should we worship images of animals. In the world today, idolatry is often imperceptible and found where something good or essential to life draws our allegiance away from God. This seduction can be a person, a relationship, an idea, a religion, a philosophy, things, money, or desire. It can also be the love of creation at the expense of people. Believers must beware of losing sight of the fundamental calling to love God, love others, build communities, and giving witness to the lost, by making creation the main thing.

With that said, we cannot err in diminishing the importance of the ecological mission. After all, our lives depend on it! So, some Christians will find this their central vocational calling, and that is good, just as creation was good when God called it into existence. Also, every Christian, church, and organization should be deeply considering how it can do everything that it does for Jesus our Lord in a way that is not destructive to creation, repairs it, and sustains it.

A third thing believers need to consider carefully is how they work with political groups concerned for creation, such as "green" parties. Green movements punctuate the globe, and this is timely in such a setting. Their ecological aspirations, in many cases, are tremendous and cohere with the gospel. However, they often have aspects of their political agenda that are repugnant to believers, such as being fiercely committed to a woman's right to abort a child.

Most also have a passionate concern for the poor and vulnerable, and this is also is to be commended. However, their answer to the problem is usually found primarily in the State. At times, they do not sufficiently recognize the need for people to have jobs and earn a living. Hence, they can often be so zealous for social justice that they bite that hand that feeds the poor. Is the State the answer? To an extent, yes, especially where wider society fails to care for creation and people. However, a purely State-led approach can lead to dependency, tax burdens that can become oppressive, and punishing those in the agricultural sector that is so important for the provision of food. What is better is the people themselves determining to live in an ecologically responsible way. The church can lead in this.

Christians who believe in ecological mission in passages like Romans 8 and Revelation 21—22 must think deeply. Yes, they should work with other groups who also care for the world (even if they do not acknowledge the Creator). However, consideration should be given to the role of the State, the broader agenda of "green parties," bringing change without overly threatening peoples' livelihoods, and how to work for the full agenda of God, faithful to the gospel. Such things are complicated and require our best thought. What seems right are churches that are "green" to the core but who are focused on the heart of God's mission.

PART THREE: ROMANS AND THE PROCLAMATION OF THE GOSPEL

The pattern of the kingdom is small beginnings like a seed that flourishes into the largest tree in the garden. We begin by greening our hearts. We green our families and homes, our churches and Christian organizations, our businesses, and other social contexts where we find ourselves. We fall in love with creation, but the Creator is our God. We ally with others in their green resolve, but we stand against their inconsistencies like the destruction of unborn people. We form Christian groups and consider how we do all this. We advocate on behalf of God's *ktisis* to the church. We include the call to creation care in the gospel we preach. We love God's world. We show grace to people who sin in this area, as in all areas of life. We do so as a critical part of our summons to proclaim Jesus that people will believe in him and be saved.

20

Social Transformation

> Important as the church is, it is, for Paul, not the ultimate aim of mission. The life and work of the Christian community are intimately bound up with God's cosmic-historical plan for the redemption of the world.[1]

MANY OF THE ARGUMENTS used in the previous two sections apply to the transformation of society. As discussed, Paul affirms the creation of the world, humankind, animals, and the whole living world. He also avers that God is sovereign over history and human society. He mentions a range of societal groupings. Obviously, individual transformation by the believer yielding to the Spirit is central to Romans. Bosch is right to state that "the fledgling Christian movement was peripheral to society, a totally negligible entity as far as size was concerned."[2] Still, as people are converted, and the faith spreads, just as the gospel brings the redemption of people by faith and social justice where injustice prevails as the transformed people of God engage in society. Hence, the gospel transforms society's structures.

THE FAMILY

In the ancient world, the family included blood relatives living together across generations, other dependents, and slaves. The household was the basic unit of society.[3] Paul gives indicators in Romans of the transformation of the family through Christ.

---

1. Bosch, *Transforming Mission*, 178.

2. Bosch, *Transforming Mission*, 175. I disagree with Bosch that this is why Paul does not critique slavery and the Roman Empire. I believe he would take up the same position today. While Christians should *always* stand with and for those oppressed, the primary task of the Christian church is the transformation of the society *from the inside rather than direct action against political rulers*. That is the point of Romans 13:4 and God's business.

3. Laansma, "Commentary on 2 Timothy," 258.

PART THREE: ROMANS AND THE PROCLAMATION OF THE GOSPEL

Marriage in Romans

The fundamental relationship in a family is husband and wife. Paul's message touches on his understanding of marriage at various points. In Romans 7, Paul refers to the seventh commandment in Romans 2:22 and 13:9 (Exod 20:14; Deut 5:18). In Romans 2:22, he critiques Jewish hypocrisy in rejecting adultery and yet committing it.

Paul begins Romans 7 using marriage to illustrate how a believer is set free from the law. He writes that "a married woman is bound by law to her husband while he lives, but if her husband dies, she is released from the law of marriage" (7:2). However, if she belongs to (*ginomai*)[4] another man while her husband is alive, she is called an adulteress (*moichalis*). Still, if her husband dies, she is free from that law and can remarry (7:3).

Paul here states the ideal of marriage found in Mark's Gospel. Some Pharisees ask Jesus concerning the legality of divorce. This discussion is backgrounded by two rabbinic schools that had different interpretations of the core verse on marriage in the law, Deuteronomy 24:1. In the verse, a man can divorce a woman for an indecency. This permission was interpreted in two ways. The harsher Shammai school understood it strictly as sexual immorality being the grounds for divorce. The Hillel school had a more liberal view, believing a man could divorce his wife for even insignificant things such as messing up dinner. Jesus takes an even harsher stance, consistent with that of the Qumran community:[5] no person should tear apart what God made one, a husband and wife.[6]

Jesus draws on Genesis 1:27: "God made them male and female" (Mark 10:6). He then cites Genesis 2:24, where a man shall leave his family home and be joined to his wife, "and the two shall become one flesh" (Mark 10:8). Jesus concludes that no one should separate two people that are married (Mark 10:9).

Likewise, Paul twice quotes Genesis 2:24, endorsing its importance in a biblical understanding of marriage. In 1 Corinthians 6:16, Paul draws on it as he directs the Corinthians away from sexual relationships with prostitutes. In Ephesians 5:31, he cites it in his instructions on marriage to the Ephesians.

Here in Romans 7, Paul affirms the Markan Jesus's stance. His use of the marriage metaphor affirms that for Paul, heterosexual, lifelong, and faithful marriage is etched into the pre-fall created order. Anyone who violates the marriage relationship is an adulterer.

Paul tacitly affirms the law "you shall not commit adultery" in Romans 13:9, where it is subsumed in the greater command, "love your neighbor." However, by placing adultery within the love command, in my view, Paul gives space for situations where love calls for a spouse to leave their marriage partner, such as violence toward

---

4. On this meaning of *ginomai*, see BDAG 199 meaning 9.
5. See CD 4:20—5:6; 11QT 17:15–19.
6. See Edwards, *Gospel According to Mark*, 299.

a spouse or children, abuse, rape, incest, and extreme acts of unfaithfulness within a marriage.

Paul also seems to suggest a more permissive view in 1 Corinthians 7:12–15, where he suggests that Christian spouses should allow unbeliever spouses to leave if they wish to leave a marriage. Where this happens, the Christian is no longer "enslaved," which may be his way of saying they can remarry, as long as it is to a Christian (1 Cor 7:39).[7]

However, loving, faithful, heterosexual marriage remains his starting point and ethical ideal. The critical point here is that the work of Christ undoes the consequences of the garden. According to Jesus, divorce was permitted due to the hardness of people's hearts (Mark 10:5). Now that Christ has come, and his people are infused with God's presence, the Spirit, they should aspire to be marriage partners who reflect the servant-heartedness of Jesus toward one another (Eph 5:22, 25).[8] They are to be filled with love, and this should shape their relationships. Romans tacitly endorses this vision. An aspect of Christian mission is standing for, living out, and proclaiming God's ideal of such faithful, loving marriages. Combined with his view on sexuality (below), it would include upholding heterosexual marriage rather than same-sex marriage within the church.[9]

Some marriages are mentioned in passing in Romans 9, including Abraham and Sarah (9:7) and Isaac and Rebekah (9:10). While it is true that Abraham had a sexual relationship with the slave Hagar (Gen 16:3–4), this is implicitly critiqued by Paul in Galatians 4:23, 29, where he speaks of Ishmael being "born according to the flesh."[10] Furthermore, the NT roundly rejects such dalliances and polygamy (1 Cor 7:2).[11]

Marriages representing this ideal are arguably mentioned in Romans 16, especially those of Prisca and Aquila and probably Junia and Andronicus (16:3–5, 7). Prisca and Aquila are never named apart from each other in the NT. They are presented as a unit, one flesh, who give of themselves for the gospel. They truly live out Paul's injunctions in 1 Corinthians 7:29–34 that marriage partners should place their

---

7. While scholars are split on this, Ciampa and Rosner are most likely correct: "*Not bound* here refers to freedom to remarry" (italics original). Ciampa and Rosner, *First Letter to the Corinthians*, 302.

8. For my view of this passage, where I see cruciform mutual servanthood as the basis for marriage and Paul re-envisaging masculinity, see Keown, "Paul's Vision of a New Masculinity," 47–60.

9. Keown, "'Biblical' View of Marriage," 10–12.

10. See, e.g., Dunn, *Epistle to the Galatians*, 246–47. "As usual in Paul, the phrase 'in accordance with the flesh' has a negative ring . . . particularly when set in contrast to 'in accordance with the Spirit' (see on 4:29), or in contrast to 'through promise', as here. Even on the surface, then, the implication is clear that Abraham's resort to Hagar was an act of weakness (see above on 2:16; also 5:13, 16–17, 19 etc.)—the *weakness of human sexual appetite* (perhaps) and longing for an heir, but particularly the attempt to bring about the fulfilment of God's extraordinary promise (Gen. 15:5–6) by ordinary human capacity" (emphasis mine).

11. See Keen, "Sexuality, Critical Issues," who notes that while there are polygamous relationships in the OT, "[i]n the first century AD, Jesus and the first Christians affirmed monogamy (e.g., Matt 19:3–6; 1 Cor 7:2; Eph 5:31; 1 Tim 3:2; Titus 1:6)."

commitment to Christ and his work above their marriage commitment. Or better, they are to love one another fully and completely (cf. 1 Cor 7:3–4), but God's purposes are their priority as they work as a team. Similarly, Junia and Andronicus are likely an apostolic couple serving God in their lives as are Philemon and Apphia in Philemon 1.[12]

Sexual Immorality

Romans 7 is, of course, not all Paul says about marriage, singleness, and sexuality. Paul's critique of same-sex relationships is evident in Romans 1:24–27. Humanity is characterized by idolatry and so under the wrath of God (1:18–23). Therefore, God has given them over to their desires, "to the lusts of their hearts for the impurity (*akatharsia*) of dishonoring their bodies among themselves" (my translation, v. 24). *Akatharsia* is broader than sexuality (cf. Matt 23:27) but is inclusive of it.[13]

Paul gives more specificity to this in 1:26–27. In Romans 1:25, he restates that the problem is idolatry, to which he responds with worship. Then, in verse 26, Paul specifies lesbian intimate relations and describes them as contrary to nature. He next describes how men give up natural relations with women, are consumed with passion for each other, and commit shameful acts with other men (v. 27). This verse calls on common knowledge of mammalian procreation through heterosexual intercourse and Genesis. It reminds readers that heterosexuality is etched into the natural created order.[14]

The first command uttered to the male and female image bearers was to "be fruitful and multiply and fill the earth" (Gen 1:28). With Romans 7, we have an explicit endorsement of marriage and its origins. Men and women become one flesh; they have children and fill the earth; this is, for Paul, essential to the natural created order. Same-sex sexual relationships cannot do this; they violate God's created intent for men and women.

If there is any doubt about this understanding of Paul here, he elsewhere considers same-sex relationships a work of the flesh that can potentially shut a person out of the kingdom of God (1 Cor 6:9–10, see also 1 Tim 1:10). As is well known, same-sex relationships were common in the Greco-Roman world, and so Paul is pushing against his culture.

---

12. While they are not clearly specified as a couple, Apphia is likely Philemon's wife (see Ehorn, *Philemon*, Phlm 2). See also 1 Cor 9:5, where the apostles and Jesus's brothers took believing wives with them as they engaged in mission.

13. Schreiner, *Romans*, 93 notes that "Paul often uses ἀκαθαρσία (2 Cor. 12:21; Gal. 5:19; Eph. 5:3; Col. 3:5; 1 Thess. 4:7) to refer to sexual sin. Paul is perhaps simply describing sexual sin in general terms in verse 24."

14. Moo, *Letter to the Romans*, 125: "Paul uses the word 'nature' in this verse as do most Jewish authors, particularly Philo, who included sexual morality as part of 'natural law' and, therefore, as a divine mandate applicable to all people."

As societies develop sexual ethics that diverge from those of the NT, an essential aspect of the Christian mission is to non-violently and with love stand against this and endorse a biblical sexual and marital ethic within God's communities. As believers engage with a world that differs from this, they may seek to resist changes to the law. If they do, they should conduct themselves with much humility, as all Christians are sexual sinners. Christians must also show grace as Christian ethics are not to be imposed on the world with more than persuasion. All sinners should be welcomed to worship in Christian communities. Most importantly, believers should retain a posture of grace toward those outside the church while upholding the Christian ethic.

Where societies are liberal concerning marriage and sexuality, Christians can learn from the first Christians who functioned in a Greco-Roman world, which was licentious to the core. They welcomed all sinners to join them. Yet, uncompromisingly, they continued to uphold their ethic within their communities. Where a person became divisive and sin was flagrantly endorsed and boasted of, they challenged those living morally bankrupt lives and expelled them (1 Cor 5). No doubt, they preached the sexual ethics of the kingdom within their communities (as references through the letters indicate).

Still, sexual ethics did not feature as a dominant aspect of the preaching of the first Christians.[15] Furthermore, they welcomed the sinful into their gatherings with love, mercy, and grace. They preached Christ and his gospel, inviting them to repent and believe and modeled a different way of living.

The Unmarried

Paul also mentions single people in Romans, especially in Romans 16. Romans 7:1–3 indicates that a divorced Christian ideally speaking, should remain single. However, as previously discussed, there may be grounds for remarriage to another believer based on the higher law of neighborly love and 1 Corinthians 7:15.

Paul himself was single, although he was possibly a widower (1 Cor 7:6–9).[16] First Corinthians 7 makes clear that where a person is single, this is a gift, and ideally, they are to remain celibate (1 Cor 7:9, 27).

---

15. Jesus sparingly spoke of sexual ethics in his preaching. It features in but does not dominate the Sermon on the Mount (Matt 5:27–32). There is no clear injunction to the first missionaries to preach on sexuality and marriage in the sending of the Twelve and seventy-two (Matt 10:1–15; Mark 6:10–11; Luke 9:3–5; 10:1–16), although it can be argued to be a component on preaching the kingdom and is perhaps implied in references to Sodom and Gomorrah. It is a part of his response to the questions on marriage (Mark 10:1–12; Matt 19:1–12) and ritual purity (Mark 7:21–23; Matt 15:19, cf. Luke 16:18). Abstinence from sexual immorality is expected of new gentile convert (Acts 15:29).

16. The term *agamos* (1 Cor 7:8) is paired with *chēra*, "widow," and through the passage, Paul pairs the husband and wife, so scholarship is concerning whether Paul is using the term as "single" or "widower" to balance *chēra*, "widow." It is likely Paul was married as a Pharisee, for this was expected. See the discussion Fee, *First Epistle to the Corinthians*, 287.

While he does not use *porn-* language in the letter, in Romans 13:13, Paul warns the Romans, single or married, not to engage in *kōmos*, *koitē*, and *aselgeia*. Instead, they are to "clothe yourselves with the Lord Jesus Christ, and do not think about how to gratify the desires of the flesh" (13:14, NIV).

Koitē can mean "bed" (Luke 11:7; Exod 10:23), the "marriage-bed" (Gen 49:4; Heb 13:4), a sexual emission (Lev 15:16; Rom 9:10), or sexual intercourse. The meaning in view in Romans 13:13 is undoubtedly sexual relationships outside of marriage.[17] The term is used negatively in Leviticus 18 and 20 of sexual intercourse with a neighbor's wife (Lev 18:20), between men (Lev 18:22; 20:13), with animals (Lev 18:23), and with a betrothed female slave (Lev 19:20).[18] While the idea of harsh punishment is God's prerogative in the NT (e.g., 12:19), Paul does not indicate a lessening of the sexual expectations of these two Levitical passages. They are premised on the creational ordinances in Genesis 1:27–28 and 2:24, and the seventh decalogue law, "do not commit adultery."

Aselgeia speaks of a "lack of self-constraint, which involves conduct that violates all bounds of what is socially acceptable, self-abandonment."[19] In the LXX and Pseudepigrapha, it is rejected as idolatrous (Sib. Or. 8:381).[20] Paul elsewhere rejects *aselgeia* (2 Cor 12:21; Gal 5:19; Eph 4:19) as do Peter and Jude.[21] Notably, the term is found in Mark 7:22 on the lips of Jesus, where he also rejects *porneia* (sexual immorality) and adultery (*moicheia*) as "evil things." For Jesus, all manner of sexual relationships other than consenting sex within a monogamous heterosexual marital relationship is immoral. Paul then, in rejecting *aselgeia* (and *porneia* and *moicheia* in other contexts), is consistent with Jesus (e.g., Matt 5:32; Mark 7:21–22), other NT writers,[22] Jewish law (e.g., Exod 20:14; Lev 18, 20),[23] and the creational ordinances of God in his repudiation of sexual relationships beyond a heterosexual marriage.

The two terms discussed above are preceded by *kōmos* (revelry) and *methē*, "drunkenness." *Kōmos* was a feast and procession celebrating the god of wine Dionysus, akin to a modern Mardi Gras. In 2 Maccabees 6:4, it is used of the debauched revelry of gentiles who "were carousing with companions and having sexual relations with women in the sacred enclosure and bringing inappropriate things inside" (LES).

---

17. BDAG 554.

18. See also negative uses in Num 5:13, 20; Wis 3:15; Sib. Or. 4:33; 5:387 (rejecting sexual relations with children); 5:393 (rejecting bestiality); T. Reu. 1:6; *Ant.* 2.55.

19. BDAG 141.

20. See also Wis 14:26; Sib. Or. 2:279; T. Jud. 23:1; Jub. 4:15; 3 Macc 2:26; *Ant.* 8:318; 15:98; 20:112; *J.W.* 1.439; 2.121; 4.562; *Mos.* 1.3, 305.

21. See 1 Pet 4:3; 2 Pet 2:2, 7, 18; Jude 4.

22. Acts 15:20, 29; 21:25; 1 Pet 4:3–4; 2 Pet 2:2, 10; Jude 4, 7; Rev 2:14, 20, 21; 9:21; 14:8; 17:4; 18:3, 9; 19:2.

23. For a discussion of later Jewish writings, see Hauck and Schulz, "Πόρνη, Πόρνος, Πορνεία, Πορνεύω, Ἐκπορνεύω," 587–90.

Similarly, in Wisdom 13:23, it is employed of idolaters who, along with other atrocities, celebrate

> raving revelries of special rituals, they no longer keep their lives of marriages pure but one destroys another by ambushes or grieves another by adulteries (LES).[24]

Philo repudiates gentiles for their festivals, which features *kōmos* amongst a range of other gross behaviors, including drunkenness (*Cher.* 92). *Kōmos* speaks of carousing and revelry,[25] and sexual immorality is a vital aspect of this. *Methē* is "drunkenness," which is also intimately linked to the sexually immoral Greco-Roman culture.

In this passage, Paul is challenging all Romans, the married and single, to be different from their world. Spouses are to be faithful to each other and not join licentious behavior. Single people are to be celibate. Central to mission is to live counterculturally, even if the world we are in is increasingly debauched. Love is to be shown to all.

There are also women named in Romans with no male names attached. They are likely unmarried, widowed, or divorced. They are spoken of commendably. Phoebe is a sister, deacon, wealthy patron to Paul and others, and prepared to bravely carry Paul's letter to Rome (16:1–2). Mary, Persis, Tryphaena, and Tryphosa are commended for their labor in the Lord (16:6, 12). Some contemporary writers have suggested the latter two women were lesbians, which is very unlikely in a letter in which Paul rejects lesbianism (1:26).[26] Rufus's mother may also be widowed and is commended for mothering Paul, implying her generous hospitality (16:13). Some of the men could also be single; however, it is more difficult to tell. The commendation of these women suggests they are role models of women who are celibate and serve God with all they have. In most cultures, the church and mission run on the labor of such special women.

Children

For Paul, the church is a family with God as Father, Jesus "the Son" and the firstborn among many brothers (8:29), and believers as siblings. They are at the same time the children of Abraham, Isaac, and Jacob,[27] and God (8:14; 9:26). They are children of promise (9:8–10) adopted into God's family with full inheritance rights (8:15–17).

---

24. See also Sib. Or. 5:394 where Rome is critiqued for *kōmos* alongside matricide, pederasty, prostitution, incest between mother and child and a father and daughter, bestiality, so that "no longer in you will virgin maidens tend the divine fire of sacred nourishing wood." This passage implies there is not a virgin remaining in the city. See also Sib. Or. 5:317. In Sib. Or. 8:118, there will be "none who are drunk (*methē*) in lawless revels (*kōmos*) or dances."

25. BDAG 580.

26. E.g., D'Angelo, "Women Partners in the New Testament," 65–86. However, she may be right to suggest that Tryphaena and Tryphosa, and Euodia and Syntyche were missionary teams. See Keown, *Philippians*, 2:313–14.

27. See 4:11, 12, 16; 9:7.

God's family includes all humankind from the nations who believe in God (4:17, 18). The children of God will be revealed at the consummation (8:19, 21, 23).

This vision of the people of God as a family is why "brothers" is his main form of address,[28] and elsewhere he speaks of Christians as brothers and sisters (16:1, 14, 23). This family should be shaped by familial and brother love (12:13), with each family member determined to ensure they do not cause their brother or sister to stumble.[29] Paul mentions Rufus's mother, who is a mother to him as well, showing how Christians can embrace one another as family (16:13). The importance of teaching children is hinted at in Romans 2:20, as long as it is not hypocritical. The family units of Romans 16 speak of whole households experiencing God's transformation (16:10, 11). One of the signs of sinful humankind is that children are disobedient to their parents (1:30), a violation of the fifth decalogue command for children to honor their parents (Exod 20:12). Paul mentions this in Ephesians 6:1, where he gives a compelling vision of the Christian family home in mutual submission and servanthood.[30] Aside from the renewal of the individual, the transformation of society begins in the family, then extending to the whole people of God.

WIDER SOCIETY

The transformation of other parts of society is found in Christian engagement with the broader world. As will be discussed in part three, chapter 24, believers are not to be extreme political agitators or revolutionaries, but without violating their fundamental commitment to obey God and his Son, are to live in submission to the State (13:1–7). This injunction presupposes a vision of the people of God transforming society from the inside out as they live as Christian communities in the carnage of a fallen world. They do not have to achieve their ends with direct political engagement but can work to build countercultural communities embodying God's virtues. They invite the world to join them, proclaiming, and modeling the life of the kingdom. As they do, the transformational power of the gospel spreads, "invading" the world and changing it.

Paul's vision of race and culture is also radically inclusive, as will be discussed (see part three, chapter 25). Where gender is concerned, in the letter, Paul does not limit the roles of men and women. The spiritual gift list of Romans 12:4–8 has no restriction on women (similarly, his other lists).[31] The sending of people to preach in Romans 10:14 is not gender exclusive. While motherhood is tacitly endorsed (Sarah and Rebekah, 9:9–10), as is fatherhood (esp. Abraham, Rom 4), women are deacons (16:1), patrons (16:2), coworkers (16:3, cf. vv. 6, 12), apostles (16:7), and arguably

---

28. See 1:13; 7:1, 4; 8:12; 11:25; 12:1; 15:14, 30; 16:17.
29. See 14:10, 13, 15, 21.
30. See Keown, "Paul's Vision of a New Masculinity," 47–60.
31. 1 Cor 12:8–10, 28–30; 13:1–3; 14:26; Eph 4:11.

overseers (Phil 1:1; 4:2–3),[32] showing their active engagement in mission and church leadership.

Romans is also intriguing from the perspective of slavery.[33] Paul begins the letter assuming his "slave" status in relation to Jesus (1:1). Assuming this position is not a demeaning of self, but a position of the highest honor because of the one he serves. Believers are redeemed from enslavement to sin to willingly serving God and his righteousness and justice (6:6, 16–22; 7:25). This enslavement is Spirit-impelled and not legally prescribed (7:6). As such, believers must "be slaves to the Lord" (12:11). They must not join the false teachers who do not do so (16:18). All this use of slave language is symbolic, yet it speaks of a willingness to take notions of ownership and apply it to the gospel.

Interestingly, a number of those named in Romans 16 have slave names. Dunn writes, "This gives a fairly clear picture of the extent to which the first Christian groups in Rome drew their strength from the lower strata of Roman society."[34] Paul, of course, was a Roman citizen, and so we see the breakdown of social barriers in the church and his mission team.

A rejection of elitism is found through Romans 12. Paul repudiates arrogance (12:3), haughtiness, intellectual arrogance, urging the Romans "to associate with the lowly" (12:16). If the people of God genuinely love one another, there is no place for such attitudes.

CITIES, REGIONS, NATIONS, AND THE WORLD

The vision of societal transformation in Romans is global. The Christian church, by the time of Romans, was an international community. Paul had traveled from Israel to the western Balkans completing his work of planting churches (15:19). He mentions the first Asian convert, Epaenetus (16:5). Paul is in Corinth, among locals with Greek names like Phoebe (16:1–2), Gaius, and Erastus (16:23), along with others with Roman names like Tertius (16:22), and Quartus (16:23). He will travel back to Jerusalem, then Rome, and then Spain to spread the gospel further (15:24–33). While the etymology of a name does not guarantee ethnicity, it is interesting that the names of

---

32. Keown, *Philippians*, 2:311–15.

33. Strictly speaking, this could have been discussed under the family as slaves were part of the family structure in Rome. I have chosen to discuss it here as the whole Empire was run on slaves who were found in the civil service, and in every part of society.

34. See Dunn, *Romans 9–16*, 894–900. Slave names include Junia, Ampliatus, Urbanus, Stachys, Aristobulus, Narcissus, Persis, Rufus, Phlegon, Hermes, Patrobas, Hermas, Philologus, Julia, Nereus, and Olympas, and potentially members of the families of the households of Aristobulus and Narcissus (which would have included slaves).

Romans 16 come from Latin,[35] Hebrew,[36] Greek,[37] and Hellenized Persian.[38] The passage testifies of a multiethnic community.

Paul is also raising funds on this trip for the poor in Jerusalem. By doing so, his trip is an international aid mission. His mission speaks of redressing economic disparity across God's world within God's people. The collection speaks of a vision of social transformation that sees the world without material inequalities. He wants next to go to Spain to take this vision of a new world to the western edge of the Empire. The concern for removing social inequalities fits with Paul's broader theology of the cosmos restored, liberated from its bondage to sin (8:19–23). One aspect of that is injustice and oppression. The vision of social transformation in Romans is genuinely inspiring. It should excite readers to desire that all people, families, villages, towns, cities, regions, states, nations, and the whole creation conformed to God's purposes. For such a dream, God's people are called to labor.

---

35. Prisca, Aquila, Junia, Ampliatus, Urbanus, Rufus, and Julia.

36. Mary, Herodian.

37. Phoebe, Epaenetus (from Asia), Andronicus, Stachys, Apelles, Aristobulus, Narcissus, Tryphaena, Tryphosa, Asyncritus, Phlegon, Hermes, Hermas, Patrobas, Philologus, Nereus, Olympas.

38. Persis means "Persian Women" in Greek.

21

Patronage and Hospitality

ONE ASPECT OF MISSION that Romans clearly endorses is the role of the wealthy in mission. This emphasis is significant as it pushes back against the idea that being wealthy is intrinsically evil. Those who are wealthy but use their possessions for God's mission are commended. Paul's view on poverty has already been touched on in the chapters on social justice and social transformation (part 3, chapters 18, 20), but some more focused comments are appropriate here.

GOD AND JESUS

The supreme patron of the world is not the emperor[1] or the gods, but Israel and the church's God.[2] Toews sees this in Romans 5:1–11, which "pictures God as the Patron who freely gives new status and privileges to the client, humanity."[3] God is superior, righteous and loving, and the person of honor, whereas humankind is the client who is weak, ungodly, a sinful enemy, dishonorable, and shameful. Yet, God "acts against all social convention and honors the shameful client."[4] He gives a new status of righteousness and the privilege of peace with God, access to him, participation in his glory, receipt of his love, reconciliation, and salvation. This significance is given through the gift of Christ's death, where counter-culturally, God the patron, took the initiative to establish a relationship based on honor. "God the Patron is a model of how patrons, the strong in the church, should relate to clients, the weak."[5] God then provides lavishly for humankind, including the beautiful grace of salvation and eternal life.

1. Jewett and Kotansky state that after Octavius's victory at Actium, "[t]he populace thus became Octavian's private clientele with him, the emperor, as the master patron." Jewett and Kotansky, *Romans*, 46.
2. Dunn, *Romans 1–8*, 264.
3. Toews, *Romans*, 143.
4. Toews, *Romans*, 143.
5. Toews, *Romans*, 143.

PART THREE: ROMANS AND THE PROCLAMATION OF THE GOSPEL

Although not found in Romans, Paul's gospel is premised on a super wealthy divine patron Jesus (in every way),[6] sacrificially giving up his inestimable riches (coming to earth), becoming poor (literally, he died naked with nothing), so that people can become rich (spiritually now, and materially in eternity). The previous sentence references 2 Corinthians 8:9, written on the same mission journey a year or so earlier as he encouraged the Corinthians to give to the Jerusalem Collection. The example of Jesus is paradigmatic for Christians and especially the wealthy. "Since Christ is *the* host, we are all guests by divine grace."[7] Believers, then, are to become hospitable patrons for the work of God. However, their patronage is to be markedly different from the wider Roman world.

COUNTERCULTURAL PATRONAGE

Paul's teaching concerning patronage and hospitality cannot be limited only to the rich. He imagines all Christians being generous to God's work and the needs of others.[8] Still, as across the biblical story, the challenge is focused on the wealthy caring for others in need.

The patronage of the wealthy Christians is not to be patterned on the Greco-Roman approach.[9] In the Roman world, a small group of elite people owned most of the wealth and property.[10] Most people then struggled to survive and sought help. When in need, they often sought a patron to assist them.

> Patrons might be asked to provide money, grain, employment or land; the better connected persons could be sought out as patrons for the opportunities they would give for professional or social advancement.[11]

The recipient became a client with the expectation that they would reciprocate their patron's generosity with gratitude and public acknowledgment, loyalty, and services that advanced the power and honor of the patron. Hence, where the patron supports the needy, the needy were expected to give back with public gratitude—a *quid pro quo* arrangement. Such patronage ran the empire and maintained the social order where the rich stayed rich as they were served by others, including slaves.

---

6. On his divinity in Paul, see esp. Rom 9:5; Phil 2:6, 9–11; Col 1:19; 2:9; Titus 2:13.

7. Witherington and Hyatt, *Paul's Letter*, 346.

8. For example, there is no limitation on Rom 12:9, 13; 13:8–10. He also commends the giving of the poor in Macedonia (2 Cor 8:2).

9. On patronage, see deSilva, "Patronage," 766–71.

10. See Downs, "Economics," 220–21. He estimates 1.5 percent of the population were elite; 6–12 percent were "middling" with an income; 2.4–10 percent needed for subsistence living; and 90 percent below subsistence level. The vast majority then lived concerned to get food, shelter, and clothing necessary merely to survive.

11. deSilva, "Patronage," 767.

Conversely, Christian "patronage" is "no strings attached," giving to the needs of others as led by the Spirit. It does include the notion of reciprocity and honor, but instead of the client or recipient repaying in kind or with service of some sort, God is trusted to repay the giver as he deems fit—primarily, in the world to come. This divine reciprocity has already been seen in God's judgment in Romans 2:6. We see it in Paul's appeals to the Corinthians for the collection he is about to take to Jerusalem as he writes to Rome. He reminds the Corinthians, "whoever sows sparingly will also reap sparingly, and whoever sows bountifully will also reap bountifully" (2 Cor 9:6).[12]

In prosperity theology, this repayment is immediate and present (and should be expected). In the gospel, God does bless in the present as his lavish generosity strengthens the believer in suffering and provision of need. He also blesses some Christians with great wealth. However, where it involves increased wealth, this is to be divested for the needs of others and God's church and mission. As he writes in 2 Corinthians 9:8: "And God is able to make all grace abound to you, so that having all sufficiency in all things at all times, *you may abound in every good work*" (emphasis mine). As believers are not under the law, there is no mention of tithing; people are to give as they are able and without compulsion (1 Cor 16:2; 2 Cor 8:3). Still, Paul delights in lavish and cheerful Christian giving (2 Cor 8:2–4, 7; 9:6; Phil 4:15–18) and fairness (2 Cor 8:13–14). The real blessings come in the eschaton, where the believer's inheritance is laid up.

SPIRITUAL GIFTS, PATRONAGE, AND HOSPITALITY

Romans is very encouraging where patronage and hospitality is concerned. Three of the spiritual gifts potentially point toward a God-giftedness in the direction of patronage and hospitality.

Service

The first is "service," *diakonia*. The term can mean "ministry," and speak of some kind of ministering, e.g., being a "deacon" (16:1).[13] Yet, across the NT, *diakon-* language is also used of serving the needs of others in hospitality, and this is the sense here.

Martha is an example in Luke 10:40. Although Jesus critiqued her in comparison to Mary listening at his feet, she was fulfilling the social requirements of a hostess caring for her esteemed guest.[14] In Acts 6:1, the term is used of the daily distribution of

---

12. Compare with Gal 6:7–8; Phil 4:17. See also Prov 11:24–25; 22:9; Luke 6:38.

13. In this sense it is used of governmental leaders who serve God (13:4); Christ (15:8); deacons (16:1; 1 Tim 3:8, 12); generally of ministers of the gospel (1 Cor 3:5; 2 Cor 3:6; 6:4; Eph 3:7; 6:21; Col 1:7, 23, 25; 4:7; 1 Tim 4:6); Satan's human servants who are false teachers (2 Cor 11:15, 23); Christ [not] a servant of sin (Gal 2:17).

14. "Her cordial reception of Jesus fits the theme of hospitality (10:4–12). She does what was

food to the widows in Jerusalem. The first Jerusalem Collection from Syrian Antioch is also called a *diakonia* (Acts 11:29; 12:25). While Paul uses *diakonia* of his whole ministry (11:13), as he does elsewhere, he describes his present Jerusalem Collection as a *diakonia* in Romans 15:31. Returning to the gift, Schreiner rightly observes: "Most likely, Paul is thinking of the gift of service in general, perhaps especially the task of rendering financial and material assistance."[15]

The use of the term for material assistance opens up the possibility that where we see the term *diakonia*, that it applies to Christian patronage, hospitality, or acts of social justice.[16] Such things as these could be in view in Romans 12:7. The Greek translates literally as "if service, in the serving." The thrust is that those with the gift of serving should see it as a *charisma* (gift) of God given by grace that they are to live out in the service of others.[17] The rich, then, should see their wealth as a gift and use it for the glory of God. Those with gifts of caring and providing hospitality should do so with a no strings attached approach, trusting God for their reward (even if not motivated by the reward but love).

Generosity

The second gift potentially in view is generosity. The Greek *ho metadidous en aplotēti* translates literally as "the one who gives in generosity." *Metadidōmi* compounds *meta* (with) and *didōmi* (give) and so yields the literal idea of "to share."[18]

In wider Greek Jewish sources, it is used of sharing in a range of different ways.[19] Commonly, it is employed of sharing what one has with another, including distributing wealth (2 Macc 1:35; Sib. Or. 3.41; *Ant*. 9.59) or sharing with someone in need.[20]

---

expected for her honored guest (see Jesus's complaints against the Pharisee in 7:36–50). Guests bring obligations in hospitality, and she pulls out all the stops." Garland, *Luke*, 453.

15. Schreiner, *Romans*, 657.

16. See also 1 Cor 16:15; 2 Cor 8:4; 9:1, 12, 13.

17. Longenecker suggests Paul "had in mind all the activities meant to build up the Christian community." Longenecker, *Epistle*, 929. Yet why should it be limited to the Christian community?

18. To "give a part of, impart, share." BDAG 638.

19. Including disseminating news (e.g., 2 Macc 8:12; Sib. Or. 7:161; T. Job 4:1; Let. Aris. 43, 309; *Ant*. 1.9; *J.W*. 2.142; *Her*. 5; *Mut*. 57); sharing the wealth of wisdom with others (Wis 7:13, cf. T. Dan 6:9; Let. Aris. 7); sharing gifts with a king (Let. Aris. 172); God bestowing generously things on people (*Ant*. 4.237); sharing food and weapons (*Ant*. 6.255); bestowing a blessing (*Ant*. 7.83); giving honor (*Ant*. 10.249); giving daughters as wives (*Ant*. 16.11); giving permission to take on the name Roman (*Ag. Ap*. 2.40); giving a plot of land for burial (*J.W*. 4.360, 381); giving people a share in eternity (*Opif*. 44, 77); Eve giving the fruit to Adam (*Opif*. 156); giving honor to created things not God (*Ebr*. 110, cf. Rom 1:23); giving a share of fame to another (*Fug*. 30); giving a pardon (*Fug*. 84); sharing in advantages gained (*Mos*. 1.315); sharing with a slave one's things (*Spec*. 1.126; *Virt*. 121); sharing in pleasure and pain (*Spec*. 2.89); to give mercy (*Spec*. 2.115; *Virt*. 141); the sun giving power to the moon (*Spec*. 2.141); to give an inheritance to children (*Spec*. 3.112); to grant freedom (*Spec*. 3.196); share in divine words spoken (*Virt*. 108); to give an opportunity to defend oneself (*Flacc*. 54).

20. Examples include sharing with an orphan (Job 31:17), the hungry (Sib. Or. 2.83), with others

Sharing in this way brings blessing (Prov 11:26; T. Zeb. 6:6). Philo's use is interesting as human sharing derives from God doing the same. Aside from a range of other ways he uses it, he likes to speak of God distributing good things to humankind,[21] and they, in kind, sharing with others in need (*Virt.* 168)—such as the poor (*Spec.* 2.71) and strangers (*Spec.* 2.119).[22] Paul uses it in Romans 1:11 of imparting, sharing, or distributing to the Romans "some spiritual gift." In Ephesians 4:28, it is applied to sharing with someone in need out of honestly gained resources.[23]

In Romans 12:8, it then speaks of one who has a special gift of sharing their wealth and possessions with others.[24] Those who do so should do it in *aplotēs*. *Aplotēs* can mean simplicity or sincerity.[25] It can have this sense here: those who have the gift of serving others should do so "sincerely," i.e., with authenticity and not for personal gain.[26] Paul's uses *aplotēs* this way of his team living sincerely before God (2 Cor 1:12), the ideal of sincere devotion to Christ (2 Cor 11:3), and of serving with a sincere heart (Eph 6:5; Col 3:22).

However, it can also more rarely mean "generosity" (*Ant.* 7.331), as in those who give lavishly to the Jerusalem Collection (2 Cor 8:2; 9:11, 12). Here, in the context of material giving, "generosity" is a better translation, despite its rareness.[27] As such, Paul is urging those in the congregation with the gift of sharing with others in need, to do so lavishly and generously.

Mercy

The final gift is mercy (*ho eleōn*). The verb *eleaō* means to show mercy to others. In Jewish Greek literature, it is found of God who shows mercy.[28] People are to reflect his

---

(T. Zeb. 6:7), with the poor (T. Iss. 7:5). It is used of sharing meat (Ep Jer 27), water (*Ant.* 1.246), an apple (*Ant.* 1.307), or food (*J.W.* 5.438; 6.307).

21. See *Leg.* 1.40; *Cher.* 86; *Det.* 101, 124, 156; *Gig.* 27, 43; *Her.* 159; *Somn.* 2.223; *Ios.* 85; *Mos.* 2.190; *Spec.* 1.49, 97, 294; 2.15; *Virt.* 125.

22. See *Ios.* 144; *Spec.* 1.120; 2.107; 3.116.

23. See also 1 Thess 2:8; Herm. Vis. 3.9, 2; 5, 3.

24. It can be taken of the office of distributing church resources, but "in simplicity" supports seeing this as personal generosity (see Moo, *Letter to the Romans*, 786). "*The patron* who provides financial support for those in need must demonstrate earnest dedication." Toews, *Romans*, 304 (emphasis original).

25. BDAG 104. All LXX uses have this sense: 2 Kgdms 15:11; 1 Chr 29:17; 1 Macc 2:37, 60; 3 Macc 3:21; Wis 1:1; Sus 63; T. Reu. 4:1; T. Sim. 4:5; T. Levi 13:1; T. Iss. 3:2, 4, 6, 7, 8; 4:1, 6; 5:1, 8; 6:1; 7:1; T. Benj. 6:7; T. Job 26:6; *J.W.* 2.151; 5.319, 529; *Opif.* 156, 170; *Mos.* 1.172. It can mean genuine piety (*J.W.* 1.111).

26. E.g., BDAG 104; Barrett, *Epistle to the Romans*, 220.

27. "On the whole, 'generosity' is the best translation so long as its motivation is kept clearly in mind." Jewett and Kotansky, *Romans*, 752. "The notion that one must give generously is probably slightly preferable since the term has this meaning elsewhere in financial contexts (2 Cor. 8:2; 9:11, 13 . . .)." Schreiner, *Romans*, 659.

28. See Ps 114:5 [116:5 Heb]; Isa 49:10; Tob 13:2; Apoc. Sedr. 15:1; T. Zeb. 7:2; T. Dan 5:9, cf. T. Ab.

mercy toward others. Showing mercy all day is the mark of a righteous person that brings blessing to one's children (Ps 36:26 [37:6]; Prov 21:26). Those who honor God show mercy to the poor, whereas those who cheat the needy provoke their creator (Prov 14:31). The Testament of Issachar 5:2 states: "Love the Lord and your neighbor; be compassionate (*eleaō*) toward poverty and sickness."[29]

Eleaō is found four times in the NT, twice in Jude 22–23, where readers are to "have mercy on those who doubt" and to other more seriously defiled sinners, to "show mercy with fear." Hence, it is an attribute linked to mission to those struggling and sinful. Paul's other use is in Romans 9:16 of God's mercy toward people based on election, grace, and faith, and not human will or exertion.[30] As such, it is an attribute of God. Here, such mercy flows over into people who show mercy toward others.

In the Epistle of Barnabas 20:2, it is explicitly applied to showing mercy to the poor. Jewett and Kotansky suggest it includes "actions to meet human need would include care for the sick, burial of the dead, or giving alms."[31] Here, it sits alongside the gifts of service and giving as another gift of care toward those in need, whether it is spiritual, mental health, economic, or relational.[32] Some are engifted with the ability to show God's mercy to those in need.

Those who do have this gift should show mercy with *hilapotēs*, which BDAG suggests means "quality or state of cheerfulness, opposite of an attitude suggesting being under duress, *cheerfulness, gladness, wholeheartedness, graciousness*."[33] It is rare, a *hapax legomenon*, and carries this meaning across all uses in Jewish Greek literature.[34] There is an allusion here to Proverbs 22:8 (LXX): "God blesses a cheerful and giving [person], and he will achieve futility for his deeds."[35] So, the one who does acts of mercy should do so cheerfully and joyfully. God will reward them.

(A) 10.13; *Ant.* 2.212; 10.242), in prayers for mercy (Sir 18:14; *Ant.* 8.115; 11.232).

29. See T. Zeb. 2:2; T. Ash. 2:6; T. Benj. 4:2, cf. *Ant.* 9.91; 12.30; *J.W.* 1.10; 6.204. It is also used of pitying someone of old age (4 Macc 6:12) or generally (4 Macc 9:3).

30. "It also reaches back into the preceding argument that all believers have been the objects of God's 'mercy' (9:15, 18; 11:30–32; cf. 12:1)." Thielman, *Romans*, 578.

31. Jewett and Kotansky, *Romans*, 754.

32. "This would include such helpful activities as feeding the hungry, caring for the sick, and caring for the aging." Mounce, *Romans*, 235. Today, this gift could "include such things as visiting the sick at home or in hospitals, visiting and helping shut-ins, comforting the dying and the bereaved, visiting and corresponding with prisoners, and sending cards to or telephoning any of these." Cottrell, *Romans: Volume 2*, 12:8: "Using the Gifts of Grace for Unselfish Service (12:3–8)."

33. BDAG 473 (emphasis original).

34. The term is quite rare, used of those who find a good woman (Prov 18:22), a charlatan entering a house (false *hilapotēs*, Pss. Sol. 4:5), in prayers and blessings to God for joyfulness (Pss. Sol. 16:12; T. Ab. (A) 20:8), eating and drinking with happiness (T. Naph. 9:2, the cheerful attitude of the sensible (*Plant.* 166; *Somn.* 2.167), and joy listening to a good teacher (*Contempl.* 77).

35. Jewett and Kotansky, *Romans*, 754. Translation LES adapted for inclusive language.

Conclusion

It must be significant that three of the seven spiritual gifts relate to acts of generosity toward others. The other four are speech and leadership gifts (prophecy, teaching, exhortation, and leadership).[36] By having three gifts emphasizing service to those in need in amongst "important" leadership gifts, Paul is challenging the Romans in a culture that was obsessed with status and rank (as we see most powerfully in Corinth, where Paul is writing). Each speaks of Christians who share with those in need and offering patronage and hospitality without expectation of reciprocation while trusting God. Examples of this in Romans could have these kinds of gifts include those who will in the future host Paul and help him on his way to Spain, Phoebe, Rufus's mother, and Gaius (15:24; 16:2, 13, 23).

LOVING HOSPITALITY

The section on ethics that follows the gifts emphasizes *agapē* love; the kind of selfless sacrifice demonstrated in the life and death of Jesus (5:8). The love of the Romans must be without hypocrisy (*anypokritos*, 12:9). The Greek can mean "impartial" (Wis 5:18). The phrase is found in Apoc. Sedr. 1:1 where the writer states that readers "should prefer nothing but sincere love" (*anypokriton . . . agapēn*, see also Apoc. Sedr. 1:25). Peter urges his Asian reader to be purified in obedience for sincere sibling-love (1 Pet 1:22). In 2 Corinthians 6:6, Paul speaks of the same kind of impartial and untainted *agapē*.[37] As such here, in urging that our love be genuine, Paul is warning about making our love a mere pretense, an outward display of emotion that does not conform to the nature of the God who is love and who has loved us.[38]

Verse 10 uses two love terms and is literally: "those-with-family-love (*philostorgos*) with sibling-[brotherly]-love (*philadelphia*) toward one another" (translation mine). *Philostorgos* compounds *philos* (love) with *storgē* (love) and speaks of the kind of love one finds in a family.[39] The second term also compounds *philos* but with *adelphos*, "brother,"[40] a term Paul uses elsewhere of Christian familial affection (1 Thess 4:9).[41]

36. Some take *proistēmi*, "leadership" as "to act as a patron," however, the term means "one who presides." Moo, *Letter to the Romans*, 786.

37. See also 1 Tim 1:5; 2 Tim 1:5 of a sincere faith. James describes the wisdom from above with it.

38. Moo, *Letter to the Romans*, 794.

39. *Philostorgos* is found of loving parents (4 Macc 15:13; Jos. Asen. 12.8), Abraham (T. Ab. (A) 1:5, see also *Ant.* 7.252; *J.W.* 1.523, 622; *Abr.* 198; *Virt.* 91, 192; *Praem.* 158), a husband for a wife (*Ant.* 11.196; 15.66), love of family (*J.W.* 7.390; *Spec.* 3.157), or more generally of affection (*Ant.* 4.135; 7.43; 15.16, 70; *Spec.* 2.40; 3.153).

40. It can be literal or figurative of a brotherly bond; see 4 Macc 13:23, 26; 14:1; *Ant.* 2.161; 4.26; 12.189; *Legat.* 87 (of the twin gods Pollux and Castor).

41. See also Heb 13:1; 1 Pet 1:22; 2 Pet 1:7; 1 Clem. 47:5; 48:1. "But the idea of *brotherly love* in such groups is not found anywhere but among the Christians." Morris, *Epistle to the Romans*, 444.

In verse 13, the church is to be a family that contributes (*koinōneō*) to those with needs (*chreia*). *Koinōneō* here has that special sense we see of giving materially (*koinōnia*) in Romans 15:26 of the Jerusalem Collection. He uses the verb *koinōneō* in Romans 15:27 of sharing spiritual blessings. The verb is also used of the Philippians sending financial gifts to Paul (Phil 4:15, cf. 1:5, 7) and students sharing their wealth with teachers (Gal 6:6).[42]

"Needs" here is *chreia*, a common and general term for the needs of others, but perhaps here with an economic twist (e.g., Eph 4:28; Phil 2:25).[43] The saints are all of God's people, sanctified in Christ, in Rome and beyond. They are to emulate what the Christians of Macedonia and Achaia have done for the Jerusalem saints in need (15:26). They are to care for those in the Roman Christian community and beyond as they engage in mission.[44]

Furthermore, in verse 13b, they are to pursue (*diōkō*) hospitality (*philoxenia*). *Diōkō* is a term drawn from hunting that has the sense of "pursue" in it, whether for malicious purposes (persecution, being pursued) or for positive things like a virtue. In Romans, Paul uses it of persecution (12:14) and of pursuing righteousness (9:30), the law (9:31), and what brings peace (14:19).[45] The verb is forceful, indicating that "we should take the initiative in this matter of hospitality."[46]

Here, the Romans are to pursue *philoxenia*. The noun compounds *philos* (love) and *xenos* (stranger) and so literally connotes the love of strangers, who are "people without a place,"[47] by showing hospitality to them. *Xenos*, "stranger," can also mean "host to strangers," and is used in this way of Gaius in Corinth (16:23).[48] Gaius, then, is an exemplar of Christian hospitality and patronage, including Paul. Hence, *philoxenia*

---

42. See also of (not) sharing in sins (1 Tim 5:22) or (not) wicked works (2 John 11); Christ sharing in flesh and blood (Heb 2:14); Christians sharing in Christ's sufferings (1 Pet 4:13).

43. Also, Phil 4:16, 19; Titus 3:14. See also Mark 2:25; Acts 2:45; 4:35; 1 John 3:17. It can be used of health needs (Mark 2:17 and parr.; Luke 9:11). Of course, if one was in poor health in the ancient world and not elite, it is very likely that person is poor as well (cf. Mark 5:26).

44. "Paul likely had in mind also the collection for the poor he was soon to take to Jerusalem (Rom 15:25–28; 1 Cor 16:1–4; 2 Cor 8–9), but his injunction here goes beyond that to enjoin a general concern all believers should have for one another." Osborne, *Romans: Verse by Verse*, 396.

45. See also of persecution (1 Cor 4:12; Gal 1:13, 23; 4:29; 5:11; 6:12; Phil 3:6; 2 Tim 3:12). Otherwise, it is used positively of seeking after love (1 Cor 14:1), to take hold of eternal life (Phil 3:12, 14), to do good to all (1 Thess 5:15), righteousness (1 Tim 6:11; 2 Tim 2:22).

46. Cottrell, *Romans: Volume 2*, 12:13: "Miscellaneous Moral Teaching (12:6–19)." He cites Lenski, *The Interpretation*, 773: "Hospitality is literally to be chased after as one hunts an animal and delights to carry the booty home." Or, as Barrett puts it, "Practise hospitality with enthusiasm." Barrett, *Epistle to the Romans*, 221.

47. Pohl, *Making Room*, 87.

48. *Xenos* is used of strangers the nations either welcomed or did not and for which they were judged (Matt 25:35, 38, 43, 44). It is also used of the burial place of strangers (Matt 27:7), strange foreign deities (Acts 17:18), foreigners (Acts 17:21), strangers to Israel and God, i.e., gentiles (Eph 2:12, 19), the faithful who were strangers in an idolatrous world (Heb 11:13), strange teachings (Heb 13:9), something stranger (1 Pet 4:12), and traveling Christians (3 John 5).

means doing what Gaius is doing, showing hospitality to others, and in ancient terms, welcoming a stranger into one's life and home.

The related *xenia* is used of a guest room, such as that which Paul hopes to use at Philemon's home (Phlm 22; Acts 28:23).[49] Coming after the appeal to contribute to the needs of the saints, this can be focused on Christian hospitality to other Christians. Interpersonal Christian relationships are in view in 1 Peter 4:9, where readers are to "show hospitality to *one another* without grumbling" (emphasis mine). These might include returnees from the Claudian expulsion,[50] Christian missionaries, those there on business,[51] refugees and runaways,[52] and locals in need, including Jewish Christians.[53]

Yet, here, in Romans, it precedes the appeal to bless persecutors in verse 14a. Hence, it could stretch as far as showing hospitality to unbelievers as well. Certainly, the latter is in view in Hebrews 13:2, where believers are to show *philoxenia* to strangers in case they are angels (cf. Gen 18).[54]

Seeing this as inclusive of unbelievers finds support in the play on *diōkō* in verses 13 and 14, where it is used of pursuing hospitality and of persecution.[55] Paul is creatively saying, "pursue showing hospitality to your pursuers." It is also supported by the citation of Proverbs 25:21–22 in Romans 12:20, where enemies are to be nourished.[56] Garrett explains the original sense of the Proverb, which included the words, "and the Lord will reward you":

> Feeding an enemy will "heap burning coals on his head" in the sense that he or she will be humiliated at having to take bread from a hated rival. The metaphor of burning coals implies intense pain; the proverb does not foresee the possibility of reconciliation with one's foe, however true and noble that may

---

49. *Zenizō*, "to receive strangers, entertain guests, surprise," is used of a lodging for guests such as that which Peter stayed in with Simon the Tanner in Caesarea Maritima (Acts 10:6, 18, 23, 32), where Paul and his group stayed at Mnason of Cyprus's house shortly after leaving Corinth to Jerusalem (Acts 21:16), where he stayed en route to Rome at the home of Publius in Malta (Acts 28:7), and "strange things" Paul teaches (Acts 17:20). It can also mean "surprised" (1 Pet 4:4, 12).

50. Jewett and Kotansky, *Romans*, 765.

51. "Hospitality as Paul has in mind involves more than just providing lodging or food for travelers, particularly traveling Christians unknown to the host." Witherington and Hyatt, *Paul's Letter*, 294. "It meant embracing this person as a member of your home." Runge, *Romans*, 283.

52. Someone like Onesimus, although, he was likely an unbeliever at the time looking for Paul (Phlm 10).

53. Witherington and Hyatt suggest the latter. Witherington and Hyatt, *Paul's Letter*, 292, 327.

54. Dunn, *Romans 9–16*, 744 notes that the two great exemplars of hospitality were Abraham (Gen 18; Philo, *Abr.* 107–114; Josephus, *Ant.* 1.196; 1 Clem. 10:7) and Job (Job 31:32; T. Job 10:1–3; 25:5; 53:3). Clement also commends Rahab's hospitality (1 Clem. 12:1).

55. Moo, *Letter to the Romans*, 798.

56. Commenting on v. 20, Dunn notes, "they should show hospitality to enemy as well as fellow believer." Dunn, *Romans 9–16*, 756.

be. Still, the implication that one should refrain from extracting vengeance is obvious.[57]

Hence, as Moo states:

> Acting kindly toward our enemies is a means of leading them to be ashamed of their conduct toward us and, perhaps, to repent and turn to the Lord whose love we embody.[58]

While being hospitable to shame an enemy is difficult for some moderns to understand, in an honor-shame culture like those of the ancient world and one in which hospitality was axiomatic,[59] it is perfectly understandable. Believers give witness to their enemies by being hospitable to them, blessing them, refusing to curse them or retaliate against, and nourishing them. As Osborne succinctly says, "Jesus' mission for the church demands that his followers practice hospitality as part of evangelism."[60]

We see the importance of being hospitable to Paul in that the virtue (*philoxenos*) is a criterion for overseers and elders (1 Tim 3:2; Titus 1:8). Similarly, a widow who wishes to receive financial support should herself "show hospitality" (*xenodocheō*, 1 Tim 5:10).

While this emphasis on hospitality is general and should characterize all believers, it cuts more deeply into the hearts and wallets of the rich—they are to share materially with those in the church who are in financial trouble. Doing so emulates Jesus (2 Cor 8:9), Zacchaeus, and the first Christians of Jerusalem.[61] The church runs on those who are rich, recognizing that they are blessed, and using their wealth for the glory of God, building God's church, and caring for those in need. Their fellowship is not to be with just their own kind but is to include the lowly (12:16, cf. Luke 14:12–14, 21).

All Christians are to respond to believers and unbelievers alike with the same love and hospitality. Authentic believers love their enemies (Matt 5:43; Luke 6:35), and love for all is emphasized in 13:8–10. Love enacted as hospitality would be necessary as:

Within Rome in particular the importance of offering hospitality to traders and travelers would be considerable."[62] Mounce adds, "In a day when inns were scarce and not always desirable, it was critical for believers to extend hospitality to Christians (and others) who were traveling."[63] Today, ample opportunities exist for Christians

---

57. Garrett, *Proverbs, Ecclesiastes, Song of Songs*, 208–9.
58. Moo, *Letter to the Romans*, 806.
59. "The obligation to provide hospitality to the stranger was deeply rooted and highly regarded in ancient society." Dunn, *Romans 9–16*, 743.
60. Osborne, *Romans Verse by Verse*, 397.
61. Luke 19:1–10; Acts 2:44–45; 4:32–37.
62. Dunn, *Romans 9–16*, 754.
63. Mounce, *Romans*, 238; Morris, *Epistle to the Romans*, 448.

to show hospitality to immigrants and refugees, and they should proactively pursue them.

Romans 14:1—15:13 deals with differences over cultural issues in the Roman Christian community. The passage endorses welcoming one another despite differences (14:1) as God and Christ have welcomed all believers (14:3; 15:7). Witherington and Hyatt observe:

> Since Christ is our exemplar and we are the church called to embody the living Word in this world, the mandate to practice hospitality toward and receive hospitality from *all* others cannot be ignored or rejected. Welcoming, that is, hospitality, "is a way of life fundamental to Christian identity."[64]

The latter verse sums up what Paul wants: "Therefore welcome one another as Christ has welcomed you, for the glory of God." In this section, eating is central. Eating together is the heart of Christian hospitality and fellowship. It was so for the ancients,[65] it is for many cultures today, and individualistic western cultures need to rediscover this. His injunctions ensure the maintenance of Christians eating together, something important elsewhere in Paul's letters.[66] Witherington and Hyatt suggest:

> Paul's concern with dietary issues and the underlying attitude of acceptance of difference that must prevail in the Christian community stems from the compelling need to maintain table fellowship in the neophyte Roman house-churches.[67]

---

64. Witherington and Hyatt, *Paul's Letter*, 346.

65. "In most ancient cultures hospitality was a prized virtue." Cottrell, *Romans: Volume 2*, 12:13: "Miscellaneous."

66. See 1 Cor 5:11; 8:1–13; 10:14–31; 11:20–34; Gal 2:11–14.

67. Witherington and Hyatt, *Paul's Letter*, 346. "This brings to light a fundamental principle of a truly Christian ethic—it is other-regarding. A Christian does not demand his or her own rights and privileges, especially when the issue is not a matter of ethical principle but rather just of personal preference . . . Since shared meals prefigure, reveal, and reflect the Kingdom, they provide 'the context for instruction on equal recognition and respect . . . to portray a clear message—that of equality, transformed relations, and a common life.' (Pohl, *Making Room*, 32). Eating was and still often remains a bounded activity and, so, when we intentionally include the other in such times, social, economic, and cultural boundaries are transcended through the relationship forged at the common table. Such is the subversive aspect of hospitality. . . . the mandate to practice hospitality toward and receive hospitality from all others cannot be ignored or rejected. Welcoming, that is, hospitality, 'is a way of life fundamental to Christian identity.' (Pohl, *Making Room*, x). Paul knew that a major portion of what we term 'sin' consists of obsession with 'otherness,' xenophobia (literally 'fear of strangers') . . . Yet, within the Christian hospitality tradition, only strangers depending on God are capable of truly welcoming other strangers . . . Christians are called to be 'strangers in the world,' (1 Pet 1:1–2; 2:17–19) aware of our own essential 'otherness' so that fear of strangers gives way to divinely enabled philoxenia ('love of strangers'). Therefore, distinctions of 'weak' and 'strong' disappear in the face of love-based hospitality. The locus of Christian citizenship is the household of God, and when we live out that identity the Lord is glorified. Indeed, the early church asserted that hospitality was 'one of the pillars of morality on which the universe rests' and considered it the primary witness of the gospel. May we who are God's guests enter into the risky but faithful proposition of loving one another through the power of the Holy Spirit, who truly is God with(in) us" (see the whole section on pp. 345–49).

PART THREE: ROMANS AND THE PROCLAMATION OF THE GOSPEL

The heart of worship is the preaching of the word and sacrament and especially the Lord's Supper. Paul is urging the believers of Rome to leave behind xenophobia, sexism, elitism, classism, ageism, generationalism, ethnocentricism, petty concerns, and the like as they meet as one family. Strangers are welcomed. The strong defer to the weak. The primary focal point of witness is the word and the table—eating together spiritually and physically.

Alongside the principles of living to one's faith understanding, non-judgmentalism, and mutual edification, Paul emphasizes the fundamental Christian ethical principle that the strong should care for the weak (15:1). In context, he applies this to the theologically strong, who understand that matters of eating and holy days are of little theological import. The weak think they do matter. In such a setting, the strong bear with the "failings" of the weak. They do nothing that will cause them to stumble, giving up their liberty for love's sake (14:15, see also 2 Cor 8). This principle also calls the wealthy to give of themselves for the poor.

EXAMPLES IN ROMANS 16

The patronage and hospitality of the prosperous punctuate Romans 16. The words of commendation (*synestēmi de hymin*)[68] for Phoebe itself is likely intended to make sure she is welcomed in Rome with appropriate Christian hospitality.[69] It also ensures the hosts that she is not there to defraud them,[70] especially as Paul knows full well the danger of this in Corinth earlier on the same trip. He may also want to make certain that he himself is trusted in Rome.[71]

Phoebe is described as a *prostatis*, a "patron of many" and Paul (16:1). The term *prostatis* is rare with this the only use in biblical Greek but indicates she is a generous benefactor (cf. Lucian, *Bis acc.* 29).[72] Fitzmyer suggests that, in addition, "*Prostatis* may be related to *proistamenos* . . . so she was perhaps a superior or at least a leader of the Christian community of Cenchreae."[73] She is clearly a wealthy woman, a leader of the church (deacon), and possibly a widow or divorcee. Her generosity and hospitality

---

68. "Paul uses *synistēmi de hymin*, the technical epistolary expression to introduce a friend to other acquaintances." Fitzmyer, *Romans*, 729.

69. Cottrell avers, "such letters could secure private hospitality." Cottrell, *Romans: Volume 2*, 16:1: "Commendation of Phoebe (16:1–2)."

70. "The Christians were noted for their hospitality, and letters of recommendation were necessary as a way of guarding against fraud." Morris, *Epistle to the Romans*, 528.

71. The verb *synestēmi* is used eight times in the same manner in 2 Corinthians (2 Cor 3:1; 4:2; 6:4, 12; 7:11; 10:12, 18; 12:11). At some point on the same mission journey, Paul's veracity was being questioned by false teachers in Corinth. He is well aware of how misunderstandings concerning money can occur.

72. "The unwillingness of commentators to give προστάτις its most natural and obvious sense of 'patron' is most striking. . . . That the word should be given full weight = 'patron, protector' (or alternatively, 'leader, ruler,' . . . is very probable, however." Dunn, *Romans 9–16*, 888.

73. Fitzmyer, *Romans*, 731.

had blessed Paul and many others.[74] Jewett and Kotansky believe she intended to fund Paul's mission to Spain.[75]

Prisca and Aquila have a church in their home, again showing their wealth and generosity.[76] They made their money from tentmaking (Acts 18:3). They also have a church in Ephesus and perhaps in Corinth, showing that they use their wealth to minister across the Roman world.[77] They had also "provided regular and extensive hospitality to Paul (Acts 18:2–3)."[78] They are examples of a married business couple who use their resources for international ministry.

The family units of Romans 16 suggest church groups, and the first person named may be the patron.[79] If so, church leaders may include Aristobulus (16:10) and Narcissus (16:11), and potentially any of the others named.

Rufus's mother, mentioned in 16:10, is described as having been a mother to Paul as well. The verse suggests that Rufus's family were well-heeled and that earlier, Paul had stayed with the family and experienced their patronage and hospitality.[80] As earlier mentioned, she may have been previously married to Simon of Cyrene, who bore Jesus's cross (Mark 15:21). His presence in Jerusalem, if he had traveled from Cyrene, could indicate he was wealthy at the time. Rufus's mother's assistance could have occurred in Jerusalem or in one of the areas Paul traveled if the family had been expelled by Claudius and had encountered Paul on his missionary journeys.[81] The Jason of verse 21 likely hosted Paul in Thessalonica (Acts 17:5–9).[82]

Patronage is evident in the greeting from Gaius in Romans 16:23 (1 Cor 1:14).[83] He is a *xenos* to Paul and the whole church. As noted earlier, the term *xenos* means "strange, a stranger, an alien," and here indicates "one who extends hospitality and

---

74. "Hospitality was likely a key element of her patronage." Walters, "'Phoebe' and 'Junia(s)'—Rom. 16:1–2, 7," 179.

75. Jewett and Kotansky, *Romans*, 89–91. Schreiner, *Romans*, 22 considers this as stretching the evidence, however, it cannot be ruled out. Jewett and Kotansky's statement that she is the only acknowledged patron (p. 22) is only true in a very specific sense, others like Gaius and Philemon were patrons for him.

76. On patronage and house churches, see Jewett and Kotansky, *Romans*, 63–69.

77. See Acts 18:2, 18, 26; 1 Cor 16:19; 2 Tim 4:19.

78. Dunn, *Romans 9–16*, 892. And perhaps Apollos (Acts 18:26).

79. However, Jewett and Kotansky argue they may be churches in apartments without a particular patron. Jewett and Kotansky, *Romans*, 966. His view that the first-named are not Christians is hardly likely (p. 967).

80. "Rufus's mother seems to have been a patroness." Witherington and Hyatt, *Paul's Letter*, 10. "To refer to Rufus's mother as "mine" indicates that she had provided hospitality and patronage in such a manner that Paul at some point in his career became virtually a member of their family." Jewett and Kotansky, *Romans*, 969.

81. Jewett and Kotansky, *Romans*, 969.

82. Moo, *Letter to the Romans*, 950.

83. Speculation that he is Titius Justus from Acts 18:7 on the basis that triple name is common lacks any evidence at all and should be treated as fanciful at best (e.g., Jewett and Kotansky, *Romans*, 980). He is not to be mistaken for the Macedonian Gaius (Acts 19:29; 20:4) or the Gaius of 3 John 1.

thus treats the stranger as a guest."[84] His home is sufficient to host Paul and the whole church,[85] suggesting a man of some means, as no doubt was Erastus, the city treasurer. If, as is likely, Erastus is the same as the man who donated the inscription in Corinth, he is likely a generous benefactor of the church and mission (part one, chapter 4). The mention of the likes of these two, Tertius (Paul's scribe),[86] and Quartus, means they are known in Rome and are also educated and potentially wealthy figures. Although we know little of them, they likely were also hospitable patrons. Tertius's work as a scribe, writing neatly and without error, was crucial to Paul's mission. He highlights the importance of administration for missional purposes. No doubt, the women of their households were active participants in the provision of the church.

CONCLUSION

Romans is a great case study in missional patronage and hospitality. It gives ample evidence of how the wealthy among the early Christians gave generously to the work of God. Doing this is vital if the church is to be healthy and if the gospel is to extend into the world.[87] Funding the church and mission is an enormous challenge for church and mission leaders. Notably, in the NT, there is no enforcement of tithing or compulsory giving. Instead, the glorious gospel is preached, and people are gripped by God's mission and the need. We need a new wave of Christian preachers who preach the message summoning the rich to the example of Christ and the challenge of funding mission to the nations. They must also be utterly transparent where money is concerned, people of utter financial integrity, and certainly not "peddlers of the gospel." Then, the wallets of wealthy Christians will be opened as their hearts are filled with a desire to give to God's mission. God's church and mission can then flourish as it should.

---

84. BDAG 684.

85. Dunn refutes that this means other traveling Christians (e.g., Schreiner, *Romans*, 808) and rightly defends this being "the whole Corinthian church." Dunn, *Romans 9–16*, 910–11. See also Jewett and Kotansky, *Romans*, 980.

86. Jewett and Kotansky, *Romans*, 979 thinks Tertius was Phoebe's scribe. Well, perhaps, but equally, he could have been a scribe of Erastus, Gaius, or Quartus. Whoever he was, he functioned as Paul's scribe for Romans.

87. "The early mission would likewise depend on such hospitality (e.g., Mark 6:8–11 pars.; Acts 16:15; 18:3; see also 16:1–2, 13, 23)." Dunn, *Romans 9–16*, 744.

22

The Sovereignty of God, Human Volition, and Mission

IN THIS CHAPTER, the vexed relationship between God's sovereignty and human volition will be discussed and applied to mission. As is known, Christian thinkers are rather polarized on this issue, with some seeing God's sovereignty as dominant and arguing for a harsh determinism (hyper-Calvinism). Others accept determinism but see a balance of human responsibility running through the text (soft Calvinism). Some see sovereignty as related to the foreknowledge of human choices (Arminianism). Yet others reduce the sovereignty of God for an open free universe in which God is aware of possibilities, but history is genuinely open dependent on human choice (Open Theism).

The relationship should be considered cautiously as the tension cannot be fully resolved.[1] Nevertheless, it must be considered as it has important implications for today's missional enterprise.

GOD IS COMPLETELY SOVEREIGN

One of the messages of Romans that is unequivocal is that God is sovereign over everything, including his mission.[2]

---

1. "The subject of predestination is confessedly very deep and mysterious: nor should it be entered upon without extreme caution, both as to the mode of stating it, and to the persons before whom it is stated." Simeon, *Horae Homileticae: Romans*, 313.

2. Schreiner rightly says of Romans 9:10–11: "Nor is it convincing to say that predestination cannot be read into the text." Also, Schreiner: "This text forges a close connection between the themes of justification and predestination, implying that they are inseparable." Schreiner, *Romans*, 499.

PART THREE: ROMANS AND THE PROCLAMATION OF THE GOSPEL

Creation and History

God created the cosmos (1:19–25). He subjugated humankind and creation to decay and death because of sin (3:23; 5:12; 8:19–23). God's action is logical because once humans sinned, they were corrupted, as is his world. Hence, they cannot be permitted to inherit eternal life for nothing corrupt can exist eternally in the realm of God and defile it. God is holy, and only that which is utterly holy can dwell permanently with him. Consequently, he consigned the cosmos to death as a consequence of sin, and because of his divine character and justice (8:20). In Romans 8:28–30, God is in control of history seen in the glorious salvation he has brought, which he predetermined.

Israel

God is sovereign over the history of Israel. He chose Abraham, not because of anything Abraham had done, but by grace (4:3; 9:8). Of his two sons, God preferred Isaac rather than Ishmael through whom to continue the line. Similarly, he selected the younger twin Jacob ahead of the older Esau (9:10–13). Not only did he elect Israel and guide the Patriarchs of Genesis, but he blessed adopted Israel with the oracles of God (3:2), the covenants, the law, and his Shekinah glory (9:4–5).

In Romans 9, we have a passage that is strongly deterministic in regards to Israel's story and salvation. Paul's overall argument is that God's word to Israel has not failed Israel and her hopes in this gospel for the salvation of all aside from law (9:6). He then demonstrates through the following verses that God's plan for human history worked out in Israel always involved election, namely, through the "children of the promise" (9:8). The line of promise in salvation history involved the choice of Isaac (not Ishmael)[3] and then Jacob and not Esau, the older son. The reason is given: God's purposes (9:11). His plans involved his sovereign choice of Jacob over Esau (9:11–13). Paul then defends the justice of God that could arguably be seen to be arbitrary (9:14). Consequently, and rightly, he defends God's freedom and the right to elect as he chooses (9:15–16). He gives Pharaoh as an example (9:18).

The point is that God is working history toward its end. For good to triumph, God chooses and intervenes based on what he deems best to achieve his ends (something we can sometimes see looking back, often, we cannot). Paul then goes on in Romans 9:19–23 to further defend God's right to do so, using the prophetic metaphor of the potter and the clay. He is the Creator! It is his world! He can do as he likes to work out his purposes and bring the world to its climax!

To hammer home his point, he uses a rhetorical question asking what if God prepared some for destruction and others for mercy. The point here is God's cosmic plan that requires such choices, and as Creator, these are his to make. He defends this from Hosea 2:23, which he sees as a prophetic prediction of God's choice to call the

---

3. Compare Gal 4:21–31.

gentiles and many Jews being lost (9:26). God has allowed Israel, in large part, to be lost in its view of righteousness by law and demand that gentiles come under the law so that they may be saved.

Jesus

Most awesomely, as the zenith of his covenantal faithfulness, God chose at just the right time to send his Son into the world, foreordained to die for the sins of humankind to liberate them from their sins (5:6; 9:5; Gal 4:4). He was born a descendant of David, but most wonderfully, he is the Son of God (1:3–4). Jesus came as God foretold in the Scriptures, filled with God's power and presence. He ministered as a servant to the Jewish people and took on himself the reproaches of humankind (15:3, 8). Born of vulnerable human flesh, he lived under the law and fulfilled it (8:4; 10:4). Yet, he was crucified. As he was not a man of sin, God raised him from the dead by the power of the Spirit and God's glory (1:3). God then seated him at his right hand as Lord (8:32). He now reigns, governing God's world on his behalf.

Spirit

The Christ, God sent the Spirit of God and Christ to dwell in those who respond by faith to the declaration of the gospel of God (5:5; 8:9). Those Jesus had called to him were empowered with this Spirit and went into the world preaching the gospel. Jesus apprehended Paul on the Damascus Road, and he joined the mission of God and became its apostle to the nations.[4]

Mission

From the day of the Edenic rupture, God has been a missional God. Now that Christ has come, and the Spirit is poured out, God guides Paul and other preachers. He filled Paul with the power to preach, to perform signs and wonders, and to gather money for the poor (15:19–33). Those who respond to God's message with faith were foreknown and predestined to do so (8:29–30),[5] and so are the called, the elect.[6] They are the elect not because they were called and *then* believed, but because they believed in God's summons.

---

4. See 1:5; 11:13; Gal 1:14–15; 2:7–9.

5. Some since Origen have argued that "God foreknew the behavior of persons, and elected them to salvation or damnation accordingly" (Toews, *Romans*, 255). He maintains this hardened into predestination in Augustine. However, as I will explain in this chapter, one does not need to soften foreknowledge and predestination but hold "free will" and predestination together in dialectical tension.

6. See 1:1, 6–7; 8:28–30, 33; 9:11, 24–26; 11:5, 7; 16:13.

Part Three: Romans and the Proclamation of the Gospel

God is guiding his mission. Ironically, the gospel exploded out of Judea because of Saul's persecution—even before he was a Christian, God used him to extend his message (Acts 8:1–4).[7] Previously I wrote:

> In a great irony, before his conversion, while he was an enemy of the gospel, God used Saul/Paul to spread the gospel by scattering the church. However, by God's sovereignty, while a horrific experience for all concerned, this scattering turned out to be positive for the mission.[8]

By the time of Romans, God's message had penetrated from Jerusalem west to the western Balkans (15:19). A church existed in Rome (1:7) that God had established through unnamed Pentecost pilgrims (Acts 2:10). Through the agency of unnamed Christians, no doubt empowered by the Spirit, the faith had reached east across the Jordan and into North Africa. Paul seeks prayer support from the Romans, knowing that prayer is critical to align mission with God's purposes (15:30–32). Paul hopes this includes his coming to Rome and then to Spain to continue the march of the gospel (1:9–13; 15:23–24).

We know from Acts and Paul's other letters that God answered the prayers of Paul and the Romans affirmatively, albeit in a circuitous route.[9] Paul went to Jerusalem and, despite death threats and imprisonments, made it to Rome (Acts 27—28). In the late first century, Clement believed he had made it to Spain, although we cannot be sure (1 Clem. Prol).

Salvation

The purpose of mission is that people are saved, and God is sovereign in salvation. Through Romans, Paul uses the language of call (*kaleō*), indicating the initiative of God. He uses it of his own call to apostleship (1:1) and of all believers' call to belong to Christ (literally: "called of Christ") and to be saints or holy ones (1:7, see also 9:24). The apostle links call with God's providence in Romans 8:28 with believers "called *according to his purpose*" (emphasis mine) and all things moving toward good for believers. Such a statement speaks of the totality of a believer's existence being shaped by God toward a good outcome, as he determines.[10] Believers are called by

---

7. One of the tremendous missional ironies is that the pre-Christian Saul unwillingly caused the expansion of the church from Jerusalem through "nobodies" into Samaria, Africa, and Syrian Antioch (Acts 8:5–40; 11:19–26). From there, the Spirit thrust Paul and Barnabas into their great western missions (Acts 13:1–4). Saul or Paul of Tarsus was inadvertently the apostle to the gentiles, before he was appointed by Christ as apostle. This is a demonstration of God's sovereignty in mission.

8. Keown, *Discovering*, 1:390.

9. Acts 23:11; 27—28; 2 Tim 1:17. Also, tradition holds he wrote seven letters from the city.

10. "Good" here indicates God's overall purposes at a cosmic level rather than at an individual level, i.e., God may allow suffering for a particular person in a particular situation, but this will be part of his overall purpose of working all things toward his intended *telos*.

God, indicating God's initiative and sovereignty. God's call is demonstrated as people respond by faith to the message. Those who do respond with faith and calling on God are the "God-called ones." Put another way, when people call on him (10:13–14), this is because they are the called ones.

Foreknown and Predestined

In Romans 8:29–30, Paul links foreknowledge, predestination, call, justification, and glorification. The verse follows the declaration of Romans 8:28 that speaks of all things working together for good for those who love God and are called according to his purpose (*prothesis*). The two verses are introduced with the conjunction *hoti*, and so is causal (for, because) giving the rationale for the previous statement of confidence. That is, verses 29 and 30 state *why* all things work for God. Namely, that God is in control of history, knows people, and calls them to ultimate glorification.

Paul here seems to assume a "foreknowing" (*proginōskō*, cf. 11:2) by God, which in the Jewish sense, is more than mere knowledge, but a relational knowing. Even so, it implies that ahead of the present time, God, in his omniscience, knows people, their hearts, choices, responses, and futures.[11] These same foreknown ones are predestined—predetermined (*proorizō*) to be transformed into the likeness of his Son i.e., to be true image bearers as Jesus is the image of God (cf. Adam typology). They are conformed to the pattern of Jesus as he lived in relentless service, sacrifice, humility, suffering, and love while people live "in Christ." The purpose (*eis* + inf.) is that Jesus might be the firstborn among many brothers and sisters. That is, Jesus is the beginning of a new humanity and new creation (cf. Romans 5 and Adam Christology above).

In Romans 8:30, those God predestined, he also called (summoned them into relationship and they accepted). Those he called, he also justified (declared righteous). Those God justified, he also glorified (gave the status of children of God; brothers and sisters of Jesus). Paul gives more grounds for confidence in Romans 8:31–39: God will have the victory, and *nothing*, no matter how heinous, can separate believers from the love of God in his Son.

The overall sense of the passage is clear. However, the problem for modern interpreters is that elucidation of the fine details is usually driven by theology and ripping texts out of context. The passage can be made to serve Arminianism if the emphasis is placed on foreknowledge and not predestination. Similarly, if one deemphasizes or redefines foreknowledge in relational terms only, and stresses predestination, it can serve hyper-Calvinism. Moreover, one can argue for a corporate non-specific

---

11. In my view, this rules out open theism as a legitimate theological option. See Ware, *God's Lesser Glory*. Schreiner asserts: "Therefore, we can be quite sure that a doctrine such as open theism is unbiblical. No branch of the Christian church—whether Catholic, Orthodox, or Protestant—has ever endorsed such a theology. It is not enshrined in any confessional statements, nor has any significant theologian ever espoused such a teaching. The universal teaching of the church throughout history is a reliable guide that should not be jettisoned." Schreiner, *Galatians*, 79.

predestination rather than a harsh individual determination, i.e., the predestination is general and corporate and does not remove individual human freedom. Likewise, Paul does not explicitly speak of predestination to salvation here, but to image bearing in Christ. As such, one can potentially avoid the difficulties of Paul's determinism by emphasizing this.

All such musings to me are futile as Paul is not answering such later questions we want to impose on the passage. He is comfortable to hold the view that all is foreknown, and all is predestined (even to an absolute degree).[12] Believers should be deeply comforted because God is in complete control of history, and *everything* is under his sovereign guidance. They can be hopeful and confident despite terrible suffering and struggle.

All this fits in with Paul's theology of a God in complete control and the world working out as he wills. Such a perspective leads some to postulate a hyper-Calvinist theology that makes a human decision and will merely something God coerces within humankind. This being so is supposedly justified because God is God and free to do as he wills. Who are we to question him as our creator (9:19–24)? However, this emphasis on God's sovereignty is only half the story in Romans and Paul.

HUMANS HAVE VOLITION AND ARE CULPABLE

If what has been discussed in the previous section is all there is to say about Romans in terms of the question of sovereignty and freedom, one could defend hyper-Calvinism from these verses. However, reading all of Romans shows that while Paul defends the sovereignty and initiative of God, he also asserts human volition and responsibility. Indeed, as much as Paul holds to the absolute sovereignty of God, he has a rich theology of human volition and will that sits within Paul's belief in a predestined world. Such a balance in his theology from a Pharisee should not surprise us, as Josephus records that the group balanced fate and human volition (Josephus, *Ant.* 13:172).

Paul's Volition

Up until the first explicit mention of predestination in Romans 8:29, Paul has referred to people acting of their own volition many times and in many ways. His own mission is to bring about the *obedience* of faith, suggesting his conscious and willing yielding to God's call on his life (1:5; 16:26). He serves God with all his heart in this mission (1:9). Under a sense of divine obligation to do so, he seeks to win a harvest of converts throughout the world and longs to come to Rome to do the same (1:14–15, cf. 1 Cor

---

12. See the quote from Josephus concerning Pharisees; they neatly balance God's sovereignty (fate) and human free will – as such, Paul continues to do this. However, priority is always given to God's action – he is the initiator from creation to redemption.

9:16).[13] He prays willingly and continually, yearning to come to Rome, despite being hindered to the point of writing (1:8–10, 13; 15:32). He knows prayer changes things, even in a predetermined world. The change that happens is etched into the story, already written.

All Are Accountable

In Romans 1:18—3:20, God is not capricious or prejudiced in his condemnation of all humankind for their sin and his wrath. All are culpable, for all have sinned. They have willingly and actively participated in idolatry, rejecting their creator (1:19–25) and participated in sexual immorality (1:26–27). They are the active participants in a range of other vices (1:28–32). It is *their* hypocrisy that is condemned for the day of wrath (2:1–11). They are the ones who sin under the law or apart from it and bear those consequences (2:12–16).

Despite having the law and their election, Jews are equally blameworthy, failing to live up to their teaching, stealing, and committing adultery, rendering their circumcisions obsolete as a means of righteousness (2:17–29). While they have the oracles of God, this only makes them more responsible and illuminates their unfaithfulness before their faithful God (3:1–4). All are under sin, participating in its decadence by their own volition (3:10–20, 23).

Faith

In Romans 3:21–31, faith in God's Son justifies. Before Paul mentions predestination, *pistis* and *pisteuō* are used forty times in Romans 1:1—8:28.[14] Faith is not defined, but Paul never states that God utterly coerces this trust, faith, or belief. Indeed, writing to a church that has never met Paul and knows only aspects of his theology, he at no point in Romans states that *saving* faith is a gift from God[15] that negates human volition.[16] What is clear is that, for Paul, while a person's choices are bound up in their

---

13. "The apostolic office means for him a commissioning for service from which he cannot by any means withdraw. It is nothing less than an *anankē* that lies on him and drives him to preach the gospel." Hahn, *Mission in the New Testament*, 99 (Greek transliterated).

14. *Pisteuō*, "believe," ten times (aside from 3:2, all concerning human faith response); *pistis*, "faith" twenty-seven times (aside from 3:3, all concerning human faith response); *apistia*, "unbelief" twice; *apisteō*, "to disbelieve" once.

15. The closest we get is Rom 12:6, where Paul states that believers have gifts that differ according to the grace given to them, and they should use them. If they have prophecy, they should use it *according to their faith*. This verse does not state initial conversion faith is a gift, but that prophecy is exercised according to the level of one's faith (the source of the faith unstated).

16. We cannot assume say that the Romans have read Eph 2:8–9, which was written from Rome some three to four years later. Ephesians 2:8–9 is used by some as a proof-text to show that faith is a gift from God, and so while it is the human of response to God, it is enabled. The verse serves the agenda of hyper-Calvinism. However, this argument is to be rejected as "faith" (*pisteōs*) is feminine

predestined salvation and God's call, they willingly act.[17] They are joined to God by *their* faith (3:28; 5:1), generated in them as the power of salvation is preached to them, they hear and believe, confess Christ's lordship, and are saved (1:16; 10:9–10, 14–17). Indeed, this has always been the case as Abraham believed God and demonstrated that belief by not wavering in his confidence in God and his promise of an heir despite him and Sarah's respective ages and the unlikelihood that they could produce a child. Instead, he grew strong due to his conviction concerning God's promises (4:1–22). Faith is not a momentary decision, but a life of choices to trust God.

Obedience

Paul holds Adam utterly culpable for his sin as he does all humankind because all have sinned (5:12–14). The right response to being justified by faith and reconciled to God by grace is active obedience, something people do by their own volition (even if in cooperation with the Spirit, 6:1–23). It is believers who are not to let sin reign in their lives by obeying their passions (6:12). They are to present themselves to God as instruments of righteousness (6:13, 19) and are to be obedient slaves to God's righteousness (6:16).

Believers do this by the power of the Spirit (7:6). Yet, it is they who must put one step after the other, walking according to the Spirit (8:4). Believers are to follow the leading of the Spirit actively (8:14). Walking is not static and passive concept but involves movement in response to God. God guides, the believer yields and obeys. They are to resist sin, putting it to death by resisting it, strengthened by the Spirit (8:13). All of this has been said before Paul declares that believers are foreknown and predestined in Romans 8:29.

Hope

As noted in the first part of this chapter, Romans 8 emphasizes the sovereignty of God. All things are shaped by God for his peoples' good. Believers are foreknown and predestined. On their own, these verses can lead us to a hyper-Calvinistic point of

---

and "gift" (*dōron*) is neuter. The gift is more likely the grace or salvation. Faith may form a portion of "this;" however, one does not need to remove human volition from the salvation transaction. This translation brings out the real meaning: "For it is by grace you have been saved through faith; and salvation by grace [this] is the gift of God; not from works, lest anyone boast . . . ."

17. "It is biblical to say that God predestines certain individuals to salvation's end-result, heaven; but it is contrary to Scripture to say that these individuals will meet the conditions for going to heaven only because God has predestined them to do so. God predestines the end, but not the means. He predestines all believers to heaven, but he does not predestine anyone to become a believer. Salvation is conditional (see 1:16), and individuals must meet these conditions by their own free-will choice. Therefore predestination itself is conditional; God predestined to heaven those whom he foreknew would meet the required conditions." Cottrell, *Romans: Volume* 1, "God Promises to Bring His Family Through Earthly Trials."

view. Yet, these verses emphasizing sovereignty are nestled in a passage that is written to comfort the suffering Romans with hope. Romans 8:17–23 speaks of the reality of suffering in the present, despite the victory of Christ.[18] Romans 8:24–25 focuses on hope. Romans 8:26–27 expresses the work of the Spirit to give hope and strength in present suffering.

Further reasons to hope are given in Romans 8:28–30: God is in control of history seen in the glorious salvation he has brought, which he predetermined. Believers are foreknown and predestined to be God's children and will be glorified. Paul gives more grounds for confidence in Romans 8:31–39: God will have the victory, and *nothing*, no matter how heinous, can separate believers from the love of God in his Son.

The point through this passage, then, is that believers should be deeply comforted because God is in complete control of history, and everything is under his sovereign guidance. Therefore, they can be hopeful and confident despite terrible suffering and struggle. Paul's purpose is not to launch debate about the mechanics of fate and freedom, but to give hope in suffering, which is inevitable for humans and especially Christians in hostile situations. He pushes hard in the direction of sovereignty to assert that even if his people can barely get through a day, "God's got this." As such, while we should explore the relationship of sovereignty and freedom, we should be wary of the fine details. The truth is, as we explore the texts, we usually find support for our biases.

Predestination Balanced by Volition

Predestination themes feature powerfully in Romans 9:1–29 and it could be said that if this was all Paul said concerning sovereignty and volition, one could arguably defend hyper-Calvinism from these verses. However, these verses are immediately followed by Paul affirming Israel's culpability. In Romans 9:30–33, Paul balances God's election and sovereignty explaining their rejection. *They* rejected Christ and the response of faith, preferring righteousness by works and law (cf. Isa 8:14; 28:16). They stumbled over Christ, and they *did not believe*. It does not say that God made them not believe. They chose to reject Christ. Their plight cannot stop Paul praying that they turn and be saved (9:1–2; 10:1). He knows that while all things are predestined, prayer changes things.

Calling on God

Again, in Romans 10:9–13, the human response of faith and verbal acknowledgment brings salvation. When a person believes and professes Christ is Lord, they do so themselves. They call on God for salvation. As discussed in more detail in part three,

---

18. For my fuller exposition of Romans 8 and suffering: Keown, "Notes of Hope in the Face of Suffering."

chapter 15, those who do respond with faith and calling on God are the "God-called ones." Thus, relationship with God involves the mutuality of the initial summons of God inviting people into a relationship with him, and their subsequent response of believing in him and calling out to him. Those that do are the called and elect. They may call on him because they are called by him, but they still willingly do so. Thus, in salvation, we have the interplay of divine sovereignty and human response, always with God's initiative. Salvation and being called involves both the prior election of God as well as the subsequent human reaching for God.

Israel's Rejection

Mention has been made of Romans 9:30–33 where Israel did not believe in Jesus and rejected him. Again, in Romans 10:14–21, Paul states that they had every chance to hear the message and *did not accept it*. Israel in rejection of Christ remains disobedient and contrary, refusing to yield (10:14–21). Their rejection is their own choice (even though it is within God's predetermined will), and as such, they can be held guilty for not accepting the message. Still, God has not rejected his people; hardened Israel have rejected him! (chapter 11). While it is a remnant chosen by grace (11:6), God's choice includes their volitional response. Much of Israel is under a spirit of stupor (11:8), but Israel is still responsible for succumbing to this and for unbelief. The consequence is that they are excluded from the olive tree of God's faithful people: "they were broken off *because* of their unbelief" (11:20, emphasis mine). They can be ingrafted to God's people if they believe in his Son (11:23). At the same time, the gentiles must beware of their own arrogance, because they too can be broken off through unbelief (11:18, 21).

In each of these previous cases, Paul does not state that Israel's failure was caused directly by God; they rejected his initiative and election purposes and so caused it by rejecting the message of Christ. It was a result of the exercise of human volition. So, in Romans 9–11, while it is true that at times, Paul uses intense election and predestination language that appears hyper-Calvinistic, we also have the human response of unbelief and the rejection of Christ. A person believes because he/she is elect, predestined to believe. Simultaneously, a person believes because they made a choice to accept the gospel and the offer of God's salvation in Christ. The two are equally valid. When a person believes by their own volition, they find that they are elect, pre-chosen.

Christian Living

Romans 12:1—15:7 is full of injunctions to obedience. In this section, there are at least fifty-eight appeals for human volitional response: twenty-nine imperatives,[19] five

---

19. Imperatives include *syschēmatizesthe* (do not be conformed) and *metamorphousthe* (be transformed, 12:2); *eulogeite* (bless, 2x) and *katarasthe* (do not *curse*, 12:14); *mē ginesthe* (do not *be wise*, 12:16); *dote* (give space for wrath, 12:19); *psōmize* (*feed* him) and *potize* (*give a drink* to him, 12:20);

hortatory subjunctives,[20] seventeen imperatival participles in the section,[21] and seven imperatival infinitives.[22] Every appeal summons them to a *willing* and determined response to God's mercies (12:1). They will all be judged by God and give account for their actions (14:10–14).

Worship and Mission

Romans 15:8–13 envisages the outcome of the gentile mission: the nations singing, praising, and rejoicing over God because of the Davidic Messiah. Expressing praise to God is an act of the will and body.

Romans finishes as it began, with Paul speaking of his determined missional work, of which it boasts (15:17). In this mission of traveling 25,000 km (15,000 mi) over land and sea,[23] by Christ's power through the Spirit, he spoke, performed miracles, and evangelized vast swathes of the ancient world (15:14–19). Paul next wishes to continue to travel to Jerusalem, to Rome, and to Spain, all volitionally, as he yearns to feed Judea's poor, preach in the capital, and build churches where Christ is not yet known (15:20–29). Again, we see his belief that prayer achieves things as he invites the Romans not only to support him in his mission (15:24) but to pray for him (15:30–32).

Romans 16 is full of people who have willingly and volitionally supported other Christians financially (16:2, 5, 13, 23), traveled across land and sea (16:1, 5, 13), been

---

nikō (do not *be overcome* by evil) and *nika* (*overcome* evil with good, 12:21); *hypotassesthō* (*be subject to* the governing authorities, 13:1); *poiei* (*do* good, 13:3); *phobou* (be afraid, 13.4); *apodote* (pay, 13:7); *opheilete* (*owe* no one anything, 13:8); *endysasthe* (*put on* the Lord Jesus Christ) and *poieisthe* (*make* no provision, 13:14); *prolambanesthe* (*welcome* the one whose faith is weak, 14:1); *exoutheneitō* (*let* no one *despise* the one who abstains) and *krinetō* (*let* not the one who abstains *pass judgment*, 14:3); *plērophoreisthē* (be fully convinced, 14:5); *krinate* (*decide* never to put a stumbling block, 14:13); *apollue* (*do not destroy* the one for whom Christ died, 14:15); *blasphēmeisthō* (do not *let* what you regard as good *be spoken of as evil*, 14:16); *katalue* (do not *destroy* the work of God, 14:20); *eche* (*keep* between yourself and God, 14:22); *aresketō* (let each of us *please* his [or her] neighbor, 15:2); *proslambanesthe* (*welcome* one another, 15:7).

20. Hortatory inclusive subjunctives include *apothōmetha* (*let us cast off* the works of darkness) and *endysōmetha* (*[let us] put on* the armor of light, 13:12); *peripatēsōmen* (*let us walk* properly, 13:13); *krinōmen* (let us not *pass judgment*, 14:13); *diōkōmen* (*let us pursue* what makes for peace and for mutual upbuilding).

21. Imperatival participles include *apostygountes* (*abhor* what is evil); *kollōmenoi* (*hold fast* to what is good, 12:9); *proēgoumenoi* (*outdo* one another in showing honor, 12:10); *zeontes* (*burn* in the Spirit) and *douleuontes* (*serve* the Lord, 12:11); *chairontes* (rejoice), *hypomenontes* (be patient), and *prokarterountes* (be constant, 12:12); *koinōnountes* (contribute) and *diōkontes* (seek, 12:13); *phronountes* (live in harmony), *phronountes* (do not be haughty), and *synapagomenoi* (associate with, 12:16); *apodidontes* (repay) and *pronooumenoi* (give thought to do, 12:17); *eirēneuontes* (live peaceably, 12:18); *ekdikountes* (never avenge yourselves, 12:19).

22. Imperatival infinitives include *hyperphronein* (do not *think of yourselves more highly*); *phronein* (*think* with sober judgment, 12:3); *chairein* (rejoice) and *klaiein* (weep, 12:15); *hypotassesthai* (be in subjection, 13:5); *tithenai* (never *to put* a stumbling block, 14:13); *bastazein* (*bear with* the failings, 15:1).

23. Schnabel, *Paul the Missionary*, "Paul's Travels: Statistics."

Part Three: Romans and the Proclamation of the Gospel

imprisoned (16:3), risked their lives (16:4), used their homes for church gatherings (16:5, 23), worked hard (16:6, 9, 11, 21), and who wrote letters (16:22). Indeed, the whole Roman church is commended for their obedience (16:19). Others who fail to obey are also held accountable and are to be watched closely (16:17–18).

LIVING IN THE DIALECTICAL TENSION

For Paul, while God is sovereign and all is predetermined to an absolute degree, within the framework of God's sovereign purposes, humans are volitional creatures who are accountable for their choices and actions.

Romans presents us with a dialectical tension between two theological premises.

1. All things are foreknown and predestined; the saved are the called and elect.
2. Within human history is human volition to decide for or against God.

God is sovereign. Yet, somehow, God's sovereignty includes personal choice which falls within the framework of his complete sovereignty. The detail is intriguing and important to consider, but it remains academic. Salvation is by election, but such an election does not preclude human volition for which people are accountable.[24]

So, can we explain this tension between God's will and human sovereignty? The answer is found in the attributes of the divine versus the human and the perspective from which one considers the story of the world.[25] Paul's God in Romans is clearly omniscient over human time—he knows it all. From the perspective of God in heaven, all was foreknown before creation, for time is a construct within his mind. Standing in the heavens, the world is like a Netflix series that God wrote and as its author and director, knows every part, for he "penned it," willed it, directed it, and observes it playing out while knowing the conclusions. He sees it in its complete sense. Hence, every decision made fits in with the story he wrote and willed.

---

24. I sometimes quip that my view is a "Calviminian" view. Overall, I affirm the Reformed view that the world is foreknown and predestined. However, living in the world, humans are volitional creatures who make decisions and choices. It feels like a world where the Arminian perspective is right. We walk in the tension of the two.

25. See Witherington and Hyatt, *Paul's Letter*, 246–49 where he discusses predestination, election, salvation, and apostasy in early Judaism. He notes that the texts that stress God's sovereignty also stress viable human choice in moral matters (e.g., Pss. Sol. 9:4; 4 Esdr. 8:55–56). He cites Rabbi Akiba: "Everything is foreseen (by God), and freedom of choice is given (to man), and the world is judged with goodness, and all depends on the preponderance of (good or ill) doing" (m. 'Abot 3.15). "While the Pharisees hold that all things are brought about by destiny, they do not deprive the human will of its own impulse to do them, it having pleased God that there should be a cooperation and that to the deliberation (of God) about destiny, humans in the case of the one who wills should assent, with virtue or wickedness." See also Josephus, *Ant.* 18.1–3. Witherington and Hyatt add: "It is not an either/or matter for Paul when it comes to viable human moral choices and God's sovereignty, but rather both/and" (p. 248).

The Sovereignty of God, Human Volition, and Mission

Yet, within the story are creatures gifted with many of his attributes, including volition.[26] We live in history, and while we can imagine standing in God's space (as I imagined myself doing in the first part of this chapter), we are limited to what people experience in every moment.[27] We are locked in space and time. We make decisions and are willful creatures. Still, our will is not completely free, for that is a myth; there are always pressures on us in any situation due to their limitations and context. Yet, we can decide, for God has willed this. When we decide, we do so by our volition within the framework of his supreme will. So, as willing creatures who can choose or not, we are active agents, and fully culpable. Yet, God knows every decision, and he also willed it. So, as Dunn says, "Divine sovereignty and human responsibility are correlative rather than antithetical."[28] Many years earlier, Spence-Jones wrote:

> Divine omnipotence combined with omniscience on the one hand, and human free-will on the other, seem indeed to human reason to be incompatible ideas; yet we are compelled to entertain both.[29]

Similarly, Osborne astutely avers,

> The debate over predestination must find a balance between these two perspectives. The key is that while God's sovereignty has priority, the two are interdependent, and I believe that God has "decreed" human choice from the beginning.[30]

The other thing that is clear about Paul's God is that he exists within time and exerts himself more palpably when he so desires, intervening as he wills, where and when he desires to. God's movement in history is seen in the life of Adam, the Patriarchs and their wives, Israel, Moses, David, the nations, and in Christ for his earthly life. He does so by his Spirit in the world and in the lives of his people. He is sovereign over the rulers across the world, ruling over every government and governing through them. They are his servants, even if they do not know this. He will bring them down as he wills, and he will raise them up. God does this all as he moves creation to its *telos*: a people of God, dwelling with God in a world freed of sin, decay, death, and every vestige of wickedness.

---

26. "We must not allow ourselves to be sidetracked by modern notions of what is or is not possible for God." Morris, *Epistle to the Romans*, 332.

27. Spence-Jones, *Epistle*, 215: "The apparent contradiction between them may be due to the failure of finite beings to comprehend infinity."

28. Dunn, *Romans 9–16*, 542.

29. Spence-Jones, *Romans*, 215. He goes on: "They have been compared to two parallel straight lines, which, according to geometrical definition, can never meet, and yet, according to the higher mathematical theory, meet in infinity; or we may take the illustration of an asymptote, which from a finite point of view can never possibly touch a curve, and yet, in analytical geometry, is found to cross it at an infinite distance." I prefer to see them as totally interwoven rather than parallel with human volition intertwined into God's predestination. There is a dialectical tension we can never explain.

30. Osborne, *Romans: Verse by Verse*, 328–29.

So, we live with three certainties. God is sovereign and entirely so. We should not water down or qualify foreknowledge, predestination, and election. They are absolute. Second, humans are volitional, responsible, and culpable beings, something we must recognize, even within a predetermined world. Humans are made in the image of God with a will and make decisions for which they are fully responsible. Third, God is present in history, seemingly moving in and out, guiding, calling, condemning, and raising up and bringing down, for he has a plan.

CONCLUDING IMPLICATIONS FOR MISSION

These three ideas go hand in hand, and while believers cannot make such a world themselves or understand a God who can be outside of time seeing it in full and engaging in time dynamically, that is okay. That is why God is God, and people are not; as Isaiah's God says, "For my thoughts are not your thoughts, your ways are not our ways and our ways are not yours" (Isa 55:8). Our right response is worship and then action on his behalf.

God's sovereignty is immensely comforting, giving his people confidence that he is in control.[31] Further, his sovereignty in mission tells Christians that whatever the mess of the world and the church, whatever the state of the mission, God is active in the situation and will bring his purposes to completion. His will cannot be thwarted. So, even though Paul, the great apostle to the gentiles, is in prison facing death, he can rejoice because the gospel is continuing to advance (Phil 1:12). He can say things like, "the word of God is not bound!" (2 Tim 2:9).

Still, as people are volitional, the summons of his people is to passionately commit to his mission each day. They should willingly participate so that people can hear the gospel, believe it, and be saved (10:6–17). All the time, believers know that God can do it without them. Indeed, he will do it without us, as no matter how important we are, the grave awaits, and the mission will go on (as in the case of Paul).

But as his people, we are to be joyful because he willed that we are who we are and where we are now. Believers know how great God is and how wonderful his salvation is. They know he is within them by the Spirit, and that they are participating in what he is doing by his power. Believers do not have to generate success when the gospel is out of season; they are called to remain faithful. God will reap a harvest when the fields are in season (2 Tim 4:2; John 4:37–38). God's children *know* that the gospel is *the* power of God for salvation for all who believe (1:16). It must be heard to be believed (10:14–17). So, they must tell the world. He will save people from all people and walks of life and will transform the world from the inside out. Amen.

---

31. "When he alludes to the subject, it is with a practical purpose; and when (as in this chapter) he speaks of God's predestination of believers to glory, his purpose is to encourage them to persevere in holiness on the ground of their assurance of God's eternal purpose concerning them, the essential human conditions being all along supposed to be fulfilled." Spence-Jones, *Romans*, 216.

23

Missional Prayer

PAUL KNOWS THAT GOD is sovereign, yet Paul is committed to prayer.[1] He knows that prayer changes things. Well, at one level, it does not, for every prayer and God's consequent response is known by God. Nevertheless, in his dynamism and ability to be over time and in time at the same time, he responds within history as people pray. Throughout Romans, which of course, is a missional letter, we see Paul's confidence in prayer and his commitment to it. We hear him cry out blessings on God and prayers for the Romans. He prays for the mission.[2]

ROMANS 1:7–10

As he does in eight of his other letters,[3] Paul ends his prescript with the blessing "Grace to you and peace from God our Father and the Lord Jesus Christ" (v. 7). He frames the letter with grace and peace from God and his Son (16:20).

Coming from Paul, this is a missional prayer. While the words are pretty much the same in the eight letters, in each, there is a slight nuance. Here, it is the prayer of a great Christian missionary who has not planted the church but recognizes its critical importance to the work of God. He writes to Rome, which governs the empire. The church there will have an enormous influence on the world, and so his prayers for them have real import. He writes to all in Rome knowing that they, like all of God's children, are both loved by God and called to be God's set apart and pure people.

Then he prays for all of them. His prayer is a blessing, asking God the Father and the Lord Jesus Christ to pour out on the Roman church grace and peace. Notably, God

---

1. "Next to the book of Psalms, there is no part of the Bible that contains such wealth of devotion, such depth of adoration, such height of thanksgiving and such width of intercession as Paul's epistles." Zwemer, "Into All the World," 164.

2. "His letters reveal Paul to be a man of prayer, engaged in continual intercession for the churches of his mission." Howell, "Mission in Paul's Epistles," 87.

3. See also 1 Cor 1:3; 2 Cor 1:2; Gal 1:3; Eph 1:2; Phil 1:2; 1 Thess 1:1; 2 Thess 1:2; Phlm 3.

is not just "the Father," he is "*our* Father," as the third-person pronoun embraces all Christians in all places and times. The pronoun speaks of intimacy and God on the side of his people.

Grace

"Grace" is *charis*, a word that, when applied to God, means his favor, beneficence, generosity, goodness, benevolence, and magnanimity. It is more of a Greek idea than peace, which invokes the Jewish notion of shalom. Here, God is the source of this grace through his Son Jesus. He is the new Adam who has undone the carnage the first Adam unleashed; he is grace embodied, who imparts the abundance of God's gift of grace to people (5:15, 17). Significantly, he uses the three-fold name which emphasizes Christ's complete sovereignty: he is Israel's Messiah, and he is Lord!

Through Romans, "grace" is used twenty-four times, which helps us see what he is praying for here. First, grace is associated with his mission calling (1:5). By asking for grace, then, in part, he is asking God to generate mission from the Romans, including a passion for sharing the gospel with the world, the works of mission, mission effectiveness, and workers for the harvest field (among other things).

Second, grace is the basis of justification (3:24; 5:17). As such, he is praying that the Roman Christians experience confidence in their status of righteousness before God. He wants them to remember that they are justified by grace and not works and not to lapse into seeking righteousness based on law or works (4:4, 16). He desires that they are strengthened in the faith that activates the verdict "justified," and that more and more people hear the gospel and experience the grace of God (cf. 4:4).

Third, having been justified by faith, grace is a sphere in which they stand (5:2). He is praying that they know this and that this will lead to boasting in the hope of God's glory, in their sufferings knowing it will strengthen them, and yielding to the love of God given to them by the Spirit.

Fourth, grace is a sovereign power that now rules and abounds to God's people in and through Jesus (5:20). It reigns through righteousness, which leads to eternal life for God's people (5:21). This status should not lead to sin, for believers are now under grace and serve righteousness (6:1, 14). Nor must they lapse into law or works observance for this quenches grace and becomes a demand and enslaves (6:15). Paul is then praying in 1:7 for the Romans to yield to the power of grace.

Fifth, grace is a word of praise, a cry of gratitude from Paul as he cries out grace to God in response to God's lavish grace. So, in Romans 6:17, he thanks God that the Roman believers are no longer captives and slaves of sin but are willingly and gratefully, slaves of the gospel. In Romans 7:25, he is grateful that through Jesus that although in anguish at his failure to live the law, he is free of its condemnation through Christ's death and the unleashing of the Spirit of life (7:25—8:4). As such, the prayer for grace in 1:7 asks that God would generate gratitude in the lives of the Romans toward God for his redemption.

Sixth, grace is linked to God's election; they are chosen by grace and not works (11:5-6). Paul wants them to recognize their election by God as a pure act of his grace. They have not earned it. It is not based on effort or merit; it is a gift. He is praying that they know this and pray for those like hardened Israel who have not responded to it.

Seventh, grace is linked to the exercise of spiritual gifts both in Paul's example and the impartation of gifts to them (12:3, 6). Paul is praying that they live by the particular graces they have been given with humility.

Eighth, grace is exercised in the act of writing the letter to the Romans, causing Paul to write in the particular boldness the letter exhibits. He is asking God that the Romans recognize the grace that generates the letter and hear in it God's favor to them, and yield to its summons to live by the gospel. Implicitly also, he is praying for the Romans that they act in a way consistent with the grace given them in Christ.

Finally, Paul ends the letter with grace, repeating the prayer of 1:7 differently (16:20). He does this in all his letters, framing his appeal with grace. Satan is still roaming free, yet to be crushed under the feet of Christ and his people. In the meantime, he prays that they will know God's favor in every aspect of their lives.

Peace

As noted, the prayer for peace asks for God's shalom. He prays for this in Romans 15:13. In Romans, peace language is found ten times. Again, by looking at these uses, we get a sense of what Paul is specifically praying. God is definitively the source of peace for Paul as he defines God as "the God of peace" in Romans 15:33 and 16:20. In Romans 15:13, peace comes in believing, which results in the Spirit abounding and producing hope in the believer.

Peace *with* God is the central dimension of the theme of peace in Romans. Those justified by faith have peace with God (5:1). Now Christians are no longer enemies, they are reconciled to him. A new covenant is signed in the blood of Jesus, and those who add their signature through faith and acknowledgment, have signed a peace treaty that God has put in place (despite having the power and every reason to smite humankind for their sin).

Paul's prayer is that they embrace this peace and live in the confidence it generates. Implicitly, he is praying that they would pass that on to others through the preaching of the gospel.

In Romans 8:6, peace of mind and heart in the believer is generated by the Spirit. Whereas humankind does not walk in the way of peace (3:17), God's people led by the Spirit do. A nuance of his prayer then is that the Romans continue in this path of peace. This peace with God, by the Spirit, overflows into peaceful relationships within the church (14:17, 19); for these, Paul is also praying. Ultimately, the believer will experience eschatological peace—an eternity with God and each other free from the threat of enemies including, sin, death, spiritual powers, and human opponents (2:10).

Just as the letter is framed by grace, it is enclosed in peace. He prays that the God of peace will be with the Romans (15:33), which is certain where there is faith. He finishes reminding them that the day is coming when the God of peace will crush Satan (16:20). His prayers bring reassurance of God's presence despite suffering and ultimate victory.

Gratitude

As in most of his letters, in Romans 1:8, Paul shifts from blessing to thanksgiving. By first praying for God's richest blessings and then turning to gratitude, Paul models the appropriate heart of the person praying. Unlike sinful humanity that fails to thank God (1:21), wanting the best for others and gratitude to God is the right human response. For Paul, thanksgiving "was almost a synonym for the Christian life."[4]

He thanks "my God," again emphasizing the believer's intimate relationship with God. He thanks him through Jesus Christ, who is the mediator between God and humankind. As Romans 8:34 intimates and Hebrews explicates, he is the High Priest of God's people. He prays for all the Romans, showing his impartiality, again reflecting the heart of God (2:11).

His reason for praying is profoundly missional: because the faith of the Romans is being proclaimed in all the world. He is grateful that the gospel is advancing north, south, east, and west. With their help, he hopes to take it further west to Spain after his trip to Jerusalem and Rome. As argued earlier, he is also giving thanks for the Roman's (and others) active evangelization, evidenced by the many gospel workers named in Romans 16.

In Romans 1:9–10, in the most solemn manner, naming God as his witness, who Paul serves wholeheartedly in his gospel mission, he speaks of his prayers for the Romans. For Paul, prayer is a core element of the life of those who recognize their summons to mission in Christ. He tells them that he prays for them unceasingly, as seen in the use of the synonyms *adialeiptōs* (v. 8) and *pantote* (v. 9).[5]

Paul uses the *adialeiptōs* twice else of his constant prayer life (1 Thess 1:2; 2:13) and urges the Thessalonians to "pray without ceasing" (1 Thess 5:17). He employs *pantote* eight other times of constant prayer.[6] As in 1 Thessalonians 1:2, he puts the

---

4. O'Brien, "Thanksgiving and the Gospel in Paul," 62. See also Carson: "If prayerlessness and ingratitude are linked with idolatry, it cannot be surprising that Paul tells believers to 'pray continually; give thanks in all situations, for this is God's will for you in Christ Jesus.'" Carson, "Paul's Mission and Prayer," 179.

5. *Adialeiptōs* means "constantly, unceasingly" (BDAG 20), while *pantote* evokes "always, at all times" (BDAG 755).

6. 1 Cor 1:4; Eph 5:20; Phil 1:4; Col 1:3; 1 Thess 1:2; 2 Thess 1:11; 2:13; Phlm 4, see also Phil 4:4;

two terms together, emphasizing his commitment to praying for others. In Romans, he prays continually that he can come to them.

Here, Paul testifies that he names the Romans in his prayer life again and again. We get a window into Paul's approach to prayer—regular, specific, targeted, and ongoing. It is likely that Paul participated in the typical Jewish pattern of prayer twice a day, at morning and evening,[7] meal-time blessings,[8] and perhaps the mid-day prayer (Acts 10:9),[9] although such statements as these suggest he probably prayed more. The many times Paul asserts his constant prayer for his converts and others like the Colossians and Romans suggests long periods of sustained prayer for others. While he has a high view of God's sovereignty, this does nothing to hinder his commitment to prayer.

His specific prayer is that, by God's will, he can come to Rome, restated twice for emphasis. The clause in Greek *ei pōs ēdē pote* is also emphatic, literally translated "if somehow now at last . . ." The clause suggests that he has asked to come to Rome many times. This desire could stretch as far back as his earlier missions in Syria, Cilicia, or as he pushed west on his first and second great Antiochian missions. As I have postulated elsewhere, it is likely he wanted most to come on his last mission when in Macedonia, just across the Adriatic from Italy. However, the Claudian edict had ruled that out, so he had sent the Jerusalem Council letters with gentiles like Luke to Rome, while he headed south to Achaia and then to Ephesus and Jerusalem.[10]

Paul had wanted to go to Rome earlier. His strategy was to plant the gospel in main urban centers, preaching in synagogues, making converts of some Jews, proselytes, and God-fearers, then establishing a community of believers, and charging them with the responsibility of taking the gospel further. Of all cities at the time, he must have longed to go to the center of his world, Rome.

In Romans 1:11–15, he builds further on his reasons for the prayer and wanting to come to Rome. He wishes to impart spiritual gifts to them, to share encouragement with them, and to preach in the city, winning more to the faith. He wants then to push west to Spain (15:24, 28).

Col 4:12; 1 Thess 3:6; 5:16.

7. Crump, "Prayer," 684. On the two prayer times see 1 Chr 23:30; Pss 5:3; 55:17; 88:13; Ezra 9:5; Dan 9:21; Jdt 9:1; Pss. Sol. 6:4. He notes that the Shema was recited at these times. These times were associated with the sacrifices that were labeled "the hour of prayer" (Acts 3:1). For Qumran, who rejected the Temple system, prayer times were associated with dawn and dusk (e.g., 1QS 10:1, 3, 11; Josephus, *J.W.* 2.128–29).

8. Crump, "Prayer," 684 notes mealtime prayers are part of Israel's traditions (Deut 8:10; Josephus, *J.W.* 2.131; 1QS 5:4–5; m. Ber. 6–8), Jesus (Mark 6:41; 8:6–7; 14:22–23 and parr.), and the early church (Rom 14:6; 1 Cor 10:30; 1 Tim 4:4).

9. Crump, "Prayer," 684 notes that the prayer in the middle of the day is another early addition (Ps 55:17; Dan 6:10; 2 En. 51:4; Acts 10:9; Did. 8:3). Often the Eighteen Benedictions (Shemoneh Esreh or Tefellah) and the Amidah (Standing) were prayed, although their role before AD 70 is uncertain.

10. Keown, *Philippians*, 1:4.

PART THREE: ROMANS AND THE PROCLAMATION OF THE GOSPEL

BLESSINGS

Through Romans, showing his worshipful posture, Paul inserts blessing statements, praising God. First, in Romans 1:25, after lamenting the idolatry of sinful humanity worshiping created things and animals rather than God the Creator, he cries out, "He is blessed forever! Amen!" He rejects idolatry by exclaiming praise to God for his glorious power to create, and the wonderful creation he has made.

Then in Romans 9:5, he cries out, "He is God over all, blessed forever. Amen!" It is disputed whether this refers to God or Christ. As I have noted earlier, the Greek supports the latter. Either way, it is another exclamation of praise to God or his Son for his supremacy over all things, people, and time.

In Romans 11:33–36, Paul cries out concerning God's wisdom and knowledge, his unsearchable judgments, and his inscrutable ways. He asks who can know God's mind or out-give him and be in his debt. He attributes God as the source of all things, the conduit of all things, and the goal of all things. Then he ends with another prayer of praise: "To him be glory forever, Amen."

THANKSGIVINGS

Attention has already been given to Paul's thanksgiving in Romans 1:8. There he uses the verb *eucharisteō*, which compounds *eu*, "good," and *charisteō*, "grace, favor," and so is a declaration of good favor on the recipient. In Romans 1:8, this is God, and Paul is responding to God's grace with grace. The verb features in Romans four more times: of sinful humanity's thanklessness before their Creator (1:8); in contrast, of Christians giving thanks for eating or abstaining from food (14:6, cf. 1 Cor 10:30; 11:24); and in Paul's case, for the Romans and Prisca and Aquila (16:4). For Paul, believers should "give thanks in all circumstances" (1 Thess 5:18).[11]

Paul also uses the noun *charis* verbally, crying out "grace be to God," which is usually translated "thanks." He does so twice in Romans. First, he cries out gratitude that the Romans have been released from enslavement to sin to obedience to the gospel (6:17). Second, he gives thanks through Jesus Christ for his deliverance from law and sin into the freedom of being in Christ, filled with the Spirit (7:25).

THE SPIRIT AND PRAYER

In Romans 8:26–27, the Spirit comes to the aid of Christians in their weakness. *Astheneia* here can be translated, "weakness, sickness," and is a standard term for points of struggle.[12] This can be general, for humanity is always universally "weak" before

---

11. See also in letter thanksgivings 1 Cor 1:4; Phil 1:3; Col 1:3; 1 Thess 1:2; 2 Thess 1:3; Phlm 4, see also 1 Cor 1:14; 14:17, 18; 2 Cor 1:11; Eph 1:16; 3:20; Col 1:12; 3:17; 1 Thess 2:13; 2 Thess 2:13.

12. BDAG 142.

God, particularly those who are in an ungodly state (5:6). Here, in 8:26, it speaks of Christians in their many struggles, for it is they who have the Spirit in them.

The Greek for "help" is *synantilambanomai*, which is only found in Greek biblical literature. The two LXX uses of the term both concern the appointment of leaders: first of other leaders coming to help bear the leadership load borne by Moses (Exod 18:22); second, of the seventy assisting Moses's managing Israel's impulsive people (Num 11:17). The only other NT use is of Martha pleading with Jesus to tell Mary to come and help her provide hospitality for Jesus (Luke 10:40). As such, here, it speaks of the Spirit coming to the aid of believers in their afflictions.

Using a causal *gar*, "because, for," Paul specifies why: believers do not know what to pray for as they should. Such uncertainty in prayer is a truth all Christians discover as they consider the complexities of life alongside discerning God's will in a given situation.

Paul then tells the Romans the help the Spirit offers. The Spirit intercedes (*hyperentynchanō*) for them with wordless (*alalētos*) groans (*stenagmos*). The Greek for "intercedes" compounds *hyper* and *entynchanō*. *Hyper* can be a prefix of intensity, as the term can mean "over and above, beyond, more than."[13] Alternatively, it can mean on "behalf of, for the sake of" believers.[14] The latter is likely as Paul uses *entynchanō* in the next verse and of Jesus's intercession for believers (8:34), and the praying of the Spirit is hardly likely to be more intense than the prayers of Jesus!

Aside from being used of Jesus's intercession (see the next section), the verb *entynchanō* is more common than the compound used in the LXX and Pseudepigrapha of a human appeal to one in authority, a sense seen in Paul's audiences with Agrippa II in Acts 25:24.[15] In that same sense of approaching a superior, it is employed of coming to God with an appeal or plea (11:2; Heb 7:25).[16]

Here, the Spirit prays on behalf of believers.[17] He does so with groans. *Stenagmos* is a term used only in Greek Jewish literature of situations of deep pain and lament. Its intensity is reflected in its only other NT use, Israel's lament in Egypt (Acts 7:34).[18] The

---

13. BDAG 1031.

14. BDAG 1030.

15. See 1 Macc 8:32; 10:61; 11:25; 2 Macc 4:36; 3 Macc 6:37; Dan 6:13; Let. Aris. 174; Mart. Pol. 17:2. Similarly, it can be used of bringing an accusation (1 Macc 10:63, 1 En. 7:6; 22:7, 15; T. Job 17:5). It also has the meaning "read" from "the idea of 'coming across' or 'encountering' a book" (BDAG 341; see, e.g., 2 Macc 2:25; 6:12; 15:39; Diog. 12.1).

16. See also Wis 8:21, 28; 1 En. 9:3, 10; 22:5, 6; 1 Clem. 56:1; Pol. Phil. 4:3; Herm. Mand. 10.3, 2; Herm. Sim. 2.6, 8.

17. The intercession of the Spirit is mentioned in Herm. Mand. 10.2, 5. "Rid yourself, therefore, of grief and do not oppress the Holy Spirit that lives in you, lest it intercede with God against you and leave you."

18. The groans of pain during childbirth (Gen 3:16; Jer 4:31; *Leg.* 3.200), sighs of lament in persecution (Exod 2:24; 6:5; Judg 2:18), a groan at someone's death (Jdt 14:16), cries of lament when Ptolemy IV Philopater (ca. 240–204 BC) tried to enter the temple (3 Macc 1:18), Israel's laments when Philopater decreed the arrest of Jews (3 Macc 4:2), in a lament at extreme sickness (Ps 6:7), the cries

adjective *alalētos* is derived from *laleō*, "to speak," and refers to something wordless or unexpressed.[19] This speaks of the Spirit in the believer, groaning, and yearning to God the Father on our behalf. Thus, even when the believer is in travail and has no idea how to pray, the Spirit is interceding with wordless lament to God.

Furthermore, the Spirit prays for believers in accordance with God's will. Hence, believers do not need to know the will of God for every situation. They can pray as led and, at times, be silent as the Spirit communes with the Father on behalf of those for they intercede. They can do so because the God who searches all human hearts is in complete accord with the mind of the Spirit.

Romans 8:26–27 are two of the most important verses for Christians in mission. So as believers look out at the world in its pain, they take comfort that the Spirit and Son (v. 34) are Father-facing, praying for them and the world. Our summons is to be "in the Spirit;" to be in harmony with these yearnings and to raise our prayers and silence to God. Such knowledge is reassuring in times of suffering. It also enables believers to be constantly in prayer, as is Paul, interceding for a world lost in sin and misery.

CHRIST'S INTERCESSION

Not only is the Spirit interceding for believers, Christ himself, exalted to the right hand of the Father, is God-facing on behalf of God's people (8:34). Paul states this in answer to the interlocuter's question, "Who is to condemn?" Implied here is the eschatological condemnation of the believer. Paul has already told the Romans that "there is no condemnation for those who are in Christ Jesus" (8:1). Hence, the answer is already known. So, trusting that the Romans now grasp this, Paul jumps to the answer: Jesus—the crucified, raised, and exalted one—is interceding for believers (us). It is stunning to imagine one person of the Trinity pleading to God on behalf of his people. Having both Spirit and Son doing this simultaneously in a harmonious chorus of prayer should give immense confidence to believers. It also reminds them that Spirit and Son are completely in sync, and as they pray and get increasingly in tune with the heart of God by the Spirit, they are also attuned to the heart of the Son.

---

of the poor (Ps 11:6 [12:5 Heb]; 30:11 [31:10 Heb]; 37:9, 10 [38:8, 9 Heb]; 101:6, 21 [103:5, 21 Heb]; 1 Clem. 15:6; Herm. Vis. 3.9, 5), the laments of exiles (Ps 78:11 [79:11 Heb]; Isa 35:10; 51:11, cf. Ezek 24:17) and at the destruction of Jerusalem (Lam 1:22), the pain of Job (Job 3:24; 23:2), moaning at past memories (Wis 11:12), the groaning of someone dying in pain (Pss. Sol. 4:14), the groan of someone in trouble (Mal 2:13), the painful lament of Jeremiah (Jer 51:33), the cries of the dead at the gates of heaven (1 En. 9:10), the pain of deep depression (T. Jos. 7:2), groanings of tear-filled repentance (Apoc. Sedr. 14:3; Jos. Asen. 10:5, 6, 7, 17), the groans of a woman sexually scorned (T. Jos. 9:4), laments not heard in heaven (T. Ab. [A] 20:14), people's lament and cries at the sacking of Jerusalem (J.W. 5.32; 6.272), the groaning of intense pain (*Leg.* 3.211).

19. BDAG 41.

Paul follows this in verse 35, asking if anything exists that can separate a believer from the love of Christ. Short answer: nothing! Well, if we accept the premise that a Christian can be severed from the olive tree of God's people or from Christ and fall from grace (11:21–22; Gal 5:4), only a person themselves can do so (and if so, this was predetermined, yet volitional). Nothing else can do this. Creation is fallen and dangerous, and spirits, enemies, and forces that repudiate God and his people abound. Pain and suffering are unavoidable as the believer's path to glory (v. 17). Physical death is also assured. Yet, nothing can sever the umbilical connection between God and the believer. Hence, the believer is "more than a conqueror" through God's love (8:37).

PAUL'S PRAYERS FOR ISRAEL (9:1–3; 10:1)

Two of the most moving moments in Romans are Paul's prayers for his people, the Israelites. These are the prayers of a Christian whose people are rejecting God despite their desperate efforts to share the gospel with them, only to be rejected. This yearning for loved ones is the pain many have felt across history and continue to feel in God's world today.

First, in Romans 9:1–3, he boldly declares that he is speaking the truth in Christ, is not lying, and is speaking from his Spirit-inspired conscience. He has "great (*megas*) sorrow (*lypē*) and unceasing (*adialeiptōs*) anguish (*odynō*) in [his] heart" for his people.

Lypē is a strong term of grief and lament used of Jesus's pain in Gethsemane (Luke 22:45) and the pain of the disciples when he died (John 16:6, 22), which can be likened to a woman in childbirth (John 16:21). It is the anguish Paul would have felt had his brother and comrade Epaphroditus died (Phil 2:27).[20]

Odynō is another term of extreme anguish and pain used of a range of things including the pain at the loss of a loved one (e.g., Gen 44:21), of being in slavery (Exod 3:7), being burned in a fire (4 Macc 14:9), facing extreme illness (Ps 40:9 [41:8 Heb]), being in Hades (Ps 114:3 [116:3]), when facing imminent death (Saul, *Ant.* 6.337), experiencing torment as did Job (Job 7:4), grief at the hanging of Eleazar (*J.W.* 7.202), and the pain of being tortured (*Flacc.* 180). "In my heart" speaks of Paul's inner being—in his mind and soul he writhes in agony for Israel.

Paul then declares he wishes he would be accursed (*anathema*) from Christ for them. The Greek often translated "wish" is, *euchomai* from which we get *proseuchomai*, the more common NT word meaning "pray." Hence, it is misleading to translate it "wish," for coming from a Jewish Pharisee with a worldview in which it is God alone who can bring a wish to pass, as in all NT uses, this is a prayer.[21] His prayer is that he might "be accursed from Christ" for the sake of his people (my brothers, my kin according to the flesh).

---

20. See also 2 Cor 2:1, 3, 7; 7:10; 9:7.
21. See also Acts 26:29; 27:29; 2 Cor 13:7, 9; Jas 5:16; 3 John 2.

Accursed is *anathema*, a term replete with meaning. In the LXX, it translates ḥē·rĕm of things or people devoted to destruction (e.g., Deut 13:15; 20:17; Josh 6:17, 18; 7:1). In the NT, it is used of a determination to destroy Paul (Acts 23:14). In 1 Corinthians 12:3, *anathema* is used of cursing Christ, something someone with the Spirit would never do.

In Galatians 1:8 and 9, Paul pronounces that those who preach a different gospel be accursed. Then, in Galatians 3:13, using different language, Christ takes the curse of the law on himself as he is accursed on the cross. With "from Christ," the term here is a prayer. In his prayer, Paul asks that he would be accursed, which is synonymous with his being destroyed. He prays this "for the sake of" (*hyper*) "my brothers, my kinsmen according to the flesh," i.e., his fellow-Israelites who are rejecting Christ. Paul uses *hyper* of Christ's vicarious death commonly in Romans and his letters (5:6, 8; 8:32).[22] So, in Galatians 3:13, Christ "by becoming a curse for (*hyper*) us," redeemed people from the curse of the law. The preposition has more than a hint of penal substitution.

So, Paul is stating that were he able, he would do what Jesus has done for humankind: take the curse of the law, sin, and death on himself to save his people. To do so, he is willing to be accursed from (*apo*) Christ. There is a sense of a prayer-wish here as Paul knows he has no power to do this, for he is flawed and human, and only Jesus has the capability of taking on the curse of the law and sin and save anyone, including recalcitrant Israel. Of course, Jesus has already done so for Israel, but hardened Israel has spurned him. Still, this prayer shows Paul identifying with Christ as he prays, and his deep desire that Israel is saved.

Paul's intercession here informs missional prayer: we pray with deep compassion and grief for our people and those of other nations, even if they are stubborn, resistant, and even violently opposed to God and us. Indeed, we are prepared to "go to hell" and back that they can "go to heaven."

Paul states his prayer for them more clearly in Romans 10:1. The desire (*eudokia*) of his heart and prayer (*deēsis*) to God for them is salvation. *Eudokia* compounds *eu*, "good" and *dokeō*, "think, consider, suppose," and so has the idea of "thinking well" of or toward someone or something, i.e., being well-disposed."

Paul's use is unusual in Jewish Greek literature, where it is usually employed of God's goodwill toward people.[23] It is utilized sparingly of words directed to God (Ps 18:15 [19:14 Heb]), to please God (Sir 2:16; 35:3; 39:18), or goodwill before the Lord (Pss. Sol. 3:4). In the NT, *eudokia* is applied mainly to God's goodwill and purpose.[24]

---

22. See also 1 Cor 1:13; 15:3; 2 Cor 5:14, 15, 21; Gal 1:4; 2:20; Eph 5:2, 25; Col 1:24; 1 Tim 2:6; Titus 2:14.

23. 1 Chr 16:10; Ps 5:13 [5:12 Heb]; 50:20 [51:18 Heb]; 88:18 [89:17 Heb]; 105:4 [106:4 Heb]; 144:16 [145:16 Heb]; Sir 11:17; Pss. Sol. 8:33; 16:12; 1 En. 1:8; Other uses include a favorable time (Ps 68:14 [69:13 Heb], sinful pleasures (Ps 140:5 [141:5 Heb]; Sir 9:12; 18:31), a lovely woman (Song 6:4), God's delights (Sir 1:27), general goodwill (Sir 15:15), satisfaction (Sir 29:23), to gain approval (Sir 32:14; 34:18; 35;16), God's pleasure (Sir 33:13; 41:4), desire to be with God (Pss. Sol. 3:4).

24. It is used of God's goodwill in Matt 11:26; Luke 2:14; 10:21; Phil 2:13. It sometimes has the

Here it carries the sense of "desire," but as with "wish" in 9:2, it is used of "prayerful desire."

The second term is one of the NT terms used exclusively of prayer: *deēsis*, meaning an "urgent request to meet a need."[25] Here, the urgent need is declared to God (*pros ton Theon*) for them, or on their behalf (*hyper autōn*). "Them" speaks of Israel in rejection of God. The purpose is "salvation," *sōtērion*. Here, their eternal deliverance from law, sin, death, and wrath is in view, i.e., eternal life.

Paul's prayers alert believers to the need to pray for the lost. No matter how and why they have rejected the gospel, believers are to "get on their knees" and raise their heartfelt desires, griefs, and anguishes to God for their salvation. The faithful sing in harmony with the chorus of prayers from the Son and Spirit to the Father for the lost. Mission begins on our knees.

ELIJAH

In Romans 11:2, Paul reminds the Romans about Elijah and the prophet's appeals to God concerning Israel who rejected his message. Paul then cites excerpts from 1 Kings 19, where Elijah cries out to God that he is the only one of God's prophets left. God replies that the prophet is mistaken for, as always, he has preserved a remnant. There are, in fact, seven thousand who have not bowed to the false god Baal (1 Kgs 19:10, 14, 18). While the point of this is to show that God has again chosen a remnant by grace and not works, this shows Elijah as a paradigm of faithfulness in life and prayer, something James affirms (Jas 5:17–18).

BE CONSTANT IN PRAYER (12:12)

Romans 12:12 is nestled in a range of commands that can quickly be glossed over because they are so tightly bunched together. Yet, each one is of critical importance. The Romans are to be devoted (*proskatereō*) to prayer. *Katareō* means to "continue without wavering in a state or condition, be strong, be steadfast, hold out, endure" (Heb 11:27).[26] Compounded with *pros*, "to," it means to endure with someone or in doing something.

In the LXX, *proskatereō* is employed to describe the effort of caring for trees (Num 13:20), enduring as one besieges a city (*Ant.* 5.130), or effort in removing foundation stones (*J.W.* 6.27). It is commonly used of devoting oneself to prayer as in the

---

sense of God's purpose (Eph 1:5, 9; 2 Thess 1:11). It is used of people holding goodwill to others in Phil 1:15.

25. BDAG 213. In Paul see 2 Cor 1:11; 9:14; Eph 6:18; Phil 1:4, 19; 4:6; 1 Tim 2:1; 5:5; 2 Tim 1:3. See also Luke 1:13; 2:37; 5:33; Heb 5:7; Jas 2:16; 1 Pet 3:12.

26. BDAG 510.

early Jerusalem community (Acts 1:14; 2:42;[27] 6:4; Col 4:2). Here, it has the sense then of "be devoted to"[28] or perhaps "stick at" prayer. The Romans, then, are to be committed to prayer as part of their Christian devotion. Obviously, this should include missional prayers.

We see the commitment for missional prayer in Jesus's injunctions to the disciples who are to pray for workers for the mission field (Matt 9:37–38). The same emphasis is found in the Jerusalem community in Acts 4. Forbidden from speaking God's word and threatened with punishment, they responded with prayer (Acts 4:23–31). After acknowledging God's sovereignty and power to create, recalling the expectation of gentile opposition from Ps 2:1–2 and Christ's death at the hands of Israel and gentiles, they prayed that God would embolden them to preach the word and perform signs and wonders through them by the power of Jesus (Acts 4:29–30). Their prayer not only caused the shaking of the room and a fresh outpouring of the Spirit (Acts 4:31), but extraordinary acts of social justice for the needy (Acts 4:32–37), a terrifying instance of God's present judgment (Acts 5:1–11), many new converts, and amazing signs and wonders (Acts 5:12–16). Despite people being afraid to join them and further persecution, their prayer resulted in renewed daily evangelism in the temple and in homes (Acts 4:29–5:42).

In Colossians 4:2–4, Paul's general appeal to be devoted to prayer is followed by a request that the Colossians pray for him and his team. He seeks prayer that despite his imprisonment, God would open doors for the word of God and that they would declare the gospel with clarity. No doubt, such missional prayer is part of what Paul has in mind.

ROMANS 15:8–13

The passage comes as a climax to the appeals for unity in diversity in Romans 14 and 15. The emphasis is on the inclusion of the gentiles and their praise of God. In verse 8, Jesus is a servant to Israel, showing God's veracity and fulfilling God's promises to Abraham.

Verse 9 shifts to the ultimate purpose of Jesus's service to Israel: "in order that the Gentiles might glorify God for his mercy." So, Jesus came not just to save Israel, but that in him and by the Spirit, the gentiles may raise their hearts and voices to God to glorify him. "Glorify" is *doxazō*, a verb associated with *doxa* (glory) and meaning to "ascribe glory to someone or something." In Jewish Greek literature and the NT, *doxa* can be used of honoring people (e.g., 2 Kgdms 10:3), the temple (e.g., 1 Esdr 8:25), or a nation (e.g., 1 Esdr 8:64; 1 Macc 15:9). As here, it is often employed of the glorification

---

27. *Proskatereō* is also used in Acts 2:42 of being devoted to apostolic teaching, the fellowship, and the breaking of bread.

28. BDAG 881.

of God, including five times in Exodus 15, the first song of praise after the Exodus (Exod 15:1, 2, 3, 11, 21).[29]

In the NT, outside of Paul, the term is used of honoring others (e.g., Matt 6:2), and often of glorifying God.[30] The first to do so after Jesus's death is the gentile Roman centurion (Luke 23:47). He is a foretaste of the gentiles hearing the gospel and glorifying God (Acts 13:48, cf. Acts 11:18; 1 Pet 2:12).

In Paul, one of the features of idolatrous humankind, locked in futile thinking and with foolish and darkened hearts, is their failure to glorify God (1:21). Believers, however, are to glorify God with their bodies (1 Cor 6:20), through radical generosity (2 Cor 9:13), and because of faithful workers like Paul (Gal 1:24).[31] Abraham also gave glory (*doxa*) to God without wavering in his faith, and so is the paradigm of the ideal response to God (4:20). Authentic faith leads to praise.

Here, Paul's particular interest is the inclusion of the gentiles and the raising of their voices to glorify God. They do so because of his mercy in the gospel of Christ. The term *doxazō* is used in this regard in some important OT texts. In LXX Mal 1:11, God's name is honored, and incense and sacrifices are made to God. Isaiah 42:10 envisages people from the ends of the earth, on the seas, and in the islands, responding to God's sovereignty by singing a new song to him. Again, in LXX Ps 85:9 (Ps 86:9 EVV), all the nations will bow down before God and glorify his name.

Paul draws on four other OT passages that anticipate the worship of the gentiles. In the citation in verse 9, David sings of the king singing praises to God among the nations (2 Sam 22:50; Ps 18:49). Transposed to the gospel, this is Jesus worshiping with his people from all the world. In verse 10, the gentiles are commanded to sing with God's people (Deut 32:43). In the context of Romans, "his people" are the Israel of faith from creation to the present setting.

In verse 11, Psalm 117:1 is cited in which *all* the gentiles are charged to "praise the Lord," and all the peoples to "extol him." Such praise is now coming to pass in Christ. Finally, in verse 12, he draws on Isaiah's prediction in Isaiah 11:1 of a descendant (root) of Jesse raised up to rule the gentiles, while the gentiles will put their hope in him. Jesus is that root of Jesse, a descendant of David, and nations are coming to the obedience of faith and praising God through him.

Paul finishes the section in prayer, describing God as the God of hope. He asks that God fill the Romans with all joy and peace that is experienced in believing. He prays this way so that by the power of the Spirit, they may overflow in hope.

---

29. See also Lev 10:3; Judg 9:9; 1 Kgdms 2:30; 1 Chr 17:18; 1 Esdr 9:52; Pss 21:24 (22:23 Heb); 49:15, 23 (50:15, 23 Heb); 85:9, 12 (90:9, 12 Heb); 90:15 (91:15 Heb); Odes Sol. 1:1, 2, 6, 11; 7:26; 14:35; Sir 3:20; 43:28, 30; Pss. Sol. 10:7; 17:5, 30, 31; Isa 5:16; 24:23; 25:1; 33:10; 42:10; 43:23; 44:23; 49:3; 66:5; Ezek 39:13; Dan 3:26, 51, 55, 56; Mal 1:11.

30. Matt 5:16; 9:8; 15:31; Mark 2:12; Luke 2:20; 5:25, 26; 7:16; 13:13; 17:15; 18:43; John 8:54; 12:28; 13:31, 32; 14:13; 15:8; 17:1, 4; 21:19; Acts 4:21; 21:20; 1 Pet 2:12; 4:11, 16; Rev 15:4.

31. Paul also uses it of honoring one another (1 Cor 12:26), the glorification of people in Christ (8:30), glorifying his own ministry (11:13), and people honoring of God's word (2 Thess 3:1).

PART THREE: ROMANS AND THE PROCLAMATION OF THE GOSPEL

ROMANS 15:30–33

Romans 15:30–33 is a direct appeal for missional prayer, something Paul does elsewhere in his letters.[32] Here, he addresses the whole church.[33] He does so through (*dia*) Christ (threefold name) and the love of the Spirit. Jesus is the conduit for his prayer to God. He is motivated by the love poured into his heart by the Spirit (5:5). He urges, exhorts, or appeals (*parakaleō*)[34] them to contend (*synagōnizomai*) with him in praying to God on his behalf.

Synagōnizomai is a *hapax legomenon* from the *agōn* nexus of terms used in athletic and military settings.[35] The prefix *syn* suggests "with, together." *Agonizomai* is used by Paul likening ministry effort to the strivings of an athlete (1 Cor 9:25), soldier (1 Tim 6:12; 2 Tim 4:7), or in a general sense (Col 1:29). Notably, it is employed to describe Epaphras's commitment to praying for the Colossians: "always *contending* on your behalf in prayers" (Col 4:12, my translation and emphasis). The compound then speaks of the Romans, gathering together in their church groupings, bowing in corporate prayer, and interceding for Paul with the kind of effort, energy, and discipline seen in top athletes or marines: they are to grapple or wrestle together in prayer.

The content of the prayer is supplied with the *hina* purpose clause in verse 31. He prays two things, both signaled by *hina*, purpose clauses. The first purpose clause has two aspects. First, that he may be delivered from the disobedient (*apeitheō*)[36] in Judea, speaking of those in Jerusalem and its orb who are not Christians. This would include, first, Jews who could hear of Paul and seek to have him killed. It may include Romans who killed Jesus and may see Paul as a threat. Both of these came to pass, although Romans protected Paul until his trial was concluded (in Rome, Acts 21:17—28:31). We will never know how much the Roman church prayed this. What we do know is that Paul's prayer-wish was answered, and by God's grace, he ended up in Rome.

---

32. See 2 Cor 1:11; Eph 6:18; Phil 1:19; Col 4:3–4; 1 Thess 5:25; 2 Thess 3:1; Phlm 22. He does not seek prayer in the chastising 1 Corinthians and Galatians.

33. The plural of *adelphos* here is inclusive: "brothers and sisters."

34. *Parakaleō* is a word Paul frequently uses in his epistolary appeals. It is pastorally creative as it is not "I command you," but has the sense "I appeal, urge, plead with, prevail upon, beseech." He uses it this way thrice in Rom 12–16 (12:1, 15:30; 16:17, cf. 12:8) and thirteen other times across his letters (overall in the NT 34x).

35. Paul uses *agōn* language elsewhere: *agōn*, "contest, struggle, fight" (Phil 1:30; Col 2:1; 1 Thess 2:2; 1 Tim 6:12; 2 Tim 4:7, see also Heb 12:1); *agōnizomai*, "to compete, struggle, fight, strive" (1 Cor 9:25; Col 1:29; 4:12; 1 Tim 6:12; 2 Tim 4:7, see also Luke 13:24; 18:36). Other terms Paul does not use include *agōnia*, "contest, anguish" (Luke 22:44); *antagōnizomai*, "to fight" (against, Heb 12:4); *epangōnizomai*, "to contend" (Jude 3); *katangōnizomai*, "to struggle against, prevail against, conquer" (Heb 11:33). See for meanings, *NIDNTTE* 1:142.

36. The ESV is overly interpretative with "unbelievers," although it is their failure to come to the obedience of believing in Jesus that is their issue (cf. John 3:36). The same kind of sense is used in Acts 14:2 and 19:9 as Jews refuse the gospel in Iconium and Ephesus. Paul uses *apeithō* in 2:8 of those who "do not *obey* the truth"; 10:1, again of Jews who are disobedient; 11:30–31, of gentiles in their former disobedience. See also Heb 3:18; 11:31; 1 Pet 2:8; 3:1, 20; 4:17.

Missional Prayer

The second aspect of the prayer is that his ministry for Jerusalem might be acceptable (*euprosdektos*) to the believers in the city (saints). He hopes they will receive the collection warmly. Some scholars dispute whether this is the case.[37] However, there is nothing in the Acts account to suggest otherwise. In fact, the converse is the case: "When we had come to Jerusalem, the brothers received us gladly" (Acts 21:17). While "the brothers" may merely describe a diverse group, more likely it is the Jerusalem believers.[38] "Us" would include the Jerusalem Collection grouping (see Acts 20:4–6).[39]

"Gladly" is *asmenōs*, a *hapax legomenon* used in Jewish Greek writings of taking delight in a building (2 Macc 4:12), gladly treating people well (3 Macc 3:15), gladly giving approval (3 Macc 5:21), and gladly listening to the law (Let. Aris. 5). While Paul does not here mention the collection (he will make an inference to it in Acts 24:17), the adverb makes clear that "Paul is received warmly by the Jerusalem Christians."[40] His warm reception is confirmed in Acts 21:20 when, after hearing Paul and his team tell them of "the things that God had done among the Gentiles through his ministry (*diakonia*)" (no doubt including the collection),[41] "they ascribed glory (*doxazō*) to God" (my translation).

The second purpose clause in verse 32 can be read consecutively or as a second aspect of the prayer. The difference is minimal. He wants to come to Rome to be refreshed in joy through the will of God. The verb *synanapausomai* can mean rest, recovery, or refreshment. The compound *syn*, "with" suggests the rich mutual encouragement of Romans 1:11. He has been hindered up to now despite praying God's will would see him in Rome (1:10). He hopes it will come to pass this time. He finishes, solemnly (*amēn*) pronouncing a blessing for God's shalom for all the Romans.

ROMANS 16:20

Toward the end of the letter, Paul asks that the grace of the Lord Jesus Christ be with all of the Romans. The prayer recalls the injunction for grace in 1:7. The letter is framed by grace.

---

37. See, e.g., Mattill, "Purpose of Acts," 116.

38. Some think "the brothers" here are Hellenistic Christians because this supposedly contradicts Romans 15:30–31 (e.g., Barrett, *Critical and Exegetical Commentary*, 2:1005). However, in Romans 15 it is "the *disobedient*" in Judea that concern him. Here, in Acts, it is "the *brothers*," indicating that this is all those. Throughout Acts, "the brothers" are "the Christians" inclusive of women (Acts 1:15; 9:30; 10:23; 11:1, 29; 12:17; 14:2; 15:1, 3, 22, 23, 32, 33, 36, 40; 16:2, 40; 17:14; 18:18, 27; 21:7; 22:5; 28:15, 21).

39. The group would at least include those named in Acts 20:3–6: Paul, Sopater (Berea, see Acts 16:21), Aristarchus (Thessalonica), Secundus (Thessalonica); Gaius (Derbe); Timothy; Tychicus (Asia), Trophimus (Asia), and Luke (see the use of "we" in Acts 20:5).

40. Peterson, *Acts of the Apostles*, 583.

41. Bock, *Acts*, 646 rightly notes the *diakonia* is likely general but would encompass the collection, especially as *diakonia* is used of the collection in Rom 15:30–31 (see also 2 Cor 8:4; 9:1, 12–13).

Part Three: Romans and the Proclamation of the Gospel

ROMANS 16:25–27

While there is some question over the originality of Romans 16:25–27, that should not detain us as it is most likely original.[42] The passage is a doxology, glorifying God, and dense with theological import and power. It speaks of the outcome of all that is done: whether the writing of Romans, Paul's mission and life, all subsequent mission, and history itself, God is glorified!

It is a long sentence beginning with "to him," repeated as "to the only wise God" and resolving on "be glory forevermore through Jesus Christ! Amen." God is the subject and object of all of history.

He is easily able to strengthen (*stērizō*) the Romans and all believers. *Stērizō* carries the meaning "to establish, strengthen."[43] Here, as in Romans 1:11,[44] it has the latter sense. Paul was writing to those *already* Christians, assuring them that the God who established them will strengthen them and enable them to stand firm to the end. The prayer speaks of God's capacity to enable their perseverance. Where a person not yet a Christian reads it, it is an invitation to believe in the God who can establish them in salvation faith.

The means and basis for this strengthening are introduced with *kata*, "in accordance with." The thing that enables them to endure is God's strengthening them in accordance with "my gospel," which of course is "the gospel." This gospel is further expounded as "the preaching (*kērygma*) of Jesus Christ." *Kērygma* is the substantive associated with *kēryssō*, "to proclaim, herald, declare."[45] It is often translated verbally, as in the ESV in the previous sentence; however, it is a noun, and it is better to retain it as a further descriptor of the gospel.[46] It should then be rendered "the proclamation/message about Jesus Christ." The phrase throws the spotlight on the center of Paul's gospel: Jesus Christ. The message Paul preaches, which is about Jesus Christ, will be the basis on which God will strengthen the Romans and all Christians. Hence, the key to perseverance is faithfulness to the gospel.

Paul reinforces the gospel emphasis in a complex *kata* "in accordance with" statement that speaks of the nature of the good news:

---

42. Metzger, *Textual Commentary*, 476–77. While the ending is missing or moved to different points, it does retain impressive manuscript evidence (𝔓61 ℵ B C D 81 1739 itar, b, d*, f, o vg syrp copsa, bo eth Clement al). I surmise it is original, but as different versions were copied for different contexts, aspects of Romans 15 and 16 irrelevant to the recipients were omitted, and hence it is moved around.

43. BDAG 945.

44. See also 1 Thess 3:2; 2 Thess 2:17; 3:3; Jas 5:8; 1 Pet 5:10; Rev 3:2. It has more the sense "establish" in 1 Thess 3:13; 2 Pet 1:12.

45. Similarly, BDAG 543.

46. Similarly, Matt 12:41; Luke 11:32 should be "the proclamation/message of Jonah"; 1 Cor 1:21: "the foolishness of the message we preach"; 1 Cor 2:3: "my message"; 2 Thess 3:13: "our message"; 2 Tim 4:17: "the message"; Titus 1:3: "the message with which I have been entrusted."

according to the revelation of the mystery that was kept secret for the times of the ages, but now has been made known having been disclosed through the prophetic writings according to the command of the eternal God to bring about the obedience of faith in all the nations." (my translation)

In this sentence, the gospel is a mystery kept secret up to the point of Christ's coming. Yet, it was in the prophetic writings but not seen and understood until Christ came (and still not recognized by many from Israel). Then, at just the right time (5:6), God commanded that what was in the prophetic writings would be disclosed and made known. The purpose is that expressed in Romans 1:5: that throughout all the nations of the world, the people would hear this gospel and would obey it by believing it.

This doxology alerts us to the importance of the theme of mission. It is about the gospel. This gospel is now unveiled for the world. The hope is that all would believe in it and the one who stands at its center, Jesus. Paul ends the letter praising God for this gospel, and his purposes worked out in salvation.

24

The State and Mission

THIS CHAPTER TAKES A cursory look at Romans 13:1–7.[1] The passage is a somewhat surprising turn considering the world of oppressive political powers in which Paul is functioning. Some see it as an interpolation as a result.[2] However, with no evidence of an interpolation, this is the easy solution, and instead, the passage gives a rich theology of the State and sits nicely in this section on relations with unbelievers.

In the passage, in the complex political context of Rome and Nero's reign,[3] Paul urges believers not to respond with resistance against Jews or the political regime.[4] They are to live in submission to the Roman state, despite it reflecting little of the ethic of God and his kingdom. Paul's thinking here suggests a broad theology inclusive of the role of the central government under God of maintaining order in each society. He speaks of rulers as God's ministers, serving him to govern his people. In the present, they are his means for the distribution of justice. Believers are not to actively resist the government but live in submission to it.

BE SUBJECT TO THE GOVERNMENT

Paul begins in Romans 13:1 using the third-person present imperative indicating a continuous state: "Let every person (soul, *psychē*)[5] be subject to the governing

---

1. This is not a technical consideration but an overview to draw out some implications for mission.

2. Kallas, "Romans xiii. 1—7:1–7: An Interpolation," 365–74.

3. See Witherington and Hyatt, *Paul's Letter*, 304–8. Issues include deflecting anti-Jewish attitudes from gentile Christians, the Claudian edict and aftermath, and Nero.

4. We should note that Paul repeats the sentiment of Rom 13:1–7 in Titus 3:1. Both Pauline passages are in sync with 1 Pet 2:13–17. Assuming a traditional authorship, dating, and setting for Titus and 1 Peter, these other two passages were written in Nero's crazy years. Hence, Paul's view is not merely for Nero's moderate years of rule. Barnett, *Paul, Missionary of Jesus*, 183 notes too that Suetonius, *Nero* 16.2 may indicate earlier persecution of Christians: "Punishment was inflicted on the Christians, a sect devoted to a new and mischievous superstition."

5. Here *psychē* is "the whole person." Moo, *Letter to the Romans*, 811.

authorities." "Governing authorities" is *exousiais hyperexousais* that connotes "highly placed authorities." While the principle seems general, the context indicates that here this refers to the State leaders;[6] in this case, the government of the Roman Empire (it applies to any government in the setting a Christian is in).[7]

"Let every person be subject" uses *hypotassō* that means "be subject to, subordinate." Elsewhere in Romans, it is used of people failing to yield to God's law (8:7) or righteousness (10:3) and on these occasions such a submission should be absolute. The other use is creation subjected to futility by God (8:20); again, this is complete and irrevocably until creation is liberated. The other Pauline uses of *hypotassō* include the spirits of prophets submitting to prophets (1 Cor 14:32), women in submission in the church (1 Cor 14:34), cosmic subjugation to God and Christ,[8] believers submitting to leaders (1 Cor 16:16) and to one another (Eph 5:21), wives submitting to husbands (Col 3:18; Titus 2:5),[9] the church submitting to Christ (Eph 5:24), and slaves submitting to masters (Titus 2:9). Here, as in Titus 3:1, it is submission to the State authorities. Titus adds that the believer is to be "obedient," with the Greek *paitharcheō* used of obedience to God (Acts 5:29, 32).[10]

The wider use and Titus 3:1 suggest that the command of Romans 13:1 should not be watered down too much to merely showing love, being passive, or non-resistant. Instead, it carries some level of obedience, compliance, and deference to the authority of the one to whom one is subject. It implies significant levels of submission (but see below). As noted above, considering the corruption and despotism of the Roman authorities, this is a remarkable statement. "Every person" here is "every soul" (*psychē*), which speaks of yielding from the inside of people's whole beings. "Every" inclusive of Christian, Jew, Roman, and others alike.

GOD HAS APPOINTED ALL GOVERNMENTS

Paul goes on with his providential theology of the State: "For there is no authority except from God, and those that exist have been appointed by God." "Appointed" is the perfect passive *tassō*, a verb which has the sense of "ordered, fixed, determined, or appointed." It is from the same nexus of terms as *hypotassō* used in the previous command to yield to the one appointed, the State. State leaders, then, are God-appointees.

---

6. Morris, *Epistle to the Romans*, 460. There is no reason to read into this use of *exousia*, spiritual forces behind them (see the discussion in Longenecker, *Epistle*, 956–59).

7. *Contra* Witherington and Hyatt: "This means submitting to a pagan and non-democratic government." Witherington and Hyatt, *Paul's Letter*, 313. Such a political anachronism is unjustified. Paul is speaking generally and so his words apply to all governments, democratic or otherwise.

8. 1 Cor 15:27, 28; Eph 1:22; Phil 3:21, see also Ps 110:1.

9. Although the verb "submit" is absent from Eph 5:22, it is implied through the participle in Eph 5:21.

10. The other use is Acts 27:21 of obeying Paul's injunction not to sail from Crete on his shipwreck trip.

The perfect tense indicates that this is a state of appointment, from the past into the present (it remains appointed). The passive is a divine passive: *God* has done this.[11]

God's divine oversight of the world political systems accords with other points in Romans where Paul sees all things under God's sovereignty (e.g., 8:28). Paul believes that all governments are God appointees. This does not endorse their behavior any more than God approves of wayward pastors and evangelists. However, they are his appointees and have been granted the opportunity to lead by God. If they fail to uphold justice and goodness, he will see them replaced.[12] While they rule, the people are to honor them, even if they appear illegitimate. Such a pattern accords with the OT story of Israel in which Pharaoh, the nations, Assyria, Babylon, Israel herself, and Medo-Persia (cf. Cyrus) were all under God's sovereignty and being used for his purposes.[13] Despite their atrocities, they were chosen by God. Where they continued to violate God's intent, they were ultimately destroyed. The world of nations that fanned out after the flood is under God's rule, and he is moving history toward its climax.[14]

NOT RESISTING THE GOVERNMENT

In Romans 13:2, Paul draws out the consequence with *hōste*, "so then, therefore." The consequence is "whoever resists the authorities resists what God has appointed." He goes on, those who resist God's appointees will incur judgment. "Resists" in the first instance is *antitassō*, which literally means "to stand against," and so "to be hostile toward, rebel, resist."

Antitassō is used in Acts 18:6 of opposition to Paul in Corinth, of God opposing the proud (Jas 4:6; 1 Pet 5:5), and the righteous person not resisting the rich oppressor (Jas 5:6).[15] Again, it is a *tassō* term, and so it implies: to stand against the one appointed by God. It means to fail to *hypotassō*, "submit." It speaks of the very opposite of the right response: instead of submitting, one resists.

The second term for "resist" is *anthistēmi*, which is synonymous with *antitassō*, with the literal sense of "stand against." Across the NT, it is used of resisting an evildoer (Matt 5:39), opposition to believers,[16] in Romans of people resisting God's will (9:19), Paul opposing Peter (Gal 2:11), believers withstanding Satan (Eph 6:13; Jas 4:7; 1 Pet 5:9), and opposition to Paul (2 Tim 4:15). The idea is then of active opposition

---

11. "This means that no governing authority exists apart from God's will and determination." Schreiner, *Romans*, 682.

12. Two OT cases in point are the reign of Eli that was ended due to corruption (1 Sam 1:1—4:18) and Saul (1 Sam 9:1—31:6).

13. Longenecker, *Epistle*, 959 notes Jer 27:5-6; Dan 4:17, 25, 32; 5:21; Sir 10:4–5; Wis 6:3.

14. See, e.g., 2 Chr 20:6; Job 12:18; Pss 22:28; 47:7-8; 52:7; 66:7; Prov 8:14-15; Isa 34:2; 40:23; Dan 2:21, 47.

15. See Varner, *James*, 492–97 for a discussion. He considers the subject is God and that this a question, which is plausible. He lists other options.

16. See Luke 21:15; Acts 6:10; 13:8, see also 2 Tim 3:8.

to the government. "Judgment" here can be divine or through the government itself. Paul then adopts a theology of living in subjection to governments rather than in opposition. He does so "to avoid any gesture of disloyalty that might jeopardize the peaceful extension of the Christian mission."[17]

THE ROLE OF THE GOVERNMENT IN JUSTICE

Paul goes on to develop his argument further in 13:3. "Rulers" is *archōn*, which is used of Jewish leaders,[18] Satan and demons,[19] gentile leaders,[20] or legal magistrates (Luke 12:58; Acts 16:19). In Paul, he applies it to secular authorities, whether Jewish or Gentile (1 Cor 2:6, 8) and Satan (Eph 2:2). Here, it is the Roman rulers and, by implication, other leaders across the world.

They "are not a terror (*phobos*) to good conduct, but to bad." *Phobos* in Romans is used for reverence to God (3:18), fear that comes from enslavement to law (8:15), and respect. Here, this has the sense of the State instilling fear.[21] In a first-century political context like Rome, where people were imprisoned in horrific conditions, flogged, beheaded (if a citizen, as per Paul later on), and crucified (if not, as per Jesus and Peter), this can rightly be translated "terror."

"Good conduct" is literally "good works" (*agathō ergō*), and so, as elsewhere, Paul is urging believers to live in society doing good works (2:7). These are those God has prepared in advance for them, equipped them for by his word, and enabled them to do (Eph 3:10; 2 Thess 2:17; 2 Tim 3:17).[22] Similarly, in Titus 3:1, Titus is to remind the Cretans to be submissive and obedient to the ruling authorities, and "be ready for every good work." Such language indicates social action and transformation. So, where the church encounters unbelievers, they are to give ethical witness to the gospel. His point is that if believers live well and do good deeds, they will not be punished. Such a statement does not guarantee good treatment, for Jews and Romans alike often punished Christians. Nonetheless, where they did, believers are to remain submissive, responding to unbelievers, including the State authorities, with blessing, hospitality, peacefulness, good works, and love (12:14, 17–21; 13:8–10). Paul then poses a question with an answer making the same point, i.e., that if a believer wants to live without fear of those in authority, they should do what is right.

---

17. Jewett and Kotansky, *Romans*, 786.

18. See Matt 9:18, 23, 34; Luke 8:41; 14:1; 18:18; 23:13, 35; 24:20; John 3:1; 7:26, 48; 12:42; Acts 3:17; 4:5, 8; 7:27, 35; 13:27; 14:5; 23:5.

19. See Matt 12:24; Mark 3:22; John 12:31; 14:30; 16:11.

20. See Matt 20:25; Luke 11:5; Acts 4:26; 14:5; Rev 1:5.

21. According to Schreiner, *phobos* here "relates to fear of punishment by civil authorities." Schreiner, *Romans*, 683.

22. See also 2 Cor 9:8; Col 1:10; 1 Tim 2:10; 5:10; 2 Tim 2:21; Titus 1:16.

"For he is God's *servant* for your good" in Romans 13:4 employs *diakonos*, a term used of Christian ministers including Paul in Romans 15:8 and Phoebe the deacon in Romans 16:1.[23] Paul sees government authorities as God's servants, his ministers. "For your good" suggests that the government exists for the good of its citizens and should hold no fear for those who conduct themselves well. On the other hand, those who do wrong should fear (*phobos*). The reason is signaled by *gar*, "because (*gar*) he does not bear the sword in vain." "Bear" is *phoreō* meaning "to carry or bear habitually or constantly," i.e., wear as clothing (cf. Matt 11:8; John 19:5; Jas 2:3).[24] The government then is both servant and soldier on God's behalf.

"The sword" is *machaira*, the same as in Romans 8:35 of those things that cannot separate a person from Christ's love. It is the short sword rather than the longer one, the *rhomphaia*.[25] This reference to the governing authorities as servants indicates that for Paul, at least, governments function on God's behalf as a means of endorsing good behavior and punishing bad.

The use of the term "sword" in a first-century setting should surely point to a government potentially utilizing the death penalty. While this is offensive to modern sensitivities, we must remember Paul's context: the death penalty was endorsed in every society and part and parcel of life. If so, the sword would be used in extreme circumstances as a deterrent, as a means of protecting society, and where the offender's crime involved the deliberate taking of a life.

Others appropriately question this on the basis that Jesus's teaching rules this out (esp. Matt 5:38–48; Luke 6:27–36). However, the injunctions of Jesus's teaching are related to relationships *within* the kingdom and community, and in a fallen world, it seems that God utilizes governments and their force. The best examples are in the OT, where we have a succession of empires mentioned above who use the sword for and against God's people. They are agents of God's justice in the world. However, where this is abused, they will be brought down. Still, on the face of it, Romans 13:4 suggests Paul may have accepted the death penalty was a part of God's way of ordering the world. Christians themselves must not take the lives of others.[26] Such things raise questions concerning whether a Christian can have a role in the State that leads to this.

We live in a world deeply influenced by Christianity in which state and church are blurred. Even in New Zealand, where the State and church are more separate than in many nations, Christian ethics are still etched into the fabric of the political, justice, education, and social systems. As such, it is unclear how Paul would respond to a democratic context where a Christian could rule a nation and where aspects of the

---

23. See also 1 Cor 3:5; 2 Cor 3:6; 6:4; 11:23; Eph 3:7; 6:21; Phil 1:1; Col 1:7, 23, 25; 4:7; 1 Tim 3:8, 12; 4:6. See also *diakonia* in Rom 12:7; 15:31.

24. BDAG 1064. Paul also uses it of bearing an image (1 Cor 15:49).

25. Plümacher, "μάχαιρα," 2:397.

26. "Whatever degree of force is in view, Paul is saying that the state is charged with doing what Christians have just been prohibited from doing." Witherington and Hyatt, *Paul's Letter*, 314.

ethics of the kingdom have become etched into the world. Such questions Christians in mission must consider carefully, come to a gospel-informed understanding and conscience position, and live faithfully to it.

"For he is the servant of God" restates the governing authorities as God's *diakonos*, "servant," used earlier in the same verse but there with an emphasis on serving for those who do good. Here the servant of God is "the avenger to bring wrath upon those who do evil."

The term for "avenger" is *ekdikos*, meaning "to rectify wrong done to another, punishing, one who punishes."[27] Its only other use is in 1 Thessalonians 4:6 of God being the avenger or punisher of those who transgress a fellow Christian in the area of sexuality. The related verb *ekdikeō*, "to avenge, punish," is used in Romans 12:19 in Paul's appeal to the Romans not to take revenge. *Ekdikēsis* meaning "vengeance, punishment," is also used in that same verse.

In context, one must link the ideas of God's wrath and the role of the government. Believers are not to avenge themselves but trust God and the governments he has ordained to act in their defense. Thus, the role of the governing authorities is to act for the benefit of society in doing good and punishing evil.

"Wrath" is not here "God's wrath" as in some translations (e.g., ESV, NET) but stands alone (NRSV, NET ["retribution"], NASB95, NKJV, NIV). The translation "wrath" then is preferable as "God's wrath" would imply that excessive or unjust punishment is still God's wrath. If so, when Paul and Peter were killed by Nero, that should be seen as God's wrath on them. Such an idea is appalling. It is the government that is the agent of wrath in this context. Ideally, they exercise judgment as God would want. However, history shows us that often governments go beyond the appropriate response. Where it happens, it is up to God to deal with the government. And he does, for all governments, without exception, fall.

WILLING SUBMISSION TO THE GOVERNMENT

In Romans 13:5, Paul draws his conclusion (*dio*, "therefore") repeating his earlier appeal for subjection to the ruling authorities in Romans 13:1. The object of subjection here is implied, not stated (lit. "in subjection"): the governing authorities. "Must" is a strong word of necessity, *anagkē*, meaning "complete obligation."[28]

"Not only because of wrath" refers back to the previous verses, where he explained that failure to submit to the State would lead to punishment. "But because of

---

27. BDAG 301.

28. BDAG 61. Used of the necessity of temptations coming (Matt 18:7), the need to go and see a field (Luke 14:18), the necessity to preach the gospel (1 Cor 9:16), a necessary law change (Heb 7:12), the necessity to make sacrifices (Heb 7:27), the need for a death so that a will can be activated (Heb 9:16), the need for copies of heavenly things to be purified (Heb 9:23), and the need to write a letter (Jude 3). It can have the meaning "distress" (Luke 21:23; 1 Cor 7:26; 2 Cor 6:4; 12:10; 1 Thess 3:7), a necessity (1 Cor 7:37), compulsion (2 Cor 9:7; Phlm 14).

conscience" suggests that there is more than mere fear involved; a transformed mind knows this to be correct, i.e., behavior in line with the gospel, the right thing to do. Such thinking reasserts the centrality of submission to the government in Paul's mind as essential to Christian living (Titus 3:1, see also 1 Pet 2:13—3:7).

FAITHFULLY PAYING TAXES

In Romans 13:6, Paul applies the general principle of submitting to the government to the payment of taxes. Tacitus notes that AD 58 was a year in which there were ongoing complaints against taxation and collectors (*publicani, Ann.* 13).[29] It is possible then that Paul may be urging the Roman Christians not to join this movement.

"Because of this" (*dia touto gar*) recalls the previous, i.e., drawing a consequence from the central Christian truth that one must submit to governing authorities outlined above. "Pay taxes" speaks of Christians submitting to government demands for taxation. It can be imperatival, "you must pay taxes," or as is likely, it is indicative, "that is why you also pay tribute."[30]

It is on the issue of taxation that Christians would interact with the government most commonly. Rome had two main types of direct taxation. The *tributum soli* taxed the cultivated land and produce. The *tributum capitis* was a poll tax taken by tax collectors that citizens did not have to pay. In Syria, which included Israel, the *tributum capitis* was 1 percent of income. Other taxes were indirect (the *vectigalia*). These included taxing the transport of goods (*portoria*) at ports or border crossings. These ranged from 2.5 to 25 percent. It was this law that people attempted to abandon in AD 58. There was also a sales taxes with slaves charged more, a manumission tax for freed slaves, and an inheritance tax.[31] Paul is urging Christians not to resist the payment of taxes.

Paul then restates that the authorities are God's servants or ministers. This time he uses the term *leitourgos* (cf. English, liturgy), which was used of those who serve in administrative or cultic service.[32] Paul uses the term of himself in Romans 15:16, and of Epaphroditus, who delivered the gift to Paul from Philippi (Phil 2:25), while the writer of Hebrews uses it of angels and priests (Heb 1:7; 8:2). It thus parallels *diakonos* above but speaks of a special sacral role before God.

---

29. See also Suetonius, *Nero*, 10.1. "Nero had promised to abolish indirect taxes because of the abuses, but his advisors did not let him do so, which led to some general consternation. There were even open protests in Rome about such taxes when Paul wrote this letter." Witherington and Hyatt, *Paul's Letter*, 315.

30. Dunn, *Romans 9–16*, 766; Moo, *Letter to the Romans*, 820.

31. See Gill, "Taxation, Greco-Roman," 1161–64.

32. *Leitourgos* is used of a political servant (3 Matt 5:5); God's servants (LXX Pss 102:21; 103:4; Sir 7:30; Isa 61:1); servants of a king (2 Kgdms 13:18; 2 Chr 9:4), a judge (Sir 10:2), a prophet (4 Kgdms 4:43; 6:15), or of the temple (2 Esdr 7:24), and ministering priests (2 Esdr 20:40).

"Attending to this very thing" uses the term *proskartereō* meaning "attend constantly," used earlier in Romans 12:12 of believers praying persistently. "This very thing" emphasizes the central role of the government in taking tax to provide public utilities for the common good. They thus serve God in the provision of an ordered civil society.

Tax and tax collectors are frequently mentioned in the NT. They frequent the Gospel narratives, despised by the people as traitors to Rome, but were people Jesus spent time with, bringing stinging criticism. He even called one (Levi/Matthew) to be an apostle and declared a chief tax collector saved.[33] Jesus also vindicated the payment of taxes when challenged on this issue (Mark 12:13–17 and parr.). One of the accusations against Jesus was that he caused people to stop paying taxes, which is patently incorrect (Luke 23:2). Paul endorses Jesus's attitude.

Paul concludes the section on submission to the government in Romans 13:7 by urging believers to give to all what is owed. The apostle here recalls Jesus teaching in Mark 12:13–17, where the implication is that Christians give to the government what is theirs. For Paul, of course, he is obligated to give the gospel to all (cf. 1:14), believers are obligated to the Spirit and not the flesh (8:12), and gentiles are to bless the Jews with material blessings (15:27). The term *opheilē*, "obligation," is used only one other time by Paul of a man's obligation to fulfill his marital duty to his wife (1 Cor 7:3). Here Paul speaks of the general principle of honoring one's obligations.

What follows is poetic parallelism with two couplets made up of two symmetrical sayings including alliteration:

A   Tribute to whom tribute is due,
Tō to phoron ton phoron
A1 tax to whom tax is due
tō to telos to telos
B   Respect to whom respect is due,
tō to phobon ton phobon,
B2 Honor to whom honor is due
tō tēn timēn tēn timēn

This verse has all the hallmarks of a saying or an adaption thereof.[34] The appeal sums up the passage. Believers are to pay taxes and tribute where it is due. They are to show respect and honor to those authorities placed over them as God's appointees.

Essential to mission is the relationship of God's people to the governments they encounter. Paul advocates blessing, peace, hospitality, nonviolence, and yielding to the demands of the State (without violating one's primary obligation to God).

---

33. See Matt 5:46; 9:9–11; 10:3; 11:19; 17:24; 18:17; 21:31–32; Mark 2:14–16; 12:14; Luke 3:12; 5:27–30; 7:29, 34; 15:1; 18:10–13; 19:2.

34. See Jewett and Kotansky, *Romans*, 801 for a range of similar sayings from the classical world (Menander, *Mon.* 1.3.7; Hesiod, *Op.* 349; Diogenes Laertius, *Lives.* 1.785; 3.83).

Part Three: Romans and the Proclamation of the Gospel

ABSOLUTE OR QUALIFIED ALLEGIANCE TO THE GOVERNMENT?

Is the compliance that Paul endorses absolute allegiance to the government, come what may? Clearly it is not, for by this stage of Romans, Paul has written eleven chapters full of reminders that God is supreme; Jesus is Messiah, the Son of God, and Lord of the world (1:4); and believers are to be led by the Spirit (8:14).[35] God is King, and Jesus is enthroned at his right hand, subjugating God's opponents (8:34). As such, a believer's allegiance is first to God, Christ as Lord, and the Spirit's direction, not to Caesar or any other governing authorities.

Paul has bemoaned idolatry whereby people fail to honor God *as* God, worshiping created things rather than the Creator (1:21–25, 30). They fail to seek God and fear him (3:11, 18, 23). To place governing authorities and the State above God is idolatry. Some degree of nationalism has its place, but it can easily elide into deifying the State at the expense of God. God becomes harnessed to nationalism, which is dangerous as state-endorsed violence can be legitimized. Believers will ultimately face God in eternal judgment, and he is their supreme ruler (2:3, 5–16; 3:19). To place the government and state above God is to dishonor him and blaspheme him among the nations (2:23–24).

Salvation is found through faith in Christ, and this has priority over all other allegiances (3:22). The life of the believer is lived to God (6:10–11, 13). They live obediently to him as his slaves bearing fruit to him by the Spirit (6:17, 22; 7:4, 6). This is the same as living led by the Spirit, not merely the whims of political powers (8:4–14). They know they will inherit the world when it is set free from its bondage to corruption (8:17–23). This freedom includes liberation from the corrupt tyrannies of oppressive powers.

As those who have acknowledged that Jesus Christ is Lord (10:9, 10), allegiance to him takes priority over all allegiances, whether one's own family, spouse, church leaders, or political authorities. Christians are summoned to present their bodies to God as living sacrifices refusing to be governed by the mindsets of their age (12:1–2). This includes rejecting the deification of the State and its leaders. Hyper-nationalism, ethnocentrism, and worship of the government in any sense is rejected. Instead, believers are to willingly and determinedly "serve the Lord as his slaves" (12:11, my translation).

Yet, believers are to recognize that the world is currently ruled by political regimes that God uses in his governance of the world (13:1–7). Hence, a believer can submit willingly to the government and its many authorities in as much as the State does not summon them to violate the core aspects of their allegiance to God: exclusive worship of the Triune God, absolute trust in him, loving one another, love for others, and giving witness to him before others.

---

35. "Caesar should be honoured but not worshiped." Green, *Evangelism*, 49.

The State and Mission

Where the government becomes an agent of persecution and seeks to demand that believers worship other gods, political rulers, or a nation itself, above God, believers can resist to the extent of refusing. Such resistance is endorsed in Revelation 13. However, they should never resist with violence; rather, they are prepared to die for their faith, they bless rather than curse their persecutors, they pray for the governing authorities (1 Tim 2:1–2), live at peace with them as best able, practice hospitality to them, never retaliate against them, and respond to their evil with good (12:13, 18–21). If they are in democratic situations, they should participate in the political system seeking to see the government lead as God would wish them to. If they are led into politics or the civil service, they should participate, without compromising their primary allegiance to God. Where their vocations bring them into advocacy or engagement with government structures, they should participate with the ethics of the gospel. Christian organizations can partner with government agencies. However, where there are corrupted governments, it is up to God to deal with them as he does.[36]

God acts in history to deal with governments as seen throughout the OT (above). In the NT, it is also reflected when Rome demolished Israel after rejecting her Messiah, as Jesus predicted (Mark 13:1–2 and parr.). It is demonstrated when Herod Agrippa I died after being declared a god (Acts 12:22–23). Soon after the writing of Romans, it will happen again when Nero will go berserk, exile and kill off opponents, and persecute Christians horrifically (*Annals* 15.44). Ultimately, in AD 68, utterly deserted, he will take his own life ending the Julio-Claudian dynasty.[37] Eventually, the Roman empire would fall.

As Paul says, God is in control of history and works it out for good for his people (8:28). Just as he did with Pharaoh at the time of the Exodus, God is raising governments of his purposes, so that ultimately his name is proclaimed in the world (9:17; Exod 9:16). God will carry out his sentence upon the earth as he sees fit (9:28; Isa 10:23). Believers are to leave that to him (12:19; Deut 32:35). God has the complex job of maintaining order across the world and in the lives of around eight billion people

---

36. Chris Wright: "They were to be good citizens and pay their taxes, but also to recall that God's mandate to the state authorities . . . was to do justice, punish wickedness and reward goodness. . . . They accepted that political authorities were there by God's appointment, but they would not have forgotten the words of the prophets, who declared that governments that perverted justice stood under God's ultimate judgment (e.g., Jer 22:1–4).

37. See Simmons, "Nero, Emperor, History of in the Primary Sources," esp. "The Burning of Rome" and "Nero's Final Years and Demise." Having earlier killed off three wives, in AD 65, after two assassination attempts, Nero sought to kill his family and closest allies. He poisoned Burrus, induced Seneca to commit suicide, and ensured the death of Seneca's brother Gallio (Acts 18:12–17). In AD 67, revolts sprang up, and Nero considered poisoning the whole Senate and releasing wild animals into the streets to terrorize people. He increased taxes for war. In AD 68, having lost control and being deserted and alone with his aides who refused to take his life for him, he stabbed himself in the throat and then Epaphroditus, his secretary, finished him off. For Paul, no doubt this was all under God's dominion, and this ended the Julio-Claudian reign.

(and growing). His purposes are beyond us, and his people trust him as he moves the world to its consummation and the age to come.

IMPLICATIONS FOR MISSION

Such a view of the government has enormous implications for mission. On the one hand, converts are to be taught to give their primary allegiance to God and his Son alone. Yet, they should also be urged to be compliant to the State as far as they are not called on to compromise their fundamental allegiance to God and Christ. In the meantime, they continue to give witness to God in their attitudes (mercy, grace, love, warmth), their actions (good deeds, hospitality, peacefulness), and their words (sharing the gospel with words full of grace and seasoned with salt, Col 4:5).

Living in the world this way is a brilliant missional strategy. While it is true the church can be too hesitant to take a stand against State oppression, equally, the church can too often get caught up in worldly politics, believing that they should seek solutions to the world's ills by involving themselves in matters of government. Of course, God raises up Christian politicians and civil servants, indeed one is mentioned in Romans; Erastus, the city treasurer (16:23). Yet, it will be God that brings the transformation of the world (through his people and governments). We should participate in the political systems as invited. We can partner with state social agencies to bring good in the world. Yet, we should not imagine that we can bring God's kingdom in through them. God will do this by his Spirit through his people and their influence.

The brilliance of God's stratagem is that it is a heart-based approach, as the politics of his kingdom involves subjects bowing the knee willingly and becoming heavenly citizens on earth (Eph 2:19; Phil 1:27; 3:20). Their hearts and minds are transformed by the Spirit, they cast influence as ambassadors of Christ and ministers of reconciliation (2 Cor 5:18, 20; Eph 6:20). As they show God's mercy to the world, do good works, participate with God's ethics in the various structures of the world, and share their faith, so that others yield. New converts are added, resources are combined, and the influence of the kingdom grows. Soon, villages, suburbs, cities, regions, countries, and the world is renewed. May it be!

Yet, then danger sets in, because as the church gains political power, the church can easily forget its place and, with an over-realized political theology, mistakenly think they run the world or can bring God's kingdom into the present. Such is the story of Christendom, where Christianity grew arrogant and became warped. God still works in history and has acted to dismantle this tenuous alliance of church and state since the Enlightenment.

Where Christendom still flourishes, as in some parts of the West today, many people in churches are at best nominal Christians, and the Christian distinctive is lost. Some are so syncretized in their faith, that they are no longer God's people even though they claim to be Christians. Many have ceased to be believers at all, having thrown off the Judeo-Christian ethic. Then, believing they have a divine right to run the world through governments, the church fights and grapples to retain control, falsely thinking they should have pride of place in the nation and run things. They forget that nations rise and fall, and yet it is God who is in control. Sometimes, we must let the heathen do what the heathen want to do. We cannot impose our ethic by force; our weapons are love, persuasion, the gospel, and good works.[38]

The believer's call is never to violate the principles of Romans 12—13: love our enemies, bless them, live at peace with them, never avenge ourselves, show hospitality to others, and respect, honor, submit to those given authority by God, and love all, without violating our allegiance to God. If we get involved in politics, the civil service, or partner with state organizations (as Erastus did at the time of Romans), we must think deeply about how we do so, yielding to the imperatives of the Sermon on the Mount and Plain (Matt 5–7; Luke 6:20–49) and Romans 12 while living within the truth of Romans 13 and Jesus as Lord. We must judge at which point the call to refuse to yield comes into play, as in Revelation 13.

What follows in Romans 13:8–14 builds on this. Believers are to show love to all others (13:8–10). They are not to participate in the sins of the heathen: revelry, substance abuse, sexual immorality, rivalry, and envy (we could add many more). As Christian soldiers, they are to don the armor of light, repudiating the darkness. Their armor is Jesus, and they live by the Spirit, not the flesh and its gross desires. They live this way individually, in marriages, bringing children up in the Lord, in their churches, in their wider communities, cities, nations, and the world. God changes the world from the inside out as people bow the knee.

In the meantime, believers must think deeply in their particular political situation and act as led by God. As Longenecker says of this passage,

> Paul sets out in abbreviated form and somewhat cryptic fashion the two major human factors that must come into play in all the decisions and practices of every believer in Jesus: (1) an evaluation of the situation in which one finds oneself (here, that of rising societal and political turmoil), and (2) the guidance provided by one's own transformed and renewed mind to think and act appropriately—with such a transformed and renewed mind brought about in a person's life by the Holy Spirit.[39]

---

38. See, e.g., 2 Cor 6:3–10; 10:1–6; 1 Thess 5:8; Eph 6:10–17.
39. Longenecker, *Epistle*, 966.

25

Culture and Cross-Cultural Mission

AT ONE LEVEL, ROMANS IS all about justification by faith and not works. It reinforces that no one can be justified before God by observing the law or any works for that matter. This message against works-righteousness is certainly how Luther and many other Protestants have read Romans and Galatians since his day. Yet, there is another side to Romans that the New Perspective on Paul has drawn to our attention: its message against all forms of ethnocentricism and racism and its summons to multiculturalism and better, interculturalism.

THE PERSPECTIVES ON PAUL AND THE LAW AND CULTURE

The Old Perspective on Paul sees the focus of Romans and Galatians as a critique of Jewish reliance on the law for righteousness. Luther saw in Romans and Galatians something similar to his battle with the Roman Catholic church with its indulgences. Similarly, Augustine combatted Pelagius's false ideas of work-righteousness a millennium prior.

The New Perspective on Paul has brought Romans and Galatians back to the context in which they were written.[1] Christianity began as a branch of Judaism.[2] Second Temple Judaism was deeply concerned that Jews were faithful to God via the law, not to *gain* righteous standing, but to *maintain* it (covenantal nomism). Gentiles could become Jews, Judaize, by placing their trust in Israel's God and going through a set of rituals, including ritual washing and circumcision (if male), for inclusion. Then, they maintained their covenantal standing through the observation of the intricacies of Jewish law and particularly boundary markers: calendric observance, especially the Sabbath, circumcision of males, food laws, and separation to maintain ritual purity.

---

1. See Schreiner, 40 *Questions about Christians and Biblical Law*, 34–40. For a fuller summary, see Yinger, *New Perspective on Paul*; Westerholm, *Perspectives Old and New on Paul*.

2. See the response of Gallio in Corinth (Acts 18:14).

CULTURE AND CROSS-CULTURAL MISSION

The first Christians were all Jews, and they continued to live faithful to the Torah. Jesus challenged aspects of it, especially including Sabbath observance,[3] ritual washing, and eating protocols.[4] As such, the first church remained very Jewish. It was likely assumed up to the Cornelius event (Acts 10—11) that circumcision was a prerequisite for inclusion in God's people. This assumption is demonstrated in the shock among Peter and the other Jewish believers when the Spirit fell on gentiles—they had not worked out the cultural implications of the gospel (Acts 10:45–46).

It was Paul who worked out the implications of the gospel for obedience to the law. He preached a gospel of God's gracious offer of justification to be received by faith and faith alone (3:22; 5:1). He recognized that the implication of Jesus's death for sin is that it is his work that saves, and a human only has to believe in him for salvation. He preached this as he engaged in mission.

Some other Jewish Christians saw removing the requirements of circumcision and law-observance as a violation of God's revelation to them through Moses and could not grasp this. So, we read in Acts 15:1 that "some men came down from Judea and were teaching the brothers,"[5] and "[u]nless you are circumcised according to the custom of Moses, you cannot be saved." We read in Acts 15:5 that some of these were Pharisees who put it this way: "It is necessary to circumcise them and to order them to keep the law of Moses."

Likely, such people had also traveled through the churches Paul and Barnabas had planted on his first Antiochian mission (Gal 1:6; 5:10). We can discern from Galatians that they were concerned about at least circumcision,[6] Jews eating with gentiles (Gal 2:11–14), and calendric observance (Gal 4:10). With their zeal for righteousness through the law, they likely advocated a range of other things, but we cannot be sure.[7]

By demanding circumcision and yielding to the laws of Moses, they were invoking two heresies. The first false idea is that salvation is gained not merely through faith, but obedience to the works of the law or any works for that matter (cf. Eph 2:8–9). This requirement is what Augustine and Luther rightly recognized and what conservative Protestantism has known ever since.

However, there is another distortion of the gospel that is equally bad. That is, by demanding Mosaic law, one is demanding that people *Judaize* (Gal 2:14), i.e., convert

---

3. Matt 12:1–12; Mark 2:23—3:4; Luke 6:1–9; 13:10–17; 14:1–6; John 5:1–18; 7:22–23; 9:1–40

4. Mark 7:1–23 and parr. At the two feeding miracles, there is no concern for cleanliness (Mark 6:30–44; 8:1–10 and parr.).

5. I have left this as masculine as circumcision is a male issue.

6. See Gal 2:3, 12; 5:2–4, 6; 6:12, 15.

7. While there is much debate over "works of the law" (3:20, 28; Gal 2:16 [3x]; 3:2, 5, 10) being merely boundary markers, as Moo, *Galatians*, 158–60, argues, this is better understood as "observing the law" in its fullest sense. He goes on: "The Reformers may have moved too quickly from this phrase to general theological conclusions about 'works'" (p. 160). Rightly he also says, "many contemporary interpreters go too far in the other direction when they insist that the phrase is "irreducibly concrete," referring *only* to the Torah, the law of Moses.

to Judaism and its complex culture. By doing so, the Judaizers were creating an elitist Christianity where there is a superior culture and to which other cultures must conform. Judaizing, inadvertently perhaps, introduces racism and ethnocentrism into the heart of the Christian faith. A gentile of whatever culture is forced to abandon large parts of their culture and become a Jew to be saved. Expecting people to Judaize privileges the Jewish culture and its protocols.

Moreover, by making circumcision a central issue, one relegates women in the church as it is all about men and their phalluses. Furthermore, focusing on race and gender matters brings all forms of elitism into view which may be why Paul includes the three social distinctions of race, gender, and social status in Galatians 3:28.

Western theology, dominated by white male theologians (like me), living in European dominated cultures, are (imperceptibly in many instances) participants in the advantages of colonialism because of their forebears and are often blind to their privilege, tacit racism, and unconscious sexism. Men like me have, for a long time, struggled to recognize these things. Often, due to this blindness, many of us who are evangelical in our theology vehemently hold onto the Old Perspective, resisting the insights of the New. So, while I remain passionate for the core understandings of the Old Perspective, if that is all we focus on, Christians miss out on the glorious corrective that has come through the New Perspective. Paul is not just vehement about grace and faith for justification and salvation rather than achieving this by any form of doing (a works soteriology). He was equally vociferous in his resistance to *any* notions of cultural and ethnic supremacy. He rejects both Jewish election presumption and arrogance (Judaizing, 2:1–5, 17–29), and the converse—gentiles claiming election priority over Jews (see 11:17–24).

While the New Perspective has been rightly critiqued for narrowing the Judaizing controversy into a merely cultural and Torah debate (which it is, but is so much more),[8] it has brought a great gift to the church. It has helped the church recognize that the Judaizers in their syncretistic demands were not merely introducing a flawed works theology but were creating a cultural heresy. They were inadvertently demanding that every gentile person subordinate themselves to the Jewish culture as understood in Second Temple Judaism. By doing so, the church would always have a dominant culture. What is more, the cultural and works heresies are fused in the questions with which the early church was grappling. We can also take note of the dangers this poses in terms of sexism, classism, and other forms of elitism.[9] We can work through the implications of these things for our setting.

---

8. See especially the twin books Carson et al., *Complexities of Second Temple Judaism*; Carson et al., *Paradoxes of Paul*.

9. These include ageism and generationalism (a big problem in western cultures).

PAUL'S RESPONSES

Three great responses to the problem of Judaizing were all catalyzed by Paul. The first is Galatians, the second is the Jerusalem Council, and the third Romans.

Galatians

The first response is Galatians, written around AD 47, before Acts 15 and the Jerusalem Council, after Judaizers had attacked Antioch and his new Galatian churches telling them what Luke records in Acts 15:1.[10] In this letter, full of passion, Paul fervently defends justification by faith (esp. Gal 2:11; 3:24). Yet, sprinkled through the letter are comments that draw out the cultural, gender, and social class implications of the problem.[11]

Paul notes that the Greek Titus did not need to be circumcised in Jerusalem and expresses his passionate resistance to the Judaizers in Jerusalem, because "God shows no partiality" (Gal 2:3–6). He critiques Peter for inadvertently forcing gentiles to Judaize by withdrawing from table fellowship with the uncircumcised (Gal 2:11–14). He boldly declares that in Christ Jesus "[t]here is neither Jew nor Greek, there is neither slave nor free, there is no male and female, for [the Galatians] are all one in Christ Jesus" (Gal 3:28). This does not destroy the distinctives of race, gender, and social class, but "[w]hat are obliterated are the barriers formed by these differences and the relative value and status among the people of God based on their differences."[12]

In Galatians 5:1—6:10, he urges the Galatians who have put on Christ (Gal 3:27) and who have received the Spirit by faith (Gal 3:2, 5), to live by the culture of the kingdom of God (Gal 5:21). The culture of God's people is premised on faith producing love, service, living the inside out life of virtue by the Spirit and not in conformity to the flesh, mutual support, the humble and gentle restoration of the sinner, humility, self-examination, sowing to please the Spirit, and perseverance in doing good to all people (Gal 5:1—6:10). The basis of the new creation is not a worldly culture imposed knowingly or unwittingly on others, but Christoformity by the power of the Spirit.[13]

---

10. On this date for Galatians, see Keown, *Galatians*, 16–32, where I agree with others that Galatians 2:1–10 aligns with Acts 11:26–30. See Longenecker, *Galatians*, lxi–lxxxviii.

11. "At the heart of Paul's defence is a clarification of what 'justification by faith' truly means. For Paul, once this doctrine was clearly understood, then the equal standing of all believers (by faith alone) before God would become clear as well." Hays, *From Every People and Nation*, 182–83.

12. Hays, *From Every People and Nation*, 186. Similarly, Bauckham: "When Paul states that in Christ there is no longer Jew, Greek, barbarian or Scythian (Colossians 3:11), what he denies is cultural privilege, not cultural diversity." Bauckham, *Bible and Mission*, 110.

13. Richard Hays: "Paul holds forth the vision of a community of faith in which all are one in Christ. . . . This is not merely a matter of an isolated slogan in Gal 3:28; it is a central theme of the letter as a whole. Jews and Gentiles are no longer divided because Christ's death brought us together. Therefore, all manifestations of racial and ethnic divisiveness are betrayals of 'the truth of the gospel.' Galatians is one of the canon's most powerful witnesses against a cultural imperialism that excluded

Part Three: Romans and the Proclamation of the Gospel

The Jerusalem Council

Just after Galatians, in AD 48–49,[14] the Jerusalem Council, made up of Paul, Barnabas, Judaizers, and Jerusalem church leaders, met to conclusively deal with the issue for the whole church. As noted above, Jewish Pharisees who accepted Jesus were advocating gentile Christians Judaize (Acts 15:1–5). No doubt horrified by their cancerous ideas that violate salvation by grace through faith *and the egalitarianism of the gospel*, Paul and Barnabas went to discuss the matter with the leaders of the Jerusalem church. They passionately defended their view.

Notably, Peter sided with Paul and Barnabas partly based on seeing the Spirit fall on the family of Cornelius. God makes no such legal demands on new gentile converts, but he gives himself to Jew and gentile alike by grace through faith (Acts 15:6–11). James agreed, and it was ruled that the gentiles should not be troubled to obey the law and circumcision (Acts 15:19). To facilitate church relationships and maintain Jewish mission, certain accommodations were made, but the gospel of grace was endorsed (Acts 15:19–35).

Romans

The third of Paul's outstanding contributions to this matter is Romans. It is a comprehensive articulation of the gospel of justification by faith for Rome and future mission. One of its challenges is its summons to all humankind that they are in the same place before God.

God is God of gentiles and Jews alike (3:29). They are all called on the same basis (9:24). Both cultural groupings are God-created (1 Cor 8:6), are both sinful, and are both justified through faith in Jesus Christ (3:22–23). There is a certain order in the exercise of God's wrath, his justification, and the giving of glory: "to the Jew first and also to the Greek" (1:16; 2:9, 10). However, this is not about status. It is merely that God called Israel to him, and they were his chosen and adopted people whom he blessed (3:1–2; 9:1–5). From them came the Messiah, God over all (9:5). Salvation came from Israel and was offered to Israel *first* as he and his disciples preached among them (10:14–21).[15] Now, this salvation is being preached to the nations and people are submitting to his lordship through the obedience of believing the word (1:5, 13; 15:18). Salvation and spiritual riches have come to them (11:11, 12; 15:27).

As in Galatians, this God does not show favoritism (2:11). There is no room in the people of God for racist or ethnocentric attitudes. There is a place for cultural

---

anyone from fellowship on the basis of criteria not rooted in the gospel." Hays, "Galatians," 195–96.

14. Based on an Acts chronology, where Acts 11:27–30 = Galatians 2:1–10. See Alexander, "Chronology of Paul," 117, 119, 122.

15. "That the Jews were the first to hear the Gospel is to Paul more than a fact of history." Barrett, *Epistle to the Romans*, 29.

differences, which are a product of the diverse and unique peoples of the word.[16] However, believers from different cultural settings are to welcome one another as God has welcomed them (14:1, 3, 18). They are not to be divided over such small cultural things. They are to live to their consciences before the Lord over small things like eating and holy days (14:3, 5–6). Knowing each person will have to give account before God, they are not to write each other off as they judge one another on small cultural points of difference (14:4, 10–12).

They are to live with an attitude of gratitude to the Lord (14:6). Love should rule their hearts, constraining their liberty to live by their culture where it causes offense (14:11–16, 20–23). Similarly, they are to be characterized by justice, peace, and joy in the Spirit despite their differences (14:17). Together, they are to serve God, knowing they are all accepted by him, approved by people, and pursue peace and mutual edification (14:18–19).

Those who fully understand the freedom they have in Christ are to lovingly serve and support those whose understanding is weaker (15:1). Accommodating others is the standpoint of the Jerusalem Council letter, which calls on the gentiles to condition their freedoms for Jewish believers locked up in their culture (Acts 15:19–20, 28–29).[17] Each member of the church is to live to build up their brothers and sisters, prepared to compromise on such things (15:2). We see this kind of attitude in 1 Corinthians 8, where believers who understand that food sacrificed to idols can be eaten (cf. Ps 24:1) but are encouraged to not eat if it may offend others (1 Cor 8:7–13).

Their ultimate example is Christ, who did not please himself but took on himself human reproach (15:3). The upshot is living in harmony, enabled by God (15:5). Their church life is punctuated by Jew and gentile praising God with one voice (15:6). Jews and gentiles are to welcome one another as Christ welcomed them, and so bring God glory (15:7). He came as a servant to his people so that gentiles from the world's cultures would worship the God of mercy (15:8).

The glorious good news is that God's vision of people of every nation and culture coming together in worship is coming to pass (15:8–12). They receive the same Spirit, who fills them with joy, peace, and hope (15:13). The gentiles are a holy offering to God (15:16), along with believing Jews. They are coming to the same obedience of faith seen in Abraham and the saints of old (15:18). Having shared in the spiritual blessings of the Jewish Messiah, Jesus Christ, they are now sharing their material

---

16. It is important to note that Gal 3:28 is preceded by Gal 3:27, where Paul says that believers baptized in the Spirit "have put on Christ" (cf. 13:14). Within the "clothing of Christ," they are still male and female, Jew or gentile, slave or free. However, their differing genders, cultures, and social statuses are now in Christ. Their lives are hidden in Christ (Col 3:2).

17. The only one of the four accommodations that transcends culture across the NT is the injunction against sexual immorality. Such a prohibition is found across the biblical narrative. The others are cultural. Paul, himself, does not appear to have a problem with eating food sacrificed to idols, meat with blood, or meat from strangled animals (1 Cor 8:1–13, 10:23–30). Paul has significant issues with sexual immorality (see part three, chapter 20).

resources with Jews in need (15:27). Little wonder Paul cries out, "May the God of peace be with you all. Amen" (15:33).

As discussed, the people named in Romans represent a multicultural community. Christ obviously was a Jewish man (9:5).[18] Men and women from Israel's past are mentioned favorably, clearly seen by Paul as God's people who will be raised in the eschaton. Jesus is a descendant of David (1:3), whose writings are referenced through the letter (4:6–8; 11:9).[19] Yet, he stresses that Abraham was a gentile when God called him, and only later circumcised (4:9–12). He mentions "the patriarchs" (9:5) and names Isaac (9:7, 10), Sarah (9:9), Rebekah (9:10), Jacob (9:13),[20] Moses and his writings,[21] Hosea (9:25–26),[22] Isaiah,[23] the sons of Korah,[24] Malachi,[25] Joel,[26] Habakkuk,[27] Job,[28] Solomon,[29] Elijah (11:2), the 7000 unnamed righteous men of Israel (11:5), and other OT writers.[30] These saints, others of faith prior to Christ, Paul, and the Jews named in Romans 16, constitute the olive tree of God's people of faith from creation into which gentiles are grafted (11:16–24).

Also discussed earlier of Paul's vision for social transformation (part three, chapter 20), Paul assumes slavery language of believers, and many of those named in Romans 16 are slave names. Where gender is concerned, the spiritual gifts lack any gender bias (12:4–8), and Paul's vision of evangelization does not preference men over

---

18. Paul also mentions Adam in 5:14 but only as a type of the one to come, Christ. It is unclear what Paul thought of his eternal destiny, although as the father of sin through whom death came, it is probable his view was negative (although we cannot be sure).

19. See also 2:6 = Ps 62:12; 3:4 = Pss 51:4; 3:13a = Ps 5:9; 3:13b = Ps 140:3; 3:18 = Ps 36:1; 3:20 = Ps 143:2; 10:18 = Ps 19:4; 11:9–10 = Ps 69:22–23; 15:4 = Ps 69:9; 15:9 = Ps 18:49; 2 Sam 22:50.

20. He refers to Esau and says God hates him, citing Mal 1:2–3. This should not be misconstrued as God's judgment on Esau, but the passage speaks of God's sovereign choice to continue the line of promise through Jacob the younger. Esau's eternal fate is up to God.

21. See 5:14; 9:15; 10:5, 19. Remembering also that Moses was considered the writer of the Pentateuch in Judaism, hence, references to the Pentateuch refer to him: 4:3, 9, 22 = Gen 15:6; 4:17 = Gen 17:5; 4:18 = Gen 15:5; 7:7 = Exod 20:17/Deut 5:21; 9:7 = Gen 21:12; 9:12 = Gen 25:23; 9:9 = Gen 18:10, 14; 9:15 = Exod 33:19; 9:17 = Exod 9:16; 10:5 = Lev 18:5; 10:6–8 = Deut 9:4 + 30:12–14; 10:19 = Deut 32:21; 11:8 = Deut 9:4; 13:9a = Deut 5:17–21/Exod 20:13–17; 13:9b = Lev 19:18; 12:19 = Deut 32:35; 15:10 = Deut 32:43.

22. See 9:25 = Hos 2:23 (2:25 LXX); 9:26 = Hos 1:10 (2:1 LXX).

23. Isaiah is named in 9:27, 29; 10:16, 20; 15:12. See also 2:24 = Isa 52:5; 3:15–17 = Isa 59:7–8; 9:20 = Isa 29:16 (45:9); 9:27–28 = Isa 10:22–23 (+ 29:10); 9:29 = Isa 1:9; 9:33 = Isa 8:14 + 28:16; 10:11 = Isa 28:16; 10:15 = Isa 52:7; 10:16 = Isa 53:1; 10:21–22 = Isa 65:1–2; 11:8 = Isa 29:10; 11:34 = Isa 40:13; 14:11 = Isa 45:23; 15:12 = Isa 11:10; 11:26–27a = Isa 59:20–21; 11:27b = Isa 27:9; 15:21 = Isa 52:15.

24. See 8:36 = Ps 44:22.

25. See 9:13 = Mal 1:2–3.

26. See 10:13 = Joel 2:32 (3:5 LXX).

27. See 1:17 = Hab 2:4.

28. See 11:35 = Job 41:11 (41:3 LXX).

29. Considering Solomon was seen as the writer of Proverbs in Jewish tradition, see 12:20 = Prov 25:21–22.

30. See also 3:14 = Ps 10:7 (9:28 LXX); 11:3 = 1 Kgs 19:10; 11:4 = 1 Kgs 19:18; 15:11 = Ps 117:1.

women. He mentions godly women, Sarah and Rebekah (9:9–10). Phoebe is a deacon, patroness, and letter-bearer to Rome (16:1-2). With Aquila, Prisca is a risk-taking coworker and church hostess (16:3, cf. vv. 6, 12). Junia is an apostle with Andronicus (16:7), and Mary, Tryphaena, Tryphosa, and Persis labor in the Lord (16:6, 12).

The Asian convert Epaenetus is mentioned (16:5), as are the Corinthians with Greek names, Phoebe (16:1-2), Gaius, and the politician Erastus (16:23), along with some with Roman names like Tertius (16:22) and Quartus (16:23). Some named in Rome are also Latin (Prisca, Aquila,[31] Junia, Ampliatus, Urbanus, Rufus, Julia). Several are Jewish (Mary, Herodian).[32] Many are Greek (Phoebe, Epaenetus, Andronicus, Stachys, Apelles, Aristobulus, Narcissus, Tryphaena, Tryphosa, Asyncritus, Phlegon, Hermes, Hermas, Patrobas, Philologus, Nereus, Olympas). One has a Greek-Persian name (Persis). These names speak of a multiethnic community in Rome that Paul wants to highlight.

Paul is also raising money from gentiles for a Jewish community in Rome from Asia, Macedonia, and Achaia (15:26-32). He wants Spaniards to be a part of this international community of believers (15:24, 28). He is obligated to the whole horde of the world's barbarians, and his vision is truly global and multicultural (1:14). No doubt he imagined the Germanic peoples and those to the east joining God's people in the future.

As in Galatians 5:1—6:10 and in other paraenetic passages,[33] Paul gives a rich vision of the culture of the kingdom in Romans 12—13. He envisages a people clothed in Christ, their races, ethnicities, languages, and cultures not eradicated, but subsumed in something more extraordinary; namely, cruciform love. Their minds are not to be shaped by the racism of their day where the world was divided Jew and gentile, Greek and barbarian, but they are now one in Christ.[34] They are to give themselves as living sacrifices, suffering and serving together in humility, love, goodness, mutual honor, zeal, hopefulness, patience, prayerfulness, generosity, harmony, joy, empathy, peacefulness, and hospitality.

As has been discussed (see part three, chapter 21), the Greek for hospitality is *philoxenia*, meaning literally "the love of strangers," and so speaks of being welcome to all, Christian and unbeliever alike (12:13, 20). Those outside the church are never to be met with violence or retribution, but welcome, blessing, and generous hospitality (12:14, 19–20). The core virtue that should shape their lives is love (13:8–10). As Gaius functioned as a *xenos* (host) welcoming the *xenos* (stranger) Paul (16:23), they are to be *xenos* to *xenos* as they welcome one another.

---

31. However, these two are likely Jews. Lampe, "Roman Christians of Romans 16," 225–26.

32. But see Lampe, who notes that Maria may be a gentile as it was a Latin *nomen*. Similarly, the names Rufus and Julia are found in Jewish inscriptions. Etymology where names are concerned is not an exact means of recognizing ethnicity. Lampe, "Roman Christians of Romans 16," 225.

33. See especially 1 Cor 12:13 and Col 3:11.

34. On the ethnic background to the NT, see Hays, *From Every People and Nation*, 157–80.

PART THREE: ROMANS AND THE PROCLAMATION OF THE GOSPEL

The gospel vision of Romans has as its end goal the people of God as one without social prejudice based on race, culture, gender, and social status. Still, it is not a completely open-ended hospitality. As formerly discussed, it does not go as far as accepting those who teach falsely (e.g., 16:17), unrepentantly engage in sexual relationships outside of marriage,[35] or cause divisions (16:17; Titus 3:10–11).[36] Still, God's people are to show all people love, do good to all people, and share Christ with them. Aside from a few extreme exceptions, all are welcome to God's table to dine, and there the strong bear with the weak in love.

ROMANS AND CROSS-CULTURAL MISSION

No discussion of mission and culture can neglect the idea of cross-cultural mission. Romans is premised on cross-cultural mission. It features Paul, a Jewish Pharisee-now-Christian missionary, born in Tarsus in Cilicia; now on yet another journey from Syria to churches he planted across ancient Asia, Macedonia, and Greece; writing to a cosmopolitan church in Italy! Furthermore, his present trip is to gather monetary gifts for a church in Jerusalem, the center of Judea in Israel. Moreover, he wants next to come to Rome and onto Spain. The backstory to Romans *is* cross-cultural mission.

Paul's Cross-Cultural Mission

It was Paul who God used to catalyze his church into cross-cultural mission. He was specifically charged to take the gospel beyond his people, the Israelites. He was well aware of this summons to cross cultures to the gentiles.[37] As Terry et al. say, "As clearly as [Hudson] Taylor understood the Lord to say, 'Go to China,' Paul understood that he was sent as a missionary to a people other than his own."[38] He was sent to invite the gentiles to the same obedience of faith as he had believed meeting Christ on the Damascus Road. Just as Jesus invited Jewish women and men to join his movement and enter his kingdom, Paul sought to do for the world.

He fulfilled this call wholeheartedly (1:9), engaging in three decades of international evangelism, preaching and planting churches in Arabia (Gal 1:17), from Jerusalem to the Adriatic Sea (15:19), and later declaring the kingdom in Rome (Acts 28:29–31). He desired to go to Spain (15:24, 28), but we are unsure he did. Others have followed and established the faith where Paul could not go. His vision was for

---

35. See 1:24–27; 7:1–5; 13:13, cf. 1 Cor 5.

36. See part three, chapter 20.

37. See 1:13; 11:11–13; 15:9, 16, 18; Gal 1:16; 2:2, 7–10; Eph 3:8; Col 1:27; 1 Thess 2:16; Acts 9:15; 22:21; 26:17, 20, 23 (cf. Isa 49:6). O'Brien, *Consumed with Passion*, 46 notes that Paul "understood his role to be that of completing the Servant's task by taking the light of the gospel 'to the nations.'" I would replace "completing" with "continuing" as Paul was under no illusions that he would not complete it in his lifetime. See Keown, "Imminent Parousia and Christian Mission," 242–63.

38. Terry et al., *Missiology*, 86.

all humankind to hear the gospel. He took the mission-vision of Jesus and put it into action.

The initial period of cross-cultural missions continued for some centuries after Paul's death. While many other parts of Europe remained resistant to Christianity,[39] by the time of Constantine (AD 311), the church was established in large portions of the Roman Empire. After this, the impulse to international cross-cultural mission continued into areas resistant to Christianity.[40]

When Europeans encountered the Americas and Oceania and their peoples, a new period of mission gained momentum.[41] With Christianity in its various denominational forms as their state religions, European nations set about both colonizing and evangelizing the new worlds. This colonial and evangelistic zeal included some going to regions known to the early Christians, yet never really evangelized with great effect, e.g., India, China, Japan, and Korea. Soon, Christianity was established in the Americas, Oceania, South Korea, and in China (albeit often suppressed).

After the failure of "civilization" seen in the World Wars of the last century, we have moved into the postcolonial era. As the influence of Western missionaries has receded in many nations, we have seen a shift in the balance of Christianity away from the West to the majority world. Now Christianity has waned in the West. The overwhelming majority of Christians are from non-Western nations.[42] The church is now genuinely multicultural.

Meanwhile, now in the period of post-colonization, with colonization and the imposition of Christianity and European cultures the subject of immense scrutiny and critique, the Western church has, to a large extent, lost its confidence in cross-cultural mission, uncertain as to how to push ahead. They are also devoting more of their attention to survival and in some instances, evangelizing their own people

---

39. For example, the gospel was no doubt shared across the European and Asian continent, but it penetrated Ireland in the early fifth century; Britain around the late sixth and seventh centuries; China in the seventh century and reintroduced in the sixteenth century; Russia in the ninth century; and Scandinavia in the mid-twelfth century.

40. Commenting on the declining Roman Empire, Tennent comments: "Christianity found new vitality outside the empire, among new people groups moving westward into Ireland and Scotland, and eastward into Arabia, Persia, and beyond. Many of the invading Germanic peoples were brought to faith in Christ Jesus. Tennent, *Theology in the Context of World Christianity*, 5.

41. See Tennent, *Theology in the Context of World Christianity*, 5–6. He notes the renewal brought by the reformation, fresh Roman Catholic impulses to mission, and Moravians and other Protestants. "From 1500 until the middle of the twentieth century millions of Europeans relocated to the New World, bringing their faith with them and spawning the birth of massive new populations, largely Christian."

42. See Tennent, *Theology in the Context of World Christianity*, 8–11. See also "Global Religious Futures." They suggest that in 2010, there were 2.2 billion Christians in the world, 31 percent of the world's population. About 26 percent was in Europe, 25 percent in Latin America and the Caribbean, 24 percent in sub-Saharan Africa, 13 percent in Asia and the Pacific, 12 percent in North America, and fewer than 1 percent live in the Middle East-North Africa region. By 2050 it is anticipated only 16 percent of Christians will be in Europe.

who have lost confidence in the gospel and as Europeans have abandoned the faith.[43] In the meantime, non-Western missions are flourishing with majority-world Christians traveling to the Western "Christian" nations to evangelize them. Additionally, immigration is changing the demographics of Western nations so that they are now no longer dominated by Europeans.[44] Indigenous peoples and those brought in from Africa, and other nations, as slaves, have quite rightly asserted their rights. Christianity is now a truly multicultural church across God's world. Yet, in traditional sending nations, many have lost a great deal of confidence.

Sadly, it also remains divided—it may be multicultural, but it is not yet intercultural. Many Christians continue to meet in cultural and ethnic church groupings. Few churches are genuinely multicultural. In Western situations like my own, too many Europeans are blind to how their gospel is harnessed to the fallacies of colonialism and Christendom. They fail to see their privilege and racial prejudice. This applies to many church cultures.

Is there still a place for cross-cultural mission today? Starting with Romans, the answer is a profound yes! God is still calling and sending missionaries like Paul to the world. There are many people and people groups who have yet to hear the gospel. The fullness of the gentiles has not yet come in! (11:25).

There remains an enormous need for Christians to cross cultural boundaries and with servant hearts, humbly work with locals to evangelize, plant churches, engage in development, social justice, social transformation, and ecological renewal, and develop Christian tertiary education and medical facilities. God needs workers to hear his summons and go into local communities and the world with the gospel. Romans 16 lists many such people in Rome. Paul likely envisages working with them in Rome, encouraging them, imparting spiritual gifts, inspiring and equipping some of them for mission at home and abroad (e.g., Spain).

However, this is no longer the Christians of the west going to civilize the heathens of the world, it is any Christian going to any place where people of other ethnicities are found. In fact, cross-cultural mission begins when we welcome the stranger into our church or small group, and as we leave the church to mingle with the people of the world.

In a place like the North Shore of Auckland, where I sit writing, this is the local businesses, homes, and the many social contexts in my area which are full of people born in other nations who now call NZ home. Every church in such a setting must be multicultural and moving in the direction of becoming intercultural, whereby cultural diversity is celebrated within the warmth of the culture of God's kingdom.

There will still be some called to go to other peoples. Some will come to the West to re-evangelize Western nations. Some will be called to leave their Western homes

---

43. See, e.g., for my own country, New Zealand: "Irreligion in New Zealand."

44. In the case of my home city, Auckland, see Tan, "Auckland More Diverse than London and New York."

and travel to people of other cultures to share Christ in the many missional tasks God's people have been given. Whereas in the past, they often went fully funded, now many will emulate Paul, Prisca, and Aquila and go as "tentmakers." They will work in "secular" vocational situations, which themselves are missional opportunities,[45] and participate with humility in local churches and with locals in mission.

Those that do have to be very culturally aware, ensuring that they take the gospel and its summons to the Christ-life without the imposition of other elements of culture. They must be well trained in contextualization and the threats of syncretism. They must be aware of their own cultural tendencies, careful not to try and convert the locals to be anything other than believers embedded in *their* culture. Wherever believers find themselves, they must not be "Judaizers" imposing their cultures, but they must allow the gospel to take root and be expressed in the cultural clothing of the given context and people. This contextualization applies to subcultures like children and youth, generational groups, and the many cultures of the world.

When the gospel establishes, it always takes on a hybrid form, a blend of the gospel and the culture into which it is embedded. If allowed to become fixed in cultural expression, the church will atrophy. The church or denomination becomes entrenched, and people mistakenly believe that the way things are done in their given context *is* the gospel.

I worship as a Presbyterian in New Zealand, and cultural issues are our biggest challenge. In an increasingly multicultural setting, our churches are full of white aging people who like their little churches with their outdated cultural norms. They are good people, but very resistant to change, and the decline of the church is plainly evident. Where this kind of thing happens, we need reformers like Paul determined to break up these limited and marginalizing cultural expressions of the gospel. We need gifted pastors who can take such churches on a journey from monoculturalism to interculturalism. Otherwise these churches will date and age and die unless new people and generations are welcomed and given space to grow and take up leadership.

Our challenge is to be people who prioritize the gospel over our cultures and allow ourselves to be transformed by its summons to love and the many expressions of the faith we will encounter in our lives. We must be rock solid in the faith, but not become wedded to non-essentials like what we eat, clothes we wear, the music we sing, the words we use to describe the gospel, our customs, and traditions. These aspects of church life must be held lightly so that they are able to be reshaped again and again by the Spirit.

---

45. See on the workshop as a place of religious discourse and mission opportunities, Hock, "Workshop as a Social Setting," 438–50; Hock, *Social Context of Paul's Ministry*.

26

Israel in God's Mission

ROMANS 9–11 DEALS WITH the great question that arises from Paul's articulation of righteousness by faith to the end of Romans 8. What is the place of Israel in God's purposes? Paul argues throughout that while God's purposes in election have seen Israel reject his Son, God has not finished with Israel. Her people who have rejected God's Messiah and have been broken off the olive tree that is God's people can be regrafted back in based on faith. Here, I will look briefly at Romans 9–11 and consider its implications for mission to Israel's people who have rejected the gospel.

ISRAEL IN ROMANS 1–8

Before coming to Romans 9–11, it is worth drawing out aspects of Paul's argument concerning Israel in Romans 1–8. First, he has pointed out that Jesus is the Davidic Messiah Israel has yearned for (1:2–4). It is in and through Messiah Jesus that God is now working out his purposes on earth.

Second, he has stated the basis on which a person is declared righteous before God: whether they are a gentile or Jew, it is by faith (1:16–17). Jews and gentiles alike are under sin (3:9), are recipients of wrath (1:18), will face the judgment of God (2:5–16; 3:19–20), and are sinful and fall short of the glory awaiting saved humankind (3:23). Although they have the law, they have failed to practice it as is required (2:12—16). Their hearts are not yet circumcised (2:25—29). Still, there are real advantages in being a Jew, as they have been entrusted with God's words (3:2) and experience multiple blessings (9:4–5). He has asserted that a Jew is not justified by observing the law, but through the law, they have awareness of sin (3:19–20).

Paul has also asserted that for all humankind, righteousness is received through faith in Jesus Christ, the sacrifice of atonement who deals with the problem of sin and wrath (3:21–24). The principle of justification by faith applies to Jew and gentile alike (3:29–30).

Romans 4 is critical to Paul's argument. He establishes that the law, works, or being a Jew were never the basis for righteous status before God. Justification has always been by faith. Buttressed by prophetic examples in Romans 1:17, 9:33, and 10:11,[1] Paul establishes this premise of faith beginning in the Genesis account of Abraham, who was justified by faith and not works (4:3; Gen 15:6). Abraham experienced the blessing that comes to those of faith that David declared years later, forgiveness of sin (4:6–8; Ps 32:1–2). Critically, Abraham did not receive this status of justification by becoming a Jew through circumcision, as he was an uncircumcised gentile when he received the declaration of justification. He is thus the father of faith for both Jew and gentile (4:9–12).

Justification by faith applies to all of history from the rupture in the garden (Gen 3) to the present and until Jesus returns. Abraham's inheritance of the world is through faith (4:13), and this is coming to pass in the gospel era as the nations submit to Christ. Abraham is the father of faith in the world (4:16–17). Now, the sin of Adam that unleashed death to humankind has been undone in Christ (5:12–21). Believers, Jew, and gentile alike, are liberated from the obligations of the law to live by the Spirit (7:1—8:4). As children of God, they are to be led by the Spirit (8:12–17).

ROMANS 9

In Romans 9:1–5, after praying that he might be condemned to destruction so that Israel be saved (which Jesus has done and Paul cannot do), Paul lists some of the privileges of being of Israel: they were adopted as God's people; God was gloriously present with them in wilderness, Tabernacle, and Temple; he has made covenants with them (esp. Noahic, Abrahamic, Mosaic, and Davidic); God gave them the precious law at Sinai along with their worship system that maintained their relationship with God. He then lands on the fundamental privilege that has recently come to pass—from Israel has come the Messiah, who is God over all (9:1–5). By climaxing here, Paul lands on their core issue—aside from messianic Jews, they have rejected Jesus as Messiah.

In my view, Romans 9:6–7 provides the key to understand all of Romans 9–11. Paul asserts that, in God's eyes, not all who are born Israelites are Israel. He then restates this, that not all children of Abraham are children of Abraham. We know from Romans 4 that it is those who are people of faith who are true Israelites. These are people with circumcised hearts (2:25–29). We can discern from Romans 4 that faith is the basis upon which a person's heart is circumcised.

In Romans 9:6–12, drawing on the stories of the Patriarchs in Genesis, Paul then defends God's faithfulness to his word through his election in history. He endorses God's sovereign freedom to elect Isaac and not Ishmael, Jacob and not Esau, as he worked out his line of promise.

---

1. See Hab 2:4; Isa 28:16 LXX.

Then, drawing on the Exodus and the creational and prophetic motif of the potter and clay,[2] in Romans 9:14–24, Paul again defends God's sovereign freedom as the creator to continue his line of election and rule history as he wills. He recalls that God was free and just to use Pharaoh that his name might be proclaimed in all the earth (v. 17). As created beings, God shows mercy to people as he wills and he hardens as he desires. Such a hardening does not rule out human volition and accountability, as for Paul, human volition and responsibility are equally aspects of his understanding of a predestined world (even if we cannot easily make sense of it, see part three, chapter 22). God has put up with people destined for destruction through history. In the present, he continues to work out his purposes to bring the called, believers, to glory, both Jews and gentiles.

He draws on prophetic texts in Romans 9:25–29 showing that God, by his sovereign election, is fulfilling his promises that people from the world will be saved into familial relationship with him, whereas Israel will experience God's wrath.

Romans 9:30–33 is crucial as it demonstrates that the problem is not a capricious, unjust God, but Israel herself who have rejected faith for works righteousness. They have failed to recognize that Jesus is the foundation of a people of God from the whole world and have stumbled over him through failing to believe in him.

ROMANS 10

Romans 10 begins with Paul again stating his prayerful desire that Israel is saved. He acknowledges their zeal and commitment to God, but failure to submit to God's righteousness by faith. They fail to see that Christ is the end of the law and that the law cannot be a basis for righteousness.

Romans 10:5–13 contrasts the idea of righteousness by the law with righteousness by faith. Paul argues that everyone, Jew or Greek, is justified by faith in Christ. He then asks in Romans 10:14–21 whether Israel has heard the gospel. He answers, they have, and God continues to hold out his hands to them in their disobedience.

ROMANS 11

Romans 11 begins with Paul asking if God has rejected Israel. He recalls a time when it appeared that the only one left in Israel was Elijah, but as always, he had a remnant of faithful people (7000 in fact). Similarly, now that Christ has come and been declared to Israel, there is a remnant of grace and not works. This remnant includes Jewish people who have heard the gospel and believe in Jesus just as the faithful in Israel believed in God before Christ's coming (people like Elijah and the 7,000).

---

2. See Gen 2:7; Isa 29:16; 64:8; Jer 18:4–6.

Romans 11:7 states the problem Israel has. They failed to obtain righteousness through law, which is implausible; the elect people of God (Jew and gentile) received it (those who believe). However, the rest were hardened.

Romans 11:11–27 answers the question of whether there is still hope for hardened Israel. His answer is a resounding, "yes!" By their sin, salvation has gone to the world, but they can still be included and experience life from the dead. He uses the image of an olive tree. Hardened Jews are likened to branches broken off through unbelief (v. 19). Yet, they can be grafted back in (vv. 23–24). "All Israel" is either all believers from history or all believing Israelites, and the difference for this discussion is minimal. What is possible is that Israelites can be saved through Jesus, their Deliverer, who can take away their sins (11:26–27).

In Romans 11:28–31, Paul states that while hardened Israelites are enemies of the Christian movement, they remain loved by God. He has not forgotten them, for his gifts and call to them as a people remain. They can experience God's mercy, as can all humankind (vv. 30–32).

MISSION AND ISRAEL TODAY

All this tells readers that God has not finished with Israel, and the mission to its people must go on. In sending his Son when he did, God created a pathway for *all* people to be saved. This status of justification is received through faith in Jesus Christ, the Lord. The church retains a spiritual debt to Israel (cf. 15:27). Israel has been, in a sense, like Jesus, been sacrificed to save the world. Part of the reason the gospel exploded into the world was Israel's rejection of it. (Ironically, it was through Saul of Tarsus that this rejection led to the gospel exploding into the gentile world as he drove the church from Israel.) God has not finished with Israel. People must hear and heed the call to share Christ with them when sent.[3]

However, Paul in Romans is crystal clear: there are not two tracks of salvation, no "bi-covenantal" theology in which there is a *Sonderweg* (special way) for Jews, and another for gentiles.[4] Before hearing the gospel of Christ, one comes to God by faith in God as revealed. Once Christ has been preached, they can come to God in one way:

---

3. "If Christ is indeed 'the surprising answer to Judaism's religious search'", if a "conflation of the Torah and Christ" is inadmissible . . . , if what matters is not Abraham's flesh but his faith (Gal 3:7; Rom 4:11, 14, 16; 9:8) . . . , if zealous observance of religion does not bring salvation (Rom 10:2), if only those who "do not persist in their unbelief" can be grafted back into the olive tree (Rom 11:23), does it not mean that Christians have a responsibility toward Jews, beyond safeguarding the peace of Jews in the world? Bosch, *Transforming Mission*, 172 notes some scholars reject that there is a need for a mission to the Jews.

4. As argued, e.g., by Gager, *The Origins of Anti-Semitism*, passim; L. Gaston, *Paul and the Torah*, passim. Schreiner, *Romans*, 616: "The theory that Paul believed that there was a *Sonderweg* (special way) of salvation for the Jews, apart from faith in Christ, comports well with modern sensibilities but is exegetically unpersuasive." See p. 616n12 for other examples of those with the view. See also Moo, *Letter to the Romans*, 740–41.

by way of faith in the Son, a faith that is generated as those destined for salvation hear the gospel.[5] In Romans 10:14–21, Paul asserts that Christ has been preached to Israel; hence, their only way to salvation is by him (unless they are completely insulated from the Christian message, which is difficult in today's world). Consequently, Christians *must* continue to engage in sharing the gospel with Israelites. Their path to God is faith in their Messiah.

The discussion thus far and especially the previous chapter also tells us very clearly that anyone who names Jesus as Lord must never lapse into anti-Semitism (or any racism of any sort). While many Bible-believing Christians find Israel's rejection of Jesus difficult, like all people, they are to be loved and treated with the grace Paul calls for in Romans 12:13–21. Many Christians also struggle to understand the way that the current government of Israel treats Palestine, seeing it as unjust. They are disturbed by some forms of Zionism. Yet, none of this means the Jewish people are to be singled out as they have been in the horrendous anti-Semitism of history.

So, it remains the call of the gospel for the church to share Christ with people physically descended from Abraham and Isaac. While we may express our views on this injustice, many other similar injustices are going on across the world. Yet, such injustices are everywhere and are usually state generated; our call is to challenge injustice evenly while loving the unjust and sharing the gospel with them. As such, and perhaps especially knowing that salvation came from the Jews, they are to be cherished and loved, and Christ shared with them.

Equally, we must beware of theologies that argue for two tracks of salvation (above). There is one way for Jew and gentile alike, faith in Jesus. We should also take care in seeking to interpret the establishment of the modern nation of Israel as a sign of the end of the age or see them as privileged above other peoples. Perhaps it is, but this does not change much—unbelieving Israel must hear the gospel. Let God bring his world to an end. God does not show favoritism (2:11).

We must carefully consider our exegesis of NT texts concerning the people of Israel, ensuring we do not read into them a false hope that in some way all Israel will turn to God. Several in Romans 11 stand out. Do Romans 11:12 and 15 speak of a final full inclusion and resurrection of Israel?[6] Or, are they statements of Paul's yearnings in which he cries out how glorious it would be *if* they did become jealous and turn? It would mean life from the dead for them, as for all humankind destined for destruction that put their faith in God and his Son.

I see these texts as articulations of the hope of the apostle who yearns for Israel to recognize Jesus and believe. That is the only way of being saved. However, I simply

---

5. "There is ultimately one people of God, and the only way to belong to it now, for Jews as much as for Gentiles, is through faith in the Messiah, Jesus of Nazareth.... Paul does not hold out any other way for Jews to be part of eschatological Israel other than the same way that Gentiles are now joining that community—only through faith in Jesus of Nazareth, the Messiah." Wright, *Mission of God*, 528.

6. An example of this is Osborne, *Romans: Verse by Verse*, 362 who states that after the mission to the gentiles is complete, "[t]hen national revival will take place, and all Israel will be saved."

do not see in the passage that Paul is stating that there *will* be some revival and all Israelites actually saved.[7]

So, does Romans 11:26 really state that all Israel's people will ultimately be saved? On the logic of Paul's theology in Romans and Galatians, for this to occur, all Israelites from all of history must believe in Jesus and do so while living. A better possibility is that this refers to all faithful Israelites like Abraham. Or is Israel here the people of God who form the olive tree of God's people, natural branches (ethnic Israelites who believe in Jesus), and those grafted in (gentiles who believe in Jesus)?

At best, for Paul's arguments in Galatians and Romans to be upheld, the final generation may believe in Jesus when he returns;[8] but is that too late? Is this really "all Israel," when "not all Israel are Israel?" Is it really faith when Jesus returns and is seen? Instead, it is certainty and no longer faith as they see him "face to face."

Such debates will go on, but these are mere digressions from the point I am making. Suffice to say; we must take extreme care to maintain the balance of Paul's theology of Jew and gentile in Romans. There is a salvation-historical order "first to the Jews," and then "also to the Greeks." Yet, the basis for both is the same: faith in Jesus.[9] So, whatever hope lies in the passage for Israel, it lies with faith in Jesus in this earthly life (after which, the writer of Hebrews tells us, they face judgment, Heb 9:27). Hence, all Jews who have heard the gospel and died without yielding to Jesus are destined for destruction (as are all gentiles—God is impartial).

Equally, we must hear other features of Romans 11. God has not rejected his people (11:1). Gentile Christians like myself must not become arrogant toward Israel; rather, we reach out to God for them in loving, yearning, contending, grief-laden, and constant prayer as did Paul.[10] We must show them the same *agapē* we are to demonstrate to all humankind. They *can* be grafted in but only if they come to believe in Jesus Messiah (11:19–23). We gentiles should be ever grateful for it was from Zion that our Deliverer came to take away our sins (11:26–27).

When a Jewish person comes to faith in Christ, they are to be warmly welcomed. If they want to continue to observe their cultural patterns of life, such as eating kosher food, worshiping on the Sabbath, circumcision, and remembering their Jewish festivals, there is no issue with such things (as long as they are not imposing them on non-Jews and separating themselves in ethnic enclaves within the church).[11] Similarly,

---

7. See the brilliant critique of such ideas in Wright, "Romans," 688–91. I echo the thoughts of Chris Wright: "Paul argues that the ingathering of the Gentiles (the 'no people') through his mission endeavors will arouse jealousy among the Jews, so that ultimately 'all Israel,' *extended and inclusive of* believing Jews and Gentiles, will share in salvation." Wright, *Mission of God*, 343 (emphasis mine, see also p. 528).

8. E.g., Osborne, *Romans: Verse by Verse*, 363; Schreiner, *Romans*, 619.

9. Schreiner, *Romans*, 616: "Paul never envisioned a salvation for Israel apart from trusting in Jesus as Messiah."

10. See Rom 9:1–3; 10:1, cf. 1:9–10; 15:30.

11. It is no different than a church gathering with vegans, vegetarians, and those who eat meat. We

other cultures will continue with a range of cultural expressions that do not threaten the core of the Christian faith. Neither should they be imposed on others. Believers should be warmly welcoming and accommodating to all who follow Jesus faithfully.

There seem to be two extremes in the Christian movement where Israel is concerned. On the one hand, some repudiate Israel and Jews with what are racist anti-Semitic attitudes. On the other, some are pro-Israel at the expense of the gospel, the supremacy and sufficiency of Christ, and the radical egalitarianism of God's kingdom. There is a third way in which, we honor Israel for our shared heritage and their faithfulness to God, for the Messiah and the OT Scriptures that came from Israel. We welcome one another in our differences. We are unified in the gospel.

Moreover, from Israel came the first apostles and Paul himself, the apostle to the gentiles. We must reach out to Israel's people with the untainted love of Christ and reject such extremes.[12] Yet, in the same way, we must honor all people for in Christ Jesus, there is neither Jew nor Greek (Gal 3:28).

---

can meet and be one allowing for such differences.

12. "Naturally, any Christian witness to Jews has to be borne in a spirit of profound sensitivity and humility, in light, once again, of the history of the Christian treatment [I would interject, "maltreatment"] of the Jews." Bosch, *Transforming Mission*, 174.

27

Romans, Mission, Theology, and Apologetics

ROMANS IS A CASE study in sharing the faith with others in one period of history. It gives us tremendous insight into what mission is, the gospel, and how to go about mission. It teaches that the mission of God is the redemption of a world and that at the heart of it is preaching the gospel that people are saved. Readers are told that it involves a range of engagement in righting the world and creation. It instructs concerning relationships with the State. The ethics of mission are laid out; supremely love. Many aspects of the gospel are affirmed, even if Romans is not "the gospel" but "an expression of the gospel" for a very particular situation. We are told that the mission is owned and outworked by the Triune God and that, equipped by vocational missionaries, all believers are to participate in the proclamation of his word.

Romans also shows us the importance of theology and apologetics in presenting Christ, whether to Christians to strengthen them, or to unbelievers that they be saved.[1] Romans is written to Christians as are all Paul's letters. Romans is a brilliant example of how to construct a persuasive argument drawing on the OT and other Jewish Greek idioms, Rabbinic exegetical approaches, Greco-Roman and Jewish rhetorical devices and thought, and present the Christian message for a given context. One of the saddest things today is to fail to be prepared to be as innovative as Paul in our theology and argumentation. Equally, it is tragic when we stop at Romans and simply unpack it

---

1. Paul uses the term *apologia*, "defence, make a defence" (*NIDNTTE* 1:361) in 1 Cor 9:3; 2 Cor 7:11; Phil 1:7, 16; and 2 Tim 4:16 (see also Acts 22:1; 25:16). He uses the verb *apologeomai*, "to . . . the faith (see also 1 Pet 3:15).

and fail to rethink the Christian story for our cultural settings.² Romans invites us to be imaginative evangelists, theologians, and apologists for the faith.³

Aside from giving insight into all manner of aspects of the gospel, the letter at times touches on arguments that can be used today. Examples include Paul's use of aspects of the cosmological and teleological arguments in 1:19—aspects of God's existence and character can be perceived from creation.⁴ He hints at the moral argument for God's existence in 2:14 and 26, recognizing that the law is (to some extent) written on gentile hearts, even if they cannot fully live it. Chapter 4 of Romans gives a hint at the fate of those who have never heard of Christ—just as Abraham was justified by faith in the God as revealed to him, others may also be so saved. His passion for grace and faith resolve the question of the basis on which a person is justified (grace through faith). Yet, having established this, he presents a strong works ethic—by the Spirit, God's people will love and do good. Romans 8:19–22 points to a world restored, rather than a world destroyed (a common view among many Christians). Paul uses diatribe to anticipate common questions of his time, which he then seeks to answer.⁵

THE FIXED POINT

Paul's genius in Romans has, as its fixed point, the story of God to this point in history and to the end of the age. Because he is so deeply immersed in years of intense study and reflection of the Jewish narrative, he intimately understands God's work in history. In particular, we see his understanding of salvation history including God's pre-existence, creation, the Rupture, the covenants, Abraham and the Patriarchs, Moses, Exodus, the wilderness, Sinai and the Law, the Conquest, Israel's life in the land, the

---

2. The Western church has rightly seen that Romans is a great missionary document, but the church has often narrowed the missionary implications of this letter to the so-called Romans Road: 'here's how you're a sinner, here's how Jesus died, here's how you are saved, and therefore, here's how you should live.' These basic truths are important, but they do not get at the heart of God's covenant purposes found in Romans." Wright, "Reading the New Testament Missionally," 191.

3. Some thinkers reject apologetics as worthless as argumentation does not convert people, e.g., Barnhouse, *God's Heirs*, 38. This is a total over-reaction for a person's conversion is a complex interplay between their situation, feelings, and thinking. Paul clearly recognized that apologetics has value, and one aspect of a person's response to God is convincing them intellectually. Of course, apologetics alone is rarely, if ever, enough, but it remains a critical aspect of evangelism in any setting. The questions vary, but Christians must always be prepared to make a defense of their faith as one component of the evangelistic process. Witherington and Hyatt, *Paul's Letter*, 3 suggest that the only apologetic section is in chapters 9–11. This is also flawed as, while the letter may not be occasioned by enemies such as 2 Corinthians and Galatians, it remains an *apologia* for the gospel of grace through faith and not law. Furthermore, there were opponents in the wider milieu who are referenced in Rom 16:17–20, in Corinth (2 Cor 10–12), affecting Philippi (Phil 3), and Asia (Col 2). The statement of Käsemann, *Commentary*, 261 that, "[w]e cannot speak either of apologetics or of controversy with specific opponents," is too limiting.

4. Cottrell, *Romans: Volume 1*, "A Universal Knowledge of God and his Law (1:18–20)."

5. Rom 2:3–4, 21–22; 3:1–9, 27–31; 4:9–10; 6:6–3, 15–16; 7:7, 13; 8:31–35; 9:14–24, 30–32; 10:8, 14–19; 11:1–7, 11; 14:4, 10. There are eighty-two questions in Romans (ESV version).

exiles, the restoration, the Prophets, the intertestamental period, and of course Christ. Christ is the center of his *apologia kai bebaiōsei tou euangeliou* (Phil 1:7), and for Paul, the central foci are his death and resurrection. The work of Christ is central because, in his death, Christ satisfied the requirements for righteousness by faith. He died as humankind's representative, substitute, and type. So, the fixed point for Paul is the story of God and the climax of that story thus far, Jesus Christ Lord and him crucified.

Paul is intimately aware of Israel's hopes of eschatological salvation, with a nexus of events tied together at the end of this age: the woes of the Messiah where evil culminates, the Messiah, God's victory over all enemies, judgment, the outpouring of the Spirit, the restoration of Israel, the rebuilding of the temple and it being filled with glory, the subjugation of the nations to God and his messianic agent, the eternal destruction of the ungodly, the resurrection, and eternal life for God's people. He knows this is to come to pass. Of course, the end has now broken into history in Jesus. The Messiah has come. Surprisingly, he has died and risen. The Spirit has been poured out. The end has begun. In the meantime, his people, Jew, and gentile, by the Spirit, united as one, are to *be* his people and work to complete his mission of bringing in the fullness of gentile and Jew.

THE TASK

Now the Messiah is seated at God's right hand. As those he sends and leads by the Spirit preach him in the nations, initiated by Paul and the early Christians, God is subduing his enemies who worship other gods and the spirits that hold the nations captive. People are yielding to him in faith. Now, a temple of God is being built, not made of stone and wood, but a people formed on and in the Messiah. Israel by faith is being extended, and the world is worshiping Yahweh. Still to come is the fullness of the Jews and gentiles coming in. This completeness will occur when God is satisfied that his mission has gone as far as it can, and the number of those predestined for eternal life and have willingly yielded to him is complete.

As has been discussed, it is commonly held that Paul believes that his trip to Spain will complete the mission, and Paul then expected Christ to return. However, such an imminent parousia is blatantly flawed.[6] Spain would represent the completion of *Paul's* mission, not that of Christ. He would then have evangelized from Jerusalem to Brigantium, on the northwestern edge of ancient Hispania. From this base, the gospel would go to the north, south, east, and when the new worlds were discovered many centuries later, west (not that Paul would know any of that). Paul writes Romans

---

6. "That Paul saw himself as a significant figure in salvation history, with a central role in the Gentile mission, is clear; but that he thought his own efforts would bring that mission to its conclusion is not clear at all." Moo, *Letter to the Romans*, 910. "But it does not follow from all this that he believed that the second coming would certainly occur after the Spanish mission." Schreiner, *Romans*, 775.

to inspire others to continue the mission once he is gone. He knows that when he does go, the Spirit and the power of God's salvation, the gospel, will remain.

When this mission is completed to God's satisfaction, Christ will return (not that Paul mentions this explicitly in Romans, see Mark 13:10; Matt 24:14). Then there will be judgment. God will then reign with his people on a world liberated from sin, decay, and death. Evil will be destroyed, including all the enemies of God and finally, death itself.

ROMANS, AN EXAMPLE OF THEOLOGY AND APOLOGETICS

Paul knows this story thoroughly, and in Romans, he lays down a reinterpretation of the story of Israel and the world that will be the basis for defending the faith for this age. Later, Augustine would return to these premises and reassert then to fend off the Pelagian heresy.[7] In the fifteenth and sixteenth centuries, inspired by Luther bravely nailing a notice on a church door, again, the gospel will be reaffirmed to overcome the indulgences of the Catholic Church.[8] Its message converted Wesley and inspired others.[9] Romans brought about the transformation of Karl Barth and Protestant theology.[10] With Galatians, it catalyzed the more recent New Perspective on Paul that has challenged a church and its academy that is undoubtedly overly Eurocentric, masculine, and blind to its biases (myself included). This fresh approach has caused the church to find afresh the need to challenge all forms of "Judaizing" in every age when the gospel is morphed to a dominant culture, and others are marginalized. Now, its message (esp. 8:19–23) is an essential plank in the church discovering the biblical summons to ecological care. Romans has inspired evangelists for centuries, and this will go on.

Still, we cannot stop at Romans. Romans did not happen by accident. God oversaw from his mother's womb the young life of Saul of Tarsus (Gal 1:15). He grew up in Tarsus (Acts 21:39), an important Cilician Roman city, where he learned the story of Israel in synagogue and home, and he engaged with the philosophies and religions of Tarsus, a city renowned for Stoicism.[11] No doubt handpicked, he studied under the great rabbi, Gamaliel (Acts 22:3, cf. Acts 5:34).[12] He was a brilliant young man who

---

7. See Cranfield, *Critical and Exegetical Commentary*, 1:35–36; Witherington and Hyatt, *Paul's Letter*, 181–84.

8. Cranfield, *Critical and Exegetical Commentary*, 1:37–38; Rasnake, *Romans*, 1.

9. Rasnake, *Romans*, 1.

10. Haacker, *Theology of Paul's Letter to the Romans*, 158.

11. Gasque, "Tarsus," 6:334. It was the hometown of the Stoic philosopher Athenodorus. Strabo claimed it outstripped Athens and Alexandria, even if it had fewer students (Strabo, *Geogr.* 14.5.131).

12. Assuming the veracity of Acts, Gamaliel's excellence as a teacher is hinted at in Paul's claims of advancing in Judaism in Gal 1:14. Chilton highlights his importance in Judaism as in m. Soṭa 9.15: "When Rabban Gamaliel the elder died, the glory of the law ceased and purity and abstinence died." Chilton, "Gamaliel," 2:904. See too Barnett, *Paul, Missionary of Jesus*, 34–36.

did not waste his youth on depravity and excess but on learning. He was a zealous Jew, passionate for his culture and traditions, advanced beyond most others (Gal 1:14). When God was satisfied he had prepared him in the petri dish of Tarsus and Jerusalem, he called him.[13] Then, he put his mind to understanding his theology afresh and apologetics: defending and confirming the gospel (Phil 1:7). The gospel was revealed to and in him, and that gospel is Christ (Gal 1:12). As he traveled, preaching, discussing, praying, praising, reading the Scriptures, observing the world around him, and thinking, thinking, thinking, he preached and wrote, and so we have Romans. Paul anticipates the great theologians, missional thinkers, and apologists who have followed him and who creatively reframed the message for their varying contexts.

The world is changing at a rate never before seen. Globalization and the internet have brought a revolution that makes the printing press look like a blip. Societies are being changed by forces coming at them from all angles. Traditional institutional structures are under threat as the people can access information from every direction, and the world is teetering. Political and natural events like conflict and pandemics create more instability. Never before has the church needed people with the brilliance of Paul to think and rethink, reframing the fixed point of our message, God and his Son in salvation history, for our times.

Romans is brilliantly written. While its exact form is elusive, it shows signs of Greek protreptic rhetoric, the ambassadorial letter form, and others. The ease with which Paul can write, drawing contemporary scholars to make such comparisons shows his familiarity with such rhetorical strategies.

Anyone can see its basic outline: God and Paul's mission; a declaration of the gospel as the power of salvation and righteousness by faith; the problem of human sin; the solution Jesus; justification by faith; reconciliation and new life in the new Adam; freedom from sin; serving God and not sin; freedom from the law and life in the Spirit; the place of Israel; how believers should live; finding unity in difference; and a postscript on the gospel mission.

He uses the media of his day, the epistle, to communicate brilliantly. He writes in Greek, with metaphors replete with meaning from Jewish and Greek sources. He uses contemporary rhetorical devices like diatribe, chiasm, and more. Throughout, Paul draws on a rich diversity of OT quotes and allusions.[14] He employs hermeneutical approaches drawn from his tradition, such as pesher and midrash. He asks rhetorical questions, employing diatribe and interlocutors to stand in the place of a critic or a Christian wanting more. While he comes back to the same ideas, he rarely says the same thing in the same way twice, reframing his argument with creative flair. All this creativity leaves readers wanting to read it again and again to grasp its depth, always

---

13. See Gal 1:15–16; Acts 9:1–18; 22:6–16; 26:12–18.

14. Käsemann, *Commentary*, 86, cogently states, "Missionary apologetics and polemics necessarily feed from a relatively fixed body of usable OT material."

finding new things with each read. He employs an amazing range of metaphors from Israel's cult, the wider society, and the world of ordinary life.

May it be that young minds dare to grapple with the biblical narrative and the likes of Romans (and Hebrews and Revelation) and do so continuing to engage with people within their churches and outside them. In this way, God can produce more female and male "Pauls" to be the apostles to the twenty-first century and beyond. May this be. Amen.

Bibliography

Alexander, Loveday C. A. "Chronology of Paul." In *DPL* 115–23.

Alexander, T. Desmond, and David W. Baker, eds. *Dictionary of the Old Testament: Pentateuch*. Downers Grove, IL: InterVarsity, 2003.

Alexander, W. M. "St. Paul's Infirmity." *ExpT* 10 (1904) 469–73, 545–48.

Allen, Roland. *Missionary Methods: St. Paul's or Ours? A Study of the Church in the Four Provinces*. London: Scott, 1912.

———. *The Spontaneous Expansion of the Church and the Causes Which Hinder It*. 3rd ed. London: World Dominion, 1956.

Arndt, William, et al. *A Greek-English Lexicon of the New Testament and Other Early Christian Literature*. Chicago: University of Chicago, 2000.

Arnold, Clinton E. *Ephesians: Power and Magic: The Concept of Power in Ephesians in Light of its Historical Situation*. Studiorum Novi Testamenti Societas—Monograph Series 63. Cambridge: Cambridge University, 1989.

Aune, David E. *Revelation 17–22*. WBC 52C. Dallas: Word, 1998.

———. "Romans as a Logos Protreptikos." In *The Romans Debate*, edited by Karl Paul Donfried, 278–96. Revised and Expanded Edition. Peabody, MA: Hendrickson, 1991.

———. "Romans as a *Logos Protreptikos* in the Context of Ancient Religious and Philosophical Propaganda." In *Paulus als Missionar und Theologe und das antike Judentum*, edited by M. Hengel and U. Heckel, 91–124. WUNT 58. Tübingen: Mohr Siebeck, 1991.

Aus, R. D. "Paul's Travel Plans to Spain, and the 'Full Number of the Gentiles' of Romans 11:25." *NovT* 21 (1979) 232–62.

Backlund, Kurt. "El, Deity." *LBD* n.p.

Bailey, Daniel P. "Suffering Servant." *EDEJ* 1257–58.

Bakken, Peter W., and David C. McDuffie. "Bibliography." https://fore.yale.edu/World-Religions/Christianity/Bibliography.

Banks, Robert J. *Paul's Idea of Community: Spirit and Culture in Early House Churches*. Grand Rapids: Baker Academic, 1994.

Bates, Matthew W. *Salvation by Allegiance Alone: Rethinking Faith, Works, and the Gospel Jesus the King*. Grand Rapids, MI: Baker, 2017.

Barclay, John M. G. *Paul & the Gift*. Grand Rapids, MI: Eerdmans, 2015.

Barker, Kenneth L. *Micah, Nahum, Habakkuk, Zephaniah*. NAC 20. Nashville: Broadman & Holman, 1999.

Barnett, Paul W. "Apostle." In *DPL* 45–51.

———. *Paul, Missionary of Jesus*. After Jesus 2. Grand Rapids: Eerdmans, 2008.

———. *The Second Epistle to the Corinthians*. NICNT. Grand Rapids: Eerdmans, 1997.

Barnhouse, Donald Grey. *God's Heirs: Romans 8:1–39*. Grand Rapids, MI: Eerdmans, 1963.

Bibliography

Barram, Michael. *Mission and Moral Reflection in Paul*. Studies in Biblical Literature 75. New York: Lang, 2006.

Barrett, C. K. *A Commentary on the Epistle to the Romans*. HNTC. New York: Harper & Row, 1957.

———. *A Critical and Exegetical Commentary on the Acts of the Apostles*. ICC. Edinburgh: T. & T. Clark, 2004.

Barth, Karl. *The Epistle to the Romans*. Translated by Edwyn C. Hoskyns. London: Oxford University, 1933.

Bauckham, Richard. *Bible and Mission: Christian Witness in a Postmodern World*. Grand Rapids, MI; Baker Academic, 2003.

———. *Gospel Women: Studies in the Named Women in the Gospels*. Grand Rapids: Eerdmans, 2002.

Beale, G. K. *The Temple and the Church's Mission*. NSBT 17. Downers Grove, IL: Apollos, 2004.

Beaulieu, Stéphane. "Deutero-Isaiah." In *LBD* n.p.

Belleville, Linda L. "Authority." In *DPL* 54–59.

Bennett, Charles E. *New Latin Grammar*. Boston: Allyn & Bacon, 1908.

Berger, Klaus. *Formgeschichte des Neuen Testament*. Heidelberg: Quelle & Meyer, 1984.

———. "Hellenistische Gattungen im Neuen Testament." *ANRW* 2.25.2 (1984) 1332–1432.

Betz, O. "σημεῖον, ου, τό Sēmeion Distinguishing Mark, Sign; Miracle." In *EDNT* 3:238–41.

Beyer, Hermann Wolfgang. "Διακονέω, Διακονία, Διάκονος." In *TDNT* 2:81–93.

Binder, H. "Die angebliche Krankheit des Paulus." *TZ* 32 (1976) 1–13.

Bird, Michael F. *Crossing Over Sea and Land: Jewish Missionary Activity in the Second Temple Period*. Peabody, MA: Hendrickson, 2010.

Black, M. *Romans*. New Century Bible. London: Oliphants, 1973.

Boa, Kenneth, and William Kruidenier. *Romans*. Vol. 6. HNNTC Nashville: Broadman & Holman, 2000.

Bock, Darrell L. *Acts*. BECNT. Grand Rapids, MI: Baker Academic, 2007.

Bornkamm, Günter. "The Letter to the Romans as Paul's Last Will and Testament." In *The Romans Debate*, edited by Karl P. Donfried, 16–29. Revised and Expanded Edition. Peabody, MA: Hendrickson, 1991.

Bosch, David. *Transforming Mission: Paradigm Shifts in Theology of Mission*. New York: Orbis, 1991.

Boston, Jonathan. "Hope in the Face of Ecological Disaster." *Stimulus* 20.1 (2013) 5–10.

Bousset, W. *Kyrios Christos: Geschichte des Christusglaubens von den Anfangen des Christentums bis Irenaeous*. Rev. ed. Göttingen: Vandenhoeck & Ruprecht, 1921.

Bowers, W. Paul. "Church and Mission in Paul." *JSNT* 44 (1991) 89–111.

———. "Fulfilling the Gospel: The Scope of the Pauline Mission." *Journal of the Evangelical Theological Society* 30 (1987) 185–98.

———. "Jewish Communities in Spain in the Time of Paul the Apostle." *JTS* 26 (1975) 395–402.

Bowley, James E. "Heroes." In *DNTB* 494–96.

———. "Pax Romana." In *DNTB* 771–75.

Bredin, Mark. *The Ecology of the New Testament: Creation, Re-Creation, and the Environment*. Colorado Springs, CO: Biblica, 2010. Kindle ed.

Briley, Terry R. *Isaiah: Volume 2*. CPNIVC. Joplin, MO: College, 2004.

Brook, G. J. "Pesharim." In *DNTB* 778–82.

Bibliography

Bruce, F. F. *1 and 2 Thessalonians*. WBC 45. Dallas: Word, 1982.

———. *The Acts of the Apostles*. Grand Rapids: Eerdmans, 1988.

———. *The Epistle of Paul to the Romans*. TNTC. London: Tyndale, 1963.

———. *Paul: Apostle of the Free Spirit*. Milton Keynes, UK: Paternoster, 1977.

Bryan, Christopher. *A Preface to Romans: Notes on the Epistle in Its Literary and Cultural Setting*. Oxford: Oxford University, 2000.

Bultmann, Rudolf. *Der Stil der paulinischen Predigt und die kynisch-stoische Diatribe*. FRLANT 13. Göttingen: Vandenhoeck & Ruprecht, 1910.

———. "Πιστεύω, Πίστις, Πιστός, Πιστόω, Ἄπιστος, Ἀπιστέω, Ἀπιστία, Ὀλιγόπιστος, Ὀλιγοπιστία." In *TDNT* 6:174–228.

Byrne, Brendon. *Romans*. Edited by Daniel J. Harrington. SP 6. Collegeville: Liturgical, 1996.

Carson, D. A., et al., eds. *The Complexities of Second Temple Judaism*. Vol. 1 of *Justification and Variegated Nomism*. Grand Rapids, MI: Baker Academic, 2001.

———. *The Paradoxes of Paul*. Vol. 2 of *Justification and Variegated Nomism*. Grand Rapids, MI: Baker Academic, 2004.

Chafer, Lewis Sperry. *Systematic Theology*. 4 vols. Grand Rapids, MI: Kregel, 1993.

Childs, Brevard S. *Isaiah: A Commentary*. OTL. Louisville, KY: Westminster John Knox, 2001.

Chilton, Bruce. "Gamaliel." In *AYBD* 2:904–6.

Ciampa, Roy E., and Brian S. Rosner. *The First Letter to the Corinthians*. PNTC. Grand Rapids, MI: Eerdmans, 2010.

Colijn, Brenda B. "The Three Tenses of Salvation in Paul's Letters." *ATJ* 21 (1990) 29–41.

Comfort, Philip W., and Walter A. Ellwell. "Rome." In *TBD* 1139–42.

Cottrell, Jack. *Romans: Volume 1*. CPNIVC. Joplin, MO: College, 1996.

———. *Romans: Volume 2*. CPNIVC. Joplin, MO: College, 1998.

Cranfield, C. E. B. *A Critical and Exegetical Commentary on the Epistle to the Romans*. ICC. 2 vols. London: T. & T. Clark, 2004.

Crump, D. M. "Prayer." In *DJG2* 684–92.

Daneel, M. L. *African Earthkeepers: Wholistic Interfaith Mission*. Maryknoll, NY: Orbis, 2001.

———. "Earthkeeping in Missiological Perspective: An African Challenge." *Mission Studies* 13.1–2 (1996) 130–88.

D'Angelo, Mary R. "Women Partners in the New Testament." *JFSR* 6 (1990) 65–86.

Danker, F. W. "Spain." In *ISBE* 4:591–92.

deSilva, David A. "Patronage." In *DNTB* 766–71.

Deissmann, Adolf. *The Religion of Jesus and the Faith of Paul*. Translated by W. E. Wilson. London: Hodder & Stoughton, 1923.

"Denmark and the Roman Empire." https://web.archive.org/web/20190107133745/http://legionord.org/index.php/artikler/denmark-and-the-roman-empire.

DeWitt, Calvin B., and Ghillean T. Prance, eds. *Missionary Earthkeeping*. Macon, GA: Mercer University, 1992.

Dicken, Frank E. "Luke." *LBD* n.p.

Dickson, John P. *Mission-Commitment in Ancient Judaism and in the Pauline Communities: The Shape, Extent and Background of Early Christian Mission*. WUNT 2:159. Tübingen: Mohr-Siebeck, 2003.

Dodd, C. H. *The Epistle of Paul to the Romans*. London: Fontana, 1959.

Donfried, Karl Paul. "False Presuppositions in the Study of Romans." In *The Romans Debate*, edited by Karl P. Donfried, 102–27. Peabody, MA: Hendrickson, 1991.

———. *The Romans Debate*. Revised and Expanded Edition. Peabody, MA: Hendrickson, 1991.

———, ed. "A Short Note on Romans 16." In *The Romans Debate*, edited by Karl P. Donfried, 44–52. Revised and Expanded Edition. Peabody, MA: Hendrickson, 1991.

Downs, D. "Economics." In *DJG2* 219–26.

Dunn, James D. G. "Romans." In *DPL* 838–50.

———. *Romans 1–8*. WBC 38A. Dallas: Word, 1988.

———. *Romans 9–16*. WBC 38B. Dallas: Word, 1988.

———. *The Epistle to the Galatians*. BNTC. London: Continuum, 1993.

Easton, M. G. "Rome." *EBD* n.p.

Edwards, James R. *The Gospel According to Mark*. PNTC. Grand Rapids, MI; Eerdmans, 2002.

Ehorn, Seth M. *Philemon*. Edited by H. Wayne House and W. Hall Harris. Evangelical Exegetical Commentary. Bellingham, WA: Lexham, 2011.

Ellis, Earle E. *Prophecy and Hermeneutic in Early Christianity*. Grand Rapids, MI: Eerdmans, 1978.

Ellwell, Walter A., and Barry J. Beitzel. "Ransom." In *BEB* 1822.

"Etruscan." https://www.britannica.com/topic/Etruscan.

European Christian Environment Network. "Bibliography of Christian Theology (Resources in English)." http://www.ecen.org/articles/theology/bibliography-creation-theology-resources-english.

Fee, Gordon D. *God's Empowering Presence: The Holy Spirit in the Letters of Paul*. Peabody, MA: Hendrikson, 1994.

———. *The First Epistle to the Corinthians*. Revised Edition. NICNT. Grand Rapids, MI: Eerdmans, 2014.

Fiore, Benjamin. "Parenesis and Protreptic." In *AYBD* 5:162–65.

Fitzmyer, Joseph A. *Romans: A New Translation with Introduction and Commentary*. AYBC 33. London: Yale University, 2008.

Fletcher, Joseph. *Situational Ethics: The New Morality*. London: Westminster John Knox, 1966.

Foerster, Werner. "Σῴζω, Σωτηρία, Σωτήρ, Σωτήριος." In *TDNT* 7:965–1025.

Forbes, Chris. "Comparison, Self-Praise and Irony: Paul's Boasting and the Conventions of Hellenistic Rhetoric." *NTS* 32 (1986) 1–30.

Ford, Coleman. "Pliny the Younger." In *LBD* n.p.

Francis, Pope. *Laudato Si'*. http://www.vatican.va/content/francesco/en/encyclicals/documents/papa-francesco_20150524_enciclica-laudato-si.html.

Friedrich, Gerhard. "Εὐαγγελίζομαι, Εὐαγγέλιον, Προευαγγελίζομαι, Εὐαγγελιστής." In *TDNT* 2:707–37.

Gabbatt, Adam. "Is Silicon Valley's Quest for Immortality a Fate Worse Than Death?" *The Guardian*, September 23, 2019. https://www.theguardian.com/technology/2019/feb/22/silicon-valley-immortality-blood-infusion-gene-therapy.

Gaffin, Richard B. "A Cessationist View." In *Are Miraculous Gifts for Today? Four Views*, edited by Richard B. Gaffin et al., 23–94. Counterpoints Bible & Theology. Grand Rapids, MI: Zondervan, 1996.

Gager, J. G. *The Origins of Anti-Semitism: Attitudes toward Judaism in Pagan and Christian Antiquity*. New York: Oxford University, 1983.

Gallagher, Robert L., and Paul Hertig, ed. *Contemporary Mission Theology: Engaging the Nations*. ASMS 53. Maryknoll, NY: Orbis, 2017.

Bibliography

Garland, David E. *1 Corinthians*. BECNT. Grand Rapids, MI: Baker Academic, 2003.

———. *2 Corinthians*. NAC 29. Nashville: Broadman & Holman, 1999.

———. *Luke*. ZECNT. Grand Rapids, MI: Zondervan, 2012.

Garrett, Duane A. *Hosea, Joel*. NAC 19A. Nashville: Broadman & Holman, 1997.

———. *Proverbs, Ecclesiastes, Song of Songs*, NAC 14. Nashville: Broadman & Holman, 1993.

Gasque, W. Ward. "Tarsus." In *AYBD* 6:333–34.

Gaston, L. *Paul and the Torah*. Vancouver: University of British Columbia, 1987.

"Gaul." https://library.laidlaw.ac.nz:2114/EBchecked/topic/227066/Gaul.

Geisler, Norman L. "Polytheism." In *BECA* 602.

"Germany." https://library.laidlaw.ac.nz:2114/EBchecked/topic/231186/Germany/58083/Coexistence-with-Rome-to-ad-350.

Gill, David William John. "Taxation, Greco-Roman." In *DNTB* 1161–66.

"Global Religious Futures." http://www.globalreligiousfutures.org/religions/christians.

Goheen, Michael W., ed. *Reading the Bible Missionally*. Grand Rapids, MI: Eerdmans, 2016.

———. "A History and Introduction to a Missional Reading of the Bible." In *Reading the Bible Missionally*, edited by Michael W. Goheen, 3–27. Grand Rapids, MI: Eerdmans, 2016.

Goldsworthy, Graeme. "Biblical Theology and the Shape of Paul's Mission." In *The Gospel to the Nations: Perspectives on Paul's Mission*, edited by Peter Bolt and Mark Thompson, 7–18. Downers Grove, IL: InterVarsity, 2000.

Gorman, Michael. *Becoming the Gospel: Paul, Participation, and Mission*. Grand Rapids, MI: Eerdmans, 2015.

Green, Joel B. "Crucifixion." In *DPL* 197–99.

Green, Michael. *Evangelism in the Early Church*. Crowborough: Highland, 1970.

Grenz, Stanley, et al. *Pocket Dictionary of Theological Terms*. Downers Grove, IL: InterVarsity, 1999.

Grindheim, Sigurd. *Introducing Biblical Theology*. London: Bloomsbury, 2013.

Guerra, Anthony J. *Romans and the Apologetic Tradition: The Purpose, Genre and Audience of Paul's Letter*. NTSMS 81. Cambridge: Cambridge University, 1995.

Gupta, Nijay K. *Paul and the Language of Faith*. Grand Rapids, MI: Eerdmans, 2020.

Guyer, Michael S. "Illyricum." In *LBD* n.p.

Haacker, Klaus. "Exegetische Probleme des Römerbrief." *NovT* 20 (1978) 1–21.

———. *The Theology of Paul's Letter to the Romans*. NTS. Cambridge: Cambridge University, 2003.

Hafemann, Scott. "'Because of Weakness' (Galatians 4.13): The Role of Suffering in the Mission of Paul." In *The Gospel to the Nations: Perspectives on Paul's Mission*, edited by Peter Bolt and Mark Thompson, 131–46. Downers Grove, IL: InterVarsity, 2000.

Hahn, Ferdinand. *Mission in the New Testament*. WMANT 13. Translated by Frank Clarke. London: SCM, 1965.

Hall, Emily. "What Is the Romans Road to Salvation?" https://www.christianity.com/wiki/salvation/what-is-the-romans-road-to-salvation.html.

Hall, J. F. "Rome." In *AYBD* 5:830–33.

Hansen, Walter G. "Rhetorical Criticism." In *DPL* 822–26.

Harris, Murray J. *Jesus as God: The New Testament Use of Theos in Reference to Jesus*. Grand Rapids, MI: Baker, 1992.

———. *The Second Epistle to the Corinthians: A Commentary on the Greek Text*. NIGTC. Grand Rapids, MI: Eerdmans, 2005.

Hauck, Friedrich, and Seigfried Schulz. "Πόρνη, Πόρνος, Πορνεία, Πορνεύω, Ἐκπορνεύω." In *TDNT* 579–95.

Hays, J. Daniel. *From Every People and Nation: A Biblical Theology of Race*. NSBT 14. Downers Grove, IL: Apollos, 2003.

Hays, Richard B. "The Letter to the Galatians." In *The New Interpreter's Bible*, edited by L. E. Keck, 11:181–348. New York: HarperSanFrancisco, 2000.

———. *The Moral Vision of the New Testament: Community, Cross, New Creation: A Contemporary Introduction to New Testament Ethics*. New York: HarperSanFrancisco, 1996.

Heide, G. Z. "What Is New about the New Heaven and the New Earth? A Theology of Creation from Revelation 21 and 2 Peter 3." *JETS* 40 (1997) 37–56.

Hendriksen, William, and Simon J. Kistemaker. *Exposition of Paul's Epistle to the Romans*. 2 vols. NTC. Grand Rapids: Baker, 1980.

Hengel, Martin. *Between Jesus and Paul: Studies in the Earliest History of Christianity*. London: SCM, 1964.

Hill, Michael. "Theology and Ethics in the Letter to the Romans." In *The Gospel to the Nations: Perspectives on Paul's Mission*, edited by Peter Bolt and Mark Thompson, 249–62. Downers Grove, IL: InterVarsity, 2000.

Hock, Ronald F. *The Social Context of Paul's Ministry: Tentmaking and Apostleship*. Philadelphia: Fortress, 1980.

———. "The Workshop as a Social Setting for Paul's Missionary Preaching." *CBQ* 41 (1979) 438–50.

Holmes, Michael William. *The Apostolic Fathers: Greek Texts and English Translations*. Updated Edition. Grand Rapids, MI: Baker, 1999.

Howell, Don H., Jr. "Mission in Paul's Epistles: Genesis, Pattern, and Dynamics." In *Mission in the New Testament: An Evangelical Approach*, edited by William J. Larkin Jr. and Joel F. Williams, 63–91. ASMS 27. Maryknoll, NY: Orbis, 1998.

———. "Mission in Paul's Epistles: Theological Bearings." In *Mission in the New Testament: An Evangelical Approach*, edited by William J. Larkin Jr. and Joel F. Williams, 92–118. 27. Maryknoll, NY: Orbis, 1998.

Hughes, Lesley. "Biological Consequences of Global Warming: Is the Signal Already Apparent." *TEE* 15.2 (2000) 56–61.

Hultgren, Arland J. *Paul's Gospel and Mission: The Outlook from His Letter to the Romans*. Philadelphia: Fortress, 1985.

Hurtado, Larry W. *Lord Jesus Christ: Devotion to Jesus in Earliest Christianity*. Grand Rapids, MI: Eerdmans, 2003.

"Irreligion in New Zealand." https://en.wikipedia.org/wiki/Irreligion_in_New_Zealand#/media/File:Religious_affiliation_in_New_Zealand_1991-2018_-_line_chart.svg.

Jervell, Jacob. "The Letter to Jerusalem." In *The Romans Debate*, edited by Karl Paul Donfried, 53–64. Revised and Expanded Edition. Peabody, MA: Hendrickson, 1991.

Jewett, Robert, and Roy David Kotansky. *Romans: A Commentary*. Hermeneia. Minneapolis, MN: Fortress, 2006.

Jones, Richard N. "Paleopathology." In *AYBD* 5:670–69.

Jørgensen, Lars. "The Warriors, Soldiers and Conscripts of the Anthropology in Late Roman and Migration Period Archaeology." In *Military Aspects of the Aristocracy in Babaricum in the Roman and Early Migration Periods*, edited by Birger Storgaard, 9–19. Publications from the National Museum. Copenhagen: Publications from the National Museum Studies in Archaeology & History, 2001.

Josephus, Flavius, and William Whiston. *The Works of Josephus: Complete and Unabridged.* Peabody: Hendrickson, 1987.

Judge, E. A. "Rome." In *NBD* 1027–29.

Kallas, J. "Romans xiii. 1–7: An Interpolation." *NTS* 11 (1964/65) 365–74.

Karris, Robert J. " Romans 14:1–15:13 and the Occasion of Romans." In *The Romans Debate*, edited by Karl Paul Donfried, 64–84. Revised and Expanded Edition. Peabody, MA: Hendrickson, 1991.

Käsemann, Ernst. *Commentary on Romans.* Edited by Geoffrey W. Bromiley. Translated by Geoffrey W. Bromiley. 1st ed. Grand Rapids, MI: Eerdmans, 1994.

———. *New Testament Questions of Today.* Philadelphia: Fortress, 1969.

Kee, Howard Clark. "Medicine and Healing." Pages in *AYBD* 4:659–64.

Keen, Karen R. "Sexuality, Critical Issues." In *LBD* n.p.

Keener, Craig S. *The Gospel of John: A Commentary.* 2 vols. Grand Rapids, MI: Baker Academic, 2012.

———. *Romans.* NCCS. Eugene, OR: Cascade, 2009.

Kellner, Menachem. "Ethics of Judaism." In *EJud* 1:250–59.

Keown, Mark J. "The Apostolic Green Imperative." In *Living on the Planet Earth: Faith Communities and Ecology*, edited by Neil Darragh, 33–40. Auckland: Accent, 2016.

———. "A 'Biblical' View of Marriage." *Candour* 10 (2013) 10–12.

———. *Congregational Evangelism in Philippians: The Centrality of An Appeal for Gospel Proclamation to the Fabric of Philippians.* PBM. Milton Keynes, UK: Paternoster, 2008.

———. *Galatians: A Commentary for Students.* Auckland: Morphe, 2020.

———. *The Gospels & Acts.* Vol. 1 of *Discovering the New Testament: An Introduction to Its Background, Theology, and Themes.* Bellingham, WA: Lexham, 2018.

———. "An Imminent Parousia and Christian Mission: Did the New Testament Writers Expect Jesus' Imminent Return?" In *Christian Origins and the Establishment of the Early Jesus Movement*, edited by Stanley E. Porter and Andrew W. Pitts, 242–63. TENTS; ECHC 4. Leiden: Brill, 2018.

———. "Is the Gay Issue a Secondary Theological Issue?" *Mark Keown* (blog), August 22, 2013. http://drmarkk.blogspot.com/2013/08/is-gay-issue-secondary-theological-issue.html.

———. "ΛΟΓΟΝ ΖΩΗΣ EPECHONTES, Holding Forth the Word of Life." In *Holding Forth the Word of Life: Essays in Honor of Tim Meadowcroft*, edited by John de Jong and Csilla Saysell, 98–117. Australian College of Theology Monograph Series. Eugene, OR: Wipf & Stock, 2020.

———. "Notes of Hope in the Face of Suffering (Rom 8:18–39)." *Stimulus*, May 2020. https://hail.to/laidlaw-college/publication/1tI5uq8/article/YeNLe05.

———. "Paul's Vision of a New Masculinity." *Colloquium* 47.1 (2016) 47–60.

———. *Philippians.* Edited by H. Wayne House et al. 2 vols. EEC. Bellingham, WA: Lexham, 2017.

———. *What's God Up To On Planet Earth?: A No-Strings Attached Presentation of the Christian Message.* Eugene, OR: Wipf & Stock, 2010.

Kim, Chan-H. *Form and Structure of the Familiar Greek Letter of Recommendation.* SBLDS. Missoula: University of Montana, 1972.

Knox, J. *Chapters in a Life of Paul.* London: A. & C. Black, 1954.

Köstenberger, Andreas J., and Peter T. O'Brien. *Salvation to the Ends of the Earth: A Biblical Theology of Mission.* NSBT 11. Downers Grove, IL: Apollos, 2001.

Kümmel, W. G. *Introduction to the New Testament.* Rev. ed. Translated by H. C. Kee. Nashville: Abingdon, 1975.

Laansma, Jon C. "Commentary on 2 Timothy." *Cornerstone Biblical Commentary* 17. Carol Stream, IL: Tyndale, 2009.

Lampe, Peter. "The Roman Christians of Romans 16." In *The Romans Debate*, edited by Karl Paul Donfried, 216–30. Revised and Expanded Edition. Peabody, MA: Hendrickson, 1991.

Lea, Thomas D., and Hayne P. Griffin. *1, 2 Timothy, Titus.* NAC 34. Nashville: Broadman & Holman, 1992.

Legrand, Lucien. *Unity and Plurality: Mission in the Bible.* Translated by Robert R. Barr. Maryknoll, NY: Orbis, 1990.

Lenski, R. C. H. *The Interpretation of St. Paul's Epistle to the Romans.* Minneapolis: Augsburg, 1936.

Liddell, Henry George, et al. *A Greek-English Lexicon.* Oxford: Clarendon, 1996.

Lipka, Michael. "7 Key Findings about Religion and Politics in Israel." https://www.pewresearch.org/fact-tank/2016/03/08/key-findings-religion-politics-israel/#:~:text=About%20eight%2Din%2Dten%20(,more%20religiously%20observant%20than%20Jews.

Little, Christopher R. *Mission in the Way of Paul: Biblical Mission for the Church in the Twenty-First Century.* Studies in Biblical Literature 80. New York: Lang, 2005.

Longenecker, Bruce W. *Remember the Poor: Paul, Poverty, and the Greco-Roman World.* Grand Rapids: Eerdmans, 2010.

Longenecker, Richard N. *The Epistle to the Romans: A Commentary on the Greek Text.* NIGTC. Grand Rapids, MI: Eerdmans, 2016.

———. *Galatians.* WBC 41. Dallas: Word, 1990

———. *Paul, Apostle of Liberty: The Origin and Nature of Paul's Christology.* Twin Brooks Series. Grand Rapids, MI: Baker, 1964.

———. "'What Does It Matter?' Priorities and the *adiaphora* in Paul's Dealing with Opponents in Mission." In *The Gospel to the Nations: Perspectives on Paul's Mission*, edited by Peter Bolt and Mark Thompson, 147–60. Downers Grove, IL: InterVarsity, 2000.

Lopez, René A. *Romans Unlocked Power to Deliver.* Springfield, MO: 21st Century, 2005.

Lüdemann, G. *Paul, Apostle to the Gentiles: Studies in Chronology.* Philadelphia: Fortress, 1984.

Magda, Ksenija. *Paul's Territoriality and Mission Strategy: Searching for the Geographical Awareness Paradigm Behind Romans.* WUNT 2:266. Tübingen: Mohr Siebeck, 2009.

Mangum, Douglas. *The Lexham Glossary of Theology.* Bellingham, WA: Lexham, 2014.

Marshall, I. Howard. "The New Testament Does Not Teach Universal Salvation." In *Universal Salvation? The Current Debate*, edited by R. A. Parry and C. H. Partridge, 55–76. Grand Rapids: Eerdmans, 2003.

———. "Who Were the Evangelists?" In *The Mission of the Early Church to Jews and Gentiles*, edited by J. Ådna and H. Kvalbein, 251–64. WUNT 127. Tübingen: Mohr Siebeck, 2000.

Marshall, I. Howard., and Philip H. Towner. *A Critical and Exegetical Commentary on the Epistles.* ICC. London: T. & T. Clark, 2004.

Martin, George. "Missions in the Pauline Epistles." In *Missiology: An Introduction to the Foundations, History, and Strategies of World Missions*, edited by John Mark Terry et al., 83–96. Nashville: Broadman & Homan, 1998.

Mattill, A. J. "The Purpose of Acts: Schneckenburger Reconsidered." In *Apostolic History and the Gospel*, edited by W. Ward Gasque and Ralph P. Martin, 108–22. Grand Rapids: Eerdmans, 1970.

McCant, J. W. "Paul's Thorn of Rejected Apostleship." *NTS* 34 (1987–88).

Meeks, Charles. "Ephraim, Son of Joseph." In *LBD* n.p.

Meinardus, Otto F. A. "Paul's Missionary Journey to Spain: Tradition and Folklore." *BA* 41.2 (June 1978) 61–63.

Melanchthon, P. *Loci communes of 1521*. In *Melanchthons Werke im Auswahl 2.1*, edited by H. Engelland, 1–163. Gütersloh: Bertelsmann, 1952.

Menoud, P. H. *Jesus Christ and the Faith: A Collection of Studies*. PTMS 18. Pittsburgh: Pickwick, 1978.

Merrill, E. H. "Image of God." In *DOTP* 444.

Metzger, Bruce Manning. *A Textual Commentary on the Greek New Testament: A Companion Volume to the United Bible Societies' Greek New Testament (Fourth rev. ed)*. 2nd ed. New York: United Bible Societies, 1994.

Meye, Robert P. "Spirituality." In *DPL* 906–16.

Michaelis, Wilhelm. "συγγενής, συγγένεια." In *TDNT* 7:736–42.

Moo, Douglas J. *Galatians*. BECNT. Grand Rapids, MI: Baker Academic, 2013.

———. *The Letter to the Romans*. 2nd ed. NICNT. Grand Rapids, MI: Eerdmans, 2018.

Moo, Jonathan. "Environmental Unsustainability and the Biblical Vision of the Earth's Future." In *Creation in Crisis: Christian Perspectives on Sustainability*, edited by R. S. White, 255–70. London: SPCK, 2009.

Morris, Leon. *The Epistle to the Romans*. PNTC. Grand Rapids, MI: Eerdmans, 1988.

Moule, Handley. *The Epistle to the Romans*. Fort Washington, PA: Christian Literature Crusade, 1975.

Mounce, Robert H. *Romans*. NAC 27. Nashville: Broadman & Holman, 1995.

Muddiman, John. *The Epistle to the Ephesians*. BNTC. London: Continuum, 2001.

Neil, Stephen. *The Unfinished Task*. London: Lutterworth, 1957.

Newman, Barclay Moon, and Eugene Albert Nida. *A Handbook on Paul's Letter to the Romans*. UBSHS. New York: United Bible Societies, 1973.

Nisbet, P. "The Thorn in the Flesh." *ExpT* 80 (1969) 125–29.

Nissen, Johannes. *New Testament and Mission: Historical and Hermeneutical Perspectives*. Frankfurt: Lang,1999.

Norris, D. Thaine. *Logos Deluxe Map Set*. Oak Harbor, WA: Lexham, 1997.

O'Brien, Peter T. *Consumed by Passion: Paul and the Dynamic of the Gospel*. Homebush West, NSW: Lancer, 1993.

———. *Gospel and Mission in the Writings of Paul: An Exegetical and Theological Analysis*. Grand Rapids: Baker, 1995.

———. "Letters, Letter Forms." In *DPL* 551–53.

———. "Thanksgiving Within the Structure of Pauline Theology." In *Pauline Studies: Essays Presented to F. F. Bruce*, edited by D. Hagner, 50–66. Exeter: Paternoster, 1980.

Osborne, Grant R. *Romans: Verse by Verse*. ONTC. Bellingham, WA: Lexham, 2017.

Packer, J. I., et al. *Nelson's Illustrated Manners and Customs of the Bible*. Nashville: Nelson, 1997.

Panjikaran, J. G. *Paul's Concept of Mission: An Exegetical and Theological Study of Romans 10:8–17*. Delhi: ISPCK, 2009.

Patzia, Arthur G., and Anthony J. Petrotta. *Pocket Dictionary of Biblical Studies*. Downers Grove, IL: InterVarsity, 2002.

Peters, George W. *A Biblical Theology of Missions*. Chicago: Moody, 1972.

Peterson, David G. *The Acts of the Apostles*. PNTC. Grand Rapids, MI: Eerdmans, 2009.

Ploutz, Paul F. *Global Warming: Handbook of Ecological Issues*. Bloomington, IN: Xlibris 2012.

Plümacher, E. "μάχαιρα, ης, ἡ *machaira* sword." In *EDNT* 2:397–98.

Plummer, Robert E. *Paul's Understanding of the Church's Mission: Did the Apostle Paul Expect the Early Christian Communities to Evangelize?* PBM. Milton Keynes, UK: Paternoster, 2006.

Pohl, C. *Making Room: Recovering Hospitality as a Christian Tradition*. Grand Rapids, MI: Eerdmans, 1999.

Porter, Stanley E. *Idioms of the Greek New Testament*. Sheffield: JSOT, 1999.

Ramsay, William M. *St. Paul the Traveller and Roman Citizen*. London: Hodder & Stoughton, 1896.

Rasnake, Eddie. *The Book of Romans*. FGS. Chattanooga, TN: AMG, 2005.

Reasoner, M. "Rome and Roman Christianity." In *DPL* 850–55.

Reed, Jeffrey T. "The Epistle." In *Handbook of Classical Rhetorical in the Hellenistic Period (330 B.C.—A.D. 400)*, edited by Stanley E. Porter, 172–92. Leiden: Brill, 1997.

Rengstorf, Karl Heinrich. "Ἀποστέλλω (πέμπω), Ἐξαποστέλλω, Ἀπόστολος, Ψευδαπόστολος, Ἀποστολή." In *TDNT* 1:398–446.

Robeck, Cecil M., Jr. "Prophecy, Prophesying." In *DPL* 755–62.

Roberts, W. Dayton. *Patching God's Garment: Environment and Mission in the Twenty-First Century*. Monrovia, CA: MARC, World Vision International, 1994.

Robinson, J. A. T. *Redating the New Testament*. Philadelphia: Westminster, 1976.

Roloff, J. "ἱλαστήριον, ου, τό *hilastērion*." In *EDNT* 2:185–86.

Rosner, Brian S., ed. *Understanding Paul's Ethics: Twentieth-Century Approaches*. Grand Rapids, MI: Eerdmans, 1995.

Rostovtzeff, M. *The Social and Economic History of the Roman Empire*. 2nd ed. Edited by Rev. P. M. Fraser. Oxford: Clarendon, 1957.

Ruether, Rosemary Radford. "Ecojustice at the Center of the Church's Mission." *Mission Studies* 16.1 (1999) 111–21.

Runge, Steven E. *Romans*. HDC. Bellingham, WA: Lexham, 2014.

Ryken, Leland, et al. *Dictionary of Biblical Imagery*. Downers Grove, IL: InterVarsity, 2000.

Sanday, W., and A. C. Headlam. *A Critical and Exegetical Commentary on the Epistle to the Romans*. 5th ed. ICC. Edinburgh: T. & T. Clark, 1902.

Schaff, Philip, ed. *Saint Chrysostom: Homilies on the Acts of the Apostles and the Epistle to the Romans*. Vol. 11 of *A Select Library of the Nicene and Post-Nicene Fathers of the Christian Church, First Series*. New York: Christian Literature, 1889.

Schaff, Philip, and David Schley Schaff. *History of the Christian Church*. 8 vols. New York: Scribner's, 1910.

Schlatter, A. *Paulus, der Bote Jesu: Eine Deutung seiner Briefe an die Korinther*. Stuttgart: Calwer, 1956.

Schmitz, Leonhard. "JUNO." In *DGRBM* 2:658–59.

———. "JU'PITER." In *DGRBM* 2:569–60.

Bibliography

———. "MINERVA." In *DGRBM* 2:1090.

Schnabel, Eckhard J. *Early Christian Mission*. 2 vols. Downers Grove, IL: InterVarsity, 2004.

———. *Paul the Missionary: Realities, Strategies and Methods*. Downers Grove, IL: InterVarsity. Kindle ed.

Schneider, G. "Ἰησοῦς, οῦ *Iēsous* Jesus." In *EDNT* 2:180–84.

Schreiner, Thomas R. *1, 2 Peter, Jude*. NAC 37. Nashville: Broadman & Holman, 2003.

———. *40 Questions about Christians and Biblical Law*. Edited by Benjamin L. Merkle. 40 Questions Series. Grand Rapids, MI: Kregel Academic & Professional, 2010.

———. *Galatians*. ZECNT. Grand Rapids, MI: Zondervan, 2010.

———. *Romans*. BECNT 6. Grand Rapids, MI: Baker, 1998.

Schweitzer, Albert. *Die Mystek des Apostels Paulus*. Tübingen: Mohr Siebeck, 1930.

Scott, James M. "Adoption, Sonship." In *DPL* 15–18.

Senior, Donald, and Carroll P. Stuhlmueller. *The Biblical Foundations for Mission*. Maryknoll, NY: Orbis, 1984.

Shead, Andrew G. "The New Covenant and Pauline Hermeneutics." In *The Gospel to the Nations: Perspectives on Paul's Mission*, edited by Peter Bolt and Mark Thompson, 33–49. Leicester: InterVarsity, 2000.

Seifrid, Mark A. "Romans." In *Commentary on the New Testament Use of the Old Testament*, edited by G. K. Beale and D. A. Carson, 607–94. Grand Rapids, MI: Baker Academic, 2007.

Silva, Moisés, ed. *New International Dictionary of New Testament Theology and Exegesis*. Grand Rapids, MI: Zondervan, 2014.

Simeon, Charles. *Romans*. Vol. 15 of *Horae Homileticae*. London: Holdsworth and Ball, 1833.

Simmons, William. "Nero, Emperor, History of in the Primary Sources." In *LBD* n.p.

Simpson, K. A. "William Hobson." https://nzhistory.govt.nz/people/william-hobson.

Smith, Gary V. *Isaiah 1–39*. NAC 15A. Nashville: Broadman & Holman, 2007.

Snodgrass, K. R. "Justification by Grace—To the Doers: An Analysis of the Place of Romans 2 in the Theology of Paul." *NTS* 32 (1986) 72–93.

Spence-Jones, H. D. M., ed. *The Pulpit Commentary: Romans*. The Pulpit Commentary. London: Funk & Wagnalls, 1909.

Stirewalt, M. Luther, Jr. "The Form and Function of the Greek Letter-Essay." In *The Romans Debate*, edited by Karl P. Donfried, 147–71. Revised and Expanded Edition. Peabody: Hendrickson, 1991.

Stowers, Stanley. *Letter Writing in Greco-Roman Antiquity*. Philadelphia: Westminster, 1986.

Swanson, James. *Dictionary of Biblical Languages with Semantic Domains: Hebrew (Old Testament)*. Oak Harbor: Logos Research Systems, 1997.

Swindoll, Charles R. *Faith That Endures: In Times Like These*. BSG. Nashville: Nelson, 1993.

Tan, Lincoln. "Auckland More Diverse than London and New York." *New Zealand Herald*, January 17, 2016. https://www.nzherald.co.nz/nz/news/article.cfm?c_id=1&objectid=11575305.

Tennent, Timothy C. *Theology in the Context of World Christianity: How the Global Church is Influencing the Way We Think About and Discuss Theology*. Grand Rapids, MI: Zondervan, 2007.

———. *World Missions: A Trinitarian Missiology for the Twenty-First Century*. ITSS. Grand Rapids, MI: Kregel, 2010.

Terry, John Mark, et al. *Missiology: An Introduction to the Foundations, History, and Strategies of World Missions*. Nashville: Broadman & Holman, 1998.

Thiede, P. "A Pagan Reader of 2 Peter: Cosmic Conflagration in 2 Peter 3 and the Octavius of Minucius Felix." *JSNT* 26 (1986) 83–91.

Thielman, Frank. *Romans*. ZECNT. Edited by Clinton E. Arnold. Grand Rapids, MI: Zondervan, 2018.

Thierry, J. J. "Der Dorn im Fleische (2 Kor. xii 7–9)." *NovT* 5 (1962) 301–10.

Thrall, Margaret E. *Commentary on II Corinthians VIII–XIII*. ICC. Edinburgh: T. & T. Clark, 2000.

Toews, John E. *Romans*. BCBC. Scottdale, PA: Herald, 2004.

Toney, Carl N. *Paul's Inclusive Ethics: Resolving Community Conflicts and Promoting Mission in Romans 14–15*. WUNT 2:252. Tübingen: Mohr Siebeck, 2008.

Towner, Philip H. "Households and Household Codes." In *DPL* 417–19.

"United Kingdom." https://library.laidlaw.ac.nz:2114/EBchecked/topic/615557/United-Kingdom/44735/Roman-Britain.

Utley, Robert James. *The Gospel According to Paul: Romans*. SGCS 5. Marshall, TX: Bible Lessons International, 1998. Logos ed.

Van Rheenen, Gerald. *Missions: Biblical Foundations & Contemporary Strategies*. Grand Rapids, MI: Zondervan, 1996.

Varner, William. *James*. . Bellingham, WA: Lexham, 2012.

Veldman, Robin Globus. *The Gospel of Climate Skepticism: Why Evangelical Christians Oppose Action on Climate Change*. Oakland, CA: University of California, 2019.

Volf, Miroslav. *Exclusion and Embrace: A Theological Exploration of Identity, Otherness, and Reconciliation*. Nashville: Abingdon, 1996.

Wallace, Daniel B. *Greek Grammar Beyond the Basics: Exegetical Syntax of the New Testament*. Grand Rapids, MI: Zondervan, 1996.

Walters, James. "'Phoebe' and 'Junia(s)'—Rom. 16:1–2, 7." In *Essays on Women in Earliest Christianity*, edited by Carroll D. Osburn, 1:167–90. Joplin, MO: College, 1993.

Walton, Steve. "Ascension of Jesus." In *DJG2* 59–61.

Ware, Bruce A. *God's Lesser Glory: The Diminished God of Open Theism*. Wheaton: Crossway, 2000.

Ware, James P. *The Mission of the Church in Paul's Letter to the Philippians in the Context of Ancient Judaism*. NovTSup 120. Leiden: Brill, 2005.

———. "The Thessalonians as a Missionary Congregation: 1 Thessalonians 1, 5–8." *ZNW* 83 (1992) 126–31.

Watson, Duane F. "Greece and Macedon." *DNTB* 421–26.

Watts, John D. *Isaiah 1–33*. WBC 24. Nashville: Nelson, 2005.

Weima, Jeffrey A. D. *1–2 Thessalonians*. BECNT. Grand Rapids, MI: Baker Academic, 2014.

Wenham, Gordon J. *Genesis 1–15*. WBC 1. Dallas: Word, 1987.

Westerholm, Stephen. *Perspectives Old and New on Paul: The "Lutheran" Paul and His Critics*. Grand Rapids: Eerdmans, 2004.

Wiefel, Wolfgang. "The Jewish Community in Ancient Rome and the Origins of Roman Christianity." In *The Romans Debate*, edited by Karl Paul Donfried, 85–101. Revised and Expanded Edition. Peabody, MA: Hendrickson, 1991.

Windisch, Hans. "βάρβαρος." In *TDNT* 1:546–53.

Winn, A. "Son of God." In *DJG2* 886–94.

Witherington, Ben, III. *The Acts of the Apostles: A Socio-Rhetorical Commentary*. Grand Rapids, MI: Eerdmans, 1998.

———. "Christology." In *DPL* 1–115.

———. "Lord." In *DJG* 485–92.

Witherington, Ben, III, and Darlene Hyatt. *Paul's Letter to the Romans: A Socio-Rhetorical Commentary*. Grand Rapids, MI: Eerdmans, 2004.

Wolter, M. *Die Brief an die Römer*. Vol. 1. Göttingen: Vandenhoeck & Ruprecht, 2014.

Wright, Christopher J. H. *The Mission of God: Unlocking the Bible's Grand Narrative*. Nottingham: InterVarsity, 2006.

Wright, N. T. *The Climax of the Covenant: Christ and the Law in Pauline Theology*. Minneapolis, MN: Fortress, 1991.

———. *Hebrews for Everyone*. London: SPCK, 2003.

———. *Justification: God's Plan and Paul's Vision*. London: SPCK, 2009.

———. *Paul and the Faithfulness of God*. 2 vols. COQG 4. Minneapolis: Fortress, 2013.

———. "Reading the New Testament Missionally." In *Reading the Bible Missionally*, edited by Michael W. Goheen, 175–93. Grand Rapids, MI: Eerdmans, 2016.

———. *The Resurrection of the Son of God*. COQG3. London: SPCK, 2003.

———. "Romans." In *The New Interpreter's Bible*, edited by Leander E. Keck et al., 10:395–770. Nashville: Abingdon, 2002.

Wuellner, W. "Paul's Rhetoric of Argumentation in Romans: An Alternative to the Donfried-Karris Debate over Romans." In *The Romans Debate*, edited by Karl P. Donfried, 152–74. Revised and Expanded Edition. Peabody, MA: Hendrickson, 1991.

Yinger, Kent L. *The New Perspective on Paul: An Introduction*. Eugene, OR: Cascade, 2011.

Yoder, John Howard. *Theology of Mission: A Believers Church Perspective*. Edited by Gayle Gerber Koontz and Andy Alexis-Baker. Downers Grove, IL: IVP Academic, 2014.

Zwemer, Samuel M. *"Into All the World": The Great Commission: A Vindication and an Interpretation*. Harrisburg, PA: Christian, 1943.

Subject Index

Aaron, 194n74, 228n147
Abba, 78n4, 81, 93, 134, 146, 193, 204, 206
Abel, 196n84, 228n147
Abimelech, 141n10
abolition (slavery), 255n26
abortion, 267
Abraham, Abrahamic, 19, 50, 50n7, 51,
    53–56, 58–59, 61, 74, 80, 87, 89, 101, 108,
    110, 122, 124–126, 136, 139–141, 143,
    165, 169n3, 172, 181, 196n84, 199n91,
    203, 213, 227n135, 228n144, 229n150,
    229n151, 239–240, 251–252, 271n10,
    275–276, 285n39, 287n54, 294, 300,
    318–319, 341–342, 349, 351n3, 353, 356
Absalom, 194n78
Abstinence (from sexual immorality), 273n15
abstinence (general), 358n12
abyss, 60, 162, 162n16, 185, 185n27, 186
acceptance, 11–12, 82, 95, 138, 156–157,
    199n91, 289
Accursed, 14, 32, 70, 180, 315–316
Achaia, 23, 35, 37n26, 38, 48, 61n15, 175,
    213n55, 234n176, 256, 286, 311, 343
Achaicus, 208n22
Achilles, 227
Acilius, 215n67
Actium, 11, 279n1
Adam, 19, 51, 54, 58, 63, 74, 87, 89, 95, 96n7,
    98, 100–101, 106n36, 118, 124n43,
    136n82, 136n83, 144n22, 164–165, 205,
    228n144, 229n148, 231n163, 238n4,
    240–241, 252, 260, 261n9, 263, 265–266,
    282n19, 297, 300, 305, 308, 342n18, 349,
    359, 364
addictions, 92, 97, 102, 134, 253
Adoption, 11, 43, 60–61, 71–72, 78, 81, 88n47,
    93, 114, 117, 127, 133n73, 133n74, 134,
    137, 141, 143, 202, 206, 231, 275, 294,
    340, 349
Adoptionism, 84n26, 88n47
Adriatic Sea, 42n39, 75, 171, 311, 344
adultery, 60–61, 151, 250–251, 274–275, 299

aedileship, 23
Aeneas, 8, 227n138
affections, 189
affinitas, 142n15
afflictions, 313
a fortiori, 67
Africa, African(s), 7, 9, 173–174, 176–178,
    260n5, 296n7, 345n42, 346
Agabus, 242
age(s), 12, 63n30, 78, 87m 93, 101, 101n24,
    112, 123, 155–156, 159–160, 172, 185n31,
    227, 300, 323, 332, 334, 352, 356–358
ageism, 203, 290, 338n9
Agrippa I, 14, 176, 218n89, 333
Agrippa II, 20, 313
Agrippina, 218n89
Ahenobarbus, 85
Alexander the Great, 9n9
Alexandria, 130n58, 174, 358
alliteration, 331
allusion(s), 33n12, 53, 54n5, 101, 109n54, 172,
    284, 359
amanuensis(es), 22, 218, 281n92
ambassador(s), 68, 208–209, 211, 334
ambassadorial letter, 27–28, 209, 359
Amidah, 311n9
Ampliatus, 26, 277n34, 278n35, 343
Ananias (of Damascus), 33, 242, 245
anathema, 60, 60n7, 86, 315–316
Andrew (disciple), 175
Andronicus, 15n27, 16, 20, 119, 209, 216n76,
    217n83, 231, 271–272, 278n37, 343
Angel(s), 60, 105–106, 152, 212, 222n108,
    247n46, 247n49, 287, 330
anger, 102–103, 116, 199
animal(s), 12, 61, 134, 260, 260n7, 262, 267,
    269, 274, 286n46, 312, 333n37, 341n17
annihilation, 163
anointed, anointing, 60, 82, 84
anointing, 60
Anthropomorphism, 63
Anthropopathism, 63

375

Subject Index

antichrist, 165, 187n42
Antinomasia, 63
antinomian, 131
Antioch (Pisidian), 50
Antioch, (Syria), 17, 34, 36, 37n26, 38, 42, 48, 218, 221, 242n19, 282, 296n7, 339
Antiochian Missions, 18, 23, 35, 36n17, 37, 38, 49, 171, 256, 311, 337
Antistrophe, 63
Antithesis, 63
antithetical, 110, 305
antitype, 54
Anti-Semitic, 14, 354
Anti-Semitism, 351n4, 352
Antonius Pius, 133n77
Antony (Mark), 11
apartheid, 255n56
Aphorism, 64
Aphrodite, 227n138
apocalyptic, 159, 246n40, 262
apodosis, 64, 187
Apollo, 11
Apollos, 25, 210n31, 216n75, 220, 225, 291n78,
Apologetics, 167, 238n4, 355, 356n3, 358-359, 359n14
Apologetic witness, 201
apologists, 356, 359
Aposiopesis, 64
apostasy, apostate, 32, 211, 304n25
Apostle(s), v, 16, 18n6, 23n8, 32-33, 37-38, 40, 43, 50n6, 55, 59, 68-70, 80n12, 85, 103, 117n18, 155n15, 167n233, 169, 171, 174n27, 175-176, 179, 182, 186, 198, 201, 203, 208, 209n25, 209n26, 211n39, 212, 217, 225-226, 229n152, 233, 244, 245n37, 246, 246n41, 246n42, 247m49, 248, 272n12, 276, 295, 296n7, 306, 331, 343, 352, 354, 361-363, 368, 370, 373
Apostleship, 28, 40, 40n35, 68, 207n18, 210-211, 244, 247n49, 296, 366, 369
Apostolic, 39, 65, 81n15, 138, 170n8, 171n15, 176n32, 209-211, 217, 225, 225n122, 231n163, 241, 262n12, 263n14, 265n24, 265n26, 272, 299n13, 318n27, 366-367, 369
Apostolic Fathers, 43n46
apostolicity, 233, 247n49
Apphia, 215, 216n76, 272, 272n12
Aqiba, Rabbi, 154n12
aqueducts, 9, 11
Aquila, 1, 14-17, 20, 25-26, 49, 119, 212, 213n54, 215-217, 219, 231, 256-257, 271, 278n35, 291, 312, 343, 347

Arabia(n), 33, 36, 37n26, 174, 176-177, 344, 345n40
Archelaus, 13
Areopagus, 51
Aristarchus, 49, 171, 215n71, 218n89, 321n39
Aristobulus, 15n27, 20, 26, 218, 218n89, 277n34, 278n37, 291, 343
Aristocracy, 10-11
Ark of the Coven 115
Armenia, 173n22
Arminianism, 293, 297, 304n24
armor, 60, 172, 254n24, 303n20, 335
ascension, 88n47, 142, 182n12, 185n30
ascetic, 31n9
Asclepius, 13
ashamed, 41, 65, 70, 77, 114, 120, 137, 179-180, 180n5, 288
Asia (Minor), Asian, 7, 23, 25n19, 35, 38, 61, 61n15, 75, 171, 175, 177-178, 213n55, 124, 216n74, 223n117, 234n176, 256, 277, 278n37, 285, 321n39, 343-344, 345n39, 345n42, 356n3
Asseverative, 64
assonance, 66
Assyria, 85-86, 177, 326
astrology, 106n106
astronomy, 228
asymptote, 305n29
Asyncritus, 20, 218, 278n37, 343
Asyndeton, 64, 66-67
atheist, 238
Athena, 8n6
Athenodorus, 358
Athens, 171, 358n11
athletics, athlete(s), 182, 320
Atlantic Ocean, 42, 177
Atonement, atone(s), 96, 109, 115-116, 118, 124, 142, 161, 348
Attitude(s), attitudinal, 12-14, 18, 50n6, 69, 73, 97-98, 109n52, 121, 143-144, 149, 151, 156, 158, 198, 203, 205, 215, 234-235, 248, 250, 252-253, 256, 258-259, 261, 277, 284n34, 289, 324n3, 331, 334, 340-341, 354, 364
augures, 12
Augustan period, 252n14
Augustine, 111, 295n5, 336-337, 358
Augustus, 7, 11, 13, 85, 133, 227
Aurelius, Marcus, 133n74
Auschwitz, 258
Authorship, vii, 2, 22, 324n4
autumn, 37
Aventine, 8n8
Azerbaijan, 173n22
Baal, 317

Subject Index

Babylon, 53, 194, 326
bacchanalia, 13
Bacchus, 13
Baetica, 222
Balaam, 229n148
Balkans, 36n16, 40, 42, 42n39, 61, 69, 75, 171, 173–174, 179, 211, 277, 296
Baltic Sea, 176–177
Baptism, baptize(d), 16, 37, 60, 88n47, 89, 99, 104, 116, 126, 143–144, 150, 188–189, 205, 252, 341n16
Barbarian(s), 40, 61, 70n47, 71, 169, 173, 176, 179, 190, 339n12, 343
Barnabas, 34–36, 48, 172, 209, 209n26, 209n27, 210n31, 211, 211n38, 222, 244, 246n42, 284, 296n7, 337, 340
Barthianism, 118
basilica, 11
baths, 11
beasts, 244n25, 260n7
beatitude, 66
beauty, 194, 240, 261
behavior(2), behaving, behavioural, 66, 97, 100, 105, 118, 121, 132, 143, 145, 149–151, 154, 155n15, 157, 253–254, 275, 295n5, 326, 328, 330
belief(s), believe(s), believed, believers, believing, x, 2, 24, 28, 30, 32, 33n12, 40–41, 42n42, 48–53, 55, 61, 63, 66, 68, 69, 71, 73, 77, 79–83, 84n25, 86, 87, 88–89, 89n53 94, 90, 92 93, 94, 96, 97, 99 108, 109–111, 114–119, 123–133, 133n71, 134–135, 137–138, 138n1, 139n2, 140–142, 142n15, 143–145, 145n24, 146–153, 153n10, 154–155, 155n16, 155n17, 156–166, 169, 172–176, 179–180, 180n4, 180n6, 182, 183–184, 186–193, 195, 196–197, 198n85, 199, 199n91, 201–206, 207n16, 208, 210, 213n55, 214, 222, 224, 231–234, 235n179, 237–238, 238n4, 240–242, 242n19, 244, 244n31, 246–248, 246n50, 248, 251, 251n11, 252, 252n12, 254, 254n25, 255–256, 256n30, 257, 260, 261–262, 264–269, 269n2, 270, 272n212, 273, 275–277, 280, 281, 284, 286n44, 287, 287n56, 288–291, 295–297, 298–299, 299n14, 299n15, 300, 300n17, 302–303, 305–306, 306n31, 308–310, 310n4, 311–315, 317, 319, 320n36, 231–327, 329, 331–335, 337, 339n11, 340–341, 341n16, 343–344, 347, 349, 350–351, 351n3, 351n4, 352–353, 353n7, 354–355, 357, 357n6, 359
bellies, belly, 66–67
bema, 60

benediction, 25
Benedictions, Eighteen, 311n9
Benefactor(s), benefactress, 22, 37, 257, 290, 292
beneficence, 54, 113, 308
benevolence, 308
Benjamin, Benjaminite, 50n7, 56
Berea(n), 37, 321n39
bestiality, 274n18, 275n24
betrothed, 274
bios, 47, 72
bird(s), 61, 260
birth, childbirth, 160, 164–165, 195n78, 198, 263, 313n18, 315, 345
birth certificate, 61, 61n14
birth pains, 159, 160, 195
bitterness, 254n22
Black Sea, 173n22
bladder stone, 61n18
blame, blameworthy, 28n39, 262, 299
blameless, 108
blaspheme(d), blaspheming, 54, 239, 332
Bless(es), blessing(s), blessedness, ix, 25, 50n7, 60, 66, 69, 74, 87, 101, 123, 136, 156, 172, 184, 187n40, 190–191, 191n66, 199, 202, 229n154, 232, 239, 254, 256–258, 262, 281, 282n19, 283–284, 284n34, 286–288, 291, 294, 302n19, 307, 310–312, 321, 327, 331, 333, 335, 340–341, 343, 348, 349
blind, blinding, blindness, 56, 61, 148n1, 240, 245, 338, 346, 358
blood, bloody, 91, 115–116, 127, 134, 161, 202, 204, 216, 250n7, 269, 286n42, 309, 341n17, 364
Boast(s), boasted, boastful, boasting, 11, 54, 79n6, 90, 109–110, 118, 137, 204, 245, 247, 250, 248, 273, 300n16, 303, 308
Body, bodies, bodily, 8, 60, 67, 80, 91, 93, 100, 102, 117–119, 130, 132–135, 139n2, 152, 150, 155n16, 163, 165, 194, 198, 205, 207, 219, 232, 235, 243, 247, 254, 272, 303, 319, 332, 359n14
boldly, boldness, embolden, 309, 315, 318, 339
born, 11, 51, 85, 107, 111, 113, 133, 173, 199, 240, 271, 295, 344, 346, 349
Bosnia, Bosnia-Herzegovina, 42n39, 171, 258
Boundary markers, 17, 107, 109–110, 141, 141n11, 143, 336, 337n7
Boundaries (cultural), 289n67, 346
Boundaries (right and wrong), 152
bow(ed), bowing 144, 161, 192, 203, 231, 317, 319, 320, 334, 335
boy, 206
branch, 17, 61, 297n11, 336, 351, 353
brave, bravely, 148n3, 275, 358

377

Subject Index

bread, 56, 287, 318n27
breath(ed), 189, 132, 232, 241
bride of Christ, 133
Brigantium, 357
Britain, Britannia, 7, 10, 176–177, 177n47, 178, 345n39
British Crown, 131
Brother(s), brotherly, 20, 31, 40, 84, 133n71, 144, 198, 205, 211, 216, 218n89, 220, 224n119, 232, 272n12, 275–276, 285n40, 285n41, 297, 315–316, 320n33, 321n38, 333n37, 337, 341
Brutus, 11
Build(s), built, upbuild, 8–9, 11, 39, 56, 94, 224n119, 233, 233n167, 233n170, 234–235, 255, 256n30, 257, 260, 265n26, 267, 276, 282n17, 303, 311, 324n119, 303n20, 335, 341, 357
Builder, 82n17
Building(s), rebuilding, 8–12, 56, 62, 86n33, 94, 190n56, 211, 224, 255, 288, 321, 357
Bulgaria, 173n22
bull, 115
burden(s), 216n74, 267
burial, buried, 50n7, 116, 205, 242, 282n19, 284, 286n48
burn(ed), burning, 33, 63n34, 91n60, 94, 207n207, 232, 287, 303n23, 315, 333n37
Burrus, 11, 333n37
butcheries, 13n20, 18

Cádiz, 177n 42
Caelian, 8n2
Caesarea Maritima, 287n49
Caesar(s) (generally), 59, 84–85, 88, 144, 188, 190, 332, 33n35
Caesar, Julius, 10, 11, 13, 59, 133, 177, 227, 227n138
Caesar, Nero, 85
Caesar, Octavian/Augustus, 11
Caesar, Titus, 85
Cain, 229n148
Caligula, 11, 14, 133
Call (on the Lord), 55, 114, 146–147, 190–193, 195–196, 199, 204–205, 231, 266, 297, 301–302
Call(s) (by God generally), 19, 33, 33n12, 53, 68, 73, 81, 87, 91, 95, 119, 146, 162, 196, 202–203, 207, 232, 252, 267, 294–297, 300, 302, 304, 306–307, 331, 335, 340, 342, 351, 359
Call (by God to mission), 36, 38, 68, 70, 73, 85, 175–176, 179, 204, 208, 210, 210n32, 211, 226, 236, 242, 244, 252, 252n16, 253–255, 257, 264, 266–267, 268, 278, 289, 289n67, 290, 296, 298, 308, 344, 346, 350–352
Calviminian, 304n24
Calvin, 241n15, 363
Calvinism, Calvinist(ic), 293, 297–298, 299n16, 300–302
Canaanite(s), 184, 196
Canaanites, 82
Cananaeus, 175
Canon, Muratorian, 43, 173
canon, 339n13
Cantabrian War, 223
Capitoline Hill, 8
Capitolium Hill, 12
capstone, 86n38
Captatio benevolentiae, 64, 212
Caribbean, 345n42
carpenter, 180
Carthage, 9
Caspian Sea, 173n22, 174, 176–177
Castor, 12, 285n40
catacomb(s), 14, 215
catacombs, 14,
catena, 54–56, 64, 96, 198
Catholic, 16, 297n11, 336, 345n41, 358
celibate, 273, 275
Cenchreae, 22, 61n15, 215, 257, 290
Cento, 64
centripetal mission, 2n6
centurion, 84, 319
Cessationism, 241
charisma, 282
charismata, 141
charismatic, 2, 94, 94n65, 225, 235, 244n32
charity, 157
charlatan, 284n34
cherubim, 115
Chiasm, 64, 359
Child, children, 61, 74, 81, 87, 90, 92–93, 102, 119, 133–134, 137, 153, 164–165, 195, 199, 202, 206, 231, 240, 250, 263–264, 267, 275, 271–272, 274–276, 282, 284, 294, 297, 300–301, 306–307, 335, 347, 349
childbearing, 8
Childbirth, 61, 164–165, 263, 313, 315
childhood, 108
China, Chinese, 177, 177n39, 177n42, 178, 235n179, 255n26, 344, 345n39
Chrestus, 14, 49
Christ, 2, 2n6, 10, 13–14, 17–18, 25–26, 29–31, 31n10, 33, 33n12, 36, 38, 40–41, 47n1, 49, 50n7, 59, 62, 66, 68, 70–71, 73, 75–83, 83n20, 83n21, 84n23, 84n25, 84n26, 84n27, 85–89, 89n51, 89n53, 89n55,

378

Subject Index

90–94, 98–99, 99n20, 100, 102–104, 106–119, 122, 124–129, 129n51, 129n52, 129n53, 130, 130n58, 131–133, 133n71, 134–140, 140n4, 141–142, 142n15, 142n16, 143, 144n19, 145, 145n26, 146, 146n28, 147–149, 149n7, 150–152, 152n9, 153–160, 160n6, 161–165, 169, 169n2, 170n9, 172–173, 176, 179–180, 183n19, 184, 184n19, 185, 185n24, 185n30, 186–187, 187n41, 187n42, 188, 188n47, 189, 189n52, 190, 190n59, 191–193, 195–200, 202–205, 207–209, 212, 214n55, 217, 222–224, 224n121, 226, 229, 229n148, 229n153, 229n154, 231n163, 232–233, 233n168, 233n169, 234, 234n175, 235, 239–243, 246, 246n41, 247, 247n46, 248, 251, 251n10, 251n11, 252, 252n12, 253–254, 254n24, 255–256, 256n30, 262, 265–266, 269, 271–274, 279–281, 283, 286, 286n48, 289, 292, 295–296, 296n7, 297–298, 300–303, 303m19, 305, 307–310, 310n4, 312, 314–316, 318–320, 320n31, 323, 325, 328, 332, 334, 339n12, 339n13, 340–341, 341n16, 342, 342n18, 343–345, 345n40, 347–351, 351n3, 351n4, 352–359

Christendom, 214, 334, 346

Christian(s), 2, 15, 17–20, 29–31, 31n9, 32–33, 33n15, 36n17, 39, 41, 43, 47–50, 50n6, 51, 53–54, 60, 69–70, 72, 75, 77–78, 79n7, 80, 81n15, 82, 90, 92–94, 98, 100, 102–103, 106, 106n35, 107, 108n49, 109, 109n54, 113, 117, 119, 122, 124–125, 132, 133n71, 136n83, 139, 142–143, 145–146, 148, 148n1, 150–151, 152n9, 153–154, 156–157, 158n20, 160, 163, 170, 170n8, 171, 174, 174n28, 174n31, 176n32, 176n33, 176n34, 176n35, 176n36, 176n37, 177n38, 177n39, 177n40, 177n41, 177n41, 177n42, 177n43, 177n44, 179, 187–189, 191, 193, 195, 195n80, 197n85, 198, 200, 200n94, 201n2, 203, 208, 209n28, 210, 212, 213, 213n54, 214n55, 217n80, 217n83, 217n87, 218, 220–222, 223n117, 225–226, 227–229, 230n156, 230n160, 231–235, 238, 241–246, 246n39, 246n40, 246n41, 247, 252–255, 255n29, 257–259, 259n2, 260, 260n4, 263n14, 265–269, 269n2, 271n11, 273, 276–277, 280–282, 282n17, 285, 285n41, 286, 286n42, 286n48, 287, 287n51, 289, 289n67, 290, 290n70, 291n79, 292–293, 296, 296n7, 297n11, 301–303, 306–309, 310, 312–314, 315, 318, 320–321, 321n38, 322, 324n3, 324n4, 324n4, 325, 327–336, 336n1, 337–338, 340, 343, 343n31, 343n32, 344, 344n37, 345, 345n40, 345n41, 345n42, 346, 351, 351n3, 352–354, 354n12, 355–356, 356n3, 357, 359, 361–364, 367, 369–371, 373

Christianity, 1, 12n16, 12n17, 13–21, 48, 51, 94, 173, 213, 215, 217n80, 242, 259, 328, 334, 336, 338, 345, 345n40, 345n41, 346

Christlike, Christlikeness, 58, 100, 107, 154–156, 232

Christoformity, 339

Christological, Christology, 54, 84, 91, 153, 204n13, 208n23, 297

chronologically, chronology, 18, 39, 191n68, 340n14

Church(es), 1, 1n4, 2, 2n4, 12, 16–20, 22, 24–26, 30–32, 35–40, 40n37, 41, 42n39, 43, 45, 47, 48n2, 49–50, 58, 61n16, 62–63, 69–70, 75, 77, 88, 88n47, 88n49, 91, 94, 97, 109n52, 119–120, 131–133, 144, 146n28, 156, 157n20, 158, 171n15, 174, 174n27, 175–176, 178, 180n2, 193, 196, 201, 201n1, 201n3, 203, 205, 207, 207n18, 208, 209n26, 210–211, 211n39, 213, 214n56, 215–218, 220–222, 222n109, 203–223, 223n115, 224, 224n119, 225, 226, 226n130, 226n131, 227, 227n133, 227n134, 229, 229n155, 230–233, 233n167, 233n169, 233n170, 235, 235n179, 235n180, 236, 236n181, 240–242, 244, 246n39, 249, 256–258, 259n2, 260, 260n5, 264n20, 265–269, 269n2, 271, 273, 275, 277, 279, 281, 283n24, 286, 288–289, 289n67, 290–291, 291n76, 291n79, 292, 292n85, 296, 296n7, 297n11, 299, 303–304, 306–307, 307n2, 309, 311n8, 320, 325, 327–328, 332, 334–341, 343–347, 351–353, 353n11, 356n2, 358–360

Cicero, 13–14

Cilicia(n), 17, 32–33, 37n26, 311, 344, 358

Circumcise(s, d), circumcision(s), 16–18, 48–49, 51, 54, 60, 66, 71, 73, 87, 91, 107, 107n42, 109–110, 140–141, 184, 185n24, 206, 244n31, 299, 336–337, 337n5, 338–340, 342, 348–349, 353

Circumincession, 94n66

circumlocution, 66

Circus Maximus, 11

Circus Nero, 11

cities, city, 8, 8n4, 9, 11–12, 12n14, 15, 17, 19, 23n14, 25–26, 32, 36–37, 39–41, 50, 75, 83, 133n72, 175, 182, 194n73, 198, 213–214, 216, 222, 226–227, 231, 257,

Subject Index

(cities, city continued)
  275n24, 277–278, 311, 292, 296n9, 311, 317, 321, 334–335, 346n44, 358
Citizens, citizenry, citizenship, 8–10, 13–14, 20n14, 23n14, 42, 85, 93, 180, 277, 289n67, 327–328, 330, 333n36, 334
civic, civil, 8, 9–10, 13, 257, 277n33, 327n21, 331, 333–335
civil wars, 10, 13
civilization, civilize(d), 179, 345–346
class(es), 9, 9n9, 20, 170, 187, 339
classical world, 331n34
classism, 290, 338
Claudian Edict/expulsion, 17, 19, 25, 31, 49–50, 107, 213, 216, 217n88, 234n177, 287, 291, 311, 324n3
Claudius, 11, 14, 14n25, 15, 17, 19, 26, 31, 49, 58, 85, 133, 157, 177, 216–217, 218n89, 291
clay, 55, 63, 101, 135, 238, 294, 350
clean, cleanliness, cleanse(s), cleansing, unclean, uncleanness, 30, 97–98, 104, 116, 136, 251n11, 337n4
Clement of Rome, 43, 49, 49n5, 171, 173–174, 287, 296, 322
Clement of Alexandria, 174n29, 174n30
Clement of Philippi, 49n5, 171
Cleopatra, 11
clergy, 224, 235
client kings, 9,
client (patronage), 279, 279n1, 280–281
Climate, 259n3
clothe, clothed, clothes, clothing, 90, 118, 155, 172, 205, 232, 255n28, 274, 280n10, 328, 341n16, 343,
code (law), 92, 107, 150–151, 255
code (household), 30, 133n72
cognate, 104, 163
cognomen, 85
Cohortative subjunctive, 64
coin(s), 8n5, 189
Collection (Jerusalem), 23, 29n3, 31, 32, 34, 38–39, 41–42, 48, 75, 135, 207, 220, 222, 226, 230, 242n18, 256, 278, 280–283, 286, 286n44, 321, 321n41
collector(s) (tax), 330–331
college, *collegia*, 12–13
colonial, colonialism, postcolonial, 200, 338, 345–346
colonies, colony, colonizing, colonization, 24n14, 222n113, 223n113, 345
Colossae, 43
comfort(s), comfortable, comforted, comforting, 81, 153, 206, 209, 301, 314, 284, 298, 298, 301, 306,

coming (first, Christ), 53, 111, 185, 185n26, 238, 280, 323, 350,
coming (judgment), 162n18
coming (second, Christ), 130, 160, 165, 174n27, 357n6,
coming (Spirit), 16,
Comitia Curiata, 8
command(s), commandment(s), 9n7, 56, 66, 76, 92, 107, 110, 111, 148n2, 150, 152, 154, 175, 181, 182n10, 183–185, 192, 206, 224, 239, 251, 252, 254n24, 270, 272, 276, 317
320, 323n34, 325
commendation, 22, 24, 25n20, 227, 275, 290n69
commission(ed), commissioning, 33n12, 40, 65, 69, 80, 138, 169, 172–173, 179, 208, 210n32, 225, 230n157, 232, 233n170, 242, 265n26, 299n13
commit(ed), committing, commitment(s), 2n6, 33n12, 39, 102, 114, 201, 209–210, 228, 236, 241, 248–249, 250–251, 256, 267, 270, 272, 274, 276, 299, 306–307, 311, 318, 320, 333n37, 350
common, 10, 12, 20, 27, 39, 50–51, 62, 66, 84, 100, 120, 149, 161, 163, 188, 201n1, 209n26,
communication, communiqués, 194, 213, 233n168
communion, 206
communism, communist, 156, 255
Communities, 42, 222, 362–363, 367, 370
communities, community, 2, 7, 10, 13n18, 14, 17n5, 30n8, 32, 39, 42n42, 49, 69, 86n33, 93–94, 107, 113, 115, 155n15, 156, 158, 171, 190n56, 190n57, 218, 222n111, 233, 233n167, 233n168, 233n170, 233n171, 235, 244n31, 249n2, 256, 256n30, 258, 267, 269–270, 273, 276–278, 282n17, 286, 289–290, 311, 318, 328, 335, 339n13, 342–343, 346, 352n5,
companion(s), 18n8, 42n40, 219, 220n100, 274
company, 42, 193, 219, 257
Comparison(s), 247n48
compassion, compassionate, 63, 252n16, 253, 284, 316
compendium, 29–30
complacency, 199
condemnation, 60, 87–88, 90, 92, 98–99, 102–104, 108, 113, 118, 126, 140, 153, 161–163, 205, 240, 251, 299, 308, 314
Conditional sentences, 64, 187
conduct, 274, 288, 327–328

380

Subject Index

confess(es), confessing, 144, 147, 180n5, 187, 187n40, 187n41, 188–189, 193, 204, 231, 300
Confession, 90, 138, 140, 144, 187–190
confessional, 297n11
confidence, confident(ly), 23, 26, 65, 81, 108, 143, 179n1, 180, 188, 221, 226, 241, 248, 250, 297–298, 300–301, 306–309, 314, 345–346
conflation, 351
Conflict(s), conflicting, 10–11, 17, 19, 30, 108, 359,
conform(ed), conformity, conformed, 87, 92, 101, 117, 137, 145, 151, 153, 155, 156, 205, 232, 240, 252, 260, 278, 297, 285, 302n19, 338, 339
Congo, 258
congregation, 212, 244n32, 283, 372
conjunction(s), 64, 66, 67, 192, 297
conquer(ed), conqueror(s), 60, 80, 82, 177, 180, 203, 315, 320
conquest, 13, 82, 177, 356
conscience(s), 30, 33, 100, 105, 142, 156–157, 160n8, 255, 315, 329–330, 341
consecrated, 116
consolation, console(s), 93, 199n93, 224
Constantine, 345
Constantinople, 230n156
construct(s), construction, 62, 180, 194, 213, 233, 241, 304, 355
consummation, 101, 106, 114, 128, 134 135, 159, 164–165, 238, 244n25, 263, 276, 334
contagion, 261
contaminated, 261
contention, 9–10, 17, 31, 49, 237
context(s), 10, 16, 20, 26, 29, 39, 48, 57, 63, 65, 73, 77, 78n3, 87, 91, 93, 98, 102, 110–111, 120, 128, 137, 141n14, 143–144, 154, 163, 179, 181–182, 186, 191–193, 194n73, 212, 217, 223n117, 224, 232, 235n180, 236, 239, 250, 252n13, 253, 255n26, 268, 274, 283n27, 289n67, 290, 297, 305, 319, 322n42, 324–325, 327–329, 336, 345n40, 345n41, 345n42, 346, 347, 347n45, 355, 359
contextual, contextually, 48, 50, 72, 78
contextualization, contextualize(d), 18, 50–51, 347
contradiction, contradictory, contradicts, 66, 106, 305n27, 321
controversies, controversy, 111, 157n20, 338, 356n3
Conversion(s), convert(s), converting, 16–17, 17n3, 18, 20, 25, 28–29, 32–33, 33n12, 35, 39, 39n33, 40n37, 41, 50–51, 55, 69, 69n46, 70, 72, 75n57, 91, 93, 107, 133, 152, 161, 179, 182n13, 197–199, 205–208, 210, 214n55, 221–223, 225–226, 227n134, 230n160, 231, 233, 233n167, 234n176, 235, 241, 244n32, 245, 264, 265n26, 269, 273n15, 277, 296, 298, 299n15, 311, 318, 334, 337, 340, 343, 347, 356n3, 358
convict, conviction(s), 50, 56, 83n20, 105, 142, 174, 174n27, 230, 241, 255, 300
convince(d), convincing, 25, 28, 25, 78, 237, 293, 303n19, 356
cooperation, 300, 304n25
copsa, 322
Corinth, 1, 14, 18, 22–23, 23n14, 24, 26, 30, 36n17, 37–38, 41, 48, 61n16, 75, 91, 210, 215, 215n65, 216n74, 218–219, 221, 226, 233, 245, 247, 257, 277, 285–286, 287n49, 290, 290n71–292, 326, 336n2, 356n2
Corinthian(s), 24–28, 31n9, 36, 37, 54, 87, 134, 136, 141n14, 146, 157, 163–164, 172, 183n66, 191n17, 208n22, 210, 216n74, 218, 220n101, 224, 224n119, 233n167, 233n168, 233n171, 234, 234n172, 245n37, 246n38, 247n44, 237n47, 237n50, 237n53, 257, 270–271, 271n7, 273, 273n16, 280–281, 285, 290n71, 292n85, 316, 320n32, 341, 343, 356n2,
Cornelius, 48, 337, 340
cornerstone, 55, 86, 86n33, 86n38, 190, 190n56, 240
coronation, 195n78
corpse, 134
corpus, 2, 18, 263
corrupt(ed), corrupting, corruption, 81, 92, 95, 96–98, 100–102, 104n31, 112, 127, 132, 134, 136, 149–150, 152–153, 164–165, 220, 232, 262, 263n18, 294, 325, 326n12, 332–333
cosmic, 54, 81, 91, 102, 117, 119, 131, 135, 137, 142, 144, 162, 164n24, 164n26, 169–171, 173, 173n24, 174–175, 195, 204, 231, 262, 262n11, 263, 269, 294, 296n10, 325
Cosmission, 265
cosmological, 356
cosmopolitan, 9, 12, 344
cosmos, 54, 84, 96, 119, 125, 134, 143, 164–165, 181, 195, 202–205, 248, 262–264, 278, 294
Council, Jerusalem, 18, 20, 35–37, 37n26, 41, 49, 58, 107, 171, 311, 339–341
council, 8, 12, 190n57
counseling, 266
countercultural, counterculturally, 94, 156, 275–276, 280
counterfeit miracles, 244, 244n26, 247

381

Subject Index

countries, country, 11, 175, 211, 215, 236, 334, 346
couple, 25, 216–217, 217n83, 272n12, 291
couplets, 331
courage, courageous, ix, 70, 148, 148n4, 216, 231
courier(s), 22, 182, 194, 208
court(s), 10, 51, 129
covenant(s), 33n12, 51, 54–55, 55n10, 58–60, 82n17, 83, 84n28, 86–87, 107n41, 109n54, 115, 120n21, 121–123, 124n43, 125–127, 130, 136, 139–140, 141n11, 152, 184, 202–204, 228n144, 244n31, 253, 294, 309, 349, 356, 356n2
covenantal, 57, 71, 87, 107, 120–121, 124n43, 125–126, 239, 295, 336, 351
Covenantal Nomism, 107n41, 141, 141n11, 336
covenantal pisticism, 141
covenanted, 261n9
Covered, covering (sin), 116, 136, 239, 249
covet, coveting, covetousness, 54, 110, 152, 250–251, 262
Covid-19, 102
coworker(s), 37–38, 41, 49, 62, 75, 215–218, 220–221, 223–225, 276
crafts, 63
crater, 117
Create(s), created, creating, v, ix, 8, 26, 74, 79, 90, 94, 99, 101, 104–105, 111, 120, 143, 147, 148n2, 149, 152, 159, 162, 165, 173, 192n70, 193, 222, 233n171, 243, 250, 258, 260–262, 263n15, 264–265, 267, 270, 272, 282n19, 294, 312, 318, 332, 338, 340, 350–351, 359
createdness, 101
creation, 51, 54–55, 61, 63, 70, 79, 79n7, 81–83, 87, 89, 93–94, 98, 101–103, 104n31, 106, 106n36, 112–113, 125, 131–132, 134–136, 136n82, 137, 143n19, 149, 149n6, 160, 164–165, 173, 175, 181, 198–199, 201–202, 231n163, 237–238, 238n6, 258–269, 260, 261n9, 263, 264n19, 267, 278, 294, 297, 298n12, 304–305, 312, 315, 319, 325, 339, 342, 355–356
creational, 124–126, 274, 350
creative(ly), 8n6, 71, 151, 193, 237–238, 287, 320n34, 359
creativity, 359
Creator, 54, 79, 101, 142, 164, 199, 201n3, 237–238, 242, 245, 253, 258–259, 260–261, 263–264, 266–268, 284, 294, 298–299, 312, 332,350
creatures, 101, 199, 260, 304–305
credal, 189

credited, 107, 140, 216
Cretans, 260n7, 327
Crete, 215, 325n10
cried, cries, 56, 134, 146, 152, 193, 206, 253, 308, 312, 313n18, 314n18, 317, 342, 352
crime, 10, 13, 187n40, 328
criminals, 20n14
crisis, 18, 259, 259n1, 369
Croatia, 42n39, 171
cross, 26, 32, 70, 82–84, 89–90, 92, 110, 117, 134, 155, 180, 183, 190, 207, 217, 233, 240, 245, 256, 291, 305, 316,
cross-cultural, 167, 336, 344–347
crucified, crucifixion, 9, 20, 20n14, 70, 76, 82–83, 85–86, 116–117, 134, 180, 183, 196, 205, 233n168, 242, 248, 295, 314, 327, 357
cruciform, 49, 75, 81, 154n14, 155–156, 271n8, 343
cruelty, 9
cult, 12–13, 60, 115, 196, 252n14, 360
cultic, 55, 57, 60, 210n32, 330
cultivated, cultivating, 156, 330
Cultural, culturally, viii, 9n9, 18–19, 30, 48–52, 72, 118, 133, 167, 172, 180, 203, 227, 242, 255–256, 266, 279, 289, 289n67, 337–339, 339n12, 339n12, 340, 341n17, 344–347, 353–354, 356
Culture(s), viii, 1, 1n4, 3, 9n9, 17, 31, 49, 70n47, 98, 137, 167, 200, 210, 222, 227, 229n155, 250, 272, 275–276, 285, 288–289, 289n65, 336, 338, 338n9, 339, 341, 341n26, 341n17, 343–347, 354, 358–359
cured, 246
curse(s), cursed, cursing, 60, 123, 184, 202, 232, 258, 261n9, 288, 302n19, 316, 333
custom(s), 10, 13, 31, 337, 347
Cynics, 27n35
Cyprian, 24
Cyprus, 18, 33–34, 36, 245, 287n49
Cyrene, 37, 217–218, 291
Cyrus, 194, 326

Damascus, 33, 33n12, 107, 129, 209, 242, 295, 344
damnation, 295n5
danger(s), dangerous, 15, 19, 20n14, 62, 98, 102, 105, 162, 176, 206, 256, 261, 267, 290, 315, 332, 334, 338
Daniel, 228n144
Danube River, 7
darkness, 62, 97, 99, 162, 162n14, 303n20, 335
Date, 2, 23–24, 37, 43n46, 54n3, 177n45, 177n47, 324n4, 339n10
daughter(s), 8n6, 88, 240, 242n19, 275, 282n24

382

Subject Index

David, 50n7, 57, 59, 68, 73, 83, 85, 88, 110, 116, 179, 191, 204, 228-229, 238-240, 295, 305, 319, 342, 349
Davidic, 55, 57, 68, 82, 86, 86n33, 122-123, 136, 190n56, 239, 303, 348-349
dawn, 160, 311n7
day(s), ix, 13, 16, 19, 29-31, 31n9, 48-49, 56, 60, 62-63, 63n31, 66, 82n17, 93, 103, 105, 109, 115, 119, 122, 130, 146, 154n13, 157, 160-162, 165, 171, 182, 184, 189, 200, 202, 206, 235-237, 241, 253-255, 255n30, 262-264, 266, 284, 288, 290, 295, 299, 301, 306, 310-311, 311n9, 336, 341, 343, 359
deacon, 22, 215, 225, 230, 257, 275-276, 281, 281n13, 290, 328, 343
dead, 68, 74, 80, 85, 89-90, 99, 111, 116-117, 124, 143-144, 150-151, 158, 161, 162, 162n18, 163, 180, 180n4, 185, 185n30, 186, 188-189, 195, 203-206, 231, 237, 242-243, 245, 284, 295, 314n18, 351-352
death, 2, 13, 15, 21, 23, 26, 29, 32, 37, 47-48, 50n7, 51, 54, 61-62, 72, 74, 80-83, 83n20, 86-92, 94-96, 96n7, 98-104, 106, 107n44, 108, 111-113, 115-118, 124, 126-127, 130-132, 134-137, 140, 142-144, 149, 149n7, 150-153, 155n16, 157, 161-165, 169n2, 170, 172, 180, 182n10, 185-187, 187n40, 191, 194n78m 195-196, 202-207, 212, 216n74, 222n108, 229n153, 230, 235, 238, 240-243, 246, 248, 251n10, 252n12, 261-264, 279, 285, 294, 296, 300, 305-306, 308, 310n18, 313, 315-319, 328-329, 329n28, 333n37, 337, 339n13, 342n18, 345, 349, 357-358
debauched, debauchery, 18, 99, 255, 274-275
debt, debtor, 40, 60, 221, 312, 351
decade, 213
decadence, 299
Decalogue, 56, 152, 251, 255, 255n27, 274, 276
decay(s), decaying, 61, 87, 96, 102, 125, 134-135, 164-165, 195, 202-204, 206, 231, 238, 241, 261, 263-264, 294, 305, 358
deceased, 12, 118
decomposed, 263
deed(s), 75, 99, 116, 136, 198, 207, 226, 235, 248, 254, 284, 327, 334
Deesis, 64
defeat, defeated, 9n8, 10-11, 82, 105-106, 160, 134, 164, 183, 195
defence(s), defend, defended, defending, defense, 10, 27n37, 28-29, 36, 40-41, 51, 88n46, 103, 150, 182, 201n2, 210, 220, 282n19, 292n85, 294, 298, 301, 329, 339n11, 340, 349-350, 355n1, 356, 358-359
defile(s), defiled, defilement, 79, 98, 116, 263, 284, 294
deforestation, 259
defraud, 290
degradation, degrades, 259, 266
deification, deifying, 332
deities, 12, 119, 188, 192, 223, 237, 286
Deity, 85, 115, 119, 144, 173, 196, 361
deliberative speech, 27-28
delight(s), delighted, 2, 107, 122, 185, 227, 266, 281, 286n46, 316n23, 321
delightful, 194
deliver(s), delivered, delivering, 23, 31, 32, 37, 39, 41-42, 59, 114n5, 135-136, 171, 208, 215, 245, 248, 320, 330, 368
Deliverer, 56, 86, 116, 135-136, 142, 204, 240, 351, 353
deliverance, 122n32, 135, 146, 219, 248, 265, 312, 317
delivery, 42, 230
Delphi, 12
demand(s), 48, 92, 161, 186, 188, 202, 237, 244n25, 244n26, 246-248, 288, 289n67, 295, 330-331, 308, 333, 338, 340
demanded, demanding, 188, 252n16, 253, 337-338
Demas, 215n71
demigods, 227
democratic, 63n35, 325n7, 328, 333
demographics, 346
demolish, demolished, 163, 259, 333
demon(s), 105-106, 162, 165, 244n25, 245, 262, 327
demoniac, 105
demonic, 98, 102, 106, 112, 185, 244n25, 249n1
Denmark, 177, 177n48m
denomination(s), denominational, 211, 225, 345, 347
deorum (pax), 12
dependency, 267
dependent, 133
dependent claus, 67
dependents, 269
depletion, 259
deposit (Spirit), 93
depravity, 116, 239, 259, 359
depression, 314n18
depth, depths, 62-63, 66, 106n37, 256, 307n1, 359
depths, 106, 185
Derbe, 321n39
derivative, 162n11

383

Subject Index

descendant(s), 54, 56, 73, 85, 101, 227n138, 239, 295, 319, 342
descended, 68, 352
descent, 50n7, 54–55, 58, 100, 133n71, 185n30, 227
desirable, 194n73, 288
desire(s), desired, desiring, 23, 26, 32, 39–40, 40n35, 41, 43, 50, 52, 70, 80, 88, 92, 97–100, 102, 107, 111, 114, 143, 145, 149–150, 170, 170n9, 173–174, 187n40, 202, 205, 210, 215, 219–220, 224n119, 226–227, 229–230, 232–233, 233n171, 235, 242, 252, 252n12, 255–256, 259, 261–262, 264, 267, 272, 274, 278, 292, 305, 308, 311, 316, 316n23, 317, 335, 344, 350
despair, 56
desperate, 114, 134, 257, 263, 315
despise(s), despised, 114, 157, 242, 255, 260, 303n19, 331
despotic, despotism, 102, 325
destined, 70n47, 95, 101, 107n44, 130, 134, 163n21, 204, 206, 350, 352–353
destiny, 165, 183, 204, 304n25, 342n18
destitution, 62
destroy(s), destroyed, 10, 82, 98, 104, 106, 112, 161, 163, 202, 205, 231, 250, 255, 261–262, 263n17, 264, 275, 303n19, 316, 326, 339, 356, 358
destroyer, 208
destruction, 57, 60n7, 79, 82, 87, 95, 98, 101–102, 104, 104n31, 105–106, 108, 113–114, 116, 130, 134, 143, 153, 160–162, 162n18, 163, 163n21, 165, 181, 183–184, 191n66, 195, 203–204, 206, 230, 235, 240–241, 250, 261–262, 263n15, 266, 268, 294, 314n18, 316, 349–350, 352–353, 357
destructive, 105, 207, 259n2, 261, 267
determination, 79, 226–227, 256, 298, 316, 326n11
determines, determined(ly), determining, determined, 2, 10, 40, 154, 172, 255–256, 267, 276, 296, 303, 325, 332, 347
determinism, deterministic, 293–294, 298
Deutero-Isaiah, 54n3
Deuteronomic, 56, 184
Deuteronomy, 55–56, 184, 186–187, 199, 270
devastation, 98, 259–260
Device(s) (rhetorical), 28, 63–67, 179n1, 191, 246n41, 355, 359
devil, 130n58
devotion, 58, 151, 283, 307n1, 318
devout, 185n26
dialectical, 295n5, 304, 305n29
dialects, 222n113
dialogical, 64
dialogue(s), 27n35, 158
Diaphora, 64
diaspora, 198, 209
Diatribe, 27, 27n35, 64, 99, 191, 198, 356, 359
dichotomy, 235, 249n1
dictation, 22
Dictator, 10
didactic letter, 27
Die(s), died, dying, 1, 19, 49, 50n7, 57, 61, 66, 70–71, 82–83, 89, 91, 99–100, 104n30, 111, 116, 118, 123–124, 135–136, 150–151, 161, 188–189, 195, 203–205, 207, 211, 228, 229n153, 231, 235, 236, 243, 240, 246, 252, 261–263, 270, 280, 284n32, 295, 303n19, 314n18, 315, 333, 347, 353, 356n2, 357, 358n12
dietary, 289
difference(s), 30, 49–52, 56, 118, 157, 190, 203, 221, 250n7, 255–256, 289, 321, 339, 341, 351, 354n11, 359
differentiation (status), 193
dignity, 230n157, 250n7
diminutive, 1n2
dine, 344
Dionysius of Halicarnassus, 7n1
Dionysus, 13, 274
Dioskouroi, 12
diplomat(s), diplomatic, 208, 217
disability, disabled, 245, 247
Disbelief, disbelieve, 247, 261, 299n14
disciple(s), 69, 175, 242, 315, 318, 340
discipleship, 173, 226, 265n26
discipline, 320
discourse(s), 27n35, 28n39, 186, 347n45
discourses,
disgrace, 79
dish, 359
dishonor(ing), dishonorable, 109, 272, 279, 332
disinherited, 236
disjunctions, 250n7
disloyalty, 327
disobedience, disobedience, disobey(ing), disobedient, 31, 55, 65, 80, 103, 136n82, 144, 144n20, 144n21, 145, 184, 186, 200, 202, 250, 276, 302, 320, 320n26, 321n38, 350
disorder, 264
dispensation, 241n16
dispersion, 175
dispute(d), 22, 24, 31, 87, 89, 120, 127n46, 138, 211n34, 217, 223n118, 312, 321
disseminating, dissemination, 2, 40n35, 212, 282n19
dissension, dissent, 99, 255

384

Subject Index

dissolution (cosmos), 164n25, 263
dissonance (cognitive), 111, 152
dissuasion, 27
distinction(s), 2, 94n66, 142, 156, 191, 209n26, 213, 250n7, 289n67, 338
distinctive(s), 96, 107n42, 109, 334, 339
distorted, distortion, distorts, 92, 97, 143, 261n9, 337
distress, 62n28, 80n12, 103, 122, 214n55, 329n28
distributed, distributing, distribution, 13, 258, 281–283, 283n24, 324
distributive justice, 120
disturbances, 14
Diverse, diversity, 51, 63, 118–119, 142, 156–158, 190n62, 205, 246n44, 318, 321, 339n12, 341, 346, 359
divide(s), divided, 23, 70, 89, 100, 109, 158, 175–176, 255, 339n13, 341, 343, 346
division(s), 19, 105, 218, 344
divination, divined, 12, 185
divine, 11–12, 33n12, 53, 65, 68, 70, 80n12, 82, 84, 84,25, 88, 91, 94n66, 131, 144, 146n29, 162, 170n7, 180, 180n6, 181, 181n7, 201, 206, 228n139, 229n154, 230n157, 238, 250n5, 255n27, 263–264, 272n14, 275n24, 280–281, 282n19, 294, 298, 302, 304, 305, 326–327, 335
Divine Passive, 65
divinity, 83, 101, 196, 280n6
divisive, divisiveness, 19, 273, 339n13
divorce, divorced, 54, 102, 151, 249n1, 270–271, 273, 275
divorcee, 290
doctrine, 29, 89n55, 105, 139n2, 153n11, 158n22, 297n11, 339n11
dogmatic, 39, 157n20
dogs, 260n7
dominance, dominate(s), dominated, dominating, domination, domineering, 7–8, 12–13, 15, 19, 39, 41, 43, 58, 60, 68–69, 72, 77, 116, 125–126, 128–129, 133, 138, 140, 150, 160, 162, 164, 172, 187, 196, 200, 224, 229, 237, 246, 249, 252n13, 254, 259n2, 273n15, 293, 338, 346, 358
dominion, 59, 96, 98, 111, 243, 259n2, 264, 333n37
Domitian, 43n46
door(s), doors, 114n6, 318, 358
dough, 56, 62
dreams, 212, 212n41
drink(ing), 62, 92, 100, 254–255, 284n34, 302n19
drugs, 246n41

drunk(en), drunkenness, 65, 99, 274–275, 275n24
dusk, 311n7
dwell(s), dwelling(s), dwelt, 92, 132, 135, 153n10, 173, 190n56, 194n73, 260, 264, 294–295, 305
dyeing, 8n6
dynamism, 307
ERE HERE
dynastic, 84
dynasty, 105n32, 333

eager, eagerly, eagerness, 40, 40n37, 45, 226, 233n171
ears, 60
arth, 2n6, 33n12, 40n34, 41, 50n7, 53n2, 57, 61, 71, 90, 96n3, 101–102, 162, 164–165, 169–170, 172, 177, 179, 181–182, 182n10, 198, 201n2, 205, 210n32, 226n129, 240, 244n28, 244n29, 253, 259n2, 261n9, 262–263, 272, 280, 319, 333–334, 348, 350
Earthkeepers, earthkeeping, 260
earthly, 32, 82, 87, 88n47, 101, 156, 305, 300n17, 353
east, eastern, eastward, 12–13, 42, 42n39, 48, 171, 174, 176–178, 222n113, 296, 310, 343, 345n40, 345n42, 357
Easter, 264n19
eat(ing), eaten, 13, 17–18, 29–31, 31n9, 48–49, 56, 61–62, 92–93, 98, 100, 105, 152n8, 157, 187n40, 194n73, 234, 255, 284n34, 289n67, 290, 312, 337, 341n17, 347, 353n11
ecclesiastical, ecclesiological, 118, 224, 235
Echoes, 53, 54, 195n80
Ecojustice, 260n4
Ecological(ly), ecology, 2–3, 164, 167, 259, 259n1, 260, 260n4, 261–262, 263n18, 264–267, 265–267, 346, 358
economic(s), 9, 12, 62, 92, 222, 259, 278, 280, 284, 286, 289
Eden, 164, 194n73, 249
Edenic, 130, 263, 295
edification, 30, 290, 341
educate(d), education, educative, 9n9, 63, 92, 218, 328, 346
effectiveness, 176, 183, 308
effectual, 146
effort(s), 32, 57, 69, 99, 143, 226, 309, 315, 317, 320, 357n6
egalitarianism, 340, 354
ego, 189n53, 229n154
Egypt, 7, 9, 53, 86, 154, 174, 177–178, 251, 313
Egyptian(s), 70, 188, 228
El, 196, 196n83, 262

Subject Index

elastic, elasticity, 50n6, 154
Elder(s), 225, 288
Eleazar, 315
elect(s), elected, election, 9, 50n7, 63n35, 74, 81, 96, 98, 103, 107n41, 119, 137n86, 146, 163, 199, 217n88, 229n229, 235, 240, 284, 294, 295n5, 299, 301–302, 304n25, 306, 309, 338, 348–350, 351
Eli, 326
Elijah, 56, 185n31, 229n149, 241, 317, 342, 350
elite, 9n7, 10, 70, 280n10, 286n43
elitism, elitist, 1, 203, 254, 277, 290, 338
Ellipsis, 65
Elymas, 245
emancipated, emancipation, 10, 14, 102, 130, 135
emancipation, 102, 130
embassy, 13
embodied, embodies, embody(ing), embodiment, 84, 86, 109, 125, 185, 234, 251, 256–257, 288–289, 308
embodying, 276
embolden, 318
Embrace(s), embracing, 80n12, 89n55, 96n6, 152n9, 250n7, 276, 287, 308, 309
emissaries, emissary, 68, 209, 211n39, 215
emission, 274
emotion(s), emotionally, 63, 255, 285
empathy, 156, 254, 343
Emperor, 11–12, 15, 17, 43n46, 81, 85, 133, 133n74, 279n1, 333n37
emphasis, emphases, 12, 17, 18n9, 22, 39, 40n34, 57, 72, 78, 83n20, 85, 95–96, 105, 106n36, 108–111, 114, 122–126, 128, 129n54, 136n36, 138–140, 144n28, 146, 149, 151–152, 159, 173, 179n1, 186–187, 188n45, 189, 192, 195n80, 204n12, 210n32, 219n99, 221, 233n168, 246n41, 250, 263, 266, 271n10, 279, 281, 283n24, 284n33, 287–288, 296–298, 302, 311, 318, 320, 322, 329, 353n7
emphasize(s), emphasized, emphasizing, 56, 71, 84, 107n41, 139, 160–161, 163n21, 171, 186, 190, 190n51, 198n86, 245, 285, 288, 290, 298, 300–301, 308, 310–311, 331
emphatic(ally), 99, 126, 139–140, 146, 150–152, 193, 198, 311
Empire(s), vii, 7, 9, 11–12, 40–41, 43, 59, 69, 77, 83, 105n32, 170n9, 177n48, 179, 194, 213, 222n112, 222n113, 269n2, 277n33, 278, 280, 307, 325, 328, 333, 345, 345n40
employer, 82
employment, 280

empower(s), empowered, empowering, v, 53, 93n63, 99–100, 107, 113n4, 123, 132, 154, 186, 196, 198, 239, 202–203, 206, 207n20, 226, 244, 247n50, 295–296
empowerer, 245
empowerment, 99, 126, 232
emulate, 56, 83, 117, 145, 154–155, 205, 226–227, 229–230, 248, 286, 347
emulated, 50, 228
emulates, 256, 288
emulating, 38, 143, 248
Emulation, 155
emulation, 157, 254
enable(s), enabled, 8, 13, 99, 107, 111, 203, 255, 289, 299, 314, 322, 327, 341
encourage(s), encouraged, encouraging, ix, 15, 39, 53, 56, 70, 92, 141, 156, 210, 216, 224n119, 226, 227, 231, 256, 259n2, 280–281, 306n31, 341, 346
encouragement, ix, 40, 69, 75, 219, 311, 321
end, endpoint (Christ, law), 112, 140, 183n19, 205, 350
end, endpoint (of the world), 132, 170
end (the), ending, 72, 78, 90, 112, 134, 159–160, 169, 180, 187, 214, 238, 254n25, 264, 294, 300n17, 322, 344, 352, 356–357
ends of the earth, 2n6, 33n12, 40n34, 41, 50n7, 53n2, 75, 177, 179, 201n2, 210n32, 226n129, 244n28, 244n29, 319
ends of the world, 61, 198
endurance, 53, 248
endure(s), endured, enduring, 56, 122n32, 163, 182, 228n146, 317, 322
enemy, enemies, enmity, 14, 56, 59–60, 60n7, 62, 70n47, 81–82, 95, 100, 105–106, 106n36, 130–131, 134, 154, 156, 160, 163n21, 164, 172, 184, 195n78, 197, 240, 252, 254, 258, 261, 264, 279, 287, 287n56, 288, 296, 309–310, 315, 335, 351, 356n3, 358
energy, 320
enforcement, 292
engage(s), engaged, engaging, engagement (missional, evangelistic), v, 3, 33, 37, 38, 40n37, 69, 75, 167, 176, 198, 210–211, 213–215, 226, 235, 254, 269, 272n12, 273, 276–277, 286, 307, 344, 346, 352, 355, 360
engaged (prayer), 307n2
engaged (politics), 276, 333
engage (sexuality), 274, 344,
engifted, 284
England, 214n56
enhanced (capacity), 92, 99
enjoy(ed), 10, 42, 216, 219

386

Subject Index

Enlightenment, 334
Enoch, 185n31, 196n84, 228
enriched, enriches, 190–191
enslaved, enslavement, enslaves, enslaving, 89, 92n61, 95n1, 99–100, 150–151, 154, 179, 251, 271, 277, 308, 312, 327
enter(ed), entering, enters, entry, 7n1, 17, 81, 83, 87, 95, 98, 109, 117, 119, 128, 136, 185, 235, 266, 284, 289, 293n1, 313, 344
entertain, entertainment, 12, 21, 287n49
enthroned, 332
enthusiasm, enthusiastic, 207n16, 286n46,
entrails, 12
entrust, entrusted, 53, 103, 142, 202, 215, 322n46, 348
environment, environmental, 259, 260, 260n4, 260n5, 262, 264n22, 265–266
envisioned, 170n8, 199n89, 353n9
envoy, 59
envy, 250, 335
eon, 238
Epaenatus, 15n27, 25, 277, 278n37, 343
Epaphras, 36n16, 38, 215n71, 320
Epaphroditus, 49, 171, 208n22, 210, 212, 215, 246n38, 315, 330, 333n37
Ephesian(s), 91, 106n38, 117, 131, 162, 172–173, 197, 208, 208n22, 210n31, 214, 222, 231, 233n169, 233n170, 237n3, 246, 270, 276, 283, 299n16, 361, 369
Ephesus, 23–24, 25n20, 26, 36n16, 38, 216, 216n74, 224, 224n121, 234n176, 237n3, 245–246, 257, 291, 311, 320n36
Ephraim, 85n32
Epictetus, 216n74
epistolary, 26, 133n71, 211, 290n68, 320n34
epithet, 84, 210
equality, 289n67
equestrian, 10
equip(ped), equipping, 40, 172, 201, 207, 225, 233, 233n167, 233n169, 233n170, 235, 327, 346, 355
equity, 252n12
Era, 12n14, 101, 110, 112, 170, 172, 184, 191, 228, 229n151, 253, 345, 349
Erastus, 23, 23n14, 37, 218, 218n93, 221, 230, 257, 277, 292, 292n86, 334–335, 343
Erastus inscription, 23, 257, 292
Erythraean Sea, 176
Esau, 229n148, 240, 294, 342n20, 349
eschatological, 61, 119, 123, 130–131, 146, 159, 174, 190, 206, 238, 262, 310, 314, 352n5, 357
eschatology, 42n39, 115, 129, 159, 160n7
Eschaton, vii, 132, 134, 159–165, 191, 191n66, 281, 342

Esquiline, 8n2
essence (divine), 94n66, 113
essential(s) (matters), 93, 117, 129, 143, 151, 157, 192, 208, 218, 241, 243, 255n27, 258, 273, 330, 331, 358
estate(s), 11, 215n67
esteem(ed), 215, 281
eternal, 165, 220, 214n55
eternal condemnation, 87, 103
eternal consequences, 162
eternal Davidic monarch, 238–239
eternal death, 80, 104
eternal deliverance, 317
eternal destination, 162
eternal destiny, 342n18
eternal destruction, 87, 102, 104, 104n31, 108, 114, 134, 161–162, 162n18, 163, 163n21, 163n22, 184, 191, 195, 230, 231, 357
eternal dwellings, 135
eternal existence, 95
eternal fate, 161, 342n20
eternal (God), 76, 79, 142, 261, 323
eternal judgment, 332
eternal life, v, 50n7, 51, 53–54, 62, 71, 87, 89, 98, 100, 103–104, 111, 113, 115, 118, 124, 132, 134–135, 142–143, 149, 161, 163–164, 191, 195, 203, 205, 207, 231, 240–241, 243, 250, 254n24, 265, 279, 286n45, 294, 308, 317, 357
eternal lostness, 163n21
eternal obliteration, 263n15
eternal outcome, 163
eternal peace, 153
eternal purpose, 306n31
eternal restoration, 263n15
eternal resurrection, 163–164
eternal separation, 98
eternal sonship, 242
eternal suffering, 163
eternal torment, 163
Eternality, 132, 142
eternity, 63n31, 130, 163, 280, 282n19, 310
ethic(s), ethical(ly), vii, 1, 3, 18, 27, 27n35, 56, 58, 91–92, 94, 100, 107, 114, 116, 118–119, 122, 125–126, 128, 142, 148, 148n1, 148n2, 148n5, 149, 149n6, 150–151, 153, 153n11, 154, 154n12, 154n14, 155–158, 201, 212n43, 218, 224, 232, 236, 252n13, 254, 254n24, 255, 264, 271, 273n15, 285, 289n67, 290, 324, 327–329, 333–335, 355–356
ethicist(s), 133n72, 148n1
Ethiopia, 174, 176, 177, 177n42, 178
Ethiopian, 173

Subject Index

ethnic, ethnicities, ethnicity, 12, 74, 80, 111, 187n40, 190n62, 203, 256, 277, 338, 339n13, 343n32, 343n34, 346, 353
ethnocentric(ism), 70, 290, 332, 336, 338, 340
Etruscan(s), 7, 7n1, 8
Etymology, 277, 343n32
eunuch, 173
Euodia, 49, 171, 216, 275n26
euphemism, 105n32
Eurocentric, 358
Europe, 7, 10, 39, 177–178, 345
European(s), 2, 7, 39n33, 177, 200, 260n4, 338, 345–346, 345n39, 345n41
evangel, 59
Evangelical, evangelicalism, 2, 57n15, 94n65, 163n21, 199n91, 338
Evangelism, vii, ix, 2, 35, 38, 40n35, 40n37, 51, 69, 69n41, 69n44, 167, 172–173, 180n2, 182n11, 188, 192–193, 201, 201n2, 207, 207n18, 207n19, 209, 209n26, 210, 210n29, 210n39, 212, 212n47, 214–217, 217n82, 226, 231–233, 233n168, 233n169, 234, 234n172, 234n173, 234n174, 234n175, 235, 235n180, 236, 238n5, 249n1, 254, 258, 260, 332n35, 265–266, 288, 318, 344, 356n3
Evangelist(s), 193, 201, 201n2, 207n18, 223n118, 232, 233, 233n167, 233n169, 233n170,
235, 256, 326, 356, 358
evangelistic(ally), 2, 32, 38, 40, 50–51, 69, 75n58, 155n15, 162, 193, 211, 213–215, 218, 223–226, 231–232, 234, 254n24, 256, 259, 345, 356
evangelization, 9, 16–17, 32, 37, 42n39, 43, 48, 51, 51n8, 72, 167, 171, 174, 193, 201, 216, 216n74, 224, 226, 235, 310, 342
evangelize(d), evangelizing, 34, 36n16, 38, 41, 43, 47n47, 69, 70, 75, 77, 169, 172–174, 176, 178, 211, 214–215, 223, 223n117, 224–226, 230, 249n1, 256, 266, 303, 345, 346, 357
Eve, 87n43, 95, 98, 136n82, 229n148, 260n7, 266, 282n19
evening, 311
evil(s), 2, 79, 80n12, 95, 97–98, 101–103, 105–106, 112, 121, 152, 152n8, 158n22, 161, 164–165, 183, 202, 241, 246n40, 254, 260n7, 261, 263, 265, 274, 279, 303n19, 303n21, 329, 333, 357, 358
evildoer(s), 187n41, 326
Evolution, xiii, 238, 238n4, 238n5, 238n6
Evolutionary Theism, 95n2
exaggeration, 65
exaltation, 30, 117

exalted, 196, 229n154, 231, 314
example(s), ix, 12, 25–26, 31, 47, 54, 56–58, 60, 64, 72, 74, 85, 90, 108, 113, 117, 120, 122–123, 139–141, 155–157, 167, 179, 187, 191, 194, 196, 198, 211, 214, 223, 225–230, 235, 237, 239, 245, 247, 254, 280–282, 285, 291–292, 294, 309, 328, 341, 345, 349, 351–352, 355, 356, 358
excellence, 117, 204, 232, 358n12
excess, 359
exclamation, 193, 312
excluded, excluding, exclusion, 24, 80, 89, 96, 99, 110, 250, 302, 339n13, 372
exclusive, 109, 111, 120, 143, 188, 192, 276, 332
exclusivism, exclusivist, 13, 199n91
excuse, excusing, 108, 160n160, 198, 238, 261
execution, 20n14
exegesis, 238n4, 352
exegetical, exegetically, 351n4, 355
exemplar(s), 286, 287n54, 289
exertion, 284
exhortation(s), 27–28, 28n40, 66, 174n27, 227n134, 232, 285
exhortatory, 28
exhorts, 27n38, 154n13, 320
exile(s), exiled 19, 41, 56, 82n17, 114, 122–123, 181, 184, 186, 195n80, 199n93, 200, 263n14, 314n18, 333, 357
exist(s), existed, existing, 24, 41, 105–106, 125, 177, 201, 238–239, 288, 294, 296, 325, 305, 315, 326, 328n11
existence, 14, 24, 79, 84, 95, 100, 106, 112, 142, 181, 187n41, 192, 201, 203, 237–238, 259, 262, 267, 296, 356
existential(ly), 104, 129
Exodus, 50n7, 53, 55, 170, 244, 251, 333, 350, 356
exorcisms, 246n41
exordium, 28
expectation(s), expected (eschatological), 68, 81n15, 83, 169, 185n31, 221, 246, 357
expectancy (life), 237, 246
expelled, 13–14, 17, 32, 49, 187n42, 198, 213, 216, 217n88, 249, 273, 291
expiation, 104, 115–117
expiatory, 116, 136
exploitation, 259n2
expulsion, 14, 14n25, 15, 17–19, 25, 31, 41, 171, 287
extinction, 259
eye(s), 2, 60, 105, 111, 155, 255n26, 349
eyewitness, 209
Ezra, 82n17, 228n144

Subject Index

face, 122, 353
factionalism, 10, 18
factions, 10
fail(s), failed, falling(s), failure, 2, 19, 74, 79–80, 81, 95, 97, 99–100, 103, 106–109, 109n52, 112, 114, 118, 122, 124, 126, 131, 149–150, 158, 160, 162–163, 181–182, 183n19, 186, 192, 195, 201–202, 228n144, 238, 253, 250, 255, 260–261, 265–267, 290, 294, 299, 303, 304n22, 305n27, 308, 310, 319, 320n36, 325–326, 329, 332, 345–346, 348, 350–351, 355–356
fairness, 252n13, 281
faith, 1, 12, 18, 30–32, 36, 39–41, 45, 48–50, 50n7, 51, 53–55, 58, 60, 60n4, 68–69, 71–77, 79–81, 83, 87, 89, 89n51, 89n53, 90–92, 94–95, 99, 99n20, 100–103, 105–120, 123–127, 127n46, 128–130, 133–134, 136, 138, 138n1, 139, 139n2, 140–141, 141n11, 141n14, 142, 142n14m 142n15, 143, 143n18, 143n19, 144–146, 152, 155, 157–158, 161, 163–165, 169, 169n2, 170–171, 173, 180n2, 183, 183n19, 184, 184n19, 185n24, 186–187, 187n42, 188–189, 190n59, 191, 191n68, 193, 195–197, 198n85, 198–199, 199n91, 200, 202–203, 206–207, 210–212, 212n48, 213, 213n49, 213n50, 214n55, 215n67, 223, 226, 227n144, 228, 228n144, 228n146, 229n149, 230, 230n158, 231, 234–235, 238–241, 243, 247n46, 248, 251, 251n11, 252, 254–255, 258, 269, 284, 285n37, 290, 295–299, 299n14, 299n15, 299n16, 300, 300n16, 301–303, 303n19, 308–311, 319, 322–323, 332–334, 336–339, 339n11, 339n12, 342, 344–345, 345n40, 345n50, 346–350, 350n3, 350n4, 352, 352n5, 353–355, 355n1, 356, 356n3, 358–359
faithful, 1n5, 2, 55, 61, 72–73, 79–81, 86n33, 91, 108, 117, 119, 125, 140–142, 146, 161, 164, 174, 187n41, 190n56, 197, 200, 232, 241, 243, 267, 270–271, 275, 286n48, 289n67, 299, 302, 306, 317, 319, 336–337, 350, 353
faithfully, 111, 329–330, 354
faithfulness, 58, 71–72, 89, 120, 120n21, 122, 124, 126, 127n46, 139, 139n2, 140, 140n4, 141–143, 148n4, 155n17, 203, 213n49, 258, 295, 317, 322, 349, 354
faithless, 74
faithlessness, 138n1
Fall (the), 95, 95n2, 96, 101, 109, 136, 136n82, 137, 143, 145, 158, 261n9, 270, 315, 348
fall away, 105, 203

fallen, 83, 90, 93, 100n23, 102, 105, 261, 263, 276, 315, 328
fallenness, 97, 172
falling, 35, 95, 247
false (falsely), 10, 18, 25n9, 25n20, 28, 29n5, 63n 37, 64, 81, 85, 95n1, 97, 99, 105–106, 143, 156, 188–189, 210, 212, 215, 218, 224n121, 235, 241, 242n19, 244n25, 244n26, 245, 247n49, 251, 260–261, 277, 281n13, 284n34, 290n71, 317, 335–337, 344, 352
Fame, 228, 228n146, 282n19
familial, 133, 153, 188, 276, 285, 350
family, 9, 9n7, 12, 29, 48, 60–61, 61n13, 81, 84–85, 88, 93, 97, 133–134, 143, 144n21, 202, 205, 215n67, 217, 218n89, 228n144, 240, 258, 269–270, 275–276, 277n33, 285, 285n39, 286, 290–291, 291n80, 300n17, 332, 333n37, 340
famine, 62
Famous(ly), 8, 20, 228n143
farming, 7–8
fascist, 156
fate(s), 161–162, 191, 298n12, 301, 342n20, 356
father(s), 8n4, 10, 24, 43, 61, 63, 68, 78n3, 79, 81, 82n17, 83, 88, 88n49, 89n55, 90–91, 93–94, 113n3, 118–119, 133, 133n69, 134, 142, 146, 153, 185n24, 187n41, 190, 190n61, 193, 204, 206, 227n134, 235, 240, 245, 275, 275n24, 307–308, 314, 317, 342n18, 349
fatherhood, 276
fatherland, 228
fauna, 61
favor (God's), 114, 308–309, 312
favorable, 316n23
favoritism, 80, 83, 101, 190, 340, 352
fear, 50n7, 81, 90–91, 93, 99, 104, 121, 153, 158, 172, 180n5, 206, 284, 289n67, 327n21, 328, 330, 332
fearlessly, 134, 235
feast(s), 13, 56, 274
Feast of Weeks, 16
fed, feed(s), feeding, 56, 100, 181, 232, 260n7, 267, 284n32, 287, 302n19, 303, 337n4, 359n14
feel, feeling(s), 156, 189, 189n53, 304n24, 356n3
feet, 61, 105–106, 172, 182, 193, 194, 194n73, 195, 203, 241, 281, 309
Felix, 23, 187n42
fellowship, 209, 256–257, 288–289, 318n27, 339, 340n13

Subject Index

female, 22, 71, 131, 216–217, 270, 272, 274, 339, 341n16, 360
feminine, 215, 217n80, 299n16
fervency, fervent(ly), fervency, fervor, 91n60, 106, 156, 205, 207, 207n16, 226, 234, 339
festivals, 31n9, 107n42, 275, 353
Festus, 23
fetiales, 12
fiat (divine), 181, 238
fictive (kinship), 133
fidelity, 58, 214
fides, 139
fiducia, 142
field(s), 171, 308, 318, 329n28
fields, 42, 211, 223, 306
fight(s), fighting, fought, 9–10, 19, 255n28, 320n35, 335
filial, 153
finance(s), financed, 8n5, 201, 211n36, 215
Financial, 62, 220
financial, 38, 75n57, 218, 220–221, 227, 282, 283n24, 283n27, 286, 288, 292
financially, 211, 222n109, 235, 303
fire, 63, 161–162, 163n22, 164n25, 181, 207n16, 223, 263, 275n24, 315
firebrand, 216
firstborn, 61, 133n71, 137, 275, 297
firstfruits, 56, 61, 207, 238
fiscal policy, 10
fish, 260n7
flattery, 218
flesh, 60, 63, 68, 81, 85, 87, 92–93, 100, 102, 104, 108, 112–113, 132, 135, 137, 143, 145–146, 153, 153n10, 163, 172, 187n42, 202, 204, 206, 247, 247n46, 247n54, 253, 255, 260n7, 262–263, 270–271, 271n10, 272, 274, 286n42, 295, 315–316, 331, 335, 339, 351n3
fleshly, 99, 150, 153
flexibility, 50n6
flock, 260n7
flogged, 327
flood, 164n25, 263, 263n14, 326
flora, 61
flourish(es), flourishing, 1, 15, 268, 292, 334, 346
foci, focus(es), focused, focusing, 1, 2, 5, 12, 19, 28, 48, 51, 54, 56–57, 72–73, 76, 92, 95, 98n18, 107, 110–112, 115, 124, 131, 159, 165, 167, 179, 183, 185, 198, 214, 220, 229, 233n155, 245, 249, 253, 254n21, 261–262, 265n26, 266–267, 279–280, 287, 301, 336, 338, 357
foe, 151, 287

follow(s), followed, following, 11, 13, 23n8, 31n9, 38, 47, 53, 62, 67n39, 75, 92, 96, 105, 111, 143, 155, 157, 159, 164, 184, 198–199, 221, 229n152, 235, 251–252, 256, 285, 294, 297, 300–301, 315, 318, 331, 335, 344, 354, 357n6, 359
follower(s), 91–92, 180, 187n42, 191, 249n2, 288
folly, 183
food(s), 13, 19, 29–30, 31n9, 42n40, 48, 62, 107n42, 157, 163, 201, 219, 219n98, 220n100, 254, 259, 267, 280n10, 282, 282n19, 283n20, 287n51, 312, 336, 341n17, 353
foolish, 40, 70, 170, 179, 199, 319
foolishness, 70n50, 180, 183, 186, 322n46
footsteps, 62
footwear, 194
forbearance, 113–114, 203, 251
force(s), forced, forcing, 9, 9n9, 10, 92n61, 96n7, 98–99, 106, 139, 157, 157n20, 172, 183, 185, 188, 195, 212n48, 223, 225, 230, 237, 239, 254n25, 261, 315, 325n6, 328, 328n26, 335, 338, 339, 359
forceful, 286
forebears, 338
foreign, foreigners, 12–13, 54, 208, 154, 286n48
foreknew, foreknowing, foreknows, foreknowledge, foreknown, 137, 202, 238, 293, 295, 295n5, 297–298, 300, 300n17, 301, 304, 304n24, 306
Forensic rhetoric (or speech), 27, 27n37, 28
forensic (justification), 120–121, 127, 129, 163n22
foreordained, 295
foresaw, foresee, foreseen, 57, 238, 287, 304n25
foreskin, 91
foretaste, 93, 319
foretelling, foretold, 241, 241n16, 242, 295
forever, forevermore, 10, 101, 122n32, 134, 149, 161, 165, 202, 204, 263, 312, 322
forgive(s), forgiven, forgiveness, 50n7, 54n5, 83, 116, 124, 135, 135n81, 136, 201, 204, 239, 251, 254n22, 349
form(s), formed, forming, 1, 8, 20n14, 24, 27, 27n31, 27n33, 27n35, 28, 33, 65, 67n39, 82–83, 87–88, 92, 94–95, 101, 110, 113, 116, 130n58, 136, 191, 205, 212, 238–239, 252n16, 257, 260, 266, 268, 276, 300n16, 335–336, 338–339, 345, 347, 352–353, 357–359
formula, 82, 146, 184, 188, 239
forthtelling, 241n16, 242
Fortunatus, 208n22

Subject Index

fortunes, 185
forum(s), 8, 11, 12
foundation, 1n1, 39, 62, 86, 90, 96, 133n72, 141, 148n1, 154–156, 190, 190n56, 251, 317,
Found(ed), founded, 8, 221, 226
founders, 19–20, 227
fountain, 201n3
France, 9–10
fraud, 290n70
free, freed, 13, 49, 70–71, 74, 81, 90, 92–93, 99, 102, 104, 111–112, 116, 118, 126, 129–132, 134–136, 149–150, 163–165, 172, 205–207, 240, 254n22, 254n25, 263, 270, 293, 305, 308–310, 330, 332, 339, 341n16, 350
freedman, freedmen, freedpeople, 14, 20, 23, 135, 231
freedom(s), 22, 31, 50n7, 51, 55, 81, 90, 92–93, 101, 104, 111, 118, 127, 130–131, 135, 137, 143, 153, 156, 161, 164–165, 202, 253, 263–264, 271n7, 282n19, 294, 298, 301, 304n25, 312, 332, 341, 349–350, 359
free will, 295n5, 298n12, 300n17, 305,
freshwater, 259
friend(s), 20, 151, 216, 235n179, 290n68
friendship, 27, 136n82
fruit(s), 25n19, 42, 61, 69–70, 93, 98, 113, 151, 151n4, 182n13, 203, 224n119, 254n24, 282n19, 332
fruitful, 272
frustrated, frustration, 93, 135, 261, 261n9, 263
fulfill, fulfill(s), fulfilled, fulfilling, fulfillment, vii, 18, 36, 42n39, 43, 45, 50n7, 53, 55–58, 66, 68, 71, 73, 83, 86, 90, 106, 108n46, 109, 112, 114, 116, 122, 125, 140–141, 149, 170n9, 172–173, 176, 182–183, 184n19, 184n20, 186–187, 199n91, 202–204, 238–241, 242n18, 242n19, 253, 264, 271n10, 281, 295, 306n31, 318, 331, 344, 350
fullness, 134, 144, 170n9, 171, 173, 175, 124, 346, 357
fund(s), funded, funding, 36, 221, 278, 292, 347
fury, 63, 102–103, 160, 162, 250
Futile, futility, 165, 284, 298, 319, 325
future(s), v, 2, 8n4, 10, 27n38, 30, 51, 63n31, 72, 90, 93, 104, 110, 114–116, 130, 142, 153, 157n20, 159, 171, 187, 219n99, 220n100, 241, 263–265, 285, 297, 340, 343, 345n42
futuristic, 159–160n7

Gades, 177n42
Gaius (2 John), 291n83
Gaius (Corinth), 23, 37, 211n36, 218–219, 221, 230, 257, 277, 285–287, 291, 291n75, 292n86, 343
Gaius (Derbe), 171, 321n39
Gaius (Macedonia), 49, 291n83,
Galahad, 229n152
Galatia, 18, 37n26, 38, 95
Galatian, 35–36, 339
Galatians (people), 48
Galilee, 10, 32
Gallio, 23, 333n37, 336n2
Gamaliel, 358, 258n12
games, 182
Garden of Gethsemane, 248
garden, 263, 265–266, 268, 271, 349
gates, 194n73, 314n18
Gaul(s), 9–10, 177, 177n41, 177n45
gay, 158, 158n21
geek, 8n6
Gehenna, 162, 162n10
gender(s), 216, 224n119, 276, 338–339, 341n16, 342, 344
genders, 341
genealogical, genealogy, 100, 196n84
generation(s), generationalism, generational, 157n20, 195, 199, 228n143, 255, 269, 290, 338, 338n9, 347, 353
generosity, generous(ly), 12, 22, 155n16, 156, 220, 232, 256–258, 275, 280–282, 282n19, 283, 283n24, 283n27, 285, 290–292, 308, 319, 343
genesis, 137, 263
genitive, 120, 126, 138, 139n2, 197n85, 233n168, 244
genius, 356
genre, 2, 22, 26–27, 45, 72
gens, 85
gentile(s), 1, 12, 17, 17n3, 18–20, 23n8, 26, 28, 30–31, 31n9, 33, 33n12, 37n23, 39–40, 43, 48–50, 50n7, 51–52, 54–57, 61, 65, 69–71, 73–75, 75n57, 76, 80, 83, 85, 87, 89n51, 96, 101, 103, 107–108, 108n46, 110–112, 114, 114n6, 115, 124, 127, 131, 138–139, 140–141, 145, 149, 160–161, 169, 169n2, 170–171, 171n12, 171n16, 173–175, 179–180, 180n6, 190, 191, 193, 195n80, 196, 203, 200, 208–210, 210n31, 210n32, 211, 211n38, 214–215, 215n71, 216, 226, 231, 234, 234n176, 244, 250–251, 256, 261, 273n15, 274–275, 286n48, 295, 296n7, 302–303, 306, 311, 318–319, 320n36, 321, 324n3, 327, 331, 336–339, 339n13, 340–341, 341n16, 342–343, 343n32, 344, 346, 348–349,

391

Subject Index

(gentile continued)
    350–352, 352n5, 352n6, 353, 353n7, 354, 356–357, 357n6
gentilicium, 85
Gentilization, 18, 31
geographer, 177
geographical, 2, 26, 61, 75, 175–176, 179
geometrical, geometry, 305
geometry, 305
Georgia, 173n22
German(s), Germanic, Germany, 174n27, 177, 177n41, 177n46, 343, 345n40
Germanicus, 85
Gezerah shawa, 65
gift(s), gifted, giftedness, 29, 32, 39–40, 40n35, 41, 54, 62, 69, 75, 75n57, 80, 89, 94, 95n1, 99, 102, 110–111, 116–119, 120, 123–124, 127, 130, 132, 134, 141–142, 142n14, 156, 202–203, 207, 207n18, 210, 210n31, 211n36, 212, 215, 217n88, 220, 224n119, 225, 228n139, 230–233, 233n167, 233n171, 234, 241, 241n15, 242, 242n29, 243, 246, 246n38, 246n41, 242–247, 253, 254n24, 256, 260n7, 264, 273, 276, 279, 281–282, 282n19, 283–284, 294n32, 285–286, 299, 299n15, 299n16, 300n16, 305, 308–309, 311, 330, 338, 342, 344, 346–347, 351
give(s), given, giver, giving, gave, v, 2, 8, 10, 19, 20, 23, 26, 48–49, 51, 55–57, 62–63, 65–66, 72–73, 77–81, 85, 87–90, 92–94, 96–97, 101–104, 106, 108–109, 112, 116, 120, 124–125, 131, 134, 137, 141–142, 148, 148n1, 149–152, 154–156, 160–161, 163–164, 174, 179n1, 186, 188, 192, 195, 198, 201–202, 202n4, 203–204, 207, 210, 214, 219, 221, 228–229, 232, 234–236, 239, 240–242, 245–247, 249, 252–253, 257, 263, 266–267, 269–272, 276–277, 279–282, 282n18, 282n19, 283, 283n27, 284, 286, 288, 289n67, 290, 290n72, 292, 294, 297–298, 298n12, 299n15, 301, 302n19, 303, 303n19, 304n25, 306, 308–309, 310n4, 312–314, 319, 321, 324, 327, 331–332, 334–335, 340–341, 343, 347, 349, 355–356
gladness, 219n98, 284, 321
Global, 71, 134, 170, 172, 256, 259, 277, 343, 345
global warming, 259, 259n1, 259n2
Globalization, 359
globe, 267
gloom, 162n14
gloria, 228
glorification, 297, 318, 319n31

glorify, glorified, glorifying, 68, 82, 90, 101, 137, 161, 205, 289n67, 297, 301, 318–319, 319n31, 322
glorious(ly), 12, 79–80, 93, 101, 103, 113, 119, 132, 135, 149, 152, 155n16, 201, 263n15, 292, 294, 301, 312, 338, 341, 349, 352
glory, 51, 57, 70, 80, 80n12, 90, 93, 95–96, 101, 109, 134–135, 137, 143, 162, 165, 170, 180n5, 190, 198, 202, 204, 228n143, 229n154, 243, 248, 260, 262, 264, 279, 282, 288–289, 294–295, 297n11, 306n31, 308, 312, 315, 318–319, 321–322, 340–341, 348, 350, 357n12, 358
God, i, iii–v, vii–xi, 1–3, 12, 15, 17, 19, 25, 31, 33, 35–36, 38–42, 45, 47–48, 50–58, 60–65, 68–165, 167, 169–175, 179–212, 216, 222–256, 258–286, 288–289, 292–337, 339–344, 346–361, 364–365, 367, 369–370, 372–373
god(s), 13, 267, 274, 317, 333
goddess(es), 8n5, 15, 83, 227n138, 252
God-fearers, 17, 50, 152n9, 222, 311
Godhead, 94, 119
godless, 89n55, 169n2
godly, 191, 198, 211, 225, 230, 248, 343
gold, 115
golden rule, 255n27
Gomorrah, 273n15
good (morally), 10, 28n40, 65, 80n12, 81, 92, 95n1, 98, 101, 103–104, 107, 110, 131, 137, 152, 152n8, 155–156, 158, 161, 181, 187, 195, 202, 220, 229, 229n152, 233–234, 254, 254n25, 256, 260, 267, 283, 284n34, 286n45, 294, 296–297, 300, 303n20, 303n21, 304n25, 312, 316, 327–329, 331, 333, 333n36, 334, 339, 344, 347, 356
good news, 41, 77, 95, 139, 151, 174, 182, 193–194, 194n78, 195, 195n78, 205, 208–209, 211, 214n55, 217, 233n169, 240, 253, 260, 322, 341
good works/deeds, 75, 172, 198, 207, 211, 226, 248, 281, 327, 334–335
Good Samaritan, 154
goodness, 99, 110–111, 124, 126, 137, 150–151, 156, 205, 250n7, 254, 304n25, 308, 326, 333n36 343
goods, 230n160, 330
goodwill, 115, 316, 316n23, 317, 217n24, 317n25
gospel, vii, 1, 1n1, 1n3, 2–3, 5, 9, 16–19, 26, 28–32, 36, 38–40, 40n34, 40n35, 42–43, 45, 47–50, 50n7, 51–60, 63, 65, 67–68, 68n4, 69–75, 75n58, 76–81, 81n15, 82, 85, 87–88, 89n51, 90, 92, 95, 95n2, 96–97,

Subject Index

101–103, 106, 112–115, 119–120, 122, 124–126, 128, 131, 134–135, 137–138, 139n2, 142n15, 143, 145–147, 156–158, 160–162, 163n21, 165, 167, 169–170, 170n5, 170n7, 170n8, 176, 179n1, 180, 180n5, 180n6, 182–187, 190–192, 192n70, 193–198, 198n87, 199n90, 199n91, 200–202, 204–205, 208, 210, 210n31, 210n32, 211, 213, 213n54, 214–218, 220, 223, 223n117, 224–227, 229–232, 233n168, 234, 234n176, 235, 235n179, 236, 240, 243, 245–246, 248–249, 251–252, 255, 258–259, 260n7, 264–271, 273, 276–277, 280–281, 281n13, 289n67, 292, 294–296, 299n13, 302, 306, 308–312, 315–319, 320n36, 322–323, 327, 329, 329n28, 330–331, 333–335, 337, 339n13, 340, 340n13, 344, 344n37, 345, 345n39, 346–356, 356n4, 357–359
Gospel(s), 2, 16n2, 40n34, 47–48, 48n3, 60n4, 68, 72, 90, 143n18, 160n7, 169, 173n24, 180n3, 180n5, 201n2, 204n11, 214n60, 217, 217n84, 230–231, 237n3, 245, 251n9, 252n16, 255n29, 259n3, 270n6, 310n4, 340n15, 362, 367
gossip, 250
govern(s), governed, governing, 9, 9n7, 77, 92, 94, 105, 110, 114, 118, 157, 161, 210n31, 241, 258, 295, 303n19, 305, 307, 324–325, 326, 328–330, 332–333
governance, 137, 332
government(s), 10–11, 60, 81, 105, 156, 202, 241, 254, 305, 324–325, 325n7, 326, 326n11, 327–333, 333n36, 334–335, 352
governmental, 254, 281n13
Governor Hobson, 131
grace, 1, 24–25, 36, 40–41, 49, 54–55, 58, 62–63, 68, 75, 80–81, 83, 87–89, 95, 99n20, 102, 104, 107, 108n46, 109n54, 110–111, 113, 116–117, 124–127, 132, 135–136, 136n82, 139, 142, 143n19, 150–152, 155, 158, 161, 173, 175, 179, 198, 202–205, 207, 211, 226, 234–235, 241, 247–248, 251–252, 252n15, 254, 268, 273, 279–282, 284, 284n32, 294, 299, 299n15, 300, 300n16, 302, 307–310, 312, 315, 317, 320–321, 334, 338, 340, 350, 352, 356, 356n3
graces, 207, 309
gracious, graciously, graciousness, 107n41, 110, 127, 143n19, 236, 240, 251–252, 254, 284, 337
graft(ed), ingraft(ed), regrafted, 55, 87, 184, 203, 302, 342, 348, 351, 351n3, 353
grain, 280

grateful(ly), gratitude, ix, 30, 69, 101, 150–151, 153, 216, 280, 308–310, 312, 341, 353
grave, 222n108, 306
Gravity, 207n20
Great Sea, 7
greatness, 205, 261
Greco-Roman, 17, 28n42, 88, 115, 133n72, 144, 148, 208, 221, 254n24, 255, 272–273, 275, 280, 330n31, 355, 365, 368, 371
Greece, 9, 9n9, 9n10, 12, 36, 42, 148n4, 171, 174, 344
greed, 97, 245, 250, 262
Greek(s), 8, 8n5, 9, 7, 12–13, 16, 18–20, 27, 27n31, 27n32, 40–41, 50n7, 54n5, 59–60, 60n7, 61, 63, 70, 70n47, 71, 77–78, 78n1, 79n6, 86–87, 101, 114, 114n5, 139, 162, 169–170, 173, 175–177, 179, 179n1, 18n21, 185, 187n37, 187n38, 190–191, 191n68, 194, 199n92, 202, 212n4, 214n55, 220, 222, 222n113, 223, 223n115, 227, 239, 239n9, 277–278, 278n38, 282–285, 290, 299, 308n13, 311–313, 315–316, 318, 321, 325, 339, 339n12, 340, 343, 350, 354–355, 359
green, greening, 259, 262n12, 263n14, 265, 265n24, 265n26, 267–268
greet(s), greeted, greetings, 19–20, 22, 22n2, 25–26, 67n39, 77, 91, 118, 132, 214n55, 212, 216, 218n92, 226, 257, 291
grief(s), grieves, grief-laden, 62n28, 275, 313n17, 315–317, 353
groan(s), groaning(s), 93, 102, 134, 206, 313, 313n18, 314, 314n18
grow(s), growing, grown, growth, 10–11, 16, 17, 19, 49, 69n46, 78, 125, 151, 158, 178, 182, 203, 207, 224, 229n155, 233, 233n167, 233n169, 334, 347
grumbling, 287
guarantee (Spirit), 93
guidance, 49, 142, 298, 301, 335
guide (God), 122n32, 238n6, 294–295, 300
guide (law), 107
guide(s), guided, (Spirit), 94, 234, 242
guidelines, 156
guilds, 12
guilt(y), guilt-driven, 71, 80, 90, 92, 96, 99, 102, 104, 137, 153, 302

Hades, 162, 162n12, 162n18, 185, 185n30, 315
Hadrian, 133n71
Hagar, 141n10, 271
hand(s), 8n4, 11, 25, 31–32, 54, 63, 61, 81, 86, 108–109, 126, 153, 161, 164, 182, 187n40, 194n75, 199n90, 209–210, 223, 225, 240,

393

Subject Index

(hand(s) continued)
  245, 254n25, 267, 295, 305–306, 314, 318, 328, 332, 334, 350, 354, 357
handiwork, 170
hanged, hanging, 32, 70, 315
Hannibal, 9n8
Hapax legomenon, 65, 257, 284, 320–321
happiness, 229n154, 284n184
hard, hardness, hardens, hardened, hardening (hearts, etc.), 61n18, 74, 90, 171, 183, 192, 194, 230, 240, 271, 295n5, 302, 309, 316, 350, 351
Harmonious, harmony, 30, 94, 131, 175, 203, 255–256, 303n21, 314, 317, 341, 343
haruspices, 12
harvest, 39–40, 50, 56, 61, 69, 77, 298, 306, 308
hate(s), hated, hatred, 62, 135, 204, 287, 342n20
haughtiness, haughty, 250, 277, 303n21
head(s), 8, 81, 84, 136, 173, 196, 200, 248, 287
heal(s), healed, healing(s), 13, 83, 92, 207, 225, 233, 237, 245–248, 263, 266
healer(s), 246
health(y), 242, 284, 286, 292
hear, heard, hearing, 2, 31, 42, 55, 57, 60, 70–71, 74, 89, 89n51, 90, 108, 119, 127, 144n21, 144n22, 147, 161, 165, 170, 173–174, 183–186, 191n68, 192, 192n70, 193, 195–197, 197n85, 198, 199n90, 199n91, 200, 202, 205, 226–227, 230–231, 234n176, 235, 240, 251, 266, 300, 302, 306–309, 314, 3:14n18, 319–321, 323, 340n15, 345–346, 350–353, 356
hearer(s), 50, 71, 73, 138–139, 193, 196, 225–227, 230
heart(s), 45, 54, 61, 80, 82, 91–93, 98, 100, 103, 107–108, 110–111, 113, 123, 128, 132, 134, 138, 141, 143–144, 151, 154–155, 160, 183–189, 195–196, 197–198, 201, 206, 226, 231, 238, 240, 242–243, 248, 251–253, 256–257, 259, 267–268, 271–272, 283, 288–290, 292, 297–298, 309–310, 314–316, 318–320, 334, 338–339, 341, 346, 348–349, 355–356
hearth, 12
heartlessness, 250
heathen(s), 75, 110, 335, 346
heaven(s), heavenly, 8n4, 60, 87, 90–91, 106n37, 119, 135, 164, 170, 172, 175, 182n10, 184–186, 194n73, 198, 199n90, 206, 230, 240, 244n25, 244n26, 247, 262–263, 300n17, 304, 314n18, 304, 316, 329, 334
Hebrew, 57, 60, 71, 82, 86, 96, 121, 153n11, 184–185, 190n56, 194, 195n78, 228n144, 228n146, 278, 283n28, 314n18, 315, 316, 316n23, 319n29
heed(ed), heeding, 103, 55, 186–187, 196, 199–200, 351
height(s), 62–63, 66, 106, 106n37, 162, 307n1
heir(s), 11, 74, 81, 84, 90, 141, 202, 205, 248, 271n10, 300, 356n3
hell, 106n37, 185, 316
Hellenistic, Hellenistische, Hellenization, Hellenized, 9n9, 27n34, 67n39, 228, 278, 321n38, 364, 370
Hendiadys, 65
henotheism, 78n1
Hera, 8n5
Heracles, 227
herald, 194, 322
heresies, heresy, 31, 247, 337–338, 358
heritage, 216, 354
Hermas, 20, 218, 277n34, 278n37, 343
Hermeneutic(al), hermeneutics, 55n10, 94n67, 215n64, 224, 359
Hermes, 20, 218, 277n34, 278n37, 343
Hero(es), heroism, heroic, 227, 227n138, 229, 229n148, 229n149, 229n150, 229n153, 229n154, 229n155, 230, 230n156, 230n157, 230n160
Herod Agrippa I, 14, 218n89, 333
Herod the Great, 20, 281n89
Herodian, 15n27, 216–217, 231, 278n36, 343
Herodotus, 7
Herods, 9, 217
heroines, 228
Hesiod, 227, 331n34
heterosexual, heterosexuality, 158, 270–272, 274
Hezekiah, 82n17, 190n56
Hillel, 154n12, 270
Hinder, hindered, hindrance(s), 173, 182, 234, 234n177, 299, 311, 321
hinterlands, 36
Hispania ulteria, 222, 357
historic(al), 26, 47, 54, 57, 78, 82, 87, 112, 176n33, 217n88, 238n4, 244, 269, 353
historicity, 238n4
history, 1n4, 1n5, 30n8, 39, 45, 48, 53–54, 57–59, 70–71, 78, 80–81, 83, 88n49, 94n67, 114–115, 128, 142, 152, 157n20, 159, 182, 199, 222, 200, 222n112, 222n113, 223, 227, 231n163, 238, 243, 245, 269, 293–294, 297n11, 298, 301, 304–307, 315, 322, 326, 329, 333, 333n37, 334, 340n15, 349–353, 354n12, 355–357, 357n6, 359
Hobson, Governor William, 131
holiness, 60, 68, 75, 79, 85, 91, 98, 131–132, 150, 306n31

394

Subject Index

holy, iv-v, 19, 30, 31n9, 48-49, 56, 60, 68, 85, 91-93, 95n1, 98, 104, 112, 115, 122n32, 131, 131n64, 132n67, 142, 143n19, 151-152, 155, 157, 174, 197, 202, 205-206, 207n16, 207n20, 210, 210n32, 230n160, 235, 238, 254-255, 264, 289n67, 290, 294, 296, 313n17, 335, 341

Holy of holies, 115

home(s), 8, 12, 19-20, 25-26, 32, 37, 104, 108, 152-153, 193, 257, 268, 270, 276, 284n32, 286n46, 287n49, 287n51, 291-292, 294, 304, 318, 346n44, 358

Hong Kong, 235n179

honor(s), honoring, 11, 50, 80n12, 83, 86, 98, 101, 134, 137, 142, 156, 190, 204, 228, 251, 276-277, 279-282, 284, 288, 303, 318-319, 326, 331-332, 335, 343, 354

honorably, honourable, honoured, 230, 254, 332

hope(s), hoped, hoping, 2, 26, 30, 39, 42, 47, 51-53, 56-57, 59, 68, 74-75, 80, 83, 86-87, 92-93, 98, 106, 114, 116, 123, 137, 142, 145, 151, 156, 161, 164-165, 173, 195, 204, 206, 218-219, 222-224, 227, 230, 237-238, 240-243, 248, 259, 261-262, 264, 287, 294, 296, 300-301, 308-310, 319, 321, 323, 341, 351-353, 357

hopeful, hopefully, hopefulness, 153, 214, 248, 298, 301, 343

hoping, 55, 185

Hortatory subjunctive, 64, 303, 303n20

Hortatory letter, 27-28, 303

Hortatory, 28

horticulturist, 62

Hosea, 229

hospitable, hospitality, 3, 37, 156, 167, 211n36, 219-221, 227, 230, 254, 257, 275, 279-281n13, 282, 282n14, 285-286, 286n14, 287, 287n51, 287n54, 287n56, 288, 288n59, 289, 289n65, 289n67, 290, 290n69, 290n70, 291-292, 288, 291, 291n74, 291n80m, 292, 292n87, 313, 327, 331, 333-335, 343-344

hospitals, 211, 284n32

host(s), hosted, hosting, 61n16, 119, 218, 230, 257, 280, 285-286, 287n51, 290-292, 343

hostess(es), 257, 281, 343

hour(s), 21, 63n31, 194, 311n7

house(s), 9, 11, 13n19, 25, 37, 49, 70, 181, 195n80, 211n39, 218-219, 227, 235n179, 284n34, 287n49, 289, 291n76

household(s), 15n27, 30, 61, 63, 133, 133n72, 213n49, 269, 276, 277n34, 289n67, 292

human(s), 19, 47n1, 50n7, 53-54, 63, 68, 73, 78, 79n7, 81-82, 87, 88n49, 90-93, 95-96, 96n5, 97, 100, 100n23, 101-107, 109, 111-113, 116, 118, 121, 123-124, 126-128, 130-131, 134, 137-138, 140-141, 141n11, 142-143, 143n19, 146, 148-149, 151-152, 155n16, 158, 160-162, 164-165, 180-181, 185, 197n85, 203, 205-207, 207n15, 208, 213, 238n5, 239, 243, 245, 249n1, 250, 250n3, 250n7, 251n10, 253, 255n27, 258-261, 261n9, 262, 264-267, 269, 271n10, 281n13, 283-284, 293-295, 298, 298n12, 299, 299n14, 299n16, 300n16, 301-302, 304, 304n25, 305, 305n29, 306n31, 310, 313-314, 316, 335, 337, 341, 350, 359

humanism, 266

humanity, 1, 47n1, 79, 81, 84, 87-88, 96, 98, 100, 102, 110, 114-116, 122, 125, 128, 130, 134, 136-137, 142, 149, 151, 199, 231n163, 250, 253, 261-262, 264, 272, 279, 297, 310, 312

humankind, 51, 55-56, 70, 79-80, 82, 87, 89-90, 97-98, 100-103, 106n36, 113, 116, 124, 124n43, 125, 136n82, 145, 149, 165, 169-170, 173, 183, 190n61, 191, 195, 203-204, 230, 238n6, 239, 243, 250-252, 259, 261-263, 269, 276, 279, 283, 294-295, 298-300, 309-310, 316, 319, 340, 345, 348-349, 351-353, 357

humble, humbling, humbly, 117, 135, 141, 154, 180, 214n55, 232, 248, 253, 339, 346

humiliated, humiliation, 30, 135, 86, 180, 243, 287

humility, 18n9, 75, 94n65, 105, 155-156, 273, 297, 309, 339, 343, 347, 354n12

humorous, 65

hunger, hungry, 62, 282n20, 284n32

hunting, hunts, 62, 286, 286n46

husband(s), 216-217, 223, 230, 234, 270, 273, 285, 325

hyperbole, 65, 170n9, 214

hyperbole

Hyper-obedience, 144

hypocrisy, hypocritical, 98, 108, 149, 261, 270, 276, 285, 299

Iberian, 222n113

Iceland, 176

Iconium, 320n36

identity, 1n1, 19, 54, 56, 84n24, 107, 116, 119, 124, 132, 142, 153, 289, 289n67

ideological, ideologies, ideology, 19, 92n61, 172, 172n17

idioms, 188n45, 239n10, 355

Subject Index

idolaters, idolatries, idolatry, idolatrous, 29, 31n9, 54, 73, 79, 79n7, 92n61, 97, 101–102, 116, 119, 143–144, 149, 199, 204, 250, 260–262, 264, 267, 272, 274–275, 286n48, 299, 310n4, 312, 319, 332, 341n17
ignorant, 200
Iliad, 227
ill(s), illness, 304n25, 315, 334
illuminate, illuminates, illuminating, illuminatory, illumined, 98, 107, 112, 152, 161, 250, 266, 299
illumined, 266
Illyricum, 42, 42n39, 43n47, 61, 66, 69, 171, 171n13, 213n55, 214n56, 221, 226, 365
image(s), 56, 59, 63, 87, 162, 181–182, 192, 260, 263, 267, 328n24, 351
image of Christ, 99, 145, 207, 232, 240
image of God, 78n4, 88, 91, 98, 106n36, 124, 132, 135, 136–137, 148n2, 153, 162, 173, 205, 238, 240, 260, 272, 297, 298, 306,
imagery, 159, 266
imagination, 59
imitation, imitatory, 148n2, 153n11, 225–226
Immanuel, 84
immigrant(s), 154, 252, 289
immigration, 346
imminent parousia, 174
Imminent parousia/return, 105–106, 106n35, 169–170, 174n27, 174n28, 174n31, 176n35, 214, 344n37, 357, 367
imminent rapture, 259
immoral, immorality, 18, 73, 97, 99, 141n10, 158, 261, 224n121, 270, 272–273, 273n15, 274–275, 299, 335, 341n17
immortal, immortality, 79, 95n2, 104, 134–135, 143, 163–164, 165, 190, 203, 212n43, 231, 241, 243n24
impartial(ly), impartiality, 70–71, 80, 80n12, 103, 161, 203, 250n5, 252, 285, 310, 353
Imperatival, imperative(s), 92, 223n118, 224, 234, 241, 262n12, 263n14, 265n24, 265n26, 302, 302n19, 303, 303n21, 303n22, 324, 330
Imperator (Augustus Caesar), 11
Imperial cult, 252n14
imperialism, 339n13
imperishability, imperishable, 135, 243, 264
imperium, 202
impiety, 97, 109n52
imports, 177
imprisoned, imprisoning, imprisonment(s), 109, 198, 224n121, 230n160, 296, 304, 318, 327
impurity, 116, 272

Imputed righteousness, 128
incantations, 246n41
incarceration, 43
incarnation, 185n25, 186
incense, 319
incest, 271, 275n24
inclusio, 66, 69, 138, 145, 210, 214
Inclusion, 51–52, 55, 65, 68, 71–72, 114, 118, 129, 133, 244n31, 318–319, 336–337, 352
inclusive, 1n3, 50n6, 64, 67, 133, 136n85, 143, 143n19, 190, 194n75, 213, 215, 224n119, 227n135, 272, 276, 284n35, 287, 303n20, 320n38, 321, 324–325, 353n7
inclusivism, 199n91
income, 280n10, 330
indecency, 270
India, Indian, 175–176m 176n32, 177, 177n42, 236n183, 345
Indigenous, 8n1, 346
individualistic, 118, 131, 135, 137, 289
Indo-European(s), 7, 222n113
indulgence(s), indulgent, 11, 102, 336, 358
Indus River, 176
industrial revolution, 12, 259
industry, 263n18
indwell, indwelling, indwells, indwelt, 80–81, 90, 99
inequalities, 278
inestimable, 280
inevitability, inevitable, 92, 96, 106, 191, 204, 230, 246, 248, 301
inferential conjunction, 192
infinite, 305n29
infinitive(s), 303, 303n20
infinity, 305n27, 305n29
Infirmity, 247n52
Influence(d), influencing, 9n9, 11, 16–18, 31n9, 47, 91, 221, 237, 259, 307, 328, 334, 345
influential, 195n80, 236
ingathering, 55, 353n7
ingrafted, 302
ingratitude, 310n4
inherit, inherited, 81, 101, 112, 136, 164, 181, 205, 263, 294, 332
inheritance, 60–61, 101, 106, 133, 275, 281, 282n19, 330, 349
iniquities, 195n80
initiative, 95, 111, 279, 286, 296–298, 302
initiator, 201, 298n12
injunction(s), 38, 56, 92, 117, 152, 155, 157, 232, 251, 271, 273n15, 276, 286n44, 289, 302, 318, 321, 325n10, 328, 341n17
injustice(s), 97, 103, 122–123, 249–252, 252n12, 253, 258, 269, 278, 352

Subject Index

Inner Sea, 176
inner (being, nature, impulse, attitude, etc.), 69, 88n49, 91–92, 98, 100, 150, 153, 158, 189, 189n53, 315
innocence, innocent, 71, 108, 111, 129, 160, 203
innovative(ly), 67, 355
inns, 288
inquiries, 236
inscription(s), 23, 257, 292, 343n32
inscrutable, 202, 312
inspirational, 226
inspire(s), inspired, inspiring, 2, 57, 67, 94, 208, 225–226, 230, 233n168, 234–236, 241, 278, 315, 346, 358
instability, 9, 359
instant, instantaneously, instantly, 135, 198, 206, 243
institution, 102, 133n72, 235, 359
instruct(s), instructed, instructing, instruction(s), 27, 29–30, 53, 56, 66, 109, 150, 175, 206, 220, 223, 255, 270, 289, 355
instrument(s), 8n6, 115, 125, 236, 252, 254n24, 300
instrumental, 217
insulae, 12
insurrectionists, 20n14
integrity, 2, 22, 24, 57, 220, 292
intellect, intellectual(ly), 9n9, 142n15, 155n16, 189n53, 227, 255, 277, 356n3
intelligence, intelligent, 8n6, 214, 228n143, 229n154
intercede(s), interceding, intercession, 59–60, 60n3, 81, 90, 93, 161, 205, 307n1, 307n2, 313, 313n17, 314, 316, 320
Intercultural(ism), 94, 203, 336, 346, 347
interlocuter(s), 27n35, 64, 109, 184, 191–192, 198–199, 314, 359
internet, 359
interpolation, 324, 324n2
intertestamental period, 357
intervened, intervenes, intervening, intervention (God), 98, 170, 234, 237, 246, 248, 294, 305
intimacy, 93, 308
intolerance, 157n20
intransitive, 233n169
invaded, invading, invasion, 9, 96n7, 261, 276, 345n40
invisible, 101, 132, 137, 173
invitation, invite(s), invited, inviting, 94, 94n68, 25, 55, 119, 146, 192, 226, 266, 273, 276, 302–303, 322, 334, 344, 356
Ionias, 217
Iran, 173, 173n22, 174, 177
Iraq, 174, 258
Ireland, 345n39, 345n40
Irenaeus, 24, 43, 164n25, 173
ironic, ironically, ironies, irony, 65, 110, 191n66, 247n48, 296, 296n7, 351
Irreligion, 346n43
irreproachable, 81
irrevocable, irrevocably, 203, 325
Isaac, 55, 229n51, 240, 271, 275, 294, 342, 349, 352
Isaiah, 42, 54–57, 83, 85–86, 86n33–37, 90, 116, 120, 123, 136, 144, 161, 164, 170, 181, 189–190, 190n56, 193–195, 195n80, 196, 200, 229, 229n149, 239–240, 262, 264, 306, 319, 342, 342n23, 362–363, 371–372
Isaianic, 86
Ishmael, 271, 294, 349
Islam, Islamic, 13, 156
island(s), 13, 42, 319
Isocolon, 65
Israel, 3, 19, 31–32, 42, 45, 48, 50–61, 68, 70–71, 74–75, 79, 81–88, 90, 96–98, 101, 107, 109, 109n52, 114–116, 121–126, 133, 135, 140–141, 145, 152, 152n9, 154, 154n13, 155, 167, 170–171, 171n16, 174, 180–181, 183–186, 187n40, 191–193, 194n63, 195, 195n80, 196, 198–199, 199n93, 200, 202, 204, 208–209, 211, 213, 228–229, 231, 238–241, 247, 251–253, 256, 260, 262, 277, 279, 286n48, 294–295, 301–302, 305, 308–309, 311, 313, 315–319, 323, 326, 330, 333, 336, 340, 342, 344, 348–352, 352n5, 352n6, 353, 353n7, 353n8, 354, 356–360
Israeli, 200n94
Israelite(s), 54, 56, 86–87, 125, 133, 140, 154n13, 184n71, 191, 199, 252, 260, 315–316, 344, 349, 351–353
Issachar, 284
Italian, Italians, 8, 8n1, 9–10, 12
Italy, 7–9, 52, 69, 311, 344
itar, 322n42
itg, 24n17
iustitia, 120, 252
iwi, 131

Jacob, xi, 54–55, 60n3, 228n144, 229n151, 240, 275, 294, 342n20, 349, 366
jails, 230n160
James, 143, 162n10, 198, 209, 211, 216n76, 246, 258, 285n37, 317, 326n15, 340
Japan, 345
jar(s), 101, 105, 135
jargon, 266

Subject Index

Jason, 37, 49, 49n4, 171, 216, 218, 230, 291

jealous, jealousy, 55, 81, 99, 114, 199, 352, 353n7

Jeremiah, 55n10, 181, 314

Jerusalem, 1, 10, 14, 16–18, 20, 23, 29n3, 31–37, 37n26, 38–43, 48–49, 58, 61, 66, 68–69, 75, 85, 86n33, 92, 107, 109n52, 146, 171–173, 175–176, 179, 184, 190n56, 198, 199n93, 207, 209, 213n54, 214n56, 216, 219–220, 222, 225–227, 230, 242, 242n18, 242n19, 246, 256, 262, 277–278, 280–283, 286, 286n44, 287n49, 288, 291, 296n7, 303, 310–311, 314n18, 318, 320–321, 339–341, 344, 357, 359

Jesse, 50n7, 57, 62, 83, 229n149, 319

Jesus, 10–11, 14, 19, 30–31, 31n10, 32–33, 33n11, 33n12, 33n15, 38, 47, 47n2, 48, 48n3, 50–57, 59, 61–63, 68–69, 69n40, 70–73, 75–78, 78n3, 79–83, 83n20, 83n21, 84, 84n23–27, 85, 85n31, 86, 86n38, 86n41, 87–88, 88n46, 88n47, 88n49, 89, 89n53, 90–92, 96, 98–100, 103–104, 107–119, 124–127, 130, 130n59, 132–133, 133n70, 134–137, 139, 139n4, 140–143, 143n19, 144, 144n22, 145, 145n24, 145–147, 149, 149n7, 150, 152–153, 153n11, 154, 154n13, 155, 155n16, 156–162, 164–165, 169, 169n2, 170, 172–175, 179–180, 180n6, 182, 182n12, 183, 183n19, 184, 184n19, 185–186, 186n34, 187, 187n41, 187n42, 188, 188n47, 189–193, 195, 195n80, 196, 198–199, 199n91, 201–202, 202n4, 203–209, 211–214, 214n55, 215, 215n71, 216, 216n76, 217, 217n88, 222, 225, 227, 227n134, 228–229, 229n155, 230–231, 231n163, 222, 235, 238–244, 244n25, 245–246, 246n41, 246n42, 247, 247n46, 249, 249n2, 251, 251n19, 252–253, 255, 257–258, 260, 260n7, 262–263, 264n19, 265, 267–268, 270–271, 271n11, 272n 12, 273n15, 274–275, 277, 280–281, 281n14, 282n14, 285, 288, 291, 295, 297, 302, 303n19, 307–310, 310n4, 311, 311n8, 312–316, 318–320, 320n36, 321–323, 324n4, 327–328, 331–333, 335, 337, 339–342, 344–345, 345n40, 348–352, 352n5, 353, 353n9, 354, 356n2, 357, 357n12, 358–359

Jewish, 1n6, 13n18, 13n19, 14, 16–17, 17n5, 18–20, 28, 31, 31n9, 32, 39, 41, 42n42, 48–50, 50n7, 53, 56–57, 59, 65–66, 70, 72, 83n20, 84n25, 92, 96, 98n18, 99, 106–107, 109, 109n54, 110, 114, 125, 127–128, 133, 133n73, 141, 144, 148–150, 152, 154, 157, 158n22, 159, 164, 171–174, 180, 184, 184n20, 185n31, 186, 188–189, 190n57, 191n68, 194, 196, 209–210, 212, 216, 220, 222n111, 227–228, 238, 240, 244, 244n25, 244n26, 256, 261–262, 270, 272n14, 274, 274n23, 282–284, 287, 295, 297, 308, 311, 313, 315–316, 318, 321, 324n3, 327, 336–338, 340–344, 350, 352–353, 355–356, 359

Jew(s), 12–15, 15n27, 16–19, 26, 30, 31n9, 32, 37n23, 39, 41–42, 48–49, 50n7, 51, 53–54, 61, 70–71, 73, 78, 80, 80n12, 86–87, 87n12, 96, 98n18, 101, 103, 107–109, 111–112, 114–115, 124, 131, 139–142, 148n2, 149, 152n9, 154, 154n13, 160–161, 169n2, 170, 172–173, 175, 180, 180n6, 185n26, 187, 190–193, 196, 198, 200, 203, 209, 209n94, 213–215, 215n71, 217, 222, 231, 244, 250–251, 256, 261, 295, 299, 311, 313, 313n18, 320n36, 324–325, 327, 331, 336–339, 339n12, 339n13, 340, 340n15, 341, 341n16, 342, 342n29, 343, 343n31, 348–351, 351n3, 351n4, 352, 352n5, 353, 353n7, 354, 354n12, 357, 359

Jezebel, 229n148

Job, 228n144, 287n54, 314n18, 315, 342

Joel, 114, 114n6, 146, 342

Johannine, 88

John Mark, 34–35, 231

John (Apostle), 48, 48n3, 138, 162n18, 164, 175

John Chrysostom, 240n156, 246n42, 286

Jonah, 228n147, 322n46

Joseph (patriarch), 60n3, 85n32, 228n144, 228n147, 364, 369

Joshua (son of Nun), 82, 181, 228n147

Joshua (Jesus), 82

journey(s), journey, 18, 23, 37, 37n26, 42n40, 43n49, 43n50, 72, 206, 214, 219, 222, 226–227, 230, 256, 280, 290n71, 291, 344, 347

joy, joyful(ly), joyfulness, joyous(ly), 31, 41, 80, 93, 134, 153, 156, 161, 194, 201, 204, 206, 219, 234, 248, 255, 262, 284n34, 306, 319, 321, 341, 343

Judah, 10, 85, 140

Judaism, 2n6, 13–17, 17n3, 17n4, 19, 21, 107, 148n2, 153n11, 154n12, 184n22, 195n80, 199n90, 201n1, 208, 229n150, 263n14, 304n25, 336, 338n8, 342n21, 351n3, 358n12

Judaize, Judaizing, 16, 18, 31, 108, 111, 152n9, 336–340, 358

Judaizers, 36, 48, 160, 247n47, 260n7, 338–340, 347

Subject Index

Judas (Iscariot), 209, 225, 242
Jude, 99n20, 216n76, 228-230, 274
Judea, 11, 13, 31-32, 41, 61, 198, 219-220, 296, 303, 320, 321n38, 337, 344
Judean, 13, 41, 135
Judeao-Christian, Judeo-Christian, 259n2, 335
Judge(s), judged, judging, 9, 50, 54, 56, 60, 71-72, 79, 88, 101, 103-105, 108-109, 117, 122, 128-129, 142, 149, 160-162, 162n18, 170, 203, 205, 250n5, 255, 203, 228n144, 250, 286n48, 303, 304n25, 330n32, 335, 341
Judgment(s), 54, 56, 60, 63-64, 73, 85-86, 90, 97-98, 98n19, 102-103, 103n26, 104-106, 109, 117, 121-122, 122n32, 123, 129-130, 146, 153, 160-162, 162n18, 163-164, 164n25, 165, 170, 172, 181-183, 190, 190n59, 194n73, 200, 203, 228n144, 240-241, 255, 263n15, 281, 303n19, 303n20, 303n22, 312, 318, 326, 327, 329, 332, 333n36, 342n20, 348, 353, 357-358
judgmentalism, 82, 108, 157, 290
judicial, 10, 60
Judith, 228n144
Julia, 20, 218, 277n34, 278n35, 343, 343n32
Julio-Claudian, 11, 105n32, 133, 333n37
Julius Caesar, 10-11, 13, 133, 227, 227n138
June, 8n5
Junia, 15n27, 16, 20, 119, 209, 216, 216n76, 217, 217n80, 217n83, 230-231, 271-272, 277n34, 278n35, 291n74, 343
Junia Theodora, 215n65
Juno, 8, 8n4, 8n5, 12
Jupiter, 8, 8n4, 8n6, 12, 78n1, 81
just (justice), 71, 78, 103, 120-121, 123, 125, 129, 148n3, 161-162, 227, 250-251, 253, 255n27, 259
justice, 2-3, 9-10, 32, 54, 60, 79-80, 85-86, 97, 103, 116, 120-121, 121n25, 122-123, 125, 148, 148n4, 157, 161, 163n22, 167, 169n2, 187n40, 198, 202-203, 227, 232, 239, 249, 249n1, 250, 250n4, 250n5, 250n7, 251, 251n10, 251n11, 252, 252n12, 252n13, 252n14, 252n16, 252n17, 253, 253n19, 254, 254n21, 254n22, 254n25, 255, 255n27, 255n28, 255n29, 255n30, 256-258, 260, 260n5, 264-265, 267, 269, 277, 279, 282, 294, 318, 324, 326-328, 333n36, 333n37, 341, 346
justification, 31n9, 39-41, 49, 50n7, 51-54, 62, 71-74, 89, 90, 93, 103, 106-107, 108n46, 110-111, 117, 120, 120n21, 123, 125, 127-128, 128n49, 129-130, 136, 139-141, 143-144, 149, 160-161, 165, 169n2, 183, 196, 200, 205, 213, 252, 293n2, 297, 308, 336-339, 339n11, 340, 348-349, 351, 359
Justified, justifies, justify, 1, 41, 47, 71, 80, 86, 89n51, 94n67, 108-111, 114, 116-117, 120, 124, 126-127, 129-130, 136, 139-140, 143-145, 161, 184n19, 187, 189, 196, 199n91, 202-204, 206, 241, 248, 258, 297-299, 300, 308-309, 325n7, 336, 340, 348-350, 356
Justin, 246n41
justly, 71, 103, 121-122
justness, 250
juxtaposition, 66

Kazakhstan, 173n22
kill, killed, killing, 20, 70, 137, 180, 187n40, 198, 215n67, 260n7, 320, 329, 333, 333n37
kin, 315n19
kind, kindness, 63, 67, 79, 80, 83, 102, 113-114, 143, 203, 250-251, 254n21, 258
king(s), 8-9, 12, 57, 60, 60n3, 71, 82, 82n17, 84, 86n36, 88, 121, 123, 201, 211, 282n19, 319, 330n32, 332
kingdom(s), 28, 59, 68, 82, 85, 93, 148, 162, 174-175, 177n47, 186n34, 201, 209, 211, 217, 228n143, 255, 263, 268, 272-273, 273n15, 276, 289, 289n67, 324, 328-329, 334, 339, 343-344, 346, 354
kingship, 122-123
kinship, 61, 133, 215
kinsman, kinsmen, kinspeople, 61, 216, 217, 316
kiss, 132, 244n25
knee(s), 170, 231, 240, 317, 334-335
knights, 229n152
koine, 42
Korah, 229n148, 342
Korea, 345
kosher, 13, 13n20, 353

labor(s), 62, 217, 217n87, 249n1, 257, 275, 278, 343
Laconia, 34
laity, 224, 235
lake of fire, 162
lamb, 260n7
lament(s) lamenting, 56, 312-313, 313n18, 314, 314n18, 315
land(s), 26, 8, 10, 36n17, 42, 82, 154, 174, 181, 182n10, 184-185, 187n41, 194, 198, 199n93, 226, 259, 280, 282, 282n19, 303, 330, 356
landowners, landowning, 10
landscape, 265

399

Subject Index

language(s), 2, 9, 13, 19, 39, 50n6, 51, 51n8, 57, 60n3, 60n7, 61–62, 63n35, 65, 67, 70, 79n6, 84, 96, 103, 106, 108, 114n5, 115–117, 120, 124–129, 129n52, 130–133, 135, 135n81, 136n85, 137–138, 140, 141n11, 143, 143n18, 144, 160–163, 163n22, 188n45, 199, 215n68, 222, 222n113, 223, 227n135, 244n32, 249, 258, 263n15, 274, 277, 281, 284n35, 296, 302, 309, 316, 320n35, 327, 342, 343

lares, 12

law(s), 2, 8n4, 12, 17–20, 30–31, 31n9, 36, 39, 41, 43, 48–49, 50n7, 51, 53–58, 60, 72–74, 79–80, 83, 86, 86n33, 89–90, 92n61, 95n1, 96–100, 103–104, 106–107, 107n41, 107n44, 108n46, 109–114, 116–118, 121, 123–129, 131, 134–136, 139–141, 141n11, 142–145, 148–152, 152n8, 152n9, 153–154, 154n13, 154n14, 155, 157–161, 183, 183n19, 184n19, 185n24n 185n26, 190n56, 196, 205–206, 213, 240–241, 252n15, 253, 254n21, 255, 261, 270, 272n14, 273–274, 281, 286, 294–295, 299, 301, 308, 312, 316–317, 321, 325, 327, 329n28, 330, 336, 336n1, 337, 337n7, 340, 348–351, 356, 356n3, 356n4, 358n12, 359

lawbreakers, 108

lawless, lawlessness, 10, 97, 116, 136, 160, 244, 275

lawyer, 154n13

law-free, 17–20, 30, 36, 41, 43, 51, 155,

laying (hands), 210, 225

lead, 38, 50–51, 57, 92, 104, 107n44, 111, 113–114, 119, 126–127, 142, 145, 150, 152, 159, 188, 198, 215, 234–235, 250n3, 255, 260, 265, 267, 300, 308, 326, 329 333

leader(s),

leader(s), 19, 22, 25, 30, 49, 172, 188, 209n28, 211, 218, 222, 223n117, 228n144, 233n167, 233n170, 281n13, 290, 290n72, 291–292, 313, 325, 327, 332, 340

leadership, 17, 81, 208, 211, 215, 225, 232, 277, 285n36, 313, 347

leading, 28, 31, 41, 51, 80, 93, 98, 107, 111, 138, 142–143, 145–146, 153, 172, 179, 215, 288, 300

leads, 81, 88, 93, 98–99, 104, 108, 143, 152, 158, 183, 207, 230, 234, 250, 254, 298, 308, 319, 328, 357

learn(ed), learning, 48, 73, 154n12, 224, 242, 273, 358–359

lesbian(s), lesbianism, 272, 275

Levi (disciple), 331

Levite, Levitical, 82n17, 274

Lewis, 363

liberal, liberalism, 189, 270, 273

liberate(d), liberating, 101, 135, 165, 202, 203, 238, 253, 254n25, 278, 295, 325, 349, 358

liberation, liberation, 2, 102, 104, 113, 165, 262, 332

libertine, 19–20

liberty, 50n6, 52, 89–90, 104, 111, 157, 253, 290, 341

library, 11

Libya, 174, 177, 177n41, 178

license, 105

licentious, licentiousness, 20, 100, 105, 111, 156, 218, 273, 275

lie, lying, 141, 251, 315

life, 1–2, 10, 12, 15, 23n8, 28–30, 40, 47–48, 50n7, 51, 53–54, 62, 70–74, 78, 80–81, 83, 86–87, 88n47, 89–90, 92–95, 95n2, 96n5, 97–100, 103–104, 106–107, 107n44, 110–113, 115, 117–119, 121, 123–126, 131–132, 134–136, 139–145, 149–151, 153–155, 155n16, 156, 158–159, 161, 163–164, 170, 181–182, 186, 188–189, 189n53, 191, 195–196, 198, 203–207, 219, 219n94, 226, 228n139, 229n154, 231–232, 233n169, 234n175, 235–237, 240–243, 244n32, 246n39, 250–251, 251n11, 252, 252n12, 252n13, 253, 254n22, 254n24, 255–256, 260–261, 265–269, 276, 279, 285, 286n45, 287, 289n67, 294, 298, 300, 305–306, 308, 310–311, 313, 317, 322, 328, 332–333, 333n37, 335, 339, 341, 347, 351–353, 356–360

lifestyle, 31n9, 264

light, 26, 52, 62, 74, 106, 113, 169, 181n7, 214, 224n119, 252, 254n24, 289n67, 303n20, 335, 344n37, 354n12

lightning, 8n4

lion, 260n7

lips, 60, 274

listen(ed), listening, 68, 141, 144n21, 162n18, 181, 185–186, 196, 281, 284n34, 321

literary, 27–28, 64, 179n1

litotes, 65, 179n1

liturgical, 156

liturgy, 330

live, v, 28, 30, 40–41, 49, 51–53, 56, 62n21, 64, 66, 71–72, 77, 79, 81–82, 90–92, 99–100, 103–105, 107–108, 111, 116, 118–119, 121–123, 125–127, 127n46, 128–132, 134–135, 138–139, 142–143, 145, 149–153, 155, 158–160, 162, 165, 183, 202–203, 205–207, 231, 239–240, 253–255, 258, 261, 262n9, 263, 265–267, 271, 275–276, 282, 289n167, 297, 299,

Subject Index

303n21, 305–306, 308–309, 324, 327–329, 332–333, 335, 337, 339, 341, 345n32, 349, 356n2, 359

lived, 11, 40, 81, 92, 100, 108–109, 112, 126, 133n72, 141, 148–149, 151, 152n9, 179, 280n10, 295, 297, 332

livelihoods, 267

lives, 8n4, 81, 99–100, 103, 111, 119, 129, 131–132, 134–135, 151, 161, 165, 183, 185n31, 199n91, 207, 216n74, 229, 235, 243, 249n1, 250, 252–253, 257, 266–267, 270, 272–273, 275, 300, 304–305, 309, 313n17, 328, 331n34, 333, 341n16, 343, 347

living, 9n10, 29n4, 58, 74–75, 80, 89–90, 92, 107, 111–112, 117, 119, 121–122, 124–126, 128, 132–133, 134–135, 137, 142–143, 143n19, 148n1, 149–150, 153, 155–158, 163, 182, 203–204, 207n20, 211, 226n13, 252–253, 254n24, 255, 261, 265, 267, 269, 271, 273, 280n10, 283, 289–290, 302, 304, 304n24, 327, 330, 332, 334–335, 338–339, 341, 343, 353

London, 346n44

Lord, ix, 22, 22n2, 29–31, 31n10, 55, 57, 59, 68, 80, 82–83, 83n21, 84, 84n23, 84n25, 84n26, 84n27, 85, 88–91, 93–94, 100, 114, 117–119, 121n25, 122n32, 123, 129n51, 129n52, 129n53, 130, 142–146, 146n27, 147, 152, 155, 157, 162, 172, 175, 180–182, 187–188, 188n47, 190 193, 195–196, 202, 204, 206–207, 211–212, 214n55, 228n143, 230–232, 240, 251n10, 255–257, 265, 267, 274–275, 277, 284, 287–288, 289n67, 290, 295, 301, 303n19, 303n21, 307–308, 316, 319, 321, 332, 335, 341, 343–344, 351–352, 357, 366, 373

lord, 8n4, 188

lords, 83

Lord's Supper, 29, 212, 290

lordship, 90, 114, 120, 140, 143–144, 147, 188, 191, 193, 195–196, 199, 204, 231, 243, 266, 300, 340

lost (salvific), 107n44, 134, 193, 204, 206, 208, 227n134, 235, 253, 267, 295, 314, 317

lostness, 163n21

Lot, 196n84, 228n147

lot(s) (by), 175

love(s), loved, beloved, loving(ly), 18–19, 30–31, 49, 52, 56, 58, 61n16, 62–63, 65, 70, 75, 78–81, 83, 85–86, 89, 89n55, 90, 92–94, 98–99, 102, 104, 106–107, 111–113, 113n3, 116, 118–119, 121, 121n25, 122–123, 125, 131, 135, 142, 150–154, 154n12, 154n13, 154n14, 155, 155n16, 156–158, 172, 184, 192, 198, 201, 201n3, 202–203, 205–207, 214, 214n55, 232, 241, 248, 251–253, 254n21, 254n24, 255, 255n28, 256, 258, 260, 262, 265, 267–268, 270–273, 275–277, 279, 282, 284–285, 285n39, 285n41, 286n45, 288, 289n67, 290, 297, 301, 307–308, 315, 320, 325, 327–328, 332, 334–335, 339, 341, 343–344, 347, 351–356

lovely, 182, 193–195, 316

lowly, 254, 277, 288

loyalty, 72, 188, 280

Lucius, 37, 37n23, 216, 218, 230

Lucius Domitius Ahenobarbus, 85

Lucius (of Cyrene, Antioch), 218

Lucius Verus, 133

Luke, 1n2, 14, 18n8, 23, 26, 36n16, 37n22, 37n23, 47, 49, 132, 162n10, 162n12, 162n16, 171, 182, 206, 209n26, 211n35, 213, 215n71, 229n155, 232, 242, 245, 311, 321n39, 339

lump of dough, 62

lunacy, 15

Lusitania, 222n113, 223

lusts, 92, 97, 134, 206, 272

Luther, 120, 129, 158n22, 241n15, 336–337, 358

Lutheran, 125–126, 372

Lycaonia, 175

Lycus Valley, 36n16

Lydia, 17n4

Lystra, 37, 51, 245

M. Acilius Glabrio, 215n67

Macedon, Macedonia, 9n8, 23, 35, 37n26, 38, 43, 49, 171, 213n55, 223n117, 223, 234n176, 256, 280n8, 286, 311, 343–344

Macedonian(s), 36n16, 49, 211n36, 218n93, 221, 256, 291n83

madness, 156

magic, 244n25

magician, 106n37

magistrates, 327

magnanimity, 308

maidens, 275n24

majesty, 228n143

Makarism, 66

Malachi, 342

malarial fever, 247

Malay Peninsula, 177

male(s), 2, 71, 78n4, 131, 217n80, 270, 272, 275, 336, 337n5, 339, 341n16, 360

malice, malicious, maliciousness, 41, 97, 247, 286

maligns, 250

Subject Index

Malta, 245, 287n49
Malta fever, 247,
maltreatment, 354n12
mammalian, 272
man, men, 32, 37, 83–84, 109n54, 55n10, 70, 78n4, 87, 109, 111, 118, 119, 136, 140–141, 148n4, 152, 160, 180, 189n53, 195n80, 196, 211, 223n118, 224, 224n119, 226, 227, 228n143, 229n153, 230–231, 234, 242, 245, 255n27, 259n2, 260, 270, 272, 274–276, 292, 295, 304n25, 307n2, 331, 337–338, 342, 344, 358
management, managing, 133n72, 313
managing, 313
mandate, 260, 272n14, 289n67, 333n36
manger, 244n25
manifest(s), manifestation(s), 131, 253, 259, 339
manipulation, 10
manumission, manumitted, 60, 130, 135, 330
manuscript(s), xii, 24, 322n41
Māori, 131
marana tha, 83n21
marble, 11
March, 16, 23
Marcion, 24, 26
Marcus Aurelius, 133n74
Mardi Gras, 274
marginalized, marginalizing, 31, 249, 252n16, 253, 347, 358
Maria, 343n32
marines, 320
marital, 273–274, 331
Marius, 10
Mark, 48, 48n2, 215n71, 217, 225n88, 241, 244–245, 248, 257, 270–271, 273–274, 286, 291–292, 311, 319, 327, 331, 333, 337, 358
mark, marks, 93, 96, 107, 244–246, 284
Markan, 270
marketplace, 31n9
marriage(s), 8n4, 8n5, 29, 29n6, 61, 97, 111, 135, 151, 158, 250, 270–271, 271n8, 272–273, 273n15, 274–275, 335, 344
married, marry, 8n5, 151, 217, 270, 273–275, 291
Martha, 281, 313
martyred, martyrs, 43, 229n152
Mary (of Bethany), 281, 313
Mary (of Rome), 15n27, 217, 230, 275, 278nn36, 343
masculine, masculinity, 78n4, 215, 217n80, 271n8, 276, 337n5, 358n30
master(s), 60, 82, 124, 151, 153, 279n1
masterful, 105

mathematical, 63n33, 305n29
maths, 63
matricide, 275n24
Mattathias, 229n150
Matthew, 47, 162n10, 162n11, 175, 241, 331
Matthias, 209
mature, maturity, 173, 233, 233n167
Mauretania, 7, 177
maxim, 154n12
meal, meals, mealtime, 61, 258, 289n67, 311
meat, 18, 31n9, 62, 283n20, 341n17, 353n11
media, 359
mediator, 310
medical, 60, 237, 346
medicine, 8n6, 237n3, 367
meditates, 91
Mediterranean Sea, 7, 40, 75, 176
mediums, 185
Medo-Persia, 194, 326
megacities, 262
meiosis, 65
Melchizedek, 196, 228, 228n147
melt, 183
member(s), 12, 36, 67, 91, 118, 195n80, 218n89, 229, 229n152, 232, 254n24, 276, 277n34, 287n51, 291n80, 341
memorandum, 27
mental, mentally, 101, 189, 206, 212n43, 284
mercantile, 9
mercies, 63, 80, 155n16, 253, 303
merciful, 57, 80, 251
mercy, 55, 57, 60, 63, 79–81, 83, 86, 101–102, 113, 115, 117, 123, 143, 145, 171, 194n73, 203, 232, 251–254, 273, 282n19, 283–284, 284n28, 284n30, 294, 318–319, 334, 341, 350–351
Merism, 66
merit, 139, 143, 199n91, 217, 229n153, 309
message(s), 26, 28, 35, 40n34, 47, 50n7, 51, 57, 68, 70, 72–73, 88, 90, 105, 138–139, 141, 145, 160n7, 162, 165, 169–170, 180, 181n7, 182–185, 185n30, 192–193, 195–196, 197n85, 198, 200, 208, 212, 215, 218, 225, 233, 233n168, 234, 266, 270, 289n67, 292–293, 295–297, 302, 317, 322, 322n46, 336, 352, 355, 358–359
messenger(s), 184, 209, 209n28, 210, 247
Messiah, 14, 32, 48, 55–56, 59, 68, 70–71, 76, 82–84, 86, 88, 90, 106, 140, 152, 159, 165, 179, 183, 185, 185n26, 186, 190, 195, 195n80, 196, 199, 303, 308, 332–333, 340–341, 348–349, 352, 352n5, 353, 353n9, 354, 357
messianic, 83n20, 84n27, 86, 106n36, 159–160, 185n31, 190, 190n57, 204, 349, 357

Subject Index

messianically, 86
metaphor(s), 51, 56, 59, 63, 89n55, 91,
    114–115, 127, 130, 133n73, 134, 163n22,
    270, 287, 294, 359–360
meteorological, 259
metonym, metonym, 66, 85n32
metropolis, 12n14, 19
middle (voice), 194, 212
Midrash, 66, 359
migraine, 247
Miletus, 246
military, 9–11, 59–60, 62, 182, 195, 208,
    223n113, 228, 320
millennial, millennium, 165, 336
mind(s), 12, 18, 29n4, 30, 41, 43, 49, 54, 59,
    61, 70, 81–82, 90, 92–93, 100, 106, 108,
    108n49. 116, 128, 137, 143, 143n18,
    151–152, 154–157, 162, 183n19, 184,
    186n43, 189, 196–197, 204, 211, 223, 225,
    229, 251n11, 253–254, 254n24, 263n18,
    282n17, 283n27, 286n44, 287n51, 304,
    309, 312, 314–315, 318, 330, 334–335,
    343, 359, 360
mindset(s), 117, 143, 210, 332
Minerva, 8, 8n6, 12
mining, 223n113
minister(s), ministered, ministering, 11, 60, 75,
    80, 90, 133, 198, 208–209, 216, 281, 291,
    295, 324, 328, 330, 334
ministries, ministry, 13, 17, 32–33, 42n39, 48,
    60, 75, 81n15, 113, 131, 155, 171–172,
    195n80, 199, 201n3, 209, 209n27, 210,
    210n32, 211, 211n34, 235n179, 242–246,
    246n41, 247–248, 281–282, 291, 319n31,
    320–321, 347n45
miracle(s), 75, 94, 197, 207, 207n18, 211,
    233n167, 237–238, 238n6, 242–244,
    244n25, 244n32, 245–246, 246n39,
    246n40, 246n41, 246n42, 249, 303, 337n4
miraculous, 237–239, 242–244, 244n32,
    245–246, 247, 258
miraculously, 245
misdeeds, 137, 206
misery, 250–251, 314
missio, 94n26
missio Christi, 205
missio Dei, 94, 201, 205–207, 265
Missio Spiritus, 206
missiological, 119, 260n5
Missiologists, 260
missiology, 94n68, 192, 344n38
Mission, i, iii, iv–ix, 1, 1n1, 1n3, 1n5, 1n6, 2,
    2n6, 3, 18, 24, 24n14, 28, 30–33, 33n11,
    33n12, 33n15, 35–36, 36n17, 37–39,
    39m29, 39n33, 40–42, 42n39, 43, 49,
    50n7, 51, 53, 57, 68–69, 72–73, 75, 75n58,
    76–77, 79n7, 83n20, 84n24, 88, 89n54,
    90–91, 94, 94n67, 96n5, 106n35, 107n44,
    118–119, 145, 149, 155, 155n15, 156–158,
    167, 169, 169n2, 170, 170n5, 170n8,
    171–173, 173n24, 174, 174n28, 174n31,
    175–176, 176n32, 176n33, 176n34,
    176n35, 176n36, 176n37, 177, 177n38,
    177n40, 177n42, 177n43, 177n44, 179,
    182, 191, 193, 197, 199, 199n90, 200–201,
    201n1, 201n2, 201n3, 202–207, 207n20,
    208–209, 209n26, 210n30, 211, 211n36,
    212–214, 214n55, 214n56, 215–222,
    22n109, 225–226, 229–230, 230n157,
    231, 231n163, 233n170, 234, 234n177,
    235, 235n180, 236, 236n181, 236n183,
    237, 241–243, 245–246, 249, 249n1,
    254, 256, 258–260, 260n5, 261n9, 262,
    263n15, 264n20, 265–267, 269, 269n1,
    269n2, 271, 272n12, 273, 275, 277–281,
    284, 286, 288, 290n71, 291–292, 292n87,
    293, 295–296, 296n7, 298, 299n13, 303,
    306–307, 307n2, 308, 310, 310n4, 311,
    314, 317–318, 322–324, 324n1, 327, 329,
    331, 334, 336–337, 339, 339n12, 340, 344,
    344n37, 345, 345n41, 346–347, 347n45,
    348, 351n3, 352n5, 352n6, 353n7,
    354n12, 355, 357n6, 358–359, 362–373
missional, v, vii–viii, ix, 1, 1n4, 1n5, 2, 5, 28,
    30, 32, 36–40, 42–43, 51, 53, 57, 69,
    94n67, 119, 122, 132, 144, 148, 155–156,
    176, 192, 203–204, 204n12, 207, 207n18,
    208, 210n31, 211, 215–216, 216n76, 217–
    219, 221, 223, 226n130, 227, 230–231,
    213n13, 232, 234, 237, 241, 245, 254, 256,
    258, 260, 262, 292–293, 295, 296n7, 303,
    307, 310, 316, 318, 320, 334, 347, 359
Missionally, 67, 204, 263n16, 264n19, 356n2
missionaries, missionary, 1, 1n1, 23, 28, 31,
    33, 33n11, 33n12, 36n17, 37, 37n26,
    42, 43n49, 43n50, 50n6, 81n15, 88,
    172, 174–175, 176n32, 186, 199, 201n3,
    204–205, 208n22, 209n26, 210, 210n32,
    212n47, 215n68, 216, 217n83, 217n87,
    218, 225, 226n130, 227n134, 236, 244,
    244n32, 260n5, 273n15, 275n26, 287,
    291, 303n23, 307, 324n4, 344–346, 355,
    356n2, 358n12, 359n14
missions, 33n13m, 33n14, 34, 70n50, 81n15,
    88n49, 94n68, 199n91, 207n20, 223n117,
    227, 231n164, 232, 242, 296n7, 311,
    345–346
Mnason, 287n49
Moldova, 173n22
monarch, 86, 190n56, 239

Subject Index

Monarchial Period, 8
monetary, money, 10, 23, 29, 38, 42n40, 219–220, 220n100, 221, 224, 256, 262, 267, 280, 290n71, 291–292, 295, 343–344
monoculturalism, 347
monogamy, monogamous, 271n11, 274
monotheism, monotheistic, 13, 78
Montenegro, 42n39, 171
moon, 282n19
moral, 12, 33n12, 98, 108, 122, 132, 148n5, 149n6, 155n15, 155n17, 157n19, 228n144, 286n46, 304n25, 356
morality, 149, 272n14, 289n67
morally, 122, 273
Moravians, 345n41
morning, 311
morph(ed), 134, 267, 358
mortal, mortality, 79, 87, 91, 93, 95n2, 100n23, 134–135, 150, 163, 204, 243, 261, 264
mos mairum, 10
Mosaic, 31n9, 107, 110, 122, 186, 254n21, 337, 349
Moses, 57, 95n1, 181, 185, 185n31, 186, 199, 228, 228n144, 229, 229n149, 240–241, 244, 246n42, 305, 313, 337n7, 342, 342n21, 356
mother, 61, 211n36, 218–219, 230–231, 257, 263, 275, 275n24, 276, 285, 291, 291n80, 358
motherhood, 276
mothering, 275
motivated, motivation(al), motives, 1, 39, 67, 90, 155–156, 172, 203, 205, 220–221, 226–224, 227, 231n163, 234, 266, 282, 283n27, 320
mountains, 122n32
mourned, 13
mouth(s), 60–61, 144, 181, 185–189
movement(s), 15, 17, 30, 32, 62, 75n58, 126–127, 150, 189n53, 209n28, 210, 225, 235, 259, 265, 267, 269, 300, 305, 330, 344, 351, 354
mud, 61, 260
multicultural(ism), 80, 203, 336, 342–343, 345–347
multiethnic, 278, 343
multi-story, 12
multitude(s), 21, 193
municipal council, 8
Muratorian Canon, 43, 173
murder, 11, 250–251
music(al), 8n6, 347
mutations, 238n6

mutual(ly), mutuality, 39, 40, 69, 75, 89–90, 111, 120, 156–157, 199, 219, 257, 271, 276, 290, 302–303, 321, 339, 341, 343
mysterious, mystery, 76, 171, 173, 202, 293n1, 323
myth, mythological, mythology, 237, 238n4, 305

nakedness, naked, 62, 280
narcissistic, 118
Narcissus, 20, 26, 218, 218n89, 277n34, 278n37, 291, 343
narrate(s), 48, 72
narratio, 28
narratival, narrative(s), 47, 48, 59, 72, 90, 95, 101, 141, 186, 213, 227, 237, 238n5, 331, 341n17, 356, 360
nation(s), 1n1, 40, 54, 61, 68, 75n58, 76, 83, 94n67, 106, 123, 144, 169, 169n2, 170n9, 171–172, 174n27, 175–177, 190n56, 195n80, 195n79, 199, 202, 204–205, 207–210, 222, 227, 239–240, 244, 253, 255n27, 258, 262–263, 276–277, 286n48, 292, 295, 303, 305, 316, 318–319, 323, 326, 328, 332–333, 335, 340n37, 341, 352, 339n11, 339n12, 343n34, 344–346, 349, 357
national(ism), 70n47, 107, 332, 352n6
natural, 17, 79, 87–88, 147, 261–262, 272, 272n14, 290n72, 353, 359
naturalist, 238
nature, 11, 24n14, 29, 31, 42, 47, 61, 70n47, 88n49, 100, 133n72, 136, 176n32, 201n3, 252, 259n2, 272, 272n14, 285, 322
Nazareth, 82, 180, 352n5
Nazism, 102, 255n26
necessity, 193, 329, 329n28
neck(s), 61, 216n74
necks, 61
necromancers, necromancy, 185–186
need, needs, needy, 245–246, 248–249, 249n1, 249n2, 252, 252n16, 254, 256–258, 267, 280, 280n10, 281–283, 283n24, 284–286, 286n43, 287–289, 317–318, 342
neighbor(s), 13, 56, 61, 100, 112, 154n12, 154n13, 157, 252, 255, 258, 270, 274, 284, 303n19
neighborly, 56, 273
neologism, 265n26
neophyte, 289
Nereus, 20, 26, 133, 218, 277n34, 278n37, 343
Nero, 11, 15, 20–21, 83, 85, 102, 133n71, 156, 218n89, 254, 260n7, 324n3, 324n4, 329, 330n29, 333, 333n37
Nerva, 43n46, 133n74
Netflix, 304

Subject Index

neuter, 300n16
Network(s), 213, 260n4
new Adam, 51, 54, 87–89, 136, 204–205, 240, 252, 260, 266, 308, 359
new creation, 83, 87, 89, 136–137, 149n6, 160, 238, 265–266, 297, 334, 339
new converts, 16–17, 40n37, 69, 69n46, 210, 221, 233, 233n167, 235, 273n15, 318, 340
new covenant, 55, 55n10, 59, 86–87, 122, 136, 309
new earth, 164, 240, 262–263
new era, 110
new heavens, 164, 240, 262
new humanity, 1, 87, 136–137, 297
new Israel, 87
new Joshua, 82
new life, 92, 99, 111, 134, 150, 252, 359
New Masculinity, 271n8, 276n30
New Perspective, 107n41, 336, 336n1, 338, 358
new song, 319
new temple, 86
New Testament, 23n17, 33n12, 107n44, 120n22, 130n59, 163n21, 169n2, 170n5, 199n93, 220n101, 232n165, 241n16, 259n1, 263n16, 264n19, 275n26, 299n13, 356n2
new way, 151, 206, 252n13
new world, 278, 345n41
New York, 346n44
New Zealand, 131, 246n39, 328, 346n43, 347
newness, 99
news, 41, 59, 77, 95, 139, 174, 182, 193–194, 194n78, 195n78, 195, 205, 208–209, 211, 213n55, 214n55, 217, 233n169, 240, 253, 260, 282n18, 322, 341, 371
Nicolaus, 17n3
night, 13, 62, 160, 182n10
Noah, 196n84, 228 n147, 261n9
Noahic, 349
nobility, 9–10
noble(s), 9, 215, 287
nobodies, 226, 296n7
noma, 85
nomen, 85, 343n32
nominal, 334
nomistic, 56
nonessentials, 52
non-judgmentalism, 156
nonmissional, 1n4
nonviolence, 156, 331
norm(s), 252, 255, 347
normal, 65, 81n15, 152n9
norms, 347
North, northern, 7, 42n39, 85, 85n32, 86, 173, 176, 181, 222, 296, 310, 346, 357

North Africa, 173–174, 177–178, 296, 345n42
North America, 345n42
North Shore, 346
Northwest, northwestern, 9, 36, 42n39, 171, 222n113, 357
notitia, 142n15
noun(s), 40n34, 67, 96–97, 114, 120, 127, 135, 138n1, 217, 226n129, 286, 312, 322
nourished, nourishing, nourishment, 219, 275n24, 287, 288
NT, xii, 2, 10, 26, 53, 58, 60n3, 65, 78, 82, 91, 106, 133, 154, 160, 162, 169, 172–173, 173n24, 176, 185, 185n30, 187, 187n41, 188, 196n84, 201, 209, 216, 219, 223n117, 224, 227–228, 228n147, 229n149, 229n151, 230, 234, 237, 241, 244, 244n32, 247–248, 262–263, 266, 271, 273–274, 281, 284, 292, 313, 315–319, 320n34, 326, 331, 333, 341n17, 343n34, 352
Nun, 82m 82n17
NZ, 94, 208, 346

oath, 187n41, –188
obedience, 36, 40, 50, 68–69, 75–76, 79–80, 87, 99–100, 107, 117n41, 138–139, 139n2, 141n11, 144n20, 144n22, 145n25, 145n26, 149n7, 155, 160n8, 185n26, 188, 195, 200, 202, 210, 214, 223, 254n24, 285, 298, 300, 302, 304, 312, 319, 320n36, 323, 325, 337, 340–341, 344
obedient, obediently, 125, 144n22, 145, 185, 300, 325, 327, 332
obey(s), obeyed, obeying, 68, 81, 92, 109, 138, 145–146, 179, 184–186, 195, 276, 300, 304, 320n36, 323, 325n10, 340
objective(ly), 79n7, 104, 118, 139n2, 140, 140n6, 197n85
obligated, obligation(s), 40, 70, 153, 156, 169, 174n27, 179, 226, 254n21, 282n14, 288n59, 298, 329, 331, 343, 349
obliterated, obliteration, 263n15, 339
obsolete, 299
occult, 106
occupation, 12
Oceania, 345
Octavian, 11, 279n1
Octavius, 279n1
offence, offend(s), offense, 83, 86, 97, 119, 234, 341
offender, 328
offensive, 328
offer, offering(s), 57, 60, 75, 75n57, 91, 99, 115–117, 155, 210n32, 211, 219, 341
office(s), 10, 12, 23n14, 233n170, 283n24, 299n13

405

offspring, 61, 74, 240
old creation, 264
old covenant, 127, 139, 202
Old Perspective, 336, 336n1, 338
Old Testament, 53, 210n32, 241n16
old way, 151
oligarchs, oligarchy, 9, 9n7, 10
olive tree, 56, 61, 115, 302, 315, 342, 348, 351n3, 353
Olympas, 20, 218, 277n34, 278n37, 343
omen(s), 185, 244
omnipotence, 101, 305
omniscience, omniscient, 297, 304–305
oneness, 119
Onesimus, 208n22, 214, 215n71, 287n52
Onesiphorus, 208n22
ontological, ontologically, ontology, 118, 119, 125, 158
Open Theism, 293, 297n11
openness, 242
opponent(s), 99, 106, 111, 165, 234n177, 247, 247n48, 260n7, 310, 332–333, 356n3
opportunities, opportunity, 2, 40n37, 57, 231, 234, 234n177, 252n12, 280, 282n19, 288, 326, 347n45
opposition, 101, 173, 247, 249n2, 318, 326–327
oppress(ed), 98, 252, 269n2, 313n17
oppression, oppressive, 105, 249–250, 267, 278, 324, 332, 334
oppressor, 326
Optimates, 10
oracle of Delphi, 12
oracle(s), 53, 142, 200, 228n143, 294, 299
oratory, 10
orcharding, orchardist, 61, 63
ordained, 224, 329
order, ordered, ordering, 9, 11, 13, 27n35, 28n39, 40, 64, 69, 79n7, 84, 90, 101, 148, 159, 175, 179n1, 224n119, 241–242, 258, 261, 263n15, 265, 270, 272, 280, 318, 324–325, 328, 331, 333, 337, 340, 353
ordinances, 121, 274
ordination, 225, 235
organically, 225
organization(s), organized, 9, 12, 225, 267–268, 333, 335
orientation, 17–18, 41, 49
Origen, 24n17, 24n18, 49n5, 130n58, 164n25, 175, 295n5
origin(s), 8, 23, 33n15, 60, 126, 130, 201n3, 209, 215, 222n113, 227n138, 237, 260, 272, 351, 364, 367, 372
original(ity), 2, 24, 25n20, 25n21, 40n34, 48n2, 76, 96, 106n36, 128, 129n54, 136, 136n83, 138, 144n21, 186n36, 188n45, 190, 194, 195n79, 204n12, 210n32, 219n99, 246n41, 271n7, 283n24, 284n32, 287, 322, 322n42
Orismus, 66
Orontes, 13
orphan(s), 252, 282n20
orthodox, 78, 297n11
Ostia, 43n49
OT, 19, 26, 42n39, 48, 53, 53n1, 54–59, 64, 82–83, 102, 104n30, 123, 139, 143, 146, 164, 170–172, 181n7, 184, 184n20, 184n23, 185, 190, 190n57, 193–194, 196, 198, 206, 228, 228n144, 230, 238–239, 241, 271n11, 319, 326, 326n12, 328, 333, 342, 354–355, 359, 359n14
otherness, 91, 289n67
outcasts, 184
outpouring (Spirit), 318, 357
outsiders, 234
overcrowded, 9
overflow(s), 309, 319
overpopulation, 259
overseers, 277, 288
oversight, 326
ownership, 277
ox, 260n7
Oxymoron, 66
ozone, 263n18

Pacific, 345n42
pagan, paganism, 31n9, 51, 97, 100, 149, 164n25, 180n4, 185–186, 199, 325n7
pain(s), painful, 56, 62n28, 150, 159–160, 164–165, 247, 254, 263, 265, 282n19, 287, 313, 313n18, 314, 314n18, 315
Pakistan, 176
palace(s), 11
Palatine, 8n2, 11–12
Paleopathology, 237
Palestine, 9–10, 23, 352
Palestinian, 9n9
Pamphylia, 34
pandemics, 359
pantheon, 15, 78, 119, 196
Paphos, 242n19
Papyrus, 24
Parabasis, 97
Parable of the Sower, 141n12
Parable of the weeds, 263
paradigm(s), 83, 155n17, 199n91, 227, 228n144, 317, 319
paradigmatic, 143, 280
paradox(es), paradoxical(ly), 66, 80, 83, 338n8, 363

Subject Index

paraenesis, paraenetic, 27, 30n8, 66, 131, 157n20, 343
paragons, 228n144
parallel(s), parallelism, 8n4, 19, 66, 69, 89n51, 162, 164n25, 188n47, 190, 263-264, 305n29, 330-331
Paranomasia, 66
Parataxis, 66
pardon, pardoned, 71, 80, 129, 282n19
Parechesis, 66
parenesis, 28, 188,
parenthesis, parenthetical, 66, 193
parents, 61, 144, 250-251, 276, 285n39
parousia, 105, 106, 106n35, 160, 169, 169n8, 170, 174n27, 174n28, 174n31, 176, 176n35, 199n89, 255, 344n37, 357
Parthia, Parthians, 174n27, 175
partiality, 80n12, 339
participate(d), participating, 12, 22, 99, 105, 116, 119, 164, 196, 201n3, 204, 208, 225, 242n20, 264-265, 299, 306, 311, 333-335, 347, 355
participation, 28, 81, 89-90, 104, 117, 150, 196, 204, 234, 255, 279
participatory, 118
participle(s), 129, 303, 303n21, 325n9
particle(s), 64, 198, 198n86
partner(s), partnered, partnership, partnering, ix, 76, 144, 215-216, 245, 270-271, 275n26, 333-335
passion, 40n36, 42n39, 52, 57, 70n48, 75, 75n57, 145, 145n23, 181n7, 183n16, 189n53, 194n76, 201n2, 207n16, 224, 226, 267, 272, 308, 339, 344n37, 356
passionate, passionately, 36, 207, 220, 225, 232, 234, 248, 259, 267, 306, 338-340, 359
passion of Jesus, 195n80
passions, 97, 134, 145, 189, 300
passive, 65, 69, 129, 212, 223-224, 239, 300, 325-326
passivity, 255
Passover, 54n7, 60, 260n5
pastor(s), ix, 50n6
pastors, 233n167, 326, 347
pastoral, 28, 30, 39, 215
pastorally, 320
Pastoral(s) Epistles, 25, 157, 173, 218n91
paterfamilias, 81
patience, patient, patiently, 63, 79, 113-114, 156, 202-203, 250, 303n21, 343
patriarchal, 55, 229n151
patriarchs, 50n7, 55, 57, 87, 122, 227n135, 294, 305, 342, 349, 356
patricians, 9
Patrobas, 20, 218, 277n34, 278n37, 343

patron(s), 223, 227, 230, 257, 275-276, 279, 279n1, 280, 283n24, 285n36, 290-292
patronage, 3, 10, 167, 218, 220-222, 231, 279, 280, 280n9, 280n11, 281-282, 285-286, 290, 290n72, 291, 291n74, 291n75, 291n76, 291n79, 291n80, 292
patroness, 8, 215, 215n65, 291, 343
Paul, v, 1-3, 11-20, 22-30, 32-43, 45, 47-73, 75-120, 123-125, 127-165, 167, 169-174, 176-177, 179-180, 182-203, 205-258, 260-266, 269-292, 294-333, 335-359, 361-373
Pauline, 1n2, 18-20, 22, 30n8, 31, 33n13, 33n14, 41, 51, 55n10, 84n27, 94, 131, 136, 163n21, 173, 206, 263, 324n4, 325
Paulines, 22, 117, 172
pax Augusta, 11
pax deorum, 12
pax Romana, 11, 228, 228n139
peace, 9, 11-12, 25, 30, 59-60, 62, 79-80, 80n12, 88-89, 92-93, 100, 105, 121, 130-131, 153, 156, 175, 190, 201, 203-204, 206, 220, 233n169, 248, 254-255, 255n27, 255n28, 256n36, 258, 262, 279, 286, 303n20, 307-310, 319, 331, 333, 335, 341-342, 351n3
peaceably, 303
peaceful, peacefulness, 93, 254, 309, 327, 334, 343
peacemakers, 157n20
peddle, peddlers of the gospel, 220, 224, 292
pederasty, 275n24
Pelagian, Pelagius, 111, 336, 358
penal substitution, 316
Peninsula, 174, 176-177
Peninsula (Arabian), 174, 176
Peninsula (Balkan), 42n39, 171
Peninsula (Malay), 177
penitence, 185n26
Pentateuch, 229n149, 342n21
Pentecost, 16-17, 20, 48, 174, 231, 296
Pentecostal, 94
people, 2, 10, 12-14, 16, 20, 25, 28, 32, 40, 47-48, 50, 52, 55-57, 59, 61, 68, 70-75, 77, 79-81, 83, 86-87, 89-90, 92-107, 109-113, 115, 117-119, 121-122, 124, 126, 128, 131-139, 141, 143-146, 149, 152, 154, 156-165, 170, 172-177, 179-181, 186, 188, 190-196, 198-205, 207-213, 215-218, 221-222, 225-232, 235-243, 245-246, 248-273, 275-278, 280-284, 286, 292, 295-298, 300-310, 312-319, 321, 323-328, 330-335, 337-360

Subject Index

peoples, 9–10, 55, 70, 82, 132, 161, 169–171, 173, 177–178, 203, 235, 258, 267, 300, 319, 341, 343, 345–346, 352
perfect, perfected, perfection, 94, 99, 109, 145, 149, 155, 158, 160n8, 185n26, 203, 239, 247, 250, 252, 288, 25–326
Perfective, 188, 188n45
perichoresis, 94, 94n66
Periphrasis, 66
perish(ing), perishability, perishable, 87, 104, 108, 135, 170, 183–184, 197, 243, 263–264
permissive, 224n121, 271
persecute(d), persecuting, 56, 108, 200, 260n7, 333
persecution, 13, 20, 62, 173, 176, 223n117, 240, 247, 286n45, 287, 296, 313n18, 318, 324n4, 333
persecutor(s), 32, 56, 232, 254, 258, 287, 333
perseverance, preservere, 129, 187, 306n31, 322, 339
Persia, 177, 177n41, 194, 326, 345n40
Persian Empire, 9, 177, 278, 343
Persian Gulf, 177
Persian(s), 70n47, 278, 278n38
Persis, 217, 230, 275, 277n34, 278n38, 343
personification, personified, personifies, 96, 98, 101, 124–126, 164, 184, 184n21, 186, 207, 252, 263
persuade, persuasion, persuasive, 26, 28n40, 225, 244, 273, 335, 355
perverted, 102, 252, 333n36
Pesher, 66, 184, 184n20, 359
Peter, 16, 138, 162n18, 175, 190, 223n117, 229n155, 246n42, 274, 285, 287n49, 326–327,
329, 337, 339–340
petition, 13, 59, 60n3
petri dish, 359
Petrine, 20
Peutinger Table, 177
phalluses, 338
Pharaoh, 141n10, 170, 181, 229n148, 294, 326, 333, 350
Pharisee(s), 32, 107–108, 111, 270, 273n16, 282n14, 298, 298n12, 304n25, 315, 337, 340, 344
Philemon, 27, 208n22, 211n36, 214–215, 216n76, 257, 272n12, 287, 291n75, 364
Philip, 175, 198, 229n155, 242n19, 244, 246n42
Philippi, 18, 49, 171, 215, 245, 330, 356n3
Philippian, 210, 220
Philippians, 27, 40n35, 40n37, 41n38, 43n47, 49n5, 69n41, 69n44, 69n46, 117, 140n7, 142n14, 145n26, 149n7, 157, 161n9, 163n21, 182n11, 182n15, 201n2, 207n18, 207n19, 208n22, 209n26, 210n30n, 210n30, 211n36, 212n47, 216n72, 217n82, 221, 233n168, 233n169, 234n172, 234n173, 234n175, 234n178, 234n180, 235, 275n26, 277n32, 286, 311n10
Philistines, 194n78
Philo, 14, 272n14, 275, 283, 287
Philologus, 20, 218, 277n34, 278, 343
philosopher, 228, 358n11
philosophical(ly), 70, 91, 92n61, 172
philosophies, 358
philosophy, 18, 267
Phinehas, 121n24, 229n150
Phlegon, 20, 218, 277n34, 278n37, 343
Phoebe, 22–24, 133n71, 208, 211n36, 214, 216, 221, 230–231, 257, 275, 277, 278n37, 285, 290, 290n69, 291n74, 292n86, 328, 343, 372
Phoenician(s), 9
Phoenicians, 9
physical, physically, 73, 80, 91, 93, 104, 112, 134, 189, 206, 219, 238, 243, 247, 255, 263n15, 290, 352
piety, 31n9, 283n25
pilgrimage, 107n42
pilgrims, 16–17, 174, 231, 296
pillars, 86n33, 190n56, 289n67
Pindar, 227
pioneer, 79
pious, 109, 199n93
Pisidia, 34
Pisidian Antioch, 50
pisticism, 141, 141n11
pitying, 284n29
plague, 13
Planet, planet(s), 96n3, 169, 266
plant, planted, planting, 16, 26, 36n16, 38, 40n37, 42n39, 43, 75, 83, 134, 171n15, 174n27, 182, 207, 211, 216–217, 226, 230, 235n179, 256, 260, 264–265, 277, 307, 311, 337, 344, 346
plantations, 9–10
planters, 216
plea, 64, 313
plead(s), pleading, 220, 313–314, 320
pleasant, 194, 194n73
please(s), pleased, pleasing, 80–81, 91, 99, 151, 153, 155, 194, 226, 236, 255–256, 303n19, 304, 316, 339, 341
pleasure(s), ix, 101, 219, 262, 282n19, 316n23
plebeians, 9
pledge, 72, 253

Subject Index

Pleonasm, 67
plight, 103, 115, 301
Pliny the Elder, 177
Pliny the Younger, 188, 188n48
plot, 216n74, 282n19
plundering, 109n52
pluperfect, 239
plural, 64, 133n71, 194, 195n80, 209, 209n27, 211, 216n75, 246n41, 320n33
pluralism, 199n91
pneumatic, 94, 100
pneumatological, 153
pneumatology, 153, 235
poet, 177n39
poetic, 331
poetry, 8n6
poison, poisoned, poisoning, 218, 260, 333n37
polemical, 184n19, 359n14
political(ly), 9, 9n7, 9n8, 10–13, 59–60, 84, 92n61, 130, 133, 133n72, 172, 188, 195, 208, 212n41, 220, 230, 234n177, 255, 255n29, 265, 267, 269n2, 276, 324, 325n7, 326–328, 330n32, 332–33, 333n36, 334, 335, 359
politician(s), 37, 218, 334, 343
politics, 10, 194, 228, 333–335
poll tax, 330
pollutants, 259
pollution, 259
Pollux, 12, 285n40
Polycarp, 175
polygamous, polygamy, 271, 271n11
Polygenism, 238n5
Polyplopton, 67
Polysyndeton, 67
polytheism, polytheist(ic), 13, 78, 78n1, 196
pomp, 180
Pompey, 10, 13
pontifices, 12
Pontus, 216
poor, 10, 13, 38, 62, 70n47, 121n25, 236, 242n18, 249n2, 252–253, 256, 267, 278, 280, 280n8, 283, 283n20, 284, 286n43, 286n44, 290, 295, 303, 314n18
Pope Francis, 259n2
populace, 11, 279n1
popular, 29, 59
Populares, 10–11
popularized, 241n15
populated, population(s), 7, 10, 12, 15, 18–20, 41, 42n42, 280n10, 345n41, 345n42
porn, 274
portending, portent, 105n32, 244
portoria, 330
ports, 22, 330

possessions, 109n52, 279, 283
possessive genitive, 120, 126
possessive gifts, 246
postcolonial era, 345
postmodern, 199n91
potter, 55, 63, 101, 238, 260, 294, 350
poverty, 62, 112, 191, 250, 256, 279, 284
power, 8n4, 9n7, 9n8, 10–11, 19, 41, 68, 70, 70n50, 71, 73, 75, 77, 79–81, 83, 85, 89, 91, 93, 96, 96n7, 98–100, 102, 106–107, 110–111, 114, 116, 118–120, 122, 132, 135, 140, 145n26, 151–153, 156, 158, 163, 170, 175, 179–180, 180n6, 181, 181n7, 182–184, 200–201, 203, 206–207, 207n16, 207n20, 208, 214n55, 226, 230–232, 233n170, 234–236, 238, 243–244, 244n32, 245, 245n37, 247–248, 261, 265–266, 276, 280, 282n19, 289n67, 295, 300, 303, 306, 308–309, 312, 316, 318–319, 322, 334, 339, 358–359
powerful(ly), 9n7, 9n9, 70, 84n26, 86n36, 93, 105–106, 109, 156–157, 158n22, 170, 182, 182n10, 191n68, 206, 226, 244, 261, 285, 301, 339n13
powerless, 116
powers, 60, 106, 106n37, 172, 172n17, 189n53, 245–246, 310, 324, 332
praenomen, 85
Praetorian Guard, 41, 182
praise(s), praised, praises, praising, 27, 28, 28n39, 57, 61, 79 80, 90, 122 123, 144, 146, 171, 187n40, 194n73, 204, 228n143, 230n160, 231, 240, 247n47, 303, 308, 312, 318–319, 323, 341, 359
praxis, 30
Pray(s), prayed, praying, 32, 48, 59, 69, 93, 135, 147, 191, 204–206, 211, 219, 221, 246, 248, 257, 299, 301, 303, 307–310, 310n14, 311, 311n9, 313–320, 320–321, 331, 333, 349, 359
prayer(s), 1, 3, 31–32, 39, 41, 43, 51, 60, 6n3, 69, 79, 90, 92–93, 122n32, 146, 146n28, 147, 156, 167, 201, 204–207, 219, 222n109, 226, 230n160, 246, 248, 257, 284n28, 284n32, 296, 299, 301, 303, 307, 307n2, 308–310, 310n14, 311, 311n7, 311n8, 311n9, 312–320, 320n32, 321–322, 353
prayerful(ly), prayerfulness, 235, 317, 34,3 350
prayerlessness, 310n4
preach(es), preached, 32, 33n12, 38–41, 43, 47–48, 50–52, 70–71, 75, 77, 88, 147, 160, 167, 169–170, 170n5, 175, 179–180, 183–186, 192–194, 198–199, 199n90, 203, 205, 209–211, 211n38, 218, 220, 223n117,

409

(preach(es), preached continued)
  223n118, 224, 224n121, 230–236, 248, 251, 253, 256, 268, 273n15, 276, 292, 295, 299n13, 300, 303, 311, 316, 318, 322n46, 329n28, 337, 340, 351–352, 357, 359
preacher(s), 119, 139, 147, 169, 185–186, 191n68, 193–194, 200, 210–212, 220, 231, 245, 292, 295
preaching, 33n12, 40, 40n34, 41–42, 42n39, 48, 50–51, 75–76, 138–139, 141, 173–175, 184, 191n68, 192–193, 198, 207, 210–212, 215–216, 22, 223, 223n117, 224, 224n121m 225–226, 232, 236, 241, 241n15, 242n19, 266, 273, 273n15, 290, 295, 309, 311, 322, 344, 355, 359
precept(s), 112, 150, 154, 157
precipitation, 181
predestination, 137, 293n1, 293n2, 295n5, 297–299, 300n17, 301–302, 304n25, 305, 305n29, 306, 306n31
predestine(s), predestined, 137, 202, 232, 238, 295, 297–298, 300, 300n17, 301–302, 304, 304n24, 350, 357
predetermined, 294, 297, 299, 301–302, 304, 306, 315
predicate, 67
predict(s), predicted, 86, 110, 164, 174n27, 196, 238, 240, 243, 333
prediction, 190, 242n19, 294, 319
Predigt, 27n36
preexistence, 88n47, 356
prejudice(s), prejudiced, 203, 205, 255n29, 299, 344, 346
premodern, 260
preparation, 32, 39, 41, 50, 72
prepare(s), prepared, preparing, 28, 32, 39, 48, 51, 83n20, 88, 101, 137, 172, 185, 188, 198, 208, 226, 254, 256, 262, 275, 294, 316, 327, 333, 341, 355, 356n3, 359
preparedness, 215, 256
preposition, 183, 316
Presbyterian, 94n65, 347
prescript(s), 67, 218n92, 307
pressure(s), 15, 99, 305
prestige, 233n170
presumption, presumptuousness, 98, 98n18, 103, 180, 217n80, 261, 338
pride, proud, 71, 75, 92, 227, 253, 326, 335
priest(s), 11–12, 82n17, 115, 206, 310, 330n32
priestess(es), 12
priestly, 12, 75n58, 210, 210n32, 211, 226, 226n129
principate, 11
priority, 80n12, 266, 272, 298n12, 305, 332, 338

prioritize, 347
Prisca, Priscilla, 1, 1n2, 14–17, 20, 25–26, 49, 119, 212, 213n54, 215–217, 219, 224, 230–231, 256–257, 271, 278n35, 291, 312, 343, 347
prison, 217, 306
prisoner(s), 32, 60, 135, 217, 284n32
privilege, 13, 279, 338–339, 346, 349
privileged, 47, 201, 352
privileges, 279, 289, 338, 349
procession, 274
proclaim(s), proclaimed, proclaiming, 26, 40, 41, 53, 69, 71–72, 89, 101, 119, 122, 165, 169–170, 173, 180, 186, 193, 195–196, 199n90, 200, 21032, 212–214, 224n121, 233n168, 234, 234n175, 245, 253, 258, 268, 271, 276, 310, 322, 333, 350
proclaimers, 47, 69, 186, 193
proclamation, 2–3, 5, 40n34, 40n35, 47–48, 50, 69, 91, 138, 141, 167, 170, 170n8, 172, 179, 183, 195n78, 206, 208, 211n34, 212, 223, 225, 232, 233n168, 248–249, 322, 322n46, 355
proconsul(s), 9, 23
proconsuls, 9
procreation, 272
procurator, 23
prodigal, 89n55
prodigy, 244
production, 22, 126, 138, 139n2, 214
profane, 14
profess(es), professed, 144, 146–147, 188–191, 196, 199, 266, 301
professing, 187–188
profession, 114, 141, 144, 146, 187–190
professional, 10, 280
professions, 138
progenitor, 87
programmatic, 121
progress, 30, 169, 173, 259, 262
progression, 231
prohibit(s), prohibited, prohibiting, 223n117, 234, 251, 328n26
prohibition(s), 98, 186, 223n117, 224, 232, 234, 341n17
Prolepsis, 67
prologue, 77, 128, 138
prominence, prominent, 8, 62, 64, 77, 107n42, 129, 176, 192, 208, 227, 230
promise(s), promised, 50n7, 53, 55–58, 61–62, 68, 72, 74, 80, 84–86, 111, 120, 122–123, 125, 134, 141, 143, 170n9, 172, 179, 181, 184, 187n41, 190, 190n56, 191, 197, 202–203, 206, 238, 240–241, 242n18, 257,

Subject Index

263, 271n10, 275, 294, 300, 300n17, 318, 330n29, 342n20, 349, 350
pronoun(s), 18n8, 67, 78n4, 308
Proof text, 139, 299n16
propaganda, 11
propagated, propagating, 117n18, 227
property, properties, 26, 280
prophecy, prophecies, 207n18, 215n64, 224n119, 232-234, 238, 241n15, 242, 242n20, 285, 299n15
prophesied, prophesy(ing), 75, 146, 224, 224n119, 240-241, 241n15, 242, 242n19
prophet(s), 50n7, 53-54, 54n3, 55-56, 68, 70-71, 73, 83, 85, 110, 121, 124, 162, 181-182, 186, 194, 195n80, 196, 200, 202, 208-209, 210n31, 229n152, 233n167, 238-241, 241n16, 242n19, 242n20, 246n41, 253, 317, 325, 330n32, 333n36, 357
prophetesses, 181
prophetic(ally), 12, 42, 55, 68, 76, 79n7, 157n20, 170-171, 181, 195n79, 212, 228n143, 238-242, 294, 323, 349-350
propitiate(s), propitiated, propitiating, 103, 118, 123, 161, 204
propitiation, propitiatory, 103-104, 115-117, 149n7, 202
propositio, 28
proposition(s), 65, 67, 289n67
propositional, 47, 129
Prosapodosis, 67
proselyte(s), 17n3, 107-108, 111, 152n9, 160, 222, 311
proselytism, 14
proselytizing, 2n6, 17
Prosopopoeia, 67
prosperity, prosperous, 11, 15, 121, 184, 191, 259, 281, 290
prostitutes, prostitution, 270, 275n24
protasis, 64, 187-188
protect(s), protected, protecting, protection, protective, 8n4, 8n5, 32, 78, 81, 86, 119, 194, 199, 290n72, 320, 328
Protestant(s), Protestantism, 125, 189, 297n11, 336-337, 345n41, 358
protests, 330n29
prototype, 260
Protreptic, 28, 28n40, 359
Provenance, 2, 22, 24, 234n178
Proverb(s), 121, 287, 288n57, 342n29
proverbially, 251
providence, 296
providential, 156, 325
Province(s), 9, 11, 25, 42n39, 222n113, 227n134

provision(s), 220, 220n100, 222, 252-253, 267, 281, 292, 303n19, 331
prudence, 148
Psalmist, 181
Psalm(s), 56, 120, 122, 182, 307n1
Psalter, 54
Pseudepigrapha, pseudepigraphal, 228, 274, 313
pseudonymous, 228
psychological, psychologically, 102, 136n82, 186, 247, 266
Ptolemies, 9
Ptolemy IV Philopater, 313n18
public, 10, 12-13, 15, 143, 180, 244, 280, 331
publicani, 330
pulpit, 193
Punic, 9,
Punic wars, 9, 9n8, 222n113
punish(es), punished, punishing, 103, 267, 327-329, 333n36
punisher, 329
punishment, 105, 199, 274, 318, 324n4, 327n21, 329
punitive, 163n22
punning, 66
pure, 37n18, 98, 149, 275, 307, 309
purified, 12, 285, 329n28
purity, 13, 17-18, 79, 91, 107n42, 118, 273n15, 336, 358n12
purpose(s), 2, 18-19, 29-32, 38-39, 42, 48-49, 50, 52-53, 67n39, 68-70, 76-77, 81, 88, 94, 101, 112, 119, 155, 163, 167, 172, 176, 181, 183, 192, 196, 202, 210n32, 226n130, 244, 251, 255n28, 256, 258, 263n15, 264, 266, 272, 278, 286, 292, 294, 296n9, 296n10, 297, 301-302, 304, 306, 306n31, 317, 317n24, 318, 320-321, 321n37, 323, 326, 333-334, 348, 350, 356n2
purposeful, 29
pursue(d), pursuing, 62, 98, 103, 109, 183, 255, 256, 286-287, 289, 303n20, 341
pursuers, 287
pursuit, 259, 264
Pythia, 12

Qal 194
Qal wahomer, 67, 194
Quartus, 37, 218, 277, 292n86, 343
queen, 8n5
quid pro quo, 280
Quintilian, 67
Quirinal, 8n2
Quirites, 8
Qumran, 190n56, 190n57, 270, 311n7
quotations, 64

411

Subject Index

quote(s), 11n12, 24, 53, 56, 83, 126–127, 170, 190, 195, 270, 298n12, 359

Rabban Gamaliel the elder, 358
Rabbi Akiba, 304n25, 358
rabbi Gamaliel, 358
Rabbinic, 154, 159, 209, 270, 355
race(s), 14, 70n47, 103, 276, 338–339, 344
race (run), 182,
races, 170, 194, 343
racial, 13, 61, 255n29, 256, 258, 339n13, 346
racism, 203, 336, 338, 343, 352
racist, 70, 340, 354
Rahab, 228n147, 287n54
rain, 8n4
rainbow, 194n73
raise(s), raised, raising, 8, 58, 80, 89–91, 93, 118, 134, 144, 150, 161, 170, 176, 186, 188–189, 191, 195–196, 200, 202–204, 206–207, 231, 235, 237, 243, 245, 252, 258, 278, 295, 305–306, 314, 317–319, 328, 333–334, 342–343
ranks, 9n7, 285
ransom, 130, 130n58
rape, 271
rapture(d), 160, 160n6, 165, 259
realism, 261n9
realm, 79n7, 124, 185n30, 186, 294
reap, 40, 281, 306
reassurance, reassuring, 310, 314
Rebekah, 55, 229n151, 271, 276, 342–343
rebel(s), 188, 262, 326
rebelled, 199
rebellion, 8, 79n7, 130, 160, 199, 261
rebellious, rebelliousness, 55, 200
rebirth, 116, 238, 263
rebuke, 27
reciprocate, reciprocation, reciprocity, 121, 221, 280–281, 285
recommendation (Letter of), 27, 290n70
recompense, 10, 122n32
reconcile(s), reconciled, reconciling, 74, 79–80, 89, 116, 127, 131, 172–173, 202, 220, 231, 266, 300, 309
reconciliation, 51, 59–60, 62, 72, 89, 101, 114, 117, 130–131, 141, 143, 164, 171–172, 252, 279, 287, 334, 359
recreate, recreation, 137, 164n25, 263n14, 264
redeem(s), redeemed, redeeming, 87, 102, 119, 122n32, 127, 130, 153–154, 263–264, 277, 316
redeemer, 201n3, 204, 229n148
redemption, 60, 72, 89, 93, 117, 124, 127, 130n59, 131, 134, 141, 143, 164, 164n26, 165, 199n93, 231, 238, 251, 264, 266, 269, 298n12, 309, 355
redemptive, 98–99, 116, 183, 204, 243, 251, 262
Reformation, 111, 345n41
reformed, 2, 10, 142n15, 304n24
Reformers, 241, 241n15, 337n7, 347
refresh(ed), refreshing, 31, 31n10, 257, 321
refreshment, 39, 75, 321
refugees, 287, 289
regent, 81, 84
regrafted, 55, 348
regulations, 31, 92n61, 107
reign(s), reigned, 11, 15, 54, 59, 82–83, 96n5, 96n7, 97–99, 122, 136, 156, 165, 172, 190, 295, 300, 308, 324, 326n12, 333n37, 358
reject(s), rejected, rejecting, 23n14, 27, 31n9, 32, 56, 70, 79, 86, 141, 149n7, 161–162, 163n21, 180, 189, 193, 195, 195n80, 197–199, 203, 209n26, 223n117, 238, 240, 242, 247n49, 270–271, 274n18, 275, 289n67, 299, 299n16, 301–302, 311–312, 315–317, 332–333, 338, 348–352, 351n3, 353–354, 356n3
rejection, 41, 50n7, 55–56, 63, 98, 101, 138, 140–141, 149–150, 196, 198–199, 202, 231, 241, 247–248, 277, 301–302, 317, 351–352
rejectors, 193
rejoice, rejoicing, 57, 61, 187n40, 224n121, 303, 303n21, 303n22, 306
relational(ly), 30, 33n12, 56, 112, 122, 130, 132, 138, 142n15, 149, 153, 156, 255, 261, 284, 297
relations, 26, 65, 272, 274n18, 289n67, 324
relationship(s), 14–15, 26, 29, 31, 39, 48, 51, 53, 55, 57, 60, 65, 70–71, 75, 80, 87, 94, 97–99, 102, 113, 118–119, 121, 123, 130–132, 136n82, 137–138, 141, 144, 148n5, 149–151, 153, 216, 221n76, 232, 236, 249, 251, 261n9, 267, 270–271, 271n11, 272, 274, 279, 287, 289n67, 293, 297, 301–302, 309–310, 328, 331, 340, 344, 349–350, 355
relatives, 216, 269
religio licita, 13
religion(s), 11–13, 30, 194, 199n91, 260n4, 267, 345, 351n3, 358
religious, 8, 9n7, 12, 31, 33n12, 60, 92n61, 172, 195–196, 199n91, 212n41, 217n88, 229n150, 258, 266, 345n42, 347n45, 351n3
religiously, 12
remarriage, remarry, 270–271, 271n7, 273
remarry, 270–271

Subject Index

remember(s), remembering, 38, 57, 79n6, 196, 229n152, 242n18, 249, 249n2, 308, 328 249, 342n21, 353
remnant, 28, 55–56, 60, 71, 74, 114, 191, 198, 200, 203, 241, 302, 317, 350
Remus, 8
renewed, 18, 55, 81, 87, 89, 101, 112, 135–137, 204, 238, 258, 262–264, 318, 334–335
renewal(s), 101–102, 131, 137, 155–156, 165, 200, 211, 263, 263n14, 265–266, 276, 345–346n41
renown(ed), 145, 217, 227, 358
repent, 273, 288
repentance, 114, 138, 143, 314n18
replacement, 23, 31n10, 199n91, 209, 225
reproach(es), 56, 240, 295, 341
reproduce, 261
reptiles, 61, 260
republic, republican, 8–12
requirement(s), 53, 55, 99, 107–108, 111, 117, 121, 155n15, 184–185, 203, 281, 337, 357
res publica, 8
rescue(s), rescued, 31, 135, 152
resist(s), resisted, resisting, 10, 55, 92, 259, 273, 300, 324, 326, 330, 333, 338
resistance, resistant, 56, 316, 324–325, 333, 338–339, 345, 347
respect, 30, 101, 255n27, 258, 289n67, 327, 331, 335
respectable, 255
rest, resting, 122n32, 257, 321
restaurants, 13n20
restoration, 164, 164n25, 165, 184, 233n170, 262n11, 263, 263n14, 263n15, 264, 339, 357
restore(s), restored, 11, 94n67, 130–131, 134, 152, 258, 262–264, 265n26, 278, 356
result(s), 10, 20n14, 47n1, 72, 86, 124, 136, 143n18, 149, 158, 180n6, 219, 239, 264, 300n17, 302, 309, 324
resurrected, 70, 80, 89, 114, 140, 165
resurrection, 29, 32, 48, 50n7, 68, 72–73, 83n20, 85, 88n47, 90, 94, 102, 104, 111, 115–117, 130n58, 134–135, 142–143, 150, 163–165, 242, 180n4, 185–186, 189, 195, 205, 207, 209, 238, 242–243, 263, 263n14, 352, 357
retaliate, retaliating, 205, 258, 288, 333
retaliation, 253
retribution, 156–157, 329, 343
retributive justice, 254
return (Claudian expulsion), 14–15, 19, 23, 31, 41, 49, 287
return (exile), 82n17, 157, 184, 194, 199

return of Christ, v, 29, 106, 107, 115, 160, 160n6, 174n27, 214, 241, 349, 353, 357–358
return (Pentecost), 48
reveal(s), revealed, revealing, 33n12, 41, 53–54, 76–77, 85, 92, 98–99, 102–104, 107, 115, 120–121, 124–126, 139, 140, 143n19, 152, 152n8, 160, 164, 170, 196, 199–200, 202, 231n163, 249–250, 261, 276, 289n67, 307n2, 351, 356, 359
Revelation, 82, 162n12, 162n16, 162n18, 164, 244n25, 246n40, 262n13, 263, 267, 333, 335
revelation, 36, 38, 73, 76, 97, 102, 146n29, 199, 247, 323, 337
revelatory, 264
revelries, revelry, revels, 65, 100, 274–275, 335
revenge, 56, 60, 232, 241, 329
reverence, 229n152, 327
reversal, 65, 243
reverse(s), 64, 84, 192, 224
reviled, 180
revival, 157n20, 352n6, 353
revive(d), 88n47, 257
revolts, 333n37
revolution, 259, 359
revolutionaries, 276
reward, rewarding, 60, 79, 103, 252n14, 282, 284, 287, 333n36
rewarder, 82
rex sacrorum, 12
rhetoric, 18–19, 28, 57, 184n21, 218, 359
rhetorical(ly), 27, 27n35, 27n37, 27n38, 28, 28n39, 63, 65, 67, 104–105, 150–151, 191n68, 223, 225–226, 230–231, 294, 355, 359
Rhine River, 7
rich(es), richest, 23n14, 62, 78, 95, 137, 101, 114, 171, 191n66, 202, 256–257, 280, 282, 288, 292, 298, 310, 321, 324, 326, 340, 343, 359
right, 9n10, 13, 14n25, 16, 48, 63, 65, 69, 81, 98, 104, 109, 111–112, 116, 120–121, 124–126, 128–129, 136, 138, 141, 147, 152, 154n14, 155n16, 160–161, 164, 191, 194, 198, 209, 220, 223n117, 223n118, 233, 246n38, 249, 251, 251n11, 253, 254n25, 258, 265, 267, 269, 275n26, 294–295, 300, 304n24, 306, 310, 314, 323, 326–327, 330, 332, 335, 357
righteous, 41, 53, 71–73, 77, 79–80, 87, 93, 96, 98, 101, 103, 105, 107–109, 111–112, 117, 120–127, 127n46, 128–130, 132, 136, 140, 143, 149, 152, 160–162, 199, 203,

413

(righteous continued)
229n153, 239, 250–251, 258, 279, 284, 297, 326, 336, 342, 348–349

righteously, 99–100, 122–123, 126, 135

righteousness, 1, 39, 41, 51, 53–54, 57–58, 60, 68n40, 71–74, 77, 79–80, 85–86, 89, 93, 95, 97–99, 102–103, 107n44, 108–111, 114–116, 120–121, 121n25, 122, 122n32, 123–129, 129n52, 131, 139–140, 143, 145, 149, 149n7, 150–151, 155, 170, 183, 183n19, 184, 184n21, 186, 189n52, 191, 195n78, 201–202, 204, 206, 208, 229n149, 238–240, 249, 252n13, 253, 254n24, 258, 261, 277, 279, 286n45, 295, 299–301, 308, 325, 336–337, 348, 350–351, 357, 359

rightful(ly), rightfully, 155n16, 250, 263–264

righting, 355

rights, 10, 14, 133, 206, 255n27, 275, 289n67, 346

riots, 216n74

ripe, ripe, 194n73, 207

rise (from death), risen, 150, 158, 186, 191, 196, 205, 209, 211, 243, 357

rise (nations), 335

risk(ed), risking, risky, 66, 216, 256–257, 289n67, 304, 343

ritual(s), 12–13, 17–19, 43, 107n42, 118, 273n15, 275, 336–337

rival(s), 245n37, 287

rivalry, 10, 18, 335

river, 222n113

road(s), 9, 33, 47n1, 62, 107, 111, 129, 169n2, 209, 234, 295, 344, 356n2

robbery, robbing, 109n52, 250

robs, 250

rock(s), 61, 83, 181

role(s), 8–10, 12, 18, 54, 68–69, 91, 93, 103, 105–106, 139, 201, 208–209, 209n26, 215, 225, 233, 233n170, 253–254, 266–267, 275–276, 279, 311n9, 324, 328–331, 344n37, 357n6

Roma quadrata, 8

Roman, vii, xi, 2, 7–20, 23, 25–26, 28, 30–31, 39–43, 45, 49–51, 54, 58, 61, 69–70, 77–78, 84–85, 88, 100, 102, 105, 115, 133, 142, 144, 148, 156–157, 163, 170, 177, 180, 182, 188, 194–195, 202, 208, 212–215, 217, 219, 221–223, 226–227, 234, 252, 254–255, 257, 260, 269, 272–273, 275, 277, 280, 282, 286, 289, 291, 304, 307–308, 310, 319–320, 324–325, 327, 330, 333, 336, 343, 345, 355, 358, 363, 365–366, 368, 370–372

Romania, 173

Romans, i, iii, iv, vii–viii, 1–2, 5, 7–12, 14–20, 22–33, 36–43, 45, 47–51, 53–64, 66–73, 75–101, 103–165, 167, 169–174, 177, 179–180, 183–186, 188–194, 196–199, 201–202, 204, 206–232, 234–235, 237–243, 245–246, 248–258, 260–267, 269–336, 339–340, 342–344, 346, 348–353, 355–373

Rome, vii, 1, 7–20, 23–26, 28–32, 37, 39–43, 48–51, 61, 68–70, 72, 75, 77, 82–84, 105, 135, 138, 156, 171, 173–175, 177, 179–180, 184, 188, 194, 198, 207, 210–211, 213–224, 226–228, 230–231, 234, 242, 256–257, 266, 275, 277, 281, 286–288, 290, 292, 296, 298–299, 303, 307, 310–311, 320–321, 324, 327, 330–331, 333, 340, 343–344, 346, 363–365, 367, 370, 372

Römer, 27n28

Römerbrief, 27n2

Romulus, 8

root(s), rooted, 1, 14, 57, 61–62, 83, 90, 148n5, 288n59, 319, 340n13, 347

rose, 82, 158, 180

rotting, 101

royal, 82, 88, 106n36, 182n10

Rufus, 15n27, 26, 119, 211n36, 217n88, 219, 230–231, 257, 275–276, 277n34, 278n35, 285, 291n80, 343, 343n32

ruin, 251, 264

rule(s), ruled, ruling, 8, 8n5, 9, 9n7, 10–11, 18–19, 31n9, 43, 57, 59, 70n47, 79, 83–84, 92n61, 108, 121, 139, 142n14, 144, 146, 149, 150–151, 157, 160n8, 189n53, 190–191, 228n143, 213, 237, 239, 255n27, 262, 266, 291n75, 297n11, 305, 308, 311, 319, 324n4, 326–329, 332, 340–341, 350

ruler(s), 9, 11, 60, 70, 83, 92, 101, 106, 143, 156, 162, 188, 232, 269, 290, 305, 324, 327, 332–333

rumors, 220

run(s), running, 82, 181–182, 214n55, 250, 275, 277n33, 288, 293, 334–335

runaways, 287

runner, 182

rupture(d), 19–20, 96, 136, 158, 295, 349, 356

Russia, 173n22, 345n39

Russian Steppe, 177

ruthless(ness), 156, 250

Rwanda, 258

Sabbath, 13, 17–19, 49, 56, 107, 107n42, 336–337, 353

Sabines, 8

Sac, 194

Subject Index

sacking, 314
sacral, 330
sacrament, 290
sacred, 12, 14, 105, 172n17, 237, 250, 274, 275n24
sacrifice(s), sacrificed, sacrificial(ly), 12, 60, 88, 90, 99, 109, 107n42, 115–117, 121, 124, 131, 137, 146, 149, 149n7, 155n16, 203, 216n744, 229n154, 254n24, 256, 280, 285, 297, 311n7, 319, 329n28, 332, 341, 341n17, 343, 348, 351
sail, 325n10
saints, 31, 57, 60n3, 132, 218–219, 229n152, 232, 234–235, 256–257, 286–287, 296, 321, 341–342
Sales tax, 330
salt, 235, 334
salvation, 2n6, 31, 33n12, 39, 40, 40n34, 41, 45, 47n1, 50n7, 51, 53, 53n2, 55, 57–58, 60n4, 62, 68, 70, 70n50, 71–74, 76–77, 79–82, 89n55, 90–91, 98–99, 99n20, 101, 103, 107–108, 110–113, 113n1, 114, 114n6m 115n10, 116–117, 119–120, 123, 125–129, 131, 137, 137n86, 138–142, 144–145, 145n26, 146, 149, 153, 158–159, 162–163, 163n21, 165, 169–170, 173, 179–180, 180n6, 181–184, 187, 187n39, 189–190n62, 191–192, 195–197, 200–201, 201n2, 202, 205–206, 210n32, 211, 226n129, 231, 231n163, 232–233, 233n168, 234, 236, 238, 244, 244n28, 244n29, 245, 248, 251, 266, 279, 294, 295n5, 296, 298, 300, 300n16, 301–302, 304, 304n25, 306, 316–317, 322–323, 332, 337–338, 340, 351, 351n4, 352–353, 353n7, 353n9, 356–357, 357n6, 359
salvific, 116, 124, 130, 140–141, 152
Samaria, 10, 32, 198, 246, 296n7
Samaritan, 154
same-sex, 272
Samuel, 181, 185, 228n147
sanctification, 60, 72, 99, 125, 131–132, 206, 252, 254n24
sanctified, sanctify, sanctifies, 75, 91, 99, 132, 210n32, 286
Sanctifier, 201n3
sanctity, 110
sand, 61
Sarah, 55, 229n151, 271, 276, 300, 342–343
sarcastic, 65
Sardinia, 9
Satan, 57, 60, 79, 93, 105, 105n32, 106, 165, 172, 203, 234n177, 241, 247, 247n46, 247n49, 260n7, 262, 281n13, 309–310, 326–327

satiate, 262
satisfaction, 202, 316n23, 358
satisfied, satisfies, satisfy, 111, 116, 123, 161, 219, 251n10, 357, 359
Saturn, 12
Saul (King), 194n78, 315, 326n12
Saul (Paul), 17, 32, 213n54, 296, 296n7, 351, 358
Sauline, 223n117
save(s), saved, saving, 40, 55, 70, 72, 74, 79–80, 83, 89–90, 92–93, 95, 98, 103–104, 107–108n46, 109–110, 113–117, 119–120, 123–125, 127–128, 131, 135, 139–144, 146, 149–153, 155n16, 161, 163, 169, 170–171, 171n12, 173, 179, 183, 187n40, 189, 191, 199, 202–205, 211, 213, 216, 226, 234–235, 244, 251, 257, 260, 264, 268, 295–296, 299–300, 300n16, 301, 304, 306, 316, 318, 331, 337–338, 348–352, 352n6, 353, 355–356, 356n2
Savior, v, 57, 82–83, 85, 85n31, 86, 119, 173, 245
Scandinavia, 177–178, 345n39
school(s), 201, 211, 270
science, scientific(ally), 200, 237
scientists, 243
Scope (of the gospel), 3, 75, 105, 108, 135, 160, 167, 169–170, 170n7, 171, 176, 231, 235, 262
Scotland, 345n40
scribal, 31n10, 48n2
scribe(s), 230, 292, 292n86
Scriptural, 157
Scripture, 229n152, 230, 300n17
Scriptures, 50n7, 53, 56, 60, 68, 73, 76, 80, 85, 96, 114, 122, 131, 142–143, 179, 189, 202, 238–239, 241, 241n15, 259–260, 295, 354, 359
scrolls, 12
sculptor, 101
Scythia, 173, 175–177
Scythian(s), 70, 173, 173n22, 177, 177n41, 339n12
sea(s), 2n6, 7, 36n17, 40, 42n39, 61, 75, 171, 173n22, 174, 176–177, 185, 220n100, 226, 259, 303, 319, 344
seal(s), sealed, 42, 93, 197
season, 306
seasoned, 33, 235, 334
seasons, 182
seat(s), seated, 60, 63, 115, 117, 161, 164, 189n53, 295, 357
secret(s), 76, 160, 160n6, 323
secretary, 22, 208, 333n37
secrets, 160

415

Subject Index

sect, 21, 324n4
sectarian, 31n9
secular, 12, 133n72, 172n17, 237, 327, 347
Secundus, 49, 49n4, 171, 321n39
security, 255n27
seduction, 267
self-centeredness, 1n4
self-destruct, 30
self-indulgent, 66
Selfish, 18, 92
selfless, ix, 156, 285
self-seeking, 98
self-supporting, 171
semantics, 188n45
seminaries, 211
Semitic, 146n27, 196
Senate, 8–12, 15, 333n37
senatorial, 9–10
senators, 11
send(s), sent, sending, 1, 18, 20, 24, 25n21, 42n40, 48, 50n7, 62, 68, 71, 77, 80–81, 84, 88, 88n49, 90, 142, 145n24, 147, 149, 152, 174–175, 181–182, 185, 191n68, 192, 193n70, 198, 200–201, 201n3, 202, 204–205, 207–209, 211, 215, 218n92, 218–220, 222, 225, 230–231, 242n19, 243, 265n26, 273n15, 276, 284n32, 286, 295, 346, 311, 344, 351, 357
sender(s), 22, 193–194, 245
Seneca, 11, 14, 14n23, 333n37
Seres, 177
sermon(s), 50, 72, 160n7, 162n18
Sermon on the Mount, 273n15, 335
Sermon on the Plain, 335
serpent, 106n36, 260n7
servant, 90, 111, 195, 195n80, 196, 199, 253, 257, 271, 281n13, 295, 318, 328–329, 330n32, 341, 344, 346
servanthood, 271n8, 276
servants, 61, 146, 156–157, 281n13, 305, 328, 330, 330n32, 334
serve(s), served, ix, 10, 81, 90, 94, 98, 103–104, 106n36, 107, 126, 139, 141, 150–152, 156, 196, 202–203, 205, 207, 229n152, 232, 233n170, 251–252, 255, 257, 275, 277, 280, 281n13, 297–298, 299n16, 303n21, 308, 310, 330–332, 341
service(s), v, 10, 31, 56, 69, 75, 79, 79n6, 81, 90, 99, 117, 130, 135, 142, 154–155, 155n16, 156, 172, 205, 208, 210, 216, 216n74, 226, 232–233, 253, 254n24, 256, 277n33, 280–282, 284, 284n32, 285, 297, 299n13, 318, 330, 333, 335, 339
servile, 20

serving, 9, 122, 179, 226, 232, 234, 253, 272, 277, 281–283, 324, 329, 343, 359
Seven (the), 225, 246n42
Seventy (elders), 313
Seventy-two (the), 209, 273n15
sex, 274
sexism, 203, 290, 338
sexual immorality, 73, 97, 99, 141, 158, 255, 261, 270–272, 273n15, 274–275, 299, 335, 341n17, 344
sexuality, 92, 132, 271, 271n11, 272–273, 273n15, 329
sexually, 275, 314
shalom, 308–309, 321
shame, 70, 86, 90, 98–99, 102, 104, 137, 151, 153, 179, 190, 204, 288
shamed, 70
shameful, 70, 137, 272, 279
Shammai, 270
sheep, 61, 193, 260n7, 263
Shekinah, 294
shelter, 280n10
Shema, 78, 192, 311n7
Shemoneh Esreh, 311n9
Sheol, 185–186
ship(s), 23, 175, 220n100, 222
shipwreck, 325n10
shock, 337
shortage, 245n37
shrines, 12
sibling(s), 61, 133n71, 137, 275, 285
Sibylline scrolls, 12
Sicarii, 188
Sicily, 9
sick, sickness, 246, 284, 284n32, 312–313, 313n18
Sierra Leone, 176–177
sighs, 313n18
sign(s), 2–3, 75, 167, 226, 238n6, 243–244, 244n25, 244n31, 245, 245n33, 245n37, 246, 246n40, 259, 276, 295, 318, 352, 359
signature, 244n31, 309
signed, 9, 130–131, 309
signer, 82n17
Silas, 18, 35, 38, 49, 209, 211n38, 212, 242n19
silence, silent, 182n10, 189, 224, 314
Silicon Valley, 243n24
silk people, 177
silkworms, 177n39
Silvanus, 210n31, 218n92
Simon Cananaeus, 175
Simon of Cyrene, 217
Simon the Tanner, 287n49, 291
simplicity, 179n1, 214n55, 283
Simul justus et peccator, 158n21

Subject Index

sin(s), 2, 19, 50-51, 54-56, 63, 73-74, 81-82, 87-93, 95, 95n1, 96, 96n5, 95n6, 95n7, 96-99, 99n20, 106-107, 107n44, 109-116, 115-119, 124, 126-127, 130, 132, 134-136, 136n83, 137-138, 140, 142-145, 149-153, 155, 158, 161, 164-165, 170, 172, 187, 187n41, 191, 195, 195n80, 202, 202n4, 203-207, 230-231, 231n163, 235, 239-240, 243, 250, 250n7, 251-252, 252n10, 252n12, 253-254, 254n24, 260-266, 268, 272, 272n13, 273, 277-278, 281n13, 286, 286n42, 289n67, 294-295, 299-300, 305, 308-310, 312, 314, 316-317, 335, 337, 342n18, 348-349, 351, 353, 358-359
Sinai, 55, 86, 152, 349, 356
sincere, sincerely, sincerity, 283, 285, 285n37
sinful, 54, 90, 97, 99-102, 110, 112, 116, 130, 132, 144-145, 190n61, 202, 204, 250, 260, 266, 273, 276, 279, 284, 310, 312, 316n23, 340, 348
sinfulness, 73, 92, 97
sing(s), singing, sang, song, 57, 61, 110, 116, 144, 191, 194,72, 199, 228, 228n143, 239-240, 288n57, 303, 316n23, 317, 319, 347
single, singleness, 272-273, 273n16, 274-275
singular, xiii, 195n80, 209n27, 223n118
sinless, sinlessness, 111, 134, 149n7
sinned, 96, 102, 111, 136, 160, 184n24, 231n163, 265, 294, 299-300
sinner(s), 47, 73, 96, 108, 128, 155, 202-203, 251, 273, 284, 339, 356
sinning, 135-136, 150
sister(s), 20, 22, 215, 218, 275-276
sisters, 31, 40, 133, 133n71, 144, 232, 276, 297, 320n33, 341
situational ethics, 154, 154n14,
skepticism, 242, 259n3, 372
skies, sky, 146, 170, 244n25
slander, 250
slaughter, 260
slave(s), 9, 12n15, 13-14, 20, 60-61, 61n13, 68, 70-71, 74, 85, 99, 116, 125, 129-131, 135, 143, 145, 150-151, 205, 208, 214-215, 218n89, 228n144, 231, 252, 254n24, 269, 271, 274, 277, 277n33, 277n34, 282, 282n19, 300, 308, 325, 330, 332, 339, 341n16, 342, 346
slavery, 60, 130, 205, 251, 253, 255n26, 264, 269n2, 277, 315, 342
slogan, 188, 339n13
slothful, 207
slums, 9
smoke, 163n22

snake(s), 245, 260n7
snare, 62
snow, 182
sober, 148n3, 303n22
social action, 327
social agencies, 338
social barriers/boundaries, 277, 289n67
social class, 339
social concern, 249n1, 258
social holiness, 132
social inequalities, 278
social injustice, 250
social justice, 2-3, 32, 121, 167, 227, 232, 249, 251-252, 252n16, 253, 256-258, 260, 265, 267, 269, 279, 282, 318, 346
social order, 167, 280
social networks, 213
social prejudice, 344
social relationships, 137, 249
social status, 338, 341n16, 344
social tensions, 255n30
social transformation, 2, 249n1, 269, 278-279, 342
Social War, 10
Social justice, 10, 222, 249-250, 258, 269, 347, 366, 370
societal, 266, 269, 277, 335
societies, 102, 261, 273
Society, 10, 96n5, 102, 133n72, 148n3, 158, 232, 252n13, 255, 255n27, 258, 265-267, 269n3, 276 277, 277n33, 288n59, 324, 327-329, 331, 360
socii, 10
Sodom, 273n15
soft Calvinism, 293
soil degradation, 259
sojourners, 154n 154n13
soldier(s), 9-10, 148n4, 177n48, 217n88, 320, 328, 335
Solomon, 195n78, 228, 228n144, 342, 342n29
Son of David, 68, 83, 179, 204
Son of God, v, 1, 2, 47n2, 48n2, 50n7, 59, 62, 68-71, 73, 78, 81-82, 84-85, 88, 88n47, 89n51, 90-91, 94, 110, 113n3, 116, 118-119, 123, 125, 133, 133n70, 137-138, 142-144, 149, 154n14, 161, 163, 174, 179, 180n4, 182, 186, 187n40, 187n42, 190, 190n61, 195-196, 202-207, 211, 227n138, 231-232, 238, 238, 240, 243, 245, 248, 251n10, 252, 275-276, 295, 297, 299, 301-302, 307-308, 312, 314, 317, 332, 334, 348, 351-352, 359
Son of Man, 32, 196

417

Subject Index

son(s), 11–12, 47–48, 60n3, 68, 82, 84–85, 88, 160, 179, 187, 217, 227n138, 228n144, 240–241, 294, 297, 342
Sonderweg, 351, 351n4
sonship, 47n2, 61, 68, 84, 84n25, 242, 133n73, 242
soothsayers, 12
Sopater, 37, 321
sorcerers, 185
Sorites, 67, 191, 191n68
sorrow(s), 195n80, 315
Sosipater, 37, 216, 218, 230
Sosthenes, 218n92
soteriological, 119, 129, 163n21, 183
soteriology, 338
soul(s), 100, 189n53, 219, 222n108, 227n134, 245, 315, 324–325
South, 18, 37, 174, 176–177, 181, 222n113, 310–311, 357
South Korea, 345
Southeast Asia, 178
South Galatia, 18, 37n26
southern Gaul, 9
southern Greece, 9
southern Russia, 173n22
sovereign, 63n35, 80–81, 85, 94, 142, 230n157, 234n177, 240, 245, 248, 269, 293–294, 296, 298, 301, 304–308, 342n20, 349–350
sovereignty, 3, 101, 167, 170n7, 235, 293, 296, 296n7, 297–298, 298n12, 300–302, 304, 304n25, 305–306, 308, 311, 318–319, 326
Sower, sowing, sows, 141, 281, 339
sows, 281
space, ix, 52, 62, 118, 188, 207, 238, 270, 302n19, 305, 347
Spain, 9, 24n14, 25, 28, 29n4, 30–32, 36n17, 39, 39n33, 40n35, 41–42, 42n42, 42n44, 43, 43n48, 43n49, 43n50, 48, 50, 52, 61n15, 68, 75, 77, 88, 88n47, 170n9, 171, 173–175, 177n41, 177n42, 191, 207, 211, 214, 218–219, 220n100, 221–222, 222n109, 222n113, 223, 226–227, 256, 277–278, 285, 291, 296, 303, 310–311, 344, 346, 357
Spaniards, 343
Spanish, 77, 211n36, 220–222, 226, 357n6
spear, 85
Spec, 2, 194, 219, 282–283, 285
specialists, 201, 224, 235
spinning, 8n6
Spirit, v, 16, 31, 34, 48–49, 51, 54, 58, 60, 60n3, 63n34, 68, 73–75, 78, 80–81, 83, 85–86, 90–91, 91n60, 92–94, 99–100, 104, 107, 111–113, 113n3, 113n4, 114, 116, 118–119, 122–126, 128–129, 131n64, 132–135, 137, 141–142, 143n19, 145–146, 151–153, 153n10, 154–156, 158n22, 159, 164, 174, 179, 182, 185–186, 191, 193, 196–198, 201–207, 207n16, 207n20, 208–209, 210n32, 211, 223n117, 225, 227, 227n134, 230–232, 233n168, 234n176, 235–236, 238–239, 242, 242n19, 243–245, 248, 253, 254n24, 255, 265–266, 269, 271, 271n10, 277, 281, 289n67, 295–296, 296n7, 300–301, 303, 303n21, 305–306, 308–309, 312–313, 313n17, 314–320, 331–332, 334–335, 337, 339–341, 341n16, 347, 349, 356–359, 361, 363–364
spirit(s), 60, 69, 91, 91n60, 93–94, 100, 105, 108, 186, 187n42, 189n53, 194, 200, 206–207, 207n16, 227, 237, 253, 257, 302, 315, 325, 354n12, 357
spiritual, 57, 62, 87, 91, 93, 104, 106, 116, 118–119, 130, 134–135, 156, 172, 172n17, 189, 189n53, 191, 198–199, 199n93, 200, 207, 210, 213n55, 219, 227n114, 229n152, 237–238, 240–241, 245n37, 246–247, 256, 263n14, 284, 286, 310, 325n6, 340–341
spiritual gift(s), 39–40, 62, 69, 75, 80, 141, 156, 210, 224n119, 225, 232–234, 241, 246, 281, 285, 309, 311, 342, 3446
Spirituality, 206n14
spiritually, 89, 134, 150, 191, 207n20, 232, 238, 255, 280, 290
Spiritus, 206
spouse(s), 151, 234, 270–271, 275, 332
spring, 23, 37
squires, 229n152
stabbed, 333n37
Stachys, 277n34, 278n37, 343
stammering, 70n47
stands, standing, 30, 41, 79–80, 96, 100–101, 103–105, 106n36, 114, 126, 149, 154, 158, 161, 176n34, 182n10, 183, 189n53, 202, 224n119, 235, 244, 249, 251, 252n16, 268, 269n2, 271, 273, 304–305, 308, 311n9, 322–323, 326, 329, 334, 336, 339n11, 352, 359
standard(s), 122, 125, 134, 150, 229n152, 312
stanzas, 63
State (the), viii, 3, 9, 12–13, 32, 49, 60, 75, 103, 105, 148, 156–157, 163n22, 167, 232, 254, 267, 276, 324–325, 327–328, 328n26, 329, 331–332, 334, 355
statesman, 148n4
statively, 239
status(es), 9n7, 13, 20n14, 53–54, 58, 71, 89, 93, 95n2, 99, 108–109, 114, 116–121, 124–133, 153, 155, 156, 161, 184, 193,

418

Subject Index

202, 277, 279, 285, 297, 308, 338–340, 341n16, 344, 349, 351
steadfast, 121–123, 317
stealing, 109n52, 299
stele, 116
Stephanas, 208n22
Stephen, 198, 244, 246n42
Stoic(s), Stoicism, 27n35, 358n11
stoicheia, 92n61, 172
Stone, 85
stone, 61, 61n18, 62, 83, 85–86, 152, 190n57, 317, 357
store(ing), 103, 160
stories, story, 7, 10, 12, 19, 45, 47–48, 50, 50n7, 51, 53–59, 64, 68n40, 69, 78, 82, 84, 87, 103, 123, 136n82, 137, 152n9, 160, 170, 180, 185, 189, 204, 213–214, 228, 238n5, 260, 265, 280, 294, 298–299, 304–305, 326, 334, 349, 356–358
storms, 8n4
Strabo, 177, 185, 358n11
stranger(s), 61, 61n16, 154, 187n41, 213n55, 232, 254, 256, 283, 286n48, 287, 287n49, 288n59, 289n67, 290–292, 343, 346
strangled, 341n17
stratagem, strategy, strategies, 1n1, 1n3, 26, 32, 208, 220, 243, 311, 334, 359
strategic, 171
straw man, 109n54
stream, 121n25
streets, 333n37
strength, 9, 122, 142n32, 192, 214n55, 244, 254n22, 277, 301
strengthen(s), strengthened, strengthening, 30, 32, 36, 38–40, 70, 76–77, 193, 224, 247, 281, 300, 308, 322, 355
strife, 250
stripes, 230n159
strive, striving(s), 212, 224n19, 320n35
strong, ix, 9, 11, 14, 17, 26, 30, 30n8, 41, 43, 49, 65, 86n36, 113, 163, 220, 222, 247, 254–255, 279, 289n67, 290, 300, 315, 317, 329, 344, 356
stronger, 41, 142, 195
structure, 2, 27n31, 45, 47, 48n3, 67, 73, 133n72, 217n80, 225, 277n33
structures, 17, 224, 235, 264, 269, 333–334, 359
struggle(s), struggled, struggling, 10, 50, 74, 90, 92–93, 111, 152, 280, 284, 298, 301, 312–313, 320n35, 338, 352
Stubborn, stubbornness, 98, 247, 316
stumble(d), stumbling, 56, 62, 70n50, 74, 83, 86, 105, 142, 180, 196, 240–241, 254–255, 276, 290, 301, 303n19, 303n22, 350

stupor, 91, 240, 302
stuttering, 70n47
style, 22, 48, 64
sub-Saharan, 68, 345
subcultures, 347
subject (sentence), 67, 212, 322, 326n15
subject, subjection, subjected, 9, 87, 96, 164–165, 204, 231, 263, 303n19, 303n22, 322, 324–325, 327, 329
subjective(ly), 71, 104, 120, 125, 139, 139n2, 140, 143
subjects, 334
subjugated, subjugating, subjugation, 83, 99, 106n36, 152, 160, 164, 202, 263, 294, 325, 332, 357
subjunctive(s), 64, 303n20
submission, submissive, 100, 105, 110, 144, 148, 156, 172, 202, 205–206, 216n74, 224n120, 240, 254, 276, 324–325, 327, 329–331
submit(ted), submitting, 16, 81, 124, 132, 156–157, 216n74, 254, 258, 325n7, 325n9, 326, 329–330, 332, 335, 340, 349–350
subordinate, 68, 188, 325, 338
subsidiary, 117, 229n155
subsidies, 12
subsistence, 280n10
substitute, substitutes, substitution, 190, 192n70, 229n151, 316, 357
suburb(s), suburban, 11, 13, 334
subversive, 24n14, 84, 289n67
succeed, success(es), 181, 244, 306
successful(ly), 39, 157
succession, successive, successor, 43n46, 63, 67, 229n152n32, 328
Suetonius, 14, 17, 20
suffered, suffering(s), 32, 41, 54, 62, 74, 80–81, 81n15, 90–93, 135, 137, 141n14, 151, 153, 160, 163–164, 180, 191n66, 195, 195n80, 196, 200, 202, 205, 216n74, 224n121, 237, 237n1, 240, 242n19, 245–248, 248n56, 260, 281, 286n42, 296n10, 297–298, 301, 301n18, 308, 310, 314–315, 343
sufficiency, 281, 354
sufficient(ly), 71, 75, 153, 156, 175, 247, 267, 292
suicide, 333n37
Sulla, 10
summon(s), summoned, summoning, 57, 68, 70–71, 122, 131, 138, 145–146, 155n16, 179–180, 191, 193, 200, 203, 208, 210, 226, 229–231, 235, 243, 268, 292, 295, 297, 302–303, 306, 309–310, 314, 332, 336, 340, 344, 346–347, 358
Sun, 12, 282n19

419

Subject Index

sunrise, 174
sunset, 174
superfluous, 67
superior(s), superiority, 60, 70, 98, 196, 279, 290, 313, 338
supernatural, 244-245
superstition, 14, 324n4
supplied, supply, 9, 72, 151, 221, 259, 320
support(s), supported, supporting, ix, 2, 10, 13, 16, 18, 24n14, 28, 31, 39, 40n35, 41, 42-43, 50-51, 55, 66, 69, 75, 77, 103, 105, 126, 128, 172, 189, 201, 211n36, 211n36, 219-222, 222n109, 222n112, 223-224, 227, 230n158, 235, 280, 283n24, 287-288, 296, 301, 303, 312, 339, 341
supporters, 10-11
supportive, 25, 29
supremacy, 85, 142, 144, 260, 312, 338, 354
supreme, 40n35, 56, 68, 82, 142, 148, 155, 188, 205, 279, 305, 332
survive, survived, 245, 280n10, 345
suspicion, 12-14, 41
Sustainability, 369
sustainability, 42n39n, 264n22
sustained, sustains, 93, 152, 173, 267, 311
suzerain, 122
sword, 60, 62, 83, 85, 182n10, 196, 206, 328, 370
syllogism, 191n68
symbol, 89
symbolic, 212n43, 277
symbolized, symbolizes, 62, 104, 116, 126, 164n25
symmetrical, 331
synagogue(s), 12-16, 19, 48, 107n42, 108, 187n42, 209, 211, 211n34, 216, 222, 311, 358
sync, 314, 324n4
syncretism, syncretistic, syncretized, 334, 338, 347
Synecdoche, 67, 194n75
Synonym(s), 125, 310
Synonymia, 67
synonymous, 67, 126, 146n27, 182-183, 316, 326
Synoptic Gospels, Synoptics, 48, 90
syntax, 31n10
Syntyche, 49, 171, 216, 275n26
Syria, Syrian, 7, 10, 13, 17, 23, 32-33, 36-37, 48, 75, 171, 174, 177, 221, 282, 296n7, 311, 330, 344
system(s), 8, 10, 92n61, 99, 196, 264, 311n7, 326, 328, 333-334, 349
Systematic, systematically, 30, 39, 241n16, 363

Tabernacle, 115, 349
table(s), 61, 63, 289, 290, 290n67, 339, 344
tablets, 152
Tacitus, 14-15, 21, 180, 215n67, 330
tactics, 106
tales, 8
targeted, targeting, targets, 57, 109, 311
Targum(s), 86, 154n13, 195, 195n80
Tarquinius Superbus, 8
Tarraconensis, 222n75, 223
Tarshish, 42
Tarsus, 296n7, 344, 351, 358, 358n11, 359
Tartarus, 162
Tautology, 67
Tax(es), taxation, taxed, taxing, 9, 15, 23, 60, 109n52, 156-157, 254, 267, 330, 330n29, 330n31, 331, 333n36, 333n27
teach(es), 32, 105, 163n21, 210n31, 224, 250n3, 287n49, 344, 355
teacher(s), 18n9, 25, 27, 83, 105, 154n13, 218, 233n167, 246n41, 277, 281n13, 284n34, 290n71, 358n12
teaching, 8n6, 28, 63, 72, 75, 88n47, 106, 130n59, 145, 153n11, 213, 215, 228, 232, 238n5, 276, 280, 285-286, 286n46, 297n11, 299, 318n27, 328, 331, 337
teachings, 148n5, 286n48
team(s), 18, 35-37, 43n47, 71, 131, 171, 211, 216-217, 220, 230, 272, 275n26, 277, 283, 318, 321
tear, tearing, 157, 163, 270, 314n18
technical, technically, 78, 114, 191, 209n28, 215n68, 217n87, 290n68, 324n1
technique, 27
technologies, technology, 192n70, 263n18
Tefellah, 311n9
teleological arguments, 356
telephoning, 284n32
telos, 112-113, 160, 296n10, 305, 331
temperance, 148n4
Temple (Jerusalem/Second), 62, 86, 86n33, 109n52, 115, 184n22, 190n56, 194, 195n80, 264n20, 311n7, 313n18, 318, 330n32, 336, 338, 338n8, 349, 357
Temple (new/renewed), 55, 86-87
Temple (Spirit), 133,
temptation(s), tempted, 92, 260n7, 329n28
tenement, 9, 12, 211n39
tension(s), 41, 43, 49, 130-132, 134, 255n30, 293, 295n5, 304, 304n24, 305n29
tentmakers, tentmaking, 29, 216, 222, 291, 347
terror, 161, 327
terrorize, 333n37
Tertius, 22, 22n2, 37, 218, 218n92, 230, 257, 277, 292, 292n86, 343

Subject Index

Tertullian, 24, 43, 173
testified, testifies, testify(ing), testifies, 54, 57, 206, 226, 239, 246n39, 278, 311
testimonies, testimony, 51, 152, 175, 180, 232
testing, 217, 242n20
tetrapods, 61
Textual variants, 24, 31n10, 48, 84, 322, 369
thank(s), 152, 204, 212, 308, 310, 312
thanksgiving(s), 79, 205, 307n1, 310n4, 312n11
thankfully, 102, 112, 141
thanklessness, 312
theatre(s), 11, 23n14
Theft, 250
theft, 250-251
theocratic, 262
theologian(s), 130n58, 148n1, 297n11, 338, 356, 359
theological, 30, 39n29, 48, 51, 58, 67, 72, 77-78, 94n66, 118, 148n5, 150, 155, 158n21, 163, 173, 215, 237, 241, 251, 290, 297n11, 304, 322, 337n7
theologically, 56, 91, 129, 150, 290
theologies, 58, 118, 259, 352
Theologoumenon, 67
theology, 3, 28, 30, 51, 57n15, 69n45, 77-78, 81n15, 88n47, 94-96, 101, 109, 111, 114-115, 117, 129, 130n59, 136, 138, 141, 143, 143n19, 148n1, 148n5, 153, 160, 162n18, 167, 173, 191, 231n163, 231n164, 241n16, 245n33, 260n4, 261n9, 262n11, 278, 281, 297n11, 298, 299, 324-325, 327, 334, 338, 345n40, 345n41, 345n42, 351, 353, 355, 358n10, 359, 364
theory, 130n58, 238n4, 305n29, 351n4
theosis, 119, 204
thesis, 53
Thessalonian, 37, 159
Thessalonians, 212n47, 214n44, 220
Thessalonica, 49, 69, 171, 218, 220, 291, 321n39
think(s), 63n33, 108n49, 109n54, 156, 170n8, 192, 199, 213, 231n164, 248n55, 256, 260, 267, 274, 290, 292n86, 303n22, 316, 321n38, 334-335, 359
thinker(s), 63, 215, 293, 356n3, 359
thinking, 51, 61, 65, 84, 97-98, 118, 125, 132, 146, 152, 200, 208, 237, 259n2, 282, 316, 319, 324, 330, 335, 356n3, 359
thirst, 62
Thirty Year's War, 157n20
Thomas, 175-176,
thorn(s), 247, 247n46, 247n49, 247n54, 248
thorns, 248

thought(s), 8n1, 59, 65, 71, 98n18, 103, 108, 116-117, 132-133, 145n25, 146n27, 148n5, 155n16, 157, 161, 185n26, 201, 225, 230n157, 267, 303n21, 306, 342n18, 353n7, 355, 357n6
threat(s), 13, 23, 95, 114n5, 162, 259, 262, 296, 310, 320, 347, 359
threaten(ed), threatening, 10, 62, 85, 259, 261, 267, 318, 354
throat, 333n37
throne, 115, 182n10, 248
thunder, 8n4
thunderbolt, 8n4
Tiber (island), 13
Tiber River, 8, 13, 13n18, 14
Tiberius, 11, 14, 133
time, 1n6, 7, 8n5, 9, 11, 13-17, 20, 23, 26, 29, 32-33, 36, 36n17, 37n20, 38, 41, 48-49, 49n5, 56, 63, 63n31, 77, 83, 101, 103, 109, 116, 141n11, 146, 152n9, 155-156, 160, 169, 170n9, 171, 173-174, 176-177, 185n26, 185n30, 186, 188n45, 190, 196, 202, 206-207, 209n26, 210-211, 219, 223n117, 224-225, 227, 234, 236, 238-239, 241-242, 248, 255n28, 256, 258, 262, 275, 277, 287n52, 291, 295-297, 302, 304-307, 311-312, 316n23, 321, 323, 330-331, 333, 335, 338, 345, 350, 356
timeless, 29
timely, 194, 194n73, 234, 267
timers, 311
timespan, 246
timing, 174n27, 234n177
Timothy, 25, 35, 37-38, 49, 179, 187, 209, 210n31, 211n38, 212, 215, 218n92, 220, 223-224, 230n118, 321n39
Timothy Keller, 193
tithing, 281, 292
Titius Justus, 17n4, 37n18, 291n83
title(s), 11, 59, 85, 210, 228n144
Titus, 129n52, 129n53, 129n55, 208n22, 215, 220, 257, 324, 325, 327, 339
Titus Caesar Vespasianus, 85
today, 2, 8n6, 13n19, 13n20, 45, 57, 59, 63, 72, 92n61, 120, 120n22, 131, 178, 194, 196, 198, 200-201, 210, 218, 230, 235, 243, 248, 253, 261, 267, 269n2, 284n32, 288-289, 293, 315, 334, 346, 351-352, 355-356
toes, 61
toil, 230n157
tolerance, 13, 63
tolerant, 254
tongue, 122, 170

Subject Index

tongues, 29, 60, 93–94, 224n119, 233n171, 244n31, 246n41
Torah, 12, 16, 82n17, 104, 106–107, 121, 143, 148, 148n2, 149–150, 152n9, 154n12, 183, 190n63, 240, 337n7, 338, 351n3
torment, 163, 315
torture(d), 188
tortured, 315
towns, 7, 278
tract(s), 47, 157n20
tractate, 27
traders, 288
trades, 8n6
tradition(s), 8–9, 28n42, 43, 49n5, 51, 55–56, 59–61, 70, 83n20, 94, 94n65, 174, 176n33, 176n34, 181, 194, 195n80, 208, 262, 289n67, 296n9, 311n8, 342n29, 347, 359
traditional(ly), 14, 20, 29, 37, 95n2, 140, 239, 244, 324n4, 346, 359
traitors, 331
Trajan, 133n74, 188
transaction, 300n16
transform(s), transformed, transforming, 11, 18, 55n10, 91–92, 94, 99, 119, 125, 128, 135, 137, 149, 155–156, 164, 172, 183, 201n3, 204–205, 208, 236n181, 243, 249n1, 265, 269n1, 269n2, 276, 289n67, 297, 302n19, 306, 330, 334–335, 347, 351n3, 354n12
transformation, 2–3, 33n12, 78, 94, 99, 128, 130, 132, 167, 207, 232, 249n1, 263, 265, 269n2, 276–279, 327, 334, 342, 346, 358
transformational, 276
transformative, 91, 120, 128
transformer, 245
transgress, 98, 329
transgression(s), 60, 97, 136, 161, 185n26
transgressor, 97
translate(s), translated, translating, 42, 60n7, 72, 91n60, 121–122, 139, 153, 163, 183, 190n56, 207–210, 212, 214, 249, 282, 311–312, 315–316, 322, 327
translation(s), 11n12, 22, 24n18, 25, 31, 38, 41–42, 56, 69, 77, 71, 85, 87, 89n53, 91n60, 98, 100, 105, 108–110, 114, 126, 136, 138, 141, 149–152, 155, 162, 179, 183, 187–188, 192–193, 195–196, 207–208, 212, 214, 217, 247, 255–256, 258, 272, 283n27, 284n35, 285, 300n16, 320–321, 323, 329, 332
translators, 223
transliterated, 299n13
transmitted, 22, 136n83, 194
transparent, 292
Transport, 62, 330

trap, trapped, 62, 84, 102, 116, 124, 134, 204, 248
travail, 134, 159, 314
travel(s), traveled, traveling, 9n10, 18, 20, 23, 31–32, 35–36, 36n17, 38, 41–42, 42n40, 42n44, 43, 48, 70, 75, 175, 179, 185, 194, 198, 207–208, 209n26, 212, 215–217 219, 220n100, 221, 223, 226–227, 230, 233n169, 242n19, 246n39, 277, 286–288, 291–292, 303, 337, 346–347, 359
travelers, 214, 231, 247, 287n51, 288
treasurer, 292, 334
treaties, treaty, 9, 59, 130, 309
Treaty of Waitangi, 131
treatise, 27, 29–30, 39
Tree of life, 95, 95n2, 266
tree(s), 56, 61–62, 70, 95, 98, 115, 141, 158, 266, 268, 302, 315, 342, 348, 351n3, 353 317
trespass(es), 60, 97, 136
trial, trials, 300n17, 320
tribal, 10
tribes, 7–8, 86n32, 174n27, 177n46
tribulation(s), 60, 159, 165
tribunes, 9
tribute, tribute, 330–331
Trinitarian, 78, 94n68, 153
Trinity, 78, 89n55, 91, 94, 94n66, 314
trip(s), 1, 8n3, 9n10, 20, 23, 25, 28, 31–32, 34–35, 37, 37n26, 38, 42–43, 92, 171, 219, 221, 235n179, 256–257, 278, 290, 310, 325n10, 344, 357
triumph(ed), 82, 195n78, 294
triumphalist, 245
Triune, 78, 88n49, 94, 94n67, 132, 201n3, 208, 332, 355
Troas, 23
Trojan, 8, 227n138
Trophimus, 246, 321n39
Trouble(d), 2, 103, 288, 314n18, 340
Troy, 8, 227
true, 73, 84–85, 107n44, 139, 142–143, 182, 188–189, 196, 228n144, 229m154, 230, 233n168, 238n5, 244–245, 245n37, 258, 263n18, 266, 271, 287, 291n75, 297, 302, 334, 349
Truly,
truly, 1, 80, 84, 229n152, 244, 271, 289n67, 339n11, 343, 346
trust(s), trusted, trusting, 72, 86, 124, 136n82, 138n1, 140–142, 142n15, 143, 149, 188–189, 189n52, 203, 215, 242, 281–282, 285, 290, 299–300, 314, 329, 332, 334, 336, 353, 353n9

Subject Index

truth(s), 8, 19, 60, 64, 67, 72, 80, 98, 103, 109, 118–119, 122n32, 145, 173, 197, 228n144, 248, 253n19, 301, 313, 315, 320n36, 330, 335, 339n13, 356n2
truthful, truthfulness, 80, 118
Tryphaena, 119, 217, 230, 275n26, 278n37, 343
Tryphosa, 119, 217, 230, 275n26, 278n37, 343
Turkey, 7, 9n10, 36, 173n22, 174, 177
Turkmenistan, 173n22
turmoil, 335
Twelve (the), 174–175, 209n26, 210–211, 225n122, 226, 273n15
twin(s), 8, 12, 285n40, 294
Tychicus, 208n22, 214, 215n71, 321n39
type(s), 28, 54, 122, 136, 190, 342n18, 357
types, 58, 229, 233n170, 330
Typological, typology, 87, 136, 297
tyrannies, 332
Tyre, 222

Ugandan, 214n55
Ugarit, 196
Ukraine, 173n22
umbilical, 315
umbrella, 146
unambiguous, 105, 162n118, 223
unashamed(ly), 180, 190, 196
unavoidable, unavoidably, 151, 243, 315
unbelief, 19, 55, 74, 118, 138, 141, 196, 240, 299n14, 302, 351n3
unbeliever(s), 41, 45, 48, 50, 72, 103, 119, 131, 135, 161–162, 189, 207n18, 219, 224, 234, 241, 254, 271, 287n52, 288, 320n36, 324, 327, 343, 355
unbelieving, 172, 223n117, 234, 256, 258, 352
unbiblical, 297n11
unblemished, 149
unborn, 268
unbreakable, 90
unbridled, 259n2
uncertainty, 8, 187, 313
uncircumcised, 66, 91, 109, 140–141, 339, 349
uncivilized, 70, 179
unclean, uncleanness, 30, 97, 116
uncomprehending, 55
unconditional, 80, 90, 228n144
uncultured, 70n47
undefiled, 91
underfoot, 250n7
underground church, 235n179
understatement, 179n1
undeserved, 62
undisputed, 22
unemployed, 10
unequivocal, unequivocally, 261, 293n9

unethical, 149
unevangelized, 50, 174, 178
unexplainable occurrences, 246n39
unexpressed, 314
unfairness, 103
unfaithful, unfaithfulness, 79, 138n1, 142, 271, 299
Unfinished, 236n183
unfulfilled, 114
ungodliness, ungodly, 56, 73, 83, 86, 89–90, 97, 102, 116, 127, 135–136, 140, 162, 162n18, 165, 169n2, 191, 203, 229, 279, 313, 357
ungrammatical, 65
unheeded, 157n20
unholy, 131–132
unified, 8–9, 49, 91, 94, 103, 255, 354
uniformity, 156
unimportant, 56, 157
unintelligible, 70n47
unique, 2, 48, 72–73, 88, 164, 247, 341
unite(s), united, 30, 119, 150, 156, 164, 172, 250n7, 252n12, 357
unity, 1n1, 30, 52, 69, 81n15, 82, 90, 94, 118–119, 142, 156–158, 224, 233n169, 254, 256, 318, 359
universal, 9, 54, 73, 96n5, 119, 127, 140, 144–145, 149, 160, 163n21, 170n7, 172, 183, 191, 211, 231n163, 239, 250, 261, 297n11, 356 n4
universalism, universalist, 163n21, 199n90
universality, 169n3
universally, 87, 99, 102, 118, 148, 148n1, 149, 154, 217, 312
universe, 164, 237, 263n15, 263n18, 265n26, 289n67, 293
universities, 211
unjust, unjustly, 250, 253–254, 258, 329, 350, 352
unjustified, 149, 325n7
unleashed, unleashes, unleashing, 96, 162, 183, 206, 235, 308, 349
unmarried, 273, 275
unmerited, 114
unnamed, 208n22, 209, 220, 296, 342
unnecessary, 64
unpalatable, 65
unpersuasive, 351n4
unprovable, 25n20
unreached, 57, 178, 191, 226
unrepentant(ly), 98, 344
unrest, 14
unrighteous, unrighteousness, 73, 97n14, 161, 122–123, 145, 162, 205
unsaved, 40, 118
unscathed, 31

Subject Index

unsearchable, 202, 312
unseen, 114
Unselfish, 284n32
unsensational, 243
unspecific, unspecified, 212, 250
unstoppable, 80
unsure, 15, 344
unsurprising, 216
Unsustainability, 264n22
unswerving, 69
untainted, 285, 354
unthinkable, 189
untouched, 222
untranslatable, 234
unusual, 227, 316
unveiled, unveiling, 76, 263, 323
unwarranted, 29n3
unwavering, 143
unwillingly, unwillingness, 144n21, 290n72, 296
upbuilding, upbuilds, 224n119, 303n20
upheaval, 227
Upheld, uphold, upholding, 70, 107–108, 110, 230n157, 240, 271, 273, 326 273, 353
Upper-class, 9n9
upright, uprightness, 10, 122, 252n13
urban, 9–10, 311
Urbanus, 119, 215, 217, 277n34, 278n35, 343
urge(d), 31, 253, 320n34, 334
urgency, urgent, 95, 106, 234n177, 255, 267, 317
urges, urging, 12, 30, 56–57, 93, 147, 155–158, 235, 256–257, 277, 283, 285, 290, 310, 320, 324, 327, 330–331, 339
usurps, 160
utilities, 331
Uzbekistan, 173n22

V

vain, 328
valid, 119, 302
valleys, 223n113
valor, 228n143
valuable, 10
value, 12, 101, 107, 149–150, 248, 260, 339, 356n3
valueless, 109
values, 18, 28n39, 156, 183, 232
vandalized, 266
variants, 84–85, 189
varied, 20, 25, 50, 258
vassal, 122
vectigalia, 330

vegans, 353n11
vegetables, 30, 62
vegetarians, 353n11
vegetation, 194n73
veiled, 76
venerate, 186
vengeance, 60, 103, 202, 241, 254n22, 288, 329
venom, 61
venture, 226
Venus, 227n138
veracity, 181, 237, 290n71, 318, 358n12
verb(s), 65, 97, 102, 104, 113n3, 114, 120, 127, 129, 135, 138n1, 163, 187, 191–192, 194, 196, 212–213, 217, 219, 221–222, 233n167, 283, 286, 290n71, 312–313, 318, 321, 325n9, 329, 355n1
verbal, verbally, 2, 40n34, 144, 188–189, 245, 301, 312, 322
verdict, 108, 130, 161, 308
vessel(s), 33, 63, 99, 101, 163, 194n73, 238
Vesta, 12
viable, 304n25
vicarious, 195, 195n80, 316
vice(s), 67, 148n3, 149, 194n75, 261, 299
victimization, 253
victims, 102
victorious, 10
victory, 8n4, 10, 81, 153, 194–195, 228, 240, 279n1, 297, 301, 310, 357
vileness, 97
villages, 278, 334
villas, 11
Viminal, 8
vindicate(s), vindicated, vindicating, 105, 129, 186, 190n59, 195, 245, 331
vindication, 196
violate(s), violated, violating, 39, 82, 97, 100, 101–102, 105, 119, 149–151, 157, 186, 224, 239, 250, 270, 272, 274, 276, 326, 331–332, 335, 340
violation, violations, 110, 255, 276, 337
violator, 97
violence, violently, 13, 82, 103, 250, 270, 332–333, 343 273, 316
virgin, 8n6, 275n24
virgin mission fields, 42, 174n27, 211
virtue(s), 56, 90, 92, 142, 148n4, 151, 156, 253–255, 276, 286, 288, 289n65, 304n25, 339, 343
virtuous, 142
visible, visibly, 89, 119, 131, 232, 244n32, 247, 249n1
vision, 1–2, 71, 78, 92, 146, 148n1, 148n5, 149n6, 155n17, 157n19, 164–165, 167,

Subject Index

169, 172–174, 216, 234n176, 240, 247, 249, 255–256, 262–263, 264n22, 271, 271n8, 276, 276n30, 277–278, 339n13, 341–345
visit(ed), visiting, 1, 12, 13n19, 25–26, 32, 37, 39n30, 50, 177, 210, 265, 282n32
visitors, 16, 234
vitality, 345n40
vocation(s), vocational, 12, 33n12, 155n15, 172, 203, 207, 211, 225, 233n167, 236, 267, 333, 347, 355
voice(s), 2, 93, 157, 170n20, 182, 184, 198, 239, 242, 318–319, 341
void, 111
volition, volitional(ly), 99, 293, 298–300, 300n16, 301–304, 304n24, 305, 305n29, 306, 315, 350
voluntarily, voluntary, 117, 151, 205, 211
votes, 10
voyages, 176
vulnerable, 237, 249, 267, 295

wages, 62
walk(s), walking, 30, 62, 92, 138, 148n2, 205, 255, 265, 300, 303n20, 304n24, 306, 309
wall, 8, 11, 82n17
wallets, 288, 292
war(s), 8n6, 12, 60, 181, 228, 258, 333n37
War of the Allies, 10
warm(th), warmly, 14, 32, 234, 321, 334, 346, 353 354
warn(s), warned, warning, 19, 55–56, 95, 99n20, 103, 105, 141, 163, 184, 203, 274, 285
warped, 92, 97, 101, 252, 334
warrior, 8, 177n48, 182n10
washing, 336–337
waste, wasteful, 255, 259, 359
watch(ed), watchful, watching, 105, 181, 192n70, 304
watchword, 157n20
water(s), 9, 89, 104, 121n25, 143, 181, 207n20, 283n20, 306, 325
wave, 292
waver, 141
wavering, 300, 317, 319
weak(ened), weaker, 26, 30n8, 31n9, 100, 142, 157, 247, 252, 254–255, 279, 289n67, 290, 303n19, 312, 341, 344
weakness(es), 81n15, 93, 206, 247, 258, 271n10, 312
wealth, 9, 9n7, 10, 180, 184, 256–257, 280, 281, 282n19, 283, 286, 288, 291, 307n1
wealthy, 10, 19, 26, 37, 218, 230, 257, 275, 279–280, 290–292

weapons, 60, 255, 282n28, 335n19
wear, 328, 347
weaving, 8n6
wedge, 249n1
weeds, 263n22
weep, 303
weighed, weight, weighted, 33n12, 148, 242, 245n33, 290n72
welcome(s), welcomed, welcoming, 1, 2, 32, 50, 75, 79, 89, 118, 193, 203, 205, 231, 255–258, 273, 286n48, 287, 289–290, 303n19, 341, 343–344, 346–347, 353–354
West, 1, 32, 42–43, 50, 61, 75, 92, 171, 177, 176, 200, 334, 345–346, 369
221–222, 235, 296, 310–311, 346, 357
Western, 10, 35–36, 38, 40, 42–43, 61, 63, 69, 75, 137, 171, 173, 177, 236, 242, 253, 259, 277–278, 289, 296, 338, 345–346, 356
westerners, 118
westward, 34, 345
whispered, whispers, 93, 157, 206
white, 338, 347
wholehearted(ly), wholeheartedness, 69, 184, 189, 192, 226, 284, 310, 344
wicked, wickedness, 71, 97, 102–103, 116, 121, 184, 286n42, 304n25, 305, 333n36
widow(s), widowed, 135, 252, 273n16, 275, 282, 288, 290
widower, 273n16
wife, wives, ix, 215–216, 216n76, 217, 223n117, 234, 270, 272n12, 273 274, 282n19, 285n39, 305, 325, 331, 333n37
wild animals, 260n7, 262, 333n37
wilderness, 260, 349, 356
Wilhelm, 369
will of God, 31, 31n20, 63, 79, 81, 93, 202, 204, 206, 208, 234n177, 298, 304, 305, 306, 310n4, 311, 313, 314, 321, 326, 326n11, 350
willed, 304–306
willful, 305
willing(ly), willingness, 110, 151, 161, 172–173, 180n5, 277, 298–300, 302–306, 308, 316, 329, 332, 334, 350, 357
win(ning), won, 10, 28, 32, 39, 39n33, 40, 40n37, 70, 75, 172, 179, 195, 223n117, 226, 233n167, 266, 298, 311
wind, 175, 182
window, 311
wine, 13, 31n9, 274
wings, 115
winter, 23
wisdom, 8n6, 12, 18, 121, 148, 180, 184n21, 202, 207n18, 233n168, 282n19, 285n37, 312

425

Subject Index

wise, 40, 70, 79, 148, 170n3, 179, 194n73, 236, 302n19, 322

Witch of Endor, 185

witness(es), witnessed, 16, 24, 48n2, 53, 60, 81n15, 94, 144, 146n28, 148, 187, 201, 209, 223n117, 235–236, 246n39, 251, 254n24, 266–267, 288, 289n67, 290, 310, 327, 332, 334, 339n13, 354n12

woes, 61, 159–160, 165, 357

wolf, 8

woman, women, 8, 8n5, 16n2, 32, 70, 78n4, 101, 118, 151, 160, 164–165, 195, 195n78, 211, 215–217, 217n84, 224, 224n119, 230–231, 234–235, 235n179, 242, 250, 267, 270, 272, 274–275, 275n26, 276, 278, 278n38, 284, 284n34, 290, 292, 314, 314n18, 315–316, 316n23, 321, 321n38, 325, 338, 342–344

womb, 358

wonder, 40, 137, 180, 244, 342

wonderful(ly), ix, 152, 216n76, 295, 306, 312

wonders, 2–3, 75, 146, 162, 167, 217, 226, 238, 243–245, 261, 295, 318

woo, 162

wood, 275n24, 357

word of God, God's word, his word, the word, 40, 40n34, 50n7, 55, 72, 74, 81, 141, 143n19, 175, 181–184, 184n21, 185–187, 189, 196–197, 202, 208, 209, 217, 226, 223n118, 230, 231n163, 232, 234–235, 240–241, 246n41, 249n1, 256, 272n14, 290, 290n72, 294, 306, 318, 319n31, 340–341, 349, 355

wordless, 206, 313–314

words, 29, 40, 56–57, 64–67, 71, 103, 105, 113, 127, 151, 164, 173, 181–182, 184, 186n34, 198, 212n40, 223n117, 232, 235, 247–248, 250, 263n18, 282n19, 287, 290, 307, 316, 325n7, 333n36, 334, 347–348

work, ix, 1n2, 2, 26, 38, 42, 49, 49n5, 54n3, 56–57, 62, 68, 72, 75, 77, 82, 90–91, 94, 101–102, 106, 113, 118, 120, 124, 127–128, 130–131, 134, 136–138, 142–143, 143n19, 145n24, 149, 153, 158, 158n22, 159, 165, 170n8, 174, 178–179, 192, 196–197, 201n3, 205–206, 208, 211, 214–215, 217, 223n118, 226, 230, 230n157, 231, 233n170, 234n176, 236, 238–239, 241, 244, 251n11, 256n30, 257, 262, 265–267, 269, 271–272, 276–277, 280–281, 292, 294, 297, 301, 303, 303n19, 307, 327, 336–338, 346–347, 350, 356–357

worked, ix, 9, 34, 37, 57, 94, 111–112, 155, 216, 219, 239, 294, 304, 323, 337, 349

worker(s), 37, 66, 77, 215n64, 217–218, 218n90, 223n118, 233n167, 235, 246n41, 260n7, 264, 276, 308, 310, 318–319, 343, 346

working, 25n21, 94, 145n26, 150, 203, 233, 294, 296n10, 297–298, 346, 348

works, 41, 49, 73, 75, 80, 82–83, 89, 97, 99, 102–103, 107–111, 114, 124, 127, 132, 136n83, 138–139, 139n2, 140–141, 143–145, 145n24, 149, 152–153, 161, 172, 177, 188–189, 189n52, 196, 202–203, 205, 211, 213, 228, 233, 238, 243, 245n37, 250, 253, 258, 260, 260n7, 286n42, 300n16, 301, 303n20, 308–309, 317, 327, 333–337, 337n7, 338, 349–350, 356

workshop, 347

world, v, 1–2, 7, 9, 9n10, 12, 30, 32–33, 42, 50, 52, 55, 57, 59–62, 68–70n50, 71, 75–76, 79–81, 81n15, 83n20, 84–85, 87–88, 88n49, 90–91, 93–94, 94n67, 94n68, 95–96, 96n7, 98, 100–103, 105–106, 112–113, 118–120, 125, 131, 133n73, 134, 136, 143–144, 148–150, 153, 155–158, 161–162, 162n18, 164–165, 167, 169–170, 170n5, 170n8, 171, 171n12, 172, 172n17, 173–180, 182, 184–186, 188, 193–196, 198–199, 199n90, 199n91, 200–201, 201n3, 202–206, 207n20, 208, 210–212, 212n48, 213–214, 214n56, 216, 226–227, 227n134, 230–233, 235–238, 238n6, 239–243, 245, 249–250, 252, 252n12, 252n14, 253, 255, 258–263, 263n14, 264–265, 265n26, 266–269, 272–273, 275–281, 286n43, 286n48, 288–289, 289n67, 291–292, 294–295, 298–299, 303–304, 304n24, 305, 305n25, 306–307, 307n1, 308, 310–311, 314–315, 319, 323–324, 326–329, 331n34, 332–335, 341, 343–345, 345n40, 345n41, 345n42, 346–347, 349–351, 351n3, 352, 355–360

World Wars, 345

worldly, 180, 334, 339

worlds, 345, 357

worldview, 48, 237, 169, 172, 265, 315

worldwide, 169, 227

worse, 184

worship, worshiped, worshiping, 55, 57, 60–61, 75, 79, 79n6, 81–82, 97, 101, 107n42, 121, 137, 142, 144, 146n28, 147, 156, 171, 188, 192, 203–205, 223–224, 232, 236, 241, 250, 252n16, 255, 257, 260–262, 267, 272–273, 290, 303, 306, 312, 319, 332n35, 333, 341, 347, 349, 353, 357

worshipers, 17

worshipful, 80, 312

Subject Index

worth, 165, 260, 348
worthless, 251, 356n3
worthy, 257
wrath, 60, 63, 73, 79n7, 80, 89–90, 95, 98, 102–104, 110–111, 114, 116, 118, 123, 130, 135, 145, 157, 160–163, 163n22, 170, 191, 202, 204, 230, 250, 254, 259, 272, 299, 302n19, 317, 329, 340, 348, 350
wrathful, 79, 104
wrestle, 320
Wretched, 152
write(s), 1, 2, 14, 19, 32–33, 38, 43, 47, 48, 50n6, 51, 71, 93, 99, 107n42, 110–111, 115, 151, 159, 170n8, 179, 181, 183, 192n79, 200, 207n16, 209, 212–214, 221, 226–227, 229n152, 232, 236, 239, 251n11, 254n25, 261–262, 262n11, 270, 277, 281, 307, 309, 329n28, 341, 357, 359
writer(s), 22, 42n42, 49n5, 53, 63–64, 196, 136n83, 140n4, 148, 154, 169, 173, 176, 220, 222, 239, 274–275, 285, 330, 342n21, 342n29, 353
writing, 7, 28, 28n42, 32, 36n17, 37–38, 42–43, 49, 56, 79n7, 91, 169, 182, 211n39, 214–215, 221, 239, 246n41, 248, 256, 261, 285, 292, 299, 309, 322, 333, 344, 346
Writings, 2, 26, 53–54, 76, 78, 95, 110, 129, 134, 162n12, 162n18, 176, 191, 191n68, 201n2, 206, 209, 212, 228–229, 229n155, 230, 262, 263n14, 274n23, 321, 323, 342
written, iv, 15, 23–32, 36, 38, 40–41, 48–49, 51, 53, 56, 72, 77, 92, 103, 107, 151–152, 163, 180, 192, 213, 215, 217, 231, 239, 280, 299, 301, 324, 332, 336, 339, 355–356, 359
wrong, 56, 65, 97–98, 112, 152, 328–329
wrongdoing, 97, 103, 137, 261, 264
wrongly, 39, 42, 98, 170
wrongs, 254n25
wrote, 12, 22, 22n2, 24, 47, 116, 171n12, 220, 264, 296n9, 304–305, 330n29, 359

xenophobia, 289n67, 290

Yahweh, YHWH, 57, 82–84, 144, 181, 188, 192, 196, 252, 357
yearn(s), yearned, yearning(s), 40, 55, 90, 101, 134, 164, 179, 199, 211, 235, 261, 263, 299, 303, 314–315, 348, 352–353
yield(s), yielded, yielding, 36, 56, 71, 92, 94, 104, 128, 132, 142–143, 143n15, 150–151, 158, 161, 173, 196–197, 197n85, 206, 208, 223n117, 232, 240–241, 252, 269, 282, 298, 300, 302, 308–309, 325, 331, 334–335, 337, 353, 357
young, younger, 84, 115, 246, 294, 342n20, 358, 360
youth, 347, 359

Zacchaeus, 288
zeal, 81, 156, 205, 207, 231–232, 337, 343, 345, 350
Zealand, 131, 246, 328, 346–347, 366, 371
zealous(ly), 51, 94, 203, 227n134, 253, 267, 351n3, 359
Zenas, 220
zenith, 57, 87, 295
Zerubbabel, 82n17
Zeus, 8n4, 12, 78n1, 81
Zion, 56–57, 61, 83, 86n36, 116, 135–136, 190, 204, 240, 262, 353
Zionism, 352

Author Index

Ådna, J., 368
Alexander, Loveday C. A., 18n6, 39n33, 340n14, 361
Alexander, T. Desmond, xi, 361
Alexander, W. M., 247n52, 361
Alexis-Baker, Andy, 373
Allen, Roland, 227n134, 361
Arndt, 361
Arnold, 106n38, 237n3, 361, 372
Aune, David E., 28n40, 262n13, 361
Aus, R. D. 42n44, 361
Avery-Peck, Alan J., xi

Backlund, Kurt, 196n83, 361
Bailey, Daniel P., 195n80, 361
Bakken, Peter W., 260n4, 361
Banks, Robert J., 361
Bates, Matthew W., 60n4, 361
Barclay, John M. G. 361, 369
Baker, David W., x
Barker, Kenneth L., 71n52, 71n53, 72, 72n54, 72n55, 72m56, 361
Barnett, Paul W., 33n11, 33n12, 209n25, 247n47, 324n4, 358n12, 361
Barnhouse, Donald Grey, 356n3, 361
Barram, Michael, 155n15, 362
Barrett, C. K. 23, 23n6, 98n18, 127n47, 140n4, 185n26, 213, 213n54, 229n153, 283n26, 286n46, 321n38, 340n15, 362
Barry, John D., x, xii, 364
Barth, Karl, 140n4, 358, 362
Bauckham, Richard, 16n2, 214n56, 217, 217n84, 339n12, 362
Beale, G. K., 264, 264n20, 362, 371
Beaulieu, Stéphane, 54n3, 362
Beitzel, Barry, J. x, 130n58, 364
Belleville, Linda L., 171n14, 362
Bennett, Charles E., 85n30, 362
Berger, Klaus, 27, 27n34, 28n42, 362
Betz, O., 244n32, 362
Beyer, Hermann Wolfgang, 60n5, 362
Billerbeck, P., xiii

Binder, H., 247n49, 362
Bird, Michael F., 2n6, 362
Black, M., x, 23n12, 362
Boa, Kenneth, 140n4, 149n7, 251, 251n8, 362
Bock, Darrell L, 321n41, 362
Bolt, Peter, 365-366, 368, 371
Bornkamm, Günter, 29, 29n3, 362
Bosch, David, 201n3, 236n181, 249n1, 269, 269n1, 269n2, 351n3, 354n12, 362
Boston, Jonathan, 259n1, 362
Bowers, W, Paul, 42n42, 201n1, 222, 222n11, 236n181, 362
Bowley, James E., 227, 227n136, 228, 228n139, 362
Bredin, Mark, 259n1, 362
Briley, Terry R, 86, 86n37, 362
Bromiley, Geoffrey W., 367
Brook, G. J., 184n20, 362
Bruce, F. F., 23, 23n7, 37n19, 199n90, 209n26, 363, 369
Bryan, Christopher, 28n42, 363
Bultmann, Rudolf, 27, 27n36, 63n63, 213n51, 363
Buttrick, George A., xi
Byrne, Brendon, 23n12, 37n25, 363

Carson, D. A.,310n4, 338n8, 363, 371
Chafer, Lewis Sperry, 241n16, 363
Childs, Brevard S., 86n36, 363
Chilton, Bruce, 358n12, 363
Ciampa, Roy E., 233n167, 233n171, 246n41, 271n7, 363
Clarke, Frank, 365
Colijn, Brenda B., 115n10, 363
Comfort, Philip W., xiii, 8n2, 363
Cottrell, Jack, 140n4, 180, 180n5, 189, 189n52, 219, 219n99, 220n100, 252n15, 284n32, 286n46, 289n65, 290n69, 300n17, 356n4, 363
Cranfield, C. E. B., 23n7, 23n9, 97, 97n17, 98n18, 105n33, 127n47, 136, 136n84,
Cranfield, C. E. B

Author Index

(Cranfield, C. E. B continued)
    136n85, 139n2, 140n4, 149n7, 171n16, 211n37, 253n19, 358n7, 363
Crump, D. M., 311n7, 311n8, 311n9, 363

Daneel, M. L., 260n5, 363
D'Angelo, Mary R., 275n76, 363
Danker, F. W., 43n48, 363
Darragh, Neil, 367
de Jong, John, 367
DeMoss, Matthew S., xiii
deSilva, David A., 280n9, 280n11, 363
Deissmann, Adolf, 363
DeWitt, Calvin B., 260n5, 363
Dicken, Frank E., 18n8, 363
Dickson, John P., 2n6, 201n1, 209n26, 210n30, 233n170, 236n181, 363
Dodd, C. H., 23n13, 363
Donfried, Karl Paul, 25n20, 29n1, 29n5, 63n37, 361–364, 366–368, 371–373
Downs, D., 280n10, 364
Dunn, J. D. G., 12n14, 14n22, 14n24, 14n25, 15, 15n28, 16n1, 19n10, 20, 20n12, 20n13, 20n15, 20n16, 22n2, 23, 23n8, 23n9, 24n15, 26n23, 26n24, 37n22, 84n26, 87n44, 89, 94n64, 96n4, 107n42, 109n52, 127n47, 140n4, 146n30, 170n4, 174, 174n25, 174n26, 188n46, 189, 189n50, 190, 190n57, 190n58, 211n38, 212n46, 121n48, 214n62, 217n79, 217n81, 217n82, 222n109, 228n144, 229n148, 229n150, 245n33, 271n10, 277, 277n34, 279n2, 287n54, 287n56, 288n59, 288n62, 290n72, 291n78, 292n85, 292n87, 305, 305n28, 330n30, 364, 373

Easton, M. G., xi, 12n15, 364
Edwards, James R., 270n6, 364
Ehorn, Seth M., 272n12, 364
Ellis, E. Earle, 215n64, 218n90, 364
Elwell, Walter A., x, xiii, 8n2, 130n58, 363–364
Engelland, H., 369
Evans, Craig, A., xi

Fee, Gordon D., 93n63, 113n4, 141n14, 233n167, 233n168, 234n172, 247n50, 273n16, 364
Fiore, Benjamin, 28n40, 364
Fitzmyer, Joseph A., 23n12, 136n82, 136n83, 140n4, 146n28, 159, 159n3, 160, 185n25, 194n71, 215n63, 215n66, 229n115, 238n5, 263n18, 290, 290n68, 290n73, 364
Fletcher, Joseph, 154, 154n14, 364
Foerster, Werner, 114n5, 364
Forbes, Chris, 247n48, 364

Ford, Coleman, 188n48, 364
Francis, Pope, 259n2, 364
Freedman, David Noel, x
Friedrich, Gerhard, 194n76, 194n77, 364, 366

Gabbatt, Adam, 243n24, 364
Gaffin, Richard B., 241n14, 364
Gager, J. G., 351n4, 364
Gallagher, Robert L., 364
Garland, David E., 183, 183n17, 233n167, 245n37, 246n38, 282n14, 365
Garrett, Duane A., 114n6, 287, 288n57, 365
Gasque, W. Ward, 358n11, 365, 369
Gaston, L., 190n63, 351n4, 365
Geisler, Norman L., 78n1, 365
Ghillean, T. Prance, 363
Gill, David William John, 330n31, 365
Goheen, Michael W., 1n4, 1n5, 94n67, 365, 373
Goldsworthy, Graeme, 57n15, 365
Gorman, Michael, 60n4, 143n18, 204, 204n11, 365
Green, Joel B., xi, 20n14, 365
Green, Michael, xi, 180n2, 332n35, 365
Grenz, Stanley, xiii, 365
Griffin, Hayne P., 173n23, 368
Grindheim, Sigurd, 130n59, 365
Guerra, Anthony J., 28n42, 365
Gupta, Nijay K., 60n4, 141n11, 143n18, 365

Haacker, Klaus, 27n27, 358n10, 365
Hafemann, Scott, 81n15, 365
Hahn, Ferdinand, 107n44, 170n5, 299n13, 365
Hall, Emily, 47n1, 365
Hall, J. F., 10n11, 11n13, 365
Hansen, Walter G., 27n37, 27n38, 28n39, 365
Harrington, Daniel J., 363
Harris, Murray J., 88n46, 247n44, 247n49, 247n50, 364–365
Hauck, Friedrich, 274n23, 366
Hawthorne, Gerald F., xi
Hays, Richard B., 89, 148n5, 149n6, 155n17, 157n19, 339n11, 339n12, 339n13, 340n13, 343n34, 366
Headlam, A. C., 23, 23n12, 37n21, 370
Heckel, U., 361
Heide, G. Z., 164n25, 366
Hendriksen, William, 128n48, 366
Hengel, Martin, 33, 33n15, 361, 366
Hertig, Paul, 364
Hill, Michael, 148n1, 366
Hock, Ronald F., 347n45, 366
Holmes, Michael William, 43n46, 366
Hoskyns, Edwyn C., 362
House, Wayne E. 364, 367

Author Index

Howell, Don H., 38, 39n29, 307n2, 366
Hughes, Lesley, 259n1, 366
Hultgren, Arland J., 1n3, 366
Hurtado, Larry W., 83n21, 84n23, 366
Hyatt, Darlene, 16n2, 140n5, 149n7, 158n22,
    171n12, 213, 213n53, 214n56, 215n65,
    217n84, 218n89, 221, 221n103, 221n104,
    221n106, 251n11, 253, 253n20, 254n25,
    280n7, 287n51, 287n53, 289, 289n64,
    289n67, 291n80, 304n25, 324n3, 325n7,
    328n26, 330n29, 356n3, 358n7, 373

Jervell, Jacob, 29n3, 366
Jewett, Robert, 23n14, 24n14, 27, 27n30,
    39n30, 42n42, 43n45, 86n41, 86n42,
    87n45, 120, 120n21, 128n48, 140n6,
    149n7, 170, 170n7, 171n16, 184n19,
    184n21, 184n22, 185n31, 188n47,
    191n67, 191n68, 192n69, 194n71,
    211n39, 215n67, 215n68, 217n88,
    220n100, 221, 221n105, 222, 222n110,
    222n112, 222n113, 223n114, 223n115,
    223n116, 228n139, 228n140, 228n141,
    229n150, 252n14, 252n16, 264, 264n21,
    264n23, 279n1, 283n27, 284, 284n31,
    284n35, 287n50, 291, 291n75, 291n76,
    291n79, 291n80, 291n81, 291n83,
    292n85, 292n86, 327n17, 331n34, 366
Jones, Richard N., 237n2, 366
Jørgensen, Lars, 177n48, 366
Josephus, Flavius, 2n6, 13, 177, 188, 194n73,
    198, 218n89, 228, 263n14, 287n54, 298,
    298n12, 304n25, 311n7, 311n8, 367
Judge, E. A., 12n14, 367

Kallas, J., 324n2, 367
Karris, Robert J., 30n8, 367
Käsemann, Ernst, 96n7, 106n37, 120, 120n22,
    125, 127n47, 140n4, 160n4, 162n15,
    170n8, 170n10, 174n25, 174n26, 185n30,
    188n44, 199n89, 212n40, 213n52,
    229n153, 356n3, 359n14, 367
Keck, Leander E., 366, 373
Kee, Howard Clark, 237n3, 367-368
Keen, Karen R., 271n11, 367
Keener, Craig S., 140n3, 180n3, 191n68,
    220n100, 255, 255n26, 367
Kellner, Menachem, 148n2, 153n11, 154n12,
    367
Keown, Mark J., iv, ix, 40n35, 40n37, 41n38,
    43n47, 49n5, 69n41, 69n44, 92n61, 96n3,
    98n19, 106n35, 136n82, 140n7, 142n14,
    142n15, 149n7, 158n21, 161n9, 163n21,
    170n8, 172n17, 172n18, 174n28, 174n31,
    176n35, 182n11, 182n15, 201n2, 207n18,
    207n19, 209n26, 210n29, 210n30,
    212n47, 216n72, 217n82, 220n101,
    232n165, 233n168, 233n169, 234n173,
    234n174, 234n175, 234n178, 235n180,
    237n1, 237n3, 242n18, 248n56, 262n12,
    263n14, 265n24, 265n26, 271n8, 271n9,
    275n26, 276n30, 277n32, 296n8, 301n18,
    311n10, 339n10, 344n37, 367
Kim, Chan-H., 27, 27n31, 367
Kistemaker, Simon J., 366
Knox, J., 23n8, 363-364, 367
Koontz, 373
Köstenberger, Andreas J., 2n6, 33n12, 40n34,
    53n2, 201n2, 210n32, 226n129, 244n28,
    244n29, 368
Kotansky, Roy David, 23n14, 24n14, 27,
    27n30, 39n30, 42n42, 43n45, 86n41,
    86n42, 87n45, 120, 120n21, 128n48,
    140n6, 149n7, 170, 170n7, 171n16,
    184n19, 184n21, 184n22, 185n31,
    188n47, 191n68, 192n69, 194n71,
    211n39, 215n67, 215n68, 217n88,
    220n100, 221, 221n105, 222, 222n110,
    222n112, 222n113, 223n114, 223n115,
    223n116, 228n139, 228n140, 228n141,
    229n150, 252n14, 252n16, 264, 264n21,
    264n23, 279n1, 283n27, 284, 284n31,
    284n35, 287n50, 291n 291n75, 291n76,
    291n79, 291n80, 291n81, 291n83,
    292n85, 292n86, 327n17, 331n34, 366
Kruidenier, William, 140n4, 149n7, 251,
    251n8, 362
Kümmel, W. G., 23n7, 368
Kvalbein, H., 368

Laansma, Jon C., 269n3, 368
Larkin, William J., 366
Lampe, Peter, 217n80, 217n83, 217n87,
    343n21, 343n32, 368
Lea, Thomas D., 173n23, 368
Legrand, Lucien, 1n1, 368
Lenski, R. C. H., 189, 189n51, 286n46, 368
Liddell, Henry George, xii, 368
Lipka, Michael, 200n94, 368
Little, Christopher R., xi, 368
Longenecker, Bruce W., 249n2, 368
Longenecker, Richard N., 26, 27, 27n25,
    27n29, 27n32, 27n33, 28, 28n41, 28n42,
    28n43, 50n6, 89n54, 128n48, 133n73,
    140n5, 211n38, 230n158, 242n18,
    252n13, 254, 254n25, 266, 266n27,
    282n17, 325n6, 326n13, 335, 335n39,
    339n10, 368
Lopez, René, 250n7, 368
Lüdemann, G., 23n8, 368

Author Index

McCant, J. W., 247n49, 369
McDuffie, C., 260n4, 361
Magda, Ksenija, 1n3, 368
Mangum, Douglas, 88n47, 368
Marshall, I. Howard, xii, 163n21, 188n43, 201n2, 368
Martin, George, 33, 33n13, 33n14, 369
Martin, Ralph P., 369
Mattill, A. J., 321n37, 369
Meadowcroft, Tim, 367
Meeks, Charles, 85n32, 369
Meinardus, Otto F. A., 43, 43n49, 43n50, 369
Melanchthon, P., 29, 29n2, 369
Menoud, P. H., 247n46, 369
Merrill, E. H., 106n36, 369
Metzger, Bruce M., 24n16, 31n10, 48n2, 322n42, 369
Meye, Robert P., 206, 206n14, 369
Michaelis, Wilhelm, 216n78, 369
Moo, Douglas J., 27, 27n26, 28n44, 31n9, 37n18, 70n49, 71n51, 87n45, 88n47, 104n29, 106n37, 108n48, 109n50, 109n51, 109n52, 109n54, 112n56, 120, 120m20, 120n23, 128n47, 139n3, 140n4, 146n28, 149n7, 154n13, 170n9, 171n15, 174n27, 179n1, 183n19, 184n21, 186, 186n32, 186n35, 190n64, 197n85, 202n5, 216n74, 217n81, 220, 220n100, 221n102, 234n117, 272n14, 283n24, 285n36, 285n38, 287n55, 288, 288n58, 291n82, 324n5, 330n30, 337n7, 351n4, 357n6, 369
Moo, Jonathan, 264, 264n22, 369
Morris, Leon, 23, 23n6, 106n37, 140n4, 174n27, 189, 189n55, 199n90, 219, 219n95, 221n106, 229n152, 251n11, 252n17, 285n41, 288n63, 290n70, 305n26, 325n6, 369
Moule, Handley, 214n55, 369
Mounce, Robert H., 22n3, 23, 23n4, 23n5, 23n10, 26n23, 26n24, 128n48, 140n4, 190n62, 217n82, 261, 261n8, 284n32, 288, 288n63, 369
Muddiman, John, 233n169, 369

Neil, Stephen, 236n183, 369
Newman, Barclay Moon, 140n4, 146n27, 369
Neusner, Jacob, xi
Nida, Eugene Albert, 140n4, 146n27, 369
Nisbet, P., 247n54, 369
Nissen, Johannes, 33n12, 169n2, 369
Norris, D. Thaine, 369

O'Brien, Peter T., 2n6, 33n12, 40n36, 42n39, 53n2, 67n39, 70n48, 75n57, 145n23, 181n7, 183n16, 194n76, 201n2, 210n32, 226n129, 244n28, 244n29, 310n4, 344n37, 369
Osborne, Grant R., xii, 140n4, 250n4, 250n5, 254n22, 265, 265n25, 286n44, 288, 288n60, 305, 205n30, 352n6, 353n8, 369
Osburn, Carroll D., 372

Packer, J. I., 11n13, 370
Panjikaran, J. G., 1n3, 370
Parry, R. A., 368
Partridge, C. H., 368
Patzia, Arthur G., xiii, 370
Petrotta, Anthony J., xiii, 370
Peters, George W., 69, 69n45, 143n19, 231n163, 131n164, 262n11, 370
Peterson, David G., 321n4, 370
Pitts, Andrew W., 367
Ploutz, Paul F., 259n2, 370
Plümacher, E., 328n25, 370
Plummer, Robert E., 180n6, 201n2, 209n28, 236n182, 370
Pohl, C., 286n47, 289n67, 370
Porter, Stanley E., xi, 188n45, 239, 239n10, 367, 370

Ramsay, William M., 247n51, 370
Rasnake, Eddie, 228n146, 229n152, 358n8, 358n9, 370
Reasoner, M., 12n16, 12n17, 14n26, 370
Reed, Jeffrey T., 208n21, 370
Rengstorf, Karl Heinrich, 208n24, 209n25, 370
Robeck, Cecil M., 241n15, 370
Roberts, W. Dayton, 260n5, 370
Robinson, J. A., 23n7, 370
Roloff, J., 116n13, 370
Rosner, Brian S., 233n167, 233n171, 246n41, 271n7, 363
Rostovtzeff, M., 222n122, 222n113, 370
Ruether, Rosemary Radford, 260n5, 370
Runge, Steven E., 287n51, 370
Ryken, Leland, x, 199n93, 370

Sanday, W., 23, 23n12, 37n21, 370
Saysell, Csilla, 367
Schaff, David Schley Schaff, 157n20, 370
Schaff, Philip, 157n20, 370
Schlatter, A., 247n45, 371
Schmitz, Leonhard, 8n4, 371
Schnabel, Eckhard J., 36n17, 176, 176n32, 176n33, 176n34, 176n36, 176n37, 177, 177n38, 177n40, 177n42, 177n43, 177n44, 201n2, 226n130, 226n131, 227n133, 303n23, 371
Schneider, G., 82n16, 371

Author Index

Schreiner, Thomas R., 28n44, 37n23, 37n24, 40n37, 96n7, 105n33, 120, 120n24, 140n4, 146n28, 154n13, 174n26, 180n5, 194, 194n74, 196n82, 207n16, 214n56, 214n59, 222n109, 230n159, 238n4, 251n10, 254n25, 272n13, 282, 282n15, 283n27, 291n75, 292n85, 293n2, 297n11, 326n11, 327n21, 336n1, 351n4, 353n8, 353n9, 357n6, 371
Schweitzer, Albert, 117n18, 371
Schulz, Siegfried, 274n23, 366
Scott, James M., 133n73, 371
Senior, Donald, 83n20, 371
Shead, Andrew G., 55n10, 371
Siefrid, Mark A., 53n1, 371
Silva, Moisés, xii, 371
Simeon, Charles, 293n2, 371
Simmons, William, 333n37, 371
Simpson, K. A., 131n63, 371
Smith, Gary V., 86, 86n33, 86n34, 190n56, 371
Smith, William, xi
Snodgrass, K. R., 108n46, 371
Spence-Jones, H. D. M., 191n68, 227, 227n135, 229n154, 230n157, 230n160, 230n161, 230n162, 255n27, 305, 305n27, 305n29, 306n31, 371
Stern, E., xi
Stirewalt, M. Luther, 27, 27n33, 371
Storgaard, Birger, 366
Stowers, Stanley, 28n42, 371
Strack, H., xiii
Stuhlmueller, Carroll, P., 83n20, 371
Swanson, James, x, 371
Swindoll, Charles R., 228n146, 371

Tan, Lincoln, 346n44, 371
Tennent, Timothy C., 70n50, 81n15, 88n49, 94n68, 199n91, 345n40, 345n41, 345n42, 371
Terry, John Mark, 344, 344n38, 369, 372
Thiede, P., 164n25, 372
Thielman, Frank, 128n47, 140n4, 185n27, 185n31, 210n31, 214n61, 215n65, 216n74, 216n77, 220n100, 233n169, 233n170, 250n3, 252n12, 252n13, 254n21, 255n28, 256n30, 258, 258n34, 284n30, 372
Thierry, J. J., 247n49, 372
Thompson, Mark, 365–366, 368, 371
Thrall, Margaret E., 247n53, 372
Toews, John E., 39n32, 64n38, 140n5, 159n2, 228n144, 252n16, 258, 258n35, 279, 279n3, 279n4, 279n5, 283n24, 295n5, 372

Toney, Carl N., 1n3, 372
Towner, Philip H., 133n72, 188n43, 368, 372

Utley, Robert James, 214n60, 251n9, 252n16, 255n29, 372

van Rheenen, Gerald, 207n20, 372
Varner, William, 326n15, 372
Veldman, Robin Globus, 259, 372
Volf, Miroslav, 80n12, 89n55, 96n6, 250n7, 372

Wallace, Daniel B., 187n37, 187n38, 239, 239n9, 372
Walters, James, 291n74, 372
Walton, Steve, 182n12, 372
Whiston, William, 367
Williams, Joel F., 366
Ware, Bruce A., 297n11, 372
Ware, James P., 2n6, 212n47, 235n180, 372
Watson, Duane F., 9n9, 372
Watts, John D., 86, 86n35, 372
Weima, Jeffrey D., 182n14, 372
Wenham, Gordon J., 146, 146n29, 372
Westerholm, Stephen, 336n1, 372
Wiefel, Wolfgang, 13n18, 17n5, 372
Windisch, Hans, 70n47, 372
Winn, A., 227n138, 373
Witherington III, Ben, 16n2, 18n6, 83n22, 140n5, 149n7, 158n22, 171n12, 204, 204n13, 208, 208n23, 213, 213n53, 214n56, 215n65, 217n84, 218n89, 221, 221n103, 221n104, 221n106, 251n11, 253, 253n20, 254n25, 280n7, 287n51, 287n53, 289, 289n64, 289n67, 291n80, 304n25, 324n3, 325n7, 328n26, 330n29, 356n3, 358n7, 373
Wolter, M., 27, 27n28, 373
Wright, Christopher J. H., 75n58, 79n7, 84n24, 96n5, 169n3, 261n9, 263n15, 333n36, 352n5, 353n7, 373
Wright, N. T., 42, 42n41, 42n43, 84n28, 108n47, 108n49, 109n53, 115n8, 120, 120n19, 120n21, 122, 122n31, 123, 124n42, 128n48, 128n49, 140n5, 148n4, 152n9, 153n10, 180n4, 204n12, 263, 263n16, 264n19, 353n7, 356n2, 373
Wuellner, W., 27, 28n39, 373

Yinger, Kent L., 107n41, 336n1, 373
Yoder, John Howard, 373

Zwemer, Samuel M., 307n1, 373

Scripture Index

GENESIS

1	70, 260
1:2	265
1:3	181n7
1:3–5	181
1:6	181n7
1:26–27	158
1:27	78, 78n4, 270
1:27–28	274
1:28	259n2, 272
1:31	101, 260
2	101, 260
2—3	263
2:7	55, 350n2
2:9	194n73
2:14	265
2:24	158, 270, 274
3	136, 349
3:8	266
3:15	106, 106
3:16	313n18
4:26	146
9:7	55n11
12–25	54
12:3	172
12:8	146n30
12:10–20	141n10
13:4	146n30
14:18	196n84
15:5	54n6, 240, 342n21
15:5–6	271n10
15:6	54n6, 65–66, 121n25, 124, 140, 239, 342n21, 349
15:7–21	140
16:3–4	271
16:4	141n10
17	54n6, 140
17:4–6	54n6
17:5	240, , 342n21
18	287, 287n54
18:10	55n11, 342n21
18:14	55n11
18:6	121n25
19:19	122n32
20:5	121n25
21:12	55n11, 342n21
21:23	121n25
21:33	146n30
24:27	122n32
24:29	121n25
25:23	55n11, 342n21
26:7	194n73
30:33	121n25
31:19–35	196
32:11	121n25
32:28	54
42:25	219n98
44:5	185n29
44:21	315
45:7	114n7
49:4	274

EXODUS

2:24	313n18
3:7	315
6:5	313n18
8:13	181
9:16	55n12, 333, 342n21
9:17	170
10:23	274
15	319
15:1	319
15:2	319
15:3	319
15:11	319
15:21	319
15:13	122n32, n33
18:22	313
20:2–3	192
20:12	251, 276

435

SCRIPTURE INDEX

(Exodus continued)

20:12–17	56
20:13	251
20:13–17	252, 342n21
20:14	251, 270, 274
20:15	251
20:16	251
20:17	54, 242n21
22:22	252
22:24	102n25
23:2	252
23:3	252
23:11	252
25:17–22	115n12
31	55
31:7	115n12
32:10–11	102n25
33:19	55n12, 342n21
34:7	122n32
35:12	115n12
38:5–8	115n12

LEVITICUS

10:3	319
11	56
11:44	132n67
11:45	132n67
15:16	274
16:2	115n12
16:7	115n12
16:13–15	115
17:11	91
18	274
18:5	183, 342
18:20	274
18:22	274
18:23	274
19:2	132n67
19:10	252
19:15	121, 252
19:18	56, 107n45, 112, 154, 154n13, 252, 342
19:20	274
19:26	185n29
19:31	185n29
19:34	154, 154n13, 251–252
20	274
20:6	185
20:13	274
23:40	194
25:42	251
26:13	251
26:26	219n98

NUMBERS

5:13	274n18
5:20	274n18
7:89	115
11:17	313
13:18	102n25
13:20	317
15:18–21	56n13
16:46	102n25
21:3	60n7
22:7	185n29
25:10–13	229n150

DEUTERONOMY

4:7	146
4:24	161
5:6–8	192
5:17–21	56, 342n21
5:18	270
5:21	54, 342n21
6:4–5	78, 192
6:4–6	252
6:11	219n98
8:3	181
8:7	185n27, 311n8
8:10	219n98
8:17	184
8:17–20	184
9:4	184, 342n21
9:4–5	184
9:4–6	121n25
9:7–8	102n25
10:16	54n8, 91
10:18	253
13:15	316
13:16	60n7
16:11	252
16:19	252
18:10–11	185
18:15–18	186
18:18–22	181
20:17	316
21:23	70, 180
24:1	54, 270
24:17	252–253
24:19	252–253
27:26	183n19
30:1	184
30:1–10	184
30:3	184
30:4	184
30:5–6	184
30:6	54n8

30:7	185
30:8	185
30:9–10	185
30:11–14	184n22
30:12	185
30:12–13	184
30:12–14	184, 184n22
30:13	185
30:14	55, 185–187
32:4	253
32:7–14	199
32:15–18	199
32:21	55, 199, 342n21
32:35	56, 83n23, 84n23, 241, 254, 333, 342n21
32:43	57, 171n11, 240n12, 319, 342n21
33:19	121
33:21	121

JOSHUA

6:17	316
6:18	316
7:1	316
	10:24n36
13:22	185n29
21:45	181
22:20	102n25
24:2	196
24:14	121n25

JUDGES

2:18	313
5:11	121n25
9:9	319

RUTH

2:14	219

1 SAMUEL

1:1—4:18	326
2:10	122n32
3:19	181
9:1—31:6	326
12:17	122
12:17–18	146
26:23	121n27, 122, 122n32
28	185
28:18	102n25

1 KINGDOMS (LXX)

2:30	319n29
9:20	194n73
31:19	194n78

2 SAMUEL

14:7	114n7

2 KINGDOMS (LXX)

1:20	194n78
1:23	194n73
10:3	318
13:18	330n32
15:11	283
18:19	194n78
18:20	194n78
18:26	194n78
18:31	194n78

1 KINGS

3:6	121n27
3:9	121n27
8:32	121n25
8:46	96n8
10:9	121n27
18:14	192
18:25	192
19	317
19:10	56
19:10–14	241, 342n30
19:14	56, 317
19:18	56, 317, 342n30

3 KINGDOMS (LXX)

1:6	194n73
1:42	195n78

2 KINGS

5:11	146n30
10:10	181
19:31	114n7
22:13	102n25
22:17	102n25

4 KINGDOMS (LXX)

4:43	330n32
6:15	330n32

1 CHRONICLES

10:9	194
16:8	146n30
16:10	316n23
17:18	319n29
18:14	131n27
23:30	311n7
24:11	82n17
29:17	121n25, 283n25

2 CHRONICLES

6:23	121n25
9:4	330n32
9:8	121n27
19:2	102n25
19:7	252
20:6	326n14
31:15	82n17
33:6	185n29
36:19	194n73
36:20	114n7
36:21–22	

EZRA

2:2	82n17
2:6	82n17
2:36	82n17
2:40	82n17
3:2	82n17
3:8	82n17
3:9	82n17
4:3	82n17
8:22	102n25
8:33	82n17
9:5	311n7
10:18	82n17

NEHEMIAH

2:20	121n25
3:19	82n17
7:7	82n17
7:11	82n17
7:39	82n17
7:43	82n17
8:7	82n17
9:4	82n17
9:5	82n17
10:10	82n17
10:37	56n13
12:1	82n17
12:8	82n17
12:26	82n17

ESTHER

1:10	187n40
7:8	181n9

PROVERBS

1:3	121n29
1:15	54n4
1:22	121n29
2:9	121n29
2:20	121n29
3:9	121n29
6:30	219n98
8	184n21
8:8	121n29
8:14–15	326n14
8:15	121n27
8:18	121n29
8:20	121n29
10:2	121n29
11:5	121n29
11:6	121n29
11:21	121n29
11:24–25	281n12
11:26	283
11:30	121n29
12:28	121n29
13:2	121n29
13:6	121n29
14:31	284
14:34	121n29
15:6	121n29
15:9	121n29
15:29	121n29
16:8	121n29
16:11	121n29
16:12	121n27
16:17	121n29
16:31	121n29
17:14	121n27
17:23	121n29
18:22	284
20:7	121n29
20:9	96n8
20:28	121n27
21:16	121n27, 121n29
21:26	284
21:21	121n29
22:8	284
22:9	281n12
25:21–22	187, 342n29
25:25	121n27

ECCLESIASTES

5:7	121n25
5:11	291n98
7:20	96n8

SONG OF SOLOMON

1:16	194n73
2:14	194n73
4:3	194n73
6:4	194n73, 316n23
6:7	194n73

ISAIAH

1:9	55, 83n23, 241n13, 342n23
1:17	253n18
1:21	121n25, 122n30
1:23	253n18
4:4	207n16
5:7	121n25, 122n30
5:16	122n32, 319n29
6:9–10	183
8:9	185n29
8:14	140n9, 301, 342n23
9:6	123n39
9:7	83n18
9:17	252
9:19	102n25
10:16	83n23
10:20–23	114n7
10:22	122
10:22–23	83n23, 114, 342n23
10:23	333
11:1	42n41, 319
11:5	123n39
11:10	57, 83, 171n11, 240n12, 342n23
11:11	114n7
11:34	83n23
12:4	146n30
12:19	83n23
13:13	102n25
16:5	83n18, 123n39
19:3	185n29
23:5	83n18
24:23	319n29
25:1	319n29
26:2	121n25
26:9	121n25
26:10	121n25
26:18	83
27:9	342n23
28:1	86
28:1–13	85
28:5	114n7
28:14	85
28:16	55, 85, 137, 140n9, 189, 190, 240, 241, 301, 342n23, 349n1
29:10	56, 240, 342n23
29:16	342n23, 350n2
30:27–28	207n16
32:16	123n40
32:16–17	121n25
32:17	123n40
33:5	122n32
33:6	121n26
33:10	319n29
33:15	83n18, 121n25, 122n30
33:17	83n18
34:14	326n14
34:23–24	83n18
35:10	314n18
37:24–25	83n18
37:32	114n7
38:19	122n32
39:8	121n25
40:8	181n7
40:9	195n78
40:13	83n23, 342n23
40:23	326n14
41:1	42n41
41:2	122n38
41:25	146n30
42:3–4	253
42:4	42n41
42:6	122n32
42:10	42n41, 319, 319n29
43:23	319n29
44:23	319n29
45:8	123n41, 184n21
45:9	342n23
45:19	122n32
45:23	56, 83n23, 104n27, 122n32, 144, 161, 170, 173, 181n9, 240, 342n23
45:24	122n32
46:3	114n7
46:10	181n9
46:12	121n25
46:13	123n41
48:1	121n25
48:3	181n9
48:18	121n25
49:1	42n41
49:3	319n29
49:6	344n37
49:10	283n28
51:5	42n41, 123n41
51:6	123n41
51:8	122n32

Scripture Index

(Isaiah continued)

51:11	314n18
51:22	102n25
52:5	54, 239, 342n23
52:7	182, 193, 194, 195n78, 240, 342n23
52:15	57, 75, 240, 347n23
52:13—53:12	195
53	90, 195n80
53:1	195, 347n23
53:13–15	196
54:14	121n25, 123n40
55:3	83n18
55:6	146n30
55:8	306
55:10–11	181n7, 184n21
55:11	181
55:11	70
56:1	121n25
57:12	121n25
58:2	121n25
58:6–7	252n16
58:8	121n25, 123n40
58:10	219n98
59:7	342n23
59:7–8	240n11, 250
59:9	121n25, 122n30
59:14	121n25, 122n30
59:17	122n32
59:20–21	56, 83, 86–87, 116, 116n17, 135, 136, 240, 347n23
60:6	195n78
60:9	42n41
60:17	121n25, 123n40
61:1	195n78, 330n32
61:3	121n25, 123n40
61:8	121n25
61:11	121n25, 123
62:1–2	121n25, 123n40
63:1	122n32, 194n73
63:5	102n25
63:7	122n32, 122n33
64:5	121n25
64:7	146n30
64:8	55
65—66	164, 262
65:1	55
65:1–2	342n23
65:2	55
65:1–2	200
65:17	262
65:17–25	240
65:18–19	262
65:20	262
65:21–25	262
66:1–2	264
66:5	319n29
66:10–12	262
66:18–23	262
66:19	42
66:24	262

JEREMIAH

1:12	181
4:2	121n25
4:4	54n8
4:31	313n18
5:16	54n4
5:28	253n18
7:5	253n18
7:20	102n25
9:23	122n32
10:10	102n25
10:25	146n30
11:16	65, 194n73
14:14	185n29
18:4–6	350n2
18:6	55
20:15	195n78
21:20	102n25
22:1–4	333n36
22:3	121n25
22:13	121n25
22:15	121n27
23:3	114n7
23:5	123n39
23:29	181, 181n7
27:5–6	326n13
27:7	121n25
30:23	102n25
31	55, 55n10
31–34	55n10
51:25	187n40
51:33	314n18

EZEKIEL

3:20	121n25
7:8	102n25
12:24	185n29
12:28	181
13:7	185n29
13:23	185n29
21:21–23	185n29
22:29	253n18
24:17	314n18
39:13	319n29
43:14	115n12
43:17	115n12
43:20	115n12

SCRIPTURE INDEX

44:30	56n13
45:9	121n25

DANIEL

2:21, 47	326n14
2:34	190
3:26	319n29
3:51	319n29
3:55	319n29
3:56	319n29
4:17	326n13
4:25	326n13
4:32	326n13
5:21	326n13
6:10	311n9
6:13	313n15
6:23	121n25
7:21–22	159n2
7:25–27	159n2
8:12	121n25
9:7	122n32
9:9	122n32
9:16	122n32
9:18	121n25
9:21	311n7
9:24	123n40
12:3b	195n80

HOSEA

1:10	241n13, 342n22
2:21	122n32, 122n33
2:23	55, 241n13, 294, 342n22
3:5	83n18
9:25–26	342
10:12	121n25
13:6	219n98

JOEL

1:19	194n73
1:20	194n73
2:11	182
2:23	122n32
2:28–29	114
2:32	55, 83n23, 114, 146, 191, 342n26
3:5	195

AMOS

3:7	181
5:7	121n25
5:24	121, 121n25
6:12	121n25
9:1	115n12
9:11	83n18
9:12	115n7

MICAH

1:2	102n25
2:1	195n78
2:14	114n7
3:11	185n29
4:17	114n7
5:7–8	114n7
5:12	185n29
5:15	102n25
6:5	122n32
6:8	252n16
6:14	219n98
7:9	122n32

HABAKKUK

2:3	71
2:4	53, 71, 126–127, 139, 184n23, 239, 342n27, 349n1

ZEPHANIAH

1:15	102n25
2:3	121n25
2:7	114n7
2:9	114n7
3:9	1146n30

ZECHARIAH

4:6	85
8:2	102n25
8:6	114n7
8:8	123n40
12:7	83n18
12:10–12	83n18
13:9	146n30
13:10	83n18

MALACHI

1:2–3	342n20, 342n25
1:11	319, 319n29
2:13	314n18
2:17	122n32
3:3	121n25
3:20	123n40

Scripture Index

MATTHEW

1:5	228n147
1:6	228n147
1:7	228n147
1:23	84
3:11	207n16
4:4	181
4:10	192
4:23	245
5:22	162n10
5:29	162n10
5:30	162n10
6:2	319
6:29	228n147
7:23	187n41
8:11	169n1
8:12	162n14
8:17	195n81
9:18	327n18
9:23	327n18
9:29	213n49
9:34	327n18
9:35	245
9:37–38	318
10:1–15	273n15
10:10	211n35
10:28	162n10
10:32	187, 187n41
11:5	253
11:8	328
11:23	162n12
11:26	317n24
11:28	257
12:1–12	337n3
12:3–4	228n147
12:18	253
12:18–21	195n81
12:20	253
12:24	327n19
12:38–39	244n25
12:39	245n36
12:39–41	228n147
12:41	322n46
12:42	228n147
13:36–40	263
14:7	187n41
15:19	273n15
15:28	213n49
16:1–4	244n25
16:4	228n147, 245n36
16:17	228n147
16:18	162n10
18:7	329n28
18:9	162n10
19:1–12	273n15
19:3–6	271n11
19:28	263
20:35	327n20
22:13	162n14
23:15	2n6, 162n10
23:23	253
23:27	272
23:33	162n10
23:35	196n84, 228n147
24:3	244n25
24:14	169n1, 214n58, 358
24:24	241, 244n25, 244n26, 244n27, 247n43
24:30	244n25
24:37–38	196n84, 228n147
25:30	162n14
25:31–46	263
25:32	169n1
25:35	286n48
25:38	286n48
25:41	106
25:43	286n48
25:44	286n48
26:45	257n33
26:48	244n25
27:27	286n48
28:18–20	169n1

MARK

1:1	47, 48n2
1:11	48n2, 195n81
1:14	186n34
1:24	132n66
3:13–19	209
6:7–13	209
9:11	48n2
10:1–2	273n15
10:5	271
10:6	270
10:8	270
10:9	270
10:45	195n81
12:13–17	331
12:31	154n12
12:33	154n12
13:1–2	333
13:4	244n25
13:8	159n2
13:10	169n1, 170n8, 199n89, 214n58, 241, 358
13:22	244n25n 244n26, 244n27
13:24–25	160n5
13:27	169n1

13:32	48n2	8:41	327n18
14:9	169n1	9:3–5	273n15
14:32–42	248	9:6	245n35
14:35	133	9:11	206n43
14:36	81, 134, 146	9:35	195n81
14:61	48n2	10:1	209
15:21	26, 217, 291	10:4–12	281n13
15:39	84, 48n2	10:10	211n35
16:7	244n25	10:15	162n12
16:20	244n25	10:16	196
		10:21	317n24
		10:25–29	154n13
		10:27	154n12

LUKE

		10:40	281, 313
1:5	228n147	11:5	327n20
1:13	317n25	11:7	274
1:53	219n98	11:16	244n25
2:1	11	11:29–30	244n25
2:12	244n25	11:29–32	228n147
2:14	317n24	11:31	228n147
2:20	319n30	11:32	322n46
2:34	244n25	11:41	228n147
2:37	317n25	11:51	196n84
2:38	199	12:5	162n10
2:29–32	195n81	12:8	187, 187n41
3:1	11	12:16	257n33
3:12	331n33	12:27	228n147
3:16	207n16	12:33	253
3:28	228n147	12:58	327
3:34–38	196n84	13:10–17	337n3
3:36	228n147	13:13	319n30
3:37	228n147	13:24	320n35
4:4	181	13:29	169n1
4:14	206n15	14:1	327n18
4:18–19	206n15	14:1–6	337n3
4:34	132n66	14:12–14	288
5:25	319n30	14:18	329n28
5:26	319n30	14:21	288
5:27–30	331n33	15:1	331n33
5:33	317n25	16:18	273n15
6:1–9	337n3	17:15	319n30
6:20–49	335	17:19	213n49
6:25	219n98	17:26–27	228n147
6:27	154	17:26–29	196n84
6:27–36	328	17:28–29	228n147
6:32–35	154	18:10–13	331n33
6:35	288	18:18	327n18
6:36	153n11	18:36	320n35
6:38	281n12	18:43	319n30
7:16	319n30	19:1–10	288n61
7:29	331n33	19:2	331n33
7:34	331n33	21:7	244n25
7:50	213n49	21:11	244n25
8:3	217	21:15	326n16
8:25	213n49	21:23	329n28
8:31	162n16, 185n28		

SCRIPTURE INDEX

(Luke continued)

21:24	169n1
22:20	195n81
22:32	213n49
22:44	320n35
22:45	315
23:2	331
23:8	244n25
23:13	327n18
23:35	327n18
23:47	319
24:10	217
24:20	327n18
24:46–49	169n1

JOHN

1:1	182
1:1–5	263
1:14	88n48, 263
1:18	88n48
1:20	187n41
1:21	186n33
1:25	186n33
1:29	169n1
1:46	180
2:18	244n25
2:11	244n25
2:18	244n25
2:23	244n25
3:1	327n18
3:2	244n25
3:11	154n12
3:14	195n81
3:16	88n48, 162n18
3:18	88n48
3:23	154n12
3:36	162n18, 320n36
4:7	154n12
4:11	154n12
4:12	154n12
4:42	169n1, 263
4:37–38	306
4:48	244n25, 244n26, 244n27, 245n36
4:54	244n25
5:1–18	337n3
5:18	192
5:22–30	162n18
5:23	190n61
6:2	244n25
6:12	219n98
6:14	186n33, 244n25
6:16	244n25
6:26	245n36
6:28	145n24
6:30	244n25
6:69	132n66
7:22–23	337n3
7:26	327n18
7:31	244n25
7:40	186n33
7:48	327n18
8:28	195n81
8:54	319n30
8:58	192
9:1–40	337n3
9:16	244n25
9:22	187n42
10:23	228n147
10:28	162n18
10:31	192
10:41	244n25
11:47	244n25
12:19	244n25
12:26	190n61
12:31	327n19
12:32	195n81
12:37	244n25
12:38	195
12:42	187n42, 327n18
12:48	162n18
14:6	89n52
14:30	327n19
16:6	315
16:11	327n19
16:21	159n2, 315
16:22	315
17:12	162n18
19:5	328
20:21	169n1
20:30	244n25

ACTS

1:8	169n1, 206n15
1:8—12:25	198
1:12–26	225
1:14	318
1:15	321n38
1:22	209
2:3	207n16
2:7	132n66
2:8–11	198n87
2:9–10	222
2:10	16, 176, 231, 296
2:11	17, 17n3, 176
2:17–21	146
2:19	244n25, 244n26, 244n27
2:20	160n7
2:22	244, 244n27, 246n42

444

Scripture Index

2:27	162n12, 162n18	7:34	313
2:31	162n12, 162n18	7:35	327n18
2:42	318, 318n27	7:36	244, 244n27, 246n42
2:43	244n27, 244n30, 245n35, 246n42	7:37	186n33
2:44–45	288n61	7:40	228n147
2:45	286n43	7:45	228n147
3	160n7, 245n35	7:55	206n15
3:1	311n7	8:1–3	198
3:1–10	246n42	8:1–4	213n54, 296
3:13	195n81	8:3	109n52
3:16	213n49	8:4	198n87, 223n117, 228n147
3:17	327n18	8:5–7	245n35, 246n42
3:21	160n7, 164	8:5–40	296n7
3:22–24	186n33	8:6	244
3:23	162n18	8:7	246
3:24	212, 228n147	8:17	225n123
3:26	195n81	8:26	176
4	318	8:26–40	234
4–5	223n117	8:29	206n15
4:2	212n44	8:30	206n15
4:5	327n18	8:32–33	195n81
4:8	206n15, 327n18	9:1–18	359n13
4:12	89n52	9:1–19	107n43
4:16	244n30	9:9	245
4:22	244n30	9:10–19	242
4:23–31	318	9:12	210n33, 225n123
4:26	327n20	9:14	146
4:27	195n81	9:15	344n37
4:29–30	318	9:17	210n33, 225n123
4:29—5:42	318	9:18	245
4:30	244, 244n27, 244n30, 195n81	9:26 30	198n88
4:31	206n15	9:28–29	33
4:32–37	288n61	9:30	32, 321n38
4:35	286n43	9:32–43	246n42
5:1–11	318	10—11	337
5:12–16	246, 318	10:1–48	234
5:15–16	246n42	10:6	287n49
5:12	244, 244n27, 244n30, 245n35, 246n42	10:9	311, 311n9
5:29	325	10:18	287n49
5:32	325	10:19	206n15
5:34	358	10:23	287n49, 321n38
6:1	281	10:24	216
6:1–6	225	10:31	206n15
6:4	318	10:32	287n49
6:5	17n3	10:38	206n15, 246n42
6:6	225n123	10:44	206n15
6:7	182, 213n49	10:45–46	337
6:8	244, 244n27, 245n35, 246n42	11:1	321n38
6:10	326n16	11:4	216n75
7	160n7	11:12	206n15
7:10	229n148	11:18	319
7:13	229n148	11:25–26	32
7:17	187n41	11:25–30	34
7:21	229n148	11:26	242
7:27	327n18	11:26–30	242n18, 339n10

445

Scripture Index

(Acts continued)		14:5	327n18, 327n20
11:27–30	38, 340n14	14:8–10	246n42
11:28	11, 206n15	14:10	245
11:28–30	209	14:12	245n34
11:29	282, 321n38	14:14	209, 211
12:17	321n38	14:17	219n98
12:22–23	333	14:20	245
12:25	282	14:22	213n49
13	50, 50n7, 160n7	14:23	225
13—14	18	15	18, 339
13:1	37, 176, 209, 218, 242n19	15:1	321n38, 337, 339
13:1–4	296n7	15:1–5	340
13:2	200n15, 242	15:1–29	36
13:3	210n33	15:3	222, 321n38
13:4	200n15, 242	15:5	3387
13:4–12	33	15:6–11	340
13:5	212n44	15:9	213n49
13:6	242n19	15:12	244, 244n27, 246n42
13:8	213n49, 326n16	15:6–11	340
13:9	206n15	15:19	340
13:9–11	242n19	15:19–20	341
13:9–12	245	15:19–35	340
13:13—14:25	34	15:20	274n22
13:16	50n7	15:22	18n7, 321n38
13:17	50n7	15:23	321n38
13:20	50n7, 13:20	15:27	18n7
13:21	50n7	15:28	206n15
13:22–23	50n7	15:28–29	341
13:26	50n7	15:29	273n15, 274n22
13:27	327n18	15:32	18n7, 242n19, 321n38
13:27–29	50n7	15:33	321n38
13:38	212n44	15:36	212n44, 321n38
13:30	50n7	15:40	18n7, 321n38
13:32	50n7	15:41	38
13:32–33	50n7	16	18n8
13:33	50n7	16:1–3	37
13:34	50n7	16:5	38, 213n49
13:35	50n7	16:6–7	206n15
13:36	50n7	16:6–8	243n176
13:37	50n7	16:6–10	223n117, 242n19
13:39	50n7	16:9	234n176
13:35	50n7	16:11—18:17	35
13:42	17n4	16:14	17n4
13:46	50n7	16:15	292n87
13:46–47	50n7	16:17	212n44
13:47	50n7, 195n81	16:18	245
13:48	319	16:19	327
13:50	17n4	16:21	212n44, 321n39
13:51	223n117	16:40—17:1	171
14	51 160n7	17	18n8, 51
14:1	210n31	17:2	211
14:2	320n36, 321n38	17:3	212n44
14:3	244, 245n34, 2466n42	17:4	17n4
14:4	209, 210n31, 211	17:3	212n44
14:3	244, 244n27, 245n34, 246n42	17:5–9	37, 49n4, 218, 291

Scripture Index

17:13	212n44	20:22–23	242n19
17:14	321n38	20:23	206n15
17:14–15	37n20	20:38	222
17:18	282n48	21:4	206n15, 242n19
17:20	287n49	21:5	222
17:21	282n48	21:7	321n38
17:23	212n44	21:9	242n19
17:31	160n7, 162n18	21:11	206n15, 242n19
18:1–2	14, 17	21:17	321
18:2	11, 16, 198n87, 213n54, 216, 257, 291n77	21:17—28:31	321
		21:20	321
18:2–3	291	21:25	274n22
18:3	26, 291, 292n87	22:5	321n38
18:5	37n20	24:17	38n28, 321
18:6	326	20:4	37, 49n4
18:7	37n18, 291n83	20:28–30	25
18:8	216n73	21—28	32
18:9	242n19	21:16	287n49
18:12–17	333n37	21:18	198
18:12–18	216n74	21:37–38	188
18:14	23, 336n2	21:39	358
18:17	17n4, 23	22	160n7
18:18	198n87, 291n77, 321n38	22—26	51
18:18–19	25	22:1	355n1
18:18–21	36	22:1–21	107n43
18:18–23	216	22:3	358
18:24—19:1	198n87, 216, 225	22:4	109n52
18:25	94	22:5	49n4
18:26	25, 216n73, 216n75, 291n77, 291n78	22:6–16	359n13
		22:21	344n37
18:27	321n38	23:5	327n18
19	38	23:8	187n41
19:1–10	223n117	23:11	296n9
19:1–20	234n176	23:14	316
19:1–41	36	24:7	23
19:6	210n33, 225n123	24:14	187n42
19:8–10	206n15	24:17	256n31
19:9	320n36	24:24	213n49
19:10	36n16, 182	24:25	162n18
19:10–120	246	25:10–12	11n12
19:11	245n34	25:16	355n1
19:11–12	246n42	25:34	313
19:21	206n15	26	160n7
19:22	37n20, 218n93	26:12–18	107n43, 359n13
19:24—20:1	216n74	26:17	344n37
19:29	49, 49n4, 291n83	26:20	344n37
20:1–3	23	26:23	212n44
20:1–6	18n8	26:29	315n21
20:3	37, 216n74	27—28	296, 296n9
20:3–6	321n39	27:21	325
20:4	37, 49n4, 198n87, 291n83	27:23–24	242n19
20:4–6	321	27:29	11n12
20:5	321n39	26:29	315n21
20:17	225	28:3–6	245
20:22	206n15	28:4	252

447

(Acts continued)

28:7	287n49
28:8	210n33, 225n123, 245, 246n42
28:9	245n34
28:15	321n38
28:15–31	41
28:21	14, 321n38
28:23	216n75, 287
28:29–31	344

ROMANS

1—3	19
1:1	22, 40, 50n7, 51n8, 59, 60–61, 61n12, 67–68, 73, 79, 90n57, 202, 205, 208, 226, 230, 232n166, 277, 295n6, 296
1:1–4	77
1:1–7	67n39, 138
1:1–15	66, 210, 224
1:1–17	51n8, 226
1:1–18	75
1:1–8:28	299
1:1–2	179
1:2	53, 60, 63n31, 70, 73, 110, 131, 202, 210, 229n149, 238
1:2–4	80, 85, 88, 348
1:4	88, 203n7, 332
1:3	50n7, 55, 59, 73, 100, 202, 204, 239, 295, 342
1:3–4	179, 204
1:3–5	73, 295
1:4	50n7, 59, 61, 63, 65, 73, 79, 83, 85, 91, 93, 142, 163n23, 202, 204, 206, 210, 242, 242n21
1:4–5	38
1:5	61, 65, 67, 75–76, 80, 124, 138, 144n22, 145, 169, 169n3, 170n7, 179, 195, 205, 211, 225, 226n128, 230, 286, 295n4, 298, 308, 323, 340
1:5–6	73, 232n166
1:6	40, 88, 205
1:6–7	295n6
1:7	19, 24, 26, 60–61, 63, 78n4, 79, 81, 85n29, 88, 113n3, 131n64, 132n65, 203, 203n6, 286, 296, 308–309, 321
1:7–10	307–308
1:8	51n8, 61, 65, 69, 77, 79n5, 79n6, 90, 101, 212, 124, 142, 169, 217, 223, 226, 310, 312
1:8–9	61n12
1:8–10	204, 257, 299
1:8–12	64
1:8–13	26
1:8–15	234
1:9	50n7, 51n8, 60, 66, 73, 88, 91n59, 179, 203–205, 207n16, 210, 226, 226n127, 226n129, 298, 344
1:9–10	310, 353n10
1:9–13	296
1:10	60, 63n31, 79, 226, 234n177, 321
1:10–12	210
1:10–15	77
1:11	18n7, 38, 61n10, 62, 75, 283, 321–322
1:11a	40
1:11b	40
1:11–12	70
1:11–15	39, 311
1:12	40, 75, 142, 190, 210, 219
1:13	40, 50, 50n7, 61, 63n31, 65–66, 179, 226, 256, 276n28, 299, 340, 344n37
1:13–14	226n128
1:13–15	40, 75, 210
1:14	61, 170, 176, 179, 190, 226, 226n127, 331, 343
1:14–15	38, 232n166, 298
1:15	24, 26, 40, 51n8, 65–66, 179, 210, 226, 234
1:15–16	50n7, 61n12
1:16a	180n5
1:16	vi, 19, 50n7, 51n8, 65, 70n50, 79, 128, 137, 139, 170, 170n7, 179, 180, 180n5, 183, 184, 190, 196, 202, 231–232, 244n32, 245, 266, 300, 300n17, 306, 340
1:16–17	41, 53, 60, 70, 73, 77, 120–121, 123, 128, 138, 139, 348
1:16–18	64
1:16—4:25	28
1:17	53, 72–73, 79n8, 107, 120, 120n21, 123–124, 126–127, 127n46, 128n50, 139–140, 184n23, 202, 239n8, 249, 342n27, 349
1:18	60, 63, 73, 79n6, 97, 102, 116n15, 128n50, 162, 170n6, 170n7, 191n65, 202, 250, 348
1:18–20	356n4
1:18–23	103, 272
1:18–32	73, 79n7, 100, 149, 250n3, 261, 264
1:18—2:1	250
1:18—3:20	73, 96, 116, 124, 128n50, 149, 152, 164, 170, 230, 250, 260, 299
1:18—11:36	29n3, 148n1
1:19	356
1:19–20	79, 101, 199, 201, 238, 261
1:19–25	73, 261, 294, 299
1:20	54, 101, 164n27, 198

448

Scripture Index

1:21	79n5, 79n6, 79n7, 190n61, 310, 319	2:10	137, 170n7, 190, 310, 340
1:21–22	204n10	2:11	67, 71, 80, 80n12, 101, 203, 250, 310, 340, 352
1:21–24	97	2:11–12	103
1:21–25	144, 262, 267, 332	2:12	97n13, 102, 104, 108, 170n6
1:22–24	54	2:12–13	160
1:23	61, 63, 79, 101, 134, 163, 164n27, 260, 282n19	2:12–15	108
1:23–25	101	2:12–16	73, 109, 299, 348
1:24	79n10, 97, 102, 116, 202, 261	2:13	79n11, 108, 127–128, 128n50, 130n56, 203
1:24–27	272, 344n35	2:14	356
1:25	60n8, 63n31, 66, 79, 79n6, 79n7, 101, 204n10, 237, 260, 272, 312	2:14–15	108, 160
1:26	79n10, 102, 202, 275	2:14–16	12
1:26–27	73, 158, 272, 299	2:15	61n11, 108, 160n8
1:26–29	261	2:16	45, 51, 54, 61n12, 63n31, 88, 142, 160–161, 203n8, 206, 271n19, 337n7
1:27	102	2:17	80, 109, 250
1:28	12, 61n11, 79n10, 97, 102, 202	2:17–18	67
1:28–31	261	2:17–24	64, 73
1:28–32	79n6, 299	2:17–29	109, 299, 338
1:29	66, 97, 128n50, 250, 262n10	2:18	109
1:29–31	64, 97, 250	2:19	2n6, 61n10, 62
1:30	61, 144, 204n10, 276, 332	2:19–20	64
1:31	66, 97, 133n71	2:20	61n11, 109
1:32	65, 79, 128n50, 182n13, 250	2:21	51n8, 63n32
2:1	66, 170n7, 250	2:21–22	61n12
2:1–2	98	2:12–24	356n5
2:1–3	105	2:22	250, 270, 276
2:1–5	64, 73, 338	2:23	97, 109
2:1–11	54, 149, 299	2:23–24	79, 332
2:1–17	67	2:24	54, 97, 158, 239, 239n8, 342n23
2:1–25	261	2:25	60, 109, 145
2:1–29	149, 261	2:25–29	54, 73, 184, 184n24, 348–349
2:1—3:8	250n4	2:26	63n33, 66, 128n50, 356
2:2	64, 79n11, 103, 203, 203n8	2:26–27	109
2:2–3	250	2:28	100
2:3	79n9, 160, 162, 203n6, 203n8, 332	2:29	54, 54n9, 79, 91, 206
2:3–14	108, 356n5	3:1	54
2:4	54, 62n23, 63, 79–80, 113, 143, 250	3:1–2	73, 340
2:5	60, 62n25, 63, 63n31, 79n9, 79n11, 98, 103, 116n15, 128n50, 160, 162, 191n65	3:1–4	299
2:5–11	103, 172, 203n8, 241	3:1–5	58
2:5–16	332, 348	3:1–9	64, 356n5
2:6	98, 108, 149, 153, 161, 281, 250, 342n19	3:2	53, 60, 62, 73, 103, 142, 202, 294, 299n14, 348
2:6–10	230	3:3	138n1, 142, 203n6, 299n14
2:6–11	64, 73	3:3–4	79
2:7	62n26, 134, 134n75, 164n24, 190, 203, 327	3:3–8	73
2:7–11	250	3:4	54, 127, 128n50, 129, 161, 170n7, 239, 239n8, 342n19
2:8	97n14, 103, 116n15, 128n50, 145, 160, 162, 320n36	3:5	64–65, 79n10, 97n14, 103, 116n15, 123, 125–126, 128n50, 161–162, 250
2:8–9	103	3:5–6	203
2:9	62, 62n28, 97n15, 170n7, 190, 340	3:6	54, 60, 79n10, 79n11, 161
2:9–10	50n7		

449

Scripture Index

(Romans continued)

3:7	60, 80, 97n12
3:8	99, 128n50, 161, 163
3:9	61, 65, 96, 96n11, 98, 108–109, 124, 127, 149, 170n6, 170n7, 190, 348
3:9–20	73
3:10	46n1, 103, 128, 250
3:10–18	54, 56, 64, 96, 240n11, 250–251
3:10–20	299
3:11–18	184n23
3:11	61n12, 79n7, 203n9, 332
3:12	170n7
3:13a	342n19
3:13b	342n19
3:13	61, 61n10, 260
3:13–14	60n9, 250n6
3:14	342n30
3:15	61, 250
3:15–17	342n19
3:16–17, 62	
3:17	309
3:18	50n7, 79n7, 203n9, 327, 342n19
3:19	60n9, 61n12, 79, 101, 108, 128n50, 170n6, 170n7, 172, 203, 332
3:19–20	108, 127, 149, 348
3:19–31	110
3:20	61n10, 61n11, 96n11, 98, 100, 109, 127, 128n50, 130n56, 161, 170n7, 203n9, 337n7, 342n19
3:21	12, 50, 53–54, 65, 79n8, 110, 124–125, 202, 229n149, 238–239
3:21–24	155, 161, 348
3:21–25	203
3:21–26	64, 140
3:21–30	50n7
3:21–31	73, 251, 299
3:21—4:25	73, 129n50
3:22	43, 79n8, 89, 118, 140–141, 128n50, 170n7, 202, 204, 332, 337
3:22–23	340
3:22–24	231
3:22–26	110
3:23	47n1, 73, 96, 97n13, 103, 108–109, 127, 137, 149, 170n6, 170n7, 172, 203n9, 243, 294, 299, 348
3:24	60, 62n26, 89, 113n1, 117, 127, 128n50, 129–130, 202, 204, 308
3:24–25	115, 142
3:24–26	79
3:25a	149n7
3:25	54, 60, 63, 97, 99n21, 113, 115n11, 128n50, 140, 202, 204, 213n50, 251
3:25b–26a	65
3:25–26	80, 124, 125–126
3:25–31	118
3:26	63, 80, 127–128, 128n50, 140n8, 141, 143, 202, 204, 251
3:27	110, 140
3:27–31	356n5
3:27—4:25	64
3:28	50n7, 99n21, 110, 127, 128n50, 140, 140n8, 161, 300, 337n7
3:29	79, 80, 190, 203, 340
3:29–30	170, 348
3:29—4:25	169n3
3:30	54n7, 78, 99n21, 127, 128n50, 140n8, 161, 203, 213n50
3:30b–c	63
3:31	64, 110, 140n8, 213n50, 240
4:1	61, 61n12, 100
4:1–2a	64
4:1–6	203
4:1–16	50n7
4:1–22	300
4:1–25	59, 74, 127
4:2	64–65, 80, 110, 128n50, 129n55
4:3	61n12, 80m, 108, 124n44, 128n50, 184n23, 196, 251, 293, 342n21, 349
4:3–4	81
4:3–6	63n33
4:4	62, 62n26, 66, 110, 239, 308
4:5	54n6, 110, 124n44, 127, 128n50, 140, 213n50
4:6	60n8, 61n12, 80, 124, 110, 128n50, 202, 229n149
4:6–8	50n7, 342, 349
4:7	66, 96n11, 97, 116
4:7–8	50n7, 54, 136, 239
4:7–9	191
4:8	65, 78, 83n23, 96n11
4:8–9	60n8
4:8–11	63n33
4:9	65, 124n44, 128n50, 213n50
4:9–10	356n5
4:9–11	108
4:9–12	54n7, 61n12, 196, 342, 349
4:10–12	54n6
4:10–16	203
4:10–20	241
4:11	62, 124n44, 128n50, 172n19, 213n50, 244n31, 275n27, 351n3
4:11–12	172n20
4:11–13	141
4:12	61, 275n27
4:13	54n6, 101, 110, 124n44, 128n50, 164, 172, 349
4:13–14	61
4:13–17a	66
4:13–18	61
4:13–20	50n7, 62n27

Scripture Index

4:14	60, 111, 141, 213n50, 351n3	5:12–21	67, 74, 87, 137, 238n5, 349
4:15	97, 103, 110, 141, 161	5:13	63, 96n11, 110
4:16	110, 113, 141, 143, 275n27, 308, 351n3	5:13–14	136
4:16–17	349	5:13–21	260
4:17	54n6, 79–80, 101, 141, 163, 164n27, 201, 203, 238–240, 242, 275, 342n21	5:14	63, 97, 97n13, 229n148, 229n149, 238, 342n18, 342n21
4:18	54n6, 275	5:14–15	54
4:18–22	203	5:15	60, 87, 89–90, 97n16, 113n1, 202, 205, 308
4:19	63n31, 213n50	5:15–17	62n26
4:20	65, 79n6, 80, 141, 204, 213n50, 240, 319	5:15–18	54
4:22	124n44, 129n50	5:15–19	238
4:22–23	63n33	5:15–20	87
4:22–24	54n6	5:16	75n58, 97n13, 97n16, 99, 104, 129n50, 163, 195n81, 240
4:23	239	5:16–21	240
4:24	50n7, 88, 163n23, 203–204, 231, 242n21	5:17	59n1, 62n24, 89, 124, 97n16, 113n1, 129n50, 134, 308
4:25	97, 129n50, 136, 161, 195n80, 202, 229, 242n21	5:18	97n16, 104, 129n50, 134n76, 161, 163, 164n24, 170n7, 243n22
5:1	50n7, 59, 89, 91n21, 126–127, 129n50, 129n55, 130, 131n62, 140n8, 160, 202, 300, 309, 337	5:18–19	149n7
5:1–2	12, 47n1, 204	5:19	65, 97n12, 128, 144
5:1–5	248	5:20	96n11, 110, 113n1, 308
5:1–10	60	5:21	50n7, 54, 59n1, 62n24, 85, 85n29, 89, 96n7, 96n11, 98, 104, 124, 113n1, 129n50, 134n75, 164n24, 205, 243, 243n22, 308
5:1–11	279, 74		
5:1–21	141	6:1	61n12, 64, 96n11, 99, 113n1, 150, 308
5:1—8:39	28, 74	6:1–2	99
5:2	113n1, 137, 202, 308	6:1–3	143
5:3	62n28, 191, 262n10	6:1–4	27n35, 74, 116
5:3–4	92	6:1–23	300
5:3–5	67, 92, 191n68	6:1—8:18	150–152
5:5	54n9, 63, 80, 86, 92, 113n3, 126, 131n64, 151, 153, 190–191, 206, 231, 266, 295, 320	6:2	96n7, 96n11
		6:3	89, 115n11, 150
5:6	50n7, 63, 89–90, 115n11, 116, 204, 295, 313, 316, 323	6:4	137
		6:3–4	126
5:6–7	229	6:3–6	205
5:6–8	67	6:4	50n7, 60, 62n21, 62n24, 78n4, 81, 89, 99, 104, 134n76, 150, 202, 231, 242n21, 243n22
5:7	128, 129n50		
5:8	47n1, 80, 89–90, 97n12, 113n3, 116, 203–204, 241, 285, 316	6:5	104, 243
5:8–9	142	6:5–6	115n11
5:8–10	115n11	6:6	50n7, 67, 116, 125, 205, 277
5:9	63, 103, 114, 115, 116, 127, 129n50, 129n55, 161–162, 191n65, 202, 204	6:6–8	150
		6:6–10	99
5:9–10	114, 204	6:7	96n11, 127, 129n50, 136
5:9–11	67	6:8	66, 89, 116, 142, 205
5:10	59, 62, 62n24, 88–89, 115, 116, 131, 134, 231	6:8–10	115n11
		6:9	50n7, 89, 163n23, 204, 243
5:10–11	130	6:10	96n11, 231
5:11	79n6, 89–90, 131, 202, 204–205	6:10–11	332
5:12	50n7, 54, 61, 87, 95–96, 96n11, 97n13, 104, 136, 164, 170, 170n7, 172, 230, 240, 244, 261, 263, 294	6:10–12	203
		6:11	61n11, 80, 89, 96n11, 118, 205
5:12–13	101	6:11–14	150
5:12–14	96, 300	6:11–18	116

451

Scripture Index

(Romans continued)

6:11–23	99
6:12	59n1, 96n11, 134, 145, 163, 252, 300
6:12–13	80
6:12–15	27n35
6:13	60, 96n11, 125, 129n50, 254n24, 300, 332
6:13–14	252
6:14	96n11, 111, 113n1, 150
6:15	20, 64, 97n13, 99, 111n55, 113n1, 150–151, 308
6:15–23	74
6:16	96n11, 129, 129n50, 144n22, 145, 254n24, 300
6:16–17	252
6:16–19	151
6:16–22	277
6:17	63n32, 65, 66, 79, 96n11, 145, 204, 300, 308, 312, 332
6:18	96n11, 125, 129, 129n50, 135n78, 136, 252n24
6:18–20	252n13
6:18–22	66
6:19	60, 97, 100, 116, 125, 129n50, 135, 252, 300
6:19–20	132
6:20	96n11, 129n50, 135n78, 252
6:21	98, 104, 137, 163m19
6:21–22	61
6:22	80, 96n11, 132n75, 135, 135n78, 136, 160, 203, 252n24
6:22–23	50n7, 132, 164n24
6:23	47n1, 62, 62n24, 62n26, 80, 85, 89, 96n11, 118, 132n75, 134, 163n19, 191, 203, 205, 241, 243
7:1	63n31, 64, 133n71, 276n28
7:1–3	54, 151, 273
7:1–4	29n6, 60, 102, 111
7:1–5	344n35
7:1–6	50n7, 74
7:1—8:4	349
7:2	270
7:2–3	61
7:3	135, 135n78, 270
7:4	80, 89, 116, 118, 133n71, 151, 163n23, 203, 205, 242n21, 276n28, 332
7:4–5	61, 151
7:5	50n7, 67, 96n11, 97, 100, 104, 110, 153, 163n19
7:6	54n9, 92, 111, 111n55, 116, 126, 151, 206, 253, 277, 300, 332
7:6–11	152
7:7	61n12, 64, 96n11, 98, 110, 356n5
7:7–9	110
7:7–12	67
7:7–25	74
7:7—8:10	253
7:8	54, 96n11
7:8–10	64
7:8–11	98
7:9	96n11
7:10	62n24, 134
7:11	96n11
7:12	67, 92, 95n1, 98, 107, 110, 128, 129n50, 131, 152
7:12–13	104, 150
7:13	64, 96n11, 97n12, 98, 152, 356n5
7:13–23	152
7:14	96n11, 98
7:14–25	111
7:15–16	67
7:16	98
7:17	96n11
7:18	65, 98, 262, 262n10
7:19	97n15
7:20	96n11
7:20–24	12
7:22	79
7:23	60, 61n10, 96n11
7:24	62, 64, 135, 152
7:25	79, 85, 90, 96n11, 98, 152, 204–205, 277, 308, 312
7:25—8:4	308
8:1	47n1, 60, 89–90, 104, 118, 126, 134n76, 161, 163, 314
8:1–2	134, 205
8:1–3	153
8:1–4	111
8:1–11	74
8:1–17	54n9, 92, 126
8:2	62n24, 90, 92, 96n11, 99, 104, 110, 118, 135, 135n78, 163n19, 206
8:2b	65
8:3	62n20, 81, 88, 96n11, 99, 100, 104, 142, 202, 204, 231
8:3b	149n7
8:3–4	117
8:4	62n21, 65, 92, 99, 129n50, 295, 300
8:4–8	153, 262
8:4–13	100, 206
8:4–14	332
8:4–16	114n55, 153
8:4–17	111
8:5	92, 100, 254n24
8:5–7	61n11
8:5–14	99
8:6	62n24, 92, 104, 131n62, 134, 134n76, 163n19, 254n24, 309
8:6–8	100

8:7	81, 325
8:7–9	203n9
8:8	81
8:9	78, 80, 90–91, 93, 100, 203, 295
8:9–10	205
8:9–11	153
8:10	66, 90, 91n59, 92, 96n11, 124n45, 129n50, 134
8:11	62n26, 88, 90, 93, 134, 137, 163, 202–204, 207, 242n21, 243
8:12	60, 133n71, 276n28, 331
8:12–13	100, 153
8:12–17	74, 349
8:13	66, 92, 100, 104, 137, 300
8:13–14	153, 206
8:14	80–81, 81n13, 92, 203, 254n24, 275, 300, 332
8:15	60–61, 63, 78n4, 81, 91, 134, 137, 146, 193, 204, 206, 231, 327
8:15–16	153
8:15–17	275
8:16	61, 81n13, 93, 202, 206
8:17	61, 81, 90, 93, 202, 205, 248
8:17–18	191
8:17–23	92, 301, 332
8:17–25	153
8:18	61n11, 63n31, 93, 137
8:18–24	264
8:18–25	149n6
8:18–40	74
8:19	81, 81n13, 202, 276
8:19–21	204
8:19–22	83, 102, 125, 164, 203, 231, 240–241, 261, 264, 356
8:19–23	61, 67, 90, 101, 131, 137, 159, 164–165, 237–238, 262–263, 278, 358
8:20	294, 325
8:21	61, 81, 135, 137, 202, 263, 276
8:22	61, 63n31, 104n31, 170n7
8:23	61, 61n14, 93, 130, 134, 207, 276
8:24	61n10, 114–115
8:24–25	301
8:26	81n13, 313
8:26–27	60, 93, 206, 248, 301, 312, 314
8:27	60, 60n3, 61n11, 63, 81, 132n65
8:27–28	202
8:28	81, 113, 170n7, 296–297, 325, 333
8:28–30	294, 295n6, 301
8:28–36	81
8:29	61, 63, 87–88, 99, 117, 132, 133n71, 137, 145, 153, 156, 202, 205, 232, 237, 240, 260, 275, 294, 298, 300
8:29–30	238, 295, 297
8:30	127, 129n50, 129n55, 161, 192, 230, 297, 319n31
8:31	61n12, 80–81, 203
8:31–32	65
8:31–35	356n5
8:31–39	297, 301
8:32	62, 88, 164, 202, 204–205, 295, 315
8:33	50n7, 63n35, 81n14, 127, 129n50, 202, 295n6
8:34	61, 63, 63n31, 81, 90, 155n11, 142, 161, 163n23, 164, 205, 231, 242n21, 310, 313–314, 332
8:34–39	104
8:35	60, 62, 62n28, 90, 113, 328
8:35–39	203, 205, 262
8:36	54, 61, 62n25, 240, 260
8:37	60, 80, 113, 203, 203n6, 315
8:38	59n1, 60, 62n24, 63n31, 66, 106
8:38–39	67, 262
8:39	61–63, 80, 90, 113, 118, 162, 164n27
9	349–350
9:1	66, 91, 118, 131n64
9:1–2	301
9:1–3	315, 353n10
9:1–5	74, 340, 349
9:1–22	210
9:1–29	301
9:1—11:36	28, 74
9:2	62n28, 317
9:2–3	211
9:3	60, 60n9, 61, 83, 90, 100n23, 133n71, 216
9:4	54, 60, 62n27, 67, 82n17, 110, 133, 137
9:4–5	50n7, 55, 294, 348
9:5	60n9, 63n31, 79n6, 82n17, 83, 87, 90–91, 100, 142, 170n7, 204, 280n6, 294, 312, 340, 342, 342n21
9:6a	74
9:6	50n7, 51n8, 61n12, 81, 182, 202, 294
9:6b	74
9:6–7	240, 349
9:6–12	349
9:6–20	54
9:6–24	240
9:6–29	64
9:6–33	74
9:7	50n7, 74, 229n151, 271, 275n27, 342, 342n21
9:7–8	61
9:7–12	55
9:7–13	59
9:8	50n7, 63n31, 81, 294, 351n3
9:8–10	275
9:8–23	74

Scripture Index

(Romans continued)

9:9	55n11, 61n12, 63n31, 229n151, 342, 342n21
9:9–10	276, 343
9:10	61, 271, 274, 342
9:10–11	203n2
9:20–13	294
9:11	50n7, 63n31, 81, 203, 294, 295n6
9:11–13	294
9:12	55n11, 342n21
9:13	62, 113n3, 229n148, 229n151, 239n8, 240, 342, 342n25
9:14	61n12, 64, 79, 97n14, 129n50, 294
9:14–24	350, 356n5
9:15	55n12, 61n12, 113n2, 229n149, 284n30, 342n21
9:15–16	294
9:15–18	80, 203n6
9:16	113n2, 284, 333
9:17	50n7, 51n8, 61, 61n12, 170, 229n148, 333, 342n21
9:18	55n12, 294
9:19	61n12, 202
9:19–14	298
9:19–21	64
9:19–23	294, 294
9:19	326
9:20	55, 61n12, 66, 101, 204, 342n22
9:20–23	63, 101, 164n27, 238, 260
9:21	61
9:21–22	101
9:21–23	63
9:22	103–104, 113, 161, 163, 191n65, 202, 241
9:22–23	64
9:23	62n23, 80, 113n2, 137, 204
9:23–24	101
9:24	65, 190n62, 203, 296, 340
9:24–26	74, 295n6
9:24–29	64
9:25	61n12, 113n3, 202, 229n149, 241n13, 342n22
9:25–26	342
9:25–28	184n24
9:25–29	55–56, 350
9:26	61n12, 202, 275, 294, 342n22
9:27	60–61, 71, 114–115, 229n149, 342n22
9:27–28	83n23, 342n22
9:27–29	74
9:28	78n3, 203n6, 333
9:29	61, 83n23, 203, 229n149, 342n22
9:30	61n12, 65, 99n21, 124n45, 129n50, 140, 198n86, 286
9:30–32	74, 82, 126, 356n5
9:30–33	50n7, 74, 301–302, 350
9:31	65, 109, 124n45, 129n50, 286
9:32	62n22, 65, 109, 140
9:32–33	61, 85, 140n9
9:33	55, 61n17, 62, 83, 137, 189, 239n8, 240, 342n22, 349
10	55, 114, 193, 198, 350
10:1	60n3, 79n5, 79n6, 114, 133n71, 204, 211, 301, 315–317, 320n36, 351n10
10:1–7	74
10:2–3	61n11
10:2	81, 203, 351n3
10:3	79n8, 124n45, 129n50, 325
10:3–6	126
10:4	12, 90, 112, 124n45, 129n50, 140, 205, 295
10:5	50n7, 67, 124n45, 129n50, 183, 229n149, 342n21
10:5–7	183
10:5–13	66, 350
10:5–17	183
10:6	61n12, 124n45, 129n50, 184
10:6–8	342n21
10:6–10	189n52
10:6–17	306
10:7	60, 162
10:8	51n8, 55, 61n12, 187, 213n50, 356n5
10:8–13	74
10:9	50n7, 80, 90, 115, 141–143, 163n23, 187n38, 202, 206, 243, 332
10:9–10	47n1, 60n9, 64, 66, 114, 144, 193, 300
10:9–11	140
10:9–13	204, 301
10:9–14	197
10:9–17	147
10:10	124n45, 126, 129n50, 332
10:11	55, 60n9, 61n12, 86, 137, 342n23, 349
10:12	62n23, 170n7
10:12–13	169n3
10:12–14	146
10:12–18	231n164
10:13	47n1, 55, 83n23, 114, 115n10, 170n7, 193, 204, 204n10, 205, 206, 342n26
10:13–14	297
10:14	51n8, 59, 276
10:14–15a	191
10:14–15	67
10:14–17	61n12, 70, 89, 89n51, 90, 138, 172, 205, 231, 266, 300, 306
10:14–18	60
10:14–19	356n5
10:14–21	74, 302, 340, 350, 352
10:15	51n8, 61, 62n20, 230n8, 240, 342n23

Scripture Index

10:16	51n8, 68, 78n3, 83n23, 145, 229n149, 342n23	11:20	140–141, 213n50, 302
10:17	51n8, 99, 141, 213n50	11:21	62, 63, 80, 121n29, 203, 302
10:17–21	64, 82	11:21–22	315
10:18	51n8, 55, 61, 170, 170n7, 184–185, 198	11:21–24	141
		11:22	63, 80, 113, 202, 203n6
10:18–21	50n7, 55–56, 184	11:22a	67
10:19	55, 199, 229n149, 342n21	11:22b–d	67
10:19–21	61n12	11:23	80, 141, 203, 302, 351n3
10:20	55, 229n149	11:23–24	184
10:21	55, 62n25, 63, 63n31	11:24	67
11	19, 350–353	11:25	61n10, 61n18, 63n31, 133n71, 171, 175, 193, 214n58, 241, 276n28, 346
11:1	50n7, 55, 59, 63–64, 199, 353	11:25–26	115n11
11:1–2	79	11:25–36	74
11:1–6	74, 203	11:26	55, 61n17, 67, 82, 97, 115, 115n10, 135, 142, 203, 229n151, 353
11:1–7	356n5	11:26–27a	342n23
11:2	60, 61n12, 63, 229n149, 297, 313, 317, 342	11:26–27	50n7, 56, 83, 87, 116, 116n17, 136, 240, 351, 353
11:3	56, 78n3, 229n149, 342n30	11:27	59, 96n11, 130
11:3–6	241	11:27	342n23 23
11:4	56, 342n30	11:28	50n7, 51n8, 61, 61n12, 62, 63n35, 64, 66, 113n3
11:5	63n31, 63n35, 71, 113n1, 121n29, 295n4, 342	11:28–31	351
11:5–6	309	11:29	81, 203, 203n7
11:6	111, 113n1, 121n29, 198, 302	11:30	79, 113n2, 121n29, 145, 203n6
11:7	50n7, 61n11, 63n35, 65, 295n4, 351	11:30–31	65, 320
11:7–10	50n7, 74, 184n34	11:30–32	50n7, 80, 284n30, 351
11:8	60, 61n10, 63n31, 69n25, 91, 202, 238n8, 240, 302, 342n21, 342n23	11:31	65, 145
		11:32	79, 113n2, 145, 170n7, 171
11:9	61, 61n12, 62–63, 69n22, 229n149, 342	11:33	69n23, 79, 103, 203n6
		11:33–34	61n11
11:9–10	56, 342n19	11:33–36	309, 312
11:10	61, 61n10	11:34	78n3, 83n23, 342n23
11:11	50n7, 64, 69n22, 97n16, 114, 199, 340, 356n5	11:35	62, 342n28
		11:36	63n31, 67, 101, 137, 170n7, 201, 202
11:11–13	344n37	12	277, 335
11:11–24	74	12—13	18, 49, 335, 343
11:11–27	351	12—15	125, 150, 155–156, 253–256
11:12	67, 69n23, 97n16, 101, 171, 175, 193, 214n58, 241, 340, 352	12:1	60, 63–64, 79–80, 90, 117, 131–132, 133n2, 133n71, 148n1, 153, 155–156, 202, 202n6, 253, 276n28, 284n30, 303, 320n34
11:13a–b	65		
11:13	171, 210n31, 226n128, 232n168, 236n128, 276n28, 295n4, 319n31	12:1–2	204, 332
11:13–14	66	12:1—15:3	28
11:15	131, 172	12:1—15:7	302
11:14	100n23, 101, 114, 199	12:1–15:13	74, 155–158
11:15	131, 134n76, 164n24, 171–172, 173n24, 243n22, 352	12:1–2	12, 75, 137, 155
		12:1—15:7	66, 302
11:16	61, 62, 132n65	12:1—15:13	129n50, 253
11:16–24	62, 342	12:2	63, 63n31, 67, 81, 101, 156, 172, 254n24, 302n19
11:17–24	64, 338		
11:18	302	12:2–3	61n11
11:18–19	61n12	12:3	61n12, 65–66, 105, 141, 207, 277, 303n22, 309
11:19	64		
11:19–23	353		

455

Scripture Index

(Romans continued)

12:3–6	80–81
12:3–8	75, 156, 202n7, 253, 284n32
12:4–5	249n2
12:4–8	232, 246, 276, 342
12:5	91, 118, 204
12:5–8	118
12:6	207, 213n50, 242, 299n15, 309
12:6–8	207, 254n24
12:6–19	286n46
12:7	63n32, 282, 328n23
12:8	80, 253, 283, 320n34
12:9	84n23, 156, 253–254, 280n8, 285, 303n21
12:9–21	75, 251
12:10	65, 137, 156, 254, 303n21
12:11	63, 67, 91n60, 94, 156, 204, 207, 232, 277, 303n21, 332
12:12	62n28, 156, 303n21, 317, 331
12:13	60n9, 61n16, 132n65, 156, 254, 256, 258, 276, 280n8, 289n65, 303n21, 333, 343
12:13–14	232
12:13–21	232, 234, 352
12:14	156, 202, 254, 285, 302n19, 327, 343
12:15	156, 254, 303n22
12:16	65, 156, 254, 277, 288, 302n19, 303n21
12:16–17	61n10
12:17	62, 97n15, 254, 258, 303n21
12:17–18	254
12:17–21	156
12:18	131, 170n7, 258, 303n21
12:18–20	62
12:19	56, 60, 61n12, 62, 78n3, 80n23, 103, 113n3, 129n50, 202, 239n8, 241, 254, 258, 274, 302n19, 303n21, 328n23, 329, 333, 342n21
12:19–20	343
12:19–21	232
12:20	56, 61–63, 62n19, 254, 258, 287, 302n19, 342n29, 343
12:21	97n15, 254, 303n19
13	156–157, 329
13:1	303n19, 324–325
13:1–2	82
13:1–4	254
13:1–6	81, 202, 241, 258
13:1–7	12, 60, 75, 102, 156, 188, 255, 176, 324, 324n2, 324n4, 332
13:1–10	232
13:2	105, 246, 326
13:3	59n1, 303n19, 327
13:4	60, 97n15, 103, 129, 269n2, 281n13, 303n19, 328
13:5	241, 303n22, 329
13:6	330
13:6–7	15
13:7	137, 254, 303n19, 331
13:8	92
13:8–10	56, 107n45, 111n55, 112, 114, 154, 156, 232, 234, 241, 254n24, 255, 280n8, 288, 327, 335, 343
13:8–14	75, 303n19, 335
13:9a	342n21
13:9	61, 61n12, 270
13:9b	342n21
13:9–10	61n16
13:9–14	255
13:10	65, 97n15
13:11	63n31, 114, 142
13:11–14	156
13:12	60, 62, 63n31, 64, 97, 103, 160, 241, 303n20
13:12–13	100
13:12–14	254n24
13:13	62n21, 61n25, 63n31, 65, 118, 274, 303n20, 347n35
13:14	85n29, 100, 102, 145, 155, 156, 205, 232, 262, 303n19, 341n16
14	18n9, 24, 49
14—15	19, 24, 26, 30
14:1	30, 65, 142, 213n50, 289, 303n19, 341
14:1–4	255
14:1—15:7	56, 75
14:1—15:12	251
14:1—15:13	30n8, 256n30
14:1—15:13	30n8, 289
14:2	30, 62n19
14:3	65, 79, 203, 289, 303n19, 341
14:3–5	18n9, 105
14:3–12	30
14:4	60–61, 64, 341, 356n5
14:5	61n11, 63n31, 303n19
14:5–6	60, 341
14:5–12	255
14:6	63n31, 79, 137, 204, 311n8, 312, 341
14:7	129n50, 131n64
14:8	205
14:9	89, 115n11, 117, 204
14:10	18n9, 60, 63, 79, 133n71, 161, 276n29, 356n5
14:10–12	172, 203, 341
14:10–13	104–105
14:10–13	172
14:10–14	303
14:11	61n12, 64, 78n3, 79n6, 83n23, 89, 144, 161, 170, 170n7, 239n8, 240, 342n23
14:11–16	341

Scripture Index

14:12	79, 161	15:12	50n7, 55, 57, 59, 59n1, 61n12, 62, 83, 229n148, 239, 342n23
14:13	18n9, 62n19, 64, 67, 105, 133n71, 254–255, 276n29, 303n19, 303n20, 303n22	15:13	80, 93, 131n62, 131n64, 206, 309, 341
14:13–16	255	15:14a	64
14:13—15:3	30	15:14	61n11, 65, 75, 133n71, 246n28
14:14	61n11, 91, 118	15:14–19	226, 303
14:15	62n19, 89, 104, 109n11, 133n71, 141, 163, 205, 276n29, 290, 303n19	15:14–31	51n8
		15:14–33	66, 77, 210, 224
14:16	61n12, 303n19	15:15	203n7, 207
14:17	59, 62n19, 82, 93, 125, 131, 202, 206, 309, 341	15:15–16	75, 80
		15:15–32	232n166
14:18	90, 90n57, 203, 205, 341	15:16	50n7, 51n8, 57, 60, 61n12, 75, 90n57, 91, 131n64, 171, 202, 204–206, 210, 210n32, 211, 226n128, 330, 341, 344n37
14:18–19	255, 341		
14:19	62, 64, 131, 286, 309		
14:20	82, 141, 163, 203, 254, 303n19		
14:20–21	62n19	15:17	82, 118, 203, 303
14:20–23	255, 341	15:17–18	205
14:21	62n19, 133n71, 254, 276n29	15:18	50n7, 75, 90, 226n128, 145, 145n22, 171, 207, 226n128, 254, 254n24, 340–341, 344n37
14:22	66, 105, 142, 303n19		
14:22–23	24, 142, 203	15:18–19	75, 211
14:23	24–25, 62n19, 96n11, 97n13, 100, 105	15:18–20	61n12
		15:18–21	210n31
15	23–24n39, 49, 352	15:19	40, 42, 51n8, 61, 61n17, 66, 80, 88, 171, 173, 179, 203, 207n18, 232, 243–244, 244n27, 277, 296, 344
15—16	24, 29		
15:1	18n9, 25, 255, 290, 303n22, 341		
15:2	61n16, 62, 303n19, 341	15:19a	42n39
15:2–3	255	15:19b	75
15:3	56, 90, 115, 142, 156, 226n128, 239n8, 240, 295, 341	15:19–20	91
		15:19–28	211
15:3–5	117	15:19–29	42
15:3–8	205	15:19–33	295
15:4	53, 56, 342n19	15:20	39n32, 51n8, 62, 75, 88, 176n32, 205, 256
15:5	79n5, 79n6, 90, 203, 341		
15:5–7	255	15:20–21	70
15:5–9	82	15:20–24	191, 226, 241
15:6	78n4, 79, 79n5, 85n29, 90, 204, 341	15:20–29	303
15:7	89, 137, 289, 303n19, 341	15:21	51n8, 57, 60, 61n10, 195, 239n8, 240, 342n23
15:7–8	156		
15:8	50n7, 60, 62n27, 80, 142, 195, 254n24, 281n13, 295, 328, 341	15:22	65
		15:23–24	42, 296
15:8–9	65, 210	15:23–29	219n99, 220n100
15:8–12	56, 64, 341	15:24	39, 42, 50, 61, 61n10, 61n15, 62n20, 69, 75, 134, 211n36, 218–219, 220, 226–227, 285, 303, 311, 343–344
15:8–13	75, 303, 318–319		
15:9	57n14, 63, 80, 203n6, 204, 239n8, 342n19, 344n37		
		15:24–33	277
15:9–11	61	15:25	23, 132n65, 256
15:9–12	56, 171, 184	15:25–26	61n17
15:9–13	240n12	15:25–27	41
15:9–31	226	15:25–28a	75
15:10	57, 61n12, 342n21	15:25–28	286n44
15:10–11	204	15:25–33	23
15:11	57, 66, 78n3, 83n23, 144, 170n7, 342n30	15:26	61–62, 132n65, 134, 229n149, 252n16, 256, 286

457

Scripture Index

(Romans continued)

15:26–32	343
15:27	191, 286, 331, 340–342, 351
15:28	42, 50, 61, 61n15, 227, 256, 311, 343–344
15:28–30	38, 226
15:28–32	242n18, 256
15:29	60n9, 191
15:30	79n5, 79n6, 85n29, 91, 92, 113n3, 133n71, 204, 207, 246n28, 320n34, 353n10
15:30–31	41, 75, 321n41
15:30–32	31, 69, 219, 296, 303
15:30–33	320–321, 321n38
15:31	23, 61, 61n17, 132n65, 139, 256, 282, 328n23
15:32	75, 81, 234n177, 299
15:33	24–25, 79, 131, 257, 309–310, 342
16	15, 19–20, 22, 24–26, 29, 45, 49
16:1	23, 25, 59n2, 60–61, 61n15, 133n71, 276, 281, 281n13, 290, 303
16:1–2	208, 214, 221, 231, 257, 275–277, 290n69, 291n74, 292n87, 343
16:1–3	37
16:1–16	198n87
16:1–23	26
16:2	91, 118, 132n65, 205, 209, 220, 257, 276, 285, 303
16:3	15, 20, 62, 90n57, 119, 216n73, 225, 276, 304, 343
16:3–5	20, 25, 215, 219, 257, 271
16:4	26, 59n2, 61, 231, 256, 304, 312
16:5	25, 38, 59n2, 61, 61n15, 89n56, 205, 216, 231, 277, 303–304, 343
16:6	62, 217, 231, 275–276, 304, 343
16:7	16, 20, 60–61, 89n56, 119, 209, 216, 216n76, 225, 271, 276, 291n74, 343
16:8	89n56, 118
16:8–10	205
16:9	119, 215, 217, 225, 304
16:10	61, 89n56, 119, 215n69, 276, 291
16:10–11	20
16:11	20, 61, 89n56, 118, 216–217, 276, 291, 304
16:12	62, 89n56, 119, 205, 217, 231, 275–276, 343
16:13	61, 63n35, 89n56, 119, 209, 219–220, 231, 257, 275–276, 285, 292n87, 295n6, 303
16:14	20, 133n71, 276
16:15	20, 132n65, 133n71
16:16	26, 59n2, 65, 91, 132, 205
16:17	31, 61n10, 62n22, 63n32, 66, 133n71, 276n28, 320n34, 344
16:17–18	18n9, 19–20, 218, 304
16:17–20	356n3
16:18	84, 90n57, 205m, 277
16:19	145, 145n22, 214, 223, 226, 304
16:20	24–25, 57, 61, 79, 85n29, 88, 105, 131, 172n21, 203, 241, 262, 307, 309–310, 321
16:21	37, 49n4, 62, 215–216, 225, 230, 304
16:22	22, 37, 91, 118, 218, 257, 277, 304, 343
16:23	23, 23n14, 37, 59n2, 60, 61n16, 133n71, 219–221, 257, 276–277, 285–286, 291, 292n87, 303, 334, 343
16:24	24
16:25	45, 51n8, 61n12, 63n31, 76, 88, 205
16:25–27	24, 322–333
16:26–27	79
16:26	61, 138, 145, 145n22, 169n3, 171, 195, 202, 298
16:27	24, 63n31, 90, 101, 137, 204–205

1 CORINTHIANS

1:1—2:16	233n168
1:1	218n92
1:2	19n11, 132, 146, 188n47
1:3	307n3
1:4	310n6, 312n11
1:9	162n17
1:10–12	220
1:12	198n87, 225n125
1:13	115n13, 316n22
1:14	23, 37, 291, 312n11
1:17–18	115n13
1:18	104n30, 115, 181n7, 183, 197, 231
1:19	104n30, 239n8
1:21	322n46
1:22	180, 244–245
1:23	70n50, 88n50, 115n13
1:27	190
1:31	239n8
2:1	69n42
2:1–4	117
2:2	115n13
2:3	322n46
2:5	213n49
2:6	327
2:7	101n24
2:8	115n13, 327
2:9	239n8
3:2	213n49
3:5	281n13, 328n23
3:4–6	198n87, 225n125
3:8	217n87
3:9	215n68, 225n124, 233n169

3:10	207n17	8:11	104n30, 105, 115n13, 141, 162n17
3:12–15	90n58	9:1	135n77
3:13	217n86	9:1–27	211n35
3:15	115n10	9:1–22	210
3:16	86–87	9:3	355n1
3:17	141, 162n17	9:5	176n32, 198n87, 216n76, 272n12
3:19	239n8	9:5–6	210n31
3:22	198n87, 225n125	9:7	260n7
4:5	90n58	9:9	239n8, 260n7
4:6	198n87, 210n31, 225n125, 239n8	9:13	69n42
4:8	191n66	9:14	212n45
4:9	210	9:16	38, 226n127, 329n28
4:12	286n45	9:19	135n77
4:16	225n126	9:19–22	50, 172, 233n167
4:17	38n27, 215n69	9:22	172
5	157	9:25	320, 320n35
5:4	207n16	9:27	141, 217n86
5:5	106n39, 115n10, 162n17	10:1	141
5:7	54n5, 106n39, 260n7	10:7	239n8
5:9–13	36, 208	10:9	104n30, 260n7
5:11	262n10, 289n66	10:9–10	141, 162n17
6:1	97n14	10:10	104n30
6:6	254n23	10:12–13	141
6:9	97n14, 141	10:14–31	289n66
6:9–10	272	10:16	115n13
6:9–11	100n22	10:23–30	341n17
6:11	129n55, 132	10:27—11:1	254n23
6:13	162n17	10:29	135n77
6:16	270	10:30	311n8, 312
6:19	86	10:31—11:1	233n167
6:20	319	11:1	225n126
7:2	271, 271n11	11:4–5	242
7:3	331	11:5	224, 224n119
7:3–4	272	11:20–34	289n66
7:6–9	273	11:24	312
7:8	273n16	11:24–25	224n119
7:9	273	11:25–26	115n13
7:11	131n61	11:26	69n42, 212
7:12–15	234, 254n23, 271	12:3	188, 188n47, 316
7:15	271	12:7	233, 23n167
7:16	115n10	12:8	233
7:21–23	135n77	12:8–10	276n31
7:22	135n77	12:9	141n14
7:26	329n28	12:9–10	246
7:27	273	12:10	242n17, 246
7:29–34	271	12:13	70, 135n77, 343n33
7:31	172	12:26	319n31
7:37	219n28	12:28–29	207n18, 210, 212, 233, 242n17
7:39	135n77, 271	12:29–30	246
8	341	12:28–30	233n167, 246n41, 276n31
8—10	24, 157	12:29	246
8:1–13	289n66135n77	12:31	233
8:4	78n2	13:1–3	156
8:6	78n2, 263, 340	13:2	141n14
8:7–13	341	13:9	242n17

(1 Corinthians continued)

14	233–234
14:1	286n45
14:5	224n139
14:5–6	242n17
14:12	224n119
14:14	207n16
14:15	207n16
14:17	224n119
14:20–25	207n18, 234
14:21	239n8
14:22	244n31
14:24–25	224n119, 241, 242n17, 254n23
14:26	224n119
14:26–29	242n17
14:26–32	224n119
14:29	242, 242n20
14:31	242
14:32	242, 242n20, 325
14:32–34	224
14:34	325
14:39	242
15	134, 163
15:2	141
15:3	99, 115, 115n13, 124, 316n22
15:3b	195n80
15:3–5	117
15:5	176n32
15:6–8	135
15:7	176n32
15:8–9	210
15:10	217n87
15:14	213n49
15:17	213n49
15:22	136, 229n148
15:24	134
15:24–28	160
15:25	172n21
15:26	134, 162n17, 172, 238n7, 261, 264
15:26–28	154
15:27	172n21, 325n8
15:28	325n8
15:32	216n74, 260n7
15:39	260n7
15:42	263
15:42–49	54
15:42–54	135
15:45	229n148, 239n8
15:45–49	87, 136
15:49	328n24
15:50	263
15:50–54	132, 238, 243n23
15:58	104n30, 217n87
16:1–4	38n28, 256n31, 286n44
16:2	281
16:6	220
16:9	216n74
16:10	215n69
16:11	220
16:12	198n87, 225n125
16:13	213n49
16:15	208n22, 282n16
16:16	217n87, 325
16:17	208n22
16:18	257
16:19	25, 198n87, 216, 257, 291n77
16:21	218n92
16:22	83n21
16:23	25n22

2 CORINTHIANS

1:1	19n11, 215n70, 218n92
1:2	307n3
1:8	216n74
1:10	135n80
1:11	219n97, 312n11, 317n25, 320n32
1:12	283
1:16	220
1:19	38, 215, 242n19
1:21–22	93
1:24	213n49, 215n68, 225n124
2:1	315n20
2:3	315n20
2:7	315n20
2:9	145n26
2:11	106n39
2:15	104n30, 115
2:17	211n35, 220, 224
2:17—7:6	220
3:1	55n10, 290n71
3:2	55n10, 244n32
3:6	281n13, 328n23
3:12–18	55n10
3:16	55n10
3:17	135n77
4:2	290n71
4:3	104n30
4:4	172
4:5	88n50, 188
4:7	101
4:7–18	93
4:7—5:5	135
4:9	104n30
4:10	115n11
4:13	213n49
4:14	69n43
5:1–10	159n1
5:7	138
5:10	131, 172

5:11	172	11:7–9	211n35
5:14	92, 316n22	11:7–10	220
5:14–15	115n11	11:8	211n36
5:15	316n22	11:8–9	220
5:17	238, 265	11:9	221
5:18	131, 334	11:13	210, 212
5:19	172, 266	11:14	106n39, 247n49
5:18–20	131n61	11:15	281n13
5:20	208, 334	11:22	210
5:21	100, 111, 149, 316n22	11:23	217n87, 281n13, 328n23
6:1	141n13	11:27	217n87
6:3–10	335n38	12:5–9	247
6:4	281n13, 290n71, 328n23, 329n28	12:7	106n39, 247n46, 247n49
6:5	217n87	12:10	329n28
6:6	285	12:11	290n71
6:12	290n71	12:12	207n18, 244, 244n27, 245, 246
7:10	315n20	12:14–16	211n35
7:11	290n71, 355n1	12:14–18	220
7:13	257	12:21	271n13, 274
7:15	145n22, 145n26	13:4	115n11
8:1–5	256	13:5	105, 141n13, 213n49
8:2	280n8, 283, 283n27	13:7	315n21
8:2–4	281	13:9	315n21
8:3	281	13:12	25n22
8:4	282n16, 321n41		
8:6–14	208n22	**GALATIANS**	
8:7	281		
8:9	191, 256, 280, 288	1:1	22n1
8:13	256	1:1–5	67n39
8:13–14	281	1:2	19n11
8:15	239n8	1:3	307n3
8:23	209, 212, 215, 225n124	1:4	316n22
9:1	282n16, 321n41	1:5	337
9:6	281	1:6	141n13
9:7	315n20, 329n28	1:7	344
9:8	281, 327n22	1:8	316
9:9	239n8	1:8–19	198
9:11	283, 283n27	1:9	316
9:12	282n16, 283	1:11–12	107n43
9:12–13	321n41	1:12	359
9:13	282n16, 283n27, 319	1:13	286n45
9:14	317n25	1:14	107n40, 358n12, 359
10—13	157	1:14–15	29, 78, 295n4
10:1–6	335n38	1:15	358
10:5	145n22	1:15–16	359n13
10:5–6	145n25	1:16	226n128, 344n37
10:6	145n22, 144n21	1:17	33, 176
10:10	247	1:18–19	33, 198n88
10:12	290n71	1:19	211
10:12–15	171	1:21	32–33
10:13–16	39n32	1:23	69n43, 286n45
10:15	69n43, 213n49, 217n87	1:24	319
10:18	290n71	2	209, 242n18
11:3	87n43, 98, 141n13, 229n148, 260n7, 283	2—3	107
11:5	212	2:1–9	198n87

461

(Galatians continued)

2:1–10	33, 198n88, 339n10, 340n14
2:2	141n13, 226n128, 344n37, 242n18
2:3	337n6
2:3–6	339
2:4	135n77
2:7	209, 226n128
2:7–9	295n4
2:7–10	172, 198, 208, 344n37
2:9	207, 209, 226n128
2:9–10	209n27
2:10	38, 242, 242n18
2:11	326, 339, 340
2:11–14	289n66, 337, 339
2:12	337n6
2:14	337
2:15–16	129
2:16	89, 129n55, 130n56, 271n10, 337n7
2:17	111, 281n13
2:20	116, 316n22
2:21	115n11
3	92
3:1	115n11
3:1–5	197
3:2	197, 337n7, 339
3:3	99
3:4	141n13
3:5	99, 197, 207n18, 245, 337n7, 339
3:6	140
3:6–29	229n151
3:7	351n3
3:8–9	139
3:10	183n19, 239n8, 337n7
3:11	127n46
3:12	183
3:13	70, 130n60, 180, 239n8, 316
3:14	213n49
3:20	78n2
3:22	89n53, 98
3:23	213n49
3:24	339
3:25	213n49
3:26	213n49
3:26–29	169n3
3:27	339, 341n16
3:27–29	172
3:28	70, 131, 135n77, 338–339, 339n13, 341n16, 354
4:3	92n61, 172, 186
4:4	111, 149, 295
4:5	134, 137, 146, 193
4:5–6	93
4:8–9	186
4:9	92n61, 172
4:10	337
4:11	141n13, 271n87
4:13	81n15
4:21–31	294n3
4:22	135n77, 239n8
4:23	135n77, 271
4:26	135n77
4:27	239n8
4:29	271, 271n10, 286n45
4:30	135n77
4:31	135n77
5	92, 158n22
5:1	111, 130, 135n77
5:1–4	141n13
5:1—6:10	339, 343
5:2–4	337n6
5:4	152n9, 315
5:6	258, 337n6
5:10	337
5:11	115n11, 286n45
5:13	99, 130, 135, 135n77, 271n10
5:13–14	154n12
5:13–25	151
5:14	107n45, 154
5:16	180
5:16–17	271n10
5:19	271n10, 272n13, 274
5:19–21	100n22
5:9–21	141n13
5:21	339
5:22	131n62
5:22–23	113, 151
5:24	115n11
6	92
6:6	286
6:7–8	281n12
6:8	104n31, 162n17
6:10	133, 213n49
6:11	218n92
6:12	115n11, 286n45, 337n6
6:13	176n32
6:14	115n11, 116
6:15	238, 265, 337n6
6:16	87
6:18	25n22, 207n16

EPHESIANS

1:1	22n1
1:2	307n3
1:4	132n68
1:5	134, 317n24
1:7	115n11, 130n60, 135n81
1:9	317n24
1:10	131n61, 172
1:10–11	164, 164n26

1:11	238n7	5:20	310n6
1:13	118, 173	5:21	325, 325n9
1:13–14	93, 172n19, 197, 231	5:21—6:9	30
1:16	312n11	5:22	271, 325n9
1:17	93	5:23	85n31, 86n40
1:20	164	5:24	325
1:21	101, 172	5:25	271, 316n22
1:22	164n26, 172, 325n8	5:31	270–271
2:1	104n28	6:1	276
2:2	172, 327	6:5	283
2:5	115n9	6:8	135n77
2:8	107, 115n9	6:10–17	106n39, 335n38
2:8–9	299n16, 337	6:12	213n49
2:10	172n20	6:13	326
2:12	286n48	6:15	172n19, 172n20, 182
2:13	115n11, 131n61	6:17	172n19, 172n20, 182, 197, 206
2:13–14	172n19	6:18	219n97, 317n25, 320n32
2:16 131n61		6:20	208, 334
2:16	115n11	6:21	208n22, 214, 281n13, 328n23
2:17	232	6:22	38n27
2:19	286n48, 334	6:23	25n22
2:19–22	86–87,		
2:20	86n38, 210n31		
3:1	226n128		

PHILIPPIANS

3:1–10	172n19
3:2	207n17
3:4–9	210n31
3:5	239, 242
3:7	281n13, 328n23
3:7–8	207n17
3:8	226n128, 344n37
3:10	327
3:12	213n49
3:17	213n49
3:20	312n11
4—6	27n35
4:2	154n12
4:6	78n2
4:9	162
4:11	172n19, 201, 207n18, 210, 210n31, 212, 233, 235, 242, 246, 276
4:11–12	172n20, 233
4:11–16	233n167
4:12	207
4:13	213n49
4:15	233n167
4:19	274
4:27	106n39
4:28	283, 286
4:30	130
4:32	135n81
5:1–2	153n11, 225n126
5:1—6:9	188
5:2	316n22
5:3	272n13

1:1	215n70, 218n92, 277, 328n23
1:2	307
1:3	312n11
1:4	310n6, 317n25
1:5	286
1:7	207n17, 286, 355n1, 357, 359
1:12	194, 306
1:12–14	182
1:12–18a	41, 41n38, 234, 234n178
1:14	69
1:14–18a	224n121
1:14–18	226n127
1:15	88n50, 317n24
1:16	355n1
1:17	88n50, 212n45
1:17–18	69n42
1:18a	41
1:18	212n45, 234, 234n175
1:19	219n97, 317n25, 320n32
1:20	86, 190
1:22	40n37, 69, 69n46, 182n13
1:25	213n49
1:25–26	43
1:27	69n43, 213n49, 33
1:27–30	235, 235n180
1:28	104n31, 162n17, 163n21
1:29	141n14
1:30	320n35
2:1–8	18n9
2:1–11	156
2:5–8	155

SCRIPTURE INDEX

(Ephesians continued)

2:5–13	117
2:6	280n6
2:6–11	30, 88
2:7	100, 195n81
2:8	115n11, 149n7
2:9–10	83n23
2:9–11	144, 161, 104n27, 280n6
2:10	162
2:10–11	56, 172
2:11	188, 188n47
2:12–13	145n26, 158
2:13	317
2:14	254n23
2:16	90n58, 217n87, 235
2:17	213n49
2:19–23	215n69
2:22	217n86
2:25	210, 212, 225n124, 286, 330
2:25–30	49, 208n22, 211n36, 220, 257
2:27	246n38, 315
3	105, 157, 218n91, 224, 356n3
3:2	260n7
3:3	87
3:3–6	108
3:6	107n40, 111, 152, 286n45
3:8	198n86
3:9	89n53
3:10	115n11, 196
3:12	286n45
3:14	286n45
3:17	225n126
3:18	115n11
3:19	104n31, 162n17, 213n49
3:20	85n31, 86n40, 115n11, 334
3:21	135, 164, 164n26, 243n23, 325n8
4:2–3	49, 277
4:3	43, 216
4:4	310n6
4:6	317n25
4:10–13	220
4:10–19	29n7, 211n36
4:15	286
4:15–16	220
4:15–18	281
4:16	220, 286n43
4:17	281n12
4:17–20	220
4:18	208n22
4:19	286n43
4:22	25n22, 41
4:23	207n16

COLOSSIANS

1:1	215n70
1:3	310n6, 312n11
1:5–27	199n90
1:6	173, 182
1:7	26, 36n16, 38, 281n13, 328n23
1:10	327n22
1:12	312n11
1:13	135n79
1:15	137, 205
1:15–17	173
1:16–17	263
1:15–20	144
1:19	88, 280n6
1:20	115n11, 131, 131n61, 164, 164n26, 173, 238n7
1:21–23	141n13
1:22	115n11, 131
1:23	173, 199n90, 213n49, 281n13, 328n23
1:24	316n22
1:25	281n13, 328n23
1:27	173, 344n37
1:28	69n42, 88n50, 173, 212n45
1:29	217n87, 320, 320n35
2	218n91, 356n3
2:1	320n35
2:6	188
2:7	213n49
2:8	92n61, 172
2:9	88, 280n6
2:10	173
2:12	213n49
2:14	115n11
2:20	115n11, 172
3:1	164
3:2	341n16
3:3	99
3:5	262n10, 272n13
3:11	70, 135n77, 173, 176, 339n12, 343n33
3:12	132n68
3:17	312n11
3:18	325
3:18—4:1	30
3:22	283
3:24	84
4	26
4:2	318
4:2–3	318
4:3–4	219n97, 320n32
4:5	334
4:5–6	235
4:7	281n13, 328n23
4:7–9	214
4:7–17	198n87, 215n71

SCRIPTURE INDEX

4:8	38n27	5:12	217n87
4:9	214	5:15	286n45
4:10	49n4, 135n81	5:16	311n6
4:10–14	37n23	5:17	310
4:11	215, 225n124	5:18	312
4:12	311n6, 320, 320n35	5:19	207n16
4:12–17	71	5:20	242
4:13	36n16	5:21	242
4:14	37n22	5:23	207n16
4:17	25n22	5:25	219n97, 320n32
4:18	218n92	5:28	25n22

1 THESSALONIANS

1:1	19n11, 37n20, 67n39, 210n31, 215n70, 218n92, 242n19, 307n3
1:2	213n49, 310, 310n6, 312n11
1:3	217n87
1:6	225n126
1:8	69, 160n6, 212, 213n49
1:8–10	214n55
1:9	69n43
2:2	320n35
2:4	217n86
2:6	37, 209
2:7	210n31
2:8	283n23
2:9	217n87, 211n35, 220
2:13	310, 312n11
2:15–16	173
2:16	344n37
2:18	106n39, 234n177
3:2	37n20, 135n80, 213n49, 225n124, 322n44
3:2–5	38n27
3:2–6	215n69
3:5	141n13, 213n49, 217n87
3:6	37n20, 213n49, 311n6
3:6–12	220
3:7	213n49, 329n28
3:10	213n49
3:12	154n12
3:13	322n44
4—5	29, 159n1
4:3–8	132n68
4:6	329
4:7	272n13
4:9	154n12, 285
4:12	254n23
4:13–18	160, 160n6
4:15	115n11
5:1	242n20
5:2	162n17, 162n17
5:8	335n38
5:10	115n11

2 THESSALONIANS

1—2	159n1
1:1	19n11, 47n20, 215n70, 218n92, 242n19
1:2	307n3
1:3	154n12, 213n49, 312n11
1:8	145
1:9	104n31, 162, 162n17
1:11	310n6, 317n24
2	160
2:3	104n31, 141n13
2:3–4	160
2:9	106n39, 244, 244n27, 247n43, 312n11
2:10	104n30
2:12	244n26
2:13	132, 310n6
2:17	322n44, 327
3	29n7
3:1	181–182, 194, 219n97, 319n31, 320
3:2	213n49
3:3	322n44
3:13	322n46
3:17	25n22, 218n92, 244n31

1 TIMOTHY

1	157
1:1	22n1
1:2–11	215
1:5	285n37
1:6	141n13
1:9	213n49
1:10	272
1:20	109n39
2:1	317n25
2:1–2	333
2:4	173
2:5	78n2
2:6	173, 195n81, 212, 316n22
2:7	69n43, 210n31, 226n128
2:10	327n22
2:11–12	224
2:13	229n148

465

SCRIPTURE INDEX

(1 Timothy continued)

2:13–14	229n148
2:13	98
2:13–14	87n43
2:16	115n10
3:1–13	225
3:2	271n11, 288
3:3	262
3:6	109n39
3:6-7	141n13
3:7	109n39
3:8	281n13, 328n23
3:9	213n49
3:12	281n13, 328n23
3:13	213n49
3:15	133
4	157
4:1	213n49
4:1–4	141n13
4:4	311n8
4:6	213n49, 281n13, 328n23
4:14	210n33, 225n123, 242n17
4:10	173, 217n87
5:5	317n25
5:8	213n49
5:10	288, 327n22
5:15	109n39, 141n13
5:17	217n87
5:18	211n35, 260n7
5:22	210n33, 225n123, 286n42
6:9	104n31, 162n17, 191n66
6:10	213n49, 262
6:11	286n45
6:12	144, 187, 213n49, 320, 320n35
6:20–21	141n13
6:21	25n22, 213n49

2 TIMOTHY

1:1	22n1
1:3	317n22
1:5	285n37
1:6	210n33, 225n123
1:8	180
1:9	101n24, 115n9
1:10	85n31, 86n40
1:12	179
1:16	208n22
1:17	296n9
2:9	182, 235, 306
2:11	115n11
2:15	217n86
2:21	327n22
2:22	286n45
2:26	106n39
3:2	144n20, 262
3:5–7	141n13
3:8	213n49, 326n16
3:10	213n49
3:11	135n80
3:12	286n45
3:16	239
3:17	327
4:1–5	215
4:2	223n118, 306
4:3	141n13
4:5	223n118
4:7	208n22, 213n49, 320, 320n35
4:11	37n22
4:15	326
4:16	355n1
4:16–17	11n12
4:17	135n80, 173, 226n128, 260n7, 322n46
4:18	135n79
4:19	25, 216, 216n73, 224, 257, 291n77
4:19–21	198n87
4:20	23, 218, 246
4:21	25n22

TITUS

1:1	22n1
1:1–4	67n39
1:2	101n24
1:3	213n49, 322n46
1:4	85n31, 86n40
1:5–9	225
1:6	271n11
1:8	132n68, 288
1:12	260n7
1:16	141n13, 144n20, 188, 327n22
2:5	325
2:9	325
2:11	173
2:13	85n31, 86n40, 88, 280n6
2:14	316n22
3	157
3:1	324n4, 325, 327, 330
3:3	213n49
3:5	115n9, 263n14
3:6	85n31, 86n40
3:7	129n55
3:10–11	344
3:13	220, 225n125
3:14	286n43
3:15	25n22

SCRIPTURE INDEX

HEBREWS

1:2	173n24, 182
1:7	330
2:1	213n49
2:4	244, 244n27, 245–246
2:8–15	173n24
2:11	190n60
2:14	213n49, 286n42
2:17	213n49
2:20	213n49
2:22	213n49
2:26	213n49
3:18	320n36
4:2	213n49
4:8	228n147
4:11–12	182
5:4	228n147
5:6	196n84
5:7	317n25
5:10	196n84
5:15	213n49
6:2	246n40
6:20	196n84
7:1–17	196n84
7:11	228n147
7:12	329n28
7:25	313
7:27	155n18, 173n24
8:2	182
8:11	173n24
9:16	329n28
9:23	329n28
9:27	353
10:24	154n12
10:38	127n46
11	228, 228n146
11:1	114, 228n147
11:4	228n147, 229n148
11:4–7	196n84
11:5	228n147
11:11	229n151
11:13	187n41, 286n48
11:16	190n60
11:24	229n148
11:27	317
11:31	320n36
11:32	228n147
11:33	320n35
11:39	213n49
12:1	320n35
12:2	190, 213n49
12:4	320n35
12:24	196n84, 228n147
12:29	161
13:1	285n41
13:2	287
13:4	274
13:7	213n49
13:8	248
13:9	286n48
13:15	187n41

JAMES

1:1	198n87
1:3	213n49
1:26—2:26	258
2	99n20
2:3	328
2:8	154n12
2:16	317n25
2:17	143
2:21	2229n151
2:25	228n147
2:26	143
3:2	96n8
3:6	162n10
4:6	326
4:7	326
5:6	326
5:8	322n44
5:14–16	246
5:16	315n21
5:17–18	317

1 PETER

1:1	198n87
1:1–2	289
1:7	190n60, 213n49
1:9	213n49
1:16	132n67
1:21	213n49
1:22	154n12, 285, 285n41
2:6	189
2:7	190
2:8	320n36
2:12	319, 319n30
2:13–17	324n4
2:13—3:7	330
2:17–19	289
2:23–25	195n81
3:1	223n117, 320n36
3:1–6	234
3:1–7	223n117
3:4	189n53
3:6	229n151
3:12	317n25
3:15	355n1

467

(Hebrews continued)

3:20	196n84, 228n147, 320n36
4:3	274n21
4:3–4	274n22
4:4	287n49
4:8	154n12
4:9	287
4:11	319n30
4:12	286n48, 287n49
4:13	286n42
4:14	257n33
4:16	319n30
4:17	320n36
5:5	326
5:9	213n49, 326
5:10	322n44
5:12	22, 218n92

2 PETER

1:5	213n49
1:7	285n41
1:12	322n44
2:2	274n21, 274n22
2:4	162n11
2:5	164n25, 196n84, 228n147
2:7	228n147, 274n21
2:10	274n22
2:12	104n31, 263n17
2:15	229n148
2:18	274n21
3	164n25
3:1–13	164
3:2	198n87
3:5–6	263
3:9	241
3:9–10	173n24
3:13	173n24
3:15	241
3:16	230

1 JOHN

1:8	96n8
1:9	187n41
1:10	96n8
2:2	173n24
2:18	160n5
2:23	187n42
3:11	154n12
3:12	229n148
3:17	286n43
3:23	154n12
4:2	187n42
4:3	187n42
4:7	154n12
4:9	88n48
4:11	154n12
4:12	154n12
4:15	187n42
4:17	162n18, 173n24
5:4	213n49

2 JOHN

1	217n88
5	154n12
7	187n42
11	286n42

3 JOHN

1	291n83
2	315n21
5	286
6	220
8	215n71

JUDE

3	320n35, 329n28
4	274n21, 274n22
7	274n22
11	229n148
13	162n14
14	186n84, 228n147
17	198n87
20	213n49
22:23	284

REVELATION

1:5	327n20
1:7	173n24
1:18	162n12
2:2	210
2:7	246n40
2:13	213n49
2:14	229n148, 274n22
2:20	229n148, 274n22
2:21	274n22
2:27	105
3:2	322n44
3:5	187n41
3:17–18	191n66
4:5	207n16
5:9–13	173n24
6:8	162n12
6:11	257n33
6:12–17	159n2

Scripture Index

7:9–11	173n24	15:1	244n25, 244n27
9:1	185n28	15:4	319n30
9:2	185n28	16:14	173n24, 244n25
9:11	162n16, 185n28	17:4	274n22
9:21	274n22	17:8	185n28
11:7	162n16, 185n28	18:3	274n22
11:15	173n24	18:9	274n22
12:1	244n25	19:2	274n22
12:2	244n25	19:20	162n13, 244n25, 247n43
12:5	173n24	20:1	185n28
13	333, 335	20:3	162n16, 185n28
13:6	246n40	20:10	106, 162n13
13:1–18	160n5	20:11–15	162n18
13:7–8	173n24	20:13	162n12
13:10	213n49	20:14	162n12, 162n13
13:12	246n40	20:15	162n13
13:13	244n25	21:1–15	173n24
13:13–14	247n43	21—22	164, 263, 267
13:14	244n25	21:4	246n40
14:6	173n24	21:8	162n13
14:8	274n22	22:2	246n40, 263
14:12	213n49	22:14	246n40
14:13	257n33	22:19	246n40
14:15–19	173n24		

Apocrypha and Pseudepigrapha

TOBIT

13:2	283n28

JUDITH

6:21	146n30
8:7	194n73
8:17	146n30
9:1	311n7
9:4	146n30
10:15	220
14:16	313n18
16:2	146n30

WISDOM OF SOLOMON

13:12	291n98
13:23	275
14:26	274n20
18:13	187n40
18:14–16	182n10
19:2	222n107

SIRACH

1:27	316n23
2:16	316
3:20	319n29
4:26	187n40
7:30	330n32
9:12	316n23
10:2	330n32
10:4–5	326n13
11:17	316n23
15:9	194n73
15:15	316n23
18:14	284n28
18:31	316n23
20:1	194n73
25:1	194n73
25:4–5	194n73
26:18	194n73
29:23	316n23
32:14	316n23
33:13	316n23
34:18	316n23
35:3	316
35:16	316n23
35:24	194n73

(Sirach continued)

39:18	316
41:4	316n23
43:11	194n73
43:28	319n29
43:30	319n29
44—50	228
44:1–3	228n143
45:13	194n73

EPISTLE OF JEREMIAH

27	283n20

SUSANNAH

63	283n25

1 MACCABEES

1:1	283n25
2:19–56	229n150
2:37	283n25
2:54	229n150
2:57	83n18
2:58	229n150
2:60	283n25
7:37	60n3
8:32	313n15
10:61	313n15
10:63	313n15
11:12	314n18
11:25	313n15
15:9	318

2 MACCABEES

1:35	282
2:25	313n15
3:14	217n88
3:15	274n18
3:22	146n30
3:31	146n30
4:12	321
4:36	313n15
4:37	146n30
5:2–6	195n80
5:18	285
6:4–3	326n13
6:4	274
6:6	187n40
6:12	313n15
6:17–20	191n68
6:23	222n107
7:13	282n19
7:37	146n30
8:2	146n30
8:12	282n19
8:21	313n16
8:28	313n16
8:36	212n42
9:17	2n6, 212n41
10:7	194n73
12:6	146n30
15:39	313n15

1 ESDRAS

4:18	195n73
4:19	195n73
4:47	220
4:60	187n40
5:58	187n40
8:25	318
8:64	318
9:52	319n29

3 MACCABEES

1:18	313n18
2:26	274n20
3:15	321
3:21	283n25
4:2	313n18
5:21	321
6:37	313n15

2 ESDRAS

7:24	330n32
12:32	83n18
20:40	330n32

4 MACCABEES

6:12	284n29
6:34	187n40
9:3	284n29
9:16	187n40
13:5	187n40
13:23	285n40
13:26	285n40
14:1	285n40
14:9	315
15:13	285n39
17:22	115n12

2 BARUCH

25:2–3	159n2

27:1–15	159n2	6:13–24	159n2
48:30–41	159n2	7:30–31	262n13
70:2–10	159n2	9:1–3	159n2
		10:6–16	159n2
		12:32	83

APOCALYPSE OF ELIJAH

5:38	262n13

JOSEPH AND ASENETH

1:6	194n73
1:8	194n73
2:19	194n73
4:4	194n73
10:5	314n18
10:6	314n18
10:7	314n18
10:17	314n18
12:8	285n39
22:7	222n108

APOCALYPSE OF SEDRACH

1:1	285
2:25	285
13:4	187n40
14:3	314n18
15:1	283n28

3 BARUCH

Pro. 2	194n73
9:6	194n73

JUBILEES

1:29	262n13
4:15	274n20
4:26	262n13

PSEUDO-PHILO (LAB)

3:10	262n13
37:17	262n13

LETTER OF ARISTEAS

5	321
7	282n19
24	187n40
43	282n19
172	222n108, 282n19
174	313n15
309	282n19

1 ENOCH

1:8	316n23
7:6	313n15
9:3	313n16
9:10	313n16, 314n18
22:5	313n16
22:6	313n16
22:7	313n15
22:15	313n15
38:2–3	195n80
39:6–7	195n80
45:4–5	262
72:1	262n13
48:1	195n80
62:4	159n2
91:16	262n13

LIVES OF THE PROPHETS

4:3	194n73

MARTYRDOM AND ASCENSION OF ISAIAH

11:2	83n18

2 ENOCH

51:4	311n9

ODES OF SOLOMON

1:1	319n29
1:2	319n29
2:6	319n29
1:11	319n29
7:26	319n29
11:16	194n73
14:35	319n29

3 ENOCH

45:5	83n18

4 EZRA

5:1–13	159n2

PSALMS OF SOLOMON

2:36	146n30
3:4	316n23, 317
4:5	284n34
4:6	273n17
4:14	314n18
6:4	311n7
8:11–13	109n52
8:33	316n23
9:4	304n25
9:6	146n30
10:7	319n29
11:1	195n78
16:12	284n34, 316n23
17:5	319n29
17:30	319n29
17:31	319n29

SIBYLLINE ORACLES

2:9	263n17
2:83	282n20
2:279	274n20
3:41	282
3:251	217n88
3:336	271n88
4:33	274n18
5:212	262n13
5:317	275n24
5:387	274n18
5:393	274n18
5:394	275n24
6:16	83n18
7:31	83n18
7:161	282n19
8:118	275n24
8:124	194n73
8:252	83n18
8:381	274

TESTAMENT OF ASHER

2:6	284n29
5:7	154n13

TESTAMENT OF BENJAMIN

4:2	284n29
6:7	283n25

TESTAMENT OF DANIEL

1:4	187n40
5:9	283n28
5:11	146n30
6:3	146n30

TESTAMENT OF GAD

2:1	187n40
4:1–7	154n13
6:1–7	154n13
6:3	187n40

TESTAMENT OF ISSACHAR

3:2	283n25
3:4	283n25
3:6	283n25
3:7	283n25
3:8	283n25
4:1	283n25
4:6	283n25
5:1	283n25
5:8	283n25
6:1	283n25
7:1	283n25
7:5	283n20

TESTAMENT OF JOSEPH

7:2	314n18
9:4	314n18
9:5	194n73
18:4	194n73

TESTAMENT OF JUDAH

23:1	274n20
24:6	146n30

TESTAMENT OF LEVI

8:16	194n73
13:1	283n25
14:5	109n52

TESTAMENT OF NAPHTALI

4:1	283n25
5:2	154n13
9:2	284n34

TESTAMENT OF REUBEN

1:6	274n18
3:4	194n73

TESTAMENT OF SIMEON

4:5	283n25
5:1	194n73

TESTAMENT OF ZEBULUN

2:2	284n29
5:1	154n13
6:6	283
6:7	283n20
7:2	283n28

TESTAMENT OF ABRAHAM (A)

1:5	285n39
10:13	284n28
16:1	194n73
16:6	194n73
20:8	284n34
20:14	314n18

TESTAMENT OF JOB

4:1	282n19
10:1–3	287n54
17:5	313n15
25:5	287n54
26:6	283n25
53:3	287m54

TESTAMENT OF SOLOMON

26:5	194n73

HISTORY OF THE RECHABITES

15:8	222n108

DEAD SEA SCROLLS

1QH 3:7–18	159n2
1QH 6:26–27	190n57
1QHa 12:22–23	195n80
1QS 4:25	262n13
1QS 5:4–5	311n8
1QS 8:7	190n57
1QS 10:1, 3, 11	311n7
4Q161 Frags. 8–10:11	83n19
4Q161 Frags. 8–10:18	83n18
4Q252 Col. 5:2–4	83n18
4Q285 Frag. 5:2	83n19
4Q285 Frag. 5:3	83n18
4Q491 Frag. 11	195n80
4Q504 Frags. 1–2, 4:6–8	83n18
4Q522 Frag. 9, 2:3	83n19
4Q491c Frag 1	195n80
11Q5 Col. 27:2	83n18
11Q14 Frag. 1, 1:3	83n18
11Q14 Frag. 1, 1:11	83n19
11Q174 Frags. 1:1, 2, 21	83n18
11QT 17:15–19	270n5
CD 3:20—5:6	270n5

PHILO

De Abrahamo, On the Life of Abraham

Abr. 66	228
Abr. 84	228
Abr. 107–114	287n54

De aeternitate mundi, On the Eternity of the World

Aet. 68	212n41

De cherubim, On the Cherubim

Cher. 86	283
Cher. 92	275
Cher. 114	263n14

De vita contemplative, On the Contemplative Life

Contemp. 77	284n34

Quod deterius potiori insidari soleat, That the Worse Attacks the Better

Det. 101	283n21
Det. 124	283n21
Det. 156	283n21

De ebrietate, On Drunkenness

Ebr. 110	282n19

Scripture Index

In Flaccum, Against Flaccus

Flacc. 54	282n19
Flacc. 180	315

De fuga et invention, On Flight and Finding

Fug. 30	282
Fug. 84	282

De gigantibus, On Giants

Gig. 27	283n21
Gig. 43	283n21

Quis rerum divinarum heres sit, Who is the Heir?

Her. 5	282n19
Her. 159	283n21

De Iosepho, On the Life of Joseph

Ios. 85	283n21
Ios. 92	212n40
Ios. 144	283n22

Legum allegoriae I, II, III, Allegorical Interpretation

Leg. 1.40	283n21
Leg. 1.56	194n73
Leg. 1.58	194n73
Leg. 2.155	14
Leg. 2.159–61	14
Leg. 3.177	194n73

Legatio ad Gaium, On the Embassy of Gaius

Legat. 87	285n40
Legat. 158	13

De migratione Abrahami, On the Migration of Abraham

Migr. 189	212n43

De vita Mosis I, II, On the Life of Moses

Mos. 1.3	274n20
Mos. 1.172	283n25
Mos. 1.195	222n108
Mos. 1.227	222n108
Mos. 1.305	274n20
Mos. 1.315	282n19
Mos. 2.65	263n14
Mos. 2.190	283n21

De mutatione nominum, On the Change of Names

Mut. 57	282n19

De opificio mundi, On the Creation of the World

Opif. 44	282n19
Opif. 77	282n19
Opif. 106	212n43
Opif. 156	282n19, 283n25
Opif. 170	283n25

De posteritate Caini, On the Posterity of Cain

Post. 84–85	184n22
Post. 124	263n14

De plantatione, On Planting

Plant. 166	284n34

De praemiis et poenis, On Rewards and Punishments

Praem. 158	285n39

Quod omnis probus liber sit, That Every Good Person is Free

Prob. 1.64	212n43
Prob. 1.71	212n43

Scripture Index

De specialibus legibus I, II, III, On the Special Laws , ,

Spec. 1.49	283n21
Spec. 1.97	283n21
Spec. 1.120	283n22
Spec. 1.126	282n19
Spec. 1.294	283n21
Spec. 1.320–23	2n6
Spec. 2.15	283n21
Spec. 2.40	285n39
Spec. 2.71	283
Spec. 2.89	282n19
Spec. 2.107	283n19
Spec. 2.115	282n19
Spec. 2.119	283
Spec. 2.141	282n19
Spec. 2.250	194n73
Spec. 3.111	219n94
Spec. 3.112	282n19
Spec. 3.116	283n22
Spec. 3.1563	285n39
Spec. 3.157	285n39
Spec. 3.196	282n19

De somniis II, On Dreams

Somn. 2.167	284n34
Somn. 2.223	283n21

De virtutibus, On the Virtues

Virt. 91	285n39
Virt. 108	282n19
Virt. 121	282n19
Virt. 125	283n21
Virt. 141	282n19
Virt. 168	283
Virt. 192	285n39

JOSEPHUS

Jewish Antiquities

1.9	282n19
1.91	222n107
1.147	177n42
1.165	228
1.183	212n41
1.196	287n54
1.230	222n108
1.246	283n20
1.307	283n20
1.328	219n94
1.325	222n107
2.10	212n41
2.55	274n18
2.64	194n73
2.83	194n73
2.96	60n3
2.161	285n40
2.212	284n28
3.126	194n73
3.206	212n41
4.3	222n108
4.24	222n108
4.26	285n40
4.135	285n39
5.99	222n108
5.130	317
5.345	212n41
6.53	222n108
6.203	212n42
6.254	222n108
6.255	282n19
6.272	222n108
6.296	194n73
6.337	315
7.43	285n39
7.83	282n19
7.188	222n107
7.252	285n39
7.331	283
8.115	284n28
8.153	194n73
8.199	212n43
8.318	274n20
9.59	282
9.91	284n29
9.92	212n43
9.251	222n108
10.61	212n43
10.92	212n43
10.249	282n19
11.8	212n42
11.59	222n108
11.66	263n14
11.67	222n108
11.135	222n108
11.196	285n39
11.222	212n42
11.229	212n42
11.232	284n28
12.20	284n29
12.65	194n73
12.165	219n94
12.181	285n40
13.105	222n108

Scripture Index

(Jewish Antiquities continued)

13.172	298
14.84	219n94
14.103	222n107
14.151	222n108
14.156	222n108
14.214–215	13
14.237	282n19
14.342	222n108
14.447	219n94
14.375	222n108
15.16	285n39
15.66	285n39
15.70	285n39
15.98	274n20
15.103	222n108
15.269	212n42
15.363	222n108
16.11	282n19
16.237	212n42
17.299–303	13
18.1–3	304n25
18.273–76	218n89
19.33	194n73
20.9	198
20.34–35	2n6
20.50	220
20.72	212n42
20.78	212n42
20.82	212n42
20.112	274n20

The Life

90	219n94

Against Apion

282.40	282n19

Jewish War

1.5	177n41
1.10	284n29
1.99	177n41
1.111	283n25
1.143	177n41
1.162	219n94
1.177	219n94
1.201	222n108
1.230	219n94
1.250	219n94
1.255	222n108
1.278	222n108
1.298	219n94
1.305	219n94
1.362	222n108
1.381	219n94
1.397	177n41
1.439	274n20
1.456	222n108
1.512	222n108
1.523	285n39
1.581	212n42
1.614	220
1.622	285n39
1.672	177n41
2.80–83	13
2.83	219n94
2.104	222n108
2.151	283n25
2.203	212n42
2.121	274n20
2.131	311n8
2.128–29	311n77
2.142	284n19
2.282	222n108
2.290	219n94
2.298	219n94
2.319	219n94
2.334	219n94
2.363	177n42
2.382	177n42
2.385	177n42
2.480	222n108
2.507	219n94
2.513	219n94
2.631	222, 222n107
5.383	222n107
5.389	222n107
3.400	222n107
3.458	219n94
4.3	222n107
4.10	222n107
4.360	284n19
4.381	284n19
4.562	274n20
4.640	222n107
4.582	212n42
5.32	314n18
5.319	283n25
5.438	283n20
5.529	283n25
6.27	317
6.204	284n29
6.286	212n43
6.272	314n18
6.307	283n20

7.9	222n107
7.90	177n41
7.202	315
7.390	285n39
7.418	188

RABBINIC LITERATURE

m. 'Abot	304n25
m. Ber. 6–8	311n8
Sipre Lev. 19:18	154n13
Sipre Deut. 161.1.3	191n68
Tg. Isa. 28:18	86n36
Tg. Isa. 42:1	195n80
Tg. Isa. 43:10	195n80
Tg. Isa. 52:13	195n80
Tg. Isa. 52:14	195n80
Tg. Isa. 53:3	195n80
Tg. Isa. 53:4	195n80
Tg. Isa. 53:10	195n80
Tg. Jer. 23:23	262n13
Tg. Lev. 19:18	154n13
Tg. Neof. Deut 30:11–14	184n22

APOSTOLIC FATHERS

1 CLEMENT

Prol.	43, 296
5:7	43
6:1	21
9:4	262n14
10:7	287n54
12:1	287n54
15:6	314n19
42:3	174
47:5	285n41
48:1	285n41
56:1	313n16
63:1	216n74

DIDACHE

8:3	311n9

DIOGNETUS

5:1–5	176

EPISTLE OF BARNABAS

20:2	284

IGNATIUS

To the Philadelphians

5:2	212
9:2	212

MARTYRDOM OF POLYCARP

17:2	313n15

POLYCARP

To the Philippians

1:2	212n44
4:3	313n16

SHEPHERD OF HERMAS

Mandate

10.2, 5	313n17
10.3, 2	313n16

SIMILITUDES

2.6, 8	313n16

VISIONS

3.9, 2	284n23
3.9, 5	314n19
5, 3	284n23

Scripture Index
Other Ancient Texts

ACTS OF PETER
3	43n49
5	175

ACTS OF PETER AND THE TWELVE APOSTLES
1:9–20	175
5:11–14	175

ARISTOTLE
Rhetorica. 1.6.132b	148n3
1.9.13.13666b	148n3

DIDASCALIA APOSTOLORUM
23	175

DIO CASSIUS
Historiae

57.18.5

DIOGENES LAERTIUS
Lives

1.785	331n34
3.83	331n34
4:27	185n31

EPICTETUS
Diatribai

4.1.77	216n74

EPISTLE TO THE APOSTLES
30	174

EUSEBIUS
Ecclesiastical History

3.1.1	175
3.49	49n5
5.18.14	185

GALEN
Natural Faculties

2.4	17

HESIOD
Works and Days (Op.)

349	331n34

HORACE
Satirae

1.4	138–43
1.5	100–101

IRENAEUS
Adversus haereses

1.10.2	43

JUVENAL
Satirae

3.62–63	13
14.96–106	180n3
14.329–31	218n89

LETTER OF PETER TO PHILIP
134:18–26	174
140:7–15	175
140:23–27	175

LUCIAN
Bis accusatus

29	290

MENANDER
Monostichoi

1.3.7	331n34

PREACHING OF PETER

3   174

PLUTARCH

Adversus Colotem

11   263n17

ORIGEN

Commentarii in evangelium Joannis 6.36   49n5

PERSIUS

Satirae

5.179–84   180n3

PLINY THE YOUNGER

Epistulae

10.96–97   188

QUINTILIAN

3.7.21   180

PLATO

Resp. 4.427e   148n3

SIMEON

Horae Homileticae: Romans   313

STRABO

Geographica

4.6.6.	185n27
11.11.1	177n39
14.5.131	358n11

SUETONIUS

Divus Claudius

25.4   14, 213n54

Divus Augustus

32.1   13

Divus Julius

84.5   13

Nero

10.	330n29
16.2	20, 21, 324n4
19.3	20

Tiberius

36   14n21

TACITUS

Annales

2.85.5	14n21
13	330
13.1	218n89
15.44.2–5	21
15.44.2–4	21
15.44.4	13

Historiae

5.1–5	180n3
5.4.1	14

TERTULLIAN

Adversus Judaeos 7   43n49

VALARIUS MAXIMUS

Facta et Dicta Memorabilia

1.3.2   14

VIRGIL

Eclogues

4.11.48   228n139

Georgics

11.11.1   177n39

www.ingramcontent.com/pod-product-compliance
Lightning Source LLC
Chambersburg PA
CBHW080531300426
44111CB00017B/2679